The Economics of Financial Markets

The Economics of Financial Markets presents a concise overview of capital markets, suitable for advanced undergraduates and for embarking graduate students in financial economics. Following a brief overview of financial markets – their microstructure and the randomness of stock market prices – this textbook explores how the economics of uncertainty can be applied to financial decision making. The mean-variance model of portfolio selection is discussed in detail, with analysis extended to the capital asset pricing model (CAPM). Arbitrage plays a pivotal role in finance and is studied in a variety of contexts, including the arbitrage pricing theory (APT) model of asset prices. Methods for the empirical evaluation of the CAPM and APT are also discussed, together with the volatility of asset prices, the intertemporal CAPM and the equity premium puzzle. An analysis of bond contracts leads into an assessment of theories of the term structure of interest rates. Finally, financial derivatives are explored, focusing on futures and options contracts.

Roy E. Bailey is a Reader in Economics at the University of Essex.

D1387480

The Economics of Financial Markets

Roy E. Bailey

CAMBRIDGE
UNIVERSITY PRESS

CAMBRIDGE UNIVERSITY PRESS
Cambridge, New York, Melbourne, Madrid, Cape Town, Singapore, São Paulo,
Delhi, Tokyo, Mexico City

Cambridge University Press
The Edinburgh Building, Cambridge CB2 8RU, UK

Published in the United States of America by Cambridge University Press, New York

www.cambridge.org
Information on this title: www.cambirdge.org/9780521612807

First published 2005
8th printing 2011

Printed in the United Kingdom at the University Press, Cambridge

A catalogue record for this publication is available from the British Library

ISBN 978-0-521-84827-5 Hardback
ISBN 978-0-521-61280-7 Paperback

The Theory of Economics does not furnish a body of settled conclusions immediately applicable to policy. It is a method rather than a doctrine, an apparatus
of the mind, a technique of thinking, which helps its possessor to draw correct
conclusions. It is not difficult in the sense in which mathematical and scientific
techniques are difficult; but the fact that its modes of expression are much less
precise than these, renders decidedly difficult the task of conveying it correctly
to the minds of learners.

J. M. Keynes

When you set out for distant Ithaca,
fervently wish your journey may be long, –
full of adventures and with much to learn.

C. P. Cavafy

Contents in brief

Contents

Figures

Preface

How can yet another book on finance be justified? The field is already well served with advanced works, many of impressive technical erudition. And, towards the other end of the academic spectrum, an abundance of mammoth texts saturates the MBA market. For the general reader, manuals confidently promising investment success compete with sensational diagnoses of financial upheavals to attract attention from the gullible, avaricious or unwary.

Alas, no one can expect to make a fortune as a consequence of reading this book. It has a more modest objective, namely to explore the economics of financial markets, at an 'intermediate' level – roughly that appropriate for advanced under-graduates. It is a work of exposition, not of original research. It unashamedly follows Keynes's immortal characterization of economic theory as 'an appara-tus of the mind, a technique of thinking'. Principles – rather than assertions of doctrine, policy pronouncements or institutional description – are the focus of attention. If the following chapters reveal no get-rich-quick recipes, they should at least demonstrate why all such nostrums merit unequivocal disbelief.

This book evolved, over more years than the author cares to admit, from lecture notes for a course in financial economics taught at the University of Essex. For reasons of space, one topic – corporate finance – has been omitted from the book, though its core insight – the Modigliani–Miller theorem – is slipped in under options (chapter 18, section 6). While the chapters are intended to follow a logical sequence, pedagogy may require a different order. Any such tensions should be straightforward to resolve. For example, chapter 2 (market microstructure) appears early but was covered later in the course. Other changes of the order in which the chapters are studied should be easy to implement. Several obvious groupings are, however, readily apparent: portfolio selection in chapters 4 and 5; asset pricing in 6 to 9; bond markets in 12 and 13; futures in 14 to 16; and options in 18 to 20.

Taxing though it may be, chapter 7, on arbitrage, is so fundamental that it deserves study as early as possible. The overused and commonly abused notion of 'efficiency' infects much of finance: here it is confronted in chapter 3, though its presence cannot escape notice elsewhere (especially in chapters 10 and 11). 'Behavioural finance' perhaps warrants greater attention than it gets. Rather than segregate the topic into a ghetto of its own, an attempt is made to disperse its message across chapters of particular relevance (especially 3, 4 and 10). No apology is offered for adhering to a conventional treatment of financial markets, eschewing as far as possible the caprice of academic fashion.

Students enrolled for the lecture course were absolved responsibility for the technical appendices, included to justify and amplify claims in the text. The appendices were much the most satisfying sections to write and, it is hoped, will interest at least those readers embarking on graduate study. Lest there be misconception that the coverage of any topic is definitive, each chapter includes brief suggestions for further reading. A student's work is never done.

The undergraduates to whom the lectures were addressed had a background in economics but most had not previously encountered the subject of finance. Consequently, while the book should be accessible to any moderately well-educated undergraduate, an acquaintance with microeconomics and quantitative methods is desirable. No more than the rudiments of differential calculus and probability theory, together with a smattering of statistics, are really necessary.

Successive generations of Essex students have contributed more to the final product than they can possibly have realized. Their toleration resembles that of opera audiences, which, in repeatedly shouting for an encore, imagine that the singer will eventually get it right. Individuals – too many to identify by name – have pointed out errors, queried obscurities and, most importantly, asked critical questions that revealed shortcomings. Attempts have been made to remedy the most glaring faults. Others undoubtedly lurk, as yet undiscovered.

A Website has been established at www.cambridge.org/0521612802. It is intended that this will form a repository for updates, feedback, exercises used in the lecture course and other supporting ancillary material. Given the unpredictable appearance, disappearance and revision of Web URLs, with a few exceptions these have been omitted from the text. The book's Website should – notwithstanding the vicissitudes of the Web – enable rapid access to relevant locations via the links listed there.

The author's procrastination in completing the manuscript would have exhausted the patience of a saint. But not of Patrick McCartan and Chris Harrison, at Cambridge University Press, the forbearance of whom has been remarkable. Persistent encouragement from Marcus Chambers and Abhinay Muthoo nudged the project back to life on countless occasions when the author would have cheerfully abandoned it. Without their unwavering support, the entire enterprise would surely have been aborted. They must, therefore, be rendered partially culpable for the appearance of the book, though they are innocent of its remaining blemishes, infelicities and errors. For these, the author accepts exclusive responsibility.

R. E. Bailey
Wivenhoe Park
November 2004

1

Asset markets and asset prices

Overview

Financial markets encompass a broad, continually evolving and not altogether clearly delimited collection of institutions, formal and informal, that serve to facilitate the exchange of assets. More to the point, the concept of an 'asset' is open to a variety of interpretations.[1] Rather than get bogged down in arbitrary classifications – and in ultimately fruitless distinctions – the nature of 'assets' and the markets in which they are traded is allowed to emerge from examples. To place the examples in context, the chapter begins by reviewing, in section 1.1, the fundamental properties of financial systems, and identifies various sorts of capital market, several of which receive attention later in the book.

The main objective of this chapter is to outline the ideas that underpin explanations of asset prices and hence rates of return. Sections 1.2, 1.3 and 1.4 describe a framework for modelling asset price determination and comment on alternative approaches.

Central to an understanding of finance is the process of arbitrage. Arbitrage trading policies seek, essentially, to exploit price discrepancies among assets. Of more interest than the policies themselves are their unintended consequences, namely the implications they have for tying asset prices together in predictable patterns. The examples in section 1.5 serve to introduce arbitrage. Its consequences emerge in several places throughout the book.

Observers and analysts of capital markets frequently seek ways to appraise the performance of the markets. The concepts of 'efficiency' introduced in section 1.7 show that different criteria can be applied in making judgements about how well the markets function.

---

[1] Perhaps it would be more accurate to use the clumsier term 'financial instrument', or possibly 'security', instead of 'asset'. But, for the purposes of this book, 'asset' is simpler and should not cause confusion.

1

1.1 Capital markets

Financial innovations are to the financial system what technological advances are to the economy as a whole. They embrace changes in the methods of doing business as well the assets traded in markets. In the broadest terms, financial innovations refer to development in the institutions of finance made in response to changes in the environment in which the institutions exist. The process of financial innovation involves institutional adaptation and evolution even when the functions of the system remain the same.

Merton and Bodie (chap. 1 in Crane et al., 1995) argue that the *functions* of financial systems change more slowly than their institutions. They propose a sixfold classification of functions.

1. *Clearing and settling payments.* Financial systems provide mechanisms that facilitate exchanges of goods and services, as well as assets, followed by settlement, transferring ownership in return for the agreed remuneration.
2. *Pooling resources and subdividing shares.* Financial systems enable multiple investors to contribute to projects that no one of them alone could afford. Also, even if a single investor could afford to fund a project, there may be incentives for diversification, each investor contributing a small portion of the project's cost and bearing a small portion of its risks.
3. *Transferring resources across time and space.* A fundamental purpose of investing is to delay consumption, for example as households accumulate wealth for retirement or for the benefit of future generations. Firms in one industry, or in one location, may seek to invest surplus funds in other industries or at other locations. Financial systems enable the assignment of these funds from households and firms with surplus resources to others that seek to acquire resources for investment and (intended) future return.
4. *Managing risk.* Financial systems provide ways for investors to exchange, and thereby to control, risks. For example, insurance enables the pooling of risks, hedging enables the transfer of risk to speculators, diversification exploits low correlations that may exist among risky projects.
5. *Providing information.* Financial systems enable *price discovery* – that is, for those who wish to trade to observe the prices (rates of exchange) at which agreements can be made. Other information, for example about expectations of future asset price volatility, can be inferred from market prices. (Chapter 19 explains how observed option prices enable inferences about the magnitude of expected asset price fluctuations in the future.)
6. *Dealing with incentive problems.* It is reasonable to suppose that contractual obligations can never stipulate the actions to be taken in every eventuality, even if every contingency could be imagined. Financial systems can help individuals to construct the sorts of contracts that fulfil their needs and to cope with the contingencies that the contracts do not explicitly take into account. For instance, the shareholders of a firm may finance its operations partly with debt, the contractual obligations for which are designed to provide incentives for the firm's managers to act in the interests of the shareholders.

What explains financial innovation (i.e. what accounts for institutional change)? There are many possible causes, including (a) technological change – e.g. advances in information technology; (b) changes in the 'real' economy – e.g. the growth of new industries and markets in South-East Asia; (c) changes in the demand for assets – e.g. ageing populations saving for retirement; and (d) changes in government regulation – e.g. the liberalization of trading rules, creating new opportunities, or new regulations providing incentives to avoid, bypass or otherwise profit from their introduction.

This book explores the operation of mature financial systems as of the early twenty-first century. While there are hints about the pattern of financial innovation, this is not a main focus of analysis. Also, the relationships between the functions of the financial system and the institutions that currently perform them remain implicit, though they should be straightforward enough to infer.

The following list of capital markets, although not comprehensive, identifies the differences among markets (differences relevant for this book, anyway) and the assets traded in them.

1. *Equity, or stock, markets.* The stock exchange is the main 'secondary' market for shares in corporations – i.e. limited liability companies.[2] It is a secondary market in the sense that the shares are already in existence, so that trade takes place between investors and need not directly involve the corporations themselves. The 'primary' market involves the issue of new shares by corporations. There are various categories of shares (e.g. ordinary shares, preference shares) but the distinctions among them are neglected here, being peripheral to the basic principles of price determination. The pattern of share prices is normally summarized by reference to particular well-known stock price averages or indexes, such as the Dow-Jones Industrial Average, Standard and Poor's 500 index, or the Financial Times Stock Exchange 100 index (see appendix 1.1).

2. *Bond markets.* These are markets for long-term securities such as government debt (known as gilt-edged securities in Britain) or corporate bonds.

   Bonds are usually regarded as less risky than shares because bonds normally oblige the issuer to promise to take specific actions at definite dates in the future. The distinction is not quite as clear as it might first seem because bond contracts can include clauses that provide for different actions in a multitude of different contingencies. Also, it is possible that the issuer of the bond will default with respect to some clause in the agreement. Even so, a typical bond is a promise to pay (a) a sequence of *coupons* (commonly twice a year) and (b) a lump sum *maturity value* (or face value) at a specified date in the future.

---

[2] If there is any distinction between 'stocks' and 'shares', it is not one of any significance here. A company's 'stock' could refer to the whole value of its equity, while 'shares' could refer to the ownership of a portion of that stock.

Bonds are commonly traded on stock exchanges in much the same way as shares. A feature of *medium-term* and *long-term* bonds is that, like shares, much of the trade is amongst investors, without the direct involvement of the issuer (government or company).

3. *Money markets*. Money markets exist to facilitate the exchange of securities such as treasury bills (commonly, three-month or six-month government debt) or other loans with a short time to maturity. Although such securities are traded in markets, any holder does not have to wait long before the issuer is obliged to redeem the debt in compliance with the terms of the contract.

4. *Commodity markets*. Markets of some form exist for almost every commodity, though financial studies are usually confined to highly organized markets for a fairly narrow range of commodities, including precious metals (gold, silver, platinum), industrial metals (such as lead, tin and copper), petrochemicals or agricultural commodities (such as cereals, soya beans, sugar and coffee). This list is not exhaustive but it does suggest that the commodities in question need to have certain physical characteristics: namely, that they can be graded according to well-defined attributes, that they are divisible into precisely defined units, and that they are storable (though often subject to deterioration over time). As will be described later, most organized commodity markets involve trading in contracts for the delivery of the stated commodity at a future date, though perhaps one very near to the present.

5. *Physical asset markets*, such as for real estate. In this case, the relevant asset for financial analysis is often a security (e.g. a mortgage) constructed to have a well-defined relationship with the physical asset (e.g. a mortgage being a loan secured against the equity of the property). It is not uncommon for mortgages to be *securitized* by financial intermediaries that issue bonds backed by (and with payoffs defined by) bundles of mortgages.

6. *Foreign exchange markets* – 'FOREX' or 'FX' markets. These are markets for one currency against another. Governments often intervene in such markets – not infrequently with disastrous consequences – to fix, or at least influence, exchange rates among currencies. Two notable features of FX markets are (a) the vast turnover of funds (often about $1.5 trillion each day in mid-2001) and (b) round-the-clock trading.

7. *Derivatives markets*. Corresponding to most of the above categories are derivative, or synthetic, securities. They are 'derivative' in the sense that their payoffs are defined in terms of the payoffs on an underlying asset or assets. The underlying asset could itself be a derivative, so that a whole hierarchy of such instruments emerges. Almost all derivatives are variants of two generic contracts.

(a) *Forward agreements*. These are contracts in which the parties agree to execute an action (typically, the exchange of a specified amount of money for a specified amount of some 'good') at a stipulated location and date in the future. For example, a forward contract might specify the delivery of 5000 bushels of domestic feed wheat to a grain elevator in Chicago, six months from the date of the agreement, at a price equal to $3.50 per bushel. A *futures* contract is a special type of forward contract designed to allow for trading in the contract itself. *Repo* contracts are combinations of loans and forward agreements. *Swaps* are sequences of forward contracts packaged together.

(b) *Options.* Options are contracts for which the holder has the right, but not the obligation, to execute a specified action at an agreed date, or over a range of dates. For example, an option might stipulate that its owner can purchase 100 IBM ordinary shares for $220 per share at any time prior to the following 30 September. Many sorts of option contracts are traded. For example, *options on futures* are options to purchase or sell futures contracts; *swaptions* are options on swap contracts. *Exotic* options encompass a variety of contracts involving non-standard terms for their execution.

1.2 Asset price determination: an introduction

1.2.1 A single asset market

The simplest economic theory of price determination applied to asset markets is that of 'supply and demand'. The prices of many assets are highly flexible, with rates of change that are rapid compared with the rates of change in the total volume of the asset in existence. At each instant of time the total stock of the asset is assumed fixed. The market price is allowed to adjust so that wealth holders, in the aggregate, are just prepared to hold the existing stock – the demand to hold the asset equals the stock in existence. Figure 1.1 depicts an equilibrium price of p^* that equates demand with the given stock denoted by $\overline{Q}$.

In some cases, it makes sense to treat the *total* stock of the asset in existence as *zero*. For example, corresponding to every futures contract there must be exactly the same volume of purchases ('long' positions) as sales ('short' positions): they net out to zero. The stock of outstanding purchases (or sales) – known as 'open interest' – will, of course, change over time, but at each instant the total of purchases and the total of sales each equals the open interest.

From this perspective, the relevant question is: what determines the demand to hold the asset? An immediate but superficial response is that the demand for an asset is determined by the same things as the demand for any good: (a) *preferences*, (b) the *price* of this and other assets, and (c) *income* (here the *stock* of wealth, not the flow of income, forms the relevant constraint). A more complete and satisfactory response involves delving beneath the surface to analyse the role of each of these elements.

1.2.2 Multiple asset markets: a more formal approach

What are the forces that determine the market prices for different assets? As a start, consider a world with many market participants – *investors* – each of whom has an initial amount of wealth available for investment.

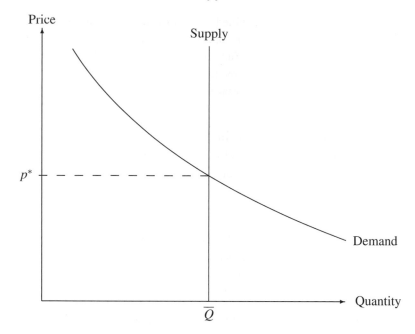

Fig. 1.1. Market equilibrium for a single asset

At each instant of time the total stock of the asset is fixed, say at $\overline{Q}$. The demand to hold the asset is depicted by the negatively sloped curve. At price p^* the market is in equilibrium – i.e. the demand to hold the asset equals the stock available to be held.

In the presence of a large number of investors, it is plausible to assume that each investor is a price taker, in the sense that no one investor has enough market power to influence prices. Each investor thus treats asset prices as parametric, though not necessarily constant over time. Initial wealth is also parametric, being equal to the sum of each asset's price multiplied by the quantity of the asset that the investor starts out with (i.e. holds as a consequence of past decisions).

Faced with given asset prices and with given initial wealth, each investor selects a portfolio in accordance with a *decision rule*. The decision rule – which can be unique to each investor – determines the number of units of each asset to hold as a function of the observed prices and initial wealth. Theories of *decision making under uncertainty* provide the necessary foundation from which each investor's decision rule is derived (see chapters 4, 5 and 11).

The *market equilibrium* at each date is defined by a set of asset prices and an allocation (portfolio) of assets among investors that, together, satisfy the following conditions.

1. Each investor's portfolio is determined according to the investor's decision rule. In particular, the chosen portfolio is optimal subject to the investor's preferences (i.e. willingness to bear risk), beliefs (about assets' payoffs) and constraints (the given level of initial wealth and, perhaps, institutional limits on permissible trades).
2. Demand equals supply; that is, the total stock of each asset equals the total demand aggregated over all investors.

Note that, in principle, some or all investors may be allowed to hold assets in negative amounts – investors may be able to 'short-sell' assets (see section 1.4.2). The main components of the approach so far are as follows.

1. At each instant of time total asset stocks (netting out assets and liabilities) are given.
2. Asset prices adjust so that existing stocks are willingly held.
3. With the passage of time asset stocks change (e.g. because companies issue new shares and debt, or repurchase shares and redeem existing debt). Also, investors revise their portfolios in response to changes in their circumstances or their beliefs about the future. As a consequence, prices change.

This is merely the skeleton of a framework and makes no definite, testable predictions. Even so, it is a useful way of viewing asset markets because most of the models in the remainder of the book emerge as special cases, each of which fits within the framework. The capital asset pricing model (see chapters 6 and 11), for instance, is perhaps the most notorious special case. It would be wrong, however, to conclude that the approach outlined above is the *only* way to model asset prices; an alternative framework, based on asset flows rather than stocks, is explored in chapter 2.

1.2.3 Rates of return

Assets are typically held because they yield – or, at least, are expected to yield – a rate of return. A general way of writing the rate of return on an asset is

$$\text{rate of return} \equiv \frac{\text{payoff } \textit{minus } \text{price}}{\text{price}} \tag{1.1}$$

where 'price' is the observed market price (or outlay on the asset) as of today, date t, and 'payoff' is the value of the asset at the next relevant point of time, date $t+1$ (where $t+1$ could be tomorrow, next month, next year or whenever). The *gross* rate of return on an asset is commonly defined as $\frac{\text{payoff}}{\text{price}}$. Thus, while the rate of return might be a number such as 0.064 (6.4 per cent), the gross rate of return would be 1.064.

An asset's payoff may have several components according to the type of asset. For a bond, the payoff is its market price at $t+1$, plus any coupons received between t and $t+1$. For a bank deposit, the payoff is the principal at t plus the interest accumulated between t and $t+1$ minus bank charges. For a company's shares, the payoff is the share's market price at $t+1$ plus the dividends, if any, paid between t and $t+1$.

Let the asset's price at t be denoted by p_t and its payoff at $t+1$ by v_{t+1}. Then the asset's rate of return between t and $t+1$, y_{t+1}, is defined by

$$y_{t+1} \equiv \frac{v_{t+1} - p_t}{p_t} \qquad (1.2)$$

where y is intended to stand for 'yield'. It is often convenient to interpret the price at $t+1$, p_{t+1}, to include any dividends or coupons received between t and $t+1$. With this interpretation, $v_{t+1} = p_{t+1}$. In words: the rate of return is the proportional rate of change of the asset's market price. Slightly more generally, the rate of return is measured by the proportional rate of change of the asset's market value (i.e. it includes flows such as dividends or coupons as well as the market price).

The *real* rate of return on an asset is defined as the rate of return measured not in units of account, 'money', as in expression (1.1), but in terms of aggregate 'real' output.[3] Call the rate of return in (1.1) the *nominal* rate of return. Then the relationship between real and nominal rates of return – often attributed to the eminent American economist Irving Fisher (1867–1947), of Yale University – can be written as

real rate of return = nominal rate of return   *minus*   rate of inflation

(See appendix 1.2 for a derivation.) More substantively, the Fisher hypothesis is commonly interpreted as the prediction that the real rate of interest is constant – that fluctuations in the nominal rate and inflation tend to offset one another.

The distinction between nominal and real rates of return is important in many branches of economics, especially monetary economics and macroeconomics (where another distinction – between actual and expected inflation – is particularly relevant). In this book the distinction between nominal and real rates of return is not prominent. Where necessary, an adjustment from nominal to real rates can be made by subtracting the rate of inflation from the nominal rate. This simple-minded approach is not intended to underrate the importance of the difference between nominal and real rates. Rather, it serves to emphasize that the determination of expected and actual rates of inflation is not studied here.

---

[3] In principle, the rate of return can be defined in the units of any commodity, service or asset. In practice, an index of aggregate output is used in an attempt to measure output as a whole.

1.2.4 The roles of prices and rates of return

The most important aspect of rates of return for decision making is that they are *forward-looking*: they depend on future payoffs. For almost all assets, the payoff is, at least in part, *uncertain* when viewed from the present, date t. For example, the prices of stocks and shares at date t can be observed at date t, but their prices at date $t+1$ are matters of conjecture.

The current, observed market price for an asset plays two distinct roles in financial economics.

1. The price represents an *opportunity cost*. An asset's price appears in the wealth constraint as the amount that has to be paid, or is received, per unit of the asset. This is the conventional role for prices in economic analysis.
2. The price conveys *information*. Today's asset price reveals information about prices in the future.

The information conveyed by prices affects investors' *beliefs* and hence their actions (portfolios selected). Investors' actions determine the demand to hold assets in the aggregate and hence influence the assets' market prices.

1.3 The role of expectations

A famous passage in John Maynard Keynes's *General Theory* illustrates the role of expectations formation in financial markets (Keynes, 1936, p. 156).

... professional investment may be likened to those newspaper competitions in which the competitors have to pick out the six prettiest faces from a hundred photographs, the prize being awarded to the competitor whose choice most nearly corresponds to the average preferences of the competitors as a whole; so that each competitor has to pick, not those faces which he himself finds prettiest, but those which he thinks likeliest to catch the fancy of the other competitors, all of whom are looking at the problem from the same point of view. It is not a case of choosing those which, to the best of one's judgement, are really the prettiest, nor even those which average opinion genuinely thinks the prettiest. We have reached the third degree where we devote our intelligences to anticipating what average opinion expects average opinion to be. And there are some, I believe, who practise the fourth, fifth and higher degrees.

Here Keynes is posing a conundrum without proposing how to resolve it. Keynes's example may seem to involve circular reasoning: asset prices affect expectations, expectations affect decisions, decisions affect prices, and so on. Regardless of whether this is circular reasoning, the puzzle pinpoints the simultaneous interactions that occur between observed prices in the present and beliefs about prices in the future.

One implication is that the demand curve drawn in figure 1.1 should be treated with the utmost caution; when a price conveys information (as well as representing an opportunity cost) a simple downward-sloping demand curve may be difficult to justify – for a higher price today could lead investors to infer that the price will be even higher tomorrow, thus encouraging a greater demand to hold the asset in anticipation of a capital gain. In the presence of such 'extrapolative expectations', the demand curve could display a *positive* slope, at least for some prices.

It is common to assume that investors have 'rational expectations'; that is, their expectations are formed with an awareness of the forces that determine market prices. Moreover, in a rational-expectations equilibrium, the forces that determine prices include the decisions made by investors. This does not imply that investors are blessed with perfect foresight, but, at least, it does exclude expectations that are systematically wrong.

The rational-expectations hypothesis, on its own, is not much help in explaining asset prices. Firstly, rational expectations make sense only in the context of a model of price determination, including assumptions about investors' preferences and the information they possess. Secondly, investors may differ in the information they can bring to bear on their decisions – there may be *asymmetric information*. Thirdly, the information available changes over time as investors learn from their experience, or forget.

It is hardly surprising, in view of all these considerations, that building expectations formation into asset-pricing theories is both (a) central to any explanation of prices and (b) fraught with complications.

In an attempt to account for some of the imponderable features of price fluctuations, Fischer Black (1986) has introduced the concept of *noise* to financial analysis. From this perspective, some investors are assumed to act in arbitrary ways that are difficult – perhaps impossible – to explain as the outcome of consistent behaviour. These investors are called *noise traders*. *Rational traders* (sometimes called 'information traders' or 'smart-money investors'), on the other hand, are assumed to behave according to more coherent precepts, or to have better information, or better ways of processing the available information, than noise traders. (Asset price determination in the presence of noise traders is examined in more detail in chapters 2 and 10.)

The noise-trader approach falls with the broader framework of *behavioural finance*, which exploits ideas from outside conventional economics, including psychology. Behavioural finance can be understood as a modelling strategy that seeks to explain many otherwise puzzling phenomena – for example, empirical evidence that appears to be incompatible with the so-called *efficient markets hypothesis* (see below, section 1.7, and chapter 3). Whether behavioural finance can do a better job than orthodox theories in this regard remains an open question. At present, behavioural finance has succeeded more as a critique of conventional models than as a constructive alternative. Consequently, orthodoxy is likely to maintain its dominance for the analysis of a range of problems, at least until a viable replacement paradigm emerges.

The acquisition and processing of information by investors is a subject that has received scant attention in financial economics. Investors are typically assumed to possess particular pieces of knowledge (e.g. of recent asset prices). Little, if anything, appears explicitly about how this information is obtained or what sense is made of it in drawing inferences about which risks are worth taking.

These aspects of the decision-making process are usually taken as given, or ignored. They can, however, be important. For instance, the accuracy of accountants' reports – derived from *past* data – are important influences on investors' expectations of *future* performance. Once confidence in past data is undermined, the repercussions can be widespread and profound; witness the response to revelations about accounting malpractice at Enron, WorldCom and other companies in 2001–2.

In constructing models of financial markets it should be recognized that different investors may behave according to many different criteria. Faced with this complexity, model builders can, perhaps, be forgiven for assuming that decision makers act *as if* their preferences and beliefs are analytically tractable.

Each investor's beliefs about assets' payoffs can be viewed as predictions made from the investor's personal model of capital markets. The 'model' implicit in behaviour is rarely – if ever – made explicit. In most applications, the 'model' is naïve – for example, that investors make decisions based on past asset prices alone to maximize a simple objective of the sort studied in chapters 4 and 5.

Some investors, however, devote great energy and skill to their portfolio choices. Instead of relying solely on past prices, they seek out potential investment opportunities, examine the strategies of individual companies, monitor the markets in which the companies operate, and study the performance of their investments with anxious vigilance. Even so, as Keynes cautions, no amount of effort can eliminate human ignorance about what the future may bring forth: 'The game of professional investment is intolerably boring and overexacting to anyone who is entirely exempt from the gambling instinct; whilst he who has it must pay to this propensity the appropriate toll' (Keynes, 1936, p. 157).

1.4 Performance risk, margins and short-selling

1.4.1 Performance risk and margin accounts

Uncertainty about the future plays a central role in economics and permeates every branch of financial analysis. A thorough treatment of uncertainty must await chapter 4, but it is useful here to distinguish between price risk and performance risk.

Price risk, or market risk, refers to the prospect that the market value of an asset will change by an unknown – though not necessarily entirely unpredictable – amount in the future. *Performance risk* refers to the prospect that a contractual obligation (e.g. the promise made to deliver an asset that the investor has agreed to sell) will not be fulfilled. Price risk receives the most attention in this book, but for the remainder of this section the focus is on performance risk.

That agreements will be honoured is taken for granted in much of economics, problems of enforcement being largely ignored. The mechanisms adopted to minimize performance risk do, however, impinge directly on some aspects of financial analysis. In particular, evidence of 'good faith' in adhering to agreements is often made via deposits in *margin accounts*. One party, or possibly both parties, to a contract may agree to deposit funds with a third party – say, a clearing house or other designated institution. These funds are returned (or form part-payment for the relevant asset) when the contract is settled. In the event of default, the deposit is used to compensate the injured party.

In many organized asset markets there are detailed, and often quite complicated, rules that determine the minimum size of margins. In other markets the provision of good-faith deposits is at the discretion of the parties themselves. The provisions might be specified as clauses in the contract or agreed more informally. Either way, it is possible for margin accounts to be used to increase an investor's exposure to price risk (relative to the investor's wealth) while simultaneously keeping performance risk within acceptable bounds.

Example: buying on margin

Consider an investor, A, who instructs a broker, B, to purchase 100 shares of company XYZ when the market price is $10 each. Suppose that A and B have an arrangement whereby A's instructions are carried out so long as B holds a margin of 40 per cent of the transaction value. Hence, in this case, A makes an immediate payment of $400 and B has effectively loaned A $600. B holds the shares as collateral against the loan to A.

Sooner or later, A will either (a) take delivery of the shares (and pay B an additional $600 plus interest and commission fees), or (b) instruct B to sell the shares (and repay the loan from B). The margin agreement works smoothly so long as XYZ's share price increases above $10. But suppose that the price falls, say, to $5. Now A owes B more than the value of the collateral, $500. If the shares are sold, and if A does not pay B an additional $100 (plus transaction costs), then B loses out. To guard against potential losses of this sort, margin accounts may require replenishing from time to time. If A does not provide additional funds when requested, then B might sell some or all of the shares to avoid realizing a loss.

A common method for managing margins is to monitor the *actual margin*, defined by

$$\text{actual margin} = \frac{\text{collateral} - \text{loan}}{\text{collateral}}$$

where 'collateral' equals the market value of the shares purchased by A and 'loan' equals the value of the loan from B to A ($600 in this example).[4] Typically, when a transaction is initiated, the actual margin equals the *initial margin* (40 per cent in the example). A *maintenance margin* is usually set somewhat below the initial margin. If the actual margin then falls below the maintenance margin, a *margin call* for a *variation margin* is made, obliging the investor to provide sufficient funds, thus raising the actual margin.[5] Thus, in this example, if the share price falls to $5, A deposits an extra $300, thereby reducing the loan to $300 and restoring the actual margin to its initial level of $40\% = (500 - 300)/500$.

The authorities in many financial markets enforce rules that govern the provision of margins. The administrative details differ across authorities and across time, and are not described here. The important point to grasp is why the margin serves to minimize the performance risk associated with trading agreements. In addition, it should be clear that trading on margin can generate very high rates of return on initial capital – and, also, very great losses. Hence, margin trading can accentuate price risk.

1.4.2 Short-sales

The notion of 'going short' or taking a 'short position' is a common one in finance. In its simplest form this refers to the action of selling an asset. For an investor who owns an asset that is sold, the action is trivial enough. What may appear more puzzling is the action of selling an asset that the investor does not own. This is the act of making a 'short-sale' or 'selling short'.

An immediate reaction might be that a short-sale is an act of deception and, hence, fraudulent. This is not necessarily the case, however, because the asset may have been *borrowed* immediately prior to the sale. Presumably, the motive of the borrower is that, at a date following the short-sale, the asset will be purchased for a lower price and returned to its lender. The short-seller then gains the difference between the sale and purchase prices.

---

[4] More formally, let m denote the margin. Let p equal the price per share, N the number of shares purchased on margin, and L the value of the loan. Then $m = (pN - L)/pN$, or $m = 1 - (L/pN)$. As p varies, so does m. If p falls, m may fall so low that the broker demands funds from the investor to reduce L and raise m.

[5] It is common to require that the actual margin be restored to its initial value, although it is possible that the investor may be obliged to restore it only to the maintenance margin threshold. The precise requirement depends on the terms of agreement between the parties to the transaction and the exchange authorities.

Whatever the motive, short-sales can and do take place without breaching codes of conduct or the law. Even so, exchange authorities commonly place restrictions on the circumstances in which short-sales are permitted. For example, the rules of an exchange might prohibit short-sales at times when the asset price is falling. In some cases, short-sales are permitted only when the most recent recorded transaction involved a price *increase* – the so-called 'uptick rule'. Exchange authorities tend to justify these sorts of rules on the ground that short-sales at times of falling, or stationary, prices would tend to exacerbate price volatility.

In addition, only a restricted group of investors may be permitted to engage in short-sales. For example, short-sales may be limited, as a privilege, to designated members – say, specialists or market makers – in an exchange. Once again, the motive is probably to limit price volatility (though it also restricts the freedom to compete). Also, by restricting the eligibility to undertake short-sales, the scope for default or dishonesty can be restrained. At the same time, conferment of the privilege to make short-sales rewards the designated exchange members for the burdens imposed by their other responsibilities. (For example, each market maker is normally obliged to ensure that investors can always succeed in trading shares on a list of companies for which the market maker is responsible.)

Not surprisingly, even when short-sales are permitted, good faith or margin deposits are normally required to insure against performance risk. Here the potential for loss arises when the borrower purchases the asset (for return to its lender) at a price *higher* than that at which it was initially (short-)sold. In this circumstance, the existence of the margin deposit serves to ensure that sufficient funds are available to enable the return of the asset to its owner, though, of course, the short-seller incurs a loss on the transaction as a whole.

Example: margins with short-sales

Suppose that investor A has an agreement with broker B that allows A to make short-sales of company XYZ's shares (the shares might be borrowed from B's own portfolio or from the portfolio of one of B's other clients). Now suppose that A instructs B to short-sell 100 shares at a market price of $10 each. B will hold the proceeds, $1000 in A's margin account, and will also demand an additional deposit of, say, $400.

Sooner or later A will return the borrowed shares by instructing B to purchase 100 XYZ shares at the ruling market price. If the price has fallen below $10, then A stands to make a profit (after allowing for the deduction of B's commission and other expenses, such as a fee for the loan of the shares). However, if the share is purchased at a price above $10, then A will make a loss – a loss that might be so large that an additional payment has to be made to B. Suppose that the shares are repurchased at a price of $16. Then A would have to pay another $200 (plus transaction costs) to B. If A defaults, then B makes a loss. To guard against this contingency, margin deposits are adjusted by margin calls in an analogous fashion to that when shares are purchased on margin.

With regard to short-sales, the actual margin is defined by

$$\text{actual margin} = \frac{\text{collateral} - \text{loan}}{\text{loan}}$$

where now 'collateral' equals the funds held in the margin account and 'loan' is the current market value of the shares that have been short-sold.[6] In the example, the initial margin is $(1000 + 400 - 1000)/1000 = 40\%$, as required.

Consequently, in the example, if the share price rises to $16 and the short-sale remains in place, a variation margin of $840 would restore the actual margin to its initial value, $40\% = (1400 + 840 - 1600)/1600$. (Once again, the rules for margins are prescribed by the relevant regulatory authorities. The detailed rules differ from market to market.)

Just as with buying on margin, short-selling can yield high rates of return but can also be very risky. Even when short-sales are permitted, the rules governing margins serve to limit the likelihood of default (performance risk), though the potential for loss (as a reflection of price risk) remains substantial.

1.5 Arbitrage

1.5.1 The arbitrage principle

Arbitrage plays a central role in financial markets and in theories of asset prices. Arbitrage strategies are – roughly speaking – patterns of trades motivated by the prospect of profiting from discrepancies between the prices of different assets but without bearing any price risk. This quest for profit has an important influence on market prices, for, in a precise sense, observed market prices reflect the *absence of arbitrage opportunities* (sometimes referred to as the *arbitrage principle*). If arbitrage opportunities are *not* absent, then investors could design strategies that yield unlimited profits with certainty and with zero initial capital outlays. Their attempts to exploit arbitrage opportunities are predicted to affect market prices (even though the actions of each investor are, in isolation, assumed not to influence prices): the prices of assets in excess demand rise; those in excess supply fall. The ensuing price changes eradicate potential arbitrage profits.

---

[6] More formally, let m denote the margin. Let p equal the price per share, N the number of shares short-sold, and C the amount of the collateral. The value of the loan from the broker to the short-seller is equal to pN, so that $m = (C - pN)/pN$, or $m = (C/pN) - 1$. Once again, m varies with p. If p increases, m may fall so low that the broker demands funds from the investor to increase the collateral, C, and thus raise m.

In its simplest form, arbitrage implies *the law of one price*: the same asset exchanges for exactly one price in any given location and at any given instant of time. More generally, arbitrage *links* the prices of different assets.

Arbitrage reasoning lies at the heart of several important contributions to financial theory. In particular, both the famous Black–Merton–Scholes theory of options prices and the Modigliani–Miller theorems in corporate finance are founded on the absence of arbitrage opportunities. The arbitrage principle also plays a role in asset price determination when combined with other assumptions. For example, arbitrage pricing theory is a consequence of marrying the arbitrage principle with factor models of asset prices (see chapter 8).

Example 1: foreign exchange markets

Suppose that the following exchange rates are observed among British pounds (£), US dollars ($) and Japanese yen (¥):

$$£1 = \$1.50$$

$$¥150 = £1$$

$$\$1 = ¥120$$

Given these exchange rates, an investor could borrow £1 and immediately sell it for $1.50; buy ¥180 with the $1.50; buy £1 for ¥150. Profit $= ¥30$, after returning the £1 loan. This is an arbitrage opportunity that, if it persists, would allow the investor to make unbounded profits. The arbitrage opportunity is sometimes called a 'money pump'. Neglecting *market frictions* – a concept examined below – such price differentials cannot persist. Market prices adjust so that the arbitrage opportunity disappears. (In this example, £1 $= \$1.50$; £1 $= ¥150$; $1 $= ¥100$ would eliminate the arbitrage opportunity.)

Example 2: a bond market

Consider a bond that promises to pay an amount v (its payoff) of, say, $115.50, one time period from today. What is the price of the bond today?

Let r denote today's rate of interest (for one-period loans) and suppose that it is equal to, say, 5 per cent. Investors will be prepared to hold the bond only if the rate of return is at least r. If the rate of the return on the bond exceeds r, investors will seek to borrow an unbounded amount, with which to buy an unlimited number of bonds. This cannot be consistent with market equilibrium in a frictionless market. Similarly, if r exceeds the rate of return on bonds, investors will seek to issue (or short-sell) an unlimited number of bonds and lend the proceeds at rate r. Again, this cannot be consistent with market equilibrium in a frictionless market.

The only market equilibrium in this idealized framework is one in which r equals the rate of return on the bond. The rate of return on the bond is defined by

$$\text{rate of return on bond} \equiv \frac{v-p}{p}$$

where p is the price of the bond today. Market equilibrium is expressed as

$$r = \frac{v-p}{p}$$

which implies that the bond price must be

$$p = \frac{1}{1+r}v = \frac{1}{1+0.05}115.50 = \$110$$

Given the interest rate of 5 per cent, a bond that pays $115.50 next period must have a market equilibrium price equal to $110 today.

1.5.2 Market frictions

Two of the most important market frictions are: (a) transaction costs; and (b) institutional restrictions on trades. The assumption of *frictionless markets* (i.e. zero transaction costs and no institutional restrictions on trades) underpins the absence of arbitrage opportunities.

Transaction costs intrude in a variety of ways. Among the most obvious are the explicit commission fees, taxes and other charges levied when trades occur. The difference between the *bid price* (at which shares can be sold to a dealer) and the *ask price* (at which shares can be purchased) might also be interpreted as a transaction cost, at least from the perspective of an investor. Other transactions costs may be less tangible but nonetheless real. For example, the time devoted to making decisions about buying and selling assets or to issuing instructions to a broker constitutes a genuine opportunity cost, even though it typically remains implicit.

Institutional restrictions take the form either of prohibitions on particular classes of trades, or of conditions that must be fulfilled before trades are permitted. For example, as already mentioned, short-sales of shares may be restricted in terms of the circumstances in which they are allowed and who is permitted to undertake them.

Other frictions are sometimes identified separately or, alternatively, subsumed within the first two. These frictions include (a) the inability of investors to borrow or lend in unlimited amounts at a common, risk-free interest rate, and (b) the availability of some assets in only indivisible units (i.e. 'lumps' that are large relative to the total stock of the asset outstanding). Conversely, in frictionless markets investors are unrestricted in their ability to borrow or lend at a given interest rate, and assets are defined in as small units as needed.

The assumption of frictionless markets is a blatant idealization. In practice, transaction costs and restrictions on trades are always present. This is no justification, however, for dismissing the relevance of arbitrage in asset price determination. For the important question is: how well do markets approximate the ideal? Some markets are good approximations. In these cases, the absence of arbitrage opportunities enables accurate predictions about patterns of asset prices.

When frictions are pervasive, few implications about asset prices can be drawn, even if arbitrage opportunities are absent. Note, however, that frictions do not necessarily impinge equally on all market participants. If the actions of those investors for whom frictions are negligible – e.g. specialist institutions and professional traders – have a significant impact on asset prices, then the observed prices are likely to reflect the absence of arbitrage opportunities. This will be so even if most investors face high transaction costs or are restricted in the trades they can execute.

Perfect and imperfect capital markets

The notion of a 'perfect' capital market – and, by implication, 'capital market imperfections' – is widely used but seldom explicitly defined. Almost all definitions would include the requirement that a perfect capital market is frictionless. In addition, it is often assumed – or taken for granted – that the markets in question are 'competitive' in the sense that the actions of individual buyers and sellers have no direct impact on prices.

Yet more conditions are commonly assumed or implied. In view of the ambiguities inherent in the usage of 'perfect capital market', the concept is avoided in this book.[7]

1.5.3 All sorts of assets

It is possible to extend arbitrage reasoning – albeit somewhat informally – to include many different sorts of asset. The components of return (or cost) from holding an asset can be classified as[8]

1. Direct, or own, return: q. For an asset such as a house this would be the utility services (shelter, privacy, etc.) for the persons dwelling in it, or the rent if it is rented out. For a bond, it would be the interest coupon. For a company's shares, it would be the dividend.

---

[7] See Stigler (1967) for perceptive insights about the nature of capital market imperfections, especially in the context of industrial organization.

[8] The classification follows Keynes's *General Theory* (1936, pp. 225–7).

2. Carrying cost: c. This is the opportunity cost of storing the asset. It is negligible for many financial assets but for physical commodities (e.g. wheat in storage or a house, which needs maintaining over time) the carrying cost is positive.
3. Convenience or security yield: ℓ. This reflects the ease with which the asset can be turned into cash without risk of loss. Keynes calls ℓ the *liquidity premium* of an asset: 'the amount ... which they [investors] are will to pay for the potential convenience or security given by [the] power of disposal' (1936, p. 226).
4. Expected capital gain or loss: g. This is the amount by which the market value of the asset changes over the ensuing time interval.

It might seem reasonable to suppose that, taking into account all four factors, every asset should yield the same return – otherwise investors would sell assets with low yields and buy those with high yields. Consequently, for any pair of assets i and j

$$q_i - c_i + \ell_i + g_i = q_j - c_j + \ell_j + g_j \tag{1.3}$$

Expression (1.3) forms the foundation for Keynes's monetary theory in an intriguing chapter of *The General Theory* entitled 'The Essential Properties of Interest and Money' (chap. 17). There is no consensus on exactly what Keynes is getting at, and the chapter remains an enigma in monetary theory.

Although it is tempting to interpret equation (1.3) as an implication of the absence of arbitrage opportunities, this is not strictly correct. The reason is that the capital gain or loss terms, g_i and g_j, are typically unknown when investment decisions are made, thus violating the requirement that arbitrage strategies are risk-free. Even so, in the presence of forward markets, a variant of (1.3) is central to the analysis of arbitrage (see chapter 14).

1.5.4 Summary of arbitrage

1. The word 'arbitrage' is often used in a loose and imprecise way. In this book its use is confined to trading strategies that (a) require *zero initial capital* and (b) are *risk-free*.[9]
2. The implications of the absence of arbitrage opportunities are most revealing when markets are *frictionless*. When frictions are not negligible, the absence of arbitrage opportunities tends to be uninformative about the pattern of asset prices.
3. The arbitrage principle applies much more widely than in the examples outlined in this section. The logic can be extended to circumstances in which asset payoffs are uncertain (chapter 7) and also to assets that yield payoffs for many periods in the future (chapter 10). It is particularly important in the study of derivatives, such as options (chapter 18).

[9] Occasionally it is necessary to examine investment strategies that are *roughly* like arbitrage in the sense that risks are small but non-zero. In these cases, the usage of the term will be qualified as *approximate* or *limited* arbitrage. The word 'arbitrage' on its own, as used here, always refers to the strict sense of being risk-free and requiring zero initial capital.

4. Arbitrage analysis places only mild requirements on investors' preferences; it is merely assumed that investors prefer more wealth to less. No assumptions are needed about investors' attitudes to risk or about their beliefs with regard to the prospects of receiving particular payoffs. In this sense, the arbitrage principle applies very generally.

5. In frictionless asset markets, the absence of arbitrage opportunities serves to *link* asset prices. In the foreign exchange example, some patterns of exchange rates can be excluded, but the absence of arbitrage opportunities on its own is silent about the *level* of each rate. In the bond market example, the bond price is linked to the interest rate; the absence of arbitrage opportunities on its own is not enough to determine both. Hence, the arbitrage principle provides a *partial* theory of asset prices.[10]

1.6 The role of time

The length of the unit time interval – say, between dates t and $t+1$ – is often left implicit in finance, as well as in economics more generally. This section seeks to clarify the several interpretations that are given to time intervals in financial economics. The simplest usage is just a convention that asset yields are expressed as rates of return *per annum* (i.e. per calendar year) even though an asset may be held for time periods greater or less than a year.

1.6.1 Measuring rates of return

Suppose that a security promises a payoff of $120 at the end of two years in return for $100 invested today. Is the rate of return equal to 10 per cent per annum? The answer depends on how frequently the return is compounded. If there is no compounding at all, then the net payoff of $20 = \$120 - \$100$ averaged over two years is 10 per cent per annum. But suppose that the return is compounded once per year; then the rate of return is less than 10 per cent per annum because part of the $20 is assumed to be paid at the end of the first year – the rate of return is approximately 9.54 per cent per annum: $120 \approx (1+0.0954)(1+0.0954) \times 100$. It is *as if* a payoff of $9.54 is received at the end of the first year, with a 9.54 per cent rate of return on $109.54 in the second year.

If the return is compounded every six months, then the annual rate is even lower at approximately 9.33 per cent: $120 \approx (1+0.0933/2)(1+0.0933/2)(1+0.0933/2)(1+0.0933/2) \times 100$.[11]

---

[10] In order to obtain definite predictions about the linkages among asset prices, the arbitrage principle on its own is often not sufficient. For example, in the Black–Merton–Scholes option price model an assumption has to be made about the random process generating stock prices – a process known as 'geometric (or logarithmic) Brownian motion' in continuous time. Given this assumption, the absence of arbitrage opportunities permits the derivation of a formula linking the option price with the underlying stock price (see chapter 19).

[11] Notice that the *six-monthly* rate is approximately $0.0466 \approx 0.0933/2$, but, by convention, rates are quoted *per annum* – i.e. 9.33 per cent.

The example shows that, even if rates of return are quoted 'per annum', their values depend on the frequency of compounding – i.e. how the payoff is accumulated over the life of the asset. There is no consensus solution to this ambiguity. A common practice in finance is to assume that the payoff on an asset accumulates *continuously* over its life. In the example above this rate – known as the 'force of interest' – is approximately 9.12 per cent per annum.

To calculate the force of interest, subtract the natural logarithm of the initial investment from the natural logarithm of the investment's payoff, then divide by the length of time between the two. In the example: $(\ln 120 - \ln 100)/2 \approx 0.0912$. It is as if the investment of \$100 at date t grows at a continuous annual rate of approximately 9.12 per cent, so that, at date T in the future, its value equals $100 \times e^{0.0912 \times (T-t)}$. Hence, for $T - t = 2$ years, $100 \times e^{0.0912 \times (2)} \approx 120$ (where 'e' is the base of the natural logarithms). A detailed explanation of the principles underlying these calculations is provided in appendix 1.3.

1.6.2 The horizon and the decision period

In studying portfolio behaviour it is important to distinguish two time intervals.

1. *Horizon.* An investor's horizon is the time between the present and the date at which investments are to be liquidated – that is, sold or turned into cash.[12]
2. *Decision period.* The decision period is the interval of time between successive dates at which decisions are made about acquiring or disposing of assets.

An investor might, for example, have a horizon of twenty years but make portfolio selection decisions every month. In the most basic models, such as those in chapter 5, the horizon and the decision period are assumed to be the same. In more complicated environments, such as those explored in chapter 11, the horizon is longer than the decision period; also, the investor can choose to liquidate capital for consumption at each decision date, or, alternatively, add to the total portfolio with savings from other sources of income.

Personal circumstances normally determine the length of an investor's horizon. For example, a twenty-year-old might have a horizon of fifty or sixty years, while that for an eighty-year-old will be much shorter.

What determines the decision period? Market frictions – in particular, transaction costs – are crucial here. In the ideal world of frictionless markets, with zero transaction costs, there is no reason why investors should not change their asset holdings at every instant of time – trading would be *continuous*. In many abstract finance models this is precisely what is assumed; a formal analytical framework has been developed to handle trading in continuous time.

---

[12] The investor's horizon might differ among assets, with some to be liquidated sooner than others, but this complication is ignored here.

Regardless of whether continuous trading is a reasonable approximation of reality, decision making is often easier to comprehend if there is a finite time, such as a month or a year, between decisions. This interval could be interpreted to reflect the presence of transaction costs, though this is not essential. Instead, it is commonly assumed (with little explicit justification) that decisions are made at discrete dates but that markets are otherwise frictionless.

1.7 Asset market efficiency

Throughout history, even to the present, financial markets have been susceptible to extreme price fluctuations, even collapse. (Some of the most notorious incidents are reviewed in chapter 10.) The potential, and sometimes actual, failure of capital markets provokes wild accusations in the popular media, especially at times of crisis. Financial economics tries to be less sensational than the media by assessing asset market performance according to standards of 'efficiency'. The concept of efficiency has several varieties in this context. The main types are these.

1. *Allocative efficiency* refers to the basic concept in economics known as *Pareto efficiency*. Briefly, a Pareto efficient allocation is such that any reallocation of resources that makes one or more individuals better off results in at least one individual being made worse off.[13]

   The so-called 'first fundamental theorem of welfare economics' states that an equilibrium with a *complete set* of *perfectly competitive* markets is Pareto efficient.[14] It is commonly assumed that the set of markets is *incomplete* – i.e. that there are many 'missing markets'. Why this is so may not be immediately obvious, but it is intimately bound up with time and uncertainty (see chapter 4). An implication of the incompleteness of markets is that any allocation of resources is almost surely not first-best Pareto efficient (even if markets are perfectly competitive). The challenging intellectual problem of studying whether allocations are second-best efficient when markets are incomplete is not examined in this book.

2. *Operational efficiency* mainly concerns the industrial organization of capital markets. That is, the study of operational efficiency examines whether the services supplied by financial organizations (e.g. brokers, dealers, banks and other financial intermediaries) are provided according to the usual criteria of industrial efficiency (for example, such that price equals marginal cost for the services rendered). Hence, studies of operational efficiency investigate the determination of commission fees, competition among financial service providers and even competition among different financial

---

[13] For a detailed introductory treatment, see, for example, Varian (2003, chap. 30). Debreu (1959, chap. 6) is definitive.

[14] The second fundamental theorem asserts that, under certain conditions (essentially, convex preferences and production technologies), any Pareto efficient allocation can be sustained as a competitive equilibrium in conjunction with an appropriate redistribution of initial resource endowments among households.

market centres. Some of these issues are reviewed in chapter 2, where it is found that operational efficiency is intimately related to informational efficiency, introduced next.

3. *Informational efficiency* refers to the extent that asset prices reflect the information available to investors. In a sense that deserves to be made more precise, markets are said to be informationally efficient if the market prices fully reflect available information. The so-called *efficient markets hypothesis* is intended to provide a benchmark for assessing the performance of financial markets in reflecting information. Although the concept of informational efficiency appears transparent enough, there are pitfalls in its application. These are studied, together with allied topics, in chapter 3.

4. *Portfolio efficiency* is a narrower concept than the others. An efficient portfolio is one such that the variance of the return on the portfolio is as small as possible for any given level of expected return. Efficiency in this context emerges from the mean-variance theory of portfolio selection – a topic studied in chapter 5.

Among the concepts of efficiency, the second and third (operational and informational efficiency) feature most extensively in financial analysis. Allocative efficiency is, in a sense, the most fundamental, in that it involves the whole economy. However, the subject is a difficult one and little is known beyond a few general – mostly negative – propositions.

Regrettably, 'efficiency' is one of the most overused and abused words in financial economics. Assertions are often made that markets are efficient or – more commonly – inefficient, little or no attention being given to the term's inherent ambiguities. For this reason, 'efficiency' as a concept in financial economics is best avoided unless accompanied by a precise characterization of its usage.

1.8 Summary

This chapter has introduced several of the main themes in financial economics – themes that provide a framework for the study of asset markets and that are explored in the following chapters.

1. Financial markets are treated as markets for stocks. Equilibrium prices are defined to be those that clear markets at each date; that is, in equilibrium, asset prices are such that existing stocks are willingly held, given the decision rules adopted by investors.

2. Investors are assumed to make their choices consistently, in accordance with their preferences, taking into account their beliefs about the future and their wealth constraints. The implications of this analysis provide the decision rules for selecting portfolios.

3. In frictionless markets the absence of arbitrage opportunities enables definite predictions about how asset prices are linked together.

4. Rates of return are typically quoted at annual rates. But investors may have horizons greater or less than a year and may revise their decisions many times before the horizon is reached.

5. Asset market efficiency is a concept open to different interpretations. Several aspects of efficiency have been introduced, the two most commonly encountered in financial economics being (a) informational efficiency (that asset prices reflect available information) and (b) operational efficiency (that asset markets function according to the tenets of industrial efficiency).

Further reading

Many textbooks in finance contain substantial amounts of introductory material. For a thorough coverage, either of the following is worth consulting: Elton, Gruber, Brown and Goetzmann (2003, chaps. 1–3); or Sharpe, Alexander and Bailey (1999, chaps. 1–3). Tobin and Golub (1998) cover much of the subject matter of financial economics with a different emphasis, namely that of placing the subject in the context of monetary economics and banking.

Students of modern finance swiftly realize that a grasp of mathematics is necessary to progress very far. Cvitanić and Zapatero (2004) offer a textbook exposition in which mathematical methods find prominence. The coverage of chapter 1 of their book is similar to that here. Subsequent chapters of the book, while in a different sequence from that adopted here, explore many of the same topics, though with significantly greater emphasis on the relevant mathematics.

The contributions comprising Crane et al. (1995) pursue in depth the functional perspective outlined in section 1.1; chapter 1 is especially interesting. A comprehensive description of financial institutions appears in Kohn (2004).

For details of stock price averages and indexes, a good starting point is *The New Palgrave Dictionary of Money and Finance* (Newman, Milgate and Eatwell, 1992), particularly the entries on 'stock market indices', 'Dow Jones indicators of stock prices' and 'Financial Times indexes'. To keep up to date with the precise rules by which the indexes are defined, the World Wide Web is a valuable resource: all the major indexes can be found via any of the readily available search engines.

A classic reference on the fundamental nature of capital markets, more important for the problems it poses than for the solutions it derives, is that by Keynes (1936, chap. 12).

Appendix 1.1: Averages and indexes of stock prices

It is common to express overall stock market trends in terms of averages or indexes of the prices of individual companies' shares. These averages are defined in a variety of ways and used for a variety of different purposes. For example, they are often used to provide a summary of share price changes on a particular day or over some time period, such as a week, month or year. Alternatively, they can be used as benchmarks against which to evaluate the performance of particular investment strategies. They also play an important role in tests of asset pricing theories (see chapters 6 and 8).

Probably the most well-known of all stock price averages is the 'Dow-Jones', the 'Dow' or – more precisely – the Dow-Jones Industrial Average (DJIA). The DJIA_t is an average of the prices of thirty large American corporations at date t. The rule for its calculation is given by

$$\text{DJIA}_t = \frac{p_{1,t} + p_{2,t} + \cdots + p_{30,t}}{30z} \tag{1.4}$$

where $p_{j,t}$ is corporation j's share price at time t. If z, in the denominator (the role of which is explained below), is set equal to unity, $z = 1$, then the DJIA_t is simply an equally weighted average of the prices for the thirty chosen corporations. The 'blue-chip' corporations selected for membership of the DJIA change only infrequently (typically as a consequence of mergers or the acquisition of one company by another). In aggregate they represent about 20 per cent of the total market value of all publicly quoted US shares.

Although the composition of the DJIA is quite stable over time, a complication arises because corporations occasionally split their shares (say, making every old share equal to two new ones) or pay dividends in the form of new shares (say, one extra share for every five shares already held).[15]

Unless the average is adjusted, a discontinuity would occur whenever such an event takes place. For example, suppose that there are just two corporations, A and B, in the index, with prices of 100 and 60 respectively. The average is thus equal to $80 = \frac{1}{2} \times (100 + 60)$. Now suppose that corporation A makes a two-for-one split. Without adjustment, the average instantly drops to $55 = \frac{1}{2} \times (50 + 60)$, though no substantive change of any sort has occurred. This is where the z factor – the *divisor* – in (1.4) comes in. The value of z is chosen so that the average does not change instantly as a consequence of the change. In this case, if $z = (50 + 60)/(100 + 60) = 11/16$, then the average remains at 80:

$$\frac{100 + 60}{2} = \frac{50 + 60}{2 \times (110/160)} = 80$$

---

[15] Stock splits are made for a variety of reasons. A common one is to make the total stock of a corporation more highly divisible and thus possible to trade in small units. Suppose, for example, that the price of a corporation's shares is $200. The smallest increment for trading is then one share, or $200. If there is a ten-for-one split, then the smallest increment is $20, a more convenient number for precise calculations that seek to avoid rounding approximations.

Of course, the average could change afterwards if investors draw inferences (favourable or unfavourable) about the motives for corporation A's stock split.

As time passes, numerous stock split and stock dividend events will occur. At each such event, the z value will be changed (typically reduced) to reflect the redefinition of units. Formally, the updating rule for divisor is as follows:

$$\text{new divisor} = \frac{\text{total of prices } \textit{after} \text{ the event}}{\text{total of prices } \textit{before} \text{ the event}} \times \text{old divisor}$$

For example, in August 2002 the DJIA divisor was reduced from 0.14445222 to 0.14418073 following Citigroup's spin-off of its subsidiary Travelers Property Casualty (TPC), an insurance company. (The shares were distributed to existing Citigroup stockholders.) By June 2004 the divisor had become 0.14090166, when (on 21 June) it was reduced to 0.13561241 as a consequence of a two-for-one split in the common stock of Proctor & Gamble.

The DJIA is an example of a 'price-weighted' index. Despite their simplicity, such indexes have drawbacks. Most importantly, they do not reflect the capital value of each corporation in the market as a whole (a very small corporation with a high share price could dominate the index). Also, price-weighted indexes are not very convenient for making systematic appraisals of portfolio strategies or testing asset pricing theories. In order to define more suitable measures, consider first a very general expression for a stock market index as of date t:

$$I_t = w_1 p_{1,t} + w_2 p_{2,t} + \cdots + w_n p_{n,t} \tag{1.5}$$

where there are n companies represented in the index and w_j denotes the weight attached to company j's share price at date t. For the DJIA, $n = 30$ and $w_j = 1/30z$.

Many stock price indexes are defined so that w_j reflects the 'size' of the company as measured by its total market value at a specified base date. Suppose that the base date is labelled as date zero, 0. For these 'value-weighted' or 'capitalization-weighted' indexes, the weights are defined as

$$w_j = \frac{X_{j,0}}{D} \tag{1.6}$$

where

$$D = p_{1,0} X_{1,0} + p_{2,0} X_{2,0} + \cdots + p_{n,0} X_{n,0}$$

where the zero, '0', subscript denotes the base date, $X_{j,0}$ denotes the total number of the jth company's shares on the base date and $p_{j,0}$ is the share price for the jth company on the base date. Here the 'divisor', D, equals the total value of all the shares in the index at the base date.

Hence, with weights defined in (1.6), the index at date t represents an average of share prices *relative to the average of prices at a base date*, each price being weighted by the number of its company's shares.

Suppose that the total number of shares changes for one or more companies. Should the 'old' number of shares outstanding be used (so that D remains unchanged), or should D be recalculated with the 'new' number? This is a standard 'index number problem', for which there is no universally accepted solution. Using the 'old' quantities corresponds to the *Laspeyres* weighting scheme, while using the 'new' corresponds to *Paasche* weighting. Most share price indexes are calculated according to the Paasche weighting scheme.

Determination of the $X_{j,0}$ (the number of shares outstanding for each company) is not as obvious as it might appear, for a portion of shares might be held under constraints that limit the opportunities for their sale. Consequently, in the construction of some indexes an attempt is made to estimate the volume of each company's shares available for trading – the so called 'free float' – by excluding the amounts of shares held by institutions, individuals or governments that, for some reason, are unlikely (or unable) to sell them.

An example of a capitalization-weighted index is the Financial Times Stock Exchange 100 ('FT-SE 100') index of the hundred largest companies, by capitalization, traded on the London Stock Exchange (LSE). Another example is Standard and Poor's 500 ('S&P 500'), index of stocks traded in New York. The FT-SE 100 was defined so that its value on 3 January 1984 equalled 1000. The S&P 500 was constructed so that its value for 1941 to 1943 equalled 10.

While indexes such as the FT-SE 100 and S&P 500 are widely used, their application is not without pitfalls. One complication is that they are often adjusted to include dividend payments. This is not, in practice, a drawback, for it allows the index value to be interpreted as the 'payoff' on a portfolio of shares with weights given by the index.

An important pitfall is that the composition of the indexes changes, sometimes quite frequently, with the passage of time. Thus, for instance, when the ranking of the largest companies quoted on the LSE changes, it becomes necessary to alter the membership of companies in the FT-SE 100 index. Quarterly reviews are made of the index – and changes can take place more often than that. Consequently, investment strategies such as 'buying the market' (where the 'market' is represented by the composition of the relevant index) are not as simple as they might at first seem. Moreover, because companies that perform poorly tend to drop out of the index, an upward 'survivorship bias' is imparted to the stock index over long periods of time.

Whatever their faults, it is possible to interpret the indexes considered so far as portfolios that investors could purchase – in principle, at least. This is not so for all indexes. For instance, it is not the case for *geometric* averages or indexes (as distinct from the *arithmetic* averages above). A geometric price-weighted average of n share prices would take the form

$$\sqrt[n]{p_{1,t} p_{2,t} \cdots p_{n,t}}$$

that is, the index equals the nth root of the product of the share prices. An example is the Value Line Composite Index of about 1700 stocks with prices quoted in New York. Notice that the index, say G_t, is normally expressed relative to some base date, 0, as follows:

$$G_t = \frac{\sqrt[n]{p_{1,t} p_{2,t} \cdots p_{n,t}}}{\sqrt[n]{p_{1,0} p_{2,0} \cdots p_{n,0}}} = \sqrt[n]{\frac{p_{1,t}}{p_{1,0}} \times \frac{p_{2,t}}{p_{2,0}} \times \cdots \times \frac{p_{n,t}}{p_{n,0}}}$$

In words: G_t equals the geometric mean of share prices relative to their values at a base date.

The expression for the value line index suggests a variant sometimes known as an *arithmetic* value line index, say A_t (as distinct form the *geometric* form above):

$$A_t = \frac{1}{n} \left(\frac{p_{1,t}}{p_{1,0}} + \frac{p_{2,t}}{p_{2,0}} + \cdots + \frac{p_{n,t}}{p_{n,0}} \right)$$

In words: A_t equals the arithmetic mean of share prices relative to their values at a base date.

While each of these indexes has its advocates, no one index dominates the rest. It is comforting, at least, that they do all tend to move in the same direction, albeit with different magnitudes.

Appendix 1.2: Real rates of return

This appendix derives an expression for the real rate of return on an asset. Let z_t denote the price level of output or 'goods' – that is, z_t can be interpreted as the amount of money that must be paid at date t, to obtain one unit of consumption. (It is assumed that there is just one sort of commodity in the economy, so that index-number problems in defining the overall price level can be ignored.) Let the symbol π_{t+1} denote the *rate of inflation* between t and $t+1$, formally defined as $\pi_{t+1} \equiv (z_{t+1}/z_t) - 1$ (or $\pi_t \equiv (z_t/z_{t-1}) - 1$). For example, if $z_t = 100$ and $z_{t+1} = 105$, the rate of inflation is 5 per cent – $\pi_{t+1} = 0.05$.

Let y_{t+1} denote the rate of return on the asset in question between dates t and $t+1$. By definition, $y_{t+1} \equiv v_{t+1}/p_t - 1$. This is the *nominal* rate of return on the asset (because the price and payoff are both denominated in units of money). For example, if $p_t = 20$ and $v_{t+1} = 24$, then $y_{t+1} = 0.20$ – i.e. 20 per cent.

The real rate of return on the asset is defined as the rate of growth of *output* achieved by investing one unit of output in the asset at date t and transforming the asset back to output at date $t+1$. That is, one unit of output is sold for money at t, the money being used to buy the asset. At $t+1$ the asset is sold for money, which is then used to buy output. The real rate of return is, then, the proportional rate of growth in the value of the asset measured in units of output rather than units of money.

At t, one unit of output is worth z_t in money. Thus, z_t could be used to purchase z_t/p_t units of the asset. Each unit of the asset is worth v_{t+1} (its payoff) in money at $t+1$. Hence, the investment in the asset is worth $v_{t+1} \times z_t/p_t$ in money at $t+1$. Now divide by the price level, z_{t+1}, to give the value of the asset at $t+1$ measured in units of output:

$$\frac{v_{t+1}}{p_t}\frac{z_t}{z_{t+1}} = (1+y_{t+1})\frac{z_t}{z_{t+1}} = \frac{1+y_{t+1}}{z_{t+1}/z_t} = \frac{1+y_{t+1}}{1+\pi_{t+1}} \tag{1.7}$$

Expression (1.7) is the amount of output at $t+1$ accumulated by investing one unit of output in the asset from t to $t+1$. The real rate of return on the asset is simply this amount minus the one unit of output invested at t:

$$\frac{1+y_{t+1}}{1+\pi_{t+1}} - 1 = \frac{1+y_{t+1}-1-\pi_{t+1}}{1+\pi_{t+1}} = \frac{y_{t+1}-\pi_{t+1}}{1+\pi_{t+1}} \approx y_{t+1}-\pi_{t+1} \tag{1.8}$$

Thus, the real rate of return equals the nominal rate of return, y_{t+1}, minus the rate of inflation, π_{t+1}; i.e. $y_{t+1} - \pi_{t+1}$. In terms of the numerical example,

$$\frac{1+y_{t+1}}{1+\pi_{t+1}} - 1 = \frac{24/20}{105/100} - 1 \approx 14.29\% \approx 15\% = 0.20 - 0.05 = y_{t+1} - \pi_{t+1} \tag{1.9}$$

Expression (1.9) becomes more accurate the smaller the rate of inflation. Alternatively, the approximation in expression (1.8) becomes an exact equality if the rates of return are defined at an instant in continuous time – that is, if the length of the time interval between t and $t+1$ is infinitesimal. Calculus reasoning then establishes that the real rate of return at t equals $y_t - \pi_t$, *exactly* (see appendix 1.3).

Appendix 1.3: Continuous compounding and the force of interest

This appendix shows how the rate of return on an asset is measured when its payoff accumulates over time at ever-increasing frequencies. The outcome is an important limiting result, known as the *force of interest*, that provides a benchmark for calculating rates of return.

Assume, following convention, that the unit time interval is one calendar year, and let r denote the annual rate of return *with no compounding*. Suppose, for example, that $r = 0.10$, i.e. 10 per cent. Then, at the end of the year, one unit of wealth grows to $1 + 0.10 = 1.10$. If the return arrives at six-monthly intervals, then the rate of return, denoted by ρ, satisfies $(1 + \rho/2)(1 + \rho/2) = (1 + \rho/2)^2 = 1.10$. The payoff now accumulates more frequently, and hence $\rho < r$ (it is approximately 9.76 per cent).

Suppose that interest is paid ever more frequently. A table of values shows the results:

Frequency		
Annually	$(1 + \rho) = 1.10$	$\rho = 0.10$
Six-monthly	$\left(1 + \dfrac{\rho}{2}\right)^2 = 1.10$	$\rho \approx 0.0976177$
Quarterly	$\left(1 + \dfrac{\rho}{4}\right)^4 = 1.10$	$\rho \approx 0.0964548$
Monthly	$\left(1 + \dfrac{\rho}{12}\right)^{12} = 1.10$	$\rho \approx 0.0956897$
Weekly	$\left(1 + \dfrac{\rho}{52}\right)^{52} = 1.10$	$\rho \approx 0.0953976$
Daily	$\left(1 + \dfrac{\rho}{365}\right)^{365} = 1.10$	$\rho \approx 0.0953226$
Hourly	$\left(1 + \dfrac{\rho}{8760}\right)^{8760} = 1.10$	$\rho \approx 0.0953107$

Notice that, as the payoff accumulates more frequently, the rate of return (measured by ρ) declines but converges to a positive number. It is possible to show that ρ converges to approximately 0.09531018 – i.e. roughly 9.53 per cent.

A sketch of how the limit is obtained is as follows. Suppose that the return is compounded n times per year (e.g. $n = 52$ for weekly compounding). Also, define $m \equiv n/\rho$ and write the total amount accumulated as

$$\left(1 + \frac{\rho}{n}\right)^n = \left(1 + \frac{1}{m}\right)^{m\rho} = \left[\left(1 + \frac{1}{m}\right)^m\right]^{\rho} \tag{1.10}$$

Increasing the frequency of compounding corresponds to a value of n (and hence m) that becomes ever larger – so that with monthly compounding ($n = 12$), weekly ($n = 52$), daily ($n = 365$), hourly ($n = 8760$), and so on. As m increases without bound, it can be proved that the term in square brackets, $(1 + 1/m)^m$, converges to $e \approx 2.7182818284$ – a positive constant.

The number 'e' appears widely in mathematics and forms the base of the natural logarithms ($\ln e \equiv 1$). There is evidence to suggest that the discovery of e may have had its origins in practical finance. (For a fascinating history of e, see Maor, 1998.)

In summary, one unit of wealth invested at a rate equal to ρ, continuously compounded (i.e. in the limit as $n \to \infty$), accumulates to e^{ρ} at the end of one unit time interval (conventionally, a year). If r denotes the rate of return *without compounding*, then by construction $1 + r = e^\rho$, or, equivalently, $\rho = \ln(1 + r)$. In this context, ρ is referred to as the *force of interest*.

Time intervals greater or less than a year (the unit value) are handled as follows. A return continuously compounded for two-year intervals at rate ρ accumulates to $e^{2\rho}$ at the end of the period. If the length of the period is $T - t$ years, from today (date t) to date T, then each unit of wealth accumulates to $e^{\rho(T-t)}$ at T, starting from t.

For a bank account or a bond, the frequency at which interest is accumulated depends on the contract between the bank and the depositor (borrower and lender in the case of a bond). It is not uncommon for interest on bank accounts to be compounded daily. Hence, the exponential form may be a close approximation, at least with frequent compounding and for interest rates that are normally experienced (i.e. not spectacularly high).

Notice that $e^{\rho(T-t)}$ can be referred to as an *interest factor*: it is the factor by which any starting principal at date t is multiplied in order to obtain its value at date T. Thus, an amount A at date t grows to $Ae^{\rho(T-t)}$ at date T. The reciprocal of the interest factor is a *discount factor*: $e^{-\rho(T-t)}$. Thus, an amount M to be received at T has a *net present value* (NPV) today (date t) equal to $Me^{-\rho(T-t)}$.

Calculating the force of interest, ρ, is straightforward. Suppose that an investment of \$200 today increases in value to \$500 in eight years' time. Then, $\rho = (\ln(500) - \ln(200))/8 \approx 0.114536$ – i.e. roughly 11.45 per cent.

More generally, suppose that an investment of A at t results in a payoff of M at date T. Then, ρ is defined such that $Ae^{\rho(T-t)} = M$. Hence, $\ln A + \rho(T - t) = \ln M$. Rearranging gives $\rho = (\ln M - \ln A)/(T - t)$. In the example, $A = \$200$, $M = \$500$, and $T - t = 8$.

To allow for price level changes, suppose that the price level of output is z_t at date t, and z_T at date T. Now, in real terms (i.e. in terms of output), an investment of A/z_t results in a payoff of M/z_T at T. Following the previous paragraph, define $\tilde{\rho}$ to satisfy $(A/z_t)e^{\tilde{\rho}(T-t)} = M/z_T$. Hence, $\ln A - \ln z_t + \tilde{\rho}(T - t) = \ln M - \ln z_T$. Rearranging gives

$$\tilde{\rho} = \frac{\ln M - \ln A}{T - t} - \frac{\ln z_T - \ln z_t}{T - t} = \rho - \pi$$

where $\pi = (\ln z_T - \ln z_t)/(T - t)$ denotes the continuously compounded inflation rate (the 'force of inflation', if you like) over the time interval t to T. Thus, the real interest rate, $\tilde{\rho}$, equals the nominal interest rate, ρ, minus the inflation rate, π.

Continuing the previous example, suppose that an investment of \$200 today increases in value to \$500 in eight years' time and, over the same interval, the price level increases from 100 to 170. Hence, $\pi = (\ln(170) - \ln(100))/8 \approx 0.066329$ – i.e. roughly 6.63 per cent. The real interest rate then equals $11.45 - 6.63 = 4.82\%$ – i.e. the nominal interest rate minus the inflation rate.

References

Black, F. (1986), 'Noise', *Journal of Finance*, 41(3), pp. 529–43.

Crane, D. B., R. C. Merton, K. A. Froot, Z. Bodie, S. P. Mason, E. R. Sirri, A. F. Perold and P. Tufano (1995), *The Global Financial System: A Functional Perspective*, Boston: Harvard Business School Press.

Cvitanić, J., and F. Zapatero (2004), *Introduction to the Economics and Mathematics of Financial Markets*, Cambridge, MA, and London: MIT Press.

Debreu, G. (1959), *The Theory of Value*, New Haven, CT, and London: Yale University Press.

Elton, E. J., M. J. Gruber, S. J. Brown and W. N. Goetzmann (2003), *Modern Portfolio Theory and Investment Analysis*, New York: John Wiley & Sons, 6th edn.

Keynes, J. M. (1936), *The General Theory of Employment, Interest and Money*, London: Macmillan (reprinted as Keynes, *Collected Writings*, Vol. VII).

Kohn, M. (2004), *Financial Institutions and Markets*, New York and Oxford: Oxford University Press, 2nd edn.

Maor, E. (1998), *e: The Story of a Number*, Princeton, NJ: Princeton University Press.

Newman, P., M. Milgate and J. Eatwell (eds.) (1992), *The New Palgrave Dictionary of Money and Finance*, London: Macmillan (three volumes).

Sharpe, W. F., G. J. Alexander and J. V. Bailey (1999), *Investments*, Englewood Cliffs, NJ: Prentice Hall International, 6th edn.

Stigler, G. J. (1967), 'Imperfections in the capital market', *Journal of Political Economy*, 75(3), pp. 287–92.

Tobin, J., and S. S. Golub (1998), *Money, Credit and Capital*, New York: McGraw-Hill.

Varian, H. R. (2003), *Intermediate Microeconomics: A Modern Approach*, New York: W. W. Norton, 6th edn.

2

Asset market microstructure

Overview

The previous chapter outlined an approach to asset price determination that focuses on *stocks*. In summary: the realized market price is such that the existing stock of each asset is willingly held by investors in the aggregate – the demand to hold the stock is equal to its supply. A second approach to price determination focuses on *flows*: the asset price is such that the flow of purchases over a short interval of time equals the flow of sales. That is, the total demand from all those investors who seek to add to their holdings of the asset equals the total supply of all those investors who seek to reduce their holdings. The two paradigms are not necessarily incompatible. Neither is necessarily right or wrong. They are just different ways of analysing the same thing – namely, what determines asset prices.

This chapter, unlike most that follow, adopts the second paradigm. Viewing prices as determined by flows of assets is particularly useful in exploring the details of how prices are set in practice and the behaviour of those who set them. Following a brief review of some basic features of market activity in section 2.1, section 2.2 studies the commonest trading mechanisms found in asset markets. Section 2.3 considers asset markets from the perspective of industrial organization and reviews the nature of competition within and between the markets.

The organization of asset markets continues to experience rapid and far-reaching institutional change. Innovations, particularly with respect to information technology, the Internet and the expansion of *e-commerce*, are largely responsible for these changes. Their impact is ongoing and yet to be fully grasped, though tentative remarks are made at relevant points in the remainder of the chapter.

Sections 2.4, 2.5 and 2.6 study some of the models that have been proposed to explain asset prices from the perspective of trade flows. The simplest of the models evades the question of *why* investors seek to trade. It treats the trade flow

33

as exogenous and explains the difference between ask prices (at which dealers sell) and bid prices (at which dealers buy) as a reflection of the inventory costs borne by dealers, together with their market power and their aversion to risk.

An alternative class of models emphasizes the motives for trade by investors that emerge from differences in information among investors, and between investors and dealers. Asset prices are then explained as the outcome of a process of competition between market participants, some of whom have better information than others about the underlying value of the assets they trade.

2.1 Financial markets: functions and participants

What is a 'market'? From an economic perspective, a *market* is any set of arrangements that enables voluntary agreements to be reached among its participants. There are three crucial elements in the definition. First, the *set of arrangements* can include diffuse, largely unorganized networks, such as foreign exchange markets, as well as highly organized institutions, such as futures markets. Second, the *agreements* need not be formal contracts, though they may be so. Third, the agreements are *voluntary*, although the coercive sanction of the law may be invoked to ensure that the agreements are implemented.

Several functions must be performed by any market.

1. To disseminate information, thus promoting *price discovery*. That is, the market should enable participants who want to buy or sell to find out the prices at which trades can be agreed.

2. To provide a *trading mechanism*, thus facilitating the making of agreements. That is, there must be a means by which those who wish to sell can communicate with those who wish to buy.

3. To enable the *execution of agreements* (sometimes known as the 'settlement function'). That is, the market should ensure that the terms of each agreement are honoured: (a) to confirm the transaction; (b) to clear the trade (ensure that the new ownership of the security is registered with its issuer); and (c) for the settlement of accounts (exchange of money). Broadly, there is a need to guard against fraud, default or other misconduct. It is in this context that the *regulation* of financial markets is particularly important.

    Many, though not all, financial exchanges are associated with a designated *clearing house* that supervises, and provides administrative procedures for, the settlement of contracts. In addition, arrangements have to be made for the safe custody of assets.

    The settlement function of financial markets is often taken for granted. Its fulfilment is relegated to the 'back office' of financial organizations. Economic theory does not have much to say about this function, except to suggest that it has the characteristics of a 'public good', with implications for the stability of the financial system as a whole.

It is noteworthy that the failure of settlement arrangements often signals the origin of many dramatic upsets in financial markets – e.g. the collapse of Barings Bank in 1995. Also, deliberations about how to organize settlements can lead to protracted controversies – e.g. over the development in the early 1990s of a settlement system for shares traded on the London Stock Exchange.

The functions of a market are, in a trivial sense, performed directly or indirectly by its participants. In addition to the authorities that regulate the markets, the participants in markets can be classified into three broad groups, according to their *motive* for trading.

1. *Public investors*, who ultimately own the assets and who are motivated by the returns from holding the assets. Public investors include private individuals, trusts, pension funds and other institutions that are not part of the market mechanism itself.
2. *Brokers*, who act as agents for public investors and who are motivated by the remuneration received (typically in the form of commission fees) for the services they provide. Under this interpretation, brokers trade for others, not on their own account.
3. *Dealers*, who do trade on their own accounts but whose primary motive is to profit from trading – rather than from holding – assets. Typically, dealers obtain their return from the difference between the prices at which they buy and sell the asset over short intervals of time.

In practice the three groups are not mutually exclusive: some public investors may occasionally act on behalf of others; brokers may act as dealers as well as holding assets of their own; and dealers often hold assets in excess of the inventories needed to facilitate their trading activities. There may be several categories of brokers and dealers distinguished by their access to, or ownership of, the market institutions. Also, in many markets there are designated dealers who have particular obligations to ensure that the trading mechanism functions smoothly. These are the so-called *market makers* or *specialists*. In return for fulfilling their obligations, market makers are normally granted privileged access to certain administrative procedures or market information.

In the financial markets that exist around the world a wide variety of forms of organization govern the interactions among market participants. The more traditional, and still widespread, exchanges are reviewed in section 2.3. During the late 1990s *electronic communications networks* (ECNs) emerged as rivals to the more traditional exchanges. In response to this challenge, organized exchanges have tended to adopt the new technologies in order to fend off encroachment from the ECNs.

The trading mechanisms employed by organized exchanges and ECNs deserve special attention, and are covered in the next section. Then, in section 2.3, the industrial organization of financial markets is explored.

2.2 Trading mechanisms

The many different trading mechanisms observed in financial markets fall roughly into two groups: *quote-driven* and *order-driven* markets. An inspection of existing markets reveals immediately that a rigid demarcation between the two types is an oversimplification. Moreover, rapid innovation (especially in the application of information technology) has led to developments that could hardly have been imagined only a few years ago. Even so, treating quote-driven and order-driven markets as distinct yields insights, as described below.

2.2.1 Quote-driven markets

Quote-driven markets, sometimes known as *dealer markets*, are those in which dealers quote *bid* and *ask* (or *offer*) prices at which they are prepared to buy or sell, respectively, specified quantities of the asset. The LSE traditionally operated in this way, although now an order-driven mechanism is available for trading in the shares of large companies. In New York, NASDAQ[1] is an outstanding example of a quote-driven market.

Dealer markets require little formal organization but need mechanisms for publicizing the dealers' price quotations, for regulating the conduct of dealers and for administering the settlement of contracts. In London the quotations are publicized on the SEAQ (Stock Exchange Automated Quotations) system, similar to NASDAQ in New York. In return for access to these facilities, the dealers must adhere to the market authority's rules, most importantly that of being obliged to quote 'firm' bid and ask prices at which they guarantee to make trades of up to specified volumes.

Figure 2.1 depicts a simplified view of the relationship between bid, p_b, and ask, p_a, prices. The horizontal axis measures the quantity, Q, of the asset traded each period. Q has a *flow* dimension: a number of units *per unit of time*. Thus, the demand, $Q^d(p)$, and supply, $Q^s(p)$, functions express the decisions of investors to *trade* (buy or sell) the asset. They are distinct from the *stock* demand and supply functions, which express the preferences to *hold* the asset. When a unit of the asset is traded, the buyer pays the ask price, p_a, while the seller receives the bid price, p_b, the difference being the *bid–ask spread*, $s = p_a - p_b$, received by the dealer.

The practice is more complicated than the diagram suggests, for in a quote-driven market different dealers often post different bid–ask spreads. Trades take place sequentially, so that the observed *transaction price* depends on whether

---

[1] NASDAQ is short for National Association of Securities Dealers Automated Quotations. Formally, NASDAQ is the information dissemination mechanism, owned and operated by the National Association of Securities Dealers.

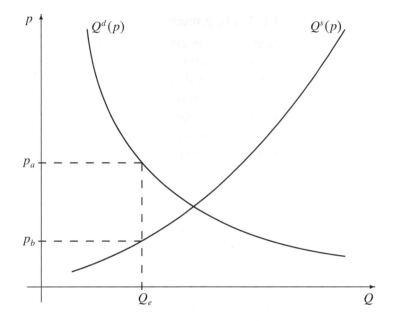

Fig. 2.1. Flow demand and supply for a single asset

The *bid–ask spread,* $s = p_a - p_b$, is the difference between the price, p_a, paid by the purchaser (the dealer's ask price) and the price, p_b, received by the seller (the dealer's bid price). At prices p_a and p_b, the flow supply of the asset equals the flow demand for the asset, resulting in a volume of trade equal to Q_e.

a sale or purchase takes place. Also, dealers may negotiate special prices for large transactions. Moreover, dealers may undertake to execute trades at the highest bid or lowest ask price (i.e. the most favourable price for the customer) currently being quoted in the market. Although in many markets the narrowest spread can be observed (in London it is known as the 'touch'), dealers could still engage in private negotiations with their clients. Thus, the actual bid–ask spread could be narrower than appears from the published quotations (or, possibly, broader for particularly large or small transactions).

2.2.2 Order-driven markets

Order-driven markets – sometimes known as *agency* or *auction markets* – include the classic Walrasian *tâtonnement* process of economic theory. In the modern literature, the mechanisms are modelled as 'double auctions', in which participants issue orders to buy or sell at a stated price. More precisely, participants issue instructions that specific actions should be taken in response to the arrival of publicly verifiable information, such as a price observation. The price is then adjusted by an 'auctioneer' until the total orders to buy equal the total orders to sell.

A market mechanism that approximates *tâtonnement* is the London gold fixing. Twice each working day, five bullion dealers meet in Rothschild's Fixing Room. The representative of Rothschild's Bank chairs the meeting and calls out a starting price. After consulting their offices by telephone, the dealers report their net purchases or sales at the stated price. The chairman aggregates the responses and, if the proposed trades do not balance, calls out a new price. The process goes on until each dealer signals acceptance with the announced price by lowering a small flag on the table around which they sit.

The London gold price fixing is an example of a *call market* mechanism. Call markets are *discrete*, or periodic, in the sense that the price is determined at a limited number of specified times. Auctions are also widely employed for new issues of government debt (e.g. British government gilt-edged securities and US treasury bills and bonds) and sometimes for initial public offerings (IPOs) of equity (e.g. Google in 2004). The call market as a mechanism in secondary markets for stocks and shares has tended to disappear, although it was employed on the Paris Bourse until the late 1980s. In recent years continuous trading systems for securities have tended to displace call markets.

In continuous auction markets, public investors direct their instructions ('orders') to brokers, requesting them to buy or sell, perhaps contingent upon observations made by the broker when the order is executed. There are many different sorts of order, the most well-known being *limit orders* (specifying purchase or sale at maximum buying prices or minimum selling prices, respectively) and *market orders* (specifying sale or purchase at the best available price). Both of these types are known as *public orders* (because they come from outside the exchange). The outstanding limit orders are generally listed in a *limit order book*. The existence of a limit order book implies an element of automaticity in matching trades, though, in practice, some element of discretion remains, particularly in determining the priority of orders. Even so, automatic trade execution systems are being introduced in financial markets, particularly in response to the opportunities offered by modern information technology. An example is the SETS (Stock exchange Electronic Trading Service) launched on the London Stock Exchange in October 1997.

In many markets, such as the New York Stock Exchange (NYSE[2]) and the Toronto Stock Exchange, there are *specialists* who are obliged to buy and sell designated shares and who can deal as principals on their own behalf.[3] The

---

[2] The NYSE operates a hybrid mechanism, in which the trading day commences with a call market to determine opening prices; thereafter, trading is continuous.

[3] Tokyo is an exception, in that market makers (*saitori*) do not trade on their own behalf.

presence of specialists serves to ensure that there is always a price at which public investors can trade.

Some markets, especially for futures contracts, traditionally operate a system of *open outcry*, in which the floor traders shout orders and communicate among one another in a *trading pit* using complicated hand signals – an example is the Chicago Board of Trade (CBOT). Advances in information technology and the consequent spread of electronic trading mechanisms have challenged the dominance of open outcry systems. Open outcry is defended in the markets that use the system, though the question of whether this is because the exchange members stand to lose if electronic trading prevails, or because open outcry genuinely offers a better service to public investors, remains unresolved.

When the object of trade is more heterogeneous than in highly organized exchanges, brokers tend to play an active role in matching buyers with sellers. Having received an order to buy or sell, the broker seeks an investor with whom to arrange an agreement. Examples of such over-the-counter markets include those for: (a) real estate (few properties being identical with any other); (b) bonds (the terms for repayment on which may have unique features); and (c) trading in blocks of shares (for the blocks may differ in the number of shares they comprise, even though the constituent shares are homogeneous).

2.2.3 *Quote-driven and order-driven markets compared*

Market mechanisms are often compared with respect to *liquidity* and *transparency*, both of which are aspects of price discovery.

'Liquidity' is defined in *The Oxford English Dictionary* as 'the interchangeability of assets and money'. Its meaning is more elusive than the definition might seem to imply, because 'interchangeability' embraces a variety of characteristics commonly associated with liquid markets. Black (1971, p. 30) asserts that

a liquid market is a continuous market in the sense that almost any amount of stock can be bought or sold immediately; and an efficient market, in the sense that small amounts of stock can be bought or sold very near the current market price, and in the sense that large amounts can be bought or sold over long periods of time at prices that, on average, are very near the current market price.

By implication, a market is *illiquid* if an offer to buy (or sell) yields no response to sell (buy) the offered quantity at the observed price. Perhaps the quantity offered is too large or too small, or the buyer (seller) would have to wait for some time for a seller (buyer) to appear.

'Transparency' is defined by the degree to which investors can observe, without delay, recent trades in the asset (although the parties to the transaction themselves may remain anonymous). Why should market participants be interested in observing other trades in the asset? Presumably, because such information is relevant for forecasting prices in the future, or for determining whether a trade is likely to be executed at, or near, the reported price.

In terms of fundamental principles, quote-driven and order-driven markets should result in the same market price if all trades are made public. In practice, however, quote-driven markets tend to be more fragmented. Different dealers quote different bid and ask prices, and deals that have been executed are not necessarily public information or may be published only with a delay. Thus, order-driven markets tend to be more transparent than quote-driven markets, the existence of a limit order book tending to make the market less fragmented. Moreover, in those order-driven markets for which the limit order book is available to public view, the pattern of trades is normally easier for participants to discern. For example, the 'consolidated tape' in New York provides information about prices and quantities that have been traded.

Which type of market is the more liquid depends on a variety of considerations.[4] For instance, in a discrete call market, investors must wait until the next price fixing takes place. This restriction is not present for continuous order-driven markets, which also have the advantage that the orders of all participants in the market are consolidated.

Even so, investors may prefer the opportunity to negotiate individual agreements with dealers in quote-driven markets. This opportunity can be of particular benefit for investors trading large blocks of shares because of the scope for negotiating advantageous terms with dealers. Also, quote-driven markets may (depending on the rules governing the publication of trades) allow an element of privacy so that deals can be kept secret, if only for a limited time.

Are liquidity and transparency always desirable? An unqualified 'yes' is probably unjustified. Keynes in *The General Theory* (1936, p. 155) boldly voices his reservations.

Of the maxims of orthodox finance none, surely, is more anti-social than the fetish of liquidity, the doctrine that it is a positive virtue on the part of investment institutions to concentrate their resources upon the holding of 'liquid' securities. It forgets that there is no such thing as liquidity of investment for the community as a whole.

Keynes has highlighted what more recent literature would call an externality: a difference between private and social benefits. Liquidity might be beneficial for any individual investor but – because of its consequences for asset price fluctuations – costly for investors in general, and perhaps for non-investors too.

---

[4] In other words, whether a market is quote-driven or order-driven may not be the most important determinant of its liquidity. Other dimensions of trading mechanisms need also to be taken into account.

Keynes clearly thought he knew the right objective, if not the best policy. 'The social object of skilled investment should be to defeat the dark forces of time and ignorance which envelop our future' (p. 155). A few pages later he makes a hesitant proposal, but then seems to withdraw his endorsement of it (p. 160).

The spectacle of modern investment markets has sometimes moved me towards the conclusion that to make the purchase of an investment permanent and indissoluble, like marriage, except by reason of death or other grave cause, might be a useful remedy for our contemporary evils. For this would force the investor to direct his mind to the long-term prospects and to those only. But a little consideration of this expedient brings us up against a dilemma, and shows us how the liquidity of investment markets often facilitates, though it sometimes impedes, the course of new investment.

This passage points to the dilemma of balancing the advantages of liquidity against the prospect that restrictions on liquidity deter wealth holders from holding risky assets (thus hindering productive investment). In the event, since Keynes's day financial markets have – if anything – become, like marriage, more 'liquid'.

Rather less has been written about the desirability of market transparency. Just as for liquidity, however, there is reason to allow that unlimited visibility of the terms and conditions of all transactions might actually deter some trades – trades that could be interpreted as socially beneficial, at least according to some criteria.

2.3 Industrial organization of financial markets

2.3.1 Control of market institutions

Not all financial markets operate within formally constituted exchanges,[5] but those that do can be divided into two categories.

1. *Mutually owned* cooperatives. In this case the exchange is organized as a club, or cooperative, controlled and managed by its members. The cooperative controls the market's facilities (e.g. computer networks or dedicated telephone links), writes the market's rule book and administers the rules. The membership typically comprises 'member firms' (dealers) but, in principle, could include brokers and public investors.
2. *Shareholder-owned* companies. In this case a company, legally distinct from the market participants, owns and operates the exchange.[6] The company's shares could be privately owned (perhaps by another company); they might be owned partly or wholly by the state. If constituted as a public company, its shares would be openly traded. The exchange's member firms may wholly or partly own its shares.

---

[5] For example, foreign exchange markets are informal networks of banks and other financial companies, which make deals with one another for buying and selling different currencies. The emerging ECNs do not necessarily have any physical location. Even formal exchanges need not have a tangible, identifiable market place where participants meet to make deals.

[6] An example is *OMgroup*, which operates Stockholmsbörsen, the Stockholm Stock Exchange, and also provides technical exchange services to other exchanges.

Many financial exchanges started life as mutually owned organizations and remained so until the late 1990s. Examples include the LSE, the NYSE, NASDAQ, the CBOT, the London Metal Exchange (LME) and the International Petroleum Exchange (IPE).

Recent years have witnessed a trend towards demutualization – a trend that gathered momentum with most of the exchanges transforming themselves into shareholder companies. The LSE, for instance, became a limited company in March 2000 and became a listed company – on the LSE – in July 2001.

The phase of demutualization was soon followed by further restructuring in the form of mergers and takeovers. For instance, the IPE, which demutualized in 2000, became in 2001 a wholly owned subsidiary of IntercontintentalExchange, based in Atlanta, Georgia. In late 2001 the London International Financial Futures Exchange (LIFFE) accepted a bid from Euronext (a company that was itself formed in 2000 from the merger of the Amsterdam, Brussels and Paris exchanges).

This upheaval in the control of financial markets reflects the changes wrought by advances in information technology (reducing the costs of share trading), regulatory reform (encouraging competition) and globalization (promoting international capital flows). From their more traditional role as 'public utilities', stock exchanges are rapidly evolving from highly regulated organizations protected with monopoly powers into firms that face competition for the services that they offer.

Should it make any difference for their survival whether the exchanges are cooperatives or shareholder-owned?

Mutually owned firms (cooperatives) tend to operate in the interests of *existing* members – or of a dominant subset of members. They tend to be appropriate forms of organization when the owners of the businesses (the exchanges) are also their customers (the member firms, dealers or brokers). Thus, the members of cooperatives might seek to reward only existing members by (a) restricting the admission of newcomers; or (b) favouring one group of members over others; or (c) discriminating against other market participants (namely non-member dealers, brokers and public investors). Also, cooperatives have a reputation for resisting innovations (such as electronic trading to displace open outcry trading) that might damage the short-term interests of existing members.

Shareholder-owned companies are more likely to be motivated by profits, made by charging fees for the use of the market's facilities. They are less likely to be anxious about the potentially adverse consequences of technological and financial innovations, and also less likely to restrain competition among those who trade on the exchange – i.e. the member firms and non-member dealers. Indeed, exchanges might even seek to stimulate such competition if it results in a greater volume of trading and profits for their shareholders.

As already noted, the exchanges themselves now also compete with one another for business (share listings and trading volume). The nature and extent of this competition is affected by regulation as well as the underlying forces of technology.

2.3.2 Regulation of financial markets

Practically all financial markets are regulated in some way or another. The regulation is typically highly complex – too complex to warrant discussion here. Very often exchanges themselves form part of the regulatory mechanism, together with the involvement of external organizations. Thus, for example, the Securities and Exchange Commission (SEC) oversees financial markets in the United States, while the Financial Services Authority (FSA) has broadly similar responsibilities in the United Kingdom.

The declared purpose of regulation is normally to protect investors from practices and conduct deemed to be unfair or improper. Most directly, the protection is intended to guard against fraud. More indirectly, regulation ostensibly seeks to foster competition, with resulting benefits for the consumers of financial services. Investors themselves would possibly favour protection against *all* losses sustained on their investments, including losses incurred when asset prices fall. Such comprehensive protection stretches beyond the bounds of regulation that has been, or is likely to be, adopted. However, when losses occur as a consequence of what is perceived to be bad advice, investors may feel justified in seeking compensation – either from those who gave the advice or from the regulators responsible for overseeing the advisers. In these circumstances, resorting to litigation will test how far the law requires investors to bear the consequences of their own decisions.

Much of the regulation in financial markets is *self-regulation*. Whatever the merits of such regulation (such as the expertise of the regulators in their own lines of business), the justification of its proponents should not necessarily be taken at face value. For regulation can have its drawbacks. These include: (a) regulatory capture, in which regulation is designed to protect the regulated institutions rather than their customers; and (b) lax regulation, such that the activities of institutions may not be properly supervised.

2.3.3 Competition within and among financial markets

As already mentioned, many financial markets approximate the competitive ideal in that market participants typically take prices as given, beyond their individual control. However, although the underlying 'commodities' (the assets) are homogeneous, the services offered by brokers and dealers may well be differentiated, offering the scope for non-price competition. Moreover, the organization of exchanges and their regulation can have the effect of restricting competition among market participants.

Competition among members of the market can be restricted in several ways.

1. It is commonly necessary for members of exchanges to be able to provide capital as a guarantee against default or fraud. The capital requirement can be interpreted as a cost of doing business, but may be used as a device to limit competition by restricting the number of members.
2. The exchange may designate individual market specialists as monopolists in specified securities, in the sense that only the specialists can trade on their own account; all other members can act only on behalf of public investors. This monopoly power is usually regarded as compensation for the obligation imposed on specialists to quote firm prices guaranteed for trade with other market participants.
3. Members of an exchange may be restricted in their trading activities outside the exchange. For example, rule 390 on the NYSE requires its members to trade listed securities on the exchange rather than the over-the-counter market. The rationale for this type of rule is, presumably, that it restricts the extent to which investors can free-ride on the price discovery function of the exchange.

The merits of restricting competition are often difficult to appraise. Those who promote the restrictions tend to emphasize the benefits for the customers, though whether the customers would agree is another matter. Sceptics will recall Adam Smith's *Wealth of Nations* (Smith, 1776, p. 144):

People of the same trade seldom meet together even for merriment and diversion, but the conversation ends in a conspiracy against the public, or in some contrivance to raise prices. [...] The pretence that corporations are necessary for the better government of the trade, is without any foundation. The real and effectual discipline which is exercised over a workman, is not that of his corporation, but that of his customers. It is the fear of losing their employment which restrains his frauds and corrects his negligence.

Smith's 'prices' in this context correspond to the charges levied by the 'workman' (a member firm) on the 'customers' (public investors). Whatever the alleged merits of restricting competition, Smith cautions that the restraints can impose burdens on those who pay the resulting prices.

Even in markets with relatively free entry, such as NASDAQ, it is possible that dealers collude to increase their profits. Circumstantial evidence suggests that imperfectly competitive practices existed on NASDAQ at least for a time (see Christie and Schultz, 1994, and Christie, Harris and Schultz, 1994). Price quotations on NASDAQ are given in 1/8 points. If dealers act competitively, it can be argued that odd-eighths quotes (i.e. 1/8, 3/8, 5/8 and 7/8) should be observed as often as even-eighths quotes. There is evidence that odd-eighths quotes appeared less frequently than even-eighths quotes during some time periods. From this the inference was drawn that dealers were colluding (tacitly or otherwise) to coordinate their quotations in an anti-competitive way. A storm of indignant dissent and protestations of innocence (as well as an inquiry by the governing body of NASDAQ) followed this allegation. From among the various counter-arguments put forward, it is worth noting that *quoted* prices are not the same as *transaction* prices; many dealers, quite in accordance with the rules, execute 'preference trades' within their quoted bid–ask spreads (see Godek, 1996).

Competition *among* financial markets may also be the object of regulation. Governments may grant monopoly status to designated exchanges requiring that all trades in specified securities must take place on the exchange. For example, in Paris all trades must be channelled through the exchange (although it is permitted for agreements to be reached off the exchange). A rationale for this sort of concentration is that it internalizes an externality: the services provided by the market mechanism are costly and there is an incentive for market participants to free-ride once the services have been provided. Sometimes the regulation is justified in terms of promoting 'fair' competition among different market centres; an example is regulatory harmonization within the European Union.

The propensity of exchanges to collude may render regulation – supposedly to restrain 'unfair' competition – unnecessary. At the same time, collusion could make regulation more desirable in order to restrain exchanges' anti-competitive practices. Advances in technology (e.g. Internet trading) can also undermine collusive practices, drive down trading costs and stimulate competition for investors' buy and sell orders.

Takeovers, mergers and joint ventures have been promoted among the more traditional exchanges as a response to increased competitive pressures. For example, negotiations for a merger of the London Stock Exchange and Deutsche Börse took place in 2000, though they were subsequently aborted for a variety of technical, regulatory and commercial reasons. The rivalry among exchanges continues, and has intensified, with the arrival of electronic exchanges such as VIRT-X.

2.4 Trading and asset prices in a call market

Among the market mechanisms described in section 2.2, a call market is one of the simplest and provides a starting point for modelling flows of trading in asset markets. In the model outlined here, market participants are divided into three groups: (a) informed investors; (b) uninformed investors (or noise traders); and (c) market makers.[7] The informed and uninformed investors are interpreted as public investors, while market makers exist to ensure that a price that balances the

---

[7] The model is the simplest variant studied in the pioneering work of Kyle (1985).

purchases and sales of public investors is realized. Members of all three groups are assumed to be risk-neutral.

Exchanges of assets among investors could take place for a multitude of reasons, here divided into two: (a) an *information motive*; and (b) a *liquidity motive*.

The information motive applies to those investors who trade because they seek to make gains (or avoid losses) on the basis of their beliefs about future payoffs from assets. The liquidity motive is a catch-all, encompassing the other reasons why investors trade. It includes circumstances in which investors sell assets to raise funds for consumption or to meet some unforeseen contingency, or when savings flows are invested in traded assets. The caprice and whims that motivate noise traders are also absorbed into the liquidity motive.

In this model, both motives are attributed to uninformed investors whose actions are exogenous and random. The total amount they trade, U, is assumed to be a Normally distributed random variable with expectation zero and variance σ_u^2 – in shorthand: $U \sim N(0, \sigma_u^2)$. (The upper-case letters U and V are used to label random variables, while their lower-case counterparts, u and v, denote the respective outcomes – i.e. values drawn from the probability distributions.)

It is assumed that there exists exactly one informed investor, whose motivation is to profit from information, albeit imperfect, about the price of the asset.[8] Both the market makers and the informed investor believe (correctly) that the value of the asset, V, is determined according to a Normal distribution with expectation μ_v and variance σ_v^2 – i.e. $V \sim N(\mu_v, \sigma_v^2)$. The informed investor's advantage is knowledge of the outcome v (i.e. not merely knowledge of the distribution from which it is drawn – information that is also available to market makers).

The market makers do not observe v but do observe the *aggregate* trade, y, of the informed and uninformed investors. Neither the informed investor nor market makers observe the amount traded by uninformed investors, but both know the distribution from which it is drawn. Market makers are assumed to be competitive, in the sense that the price is chosen to maximize expected profit (conditional on y) such that the *level* of expected profit is zero – zero expected profit is the highest that can be achieved. (This implication would follow from assuming free entry into the market-making business.)

The steps in price formation are as follows.

1. The informed trader learns v and chooses the amount of the asset to trade, x, so as to maximize expected profits (being uncertain about the size of the uninformed investors' trade and the price chosen by the market makers, but knowing the market makers' behavioural rule).

---

[8] The 'value' and market price are not generally equal, as should become clear.

2. The trade of the uninformed investors, u, is determined randomly as a drawing from $N(0, \sigma_u^2)$.
3. Upon the receipt of the batch of market orders from investors, $y = u + x$, the market makers set the price.

Kyle (1985) now shows that the market price, $p(y)$, and the amount traded by the informed trader, $x(v)$, are given by

$$p(y) = \mu_v + 2\frac{\sigma_v}{\sigma_u}y \qquad x(v) = \frac{\sigma_u}{\sigma_v}(v - \mu_v) \tag{2.1}$$

Market makers observe the aggregate trade, y, but cannot infer its components, u and x, separately. Hence, the equilibrium price depends on y alone, not on u and x. The market makers are aware, however, of the way in which the informed trader processes knowledge of v. Also, the informed trader knows the mechanism by which market makers set the price.

What insights can be gleaned from this model?

1. The model shows how an asymmetry of information can generate trade and how market makers can set prices to equilibrate the market even though they have less information than the informed investor. (The market makers do observe the total volume of trade, y – a number which is not known by, or at least is irrelevant for, the uninformed investors.)
2. Suppose that the informed trader is 'important' in the sense that σ_v is large relative to σ_u. Then, if market makers observe a large positive y, the price rises significantly above μ_v. The reason is that market makers infer that, in this case, a large y means that the informed trader has information that v is high, and thus seek to avoid losses by setting a high price. But the informed trader knows that the uninformed investors don't vary their trade much (small σ_u). Hence, when v is known to be high, the informed trader limits the size of $x(v)$ (see equation (2.1)) – otherwise the market makers would raise the price above the level that maximizes the informed trader's expected profit.

   Conversely, suppose that uninformed traders are important, in the sense that their trade varies a lot – i.e. σ_u is large relative to σ_v. Now the price varies *less* with respect to aggregate trade, y, because the market markers recognize that most of the variation in trade comes from random fluctuations in uninformed investors' trades. At the same time the informed investor can exploit the 'smokescreen' of random trades from the uninformed investors and will issue a higher demand $x(v)$ (for each level of v), because the market makers will be less able to disentangle the trade of the informed investor from the uninformed investors. (Remember that the market makers observe only y, not its two components – the separate trades of the informed and uninformed investors.)
3. The model can be interpreted as a theory of *insider dealing*, the informed investor being the 'insider'. Despite the presence of an insider, Kyle shows that the asset

market is efficient in the sense that the market price equals the expectation of V *conditional on* y. This equilibrium is *semi-strong form* efficient in the sense that the market price reflects (is a function of) all publicly available information – y is public information, being known to all participants. *Strong form efficiency* would require that price equals v, but this almost surely never occurs in the presence of uninformed investors (i.e. $\sigma_u > 0$) – and, if no uninformed investors are present, all insider trades would immediately, and fully, reveal the insider's knowledge. (See chapter 3, section 3.3, for a discussion of semi-strong and strong form efficiency.)

Kyle's simplest model, outlined above, can be generalized in a number of ways without destroying its main insights. Kyle (1985) pursues the approach further by allowing for a sequence of auctions and, in the limit, to a model of continuous trading. Extensions to allow for more than one informed investor, however, do raise important questions about the impact of information. With more than one informed investor, there will be a tendency for competition among them to reveal their knowledge indirectly by affecting prices. Hence, the incentive to acquire information is blunted, if not eradicated. (See O'Hara, 1995, pp. 106–12.) Also relevant is the Grossman–Stiglitz paradox, outlined in chapter 3, page 71, below.

Kyle's approach, focusing as it does on order-driven mechanisms, does not address the determination of bid–ask spreads and the sequential formation of transaction prices in dealer markets. These are the subject of the next two sections, beginning with the role of inventory costs in section 2.5, returning to informational issues in section 2.6.

2.5 Bid–ask spreads: inventory-based models

Explanations of the bid–ask spread fall into two groups: inventory-based theories, and information-based theories. In each case market participants are classified into market makers and public investors. Market makers are assumed to be dealers who quote bid and ask prices at which they guarantee to buy and sell the asset (if the size of each order falls within a pre-announced range). Public investors are subdivided into informed and uninformed investors as in the previous section, though this distinction is relevant only for the information-based models.

The framework studied here abstracts from reality in a number of ways. Dealers who are not market makers are ignored. Brokerage services are not treated separately from the services of market makers. Hence, the bid–ask spread should be interpreted as including all transaction costs (such as commission fees and taxes). Also, phenomena such as deals made within quoted spreads and special arrangements for large block orders are neglected.

In both inventory-based and information-based theories, public investors are assumed to arrive at the market in a random flow and to issue orders to buy or sell one unit of the asset. The market makers execute buy orders at the ask price and sell orders at the bid price. Price quotations are then changed according to some rule, studied below, according to the market makers' observations of orders to buy or sell the asset.

Inventory-based models view the price quotations as determined by the need for market makers to hold inventories of the asset to satisfy the flow of demands and supplies from public investors. The main influences on the bid–ask spread are assumed to be these.

1. *Costs of holding inventories*. There is an opportunity cost of holding inventories, in the sense that the funds could be invested elsewhere. For physical assets (e.g. soya beans or precious metals) the cost of storage may be important, though storage costs are probably negligible for most financial assets.
2. *Market power*. To the extent that competition among market makers is restricted, the exploitation of their market power implies that bid prices are lower, and ask prices higher, than otherwise. Also, the costs associated with the privileges of being a market maker (e.g. the obligation to quote firm prices or the need to fulfil minimum capital requirements) would be covered by the bid–ask spread.
3. *Risk aversion*. Market makers, because of their obligations to the market authorities, or concern for their reputations, or for other reasons, may seek to avoid the prospect of zero inventory.

Other than implying the existence of a non-zero spread, the predictions of inventory models are rather weak.

1. It can be shown that the transaction prices, at which trades actually take place (the bid price when the market maker buys and the ask price when the dealer sells), say $p_t, p_{t+1}, p_{t+2} \ldots$, are such that their differences Δp_{t+1}, Δp_{t+2}, etc. are *negatively* autocorrelated. That is, increases tend to be followed by falls and vice versa (see Roll, 1984).
2. It can be shown that the size of the spread is a decreasing function of the volume of inventory. Note, though, that a market maker's volume of inventory is, itself, the object of choice. Hence, this implication is, in itself, not very revealing.

In spite of their weaknesses, inventory models are of value if sufficient detail is known about the market in question (e.g. about the random pattern of order flows). This knowledge could then be used to obtain more definite, testable, predictions.

2.6 Bid–ask spreads: information-based models

The information-based models studied in this section take it for granted that inventories are always adequate and that the costs of holding them can be ignored. Instead, the analysis highlights (a) the asymmetry of information between informed and uninformed investors, and (b) the assumption that market makers cannot observe whether the orders they receive come from informed or uninformed investors.

In order to focus attention on the informational aspects of price determination, assume that each market maker incurs zero transaction costs, is risk-neutral and has no market power. Thus, the framework is similar to that of Kyle (1985), studied in section 2.4. Here, however, there may be multiple informed investors, though the size of each order is assumed fixed at one unit of the asset. The market makers are assumed to receive orders sequentially, one at a time, in a random flow from either informed or uninformed investors.

When a market maker receives an order, it may have come from an insider who, by definition, knows more about the value of the asset than the market marker (and, thus, profits at the market maker's expense).[9] Alternatively, the order may have come from an uninformed investor who, by definition, is trading for some reason other than to exploit information about the value of the asset. In this framework, if only informed investors participate in trade, the market makers cannot survive and the market will collapse. But if the market makers have some knowledge, albeit imperfect, about the composition of the order flow then the market can be viable. In particular, the market makers are assumed to know the probability that an uninformed investor has issued an order.

One implication of the analysis is that each market maker will quote a non-zero bid–ask spread. To understand why this is so, consider the gains or losses made by market makers in trading with informed and uninformed investors, respectively.

In trading with *informed* investors, each market maker incurs an expected loss – by assumption, the informed traders know something that the market makers do not.

In trading with *uninformed* investors, each market maker would earn zero expected profits *if the bid price equals the ask price*. (This is because, by assumption, the market makers have no information advantage over the uninformed investors.) Hence, by quoting ask prices in excess of bid prices, the market makers can, on average, gain in their dealings with uninformed investors. This expected gain offsets the expected loss from trading with informed investors.

As in section 2.4, it is assumed that competition among market makers ensures that they break even on average – i.e. make zero expected profits. (This is a reasonable assumption in the presence of free entry, the absence of transaction costs and risk-neutral market makers.) Hence, equilibrium bid and ask prices

---

[9] Strictly, the value of the asset is a random variable even for informed investors. Their advantage is that they learn the outcome of the random variable before acting, whereas the market makers and the uninformed investors know only the distribution, not the outcome.

are determined such that the expected profit of market makers from uninformed investors just balances the expected loss from informed investors.

Not only is it possible to account for a non-zero spread, but *learning* can be built into the evolution of prices. The orders to buy or sell received by market makers contain partial information about the value of the asset – information that the market makers exploit in revising their bid and ask prices over time. It is this insight that is central to the contribution of Glosten and Milgrom (1985).[10]

Before trading commences at each date, every market maker begins with a *prior* belief about the asset's value. This prior belief is an input into the setting of bid and ask prices. An order to buy or sell is then observed and the market maker's beliefs are updated. Formally, the market maker is assumed to behave in accordance with Bayes' Law to obtain updated, or *posterior*, beliefs about the asset's value. These updated beliefs form the prior beliefs at the next trading date.

Several interesting implications follow from the analysis.

1. It can be shown that the transaction price follows a *martingale*.[11] (The transaction price is the bid price in the event of a sale to a market maker, or the ask price in the event of a purchase from a market maker.) Notice that the relevant set of information for this martingale is the set available to the market makers, not that of the informed investors. Notice also that, in principle, it is possible to compare the inventory-based approach with the information-based approach: the former predicts that the differences in transaction prices are negatively serially correlated, while for a martingale the differences are uncorrelated.

2. Given that (a) the informed investors know the probability distribution of the asset's value and (b) the market makers' beliefs are updated according to Bayes' Law, it then follows that the market makers' beliefs eventually converge to the probability distribution of the asset's value. That is, in a sense, the 'truth' is eventually revealed by the process of trade. This does not mean that a unique value for the asset is revealed, but, rather, that the probabilities associated with each possible asset value become known to the market makers and, hence, are reflected in market prices. In other words, the asset market is *semi-strong* form efficient at each date but tends in the limit to being *strong* form efficient as the sequence of trading dates becomes unbounded, so long as the underlying probability distribution of the asset's value remains unchanged. (See chapter 3, section 3.3, for a discussion of semi-strong and strong form efficiency.)

3. It is possible for the market to fail altogether in the sense that the market makers set the bid–ask spread so wide that no trade takes place. This can occur if there are too many informed investors relative to uninformed investors. Given that the dealer always makes a loss when trading with informed investors, it is possible that the

---

[10] A detailed survey of Glosten and Milgrom's model together with subsequent work appears in O'Hara (1995).
[11] See chapter 3, page 57, for a discussion of random walks and martingales.

bid–ask spread needed for the dealer to break even, on average, would have to be so wide that no one would wish to trade. This is an extreme example of 'adverse selection', in which the existence of asymmetric information destroys opportunities for mutually beneficial trades. (See Akerlof, 1970, for the pioneering analysis of market failure as a consequence of adverse selection.) Herein lies a possible explanation for the emergence – and disintegration – of asset markets.

Useful though it is, the framework outlined above is simplistic and needs extension in numerous ways, just three of which are as follows:

1. The model could be generalized to allow investors to choose the number of units of the asset they trade. This would enable predictions to be made about the impact of trade flows on asset prices, and also enable the study of the implications of transactions in large blocks of shares that often arise in institutional trades.
2. The model could be generalized so that informed investors take into account the effects of their actions on prices, thereby permitting strategic interactions between the informed investors and the market makers.
3. The flow of trade from uninformed investors has been assumed to be exogenous in the above. Although, by definition, uninformed investors cannot exploit information they don't have, they could choose the times of their trades. In this way it may be possible for uninformed investors to benefit, at least partially, from the information revealed by the actions of informed investors (see O'Hara, 1995, chap. 5).

These extensions make it possible to apply the information-based framework to more realistic conditions and also to generate definite predictions about price patterns. The main message of the information-based models remains, however, that the bid–ask spreads need not simply reflect the costs of doing business but also – and perhaps more importantly – that they depend on information asymmetries that exist among the investors, each of whom seeks to exploit available knowledge about the asset's value.

2.7 Summary

The study of the microstructure of asset markets is important for the insights it yields about how asset prices are formed and evolve.

1. Asset markets (in common with other markets) enable price discovery, provide a trading mechanism, and support the settlement of contracts.
2. Existing asset trading mechanisms are complex, though there is a handy distinction between quote-driven and order-driven markets. In principle, both mechanisms could provide the same degree of liquidity and transparency. In practice, quote-driven markets tend to be more liquid but less transparent than order-driven markets. Liquidity and transparency are normally regarded as desirable qualities, though their desirability should be accepted only with caution.

3. The rules and regulations of exchanges affect the competition among market partic-ipants and the services offered to public investors. A trade-off may exist between the competition among market members and the quality of service provided to public investors.

4. Asymmetries in information among investors can have an important impact on asset prices. The market mechanism can affect (a) the dissemination of new information and (b) the extent to which the information is reflected in transaction prices.

5. The inventory approach to bid–ask spreads explains the spreads with reference to the costs of doing business, the market power of dealers and their aversion to risk.

6. The information-based studies of bid–ask spreads focus on information asymmetries in explaining the size of spreads. Here, wide spreads (high ask prices relative to bid prices) reflect the importance of investors, whose information is superior to that of the market makers, whose responsibility it is to quote prices at which trade can take place.

Further reading

Spencer (2000, chaps. 4–6) surveys the literature on asset market microstructure and provides a concise overview of financial regulation. Harris (2003) provides a detailed description of the institutional aspects of asset trading, especially in US markets.

O'Hara (1995) presents a comprehensive and detailed analysis of the mecha-nisms by which asset prices are set, together with a bibliography of the litera-ture. Further insights appear in O'Hara (2003). On auctions, Klemperer (2004) provides an excellent entry point to the modern literature.

Spulber (1999) analyses firms as intermediaries in a broad context that encom-passes brokers and dealers in asset markets. For research on the industrial orga-nization of financial markets, Pirrong (1999, 2000) offers both theoretical and empirical insights. Lo (1996, especially chaps. 1, 2 & 7) is also worth consulting.

References

Akerlof, G. (1970), 'The market for lemons: qualitative uncertainty and the market mechanism', *Quarterly Journal of Economics*, 84(3), pp. 488–500.

Black, F. (1971), 'Towards a fully automated exchange, part I', *Financial Analysts Journal*, 27(4), pp. 29–34.

Christie, W. G., J. H. Harris and P. H. Schultz (1994), 'Why did NASDAQ market makers stop avoiding odd-eighth Quotes?', *Journal of Finance*, 49(5), pp. 1841–60.

Christie, W. G., and P. H. Schultz (1994), 'Why do NASDAQ market makers avoid odd-eighth quotes?', *Journal of Finance*, 49(5), pp. 1813–40.

Glosten, L. R., and P. R. Milgrom (1985), 'Bid, ask and transactions prices in a specialist market with heterogeneously informed traders', *Journal of Financial Economics*, 14(1), pp. 71–100.

Godek, P. E. (1996), 'Why NASDAQ market makers avoid odd-eighth quotes', *Journal of Financial Economics*, 41(3), pp. 465–74.

Harris, L. (2003), *Trading and Exchanges: Market Microstructure for Practitioners*, New York: Oxford University Press.

Keynes, J. M. (1936), *The General Theory of Employment, Interest and Money*, London: Macmillan (reprinted as Keynes, *Collected Writings*, Vol. VII).

Klemperer, P. (2004), *Auctions: Theory and Practice*, Toulouse Lectures in Economics, Princeton, NJ, and Woodstock, UK: Princeton University Press.

Kyle, A. S. (1985), 'Continuous auctions and insider trading', *Econometrica*, 53(6), pp. 1315–35.

Lo, A. W. (ed.) (1996), *The Industrial Organization and Regulation of the Securities Industry*, Chicago: University of Chicago Press.

O'Hara, M. (1995), *Market Microstructure Theory*, Oxford: Blackwell.
 (2003), 'Liquidity and price discovery', *Journal of Finance*, 58(4), pp. 1335–54 (presidential address to the American Finance Association).

Pirrong, S. C. (1999), 'The organisation of financial exchange markets: theory and evidence – costs and benefits', *Journal of Financial Markets*, 2(4), pp. 329–57.
 (2000), 'A theory of financial exchange organisation', *Journal of Law and Economics*, 43(2), pp. 437–71.

Roll, R. (1984), 'A simple implicit measure of the effective bid–ask spread in an efficient market', *Journal of Finance*, 39(4), pp. 1127–40.

Smith, A. (1776), *An Inquiry into the Nature and Causes of the Wealth of Nations*, Chicago and London: University of Chicago Press (ed. E. Cannan, 1904).

Spencer, P. D. (2000), *The Structure and Regulation of Financial Markets*, Oxford: Oxford University Press.

Spulber, D. F. (1999), *Market Microstructure: Intermediaries and the Theory of the Firm*, Cambridge: Cambridge University Press.

3

Predictability of prices and market efficiency

Overview

October. This is one of the peculiarly dangerous months to speculate in stocks in. The others are July, January, September, April, November, May, March, June, December, August, and February.

Mark Twain, *The Tragedy of Pudd'nhead Wilson*, 1894, chap. 13.

The extent to which asset prices in the future can be predicted on the basis of currently available information is a matter of great significance to practical investors as well as academic model builders. For academic researchers, the objectives are to obtain an understanding of the determination of prices and to find ways of assessing the efficiency of asset markets. For investors, the objective is to exploit their knowledge to obtain the best rates of return from their portfolios of assets.

The quest for profits implies, in an important though imprecise sense, that market prices should reflect all available information. If investors detect an opportunity to profit on the basis of information, then their actions (collectively, not necessarily in isolation) cause prices to change until the profit opportunity is eliminated. Considerations such as these motivate the famous martingale and random walk models studied in section 3.1.

Section 3.2 discusses much the same material, in the context of informational efficiency as introduced in chapter 1, while section 3.3 studies in more detail the differing patterns of information. Section 3.4 reviews several of the common asset market 'anomalies', so named because they are difficult to explain by conventional means and, hence, are often regarded as evidence of inefficiency. Finally, 'event study' analysis, outlined in section 3.5, serves to illustrate applied research on asset market efficiency.

3.1 Using the past to predict the future

3.1.1 Martingales and random walks

Perhaps the oldest and most well-known model of asset prices, the 'martingale' model has its origins in a system of gambling and is given a precise rendering by the mathematical theory of probability. In its simplest form the martingale model of asset prices can be written

$$E[p_{t+1}|\Omega_t] = p_t \tag{3.1}$$

where p_t denotes the price of an asset (say, one unit of a company's stock) at date t and Ω_t is a set of information available at date t.

For the moment, assume that Ω_t comprises all the past prices of the asset – i.e. $\Omega_t = \{p_t, p_{t-1}, \ldots\}$. In some applications, Ω_t is assumed to contain additional information (e.g. the prices of other assets, or companies' earnings data). The crucial features of Ω_t are: (a) that it contains only things that are known at date t; and (b) that it contains, at least, all current and past prices of the asset.[1]

Expression (3.1) asserts that the asset price evolves according to a random, or stochastic, process that can take any form except that the expectation of next period's price, conditional on information available today, equals today's price. This may appear innocuous enough. It is not. For, in general, a conditional expectation, $E[p_{t+1}|\Omega_t]$, depends on all the conditioning information (i.e. every element of Ω_t). For example, the expected value of the price of Microsoft's shares, conditional upon last year's rate of growth in the world economy, will, in general, differ according to whether the rate of growth was 1 per cent, or 2 per cent or 0 per cent. The martingale model asserts that this is not so and that *all* the information available as of date t is encapsulated in p_t alone – as a result of investors' actions, the information that influences their decisions is somehow reflected in p_t.

If the activity of investing is likened to gambling, then the ownership of the asset is viewed as participation in a *fair game*, in the sense that the expected gain or loss is zero. From (3.1)

$$E[p_{t+1} - p_t|\Omega_t] = 0 \tag{3.2}$$

In summary, the assumptions that imply that the asset price evolves according to (3.1) or (3.2) are: (a) investors believe that holding the asset is just like playing a fair game; and (b) they have access to the information contained in the set Ω_t.

---

[1] It is important in deriving the predictions of the theory that information acquisition also requires 'perfect recall' (no forgetfulness) – i.e. that information, once in Ω_t, does not subsequently disappear.

As expressed so far, the martingale hypothesis predicts that the expected rate of return on an asset equals zero: $E[p_{t+1} - p_t | \Omega_t]/p_t = 0$. Investment may or may not be interpreted as gambling, but, regardless of whether it is, most assets are assumed to yield non-zero – usually positive – expected returns.[2] Hence, (3.1) is replaced with the assumption that

$$E[p_{t+1}|\Omega_t] = (1+\mu)p_t \qquad (3.3)$$

where μ is a constant. (In probability theory, if $\mu > 0$, (3.3) is known as a *sub*martingale. For assets with limited liability, it is reasonable to assume at least that $\mu \geq -1$. Typically it is assumed that $\mu > 0$.)

Rearranging equation (3.3) gives

$$\mu = \frac{E[p_{t+1}|\Omega_t] - p_t}{p_t} \qquad (3.4)$$

so that μ can be interpreted as the expected rate of return from holding the asset, conditional upon information set Ω_t. In expression (3.4) it is assumed that the asset's payoff at date $t+1$ is equal to p_{t+1} – that is, any dividends or coupons are absorbed in the price. Alternatively, dividends or coupons can be treated explicitly by including another term in the numerator of (3.4).

The interpretation of μ as the expected rate of return can be seen more clearly by writing the rate of return, r_{t+1}, as

$$r_{t+1} = \frac{p_{t+1} - p_t}{p_t} \qquad (3.5)$$

It is important to recognize that r_{t+1} is assumed to be *random* – i.e. r_{t+1} takes on different values, each value being assigned a probability. The theory is silent about how the probabilities are assigned to the values of p_{t+1} and, hence, r_{t+1}. The probabilities might be interpreted as reflecting the 'true' underlying mechanism governing asset price fluctuations. But, if this seems puzzling (who or what determines truth in this context?), the probabilities could be interpreted

---

[2] No position is taken here about whether gambling should be condemned on moral grounds or whether it should be viewed as reckless or imprudent behaviour. Often those who promote the purchase of securities are keen to distinguish investing from gambling, perhaps to avoid potential condemnation. It is argued, for instance, that investment in stocks and shares differs from gambling because firms' equity represents 'real', 'productive' capital. While this may be true, a positive return on that capital is not guaranteed. Uncertainty about future gain or loss is obviously not attenuated merely by branding the commitment of funds as investment (good) rather than as gambling (bad). Alternatively, investing is sometimes distinguished from gambling on the ground that gambling is the mindless casting of money to fortune, while investment does – or at least *should* – involve exercising judgement and effort in the evaluation of various contingencies. From this perspective, betting on a horse race is not gambling if the punter devotes time to assessing the form of the horses and their riders.

as expressing degrees of belief about asset prices held by investors.[3] In any case, to repeat, the hypothesis is silent on this matter.

Given that p_t is an element of Ω_t (so that p_t is non-random with respect to Ω_t),

$$E[r_{t+1}|\Omega_t] = \frac{E[p_{t+1}|\Omega_t] - p_t}{p_t} = \mu \tag{3.6}$$

The force of the martingale hypothesis is the assumption that μ is a constant, in particular that μ does not vary with any element of Ω_t. This implies, using a fundamental identity in probability theory (the 'law of iterated expectations'), that the *unconditional* expectation of r_{t+1} equals the *conditional* expectation, and both equal μ:

$$E[E[r_{t+1}|\Omega_t]] = E[r_{t+1}] = \mu \tag{3.7}$$

The expected rate of return conditional on information available at date t equals the unconditional expectation of the rate of return. Thus, the information available at date t is of no value in predicting $r_{t+1}, r_{t+2} \cdots r_{t+k} \cdots$

There are several other ways of expressing the martingale model. For instance, from (3.7), $E[r_{t+1}|r_t] = \mu$ (because r_t is calculated from p_t and p_{t-1}, both of which are elements of Ω_t). Indeed, the reasoning can be extended to conclude that $E[r_{t+k}|r_t] = \mu$ for all $k \geq 1$ – that is, for all dates beyond the present. Similarly, $E[r_{t+k}|r_t, r_{t-1}, \ldots] = \mu$ (because Ω_t contains all past prices of the asset, from which its past rates of return are calculated).

Another way of writing (3.6) is

$$r_{t+1} = \mu + \varepsilon_{t+1}$$

where $E[\varepsilon_{t+1}|\Omega_t] = 0$. This turns out to be convenient in many applications.

The martingale model places only mild restrictions on the random process governing asset price changes – crudely, that the rate of return at one point of time (proportional change in the asset's price) provides no information about the rate of return at any later date, or, less crudely, that the rate of return is uncorrelated with any function of the return at any later point of time.

Most studies of asset prices stemming from the martingale model impose additional restrictions on the underlying probability distributions in order to obtain testable restrictions. The result is a set of *random walk* models that differ among one another according to the assumptions made about ε_t (or, equivalently, about r_t or p_t).

---

[3] Of course, the investors' beliefs could be the same as the true probabilities. It is legitimate, however, to be sceptical about what meaning can be attached to the notion of 'true' probabilities or the 'true' underlying mechanism in this context. The martingale model is, after all, just a model – an abstract idealization that provides a more or less accurate representation of events in the world. From this perspective, it makes little sense to dignify any model and its probabilities as being 'true'. The model – *any* model – is just a handy fiction, that's all.

Two of the commonest additional restrictions are (i) that the ε_{t+k} are *statistically independent* of one another for all $k \neq 0$, and (ii) that the ε_{t+k} are statistically independent *and identically distributed* for all $k \neq 0$. It can be shown that (i) implies, but is not implied by, the martingale hypothesis – hence (i) is a genuine restriction on the martingale hypothesis. Also, it is obvious that (ii) presents yet another restriction (because in (i) the distributions are not required to be identical).

The additional restrictions made to derive the random walk models provide greater scope for evidence to contradict the models. That is, for some sets of data, the random walk models might be rejected while the martingale is not. However, the random walk models do not have quite the same appeal as the less demanding martingale, because it is not altogether clear *why* the additional restrictions should hold. Even so, the random walk models are easier to test and, hence, are popular devices for exploring the data.

The models outlined so far are such close siblings that in what follows they are referred to, rather imprecisely, as the 'random walk hypothesis' (i.e. the distinctions among the variants are neglected).

Other models of asset prices

In order to make further progress in understanding asset prices, it is often necessary to make yet more restrictive assumptions about the underlying probability processes. The most famous of these is the assumption of *geometric Brownian motion* (gBm) – widely used in the study of financial derivatives, especially options.[4]

The mathematics of gBm are rather intricate but the basic ideas can be expressed as follows. Define the log-price difference as $y_{t+1} \equiv \ln p_{t+1} - \ln p_t$, where 'ln' denotes the natural logarithm operator. Now y_{t+1} can be interpreted as being approximately equal to the rate of return on the asset, defined above in equation (3.5): $r_{t+1} = (p_{t+1} - p_t)/p_t$ (the approximation being closer the smaller the rate of return or the shorter the time interval).

The gBm assumption implies not only that the asset's rate of return, approximated by y_{t+1}, is identically and independently distributed across time but also that y_{t+1} obeys the *Normal distribution*, a cornerstone of probability theory. In fact, gBm goes even further and assumes that the rate of return is independently, identically and Normally distributed no matter how short the interval between price observations. More formally, suppose that $s > 0$ denotes an interval of time,

---

[4] Geometric Brownian motion is also variously known as logarithmic Brownian motion or as the logarithmic Wiener–Einstein process.

perhaps arbitrarily small, then $y_{t+s} \equiv \ln p_{t+s} - \ln p_t$ is distributed Normally and independently of the log-price difference for every other time interval.

Being based on the Normal distribution, gBm is defined by two parameters: an expectation or 'drift' parameter, μ, and a variance or volatility parameter, σ^2.[5] The values of these parameters, particularly σ^2, have been subjected to a great deal of empirical scrutiny. In addition, models in which volatility, σ^2, changes over time or may even be infinite attract great interest in applied finance.

3.1.2 Empirical evidence

From the early twentieth century to the present many tests have been made of the random walk hypothesis of stock market prices in all its variants. Following the advent of inexpensive computers and the accumulation of plentiful data, the scope for such tests increased dramatically. Consequently, the ingenuity and energy of applied statisticians have resulted in the agglomeration of a bewildering mass of empirical evidence.

Many of the test methodologies share a common theme, namely to investigate the covariances of asset returns between different points of time. That is, the tests are based on covariances such as $\text{cov}(r_t, r_{t-s})$, for $s \neq 0$. The martingale hypothesis implies that $\text{cov}(r_t, r_{t-s}) = 0$, for $s \neq 0$. Indeed, appendix 3.1 shows that $\text{cov}(r_{t+1}, f(x_t)) = 0$ for every $x_t \in \Omega_t$ (i.e. x_t is any information known at date t) and where $f(\cdot)$ is any function of x_t. In a statistical sense, pairs of variables for which the covariances are zero are called 'orthogonal'. Hence, these procedures are known as *orthogonality tests*. They are common in applied econometrics.

More concretely, many of the tests are based on sample autocorrelation coefficients using a time series of data on an asset or portfolio of assets.[6] The martingale and random walk models predict that all these autocorrelations equal zero. Given a sample of data, the autocorrelations can be computed, together with formal statistical tests of the null hypothesis that they are equal to zero.

As with much empirical work, the statistical results are mixed.[7] The tests do, however, provide at least some evidence that the autocorrelations are non-zero, thus tending to reject the random walk hypothesis in one or other of its forms. That is, the evidence suggests that future asset prices are *predictable*, albeit with

---

[5] Formally, the expected value of y_{t+s} equals μs and the variance of y_{t+s} equals $\sigma^2 s$ – the expectation and variance are proportional to the length of the time interval. See Ross (2003, chap. 3) for an introduction to geometric Brownian motion.

[6] The autocorrelation coefficient between r_t and r_{t-s} is defined as the ratio of $\text{cov}(r_t, r_{t-s})$ to the product of the standard deviations of r_t and r_{t-s}, respectively. In applied work, the rate of return is often calculated as the difference in the logarithm of prices in adjacent periods – i.e. $r_t = \ln p_t - \ln p_{t-1}$. This can be interpreted as either (a) an approximation to the proportional rate of change of the asset's value, or (b) an exact measure of the continuously compounded rate of change over the interval $t-1$ to t.

[7] A thorough review of the evidence appears in Campbell, Lo and MacKinlay (1997, chap. 2).

error, from present and past asset prices. There is evidence that measured rates of return for *portfolios* of shares are positively autocorrelated over short intervals of time (i.e. high rates of return tend to be followed by high rates of return and vice versa, over periods of several months).

For the individual assets that comprise portfolios, the evidence tends to be more supportive of the random walk hypothesis. Negative autocorrelations of returns are commonly estimated, though they are often found to be insignificantly different from zero. The two sets of results are compatible if – as is observed – rates of return are positively correlated across the individual assets, some of the non-zero correlations being contemporaneous (i.e. for the same time interval), others being non-zero across both assets and time.

The random walk models presented above are silent about the correlations of rates of return across different assets. This weakness is addressed in more sophisticated models of asset prices, where correlations of returns across assets play an explicit, indeed vital, role. (This is so, for example, in the capital asset pricing model, discussed in chapter 6.)

Over longer intervals of time – several years or decades – there is evidence of *mean reversion*; i.e. 'long-horizon returns' are such that assets with low average returns tend to experience a rise in return, and conversely for assets with high average returns (returns being measured relative to a market average). This pattern of predictability is, of course, incompatible with the martingale and random walk models. But, beware. Small sample sizes (few observations) necessarily limit the inferences that can be drawn from studies of long-horizon returns.

Statistical inferences based on small samples are less reliable than for large samples. Even large samples may be of limited usefulness if a 'regime shift' (e.g. an abrupt technological change, a war or other political upheaval) is deemed to have altered crucial underlying parameters. As Paul Samuelson puts it (in a slightly different but closely related context; Samuelson, 1994, p. 17, italics in original):

We have only *one* history of capitalism. Inferences based on a sample of one must never be accorded sure-thing interpretations. When a thirty-five-year-old lost 82% of his portfolio between 1929 and 1932, do you think it was fore-ordained in heaven that later it would come back and fructify to +400% by his retirement at 65? [...]

It is a dogma, not a guaranteed fact, that financial data are generated by a *stationary probability* process. [...] The art of practical decision-making is to try to glean from experience what aspects of it are likely to have relevance for the future. The Bible tells us, 'There is a time to remember, and a time to forget'. But the Good Book does not inform us just how to ascertain those times.

Samuelson is careful not to dismiss statistical analysis as worthless but reminds us, yet again, that statistics should always be used with caution. In particular, making inferences from past data about the future is a much more delicate process, and more prone to error, than its practitioners commonly admit.

Tests of geometric Brownian motion have focused on (a) estimation of the volatility parameter, and (b), more generally, on whether the Normal distribution accurately models the observed data on log-price differences.

The evidence on volatility is clear: studies of the σ^2 parameter agree that it is not constant but varies across time for most assets. There is no consensus, however, about how its variations are best modelled. Many attempts have been made but no convincing empirical model of σ^2 has yet been found (and won't be until a plausible theory of variations in σ^2 becomes available to guide empirical studies).

The evidence on Normality also tends to tell against the assumption. While gBm appears to accord with the data for much of the time, observed asset prices are notoriously subject to occasional 'spikes' – sudden large price changes of a large magnitude either upwards or downwards. These phenomena lead to the inference that empirical frequency distributions of log-price change data have 'fat tails' – meaning that, compared with the Normal bell-shaped probability density curve, very high and very low observations are more common than would be predicted from a Normal distribution. Once again, many attempts have been made to develop models that account for such patterns of data, but none, as yet, commands widespread support as a replacement for gBm.

3.1.3 Security analysis

Investment managers and consultants often rationalize their success – or at least their survival – by being able to detect patterns in asset prices from which they can profit. That such patterns might occur is consistent with the evidence on random walks, and the endeavour known as 'technical analysis', or 'charting', involves the design of trading rules to exploit the profitable opportunities implied by the patterns.

Technical analysis forms one branch of security analysis. A second branch, sometimes referred to as 'fundamental analysis', focuses on predicting asset prices by identifying the underlying, so-called 'fundamental', determinants of rates of return.

Another illustration of security analysis is the claim that security returns are 'mean reverting' – that is, if a company's shares are highly priced (according to some – commonly unspecified – criterion) then they are likely to fall in the future; and conversely for companies the share prices of which are unusually low. It seems that such considerations might have influenced even Keynes in his investment decisions: 'My central principle ... is to go contrary to general opinion, on the ground that, if everyone agreed about its merits, the investment is inevitably too dear and therefore unattractive' (quoted in Skidelsky, 2000, p. 171).

From a casual viewpoint, claims that technical analysis enable profitable investment strategies are often interpreted as evidence of asset market 'inefficiency' – on the argument that fundamental analysis provides the benchmark for efficiency, and that fundamentals fail to explain patterns in asset prices. Allegations like this are widespread in finance. They can be misleading and require the detailed scrutiny undertaken below, in section 3.2.

3.2 Informational efficiency

3.2.1 Informational efficiency and the efficient market hypothesis

The concept of efficiency mentioned in the previous section is that of *informational* efficiency, introduced briefly in chapter 1. A standard definition is as follows.

A capital market is said to be efficient if it fully and correctly reflects all relevant information in determining security prices (*New Palgrave Dictionary of Money and Finance*, Newman, Milgate and Eatwell, 1992, Vol. I, p. 739).

The definition may seem precise enough at first glance, but it is incomplete and needs careful dissection to avoid misinterpretation. The two crucial phrases are 'fully and correctly reflects' and 'all relevant information'.

Beginning with the second phrase, it is necessary to be clear about what constitutes 'relevant' – and, by implication, *ir*relevant – information. From the perspective of efficiency, the set Ω_t (see above) comprises the relevant information. While past and current asset prices are, almost invariably, deemed suitable for inclusion in Ω_t, it may be appropriate to include other information as well. Conclusions about efficiency could differ according to what is included in, or omitted from, Ω_t.[8]

Hence, it is important to stipulate the composition of Ω_t when drawing inferences about efficiency. Section 3.3 outlines a standard classification for different compositions of Ω_t. The question remains, however: which particular set Ω_t should be used in assessing efficiency? Or, expressed differently, conclusions about the efficiency of asset markets (in the sense of the definition above) are *conditional* on the postulated set of relevant information.

---

[8] For example, it might be found that a company's share price is not correlated with its past earnings. This could be evidence of inefficiency if prices should reflect past earnings. But if past earnings are irrelevant – say, because the future is what matters, not the past – then the evidence is consistent with efficiency.

Sometimes fundamental information – and *only* fundamental information – is assumed to be included in Ω_t. This condition is a typical requirement in most versions of the *efficient markets hypothesis* (EMH). That is, evidence supports the EMH if and only if asset prices 'fully and correctly reflect' fundamental information. But this begs the question of what is, and what is not, 'fundamental' information. Without a criterion for separating what is fundamental from what is not, the distinctiveness of the EMH evaporates. Sometimes the EMH is expressed loosely without specifying what belongs to Ω_t – a looseness that broadens the generality of the EMH while doing nothing to resolve its ambiguity.[9]

In this context, the ideas of behavioural finance can be invoked to provide alternatives to the EMH. Thus, for example, noise traders can be treated as investors who do not use fundamental information or who otherwise fail to use it 'fully and correctly'. Interpreted in this way, noise trading is part of a general approach to studying the role of information (see Shleifer and Summers, 1990, or Shleifer, 2000, chap. 2).

Turning to the first phrase, 'fully and correctly reflects', a way must be found of distinguishing between those configurations of asset price changes that fully and correctly reflect the set of information, Ω_t, and those that do not. A model is needed to translate the information into predictions with which the observed asset prices can be compared. (The 'model' can be understood to comprise both (i) the information set *and* (ii) the theory linking information and the predictions. It seems clearer, here, to distinguish between the two rather than to lump them together.)

3.2.2 *Appraising efficiency: methodology*

The most important point established so far is that statements about whether asset markets are efficient, or inefficient, invariably rely on the criteria chosen to characterize efficiency – a trivial point but one that, when overlooked, is a source of confusion. Why? Simply because markets may be judged as efficient according to one set of criteria but inefficient according to another.

Where do the criteria for efficiency come from? They come from models of asset prices and associated information sets that together provide criteria for efficiency. Testable hypotheses about the patterns of prices compatible with efficiency are then derived from each model and information set. *These hypotheses depend on the chosen model and information set – and hence on the criteria for efficiency.*

---

[9] Scant attention is paid in finance as to whether information is reliable or, indeed, to address profound questions about how decision makers make sense of the knowledge that they have somehow acquired. If such matters are regarded as irrelevant or inconsequential, reflection on Bertrand Russell (2001) should serve to induce salutary discomfort about the analysis of informational efficiency.

Given a sample of data (typically observed prices and other relevant asset market indicators), statistical tests can be made of the hypotheses. If the hypotheses are rejected, the evidence favours inefficiency. If the hypotheses are accepted, the evidence favours efficiency.[10] This programme for assessing market efficiency is summarized in figure 3.1.

The relevance of an underlying model is asserted boldly by Eugene Fama:

The Theory [of asset market efficiency] only has empirical content ... within the context of a ... specific model of market equilibrium, that is, a model that specifies the nature of market equilibrium when prices 'fully reflect' available information (Fama, 1970, pp. 413–14).

... market efficiency per se is not testable. It must be tested jointly with some model of equilibrium, an asset-pricing model (Fama, 1991, pp. 1575–6).

Every appraisal of asset market efficiency depends upon a model of asset prices. Some researchers regard this requirement as trivially obvious. Others leave the model implicit or overlook the requirement. But a model is necessary to provide the criteria for distinguishing market efficiency from inefficiency. Even if the criteria are not stated, they are present. Even if a model is not formally adopted, it is implicit in the analysis. Why bother to make the model explicit? Because the inferences drawn from the evidence depend upon it.

Dependence on a model does not mean, of course, that all models are equally acceptable. Rather, it means that the conclusions about efficiency or inefficiency are neither more nor less reliable than the underlying model from which they are obtained.

Some models need few assumptions. For example, the absence of arbitrage opportunities is compatible with a broad range of investment strategies. The problem is that there are few instances when arbitrage reasoning can be applied unencumbered by considerations of risk or market frictions, with the consequence that whether or not a genuine arbitrage opportunity exists often remains in doubt.[11] Other models (a) rely on more assumptions, (b) can be applied to a broader range of phenomena and, consequently, (c) are more liable to rejection when confronted with the evidence.

Exactly what constitutes a convincing model is open to debate. For some people, a convincing model is one that accords most closely with observed behaviour, no matter how bizarre, crazy or misguided that behaviour appears to be. For others, a convincing model is one founded on how individuals ought

---

[10] For many careful statisticians, hypotheses are either rejected or *not rejected*. If the evidence does not reject a hypothesis, it does not mean that the hypothesis should be accepted, rather that the evidence is not against it.

[11] The same point is made, but from a rather different perspective, in Shleifer (2000, pp. 3–5, and chap. 4), where the concept of *risky*, or 'limited', arbitrage is introduced. The nature and implications of arbitrage are considered later, in chapter 7.

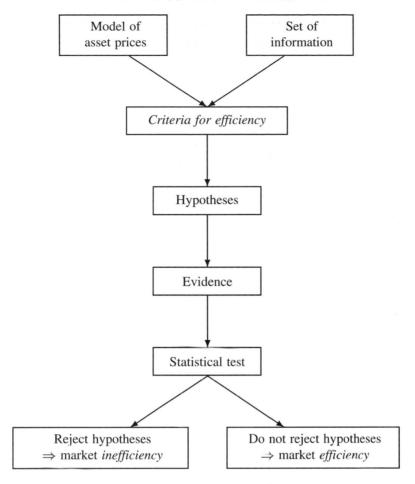

Fig. 3.1. A method for appraising asset market efficiency

Appraisals of market efficiency involve examining whether evidence about asset prices is compatible with criteria for efficiency. A model of asset prices, together with an assumed information set, generates the criteria. The criteria, in turn, provide testable hypotheses that, when confronted with evidence, enable inferences to be drawn.

to act, according to some set of normative behavioural criteria. In either case, a priori, theoretical considerations are unavoidable – and for the sake of clarity, at least, should be made explicit.

Suppose that a model is chosen as a benchmark to express asset market efficiency. If tests based on observed patterns of asset prices do not reject the hypotheses derived from the model, it is tempting to conclude that the asset market in question is informationally efficient. But (this is Fama's point) such an inference is inextricably bound up with the chosen model. Another model might generate different (even exactly contrary) inferences.

Different models are not necessarily incompatible with one another, of course. They may even make the same predictions (i.e. be observationally equivalent). In such circumstances, tests of efficiency are more robust because the results are not dependent on a single model. But it is not possible to escape reliance on some a priori modelling, no matter how widely applicable it might be.

A practical warning: every statistical test is susceptible to the well-known type I and type II errors (respectively, that a true hypothesis is rejected, and that a false hypothesis is not), though it is the investigator's responsibility to control these as far as possible. A particular weakness of many tests of market efficiency is that the *alternative* often remains unspecified or loosely defined. Thus, the question of which hypothesis finds favour when market efficiency is rejected is commonly ignored.

Relative efficiency

A neglected issue (both here and in the literature) is whether one market is more or less efficient than another (keeping in mind the caveats outlined above). That is, there is a question of *relative*, or *comparative*, efficiency. Comparisons might be between different market locations (e.g. Frankfurt versus New York), or different parts of the same market (e.g. bonds versus equities) or the same market at different points of time (e.g. Tokyo in 1990 and Tokyo in 2005).

In order to make inferences about relative efficiency, ways must be found of ranking various degrees of *in*efficiency. Market efficiency is then interpreted as an *absolute* characteristic – an absolute that is never attained in practice. Very little is known about relative efficiency. Much more research is needed before any confident inferences can be made, both about whether the concept is itself interesting and, if so, about the outcome of comparisons made according to any given set of efficiency criteria.

Summary

Tests of efficiency cannot be separated from the models and the information sets on which their predictions are conditioned. Appearances can deceive; *a test of efficiency is not model-free merely because the model is left implicit.* This does not mean that tests of efficiency are impossible or worthless. It does mean that the conclusions about efficiency must be conditional on the model that provides the criteria for efficiency – the conclusions can never be incontrovertible. Hence, the bold question 'are financial markets efficient?' is, at best, a rhetorical device to initiate debate. Unequivocal answers deserve to be treated with the utmost suspicion.

3.2.3 Beating the market

Informational efficiency is often defined in terms of the profits that could be made by exploiting information: 'A market is efficient with respect to a particular set of information if it is impossible to make abnormal profits (other than by chance) by using this set of information to formulate buying and selling decisions' (Sharpe, Alexander and Bailey, 1999, p. 93). Similarly: '... efficiency with respect to an information set, ϕ, implies that it is impossible to make economic profits by trading on the basis of ϕ' (*New Palgrave Dictionary of Money and Finance*, Newman, Milgate and Eatwell, 1992, Vol. I, p. 739; the symbol ϕ denotes the same set as the Ω_t used here).

In the quotations, 'abnormal profits' and 'economic profits' (both can be understood to mean the same thing) must be determined according to some criterion or another. They are not model-free; i.e. in common with every other test of efficiency, there must be a benchmark against which to make judgements about efficiency or inefficiency.[12]

In this approach to efficiency, the model provides the prediction of what constitutes 'normal profits'. If a sample of asset prices is found for which profits higher than normal can be obtained, these definitions imply that the market is inefficient (at least for the sample of data under investigation). Alternatively, the evidence could be interpreted as implying that the data reject the model (together with its information set) from which the prediction is derived.

In a similar vein, 'beating the market' corresponds to market inefficiency if decision rules (investment strategies) can be constructed to yield abnormally high profits. To 'beat the market' presumably means that there are criteria that define (a) the set of permissible decision rules and (b) the benchmark against which the rules are to be judged. This is where the model and information set are relevant.

If, for example, one decision rule provides a higher rate of return than another, and the latter represents 'the market' return, then the market has been beaten and is judged to be inefficient. Different representations of what constitutes the market lead, of course, to different conclusions. For example, 'the market' rate of return in a stock exchange might be interpreted as the rate of return on a portfolio of all the stocks traded in the market (suitably weighted according to each asset's share of the aggregate market capitalization). But, as will be shown in a later chapter, many models of asset markets predict the existence of a trade-off between return and risk. Returns that are higher than the market average can be obtained by holding a greater proportion of risky assets than is representative of the market.

---

[12] In constructing a benchmark, transaction costs could be important. For instance, a market may be inefficient according to a particular set of criteria but, in the presence of transaction costs, abnormal profits may not be available. Some benchmarks for efficiency assume that transactions costs are zero; others allow such costs to be positive.

It would be absurd to infer that the prospect of making higher-than-average returns, in compensation for bearing risk, implies that the market is inefficient.

Instead, it makes more sense to construct a model of the trade-off between expected return and risk (suitably defined) and then to test whether the data on prices are compatible with the predicted trade-off. If the data are compatible with the trade-off, this is evidence in support of efficiency – conditional upon the adopted model, of course. If the data are not compatible, then either the market is inefficient or the model is inappropriate (or both).

Note also the role of the information set. It may be reasonable to assume that more information is better than less for any individual investor who seeks to achieve the highest rate of return, given the actions of everyone else.[13] As already emphasized ad nauseam, definitions of efficiency are conditional upon the set of information (as well as, or in combination with, the chosen model).

What has not yet been addressed is the role or significance of informational *asymmetries* – i.e. circumstances in which some investors are assumed to possess superior information compared with others. The existence of informational asymmetries could in itself be interpreted as an attribute of inefficiency, though this is not common in the literature. Instead, the implications of such asymmetries, not merely their existence, for asset prices has attracted attention – as outlined in the next section.

3.3 Patterns of information

3.3.1 Weak, semi-strong and strong form efficiency

It has already been suggested that different information sets could lead to different, and possibly contradictory, conclusions about efficiency even in the context of what is otherwise the same model. To avoid confusion, it is helpful to link each claim about efficiency with the information set on which the claim is based. A conventional classification is as follows.

- *Weak form efficiency.* Here, the relevant set of information comprises all current and past prices (equivalently, rates of return) for the assets being studied. The simplest of the random walk models reviewed above (section 3.1.1) provide examples of weak form efficiency.
- *Semi-strong form efficiency.* This asserts that the asset market is efficient relative to all *publicly available* information. The rationale here is that there are sufficient investors who act upon publicly available information for their actions to result in observed prices that reflect the information.

---

[13] This sentence has been worded to avoid a trap: more information could benefit an individual investor but might make *everyone* worse off if the information becomes widely available and if, as a consequence, asset prices change when all investors act in their own, isolated, best interests.

As with every other test, it is necessary to use the information in the context of a chosen model of the asset market. The distinctive problem with respect to semi-strong form efficiency is to determine what constitutes 'public information'. This is more ambiguous than it first seems, for there may be wide disparities of information among investors according to how much effort they make to collect information (even if the information is in the public domain). Hence, inferences about efficiency could be contradictory depending on which information is deemed to be 'publicly available'.

- *Strong form efficiency.* Here, the assertion is that the market for an asset is efficient relative to *all* information. For an asset market to be efficient in this sense, even private information would be reflected in asset prices.

  Presumably, strong form efficiency follows from the hypothesis that any investor with private or *inside* information seeks to profit from that information. Strong form efficiency then requires that the actions of such privileged investors affect prices sufficiently quickly that the pattern of observed prices is as predicted by the model.

3.3.2 The Grossman–Stiglitz paradox

Up to this point, the distribution of information among all investors has been taken as given, determined exogenously and separate from the mechanism of price formation. If, however, investors with superior information can exploit their advantage, there is an incentive to acquire information.

If information is freely available, it is reasonable to assume that it is shared equally – that is, information is symmetric though not generally perfect.[14] This being so, and ignoring frictions in the price-setting mechanism, many models of asset markets predict that prices fully reflect the information that is available and common to all investors.

Suppose, instead, that information is costly to acquire. It is then plausible to assume that investors collect information up to the level that marginal cost equals the marginal benefit from acquiring it. Now, if the actions of the informed investors are fully reflected in asset prices, it would be to the advantage of any one investor to infer the information from the observed market price rather than to incur the cost of acquiring it. But every investor is in the same position as any other in seeking to infer the information from the observed price. Hence, no individual investor has an incentive to bear the cost of obtaining the information.

---

[14] 'Perfect information' could be understood to mean that prices in the future are known at the outset – i.e. with perfect foresight. More generally, perfect information could mean that all investors act as if they know the random process that generates future asset prices. The pitfalls in making sense of such an assumption are noted above, in footnote 3. Geanokoplos (1992) discusses the more profound issue of how information becomes 'common knowledge' when decision makers observe and take into account the decisions of others.

If no investor is prepared to bear the cost, the asset price cannot reflect the information that has not been collected.

This is the Grossman–Stiglitz paradox: if market prices reflect the information there is no incentive to collect it – just observe the prices. Only if prices do not fully reflect the information is there an incentive to expend resources in collecting it. In summary, Grossman and Stiglitz argue that 'because information is costly, prices cannot perfectly reflect the information which is available, since if it did, those who spent resources to obtain it would receive no compensation' (Grossman and Stiglitz, 1980, p. 405).

The implication of the Grossman–Stiglitz paradox is that strong form efficiency is a rare occurrence, likely to be observed only when all information is freely (hence symmetrically) available. More importantly, the paradox suggests that asymmetric information is probably commonplace in asset markets. This being so, investigations of asset market efficiency should explicitly allow for investors to act on the basis of different information sets. Yet again, modelling considerations are unavoidable in drawing inferences about informational efficiency. A framework suitable for analysing the propagation of information among investors – and consequently to prices – was explored above, in chapter 2.

3.4 Asset market anomalies

For a phenomenon to be an anomaly there has to be 'conventional wisdom' that the phenomenon violates. The conventional wisdom in this context is that certain patterns of asset prices should be observed. The phrase 'should be observed' is the warning that a model is lurking near, though perhaps below, the surface.

3.4.1 A catalogue of popular anomalies

There follows a list – representative, not encyclopedic – of asset price anomalies.

1. *Calendar effects.*
   (a) *The January* (or 'turn-of-the-year') *effect.* The shares of many small companies (those with a smaller-than-average market capitalization) tend to experience above-average returns in January, especially in the first half of the month.[15]
   (b) *The September effect.* It has been calculated that $1 invested in US stocks in 1890 would have grown to $410 by 1994 if the month of September had been excluded (i.e. selling in late August and buying back in early October). This is about four times the increase if the $1 had been invested for the whole of each year.[16]

---

[15] 'The turn-of-the-year effect occurs in the US with a very high degree of regularity, although since it became widely publicized in the 1980s, the effect seems to have diminished in magnitude' (*New Palgrave Dictionary of Money and Finance*, Newman, Milgate and Eatwell, 1992, Vol. III, p. 705).

[16] Based on calculations by J. J. Siegel (*Economist*, 1995).

(c) *Week-of-the-month effect*. Shares tend to show above-average returns in the first half of the month.

(d) *Monday blues*. Rates of return on many shares tend to be negative each Monday.

(e) *Hour-of-the-day effect*. On Monday mornings shares tend to show below-average returns in the first forty-five minutes of trading but higher-than-average returns during the early trading period for other days of the week.

2. *Weather and stock markets*. There is evidence that asset prices are positively correlated with sunny days. In a study of stock markets in twenty-six cities around the world for 1982 to 1997, Hirshleifer and Shumway (2003) find evidence that, the cloudier the weather on any day, the greater the likelihood of a fall in stock prices that day.[17] The magnitude of the price fluctuations is, however, sufficiently small that even modest transaction costs tend to outweigh the gains from trading strategies designed to exploit the effect of weather.

Is the association of cloudiness with asset prices an anomaly? It may seem implausible that the weather should affect investors' behaviour, but that there is evidence of such an effect is not as bizarre as it might seem. Psychological studies readily provide evidence that weather affects mood and, if mood influences trading decisions, then it is hardly surprising that asset prices are correlated with the weather. Is such investor behaviour 'irrational' (with results that could be interpreted as evidence of asset market inefficiency)? If the weather affects individual preferences and individuals respond consistently to their preferences, it hardly behoves economists (or anyone else, for that matter) to condemn the resulting actions as irrational.

3. *The small-firm effect, or size effect*. Evidence has been produced that small companies earn higher returns than predicted by models such as the CAPM (introduced later, in chapter 6). Reflecting on this finding, Black comments (1993, p. 37):

... it's a curious fact that just after the small-firm effect was announced, it seems to have vanished. What this sounds like is that people searched over thousands of rules until they found one that worked in the past. Then they reported it, as if past performance were indicative of future performance. As we might expect, in real-life, out-of-sample data, the rule didn't work any more.

4. *The high earnings/price ratio effect*. Companies with a high ratio of earnings to stock price appear to have shares that earn excess returns (again, measured against a common benchmark such as the CAPM). There is some disagreement about whether or not this is the 'size effect' in another guise.

5. *The closed-end mutual fund paradox*. A closed-end mutual fund is essentially a bundle of other securities that could themselves be purchased and sold individually.[18]

---

[17] See also Saunders (1993). For contrary evidence, see Loughran and Schultz (2004).

[18] The main difference between closed-end mutual funds (or investment trusts, as they are known in Britain) and the more well-known open-ended mutual funds (open-ended investment companies, or unit trusts in Britain) is that closed-end mutual fund shares are traded in the secondary market. Open-end fund shares are exchanged directly with the trust managers at values that reflect the current market prices of the component assets. Hence, the outstanding capital of open-end funds varies with new subscriptions and redemptions while that of closed-end mutual funds changes as a consequence of management decisions approved by the fund's shareholders. Also, closed-end mutual funds have discretion to borrow, thus creating leverage for their owners.

The closed-end mutual fund paradox stems from the observation that the market value of the funds often diverges from the current market value of their net assets. Consequently, the paradox is sometimes interpreted as a violation of the 'Law of One Price' (the prediction that two identical assets command the same market price).

Newly formed funds often sell at a premium above the value of the underlying assets, but the shares of those that remain in existence after several years frequently trade at significant discounts (that is, at prices below their net asset values). Most models of asset prices predict that, apart from a margin to allow for management expenses, the value of each fund should equal the sum of the values of the assets in the fund, net of any borrowing. Otherwise, if the shares of a fund trade at a significant discount, profits could be made by acquiring a controlling interest in the fund and winding it up (or by turning the company into an open-ended mutual fund).

There is evidence that, following publicity about the paradox, discounts on closed-end mutual funds declined, though they have not disappeared altogether. Also, the discounts tend to differ among funds in ways that prove hard to explain.

6. *Initial public offerings* and *seasoned equity offerings* (SEOs). Distinctive patterns of share price fluctuations have been documented following IPOs, when companies issue publicly traded equity for the first time. Initial returns on the shares, in the weeks immediately following an IPO, tend to be high (though the size of the short-term gain is thought to vary cyclically across time). Over time-spans of several years the shares of IPOs are observed, on average, to underperform relative to conventional market benchmarks. The price patterns for SEOs – shares issued to raise additional funds for an existing publicly traded company – are not dissimilar, though perhaps less pronounced.

Three questions have been proposed for appraising the significance of anomalies.[19]

1. Is the anomaly 'real', in the sense of arising repeatedly in similar circumstances, rather than a one-off quirk or oddity?
2. Is there a mechanism that could explain the anomaly?
3. Does the anomaly represent a substantive phenomenon, of importance, rather than a mere curiosity?

A feature of many financial anomalies is that they tend to disappear soon after evidence of their existence enters the public domain. An example is the small-firm effect – and also, to an extent, the closed-end mutual fund paradox. The tendency of anomalies to evaporate may occur either because they signal profitable investment opportunities, which disappear when they become widely known, or because they were never genuine, in the sense that only a few studies could detect their presence.

---

[19] V. S. Ramachandran put forward the criteria in his BBC Reith Lectures (Ramachandran, 2003, p. 73). Although Ramachandran's lectures were on neurophysiology, his criteria are relevant here too.

As for the second question, the very *absence* of a mechanism, or theory, to account for a phenomenon in finance is commonly the justification adduced for identifying it as an anomaly. Thus, 'exceptions to the current body of knowledge may be incorporated into that body of knowledge and become tomorrow's conventional wisdom' (*New Palgrave Dictionary of Money and Finance*, Newman, Milgate and Eatwell, 1992, Vol. III, p. 573). But, in finance at least, there is more to anomalies than this, given that they are typically supposed to represent asset market inefficiencies – an explanation for an observed phenomenon could be accepted as conventional wisdom yet remain excluded from the realm of models that express market efficiency. (This appears to be so for many models in behavioural finance.)

Finally, there is the question of whether phenomena that satisfy the first two criteria are of substantive significance. In some cases, such as the price patterns observed after IPOs, it is generally accepted that the consequences can have an important impact on the companies issuing shares and their promoters. However, others – such as some of the calendar effects or weather effects – probably add little to an understanding of financial principles or have negligible impact on decision making. Moreover, even if they might potentially be substantive, their magnitudes may be so small (relative, say, to transaction costs) that their impact can safely be ignored.

In summary, the study of anomalies provides a fruitful way of learning more about financial systems, but rather as a spur to further analysis and investigation than as an end in itself.

3.5 Event studies

An 'event study' refers to a particular method of testing predictions derived from a model. The 'event' being studied is a well-defined incident, such as a takeover bid by one company for another. Associated with the event are observations such as, for example, data on the companies' share prices near to the date of the event. These observations are compared with the predicted outcome for the type of event under investigation. Inferences can then be drawn about whether the data are consistent with the model's predictions. Statistical test procedures provide the formal criteria for deciding whether the predictions are compatible with the data.

Event studies are widely used in assessments of market efficiency, but they could be, and have been, employed in many other contexts. In the market efficiency applications, the chosen model embodies the criteria for efficiency. If the predictions are borne out in the data, this is interpreted as evidence in support of efficiency (conditional on the criteria, of course). Conversely, if the data and predictions are incompatible, this is evidence of inefficiency (again, given the specified criteria).

Near to midnight on 14 April 1912 the ocean liner *Titanic*, on her maiden voyage, struck an iceberg in the north Atlantic and sank – an event that startled the world. The loss of the *Titanic* was, presumably, unanticipated by investors in the vessel's parent company, the share price of which fell when the news broke. Khanna (1998) addresses the question of whether the fall in the price of the company's shares accurately reflected the loss incurred as a result of the disaster. After allowing for the insured portion of the loss and for overall stock market price movements, Khanna's calculations suggest that the reduction in the market value of the company approximated the loss that it sustained. While the result can be interpreted as evidence of market efficiency, Khanna is careful to caution that such an inference has been made using a sample containing just a single observation.

Stock splits provide more readily available opportunities for event studies. A 'stock split' involves a redefinition of the units in which a company's stock is measured – for example, each existing share becomes two new shares in a two-for-one split. Most models of asset prices predict that stock splits should have no effect on the company's total market value. This implication follows simply from the recognition that a stock split does not, in itself, change any real asset of the company; it is merely a bookkeeping exercise (albeit one that is made for a purpose: typically, that it enables the equity of the company to be traded in smaller units).

Suppose that, when a stock split occurs, the market value of the company is observed to increase. (Such observations are, apparently, quite common.) Is this evidence of market inefficiency? The answer depends partly on how carefully the test has been made. For it could be that the event (the stock split) and the observations (higher share prices) are both consequences of a third influence, such as improved company profitability. Of course, the tests can and should be designed to control for the simultaneous occurrence of all relevant factors. Even so, the omission of potentially relevant explanatory variables should be a warning against making careless and extravagant inferences from event studies.

Event studies are instructive because the models upon which they rely are typically widely applicable and, hence, yield uncontroversial predictions. Fama (1991, p. 1602) concludes that 'event studies are the cleanest evidence we have on efficiency (the least encumbered by the joint-hypothesis problem). With few exceptions, the evidence is supportive.' By 'joint-hypothesis problem' Fama refers to the impossibility of separating appraisals of market efficiency from the assumed model of asset prices. Fama's assertion about the 'cleanest evidence' can be understood to mean that the evidence is compatible with many different models of asset price determination – i.e. the results are robust to the choice of model.

Stock splits are prominent in event studies because most models predict that splits, on their own, have no effect on the company's market value. There is, thus, a broad consensus about what should be observed if the market is efficient. Other event studies tend to involve rather more controversial models.

For example, suppose that a company executes a debt-for-equity swap – the company issues bonds and uses the funds to buy back some of its equity. The Modigliani–Miller theorem predicts that such a swap should have no effect on the total market value (equity plus debt) of the company.[20] But suppose that it is observed that debt-for-equity swaps are correlated with an *increase* in the market value of the company. What inference can be drawn? Perhaps the Modigliani–Miller theorem is invalid – not in the sense that its logic is at fault, but because its predictions follow from assumptions that are themselves implausible. Is this evidence of market inefficiency? Yes, if the assumptions of the Modigliani–Miller theorem define the criteria for efficiency. No, not necessarily, if other criteria are used to characterize efficiency. Another possibility is that the Modigliani–Miller theorem does hold but the swap occurred concurrently with some other event that affected the company's market value (e.g. news about its profitability). This sort of problem has already been described in the context of stock splits.

In summary, although the elegant methodology of event studies yields valuable evidence about asset market efficiency, it does not differ in principle from other tests. If event studies do have a distinctive advantage over other methods, it is largely because they offer an opportunity to make clear, unambiguous inferences applicable to broad classes of models. From a formal statistical perspective, however, sample sizes tend to be small and, hence, the tests are more vulnerable to errors of inference.

3.6 Summary

Every investor would like to possess the capacity to forecast asset prices better than anyone else. Almost all investors are doomed to disappointment. This chapter has sought to explain why. The most important reasons are these.

1. Tests of market efficiency, or inefficiency, are always tests of models that are chosen to represent efficient markets.
2. The martingale and random walk models of asset prices are motivated by the supposition that investors seek to exploit any profit opportunities and that prices adjust in response. This being so, asset prices should be unpredictable on the basis of currently available information.

---

[20] See chapter 18, section 18.6, for a statement of the Modigliani–Miller theorem.

3. Much of the empirical evidence finds against the random walk models and, hence, implies that prices are, at least to some extent, predictable. The patterns of predictability do, however, themselves vary across time.

4. Appraisals of asset market efficiency often rely on random walk models. Given the evidence, the implication follows that asset markets are *in*efficient. Such a conclusion is premature because other models might, arguably, provide more suitable criteria for efficiency.

   Even when the evidence favours a random walk model, it is not safe to conclude that markets are efficient. Why not? Because the evidence may be compatible with models that are considered to represent *in*efficiency (see chapter 10, section 10.3. As a result, claims about efficiency, or inefficiency, should be treated with caution, especially when they are unaccompanied by a statement of the criteria adopted to separate efficiency from inefficiency.

5. Judgements about informational efficiency also need to take heed of the different quantities and qualities of information available to predict asset prices. Moreover, in some contexts the existence of asset market equilibrium may require the presence of asymmetries of information across investors.

6. Asset price anomalies highlight phenomena that are incompatible with conventional wisdom. Some anomalies survive but, once publicized, the phenomena may disappear, or be absorbed into conventional wisdom.

7. Event studies provide a flexible and attractive method for studying propositions about asset prices in general and informational efficiency in particular. While not model-free, event studies can often be designed to be compatible with many different models of asset prices.

Further reading

The statistical analysis of asset prices from the time series perspective of section 3.1 has a long and illustrious history. An excellent, though advanced, survey of modern research is provided by Campbell, Lo and MacKinlay (1997, chap. 2).

The history of empirical studies exploring the randomness, or otherwise, of stock prices is intertwined with arguments about efficiency. For a collection of early influential contributions, particularly Louis Bachelier's pioneering thesis on the *Theory of Speculation* (presented in 1900), see Cootner (1964). Mandelbrot (1997, 2000) provides an illustration of ongoing research pursuing one potentially fruitful line of inquiry – the multifractal modelling of asset price fluctuations.

Most finance texts discuss asset market efficiency, though not all acknowledge its reliance on a priori model building. Among the more reliable textbooks is that by Elton, Gruber, Brown and Goetzmann (2003, chap. 17). The early survey papers produced by Fama (1970, 1991) contain many valuable insights, as does Fama (1998). In the more recent popular literature, Shiller (2000) presents a forthright critique of stock markets from the perspective of an acknowledged expert. Shiller (2003) and Malkiel (2003a) bring the debates up to date from contrary viewpoints.

The voluminous body of work on asset market anomalies continues to expand, with the addition of newly discovered oddities in price patterns. Useful starting points are the entries on 'stock market anomalies', 'going public' and 'seasoned equity issues' in *The New Palgrave Dictionary of Money and Finance* (Newman, Milgate and Eatwell, 1992). For discussions of closed-end mutual funds, see Lee, Shleifer and Thaler (1990), Malkiel (2003b) and, in particular, Shleifer (2000, chap. 3). Fama (1998) provides a critical assessment of anomalies and their links with informational efficiency.

A seminal contribution to the analysis of stock splits and event studies is that of Fama, Fisher, Jensen and Roll (1969). For a careful exposition of the methodology of event studies in finance, with several illustrations, see MacKinlay (1997) or Campbell, Lo and MacKinlay (1997, chap. 4).

Appendix 3.1: The law of iterated expectations and martingales

This appendix explains why the martingale result, $E[r_{t+1}|\Omega_t] = \mu$, where μ is the unconditional expectation of r_{t+1}, implies that $\text{cov}(r_{t+1}, f(x_t)) = 0$, for any function $f(\cdot)$ and any $x_t \in \Omega_t$.

The result follows directly from the 'law of iterated expectations' in probability theory. The law of iterated expectations states that

$$E[E[Y|X]] = E[Y] \tag{3.8}$$

where X and Y are any two random variables (with finite expectations). The expression $E[Y|X]$ denotes the expectation of Y conditional upon a given value of X. The value of $E[Y|X]$ depends on the value of X.

Now it is possible to compute the expectation of $E[Y|X]$ with respect to the random variable X. (That is, $E[Y|X]$ is treated as a random variable – because X is random – and its expectation is calculated.) The law of iterated expectations, (3.8), asserts that this expectation of the conditional expectation equals the *unconditional* expectation of Y.[21]

To show that $\text{cov}(r_{t+1}, f(x_t)) = 0$, begin with the conditional expectation of r_{t+1}:

$$E[r_{t+1}|f(x_t)] = \mu \tag{3.9}$$

---

[21] See Grimmett and Stirzaker (2001, especially chaps. 3, 4 & 12) for a thorough analysis of conditional expectations and the mathematical theory of martingales.

where $E[r_{t+1}] = \mu$, $x_t \in \Omega_t$ and, hence, $f(x_t) \in \Omega_t$. For notational convenience define z_t as $z_t \equiv f(x_t)$, with expectation $\mu_z \equiv E[z_t] = E[f(x_t)]$. Therefore, (3.9) can be written $E[(r_{t+1} - \mu)|z_t] = 0$.

The covariance between r_{t+1} and z_t is defined by

$$\text{cov}(r_{t+1}, z_t) \equiv E[(r_{t+1} - \mu)(z_t - \mu_z)]$$

which is shown to equal zero as follows:

$$E[(r_{t+1} - \mu)(z_t - \mu_z)] = E[E[(r_{t+1} - \mu)(z_t - \mu_z)|z_t]] \qquad (3.10)$$

$$= E[(z_t - \mu_z)E[(r_{t+1} - \mu)|z_t]] \qquad (3.11)$$

$$= E[(z_t - \mu_z)0]$$

$$= 0$$

Equation (3.10) applies the law of iterated expectations, with $Y = (r_{t+1} - \mu)(z_t - \mu_z)$ and $X = z_t$. In (3.11), $(z_t - \mu_z)$ can be factored out of the expectation because, by construction, it is constant with respect to the *conditional* expectation. The result then follows from the hypothesis that $E[(r_{t+1} - \mu)|z_t] = 0$. Hence, as claimed, $\text{cov}(r_{t+1}, f(x_t)) = 0$. Note that $f(x_t)$ includes any function of any of the information in Ω_t. Hence, it certainly implies that $\text{cov}(r_{t+1}, r_t) = 0$, as asserted.

References

Black, F. (1993), 'Estimating expected return', *Financial Analysts Journal*, 49(5), pp. 36–8.

Campbell, J. Y., A. W. Lo and A. C. MacKinlay (1997), *The Econometrics of Financial Markets*, Princeton, NJ: Princeton University Press.

Cootner, P. H. (ed.) (1964), *The Random Character of Stock Market Prices*, Cambridge, MA: MIT Press.

Economist, The (1995), 2 September, p. 108.

Elton, E. J., M. J. Gruber, S. J. Brown and W. N. Goetzmann (2003), *Modern Portfolio Theory and Investment Analysis*, New York: John Wiley & Sons, 6th edn.

Fama, E. F. (1970), 'Efficient capital markets: a review of theory and empirical work', *Journal of Finance*, 25(2), pp. 383–417.

   (1991), 'Efficient capital markets II', *Journal of Finance*, 46(5), pp. 1575–1617.

   (1998), 'Market efficiency, long-term returns and behavioral finance', *Journal of Financial Economics*, 49(3), pp. 283–306.

Fama, E. F., L. Fisher, M. Jensen and R. Roll (1969), 'The adjustment of stock prices to new information', *International Economic Review*, 10(1), pp. 1–21.

Geanakoplos, J. (1992), 'Common knowledge', *Journal of Economic Perspectives*, 6(4), pp. 53–82.

Grimmett, G., and D. Stirzaker (2001), *Probability and Random Processes*, Oxford: Oxford University Press, 3rd edn.

Grossman, S. J., and J. E. Stiglitz (1980), 'On the impossibility of informationally efficient markets', *American Economic Review*, 70(3), pp. 393–408.

Hirshleifer, D., and T. Shumway (2003), 'Good day sunshine: stock returns and the weather', *Journal of Finance*, 58(3), pp. 1009–32.

Khanna, A. (1998), 'The *Titanic*: the untold economic story', *Financial Analysts Journal*, 54(5), pp. 16–17.

Lee, C. M. C., A. Shleifer and R. H. Thaler (1990), 'Anomalies: closed-end mutual funds', *Journal of Economic Perspectives*, 4(4), pp. 153–64.

Loughran, T., and P. H. Schultz (2004), 'Weather, stock returns, and the impact of localized trading behavior', *Journal of Financial and Quantitative Analysis*, 39(2), pp. 343–64.

MacKinlay, A. C. (1997), 'Event studies in economics and finance', *Journal of Economic Literature*, 35(1), pp. 13–39.

Malkiel, B. G. (2003a), 'The efficient market hypothesis and its critics', *Journal of Economic Perspectives*, 17(1), pp. 59–82.

(2003b), *A Random Walk Down Wall Street*, New York: W. W. Norton, revised and updated edition.

Mandelbrot, B. B. (1997), *Fractals and Scaling in Finance: Discontinuity, Concentration, Risk*, New York: Springer.

(2000), *Cartoons of the Variation of Financial Prices and of Brownian Motions in Multifractal Time*, Cowles Foundation Discussion Paper no. 1256, Yale University.

Newman, P., M. Milgate and J. Eatwell (eds.) (1992), *The New Palgrave Dictionary of Money and Finance*, London: Macmillan (three volumes).

Ramachandran, V. S. (2003), *The Emerging Mind: The BBC Reith Lectures 2003*, London: Profile Books.

Ross, S. M. (2003), *An Elementary Introduction to Mathematical Finance: Options and Other Topics*, Cambridge: Cambridge University Press, 2nd edn.

Russell, B. (2001), *The Problems of Philosophy*, Oxford: Oxford University Press (first pub. 1912).

Samuelson, P. A. (1994), 'The long-term case for equities. And how it can be oversold', *Journal of Portfolio Management*, 21(1), pp. 15–24.

Saunders, E. M. (1993), 'Stock prices and Wall Street weather', *American Economic Review*, 83(5), pp. 1337–45.

Sharpe, W. F., G. J. Alexander and J. V. Bailey (1999), *Investments*, Englewood Cliffs, NJ: Prentice Hall International, 6th edn.

Shiller, R. J. (2000), *Irrational Exuberance*, Princeton, NJ, and Oxford: Princeton University Press.

(2003), 'From efficient markets to behavioral finance', *Journal of Economic Perspectives*, 17(1), pp. 83–104.

Shleifer, A. (2000), *Inefficient Markets: An Introduction to Behavioral Finance*, Oxford: Oxford University Press.

Shleifer, A., and L. H. Summers (1990), 'The noise trader approach to finance', *Journal of Economic Perspectives*, 4(2), pp. 19–33.

Skidelsky, R. (2000), *John Maynard Keynes*, Vol. III, *Fighting for Britain, 1937–1946*, London: Macmillan.

4

Decision making under uncertainty

Overview

It is universally acknowledged that uncertainty is pervasive in everyday life and, hence, in economic decision making. What is not universally accepted, however, is how to explain decision making under uncertainty, all the candidate models being recognized as unrealistic for some reason or another. By their nature, of course, all models are abstractions and, in some degree, unrealistic. A particular difficulty with uncertainty is that every model proposed, up to the present, has been the target of penetrating criticism. That said, the *expected utility hypothesis* (EUH), outlined in section 4.2, remains the most popular approach to uncertainty in economics. Two close relatives of the EUH, also studied in this chapter, are: (a) the *state-preference* model, and (b) the *mean-variance* model.

The expected utility hypothesis can be interpreted as a special case of the state-preference model (though such an interpretation is not mandatory). Similarly, the mean-variance model (studied in section 4.4) can be interpreted as a special case of the EUH. Thus, the three approaches form a hierarchy, with state-preference being the most general and mean-variance the least. The reason why all three deserve consideration is simple: more general models are applicable to a broader range of phenomena but make fewer definite predictions; more special models apply more narrowly but make more definite (and, hence, testable) predictions.

Section 4.3 digresses from the main theme to review briefly some of the influential but less mainstream approaches to decision making under uncertainty.

Risk and uncertainty

Frank Knight (1885–1962), in his classic *Risk, Uncertainty and Profit* (1921), distinguishes between the concepts of risk and uncertainty. He applies the notion of risk to those unknown events for which 'objective probabilities' can be assigned.

Uncertainty, on the other hand, Knight applies to events for which such probabilities cannot be assigned, or for which it would not make sense to assign them. Keynes takes a similar view (1936–37, pp. 213–14):

> By 'uncertain' knowledge ... I do not mean merely to distinguish what is known for certain from what is only probable. The game of roulette is not subject, in this sense, to uncertainty; [...] The sense in which I am using the term is that in which the prospect of a European war is uncertain, or the price of copper and the rate of interest twenty years hence, or the obsolescence of a new invention. [...] About these matters, there is no scientific basis on which to form any calculable probability whatever. We simply do not know.

Had he lived in a later age, Keynes might have added climate change to his list, along with its associated environmental catastrophes.

Following Knight, a game of chance is risky because, although the outcome of any one trial is unknown in advance, repetition of the game a large number of times enables observed relative frequencies to be interpreted sensibly as objective probabilities. Uncertain events, by contrast, are those that cannot be repeated in any controlled way, thus rendering the calculation of relative frequencies difficult, if not impossible. Even worse, the very definition of the uncertain event may be problematical – few, in Keynes's time, could have conceived of global warming or could have described its potential consequences.

These difficulties need not imply, however, that probabilities have no role in the analysis of uncertainty. For it can be shown that, if individuals act in accordance with a set of well defined conditions (axioms briefly reviewed in section 4.2), their decisions are made *as if* they assign probabilities to uncertain events. Here it is appropriate to interpret the probabilities as *subjective* degrees of belief, because there need be no consensus about how the probabilities are assigned to events. Hence, there is no compelling reason why individuals should agree on the probability that any particular event will occur.

Some phenomena (for example, death rates in large populations), while not susceptible to repetition as in games of chance, do involve enough averaging over individual outcomes to permit the accurate estimation of probabilities. Insurance contracts (e.g. for life insurance) can then be negotiated, and insurance markets become viable.

Insurance markets aside, most financial markets involve uncertainty rather than risk, in the sense that relative frequencies are not readily available to estimate probabilities. Even so, a strict distinction between risk and uncertainty is not upheld here, the words 'risk' and 'uncertainty' being used interchangeably. A distinction between the two is not crucial. Indeed, it may even be a hindrance to clear thinking.

Most applications in finance permit the estimation of probabilities from past data or other information. In some circumstances the estimates are likely to be reliable, less so in others.[1] Financial analysis is thus typically located somewhere along the spectrum between two polar extremes – with events allowing the calculation of relative frequencies at one end of the spectrum, and unique, unforecastable phenomena at the other.

4.1 The state-preference approach

4.1.1 Modelling uncertainty

The state-preference approach comprises three basic ingredients.

1. *States of the world,* denoted by the set $S = \{s_1, s_2, \ldots, s_\ell\}$, where each s_k is interpreted as a label for the description of some contingency that could occur. It is assumed that exactly one state *will* occur, though decision makers do not know, at the outset, which one. The description of each state is complete and exhaustive, in the sense that all the relevant information is provided for the decision problem being studied. In its application to asset markets, each state specifies the payoffs of every asset, or, at least, provides enough information for the payoff in every state to be determined.

2. *Actions,* which describe all relevant aspects of the decisions that are made prior to the state of the world being revealed. In portfolio selection, an action is described by the choice of a particular collection of assets. One action might be to hold all wealth in cash; another might be to put half into the shares of one company and half into the shares of a second; another might be to borrow $1000 and invest the dollars in euros; and so on.

3. *Consequences,* which express the outcomes of an action corresponding to each state of the world. In portfolio selection, the consequence of an action (a chosen portfolio) is represented by a list, each element of which is the total value of the portfolio in the corresponding state. This total value is termed *terminal wealth.* Terminal wealth is determined only when the state is revealed and, hence, differs across states.

   More generally, the consequence in any one state (given the decision maker's action) could be represented as a 'bundle of goods' (a vector), the elements of which depend on the realized state and the individual's action. In portfolio analysis, the consequence is simplified by aggregating the elements of the vector (each asset's payoff) – a simplification that would not be appropriate if, for instance, the investor has preferences about various distinctive, non-pecuniary, aspects of assets' payoffs (e.g. a work of art might be the source of pleasure to its possessor quite separate from its capacity to yield a return in the form of an increase in its price).

---

[1] In his provocative book *The New Financial Order,* Shiller (2003) proposes the introduction of markets for several new financial instruments, with payoffs dependent on events the probabilities for which are difficult to infer (notwithstanding the accumulation of voluminous data).

Thus, if c denotes a consequence and a denotes an action, then the three components of the theory are related by a function of s_k and a such that $c = f(s_k, a)$. Formally, the function $f(\cdot, \cdot)$ maps states and actions into the space of consequences. In portfolio selection, the function simply links the amount of each asset held (the action) to each asset's payoff in every state, and hence to the consequence (terminal wealth).

In the state-preference model, each individual is assumed to possess preferences defined over consequences, or (with little loss of generality) the individual has a utility function the value of which serves to rank all the possible consequences.[2] Formally, the utility function can be expressed as

$$\mathcal{U} = U(f(s_1, a), f(s_2, a), \ldots, f(s_\ell, a)) \tag{4.1}$$

where the function $U(\cdot, \cdot, \ldots, \cdot)$ is allowed to differ across individuals.

Remember that, at the time when the action is taken, it is not known which state will occur. The individual's decision problem is to maximize utility, $\mathcal{U}$, by choosing a feasible action (i.e. an action that obeys whatever constraints the individual faces). In the portfolio application, a feasible action is a portfolio that satisfies the individual's wealth constraint (the total net value of assets cannot exceed initial wealth) and, perhaps, other constraints (e.g. an upper limit to the amount that the individual can borrow, or a restriction to hold only non-negative amounts of some or all assets).

Although only a single future date is assumed below, a 'tree diagram' illustrates how a sequence of dates can be studied; see figure 4.1.

At date 0, 'today', investors have to make decisions not knowing which of the six states, $S = \{s_1, s_2, \ldots, s_6\}$, will occur at date 2. At date 1 it becomes known that one of the *events*, (subsets of S) $\{s_1, s_2\}$, $\{s_3, s_4\}$ or $\{s_5, s_6\}$, has occurred. Finally, at date 2 the state is revealed.

Pursuing the example further, suppose that there is just one asset that changes in value between dates 0 and 1 by $+2$, 0 or -2, depicted by the three branches in figure 4.1. Between dates 1 and 2 the change is either $+5$ or 0, depicted by the pairs of branches between dates 1 and 2 in figure 4.1. Hence, the set of states at date 0 is $S = \{+7, +2, +5, 0, +3, -2\}$, exactly one of which occurs at date 2.

For simplicity, in what follows it is assumed that investors make decisions with respect to a single future date at which time the occurrence of precisely one state

---

[2] Given conditions well known in choice theory, a utility function can be constructed to represent preferences. The assumptions needed are, in summary, that the preference ordering is complete (on a closed convex outcome set), reflexive, transitive and continuous. See Varian (2003) for an introductory treatment. A concise, rigorous analysis appears in Debreu (1959, pp. 56–9).

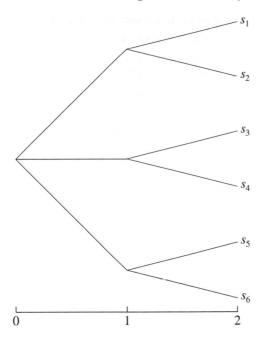

Fig. 4.1. States in a two-period world

From the perspective of date 0 there are six states, one of which will occur at date 2. At date 1 partial information is revealed about the state, in particular whether it will be one of (s_1, s_2) or (s_3, s_4) or (s_5, s_6).

is realized. The payoffs on the n assets in the ℓ possible states can be arranged in a *payoff array*, as follows:

	Assets			
	1	2	...	n
State 1	v_{11}	v_{12}	...	v_{1n}
State 2	v_{21}	v_{22}	...	v_{2n}
	$\vdots$	$\vdots$	$\vdots$	$\vdots$
State ℓ	$v_{\ell 1}$	$v_{\ell 2}$	...	$v_{\ell n}$

where rows correspond to states and columns correspond to assets. Thus, v_{kj} is the payoff to a unit of asset j if state k occurs.

Let p_j denote the price of asset j observed today (when the portfolio decision is made). Then the rate of return on asset j in state k is defined by

$$r_{kj} = (v_{kj} - p_j)/p_j = (v_{kj}/p_j) - 1$$

The *gross* rate of return on asset j, R_{kj}, is defined by $R_{kj} \equiv (1 + r_{kj}) = v_{kj}/p_j$.

In constructing the payoff array it is assumed that there is a finite number, ℓ, of possible states and a finite number, n, of assets. In practice, it makes sense to interpret ℓ as an exceedingly large number (consider all the different sets of circumstances that could conceivably occur). Formally, it is possible to allow the number of states to be infinite, but to do so would require more subtle mathematics than studied here. There could also be a large number of different assets. Moreover, in some applications the number, n, of assets is *endogenous* – that is, chosen by institutions or investors (who, for example, may be able to create *derivative* securities with payoffs based on other assets). For the remainder of this chapter, however, the number of securities is assumed to be given and fixed exogenously.

A risk-free asset, if one exists, by definition has the same payoff in each state. In what follows the risk-free asset is denoted with subscript 0, with payoff v_0 in every state and rate of return $r_0 = (v_0/p_0) - 1$.

Suppose that there exists an asset that has a positive payoff of one unit of wealth in a particular state, say k, and zero in every other state. This asset could play the role of an 'insurance policy', the purchase of which allows the investor to offset any adverse consequences in state k, and only in state k. Now assume that one such asset exists *for every state*. Investors can then insure against the adverse consequences of every possible contingency. This does not mean that uncertainty vanishes but, rather, that the array of available assets is so extensive that every separate state can be targeted. Conditional on the occurrence of any state, investors could be certain of obtaining a known payoff, the cost of which is the asset's price (or 'insurance premium'). The presence of such an asset for every state is sufficient for the existence of a *complete* set of asset markets. Otherwise, asset markets are said to be *incomplete*. Completeness is an idealization, rarely claimed to be encountered in practice. It does, however, have important implications for asset market equilibrium, and hence is useful as a benchmark against which more realistic circumstances can be evaluated. (The implications of asset market completeness are explored further in section 4.2 and appendix 4.3.)

4.1.2 Decision making under uncertainty

To make the portfolio decision more definite, denote terminal wealth as W_k, where the subscript k denotes the state. The investor's utility function is defined over the consequences, W_k, $k = 1, 2, \ldots, \ell$:

$$\mathcal{U} = U(W_1, W_2, \ldots, W_\ell) \tag{4.2}$$

Compare (4.2) with (4.1): $W_k \equiv f(s_k, a)$.

In comparison with standard consumer theory, the utility function, (4.2), may look peculiar because exactly one – and only one – state will actually occur. But, in the presence of uncertainty, the investor must make a decision *before* the state is revealed, and hence must weigh up the consequences across all the conceivable states – it is *as if* the investor is choosing all $W_1, W_2, \ldots, W_\ell$ (only one of which will be obtained).

The wealth constraint states that the investor's outlay on assets equals initial wealth:

$$p_1 x_1 + p_2 x_2 + \cdots + p_n x_n = A \tag{4.3}$$

where A is initial wealth and $x_1, x_2, \ldots x_n$ denote the number of units of each asset in the portfolio, so that $p_j x_j$ is the amount of wealth devoted to asset $j = 1, 2, \ldots, n$. (Strictly, the constraint should assert that the outlay on assets is *no greater than* initial wealth, but the inequality can safely be ignored if the investor always prefers greater terminal wealth to less – an assumption that is maintained throughout.)

The value of A is assumed to be given and can be interpreted as the sum of the number of units of each asset that the investor initially holds multiplied by its price.[3] According to the investor's circumstances, other constraints (e.g. non-negative holdings of assets, $x_j \geq 0$ for all j) could be imposed, but they are neglected here.

The portfolio is linked to terminal wealth via the payoffs of each asset in each state of the world:

$$W_k = v_{k1} x_1 + v_{k2} x_2 + \cdots + v_{kn} x_n \qquad k = 1, 2, \ldots, \ell \tag{4.4}$$

which is the sum of the payoff of each asset multiplied by the chosen amount of the asset. Equation (4.4) identifies the explicit form for $f(s_k, a)$ in the portfolio selection problem.

In summary, each investor chooses $x_1, x_2, \ldots, x_n$ to maximize

$$\mathcal{U} = U(W_1, W_2, \quad , W_\ell)$$

subject to

$$p_1 x_1 + p_2 x_2 + \cdots + p_n x_n = A$$

where

$$W_k = v_{k1} x_1 + v_{k2} x_2 + \cdots + v_{kn} x_n \qquad k = 1, 2, \ldots, \ell$$

---

[3] The value of A can be written as the market value of initial holdings of assets: if the investor holds $\omega_1, \omega_2, \ldots, \omega_n$ at the outset, then $A = p_1 \omega_1 + p_2 \omega_2 + \cdots + p_n \omega_n$. The important point is that, whatever the construction of A, it is parametric – i.e. not chosen by the investor.

The result is a portfolio decision in which the amount of each asset held depends on asset prices, initial wealth and preferences – just as, by analogy with consumer theory, the demand for goods depends on their prices and the consumer's income.

The analysis can be extended to cover a multiperiod horizon, generalizing the single-period decision problem described so far. Now the level of terminal wealth must be indexed by *date* as well as state, so that W_{kt} denotes the level of wealth in state k at date t. Note that 'state k at date t' would express the information available to the individual at date t; more information would be revealed as time passes. In the multiperiod generalization, preferences (and, hence, utility) depend on the levels of wealth in all states and at all dates. Also, the wealth constraint must be modified to reflect the opportunities for the investor to transfer wealth from one date to the next. This, more complicated, multiperiod decision problem is reserved for chapter 11.

The state-preference framework is useful as an abstract tool for understanding the fundamentals of decision making under uncertainty, but it is more special than it might at first appear. For example, the set of states, S, is given exogenously; it cannot be affected by the actions of any of the investors. Also, it might seem implausible to assume that investors are capable of ordering *every* possible consequence of their actions across what may be a vast number of states. Consequently, the state-preference model is not as widely applicable as it might at first seem.

Whether viewed as general or as special, the state-preference model yields few testable predictions and, hence, is of limited worth. One way to proceed (the route adopted here) is to specialize the theory, in particular, by restricting the range of preferences or beliefs according to which investors make decisions.

4.2 The expected utility hypothesis

4.2.1 Assumptions of the EUH

Although it might seem natural that a numerical probability is somehow associated with each state of the world – as a measure of the likelihood of the state's occurrence – such an association is by no means necessary. Indeed, the notion of probability is completely absent from the analysis in the preceding section. In view of the doubts about the concept of probability expressed early in this chapter, its absence can be understood as a strength, not a weakness, of the state-preference model. However, one way in which the state-preference model can be modified to yield more definite implications is to permit a role for probability.

One such approach – the most popular – is that based on the expected utility hypothesis. One aspect (not the only one) of the EUH is that probabilities are assigned to states of the world. By attaching a probability to each state, the EUH enables a distinction to be drawn between the decision maker's *beliefs* (expressed by probabilities) about which state will occur and *preferences* about how the decision maker orders the consequences of different actions.

The EUH can be presented in a variety of ways.[4] The approach adopted here begins by assuming that decision makers (investors) act in accordance with an ordering of actions (portfolio choices). The implications of the EUH then emerge by imposing a particular set of conditions on the orderings of actions. These conditions – or axioms, or assumptions – are not studied in detail here but can be summarized as follows.[5]

1. *Irrelevance of common consequences.* Consider an event (a set of one or more states) and compare actions with consequences that differ among states *in* the event but with consequences that are identical (i.e. common) to one another for states *not in* the event. The first assumption is that the decision maker orders the actions independently of the common consequences for states not in the event.[6]

   An example should make the rather convoluted statement of the condition more transparent. Consider circumstances in which there are three possible states and two pairs of actions: *A* and *B*, and *A'* and *B'*. (Think of the actions as portfolio decisions with uncertain payoffs – i.e. outcomes that differ across states.) Suppose that the payoff array is as follows.

	Actions			
	A	*B*	*A'*	*B'*
State 1	10	0	10	0
State 2	0	10	0	10
State 3	20	20	0	0

Notice that *A* and *A'* (and *B* and *B'*) differ only with respect to the payoff in state 3 (which is equal at twenty for *A* and *B*, and at zero for *A'* and *B'*, respectively).

The 'irrelevance of common consequences' asserts that any decision maker who prefers *A* to *B* will prefer *A'* to *B'*, and conversely. Roughly speaking, if action *A* is preferred over action *B* when the common consequences for states *outside* the event are 'favourable', then action *A* remains preferred over action *B* when 'favourable' is

---

[4] Most expositions of the EUH assume at the outset that probabilities (be they objective or subjective) can be assigned to states. Others demonstrate the existence of probabilities as an implication of the theory. (Strictly, probabilities are assigned to sets of states known as events. Such a procedure resolves a technical problem that arises when there are an infinite number of states. It can be ignored where the number of states is finite, as is assumed to be the case here.)

[5] A precise statement of the three axioms, together with a careful analysis of their implications, can be found in Marschak and Radner (1972, chap. 1). A classic exposition, elegant as well as precise, is that of Savage (1954).

[6] Note that the consequences in states outside the event are identical across *actions*, not across the *states* outside the event. They are the same for each action, not necessarily for each state.

replaced by 'more favourable', or 'less favourable' or whatever (i.e. when *A* becomes *A'* and when *B* becomes *B'*). Although this condition may seem innocuous, it is one of the most contentious assumptions of the EUH, and has been the source of intense controversy.

2. *Preferences are independent of beliefs.* Consider the consequences in any particular state (i.e. in one *row* of the payoff array). The second assumption asserts that preferences over consequences for the given state are independent of the state in which they occur. Less formally, the decision maker cares only about the consequence, not the label of, or index of (say, a subscript '*k*'), the state in which it is received. In other words, a terminal wealth of $100,000 has the same personal value to an investor whether it is received as a consequence of a stock market boom or in a depression (boom and depression being identified as two separate states). One way of interpreting this condition is that it requires the definition of a state to be complete, in the sense that there are no hidden attributes of a state that might influence a decision maker's action separately from, and in addition to, the consequences of that state.

3. *Beliefs are independent of consequences.* The third assumption asserts (again, somewhat imprecisely) that the decision maker's degree of belief about whether a state will occur is independent of the consequences in the state.[7] Thus, the decision maker's belief about whether it will rain tomorrow is independent of whether a million dollars, or one dollar, or nothing, will be received in the event of rain tomorrow.

Together with the assumption of a complete ordering of actions and some purely technical assumptions, the three conditions imply that: (a) the decision maker acts as if a *probability* (a real number between zero and unity) is assigned to each state; (b) there exists a function – the *von Neumann–Morgenstern utility function* – that is dependent only on the outcomes; and (c) the decision maker orders the actions according to the *expected value* of the von Neumann–Morgenstern utility function.

Formally, using the notation of the state-preference approach, the EUH implies that

$$\mathcal{U} = U(W_1, W_2, \ldots, W_\ell)$$
$$= \pi_1 u(W_1) + \pi_2 u(W_2) + \cdots + \pi_\ell u(W_\ell) \tag{4.5}$$

where π_k is the probability that the individual investor assigns to state s_k. The function $u(\cdot)$ is the von Neumann–Morgenstern utility function. Notice that the $u(\cdot)$ is the same for all states, though the value of its argument, W_k, generally differs across states. Both the probabilities and the von Neumann–Morgenstern utility function are allowed to differ across investors. It is assumed,

---

[7] This statement is imprecise because 'degree of belief' is undefined. Formal statements of the assumption are precise but they require construction of a more detailed analytical apparatus than is warranted here.

however, that $u'(W) > 0$ for all relevant levels of W – i.e. investors prefer more wealth to less.

By definition, the expected value of the von Neumann–Morgenstern utility function is just the expression given by (4.5), hence justifying the title, *expected utility hypothesis.* A common notation is to let W (note the absence of a subscript) denote a label for wealth as a random variable. A random variable can be understood as a list, each element of which is an outcome – W_k in this case – together with its associated probability, π_k, one pair for each state, $k = 1, 2 \ldots, \ell$. Then the EUH is written compactly as stating that actions are ordered according to $E[u(W)]$, where $E[\cdot]$ denotes the operation of summing over the product of probabilities and utilities.

In summary, the EUH asserts that actions are chosen to maximize expected utility:

$$E[u(W)] \equiv \pi_1 u(W_1) + \pi_2 u(W_2) + \cdots + \pi_\ell u(W_\ell)$$

4.2.2 Remarks on the EUH

1. Ever since the EUH was made famous by John von Neumann and Oskar Morgenstern in their pioneering *Theory of Games and Economic Behavior* (1944), it has been the subject of intense discussion and scrutiny.

   As the title of von Neumann and Morgenstern's book suggests, they applied the EUH to games of chance and – more to the point – as a *normative* theory, a theory of how the participants in games ought to behave. In finance, however, it is typically invoked as a *positive* theory – that is, to explain how individuals actually behave. Unfortunately for the theory, persuasive evidence has accumulated from many studies that individuals often violate one or more of the EUH assumptions. The significance of this evidence is a matter of debate, and several alternative theories have been put forward. None of them has, however, yet achieved the level of acceptance (albeit, grudging) of the EUH.

   Also, it can be argued that, in evaluating a theory, more weight should be placed on the extent to which evidence accords with its predictions and less on the validity – or otherwise – of its assumptions. Whatever the merits of this standpoint (and it is not a consensus view), the EUH remains one of the cornerstones of decision making in general, and of portfolio selection in particular.

2. One implication of the EUH is that individuals act *as if* they assign probabilities to states of the world. The existence of probabilities is deduced, not assumed at the outset.[8] It is not necessary to rely on the existence of objective probabilities nor to assume that decision makers have any conscious awareness of the notion of probability. Both of these consequences provide solace for model builders in financial

---

[8] Even so, as already noted, expositions of the EUH commonly do assume the existence of objective probabilities. The formal logic of the EUH is the same either way.

theory, if only because the opportunity to engage in repeated experiments (of the sort needed to justify objective probabilities) is, at best, a convenient fiction.

While the concept of 'subjective' probability is arguably more attractive than 'objective' probability in explaining individual behaviour, it is adopted here as a modelling strategy rather than as an statement of dogma. Some problems may be easier to solve, or to comprehend, by assuming the existence of underlying 'true', objective, probabilities attached to states of the world. Whatever the approach, in empirical applications it is necessary to find observable counterparts to some, at least, of the theoretical concepts. For instance, asset price observations provide the raw material for estimating probabilities, or – more commonly – sample statistics (e.g. means and variances) corresponding to probability distributions, the values of which individuals could (possibly, even, should) use in making their decisions.

3. *Attitude to risk.* The individual's attitude towards risk is expressed by the $u(\cdot)$ function. When the argument of the function is wealth, W, $u''(W) < 0$ defines *risk aversion* (the marginal utility of wealth, $u'(W)$, is decreasing in wealth), $u''(W) > 0$ defines *risk loving* (marginal utility of wealth is increasing) and $u''(W) = 0$ defines *risk neutrality* (constant marginal utility of wealth).

Risk-loving and, to a lesser extent, risk-neutral attitudes to risk lead to extreme forms of behaviour that are seldom observed. Hence, most applications of the EUH focus on risk-averse preferences. Two popular indicators of the degree of risk aversion are available as (a) the index of *absolute* risk aversion, $-u''(W)/u'(W)$, and (b) the index of *relative* risk aversion, $-Wu''(W)/u'(W)$.

4. *Popular functional forms.* Although some properties of individual behaviour can be derived from the EUH, more definite predictions can be obtained if $u(W)$ takes a particular functional form.

The most popular functional form of $u(W)$ in finance, and economics generally, is the *iso-elastic* function, expressed by

$$u(W) = \begin{cases} W^{1-\gamma}/(1-\gamma) & \text{for } \gamma \neq 1 \\ \ln W & \text{for } \gamma = 1 \end{cases} \tag{4.6}$$

(The popularity of this functional form stems from its analytical tractability, not because there is much evidence that it corresponds to individual behaviour.) In this case, the index of relative risk aversion is equal to the parameter γ; hence, it is commonly known as the *constant relative risk aversion (CRRA) utility function*. Risk neutrality corresponds to the case $\gamma = 0$, with $\gamma > 0$ corresponding to risk aversion.

A second functional form sometimes assumed is $u(W) = 1 - e^{-\phi W}$, where $\phi > 0$. In this case, the parameter ϕ equals the coefficient of absolute risk aversion and, hence, the function is known as the *constant absolute risk aversion (CARA) utility function*.

A third functional form – perhaps the simplest – is the *quadratic*: $u(W) = W - bW^2$, where $b > 0$ is a parameter expressing preferences. The implications of this form are explored below, in section 4.4.

4.2.3 Portfolio selection in the EUH

Formally, the portfolio selection problem can be stated as: choose the portfolio of assets to maximize expected utility subject to the wealth constraint. That is, the investor chooses $\{x_1, x_2, \ldots, x_n\}$ to maximize $E[u(W)]$ subject to the wealth constraint, (4.3), above.

This is the static, or one-period, portfolio selection problem: it does not address the issues of (a) revising decisions with the passage of time, or (b) the possibility that the investor wishes to consume some wealth (or add to wealth by saving non-asset income) before the terminal date. (These are studied in chapter 11. Remarkably few alterations of the principles outlined below are required to cope with these extensions.)

In portfolio theory it is usual to express the analysis in terms of *rates of return* and *proportions* of initial wealth invested in assets. Thus, terminal wealth is written

$$W = (1 + r_P)A \tag{4.7}$$

where r_P is the rate of return on the portfolio as a whole – that is, a weighted average of the rates of return, each weight being the proportion of initial wealth invested in the relevant asset. The details of the notation are reserved for appendix 4.1. It is important to remember that W and r_P in equation (4.7) differ across states. The k subscript has been omitted to reduce notational clutter. Initial wealth, A, by definition, does not differ across states.

In some parts of the analysis, depending on context, it is appropriate to assume the existence of a risk-free asset – an asset that yields the same rate of return, say r_0, in every state. Being constant across states, r_0 is non-random.

The *excess* rate of return on asset j over the risk-free rate is defined as $r_{kj} - r_0$. This is usually written slightly more compactly as $r_j - r_0$, omitting the state subscript.

The fundamental valuation relationship

Every portfolio that maximizes expected utility must satisfy a condition called the *fundamental valuation relationship* (FVR). This relationship crops up whenever the maximization of expected utility is the goal, although its appearance may differ slightly according to the context. The FVR really is *fundamental* in finance.

The FVR is the *first-order condition* for maximizing expected utility. More precisely, the FVR is the *set* of first-order conditions, one for each asset. In its most general form the FVR is written as

$$E[(1 + r_j)H] = 1 \qquad j = 1, 2, \ldots, n \tag{4.8}$$

where H is a 'random variable' in the sense that it varies across states.

What is this H variable? It depends on the context. In the static portfolio problem outlined so far it takes one form (explained below). In intertemporal portfolio planning it takes another.

To obtain an intuitive grasp of the FVR, consider the one-period, static portfolio problem in which the investor seeks to maximize the expected utility of wealth. Suppose that the investor devotes one additional unit of wealth to asset j. The payoff is $(1 + r_j)$ and the increment to utility is $(1 + r_j)u'(W)$. This varies across states, the increment to *expected* utility being $E[(1 + r_j)u'(W)]$. (In words: weight the utility increment in each state by the state's probability and sum over the states.)

At a maximum of expected utility it is necessary that the expected utility increment is the same, say λ, for each asset, so that

$$E[(1 + r_j)u'(W)] = \lambda \qquad j = 1, 2, \ldots, n \qquad (4.9)$$

Why? Because, if (4.9) does not hold, then expected utility can be increased by shifting wealth from those assets with low values of $E[(1 + r_j)u'(W)]$ to those with high values. Only when equality holds for every asset can expected utility be at a maximum.[9] A formal derivation of the FVR is outlined in appendix 4.2.

In view of the previous paragraph, the symbol λ can be given a simple interpretation. It is the increment to expected utility resulting from a small increase in initial wealth – i.e. the expected marginal utility of wealth, $E[u'(W)]$. At a maximum of expected utility, the expected *marginal* utility of wealth must equal the increment to expected utility from a small change in the holding of any asset; otherwise, expected utility is not at a maximum. The adjective 'small' is required because λ, although the same for all assets, is not generally constant when wealth changes. Hence, changes in initial wealth lead to changes in λ itself.[10]

Finally, divide both sides of (4.9) by λ and observe that the FVR holds with $H \equiv u'(W)/\lambda$.

Another way to write the FVR, convenient in the presence of a risk-free asset, is

$$E[(r_j - r_0)H] = 0 \qquad j = 1, 2, \ldots, n \qquad (4.10)$$

To obtain this expression, write equation (4.8) with r_0 instead of r_j, subtract from the equality involving r_j and rearrange to give (4.10). Now the λ cancels out and H can be replaced by $u'(W)$.

---

[9] Note that (4.9) necessarily holds only if the investor can hold negative as well as positive amounts of each asset – i.e. if short-selling is permitted. Suppose that short-selling is prohibited, so that negative holdings are not allowed. Now it is possible that the investor's portfolio is forced to a 'corner' at which a zero amount of some asset is held, when the investor would prefer to short-sell the asset. In this case, the equality (4.9) must be replaced by an *inequality* to reflect the extra constraint of no short-sales.

[10] Formally, all these derivations involve limits as the change in initial wealth, A, becomes infinitesimal. This enables the differential calculus to be applied. The intuition remains valid – though approximate – for finite changes.

The FVR provides a set of *necessary* conditions for a maximum. The *second-order* conditions, together with the FVR, provide necessary and *sufficient* conditions that a solution of the FVR constitutes a maximum of expected utility. The second-order conditions are straightforward to interpret in the static portfolio problem. They amount to the requirement that $u''(W) < 0$; that is, that the investor is *risk-averse*.

If the investor is a risk lover, $u''(W) > 0$, there is generally no solution at all to expected utility maximization unless some extra (and perhaps arbitrary) constraints are imposed on the investor's choices. Risk neutrality, $u''(W) = 0$, provides a knife-edge case, considered below.

In order to calculate the amounts of each asset in an investor's optimal portfolio, it is necessary to assume that the utility function (and hence H) takes a particular functional form – e.g. the constant relative risk aversion function, (4.6), above. However, even with a specific function to represent utility, explicit solutions are not generally available without making additional assumptions.

Note that the value taken by H differs across states. The values of H differ also across investors. There is, however, a special case – important in some applications – for which H is equal across investors (though not across states) in market equilibrium. This result holds when (a) investors are *unanimous* in their beliefs (they agree on the probability assigned to each state), and (b) asset markets are *complete* (in the sense defined in section 4.1.1). Appendix 4.3 demonstrates why H is the same for every investor under these conditions.

Risk neutrality

The case of risk neutrality, $u''(W) = 0$, is more interesting than might first appear. Risk neutrality implies that the marginal utility of wealth is independent of wealth – say $u'(W) = c$, a positive constant. This means that (4.10) can be written as

$$E[(r_j - r_0)u'(W)] = 0$$
$$cE[(r_j - r_0)] = 0$$
$$E[(r_j - r_0)] = 0$$
$$E[r_j] = r_0 \qquad j = 1, 2, \ldots, n \qquad (4.11)$$

because the c is the same for each state and can be cancelled out. Expression (4.11) does not involve any choice variable (that is, any x_j) of the individual; it either holds or it does not. If it does not hold, the investor would seek to borrow at r_0 and invest an unbounded amount in any asset for which $E[r_j] > r_0$; and short-sell an unbounded amount of any asset for which $E[r_j] < r_0$, the proceeds being invested at the risk-free rate, r_0. This is just a way of acknowledging that there exists no solution to the maximization problem unless (4.11) holds; i.e. the expected return on every asset equals the rate of return on the risk-free asset. In such an equilibrium, risk-neutral investors are indifferent about which assets they hold. (Obviously, other equilibria could exist if restrictions are imposed on investors' decisions – e.g. an upper limit on the amount of borrowing at the risk-free rate or limits on short-sales.)

To an outside observer, a world of uncertainty with risk-neutral investors would look rather like a world of certainty (in which asset payoffs, by definition, would not differ across states). But note that (4.11) involves an expectation. Exactly one state will be realized, and almost surely the actual excess return for asset j will be negative or positive (not zero). The expectation may be equal to r_0 but the actual outcome, when the state is revealed, may well differ. The appearance of certainty in a world of risk-neutral investors is potentially deceptive: risk is present (the future is unknown) even if investors choose to ignore it.

4.3 Behavioural alternatives to the EUH

While the EUH plays a pivotal role in decision making under uncertainty, its pre-eminent status is insecure. Some criticisms of the EUH have already been mentioned; they apply much more broadly than to finance, or even to economics as a whole. At the heart of scepticism about the EUH is its incompatibility with observations of individual behaviour, especially evidence deriving from experimental studies in which candidates are asked to make decisions in controlled, but artificial, circumstances involving risk.

As a consequence of the apparent failure of the EUH, several alternatives have been devised. The main objective has been to construct more plausible descriptions of individual behaviour, less emphasis being given (a) to normative (i.e. prescriptive) theories, and (b) to developing testable predictions about, for example, the quantities held of particular assets. Instead, attention tends to centre on the impact of heuristic 'rules of thumb' in decision making. Also, *framing* – the way in which a decision problem is presented – is allowed to affect the resulting decision.

While it is easy to criticize any theory such as the EUH as being unrealistic, it is more challenging to propose an alternative that is testable – i.e. a theory that goes beyond a *post hoc* rationalization of some observed phenomenon. Even so, active research in behavioural finance is beginning to identify credible explanations that can outperform the EUH.

Almost all proposed replacements for the EUH can be viewed, in one way or another, as reflecting *bounded rationality* – that decision makers are unable to process all the information needed to determine their actions in accordance with, say, the EUH. From this perspective, individuals accept (consciously or otherwise) that they cannot adhere to the prescriptions of the EUH, even if they wish to do so. Decision makers have to tolerate imperfect approximations to the ideal.

The approximations take one of a host of forms. For instance, it is possible that the decision maker is internally consistent, in the sense that the assumptions of the EUH are satisfied but that the probabilities used to weight utility levels embody systematic errors – errors that the decision maker would avoid if only they could be detected and recognized as such. The theory of *cognitive dissonance* postulates that individuals experience difficulty in coping with new information of a sort that implies that earlier decisions, based on erroneous beliefs, have led to mistaken actions: the individual avoids revising beliefs that have unpalatable consequences for past decisions. As a result, a reliance on beliefs that are known to be wrong tends to distort decisions.

Two distinct, though closely related, approaches – *prospect theory* and *regret theory* – modify the EUH's objective function, $E[u(W)] \equiv \pi_1 u(W_1) + \pi_2 u(W_2) + \cdots + \pi_\ell u(W_\ell)$, by replacing either, or both, of the probability weights and the von Neumann–Morgenstern utility function.

In *prospect theory*, 'true' (or objective) probabilities are assumed to exist but are replaced with decision weights. Individuals' decision weights reflect mistakes in assessing probabilities, the desirability of outcomes in particular states, or ambiguities in the interpretation of which state has occurred. It is typically assumed, for instance, that decision weights *over*-weight low probabilities – i.e. the decision weight assigned to a rare event exceeds its probability. However, discontinuities in the relationship between probabilities and decision weights tend to occur for events with very low and very high probability. Events for which the probability approaches zero may be ignored (decision weight $= 0$), while those with high probability are regarded as certainties (decision weight $= 1$).

Also, in prospect theory the utility function is replaced by a 'value function', say $z(W)$, which is assumed to have the form depicted in figure 4.2. The important attributes of the value function are: (a) it is a continuous, increasing function of wealth; (b) there exists a kink at a 'reference point' or *status quo* point, S (which can be identified with the individual's initial wealth, so that $W^* \equiv A$); (c) for wealth in excess of W^*, the individual is risk-averse ($z(\cdot)$ is concave from below – i.e. $z''(W) < 0$); and (d) for wealth less than W^*, the individual is a risk lover ($z(\cdot)$ is convex from below – i.e. $z''(W) > 0$). These properties, together with the weights that replace probabilities, generate predictions that – arguably – accord more closely with the evidence from individual experiments than the EUH.

Unlike prospect theory, *regret theory* retains the 'true' EUH probabilities but amends the von Neumann–Morgenstern utility function in such a way that the

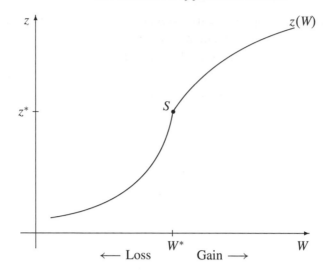

Fig. 4.2. The value function, $z(W)$, in prospect theory

The value function in prospect theory replaces the von Neumann–
Morgenstern utility function. It is assumed that there is a kink at
the 'reference point' or *status quo* point, S, with initial wealth, W^* –
what decision makers care about are *changes* in value. The value function exhibits risk aversion for wealth greater than W^*, and risk-loving
behaviour for wealth less than W^*.

decision maker compares the outcome in each state with outcomes in other states
that might have occurred but didn't. Thus, once a state is revealed, the individual
may regret – or rejoice about – whatever action was chosen prior to the resolution
of the uncertainty. Being aware that such a reaction will occur, the decision
maker's chosen action will take into account its potential impact. Once again, the
predictions of the theory are found to be consistent with experimental evidence
in ways that those of the EUH are not.

More radical departures from the EUH originate from psychology rather than
conventional economic reasoning. The theories attempt to incorporate a wide
range of behaviour, from the propensity of individuals to be overconfident about
their decisions, to a reliance on blatantly irrelevant information, through to a
penchant for guidance from superstition or even magic.

Many commentators about the world of finance go so far as to argue that a
substantial proportion of investors are completely irrational, at least for some
intervals of time. This need not imply that behaviour is beyond explanation,
though it does suggest that some events are difficult – perhaps impossible – to
analyse successfully with conventional tools. Psychological theories of the sort

reviewed above are typically invoked to rationalize aberrant behaviour, extreme price fluctuations or extraordinary incidents, rather than as expressions of normal behaviour (see chapters 10 and 11). Arguably, the theories warrant a more central position in finance than they have achieved. While undermining the pre-eminence of the EUH, as yet, however, they have not displaced it.

4.4 The mean-variance model

4.4.1 The mean-variance approach to decision making

Even if the EUH is accepted as a reasonable expression of the decision maker's objective, for many purposes it remains too general, unless a specific form is assumed for the von Neumann–Morgenstern utility function. One of the simplest is that $u(\cdot)$ is *quadratic* in wealth.

If the von Neumann–Morgenstern function is quadratic, then expected utility can be written as a function of the expected value (mean) of terminal wealth and the variance (or its square root, the standard deviation) of terminal wealth; hence the name 'mean-variance analysis' for a framework that greatly facilitates the construction of optimal portfolios.[11]

More formally, denote the expected value of terminal wealth by $E[W]$ and its variance by $var[W] \equiv E[(W - E[W])^2]$. Then, if the function $u(\cdot)$ is quadratic, the expected value of $u(W)$ is a function of $E[W]$ and $var[W]$:

$$E[u(W)] = F(E[W], var[W]) \qquad (4.12)$$

where $F(\cdot, \cdot)$ is a function to be specified.

4.4.2 Remarks on mean-variance analysis

1. It is shown in appendix 4.4 that the function $F(\cdot, \cdot)$ must take a particular form if it is derived from a quadratic von Neumann–Morgenstern utility function. It is written more generally in (4.12) because the mean-variance objective can be justified on grounds other than as the expected value of a quadratic utility function.

2. There are at least three ways of justifying the mean-variance objective.

   (a) From the EUH, if the von Neumann–Morgenstern utility function is *quadratic* in wealth, as already suggested.[12] A quadratic approximation to a general utility function could also justify mean-variance analysis.

---

[11] The origin and early development of mean-variance analysis in the 1950s is credited to Harry Markowitz, who shared the Nobel Memorial Prize in 1990 for his contributions to financial theory and practice.

[12] A quadratic utility function may exhibit diminishing marginal utility for some levels of wealth but cannot be monotonic throughout – the function reaches a maximum at a finite level of wealth and thereafter declines. For this reason, if a quadratic utility function is specified, the level of wealth is assumed not to exceed the level at which the function reaches its maximum.

(b) From the EUH, if the rates of return are determined according to a multivariate *Normal distribution*.[13] The points to note in obtaining this result are that: (i) Normal distributions are characterized entirely by their means (expectations), variances and covariances; and (ii) linear combinations of Normal random variables are also Normal (hence, terminal wealth, or the rate of return on a portfolio of assets with Normally distributed returns, is also Normally distributed).

(c) Directly on the grounds that such a criterion is plausible, without recourse to more basic assumptions such as those of the EUH.

3. What is so special (i.e. restrictive) about mean-variance analysis? At first sight, mean-variance analysis might appear to provide simply a definite form of the EUH. It is common, after all, to express random variables in terms of their means and variances. However, some important aspects of probability distributions cannot be expressed by means and variances. For instance, any *skewness* in the distribution is ignored.[14]

A less obvious feature of probability distributions, not captured by the variance, is the tendency for some random variables to be concentrated either near to, or far from, their means. An index of this tendency is the distribution's *kurtosis*.[15] There is evidence that the distributions of many asset prices and rates of return have 'fat tails' – i.e. that extreme values, or outliers, occur more frequently than consistent with Normal random variables.

The upshot is that mean-variance analysis is compatible only with a restricted class of random variables. To the extent that asset payoffs (and, hence, rates of return) do not conform with these restrictions, mean-variance analysis is liable to result in misleading conclusions. It could be, of course, that investors choose to ignore the presence of skewness and kurtosis (perhaps as a consequence of maximizing a quadratic von Neumann–Morgenstern utility function).

4. In most, though not all, mean-variance models the objective is written as a function of the expected value and variance of the *rate of return* to wealth rather than the level of wealth. The rate of return on wealth is defined as $r_P \equiv (W - A)/A$, where A is initial wealth, as previously defined. The expectation and variance of r_P are written as $\mu_P \equiv \mathrm{E}[r_P]$ and $\sigma_P^2 \equiv \mathrm{E}[(r_P - \mu_P)^2]$, respectively (where the subscript P is intended to

---

[13] While sufficient, Normality is not necessary – a broader class of distributions also implies a mean-variance objective for EUH investors. Chamberlain (1983) provides an exhaustive characterization of the relevant probability distributions. Further contributions appear in Meyer (1987), Levy (1989), Sinn (1989) and Meyer (1989). For empirical evidence, see Levy and Duchin (2004).

[14] Skewness is, formally, a property of the third moment of the probability distribution and reflects, roughly, the tendency of the random variable to fall systematically either below (left-skewed) or above (right-skewed) its mean. A skewed distribution is *non-symmetric*.

[15] Kurtosis is a property of the fourth moment of the probability distribution. The Normal distribution provides a benchmark and is said to be 'mesokurtic'. Distributions with more probability than the Normal in the tails are known as 'leptokurtic', and with less as 'platykurtic'. The diagnosis of skewness and kurtosis is often difficult in practice. For example, the presence of kurtosis may be confused with a variance that varies across time. See Engle (2004).

stand for 'portfolio' – i.e. the portfolio that results in the terminal wealth level W).[16] Expressed in this way, the mean-variance criterion can be written as

$$G(\mu_P, \sigma_P^2) \qquad (4.13)$$

Starting with (4.13) has the attraction that the objective is independent of the investor's initial wealth. However, this form of the objective is not directly comparable with that of the EUH because the level of initial wealth, A, has been absorbed in going between $F(\cdot, \cdot)$ and $G(\cdot, \cdot)$ (see appendix 4.4 for details). Thus, for instance, to predict how changes in A affect investors' portfolio choices, it is necessary to revert to (4.12), in which A appears explicitly.

5. It is common to interpret the variance of return, σ_P^2 (or, equivalently, the standard deviation, σ_P), as expressing the *risk* of the portfolio. Natural though it may seem, this representation is adopted only provisionally. In chapter 6 a different interpretation of risk, based on asset market equilibrium, is proposed.

To make sense of the trade-off between expected return, denoted by μ_P, and risk, expressed by σ_P, it is assumed that $G(\mu_P, \sigma_P^2)$ is increasing in μ_P and decreasing in σ_P.[17] In words, expected return is a 'good' and risk is a 'bad'. Also, it is assumed that the curves for which $G(\mu_P, \sigma_P^2)$ is constant in μ_P, σ_P space (the indifference curves), are convex from below. See figure 4.3.[18]

The justification for the convex-from-below shape of the indifference curves can be made on several grounds: (a) intuitive plausibility – that it seems reasonable that, at higher *levels* of risk, the greater are the increments to expected return needed to compensate for *increments* in risk if the decision maker's utility is kept constant; (b) as an implication of a quadratic von Neumann–Morgenstern utility function that is increasing in wealth; and (c) to draw the indifference curves otherwise would lead to predictions that are inconsistent with commonly observed behaviour.[19]

A particular form of the $G(\mu_P, \sigma_P^2)$ function that satisfies the conditions above is given by

$$G(\mu_P, \sigma_P^2) = \mu_P - \alpha\sigma_P^2 \qquad (4.14)$$

where $\alpha > 0$ is a parameter that represents the investor's preferences.[20] The magnitude of α reflects the investor's attitude to risk (as expressed by the variance, σ_P^2).

---

[16] In terms of $E[W]$ and $var[W]$, $\mu_P = (E[W] - A)/A$ and $\sigma_P^2 = var[W]/A^2$.

[17] Formally, the first partial derivative of G with respect to μ_P is positive, $\partial G/\partial \mu_P > 0$; and the first partial derivative of G with respect to σ_P^2 is negative, $\partial G/\partial \sigma_P^2 < 0$. For the purposes of these qualitative conditions, it does not matter whether the standard deviation, σ_P, or the variance, σ_P^2, is used to represent risk.

[18] Note that it matters that σ_P, not σ_P^2, is used in the figure. More formally, the 'convex from below' property of indifference curves follows from assuming that $G(\mu_P, \sigma_P^2)$ is *quasi-concave* in μ_P and σ_P. In this context, a function is quasi-concave if a straight line joining any two points on any given indifference curve lies nowhere below the indifference curve.

[19] For example, if the indifference curves are drawn as *concave* from below, the investor would always 'plunge', in the sense of holding either the least risky or the most risky feasible portfolio. Investors rarely behave in this way. Hence, such indifference curves would not seem to provide a plausible foundation for observed behaviour. Note that, even with convex-from-below indifference curves, investors might still plunge (depending on the means and variances of returns), but, at least, they are not guaranteed to do so.

[20] Portfolio selection to maximize $\mu_P - \alpha\sigma_P^2$, as in (4.14), can be shown to maximize expected utility if (a) assets' rates of return are Normally distributed, and (b) the von Neumann–Morgenstern utility function satisfies constant absolute risk aversion – i.e. $u(W) = 1 - e^{-\phi W}$, where $\alpha = \phi/2$.

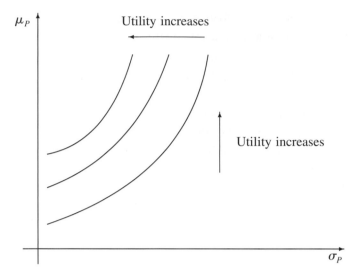

Fig. 4.3. Indifference curves in μ_P, σ_P space

In mean-variance analysis the investor's preferences can be expressed by indifference curves in the plane of expected return, μ_P (a 'good'), and standard deviation of return, σ_P (representing risk, a 'bad'). Points to the north-west, depicting higher expected return and lower risk, are more preferred to points in the south-east.

In particular, sometimes $1/\alpha$ is referred to as a measure of the investor's *risk toler-ance*. If $\alpha = 0$, risk has no influence: the investor is wholly tolerant of risk. At the other extreme, if α is very large (formally, $\alpha \to \infty$), the investor becomes extremely *in*tolerant to risk. To see this, divide through (4.14) by α and then allow $\alpha \to \infty$. The objective function then becomes $-\sigma_P^2$, the maximization of which is equivalent to minimizing risk, irrespective of expected return.[21]

4.4.3 The FVR in the mean-variance model

What form does the FVR take in the mean-variance model? Appendix 4.5 shows that, in this case, the FVR can be written as

$$\frac{\mu_j - r_0}{\sigma_{jP}/\sigma_P} = \frac{\mu_P - r_0}{\sigma_P} \qquad j = 1, 2, \dots, n \qquad (4.15)$$

---

[21] While plausible enough, this argument is imprecise. A more rigorous treatment specifies the objective function as $G(\mu_P, \sigma_P^2) = \gamma\mu_P - \alpha\sigma_P^2$, where $\gamma > 0$ is another parameter. The investor's preferences with respect to risk are now captured by the ratio γ/α. As $\gamma \to 0$ for given $\alpha > 0$, $\gamma/\alpha \to 0$: in words, the investor becomes extremely intolerant to risk. In graphical terms, the indifference curves become vertical and the investor acts to minimize risk no matter what the expected return.

where σ_{jP} denotes the covariance between the rate of return on asset j and the rate of return on the portfolio as a whole. This important set of equalities lies at the core of mean-variance analysis and is studied in detail in chapter 5. In particular, it is shown there that σ_{jP}/σ_P equals the increment to risk (as expressed by σ_P) associated with an incremental change to the proportion of asset j in the portfolio. Thus, the FVR states that each asset's expected rate of return in excess of the risk-free rate, $\mu_j - r_0$, per unit of its contribution to overall risk, σ_{jP}/σ_P, is the same for all assets – a necessary condition for a mean-variance optimum.

Notice that the investor's *preferences* (attitudes to risk) do not appear in expression (4.15). The equalities depend only on *beliefs* (expressed in terms of means, variances and covariances of assets' rates of return). This does not mean that preferences are irrelevant but, rather, that there is a sense in which the role of preferences is separate from the role of beliefs. For a mean-variance investor, portfolio selection can be understood as the outcome of a two-stage process.

1. Choose a portfolio that satisfies the FVR conditions, (4.15). It is shown in chapter 5 that this portfolio takes a very special form, consisting of exactly *two* 'special' assets, which are themselves portfolios of assets. If a risk-free asset is available, one of the two special assets can be chosen to comprise just the risk-free asset alone. Investor preferences are not relevant in constructing the special assets; their composition depends only on means, variances and covariances that can, in principle, be estimated from observed data.
2. According to investor preferences, choose the optimal portfolio that optimizes these preferences – i.e. choose the portfolio that reaches the highest feasible indifference curve.

The practical importance of this approach is that it is often reasonable to assume that the first stage is the same for all investors who have the same information, while investors can be allowed to possess their own, unique preferences (expressing attitudes to risk) in the second stage.

4.5 Summary

Three approaches to the study of uncertainty lie at the core of this chapter.

1. *State-preference analysis.* The state-preference model provides a general framework for understanding decisions under uncertainty. A 'state of the world' represents a complete description of all the relevant information (e.g. asset prices, company profitability, technology, the weather, etc.) needed for a decision maker to evaluate unknown future outcomes. Decisions are made before the state is revealed, and, once it is revealed, all uncertainty is resolved. Decision makers are required to be able to order their actions in a consistent way but, beyond this, little is assumed about their behaviour. The drawback is that the model yields few, if any, testable predictions. It is too general to handle many practical problems.

2. *Expected utility hypothesis.* The EUH can be interpreted as a specialization of the state-preference approach that (a) enables the use of probabilities to express beliefs, and (b) characterizes preferences about uncertain outcomes with a von Neumann–Morgenstern utility function that depends on the outcome (say, the level of wealth) but that is the same function for all states. The EUH leads to the *fundamental valuation relationship*, $\mathrm{E}[(1+r_j)H] = 1$, a condition necessary for the maximization of expected utility in portfolio theory.

   The EUH is the cornerstone of the economics of decision making under uncertainty, but evidence on individual behaviour contradicts its predictions (and, by implication, some of its assumptions). Moreover, the EUH's predictions, whether contradicted or not, are not sufficiently definite for most portfolio studies, unless a specific functional form for the von Neumann–Morgenstern utility function is assumed.

3. *Mean-variance analysis.* Because means and variances are routine to estimate and interpret, the mean-variance model is directly applicable to practical portfolio selection problems. The model is, however, highly restrictive; indeed, so restrictive that empirical evidence often casts doubt on its validity (for example, the model ignores skewed distributions of asset returns). Even so, mean-variance analysis provides the foundation for the capital asset pricing model (studied in chapter 6), one of the most well-known (though frequently disparaged) models of asset prices.

Attempts have been made to overcome the inadequacies of these three approaches, mainly by appeals to behavioural theories of choice under uncertainty that are more commonly found in psychology than economics. Important though the alternatives are, their emergence has not yet served to displace the more orthodox models studied in this chapter.

Further reading

The economic theory of decision making under uncertainty extends far beyond finance. Most of the contributions to the economics literature were not, and are not, directed primarily to problems in finance such as portfolio selection. Intermediate microeconomics texts such as those by Varian (2003, chaps. 12 & 13) provide an elementary starting point. An exposition of the expected utility hypothesis (together with some alternative approaches to decision making under uncertainty, such as 'safety first' and 'stochastic dominance', not covered here) appears in Elton, Gruber, Brown and Goetzmann (2003, chaps. 10 & 11). Bernstein (1996) offers an informative and entertaining account of the emergence and development of ideas about uncertainty. For rigorous analyses of uncertainty in modern finance, see Lengwiler (2004, especially chaps. 2–5) and Cvitanić and Zapatero (2004, chap. 4).

   The axiomatic foundations of the EUH have been intensively researched for many years. Concise overviews of the literature are to be found in *The New*

Palgrave Dictionary of Money and Finance (Newman, Milgate and Eatwell, 1992: 'expected utility hypothesis', Vol. I, pp. 856–62; and 'uncertainty', Vol. III, pp. 712–19). The entry on 'state preference approach' (Vol. III, pp. 530–2) is also worth consulting.

Most derivations of the EUH begin by assuming the existence of probabilities. Although careful not to make claims of originality, Marschak and Radner (1972, chap. 1) develop a clear and comprehensible account in which probabilities emerge as part of the solution, and are not assumed to exist at the outset. Arrow (1971, especially chaps. 1–4) provides what remains one of the finest treatments, at an advanced level, of both the foundations and applications of the theory of choice under uncertainty. For insightful discussions of the controversies about the EUH axioms, see Drèze (1974) and Ellsberg (2001).

Excellent starting points for behavioural finance are the analyses by Shiller (1999) and Kahneman (2003). Also worth consulting are Epstein (1992) and Olsen (1998). These references discuss applications that go beyond the coverage of this chapter to include topics relevant for chapters 10 and 11. Among the many contributions not specifically directed to finance, those by Tversky and Kahneman (1974), Kahneman and Tversky (1979), Loomes and Sugden (1982) and Starmer (2000) deserve careful attention. Shiller (2000) applies the principles of behavioural finance in a perceptive analysis of the US stock market boom of the late 1990s.

Appendix 4.1: Useful notation

This appendix outlines convenient ways of expressing wealth and rates of return that are handy in concise presentations of portfolio theory. It uses no more than simple algebraic manipulations.

For brevity, the subscript k (denoting the state of the world) is omitted. Terminal wealth can then be written as

$$W = \sum_{j=1}^{n} v_j x_j$$

where the expression $\sum_{j=1}^{n}$ means 'sum up over the j from 1 to n'. Often the $j = 1$ and n are omitted when it is clear what is being summed and what its range is.

Now substitute the relationship used to define the rate of return on asset j: $v_j = (1 + r_j)p_j$. Remember that r_j varies with the state but p_j is observed at the outset and hence does not. Hence

$$W = \sum_{j=1}^{n} (1 + r_j)p_j x_j \tag{4.16}$$

Suppose that initial wealth is positive: $A > 0$. This being so, much of portfolio theory can be presented in terms of the *proportion* of initial wealth invested in asset j, denoted by a_j, where $a_j \equiv p_j x_j / A$. By definition, all the $a_1, a_2, \ldots, a_n$ must add up to unity: $\sum a_j = 1$.

Now it is possible to construct an expression for the rate of return on the whole portfolio, $(W - A)/A$, or $(W/A) - 1$, as follows:

$$W = \sum (1 + r_j) p_j x_j \qquad \text{from (4.16)}$$

$$= \sum (1 + r_j) a_j A \qquad \text{from the definition of } a_j$$

$$\frac{W}{A} = \sum (1 + r_j) a_j \qquad \text{dividing through by } A$$

$$r_P \equiv \frac{W - A}{A} = \sum r_j a_j \qquad \text{using } \sum a_j = 1$$

Thus, the rate of return on the portfolio, r_P, equals the weighted sum of the rates of return on each asset, the weights being the portfolio proportions. Note that the rate of return is uncertain because r_j, *not* a_j, varies across states.

Finally, suppose that $A = 0$. This will be the case for arbitrage portfolios, which by definition use zero initial wealth. It is not possible to divide by A and it is convenient to define $y_j \equiv p_j x_j$, the total investment in asset j. (In a non-trivial portfolio constructed from zero initial wealth, y_j will be positive for some assets, negative for others.) Thus

$$W = \sum (1 + r_j) y_j \qquad \text{using } y_j \equiv p_j x_j$$

$$= \sum y_j + \sum r_j y_j$$

$$= \sum r_j y_j \qquad \text{because } A = \sum y_j = 0 \text{ by assumption}$$

In this case, r_P cannot be defined as above because the denominator, A, is zero.

Appendix 4.2: Derivation of the FVR

Designate the risk-free asset as 'asset 0', with payoff v_0 in every state. The FVR is obtained by solving the problem: choose $x_0, x_1, x_2, \ldots, x_n$ to maximize $E[u(W)]$ subject to $p_0 x_0 + p_1 x_1 + p_2 x_2 + \cdots + p_n x_n = A$, where x_0 is the investment in the risk-free asset. Consider the Lagrangian expression

$$\mathcal{L} = \pi_1 u(W_1) + \pi_2 u(W_2) + \cdots + \pi_\ell u(W_\ell)$$

$$+ \lambda (A - p_0 x_0 - p_1 x_1 - p_2 x_2 - \cdots - p_n x_n)$$

where $W_k = v_0 x_0 + v_{k1} x_1 + v_{k2} x_2 + \cdots + v_{kn} x_n$. Partially differentiating the Lagrangian with respect to x_j and λ provides the first-order conditions:

$$\pi_1 v_0 u'(W_1) + \pi_2 v_0 u'(W_2) + \cdots + \pi_\ell v_0 u'(W_\ell) = \lambda p_0$$

$$\pi_1 v_{11} u'(W_1) + \pi_2 v_{21} u'(W_2) + \cdots + \pi_\ell v_{\ell 1} u'(W_\ell) = \lambda p_1$$

$$\vdots$$

$$\pi_1 v_{1j} u'(W_1) + \pi_2 v_{2j} u'(W_2) + \cdots + \pi_\ell v_{\ell j} u'(W_\ell) = \lambda p_j$$

$$\vdots$$

$$\pi_1 v_{1n} u'(W_1) + \pi_2 v_{2n} u'(W_2) + \cdots + \pi_\ell v_{\ell n} u'(W_\ell) = \lambda p_n$$

$$p_0 x_0 + p_1 x_1 + p_2 x_2 + \cdots + p_n x_n = A$$

In a more compact form, the first-order conditions can be written as

$$E[v_j u'(W)] = \lambda p_j \qquad j = 0, 1, 2, \ldots, n$$

Now divide through each equation by its respective p_j:

$$E[(v_j/p_j) u'(W)] = \lambda \qquad j = 0, 1, 2, \ldots, n$$

and remember that, by definition, $r_j = (v_j/p_j) - 1$, so that

$$E[(1 + r_j) u'(W)] = \lambda \qquad j = 0, 1, 2, \ldots, n$$

which is the FVR for the one-period portfolio problem.

Appendix 4.3: Implications of complete asset markets

This appendix shows that, if two conditions are satisfied, the H random variable in the FVR does not depend on preferences; that is, it is the same for every individual investor irrespective of the investor's von Neumann–Morgenstern utility function. The two conditions are (a) unanimity of beliefs and (b) a complete set of asset markets. Unanimity of beliefs asserts that all investors behave as if they attach the same probability to each state. The result can be demonstrated once the term 'complete set of asset markets' has been defined.

Definition of a complete set of asset markets: there exists a complete set of asset markets if it is possible to construct ℓ distinct portfolios – one for each state – such that each portfolio has a payoff of one unit of account in precisely one state and zero in every other state. Thus, for every state it is possible to obtain a unit payoff in that state and that state alone. Each of these portfolios can be regarded as an asset in its own right, here called an 'Arrow security'.[22]

---

[22] So named for its originator, Kenneth Arrow (see Arrow, 1963–64).

Formally, an *Arrow security* has a payoff of one in exactly one state and zero in every other. Thus, completeness of asset markets is equivalent to the existence of ℓ distinct Arrow securities – one for each state.

Assume that there exists a complete set of asset markets. To keep the notation simple (and for no other reason), suppose that the completeness is represented by the presence of ℓ Arrow securities labelled $j = 1, 2, \ldots, \ell$ (there may be lots of other securities as well, labelled $j = \ell + 1, \ell + 2, \ldots, n$). By construction, each Arrow security, j, has payoffs

$$v_{kj} = \begin{cases} 1 & \text{if } k = j \\ 0 & \text{if } k \neq j \end{cases}$$

Also by construction, the rate of return on an Arrow security satisfies $(1 + r_{kj}) = 1/p_j$ if $j = k$, and $(1 + r_{kj}) = 0$ otherwise.

Consider the FVR written out in full for any asset j:

$$(1 + r_{1j})H_1\pi_1 + (1 + r_{2j})H_2\pi_2 + \cdots (1 + r_{\ell j})H_\ell\pi_\ell = 1 \qquad (4.17)$$

Note that all investors agree on the rate of return in each state and, from the assumption of unanimity of beliefs, the probabilities $(\pi_1, \pi_2, \ldots, \pi_\ell)$ are the same for all investors.

The reasoning so far allows the H_k to differ across individuals in accordance with their preferences (how they subjectively value the payoffs in different states).

Now consider equation (4.17) for the Arrow securities alone. By the definition of Arrow securities, (4.17) specializes to

$$(1 + r_{jj})H_j\pi_j = 1$$

$$\frac{1}{p_j}H_j\pi_j = 1$$

$$H_j = \frac{p_j}{\pi_j} \qquad j = 1, 2, \ldots, \ell \qquad (4.18)$$

By construction, the right-hand side of (4.18) is the same for every investor. Hence, H_j is the same for every investor – the result asserted at the outset. Notice that (4.18) is a consequence of *asset market equilibrium* (under the stated conditions), not a feature of individual investors' preferences.

Appendix 4.4: Quadratic von Neumann–Morgenstern utility

Any quadratic von Neumann–Morgenstern utility function can be written in the form

$$u(W) = W - bW^2 \qquad (4.19)$$

where $b > 0$ is a parameter characterizing preferences. (The multiplication of (4.19) by any positive constant and the addition of any constant would leave unchanged all decisions based on expected utility.) In order to ensure that utility is increasing over the relevant range of wealth, b is assumed to satisfy $b < 1/(2W_k)$ for W_k in every state $k = 1, 2, \ldots, \ell$.

Taking the expectations in (4.19):

$$E[u(W)] = E[W] - bE[W^2] = E[W] - b(\text{var}[W] + E[W]^2)$$

which is the form the mean-variance criterion takes when derived from a quadratic utility function.

To obtain the relationship between $F(\cdot, \cdot)$ and $G(\cdot, \cdot)$, notice that terminal wealth can be written as $W = (1 + r_P)A$. Hence, $E[W] = (1 + \mu_P)A$ and $\text{var}[W] = \sigma_P^2 A^2$, so that

$$G(\mu_P, \sigma_P^2) \equiv F((1 + \mu_P)A, \sigma_P^2 A^2)$$

Appendix 4.5: The FVR in the mean-variance model

To obtain the FVR in the mean-variance model, note that marginal utility is given by differentiating (4.19): $u'(W) = 1 - 2bW$. Also, recall that for any two random variables, X and Y, $E[XY] = E[X]E[Y] + \text{cov}[X, Y]$, from the definition of covariance. A sketch of the derivation of the FVR is as follows:

$$E[(r_j - r_0)u'(W)] = 0$$

$$E[(r_j - r_0)]E[u'(W)] + \text{cov}[(r_j - r_0), u'(W)] = 0$$

$$(\mu_j - r_0)E[u'(W)] - 2bA\sigma_{jP} = 0 \qquad (4.20)$$

where $\sigma_{jP} \equiv \text{cov}[r_j, r_P]$. Note that $\text{cov}[(r_j - r_0), u'(W)] = \text{cov}[r_j - r_0, 1 - 2bW] = E[(r_j - r_0 - \mu_j + r_0)(1 - 2bW - 1 + 2bE[W])] = -2bE[(r_j - \mu_j)(W - E[W])] = -2bAE[(r_j - \mu_j)(r_P - \mu_P)] = -2bA\sigma_{jP}$, using $W = (1 + r_P)A$.

If condition (4.20) holds for any asset j, it must also hold for the portfolio as a whole (the portfolio can be interpreted as a single, composite asset):

$$(\mu_P - r_0)E[u'(W)] - 2bA\text{cov}[r_P, r_P] = 0$$

$$(\mu_P - r_0)E[u'(W)] - 2bA\sigma_P^2 = 0 \qquad (4.21)$$

since $\sigma_P^2 \equiv \text{var}(P) = \text{cov}[r_P, r_P]$. Now rearrange (4.20) and (4.21), cancelling out $E[u'(W)]$ and $2bA$, to give

$$\frac{\mu_j - r_0}{\sigma_{jP}/\sigma_P} = \frac{\mu_P - r_0}{\sigma_P} \quad j = 1, 2, \ldots, n$$

which is a standard expression for the FVR in mean-variance analysis.

References

Arrow, K. J. (1963–64), 'The role of securities in the optimal allocation of risk-bearing', *Review of Economic Studies*, 31(2), pp. 91–6 (also published as chap. 4 in Arrow, 1971).

——— (1971), *Essays in the Theory of Risk-Bearing*, Amsterdam: North-Holland Publishing.

Bernstein, P. L. (1996), *Against the Gods: The Remarkable Story of Risk*, New York: John Wiley & Sons.

Chamberlain, G. (1983), 'A characterization of the distributions that imply mean-variance utility functions', *Journal of Economic Theory*, 29(1), pp. 185–201.

Cvitanić, J., and F. Zapatero (2004), *Introduction to the Economics and Mathematics of Financial Markets*, Cambridge, MA, and London: MIT Press.

Debreu, G. (1959), *The Theory of Value*, New Haven, CT, and London: Yale University Press.

Drèze, J. H. (1974), 'Axiomatic theories of choice, cardinal utility and subjective probability: a review', in J. H. Drèze (ed.), *Allocation under Uncertainty: Equilibrium and Optimality*, London: Macmillan, chap. 1.

Ellsberg, D. (2001), *Risk, Ambiguity and Decision*, New York and London: Garland Publishing.

Elton, E. J., M. J. Gruber, S. J. Brown and W. N. Goetzmann (2003), *Modern Portfolio Theory and Investment Analysis*, New York: John Wiley & Sons, 6th edn.

Engle, R. F. (2004), 'Risk and volatility: econometric models and financial practice', *American Economic Review*, 94(3), pp. 405–20.

Epstein, L. (1992), 'Behavior under risk: recent developments in theory and applications', in J. J. Laffont (ed.), *Advances in Economic Theory*, Cambridge: Cambridge University Press, chap. 1.

Kahneman, D. (2003), 'Maps of bounded rationality: psychology for behavioral economics', *American Economic Review*, 93(5), pp. 1449–75.

Kahneman, D., and A. Tversky (1979), 'Prospect theory: an analysis of decision under risk', *Econometrica*, 47(2), pp. 263–91.

Keynes, J. M. (1936–37), 'The general theory of employment', *Quarterly Journal of Economics*, 51(2), pp. 209–23 (also published in Keynes *Collected Writings*, Vol. XIV, pp. 109–23).

Knight, F. H. (1921), *Risk, Uncertainty and Profit*, Boston: Houghton Mifflin.

Lengwiler, Y. (2004), *Microfoundations of Financial Economics*, Princeton Series in Finance, Princeton, NJ, and Woodstock, UK: Princeton University Press.

Levy, H. (1989), 'Two-moment decision models and expected utility maximization: comment', *American Economic Review*, 79(3), pp. 597–600.

Levy, H., and R. Duchin (2004), 'Asset return distributions and the investment horizon', *Journal of Portfolio Management*, 30(3), pp. 47–62.

Loomes, G., and R. Sugden (1982), 'Regret theory: an alternative theory of rational choice under uncertainty', *Economic Journal*, 92, pp. 805–24.

Marschak, J., and R. Radner (1972), *Economic Theory of Teams*, New Haven, CT: Yale University Press.

Meyer, J. (1987), 'Two-moment decision models and expected utility maximization', *American Economic Review*, 77(3), pp. 421–30.

(1989), 'Two-moment decision models and expected utility maximization: reply', *American Economic Review*, 79(3), p. 603.

Newman, P., M. Milgate and J. Eatwell (eds.) (1992), *The New Palgrave Dictionary of Money and Finance*, London: Macmillan (three volumes).

Olsen, R. A. (1998), 'Behavioral finance and its implications for stock-price volatility', *Financial Analysts Journal*, 54(2), pp. 10–18.

Savage, L. J. (1954), *The Foundations of Statistics*, New York: John Wiley & Sons.

Shiller, R. J. (1999), 'Human behavior and the efficiency of the financial system', in J. B. Taylor and M. Woodford (eds.), *Handbook of Macroeconomics*, New York: Elsevier, Vol. IC, chap. 20, pp. 1305–40.

(2000), *Irrational Exuberance*, Princeton, NJ, and Oxford: Princeton University Press.

(2003), *The New Financial Order: Risk in the 21st Century*, Princeton, NJ, and Oxford: Princeton University Press.

Sinn, H.-W. (1989), 'Two-moment decision models and expected utility maximization: comment', *American Economic Review*, 79(3), pp. 601–2.

Starmer, C. (2000), 'Developments in non-expected utility theory: the hunt for a descriptive theory of choice under risk', *Journal of Economic Literature*, 38(2), pp. 332–82.

Tversky, A., and D. Kahneman (1974), 'Judgment under uncertainty: heuristics and biases', *Science*, 185, pp. 1124–31.

Varian, H. R. (2003), *Intermediate Microeconomics: A Modern Approach*, New York: W. W. Norton, 6th edn.

von Neumann, J., and O. Morgenstern (1944), *Theory of Games and Economic Behavior*, Princeton, NJ: Princeton University Press.

5

Portfolio selection: the mean-variance model

Overview

This chapter explores in greater depth than chapter 4 the study of portfolio decisions when investors act to optimize a *mean-variance* objective function.

In addition to its significance as a testable theory of asset demand, mean-variance analysis plays two other roles: (a) it provides a method for the practical construction of portfolios; and (b) it forms the foundation for the capital asset pricing model, the subject of chapter 6.

Although mean-variance analysis and the CAPM are close relatives, it is important to distinguish between the two. Mean-variance analysis provides a theory of individual behaviour regardless of whether the market, as a whole, is in equilibrium. The CAPM, building on mean-variance analysis, provides a theory of asset prices in market equilibrium.[1] This chapter addresses only the former problem – of individual behaviour – and is silent about the implications of market equilibrium for asset prices.

The analysis in this chapter proceeds in a sequence of steps, each of which builds on the previous one. The steps are summarized as follows.

1. A review of the basic concepts of mean-variance analysis.
2. The choice between two risky assets: the objective here is to construct a frontier between the expected rate of return on each portfolio and the portfolio's standard deviation of return. No risk-free asset is available.
3. The choice among many risky assets, again excluding risk-free lending or borrowing. The portfolio frontier is found to take the same form as in the two-asset case, and an important proposition – the first mutual fund theorem – is explained.

---

[1] Market equilibrium refers here to an equality between the total of investors' demands to hold assets and the aggregate stocks available to be held.

4. The choice among many assets when a risk-free asset is available. In this case, the portfolio frontier takes a simple linear form, hence justifying the second mutual fund theorem.

5. Optimal portfolio selection: here the selection of an optimal portfolio from among the efficient portfolios is examined.

Risk. In this chapter, the *standard deviation* (or, equivalently for this purpose, variance) of an asset's rate of return is used to measure the *risk* associated with holding the asset. As noted in chapter 4, this association should be treated as provisional. Subsequent chapters argue that it needs to be qualified: there may exist other, more suitable, measures of an asset's risk than its standard deviation of return.

Absence of market frictions. In common with much of financial theory, it is assumed that market frictions (transaction costs and institutional restrictions on trades) can be ignored. Just how restrictive this assumption is, of course, depends on the severity of the frictions in any particular application. The treatment here requires, at least, that market frictions do not impinge in a significant way on the portfolio selection decisions of investors.

5.1 Mean-variance analysis: concepts and notation

5.1.1 The mean-variance objective

Each investor who acts according to a mean-variance objective is assumed to choose a portfolio that maximizes

$$G = G(\mu_P, \sigma_P^2)$$

subject to the constraint that the total value of assets (calculated at initial prices) does not exceed initial wealth The expected (or mean) rate of return on the portfolio is denoted by μ_P. Risk is measured by σ_P, the standard deviation of the rate of return on the portfolio. Pairs of μ_P and σ_P for which $G(\mu_P, \sigma_P^2)$ is constant define *indifference curves* (examined later, in section 5.5; see also chapter 4, page 103).

In this chapter, the investor is assumed to make exactly one portfolio decision; a decision that (for whatever reason) remains unchanged for the whole of the time period being studied. What happens after the decision has been made is ignored. (More complicated decisions involving revisions to portfolios – and other relevant choices – are explored in chapter 11.)

As explained in chapter 4, a mean-variance investor's optimal portfolio selection can be split logically into two steps. *First*, the portfolio frontier, comprising those portfolios for which σ_P^2 is minimized for each μ_P, is constructed.[2] *Second*, a choice is made from among the frontier portfolios so as to maximize the objective, G, in accordance with preferences, expressed by the investor's own, personal $G(\cdot, \cdot)$ function. Assuming that the objective function is increasing in expected return and decreasing in risk, only a portion of the portfolio frontier – the efficient portfolio set – is relevant in the second step.

The expected return and standard deviation of portfolio return encapsulate the investor's beliefs about the rates of return on individual assets: by varying the composition of the portfolio, the investor effectively chooses μ_P and σ_P. The constraint on the investor's portfolio choices is called the *portfolio frontier*; it is expressed in terms of μ_P and σ_P, rather than directly in terms of the amount of each asset held.

The mean-variance model acquires its practical relevance because means, covariances and variances[3] of rates of return can be estimated from past observations on asset prices or from other relevant information. That is, *experience* (typically, price observations) can be used to represent an investor's *beliefs* in a way that involves standard statistical methods – methods that would not necessarily be applicable in other models of portfolio selection. Armed with estimates of means and variances, it is a routine matter to calculate the portfolio frontier.

In what follows, a distinction should be drawn between the theoretical concepts (of means and variances) and the *estimates* that are made of them. They are different things: the estimates are observable counterparts of the unobservable theoretical concepts. In practical calculations of portfolio frontiers, it is necessary to use numerical values (i.e. estimates) of means and variances. These can be obtained using a variety of methods. Calculations based on past data may be the most convenient way to estimate the means and variances. But individuals may differ in their beliefs (perhaps they differ in their available information, or in how they process it) and there is nothing that compels individuals to use one method rather than another in forming their estimates. Indeed, from the standpoint of economic analysis, investors may be assumed to act only *as if* they choose according to a mean-variance criterion; there is no reason why they should be *consciously* aware of means and variances.

If all investors have access to the same information, and if this information is the set of past rates of return on the assets, then, arguably, all investors should possess common beliefs and, hence, should arrive at the same estimates of the means and variances. (More precisely, what is important is whether investors act

---

[2] The diagrammatic treatment is given in terms of σ_P rather than σ_P^2. Given that the standard deviation is the positive square root of the variance, minimizing one is equivalent to minimizing the other. Hence, it is a matter of convenience about which to minimize.

[3] From now on, 'variances' should be understood to include covariances, unless indicated otherwise.

as if they agree. Whether they could or would acknowledge that they agree is another matter, irrelevant in this context.)

To postulate that investors agree about means and variances is restrictive, however, and is not needed in this chapter; the focus of attention is on the decisions of a single investor. The question of whether investors act as if they share the same beliefs about the means and variances of assets' returns becomes important in the theory of market equilibrium, involving as it does interactions among all investors.

5.1.2 Notation

The following notation is used throughout the remainder of this chapter, and also in chapter 6.

r_j = rate of return on asset $j = 1, 2, \ldots, n$ (each r_j is a random variable).

$\mu_j = \mathrm{E}[r_j]$, expected rate of return on asset j.

$\sigma_{ij} = \mathrm{cov}(r_i, r_j) \equiv \mathrm{E}[(r_i - \mu_i)(r_j - \mu_j)]$, covariance between the rates of return r_i and r_j.

$\sigma_j = +\sqrt{\sigma_{jj}}$, standard deviation of return on j, where $\sigma_{jj} = \mathrm{var}(r_j) \equiv \mathrm{E}[(r_j - \mu_j)^2]$.

$\rho_{ij} = \sigma_{ij}/(\sigma_i \sigma_j)$, correlation coefficient between returns on assets i and j.

$a_j = p_j x_j / A$, proportion of portfolio invested in asset j, with $\sum_j a_j = 1$.

r_0 = rate of return on *risk-free* asset, $\mu_0 \equiv r_0$.

In the following, a subscript i or j refers to a single asset while an upper-case subscript (e.g. P or Z) refers to a portfolio of several assets. A *portfolio* is defined as a vector, or list, of asset holdings, $x_0, x_1, x_2, \ldots, x_n$, chosen subject to the constraint $\sum p_j x_j = A$, where A denotes initial wealth. The portfolio is more conveniently written in terms of proportions: $a_0, a_1, a_2, \ldots, a_n$. In this representation asset prices and initial wealth are hidden in the background. The expected rate of return and variance of the rate of return on any portfolio, P, take the form

$$\mu_P = \sum_j a_j \mu_j$$

and

$$\sigma_P^2 = \sum_{i=1}^{n} \sum_{j=1}^{n} a_i a_j \sigma_{ij}$$

The range of j in the above summation for μ_P is $j = 1, 2, \ldots, n$ when there is *no* risk-free asset, and $j = 0, 1, 2, \ldots, n$ when there is a risk-free asset. It should be clear from the context which is intended.

5.2 Portfolio frontier: two risky assets

The case of two risky assets (with no risk-free asset) is a handy building block for the general case of n assets. In figure 5.1 the two end points mark the expected returns and standard deviations of the two assets; the curved line joining them is the portfolio frontier. Note that the frontier must pass through the two dots marked 'Asset 1' and 'Asset 2' because, with just two assets to choose between, both are on the frontier: depending on the investor's preferences, total wealth could be devoted entirely to one of the assets. The goal here is to understand how the frontier is constructed. Having grasped the two-asset model, the general case of $n > 2$ assets can be understood with little extra effort.

Define $a = a_1$ so that $(1 - a) = a_2$. Then, from the definitions of expectations and variances,

$$\mu_P = a\mu_1 + (1-a)\mu_2$$
$$\sigma_P^2 = a^2\sigma_{11} + 2a(1-a)\sigma_{12} + (1-a)^2\sigma_{22}$$
$$= a^2\sigma_1^2 + 2a(1-a)\rho_{12}\sigma_1\sigma_2 + (1-a)^2\sigma_2^2$$

Note that $\sigma_{11} \equiv \sigma_1^2$, $\sigma_{22} \equiv \sigma_2^2$, $\sigma_{12} \equiv \rho_{12}\sigma_1\sigma_2$.

Consider the special cases for which the correlation between the two rates of return takes on extreme values: $\rho_{12} = \pm 1$:

$$\sigma_P^2 = a^2\sigma_1^2 \pm 2a(1-a)\sigma_1\sigma_2 + (1-a)^2\sigma_2^2$$
$$= (a\sigma_1 \pm (1-a)\sigma_2)^2$$
$$\sigma_P = |a\sigma_1 \pm (1-a)\sigma_2|$$

Hence, bearing in mind that the standard deviation, σ_P, must be non-negative (by definition),

$$\rho_{12} = +1 \Longrightarrow \sigma_P = a\sigma_1 + (1-a)\sigma_2$$
$$\rho_{12} = -1 \Longrightarrow \sigma_P = (a\sigma_1 - (1-a)\sigma_2) \geqq 0 \text{ for } a \geqq \frac{\sigma_2}{\sigma_1 + \sigma_2}$$
$$\rho_{12} = -1 \Longrightarrow \sigma_P = -(a\sigma_1 - (1-a)\sigma_2) > 0 \text{ for } a < \frac{\sigma_2}{\sigma_1 + \sigma_2}$$

The expressions above trace out lines in the (μ_P, σ_P) plane after eliminating a, using the definition $\mu_P = a\mu_1 + (1-a)\mu_2$. The three lines are depicted in figure 5.2.

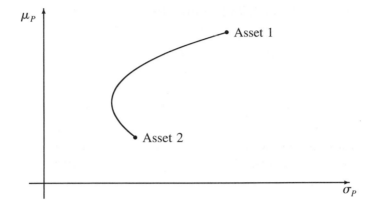

Fig. 5.1. The efficiency frontier with two assets

The portfolio frontier depicts the minimum σ_P for each level of μ_P. It is shown here for non-negative combinations of two assets. For a zero proportion of asset 2 in the portfolio, the frontier is located at the point labelled 'Asset 1'. Similarly, for a zero proportion of asset 1 in the portfolio, the frontier is located at the point labelled 'Asset 2'.

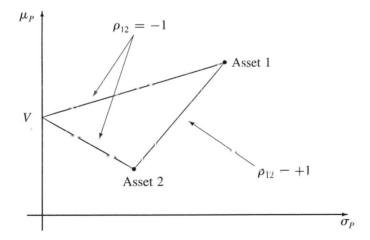

Fig. 5.2. The efficiency frontier with two assets and $\rho_{12} = \pm 1$

The portfolio frontier depends, among other things, on the correlation between the assets' rates of return. At one extreme, $\rho_{12} = +1$, the frontier is the line segment joining points labelled 'Asset 1' and 'Asset 2'. At the other extreme, $\rho_{12} = -1$, the frontier consists of two line segments, from 'Asset 2' to V, and from V to 'Asset 1'.

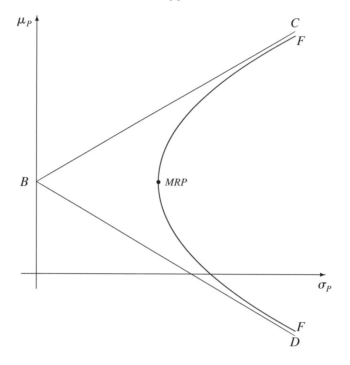

Fig. 5.3. The efficiency frontier allowing for short-sales

The frontier *FF* allows for all possible combinations of assets in the portfolio (such that their proportions sum to unity) including a negative proportion (short-sale) of one or other asset. The positively sloped portion of *FF* approaches but never reaches the ray *BC*. The negatively sloped portion of *FF* approaches but never reaches the ray *BD*. The point marked *MRP* (minimum risk portfolio) identifies the portfolio for which σ_P is smallest for all possible values of expected return (for this portfolio, $\mu_{mrp} = B$).

Remarks

1. For all values of the correlation coefficient, ρ_{12}, strictly greater than -1 and strictly less than $+1$, the frontier is non-linear. For non-negative holdings of both assets it is the line depicted in figure 5.1, lying within the triangular region bounded by the lines in figure 5.2.

2. Extension of the portfolio frontier beyond the points given by $a = 1$ or $a = 0$ involves the *short-sale* of one of the assets (the resulting funds being used to purchase the other).

3. It can be shown that the relationship between the expected return on the portfolio, μ_P, and the *variance*, σ_P^2, is a *parabola*. Usually, as here, the graph is drawn using the *standard deviation* σ_P, in which case the relationship between μ_P and σ_P is a *hyperbola*.

   This hyperbola takes the form depicted in figure 5.3 on page 120. Note that the frontier approaches, but never intersects, the two rays *BC* and *BD* as σ_P tends to infinity. The point *MRP* on the frontier, for which σ_P is at a minimum when ranging over *all* expected return values (i.e. not for a given μ_P), is called the *minimum risk portfolio*.[4] The expected rate of return corresponding to *MRP* is denoted by point *B* in figure 5.3. For later reference, let μ_{mrp} denote the expected rate of return on the minimum risk portfolio. Also for later reference, note that the MRP is optimal only for investors whose preferences, expressed by $G(\mu_P, \sigma_P^2)$, focus entirely on risk and give zero weight to expected return. Every investor who is prepared to tolerate higher risk for a higher expected rate of return would choose a portfolio with greater risk than that of the MRP.

4. The upward-sloping arm of the frontier defines the set of *efficient* portfolios – i.e. an efficient portfolio is one for which μ_P is maximized for a given σ_P. As already noted, if $G(\mu_P, \sigma_P^2)$ is increasing in expected return and decreasing in risk, the choice of an optimal portfolio will always be made from the efficient set.

5.3 Portfolio frontier: many risky assets and no risk-free asset

Suppose that there are $n > 2$ risky assets (with no risk-free asset). The shape of the portfolio frontier is the same as for the two-asset case (it is a hyperbola). Including additional assets allows for increased diversification – i.e. the attainment of at least as low a level of risk for each level of expected return. The frontier with a larger number of assets is located to the left of the frontier with fewer assets. (More precisely, the frontier is nowhere to the right when additional assets are available. This allows for the possibility that the additional assets have returns that are perfectly correlated with combinations of existing assets, and hence do not affect the trade-off between μ_P and σ_P.)

It is assumed from now on that the n assets are 'genuinely different', in the sense that the return on no asset can be formed as a linear combination of the returns on other assets. *Composite* assets created as portfolios (linear combinations) of existing assets play an important part in what follows, but for convenience they are excluded from the list of n underlying assets.

To gain some intuition for the multiple-asset case, imagine starting with two assets. Then form an *efficient* portfolio of the two. This portfolio has a random return (with an expectation and a variance) that depends on the proportions of the two assets held in it. Now treat this portfolio as if it is a single asset. This composite asset is rather like a simple 'closed-end mutual fund' in the United States or 'investment trust' in Britain. The composite asset can be identified with a point on the efficient frontier for the two underlying assets, the location of the point being determined by the asset proportions in the portfolio.

---

[4] This terminology is convenient but could be misleading: all points on the frontier depict points of minimum risk for a *given* expected return, μ_P. The *minimum risk portfolio* is defined without holding μ_P given at a specified level. The *MRP* identifies a portfolio with *global* minimum risk.

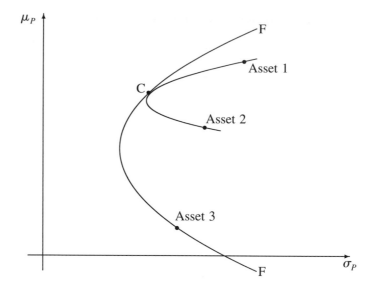

Fig. 5.4. The efficiency frontier with three assets

If a third asset becomes available, it is possible to construct a frontier *as if* for two assets, one of which is a composite of assets 1 and 2 (such as marked by point C), the other being asset 3. The line FF depicts the overall portfolio frontier only if asset 3 on its own happens to be the portfolio with minimum σ_P when μ_P is set equal to μ_3, the expected rate of return on asset 3. (In general, frontier portfolios contain non-zero proportions of at least two assets so that 'Asset 3' lies strictly inside, not on, the boundary of the frontier.)

By including a third asset along with the first two, the portfolio selection problem can be analysed just as if the choice is between the composite asset and the third asset. All of the analysis of the previous section applies, the result being depicted in figure 5.4.

Beware. While the analysis so far is suggestive, it is incomplete and could be misleading, for the line FF in figure 5.4 is *not* necessarily the frontier in the three-asset case. The reason is that FF denotes the frontier only for cases in which a single asset – asset 3 in figure 5.4 – lies on the frontier. In general, the portfolio frontier lies to the left of FF: an individual asset, while on its own constituting a *feasible* portfolio (all initial wealth could be invested in a single asset), is typically not on the frontier, with $n > 2$ assets.

Despite this warning, it is reasonable to suppose that a pair of composite assets – mutual funds – can be constructed from subsets of any number $n > 2$ of assets, and that these two composite assets can be used to trace out a frontier. There are many such pairs, each of which generates its own frontier. The portfolio frontier for the n asset problem is that which is the 'furthest to the left' in the μ_P, σ_P plane. The upshot, explored further below, is that it is possible to trace out the portfolio frontier as if there are exactly two assets, which are themselves composites of the individual assets. (Note that both composite assets may need to include a non-zero amount of every individual asset.)

The formal optimization problem from which the portfolio frontier is constructed is as follows: for a given value of μ_P, choose portfolio proportions, $a_1, a_2, \ldots, a_n$, to

$$\text{minimize } \sigma_P^2 = \sum_{i=1}^{n} \sum_{j=1}^{n} a_i a_j \sigma_{ij}$$

$$\text{subject to } \mu_P = \sum_{j=1}^{n} a_j \mu_j \text{ and } \sum_{j=1}^{n} a_j = 1$$

A separate minimization is carried out for each given value of μ_P so that, as μ_P is changed, the frontier is traced out. (Appendix 5.2 offers a formal analysis.)

The description of the portfolio frontier above hints at the *first mutual fund theorem* (or *first separation theorem*) of portfolio analysis.[5] A precise statement of the theorem is: given the existence of $n \geq 2$ assets, the random rates of returns on which can be expressed entirely by their means and variances, there exist two mutual funds (composite assets) such that the expected rate of return and variance of *every* frontier portfolio can be obtained by holding only the two mutual funds. That is, for any arbitrary frontier portfolio, the two mutual funds alone can be combined to form a portfolio that has the same expected rate of return and the same variance as the arbitrarily chosen frontier portfolio.

In order to gain some intuition for the importance of the first mutual fund theorem, consider an investor whose beliefs can be expressed in terms of means and variances and who seeks to choose a portfolio that maximizes $G(\mu_P, \sigma_P^2)$. The investor's beliefs are expressed by

μ_1	μ_2	μ_3	$\cdots$	μ_n
σ_{11}	σ_{12}	σ_{13}	$\cdots$	σ_{1n}
	σ_{22}	σ_{23}	$\cdots$	σ_{2n}
		σ_{33}	$\cdots$	σ_{3n}
			$\cdots$	$\vdots$
			$\cdots$	σ_{nn}

---

[5] Although the mutual fund theorems of portfolio analysis are most commonly found in mean-variance analysis, they appear in more general treatments involving broader classes of preferences and distributions of asset returns.

Suppose that the number of assets, n, is very large (say, 1000) and that the investor finds it too complicated and wearisome to choose among the n assets in maximizing $G(\mu_P, \sigma_P^2)$.

Thus, suppose that the information about beliefs (means, variances and covariances) is handed to an expert. The expert does some calculations and replies (correctly) that the investor can achieve a maximum of $G(\mu_P, \sigma_P^2)$ by choosing between just two assets – say, A and B – that are themselves portfolios (mutual funds) of the original n assets. The investor's portfolio choice problem – maximization of $G(\mu_P, \sigma_P^2)$ – is thus dramatically simplified. Note the following.

1. The expert needs to know *nothing* about the investor's preferences, $G(\mu_P, \sigma_P^2)$. Hence, the same pair of assets, A and B, could be used to locate the optimum portfolio for *every* investor who shares the same beliefs (means, variances and covariances).

2. The first mutual fund theorem guarantees that the expert is right to claim that the problem simplifies to the choice between two assets (so long as the expert makes no mistakes in the calculations).

3. The expert creates the two assets as follows. (a) For any level of portfolio expected return, μ_P, choose the portfolio that minimizes σ_P^2. By construction, the solution pair (μ_P, σ_P) lies on the portfolio frontier. (b) Hence construct two portfolios, A and B, *on the frontier* corresponding to *any* two different levels of μ_P.

4. With a knowledge of $\mu_A, \mu_B, \sigma_A^2, \sigma_B^2, \sigma_{AB}$ (means, variances and covariance of returns for A and B), the investor can construct exactly the same portfolio frontier as for the original n assets. An optimal portfolio comprising just A and B is then chosen to maximize $G(\mu_P, \sigma_P^2)$ from among the frontier portfolios.

While the discussion above is intended to motivate the mutual fund theorem, it is not a proof. A sketch of a proof is as follows. *First*, it can be shown that there is a unique portfolio of the n assets corresponding to each point on the frontier.[6] *Second*, choose any distinct pair of frontier portfolios: these correspond to the mutual funds referred to in the theorem. *Third*, the expected return on any arbitrary frontier portfolio can be expressed as a portfolio constructed from the mutual funds.[7] *Fourth*, it is possible to show that the newly constructed portfolio satisfies exactly the same first-order (variance-minimizing) conditions as the arbitrarily chosen portfolio. *Fifth*, because the constructed portfolio satisfies the same conditions, it defines the same point on the frontier and hence has the same variance. *Finally*, as far as mean and variance are concerned, the arbitrary portfolio and the portfolio constructed from the mutual funds are identical. Hence,

[6] Uniqueness follows from the assumption that all n assets are 'genuinely different' in the sense that there are no linear dependences among their random rates of return.

[7] For example, suppose that the expected returns on the mutual funds are 10 per cent and 20 per cent, respectively. Let the expected return on some other portfolio be μ_P. Then the portfolio of mutual funds needed to obtain μ_P is found by solving: $\mu_P = 0.10\theta + 0.20(1-\theta)$ for θ. In this example, $\theta = 2 - 10\mu_P$.

the first mutual fund theorem holds: any frontier portfolio can be constructed from the two mutual funds.

5.4 Portfolio frontier: many risky assets with a risk-free asset

5.4.1 Efficient portfolios

In the presence of a risk-free asset and any number of risky assets, the set of efficient portfolios is a straight line. In figure 5.5 the efficient portfolios lie along the line $r_0 Z E$, where r_0 is the risk-free rate of return and Z is the point of tangency between a ray from r_0 and FF (the frontier for portfolios of risky assets only). The set of efficient portfolios is obtained by minimizing the portfolio risk, σ_P, for each given expected portfolio return, μ_P.

The point of tangency depicted by Z in figure 5.5 identifies the efficient portfolio for which the proportion of the risk-free asset is zero. Efficient portfolios to the left of Z, along $r_0 Z$, include a positive proportion of the risk-free asset, while those to the right, along ZE, involve a negative proportion (i.e. borrowing to finance the purchase of risky assets).

The formal optimization problem from which the set of efficient portfolios is constructed is as follows: for a given value of μ_P, choose portfolio proportions, $a_0, a_1, a_2, \ldots, a_n$, to

$$\text{minimize } \sigma_P^2 = \sum_{i=1}^{n} \sum_{j=1}^{n} a_i a_j \sigma_{ij}$$

$$\text{subject to } \mu_P = \sum_{j=1}^{n} a_j \mu_j + a_0 r_0 \text{ and } a_0 + \sum_{j=1}^{n} a_j = 1$$

A separate minimization is carried out for each given value of μ_P so that, as μ_P is changed, the efficient set is traced out. (See appendix 5.3 for a formal analysis.)

Remarks

1. *Why is the set of efficient portfolios a straight line?* An intuitive argument is as follows. First, construct the frontier, FF, for risky assets alone, as described in the previous section. Next, plot the rate of return, r_0, for the risk-free asset on the vertical axis of the (μ_P, σ_P) diagram and connect this with a ray to *any* point on the frontier FF. Points along this ray depict the expected return and risk for portfolios comprising the risk-free asset and the portfolio of risky assets given by the chosen point on the FF frontier. Lower levels of risk can be attained (for each level of expected return) by pivoting the ray through r_0 to higher and higher points along FF, until the ray is *tangential* with FF. No further reduction in risk is feasible (for a given expected return and the frontier, FF, that is). The set of efficient portfolios for all assets including the risk-free asset is then the ray formed from this tangency – i.e. the line $r_0 Z E$ in figure 5.5.

2. *Must such a tangency (on the positively sloped portion of FF) always exist?* No. A necessary and sufficient condition for the existence of the tangency depicted in

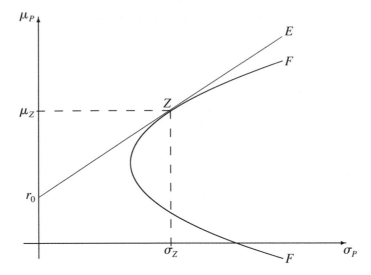

Fig. 5.5. Efficient portfolios with a risk-free asset

When a risk-free asset, with rate of return r_0, is available the portfolio frontier becomes the ray r_0ZE, starting at r_0 and tangential to FF at Z. To the left of Z, along r_0Z, efficient portfolios contain a non-negative proportion of the risk-free asset. To the right of Z, along ZE, efficient portfolios involve borrowing at the risk-free rate.

figure 5.5 is that $r_0 < \mu_{mrp}$; i.e. the risk-free interest rate must be less than the expected rate of return on the portfolio of risky assets with minimum risk. (See figure 5.3 on page 120, where point B corresponds to μ_{mrp}.)

What happens if $r_0 \geqq \mu_{mrp}$? Suppose that $r_0 > \mu_{mrp}$. In this case, it can be shown that the investor would choose to *short-sell* a portfolio of risky assets and invest the proceeds in the risk- free asset.[8] The set of efficient portfolios remains a positively sloped straight line through r_0, the risk originating in the payoffs from the assets that have been short-sold.

Suppose that $r_0 = \mu_{mrp}$. In this case, it can be shown that the investor could choose a portfolio of risky assets such that $\sum_{j=1}^{n} a_j = 0$ (i.e. with some assets short-sold and some positive holdings) to yield an expected return equal to r_0 and zero risk, $\sigma_P = 0$. There is no optimal solution in this case; the investor perceives that there exists a portfolio of risky assets that has precisely the same mean-variance properties as the risk-free asset.[9]

---

[8] The portfolio that would be short-sold can be identified with the point of tangency between a ray from r_0 and the lower, negatively sloped, arm of the FF frontier. For a detailed exposition, see Huang and Litzenberger (1988, pp. 78–80).

[9] It is tempting to interpret the basket of risky assets in question as being an arbitrage portfolio: a zero outlay of initial capital on risky assets yields a risk-free return. As the analysis in chapter 7 shows, this temptation should be resisted, for here the absence of risk is *conditional* upon the investor's perceptions of the means and variances of assets' returns. Arbitrage in the strict sense of chapter 7 is not conditional on this information.

While $r_0 \geqq \mu_{mrp}$ *could* conceivably hold for an individual investor, market equilibrium is inconsistent with this inequality holding for every investor; some investor has to be prepared to hold the assets sold by others. In summary: the circumstances for which $r_0 \geqq \mu_{mrp}$ are pathological – unusual, to say the least. From now on it is assumed that $r_0 < \mu_{mrp}$.

3. *Second mutual fund theorem (second separation theorem) of portfolio analysis.* Under the same conditions as for the first separation theorem and in the presence of a risk-free asset, *any* efficient portfolio can be attained by holding at most two assets, one of which is the risk-free asset and the other is a mutual fund. Not just any mutual fund will do. It must be a portfolio chosen from those in the efficient set (any one of these will do).

   To understand why the theorem holds, suppose that the mutual fund is chosen to be the efficient portfolio with expected return μ_Z and risk σ_Z (point Z in figure 5.5). Now *any* efficient portfolio (i.e. along the line $r_0 ZE$) can be formed as a combination of this mutual fund and the risk-free asset.

4. Note that the efficient set is a straight line only if the investor can borrow and lend at the same risk-free rate, r_0. Suppose, instead, that the investor can lend at a rate r_0^L, lower than the rate, r_0^B, at which funds can be borrowed. Now the set of efficient portfolios has three segments (see figure 5.6).

   For low levels of expected return and risk (such that the investor holds a positive amount of the risk-free asset), the efficient portfolios are located on the ray from r_0^L tangent to *FF* at point Y. Points beyond Y are irrelevant because, by assumption, the investor cannot *borrow* at rate r_0^L.

   For high levels of expected return and risk (such that the individual borrows in order to invest in risky assets), the efficient portfolios are located on the line segment to the right of Z. Formally, Z is defined by the ray through r_0^B that is tangent to *FF*. Points between r_0^B and Z are irrelevant because, by assumption, the investor cannot *lend* at rate r_0^B.

   At intermediate levels of expected return and risk, the investor neither borrows nor lends (initial wealth being invested entirely in risky assets) and the efficient portfolios are located along *FF* between Y and Z. Thus, the whole set of efficient portfolios is depicted by the connected line segments, $r_0^L Y$, *YZ* and *ZE*.

5.4.2 *The trade-off between expected return and risk*

In mean-variance analysis, the investor chooses between *efficient portfolios*, where an efficient portfolio is one for which expected return is maximized for a given level of risk (standard deviation of portfolio return, σ_P). The following paragraphs show how the efficient portfolios can be characterized in terms of assets' means and variances. This is accomplished by deriving expressions for the increment to expected return and risk in response to incremental variations in the amount of an asset in the portfolio.

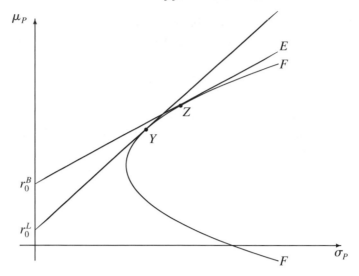

Fig. 5.6. Efficient portfolios with different lending and borrowing rates

If the rate at which funds can be borrowed, r_0^B, exceeds the rate at which funds can be lent, r_0^L, the frontier comprises three segments: $r_0^L Y$ (some funds are lent), YZ (neither lending nor borrowing), ZE (funds are borrowed for investment in risky assets).

Suppose that an investor holds a portfolio labelled by P; this portfolio need not be efficient, it is just any feasible portfolio of assets. Denote its expected return and risk by μ_P and σ_P, respectively. Now suppose that a small increase is made in the holding of asset j, the necessary funds being borrowed at the risk-free interest rate. The quantity of each of the other assets remains unchanged. Denote the increase in the proportion of j in the portfolio by Δa_j (and, by construction, $\Delta a_0 = -\Delta a_j$).

Expected return. The change in the portfolio's expected return is the difference between the expected return on asset j and the risk-free rate of interest, r_0, multiplied by the change in the proportion of asset j:

$$\Delta \mu_P = (\mu_j - r_0)\Delta a_j \tag{5.1}$$

Risk (standard deviation). Calculation of the change in the risk of return on the portfolio, $\Delta \sigma_P$, involves more effort. The derivation in appendix 5.4 shows that

$$\Delta \sigma_P = \beta_{jP}\sigma_P \Delta a_j \qquad \text{where} \qquad \beta_{jP} = \frac{\sigma_{jP}}{\sigma_P^2} \tag{5.2}$$

(Strictly, (5.2) is an approximation that approaches an equality in the limit as Δa_j tends to zero.) The symbol σ_{jP} denotes the *covariance of the return on asset j with the whole portfolio*. Formally, $\sigma_{jP} = \sum_{i=1}^{n} a_i \sigma_{ij}$. Equation (5.2) shows that $\beta_{jP}\sigma_P$ can be interpreted as the increment to overall portfolio risk resulting from an increment to the proportion of asset j held in the portfolio – i.e. $\Delta\sigma_P/\Delta a_j$.

The β_{jP} term plays a central role in the capital asset pricing model (chapter 6), which is why equation (5.2) is written the way it is. In words, β_{jP} captures the relationship between variations in the rate of return on asset j and the rate of return on the whole portfolio, P. Note especially that the change in σ_P associated with a change in asset j is not equal to σ_j (the standard deviation of the rate of return on asset j). Why not? Because asset returns may be correlated with one another and these correlations must be taken into account. The influence of the correlations is encapsulated in β_{jP}.

Efficient portfolios. It is possible now to obtain a necessary condition that must be satisfied if P is to represent an *efficient* portfolio. If P is efficient, it must be the case that a small change in the portfolio proportion of any asset must disturb the expected return per unit of risk by the same amount for all assets. That is, $\Delta\mu_P/\Delta\sigma_P$ must be equal for all assets. Taking the ratio of (5.1) and (5.2), it follows that $(\mu_j - r_0)/\beta_{jP}\sigma_P$ must be equal for all assets $j = 1, 2, \ldots, n$. Otherwise, it would be possible to obtain a higher expected return with no higher risk, contradicting the hypothesis that P is efficient.[10]

Finally, note that the slope of the trade-off between the expected return and risk for the whole of any efficient portfolio, P, is equal to $(\mu_P - r_0)/\sigma_P$. The reason for this is that the portfolio P can itself be interpreted as a single composite asset for which the necessary condition must hold. The rate of return on the whole portfolio must, by definition, always be perfectly positively correlated with itself, so that $\beta_{PP} = 1$, and the result follows.

The above analysis can be summarized by writing down the conditions that must necessarily hold for every *efficient* portfolio, P:

$$\frac{\mu_1 - r_0}{\beta_{1P}\sigma_P} = \frac{\mu_2 - r_0}{\beta_{2P}\sigma_P} = \cdots = \frac{\mu_n - r_0}{\beta_{nP}\sigma_P} = \frac{\mu_P - r_0}{\sigma_P} \tag{5.3}$$

Notice that the σ_P terms in the denominator could be cancelled out in (5.3).

---

[10] It is, of course, not permissible to divide by β_{jP} if $\beta_{jP} = 0$. This case (which is of some interest in chapter 6) can be handled without difficulty because it can be shown that, if $\beta_{jP} = 0$, the expected rate of return on asset j equals the risk-free rate, $\mu_j = r_0$. Also ignored are 'corner solutions' that arise when a zero quantity of some asset is held in an efficient portfolio. These cases – which can occur if short-sales (i.e. negative asset holdings) are prohibited – involve replacing the first-order equalities with inequalities.

Equation (5.3) holds for every efficient portfolio. Hence, it holds for Z, the portfolio comprising only risky assets. Equation (5.3) then becomes

$$\frac{\mu_1 - r_0}{\beta_{1Z}} = \frac{\mu_2 - r_0}{\beta_{2Z}} = \cdots = \frac{\mu_n - r_0}{\beta_{nZ}} = \mu_Z - r_0 \qquad (5.4)$$

Note that the common term, σ_Z, has been cancelled out in going from (5.3) to (5.4). This is just for convenience. Conditions (5.4) are very important. They lie at the heart of the CAPM. But there is more to the CAPM than the equalities of (5.4). The extra conditions are studied in chapter 6.

5.4.3 The Sharpe ratio and risk-adjusted performance

The Sharpe ratio (named after its originator, William Sharpe) for any asset, or portfolio of assets, j, is defined by

$$s_j = \frac{\mu_j - r_0}{\sigma_j}$$

In words, s_j denotes the expected excess return on asset j normalized by its standard deviation. In practice, the Sharpe ratio would be measured by substituting the sample mean rate of return for μ_j and the sample standard deviation for σ_j. It provides a way of comparing assets with differing expected returns and risks (risk being identified with the value of σ_j).

For a graphical interpretation, figure 5.7 reproduces figure 5.5, with the FF frontier omitted. Consider any asset, say asset 1, and draw a ray from r_0 on the vertical axis to the point labelled A_1 (μ_1, σ_1). The slope of this line equals the Sharpe ratio for asset 1, $s_1 = (\mu_1 - r_0)/\sigma_1$. The point A_2 identifies a second asset with a lower Sharpe ratio.

Suppose that s_e denotes the Sharpe ratio for an efficient portfolio. All efficient portfolios share the same Sharpe ratio, which equals the slope of the line segment r_0E in figure 5.7. From the diagram it can be seen that $s_P \leqq s_e$ for *any* asset or portfolio of assets, P, whether or not P is efficient.

The risk-adjusted performance (RAP) is derived from the Sharpe ratio (see Modigliani and Modigliani (1997)). To define the RAP, suppose that a 'benchmark portfolio' is identified. In principle, this can be any portfolio, but typically it denotes a portfolio composed of a broad range of assets. Let σ_B denote its standard deviation of return. The RAP for any asset j is defined as

$$RAP_j = r_0 + \frac{\sigma_B}{\sigma_j}(\mu_j - r_0)$$

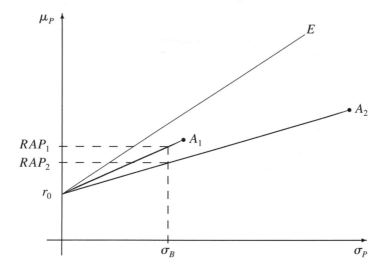

Fig. 5.7. The Sharpe ratio and risk-adjusted performance

The Sharpe ratio for any asset is the slope of a line from r_0 to the point in the (μ_P, σ_P) plane given by its expectation and standard deviation of return. The risk-adjusted performance, RAP, of any asset equals the hypothetical expected rate of return when its standard deviation of return is normalized to some benchmark level – say, σ_B.

or $RAP_j = r_0 + \sigma_B s_j$, substituting j's Sharpe ratio. In words, RAP_j would be the expected rate of return on asset j if its risk equalled that of the benchmark but its Sharpe ratio remained unchanged. Notice, for the illustration in figure 5.7, the Sharpe ratio for asset 1 exceeds that of asset 2 even though asset 2 has a higher expected rate of return.

In practice, sample means and variances are substituted for the theoretical values and RAP values are calculated to compare the performance of assets (or portfolios of assets) relative to the benchmark portfolio.

5.5 Optimal portfolio selection in the mean-variance model

What we have done so far is to trace out the portfolio frontier and identify the set of efficient portfolios. With agreement about means and variances, the efficient set of portfolios is the same for each investor. There is still scope, however, for different investors to choose different portfolios. The reason is that investors can differ in their preferences, commonly interpreted (in portfolio selection) as reflecting different investors' attitudes to risk.

In view of the mutual fund theorems outlined in previous sections, it is sufficient to assume that the portfolio is selected as a combination of exactly two assets.

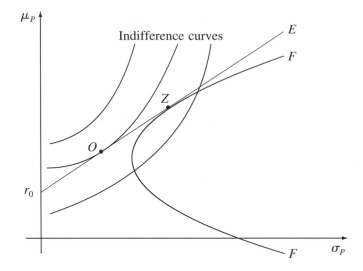

Fig. 5.8. Optimal portfolio selection

The indifference curves express the investor's preferences among different values of μ_P and σ_P. The most preferred (i.e. optimal) portfolio
lies on the highest indifference curve that is attainable subject to being
feasible (i.e. on or below the $r_0 ZE$ line, denoting the efficient set). For
the preferences shown here, the optimum is at point O.

Consider the case in which a risk-free asset is available. In figure 5.5 the set
of efficient portfolios is represented by the straight line passing through r_0 and
tangent, at Z, to the portfolio frontier (for risky assets). See figure 5.8, in which
the efficient portfolio set is depicted by the line $r_0 ZE$ tangent to the frontier FF
at Z, the efficient portfolio comprising only risky assets.

Any efficient portfolio can be constructed as a combination of the risk-free asset
and the portfolio of risky assets depicted by the point Z. Given the indifference
curves shown in figure 5.8, the optimum portfolio is depicted by point O.

The trade-off between μ_P and σ_P, expressed by the line $r_0 ZE$ in figure 5.8,
can be written as

$$\mu_P = r_0 + \frac{\mu_Z - r_0}{\sigma_Z} \sigma_P$$

That is, the relationship between μ_P and σ_P is linear, with intercept r_0 and slope
equal to $(\mu_Z - r_0)/\sigma_Z$.

Suppose now that preferences can be expressed as $G(\mu_P, \sigma_P^2) = \mu_P - \alpha \sigma_P^2$,
where $\alpha > 0$ expresses attitude to risk and, hence, can differ between investors.
(Recall the discussion in chapter 4, pages 103–04.)

Assuming that preferences take this form, it can be shown that the proportion of initial wealth invested in the risky asset, q, is given by

$$q = \frac{\mu_Z - r_0}{2\alpha\sigma_Z^2} \tag{5.5}$$

(See appendix 5.5 for the derivation.)

Although this formula holds only for the objective function $G(\mu_P, \sigma_P^2) = \mu_P - \alpha\sigma_P^2$, it is useful in practical applications. The result confirms intuition that: (a) the greater the excess expected return, $\mu_Z - r_0$, the greater the holding of the risky asset; (b) the riskier the risky asset (i.e. the higher the level of σ_Z^2), the lower the holding of the risky asset; and (c) the greater the risk tolerance (i.e. the smaller is α), the higher the holding of the risky asset.

5.6 Summary

This chapter has shown that the following implications can be derived for investors whose beliefs about asset returns are expressed in terms of means and variances.

1. The portfolio frontier for risky assets alone is obtained by minimizing risk, σ_P or σ_P^2, for each level of expected return, μ_P, and is a hyperbola in the (μ_P, σ_P) plane. Consider any two distinct portfolios, A and B, on the frontier. Then every portfolio on the frontier can be expressed as a combination of A and B. The *efficient* portfolios are frontier portfolios for which expected return is maximized at a given level of risk.
2. When a risk-free asset is available, the set of efficient portfolios is described by a straight line, with intercept at the risk-free rate and tangential to the risky asset frontier. Every efficient portfolio can be expressed as a linear combination of any two distinct efficient portfolios. The conditions that characterize the set of efficient portfolios form the basis for the CAPM, studied in chapter 6.
3. The set of efficient portfolios depends only on investors' beliefs about rates of return (expressed by means and variances), not on preferences with respect to risk. Investors with different risk preferences select different portfolios but always choose a member of the efficient set.

Further reading

There exist many expositions of mean-variance analysis at various levels and directed towards different audiences. For readers seeking a more extended, management-oriented approach, the following are representative: Grinblatt and Titman (2001, chaps. 4 & 5); Sharpe, Alexander and Bailey (1999, chaps. 7–9). An excellent exposition appears in Elton, Gruber, Brown and Goetzmann (2003, chaps. 4–6). At a more advanced level, a rigorous treatment can be found in

Huang and Litzenberger (1988, chap. 4). This reference is particularly useful for sorting out awkward special cases. An early and not very well-known analysis of the portfolio frontier, still worth attention, is provided by Merton (1972). The most comprehensive and detailed examination of mutual fund theorems remains that of Cass and Stiglitz (1970).

Appendix 5.1: Numerical example: two risky assets

The following example corresponds to section 5.2 and focuses on the special cases of perfect positive and negative correlations between assets' rates of return. Suppose that $\mu_1 = 0.25$, $\mu_2 = 0.50$, $\sigma_1 = 0.20$ and $\sigma_2 = 0.40$. Hence

$$\mu_P = 0.25a + 0.50(1-a)$$
$$= 0.50 - 0.25a$$

The special cases, $\rho_{12} = \pm 1$, result in

$$\rho_{12} = +1 \implies \sigma_P = 0.20a + 0.40(1-a)$$
$$\rho_{12} = -1 \implies \sigma_P = (0.20a - 0.40(1-a)) \geq 0$$
$$\text{for } a \geq \frac{0.40}{0.20 + 0.40} = \frac{2}{3}$$
$$\rho_{12} = -1 \implies \sigma_P = -(0.20a - 0.40(1-a)) \geq 0$$
$$\text{for } a \leq \frac{0.40}{0.20 + 0.40} = \frac{2}{3}$$

For $\rho_{12} = +1$

$$\sigma_P = 0.20a + 0.40(1-a) = 0.40 - 0.20a$$
$$a = \frac{0.40 - \sigma_P}{0.20}$$
$$\mu_P = 0.50 - 0.25\left(\frac{0.40 - \sigma_P}{0.20}\right) = 1.25\sigma_P \tag{5.6}$$

For $\rho_{12} = -1$ and $a \geq 2/3$

$$\sigma_P = 0.20a - 0.40(1-a) = 0.60a - 0.40$$
$$a = \frac{\sigma_P + 0.40}{0.60}$$
$$\mu_P = 0.50 - 0.25\left(\frac{\sigma_P + 0.40}{0.60}\right) = \frac{1}{3} - \frac{5}{12}\sigma_P \tag{5.7}$$

For $\rho_{12} = -1$ and $a \leqq 2/3$

$$\sigma_P = -0.20a + 0.40(1-a) = 0.40 - 0.60a$$

$$a = \frac{0.40 - \sigma_P}{0.60}$$

$$\mu_P = 0.50 - 0.25 \left(\frac{0.40 - \sigma_P}{0.60} \right) = \frac{1}{3} + \frac{5}{12}\sigma_P \qquad (5.8)$$

The equations (5.6), (5.7) and (5.8) define the three sides of the triangle in a diagram such as figure 5.2 on page 119.

Appendix 5.2: Variance minimization: risky assets only

This appendix explores the properties of the portfolio frontier when the investor chooses among n risky assets, beginning in A.5.2.1 with the formal minimization of portfolio variance. Appendix section A.5.2.2 offers a graphical interpretation, while A.5.2.3 describes a special case (relevant for the capital asset pricing model, chapter 6) that compares portfolios, the rates of return on which are uncorrelated.

A.5.2.1: The portfolio frontier

Form the Lagrangian

$$\mathcal{L} = \sum_{i=1}^{n} \sum_{j=1}^{n} a_i a_j \sigma_{ij} + \gamma \left(\mu_P - \sum_{j=1}^{n} \mu_j a_j \right) + \lambda \left(\sum_{j=1}^{n} a_j - 1 \right)$$

where γ and λ are Lagrange multipliers.

Noting that the minimization is carried out for each value of μ_P, the first-order conditions are found by partially differentiating $\mathcal{L}$ with respect to $a_1, a_2, \ldots, a_n, \gamma, \lambda$, and setting the resulting expressions to zero:

$$\frac{\partial \mathcal{L}}{\partial a_j} = 2 \sum_{i=1}^{n} a_i \sigma_{ij} - \gamma \mu_j + \lambda = 0 \qquad j = 1, 2, \ldots, n \qquad (5.9)$$

$$\frac{\partial \mathcal{L}}{\partial \gamma} = \mu_P - \sum_{j=1}^{n} \mu_j a_j = 0 \qquad (5.10)$$

$$\frac{\partial \mathcal{L}}{\partial \lambda} = \sum_{j=1}^{n} a_j - 1 = 0 \qquad (5.11)$$

The second-order conditions are messy and not very revealing. Given the quadratic minimand (i.e. the variance, σ_P^2) and the linear constraints, it is tedious, though not difficult, to check that the second-order conditions are indeed satisfied.

The optimum portfolio proportions can be found by solving the $n+2$ first-order conditions for the portfolio proportions and the values of γ and λ. Instead of deriving the explicit solution, it is more instructive to interpret the first-order conditions. Multiply through (5.9) by a_j and sum over j to give

$$2\sum_{j=1}^{n}\sum_{i=1}^{n}a_j a_i \sigma_{ij} - \gamma\sum_{j=1}^{n}a_j(\mu_j - \omega) = 0 \tag{5.12}$$

where $\omega \equiv \lambda/\gamma$.

Substituting from (5.10) and (5.11) into (5.9) and (5.12) and rearranging gives

$$\sigma_P^2 = (\gamma/2)(\mu_P - \omega) \tag{5.13}$$

$$\sigma_{jP} = (\gamma/2)(\mu_j - \omega) \quad \text{for } j = 1, 2, \ldots, n \tag{5.14}$$

where $\sigma_{jP} = \sum_{i=1}^{n} a_i \sigma_{ij}$ is the covariance of the return from asset j with portfolio P. Combining (5.13) and (5.14) to eliminate γ yields a condition that must hold for all portfolios on the frontier:

$$\frac{\mu_j - \omega}{\sigma_{jP}} = \frac{\mu_P - \omega}{\sigma_P^2} \quad \text{for } j = 1, 2, \ldots, n$$

Given that the first-order conditions are linear in a_j, the solution for the variance-minimizing value of each a_j is unique. A sketch of this result is as follows. From (5.14) solve for the a_j as functions of σ_{ij}, μ_j $(i, j = 1, 2, \ldots, n)$, γ and ω. That this solution is unique follows from the linearity of the equations and the assumption that there are no exact linear dependencies among the returns on the n assets (i.e. the assets are genuinely different from one another). Next, substituting the a_j into the two constraints and rearranging yields a unique solution for each of γ and ω as a function of the σ_{ij}, μ_j and μ_P.

Finally, substitute the values of γ and ω back into the initial solutions for a_j, which now become functions of the σ_{ij}, μ_j and μ_P as required (i.e. γ and ω have now been eliminated). The resulting expressions for a_j are messy and not otherwise needed here; hence, they are omitted.

A.5.2.2: A graphical interpretation

An interpretation of ω can be given with reference to figure 5.9. Choose an efficient portfolio and denote it by P. The slope of the frontier, $d\mu_P/d\sigma_P$, at

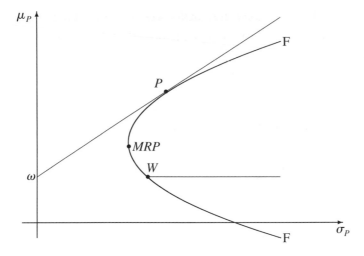

Fig. 5.9. The portfolio frontier with risky assets

Choose any portfolio on the frontier – say, P – and draw a straight line tangent to FF. The line intersects the vertical axis at a point such as ω. All feasible portfolios (i.e. on or within FF) with an expected return equal to ω (i.e. along the horizontal line starting at W) have rates of return that are uncorrelated with the return to portfolio P.

P is equal to $(\mu_P - \omega)/\sigma_P$. This result can be obtained by, first, invoking the envelope theorem to obtain $d\sigma_P^2/d\mu_P = \gamma$.[11] Hence,

$$\frac{d\sigma_P^2}{d\mu_P} = \frac{d\sigma_P^2}{d\sigma_P}\frac{d\sigma_P}{d\mu_P} = 2\sigma_P\frac{d\sigma_P}{d\mu_P} = \gamma \tag{5.15}$$

Rearranging gives

$$\frac{d\mu_P}{d\sigma_P} = \sigma_P\frac{2}{\gamma} = \sigma_P\frac{\mu_P - \omega}{\sigma_P^2} = \frac{\mu_P - \omega}{\sigma_P} \tag{5.16}$$

where (5.13) has been substituted to eliminate $2/\gamma$.

---

[11] In this context the envelope theorem implies that $d\sigma_P^2/d\mu_P = \partial\mathcal{L}/\partial\mu_P$, where the total derivative serves as a reminder that the minimizing portfolio proportions and the Lagrange multipliers change in response to an incremental change in μ_P. A derivation from first principles – tantamount to proof of the envelope theorem – involves totally differentiating $\mathcal{L}$ with respect to μ_P, allowing for changes in the optimal portfolio proportions in response to the change in μ_P. Substitution from the first-order conditions then yields $d\sigma_P^2/d\mu_P = \gamma$. For treatments of the envelope theorem, see Samuelson (1947, pp. 34–6), or *The New Palgrave Dictionary of Money and Finance* (Newman, Milgate and Eatwell, 1992, Vol. II, pp. 158–9).

A.5.2.3: Portfolios with uncorrelated returns

In the capital asset pricing model (see chapter 6, section 6.6) it is necessary to identify portfolios, the rates of return on which have a zero correlation with any given frontier portfolio. The following derivation shows that all such portfolios have an expected return equal to ω. (While the value of ω depends on the frontier portfolio, this dependence is not made explicit in the notation.)

Consider any portfolio (it need not be on the frontier) denoted by W with asset proportions $w_1, w_2, \ldots, w_n$, rate of return $r_W = \sum w_j r_j$ and expected rate of return $\mu_W = \sum w_j \mu_j$ (see figure 5.9). The asset proportions in frontier portfolio P are denoted by $a_1, a_2, \ldots, a_n$, with rate of return $r_P = \sum a_j r_j$ and expected rate of return $\mu_P = \sum a_j \mu_j$.

The covariance between r_P and r_W, $\mathrm{cov}(r_P, r_W)$ is given by

$$
\begin{aligned}
\mathrm{cov}(r_P, r_W) &= \mathrm{E}[(r_P - \mu_P)(r_W - \mu_W)] \\
&= \mathrm{E}\left[\sum_{i=1}^{n} a_i(r_i - \mu_i) \sum_{j=1}^{n} w_j(r_j - \mu_j)\right] \\
&= \sum_{i=1}^{n}\sum_{j=1}^{n} a_i w_j \sigma_{ij} \\
&= \sum_{j=1}^{n} w_j \sum_{i=1}^{n} a_i \sigma_{ij} \\
&= \sum_{j=1}^{n} w_j \sigma_{jP} \\
&= (\gamma/2) \sum_{j=1}^{n} w_j(\mu_j - \omega)
\end{aligned}
\tag{5.17}
$$

where the last equality follows from (5.14) because P denotes a frontier portfolio.

If r_P and r_W are uncorrelated, $\mathrm{cov}(r_P, r_W) = 0$. It then follows from (5.17) that $\mu_W = \omega$ (because $\sum w_j(\mu_j - \omega) = \mu_W - \omega \sum w_j$, and portfolio proportions sum to unity). Referring back to figure 5.9, the expected return on any portfolio uncorrelated with P is equal to ω. These portfolios are located along the horizontal line beginning at point W.

It is now possible to demonstrate that the expected return, μ_{mrp}, on the portfolio with global minimum risk (depicted by *MRP* in figure 5.9) must satisfy $\mu_{mrp} > \omega$, given that $\mu_P > \mu_{mrp}$ (because P is on the upward-sloping portion of *FF*). Construct a new portfolio with proportion θ of the portfolio denoted by P and

$(1-\theta)$ of W. From the first mutual fund theorem, *any* frontier portfolio can be constructed by an appropriate choice of θ. Let S denote the variance of the rate of return on this portfolio, so that

$$S = \theta^2\sigma_P^2 + (1-\theta)^2\sigma_W^2$$

where σ_P^2 and σ_W^2 are the variances corresponding to P and W, respectively. Note that no covariance term appears because, by construction, the returns on P and W are uncorrelated.

The variance on the *MRP* portfolio is found by choosing θ to minimize S. Differentiating with respect to θ and setting the resulting expression to zero provides the first-order condition

$$\frac{dS}{d\theta} = 2\theta\sigma_P^2 - 2(1-\theta)\sigma_W^2 = 0$$

The second-order condition for a minimum, $d^2S/d\theta^2 = 2(\sigma_P^2 + \sigma_W^2) > 0$, is certainly satisfied. The first-order condition can readily be solved to give $\theta_{mrp} = \sigma_W^2/(\sigma_P^2 + \sigma_W^2)$. Therefore, $0 < \theta_{mrp} < 1$. Hence, it follows that $\mu_{mrp} = \theta_{mrp}\mu_P + (1-\theta_{mrp})\omega > \omega$ as claimed, and as depicted in figure 5.9.

Appendix 5.3: Variance minimization with a risk-free asset

Although the analysis in the presence of a risk-free asset closely resembles that in its absence, the outline below is self-contained as far as it goes.[12] It is instructive to recognize that ω and r_0 play exactly analogous roles (see appendix 5.2).

Note that $a_0 = 1 - \sum_{j=1}^n a_j$, so that

$$\mu_P = \sum_{j=1}^n \mu_j a_j + a_0 r_0$$

$$= \sum_{j=1}^n \mu_j a_j + \left(1 - \sum_{j=1}^n a_j\right) r_0$$

$$= \sum_{j=1}^n (\mu_j - r_0)a_j + r_0$$

Form the Lagrangian

$$\mathcal{L} = \sum_{i=1}^n \sum_{j=1}^n a_i a_j \sigma_{ij} + \gamma\left(\mu_P - \sum_{j=1}^n (\mu_j - r_0)a_j - r_0\right)$$

[12] The second-order conditions are ignored for exactly the same reason as in appendix 5.2.

where γ is a Lagrange multiplier. The value of μ_P is a parameter in this optimization – i.e. a separate minimization is carried out for each value of μ_P.

The first-order conditions are found by partially differentiating the Lagrangian, $\mathcal{L}$, with respect to $a_1, a_2, \ldots, a_n, \gamma$ and setting the resulting expressions to zero:

$$\frac{\partial \mathcal{L}}{\partial a_j} = 2 \sum_{i=1}^{n} a_i \sigma_{ij} - \gamma(\mu_j - r_0) = 0 \qquad j = 1, 2, \ldots, n \qquad (5.18)$$

$$\frac{\partial \mathcal{L}}{\partial \gamma} = \mu_P - \sum_{j=1}^{n} (\mu_j - r_0) a_j - r_0 = 0 \qquad (5.19)$$

The optimum portfolio proportions (one set for each value of μ_P) are found by solving these $n+1$ conditions for the portfolio proportions and the value of γ. Multiply through (5.18) by a_j and sum over j to give

$$2 \sum_{j=1}^{n} \sum_{i=1}^{n} a_j a_i \sigma_{ij} - \gamma \sum_{j=1}^{n} a_j (\mu_j - r_0) = 0 \qquad (5.20)$$

Substituting from (5.19), equations (5.20) and (5.18) can be written as

$$\sigma_P^2 = (\gamma/2)(\mu_P - r_0) \qquad (5.21)$$

$$\sigma_{jP} = (\gamma/2)(\mu_j - r_0) \quad \text{for } j = 1, 2, \ldots, n \qquad (5.22)$$

where $\sigma_{jP} = \sum_{i=1}^{n} a_i \sigma_{ij}$ is the covariance of the return on asset j with the return on the portfolio P.

Elimination of γ from (5.21) and (5.22) yields

$$\frac{\mu_j - r_0}{\sigma_{jP}} = \frac{\mu_P - r_0}{\sigma_P^2} \quad \text{for } j = 1, 2, \ldots, n \qquad (5.23)$$

Inserting the definition of $\beta_{jP} \equiv \sigma_{jP}/\sigma_P^2$, equations (5.23) provide the necessary conditions that hold for all efficient portfolios (see (5.3) on page 129 in section 5.4).

Appendix 5.4: Derivation of $\Delta \sigma_P = \beta_{jP} \sigma_P \Delta a_j$

The standard deviation of the return on any portfolio is defined by

$$\sigma_P = \left[\sigma_P^2\right]^{\frac{1}{2}} = \left[\sum_{i=1}^{n} \sum_{j=1}^{n} a_i a_j \sigma_{ij}\right]^{\frac{1}{2}}$$

Partially differentiate with respect to a_j to give

$$\frac{\partial \sigma_P}{\partial a_j} = \frac{1}{2} \left[\sum\sum a_i a_j \sigma_{ij} \right]^{(\frac{1}{2}-1)} \left[2 \sum_{i=1}^{n} a_i \sigma_{ij} \right]$$

$$= [\sigma_P^2]^{-\frac{1}{2}} \sigma_{jP} = \frac{\sigma_{jP}}{\sigma_P} = \frac{\sigma_{jP}}{\sigma_P^2} \sigma_P$$

$$= \beta_{jP} \sigma_P \tag{5.24}$$

Therefore, using Δ to denote small, discrete, changes, (5.24) can be approximated by $\Delta\sigma_P \approx \beta_{jP}\sigma_P\Delta a_j$, which appears as an equality – expression (5.2) on page 128 in section 5.4.2.

Appendix 5.5: The optimal portfolio with a single risky asset

Suppose that the investor chooses a risk-free asset and a single risky asset with expected return μ_Z and variance of return σ_Z^2. (Typically, the risky asset will itself be a portfolio of individual risky assets.) Let q denote the proportion of the portfolio invested in the risky asset. It follows immediately that the expectation μ_P and variance σ_P of returns on the whole portfolio are

$$\mu_P = q\mu_Z + (1-q)r_0 \quad \text{and} \quad \sigma_P^2 = q^2\sigma_Z^2 \tag{5.25}$$

because the variance of the risk-free rate of return is zero.

In this case it is possible to obtain a very simple form for the trade-off between μ_P and σ_P. From (5.25), $\sigma_P = q\sigma_Z$ and $\mu_P = r_0 + (\mu_Z - r_0)q$. Eliminating q gives

$$\mu_P = r_0 + \frac{\mu_Z - r_0}{\sigma_Z}\sigma_P \tag{5.26}$$

as described above in section 5.5. Note that the investor's optimization problem can be viewed as one of choosing μ_P and σ_P to maximize $G(\mu_P, \sigma_P^2)$ subject to the constraint (i.e. the trade-off) given by (5.26).

Given the functional form $G(\mu_P, \sigma_P^2) = \mu_P - \alpha\sigma_P^2$, the maximization is achieved by eliminating μ_P and σ_P using (5.25) – that is

$$G = q\mu_Z + (1-q)r_0 - \alpha q^2\sigma_Z^2$$

Differentiating with respect to the investor's choice variable, q, and setting the resulting expression to zero yields the first-order condition

$$\mu_Z - r_0 - 2\alpha q\sigma_Z^2 = 0 \tag{5.27}$$

The second-order condition for a maximum, $d^2G/dq^2 = -2\alpha\sigma_Z^2 < 0$, is satisfied if $\alpha > 0$, as assumed.

Rearranging the first-order condition, (5.27), to solve for q results in equation (5.5) on page 133.

References

Cass, D., and J. E. Stiglitz (1970), 'The structure of investor preferences and asset returns, and separability in portfolio allocation: a contribution to the pure theory of mutual funds', *Journal of Economic Theory*, 2(2), pp. 122–60.

Elton, E. J., M. J. Gruber, S. J. Brown and W. N. Goetzmann (2003), *Modern Portfolio Theory and Investment Analysis*, New York: John Wiley & Sons, 6th edn.

Grinblatt, M., and S. Titman (2001), *Financial Markets and Corporate Strategy*, New York: McGraw-Hill, 2nd edn.

Huang, C.-F., and R. H. Litzenberger (1988), *Foundations for Financial Economics*, Englewood Cliffs NJ: Prentice Hall.

Merton, R. C. (1972), 'An analytic derivation of the efficient portfolio frontier', *Journal of Financial and Quantitative Analysis*, 7(4), pp. 1851–72.

Modigliani, F., and L. Modigliani (1997), 'Risk-adjusted performance: how to measure it and why', *Journal of Portfolio Management*, 23(2), pp. 45–54.

Newman, P., M. Milgate and J. Eatwell (eds.) (1992), *The New Palgrave Dictionary of Money and Finance*, London: Macmillan (three volumes).

Samuelson, P. A. (1947), *Foundations of Economic Analysis*, Boston: Harvard University Press.

Sharpe, W. F., G. J. Alexander and J. V. Bailey (1999), *Investments*, Englewood Cliffs, NJ: Prentice Hall International, 6th edn.

6

The capital asset pricing model

Overview

A core objective of asset market theory is to explain the risk premium, $\mu_j - r_0$ (the expected rate of return minus the risk-free rate), for each asset. One of the most widely discussed explanations is that provided by the *capital asset pricing model*.

The CAPM extends the mean-variance model of portfolio selection for an isolated individual investor to the market as a whole. It addresses the question: if all investors behave according to a mean-variance objective and if they all have the same beliefs (expressed by the means and variances of asset returns), then what can be inferred about the pattern of asset returns when asset markets are in equilibrium (in the sense that 'supply = demand' for each asset)? Equilibrium does not require that prices are constant across time; it assumes that at each point of time prices adjust so that the demand to hold each asset equals its total stock.

The static version of the CAPM in the presence of a risk-free asset is sometimes known as the Sharpe–Lintner model, named after its originators in the 1960s.[1] If a risk-free asset is absent, the CAPM is referred to here as the 'Black CAPM' after its originator, Fischer Black.

The steps in this chapter, listed according to section, are as follows.

1. *Assumptions of CAPM*. The conditions underlying the CAPM's predictions are outlined in section 6.1.
2. *Asset market equilibrium*. Section 6.2 places each investor's portfolio selection decision in the context of market equilibrium. All investors are shown to select portfolios that are located along the *capital market line*.
3. The *characteristic line and the market model* (section 6.3). Associated with each asset is a linear relationship – the *characteristic line* – between its expected rate of

---

[1] Sharpe shared the Nobel Memorial Prize in 1990 for his innovative work on the CAPM and portfolio theory.

return and the expected return on the portfolio representing the market as a whole. The characteristic line resembles an implication of the so-called 'market model' of asset returns.

4. The *security market line* (section 6.4) is one of the most well-known implications of the CAPM. It provides the focus for many applied studies of the CAPM.

5. *Risk premia and diversification.* In section 6.5 the concept of 'risk' in the CAPM is explored, together with its relationship to diversification, construed as a strategy to reduce risk.

6. *Extensions.* The implications of restrictions on investors' ability to borrow or lend unlimited amounts at a risk-free interest rate are examined in section 6.6. Some other extensions to the CAPM are also sketched.

6.1 Assumptions of the CAPM

Many expositions of the CAPM present a long list of assumptions from which the predictions of the model are derived. The assumptions can be condensed into three sets of conditions: (1) that asset markets are in equilibrium (in the sense that markets are frictionless and that prices adjust so that the existing stock of each asset is willingly held); (2) that all investors behave according to a mean-variance criterion (see chapter 5); and (3) that investors base their decisions on the same values of means, variances and covariances – the investors are said to have *homogeneous beliefs*. In more detail, the assumptions are as follows.

1: Asset markets are in equilibrium

(a) Frictionless markets. This assumption has two elements: (i) zero transaction costs; and (ii) no institutional restrictions on asset trades (e.g. short-sales are allowed). This assumption is, of course, an idealization, hardly ever likely to be strictly satisfied in practice. Its relevance is to signal that the predictions of the CAPM are more likely to be accurate if frictions are small than if they impinge significantly on investors' decisions.

(b) Investors can borrow or lend unlimited amounts at the risk-free rate of interest. This assumption could be interpreted as an implication of frictionless markets but is noted separately to highlight its presence. It is abandoned in the Black CAPM.

(c) Assets are divisible into any desired units. In principle, investors should be able to hold $10, or $1, or 1 cent of any asset. The implication is that the predictions of the CAPM are unlikely to be accurate if there exist indivisible assets that consume a large proportion of each investor's initial wealth.

(d) All assets can be bought or sold at observed market prices.

(e) Investors are price takers: the decisions of any one investor do not affect asset prices. This condition states that no investor can exert monopoly power; asset markets are assumed to be competitive.

(f) Taxes are neutral. What is relevant for the following analysis is not so much the common assumption that taxes are zero but, rather, (i) that all investors face the same tax rates and (ii) that tax rates are the same for all sources of investment income, in particular for capital gains and dividends.

2: Mean-variance portfolio selection

(a) All investors behave according to a single-period investment horizon. That is, their objectives focus on the value of terminal wealth at a specified date in the future, no revisions to chosen portfolios being permitted during the intervening time period. This restriction is relaxed in chapter 11.
(b) All investors select their portfolios according to a mean-variance objective.

3: Homogeneous beliefs

All investors use the same estimates of the expectations, variances and covariances of asset returns. This condition is maintained throughout. It could be relaxed, but only at the expense of greater complexity and burdensome notation.

6.2 Asset market equilibrium

6.2.1 Market equilibrium in the CAPM

The notation used here is that of chapter 5. Recall that the condition that defines portfolio equilibrium for each investor is (see chapter 5, section 5.4.2)

$$\frac{\mu_j - r_0}{\beta_{jZ}} = \mu_Z - r_0 \quad \text{where} \quad \beta_{jZ} = \sigma_{jZ}/\sigma_Z^2 \quad \text{for } j = 1, 2, \ldots, n \qquad (6.1)$$

and where Z denotes the *efficient* portfolio consisting of only risky assets. Let $z_1, z_2, \ldots, z_n$ denote the proportions of risky assets in the Z portfolio. By construction, $\sum_{j=1}^{n} z_j = 1$ (i.e. $z_0 = 0$ – that is, the risk-free asset is not held in Z). The assumption of homogeneous beliefs implies that all expected returns, variances and covariances are identical across investors. Hence, β_{jZ} is the same across investors for each asset, j. Consequently, z_j is the same across investors for each asset, j.

Let $i = 1, 2, \ldots, m$ index the investors in the market. The value of investor i's holding of asset j is then equal to $z_j B_i$, where B_i is the total value of the investor's holding of all risky assets – B_i equals initial wealth A_i minus investor i's holding of the risk-free asset (or, plus the value of borrowing at the risk-free rate). The *equilibrium* total market value of asset j equals the sum across investors of the value of the asset j demanded:

$$p_j X_j = \sum_{i=1}^{m} z_j B_i = z_j \sum_{i=1}^{m} B_i = z_j B \quad \text{for } j = 1, 2, \ldots, n$$

whcre $p_j X_j$ is the total market value (price *times* quantity) of asset j, and B is the total market value of *all* holdings of risky assets (i.e. B equals the sum of the B_i over all investors). In market equilibrium

$$z_j = \frac{p_j X_j}{B} \equiv m_j \qquad \text{for } j = 1, 2, \ldots, n$$

Market equilibrium implies that asset prices adjust such that the share, z_j, of each asset in the risky asset portfolio of every investor equals the share of that asset in the whole market, $p_j X_j / B$, the market portfolio. From now on, m_j is used to denote the value of z_j *in market equilibrium.*[2] Also, write β_{jP} as β_j when P is the market portfolio – i.e. $\beta_j \equiv \beta_{jM}$.

Summary: the proportion of each risky asset in the efficient portfolio comprising exclusively risky assets is the same for every investor. That this portfolio is identical for all investors follows from the assumption of homogeneous beliefs. In market equilibrium, existing stocks of assets are willingly held. Hence, the proportion of each asset in this portfolio equals its share in the market as a whole.

More formally: *the proportion, z_j, of each risky asset, j, in the risky asset portfolio, Z, is the same for every investor, and this proportion is equal to the share, m_j, of the market value, $p_j X_j$, of asset j in the total market value, B, of all risky assets.*

6.2.2 Capital market line

The *capital market line* (CML) is depicted in figure 6.1 as the ray drawn from the risk-free interest rate, r_0, tangential to the portfolio frontier for risky assets, FF. The point of tangency is denoted by M, (μ_M, σ_M).

Figure 6.1 is constructed as follows. The assumption of homogeneous beliefs implies that FF is identical for every investor. Together with a common r_0 for each investor, this implies that the efficient set of portfolios is the same for every investor. Thus, as explained above, the efficient portfolio comprising exclusively risky assets is the same for every investor – in figure 6.1 the point M depicts its expected rate of return, μ_M, and standard deviation of return, σ_M.

The CAPM does not imply that each investor's entire portfolio (including the risk-free asset) contains the same proportion of each asset as that for every other investor, only that asset proportions are equal for assets belonging to the efficient portfolio in which the risk-free asset is absent (recall that this is the portfolio denoted by Z in the mean-variance analysis). The CAPM predicts that different investors hold different proportions of the risk-free asset depending on

---

[2] The proportion of asset j in the market portfolio, m_j, should not be confused with m, the number of investors.

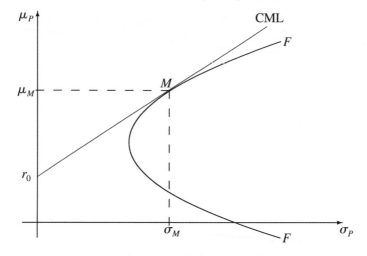

Fig. 6.1. The capital market line

The CML depicts the locus of efficient portfolios in market equilibrium if all investors share the same beliefs about means and variances. The CML passes through r_0 on the vertical axis and is tangent at M to FF, the portfolio frontier for risky assets alone. Point M identifies the market portfolio, in which the share of each risky asset equals its share in the whole market.

their attitudes to risk; their optimal portfolios are located along the CML, not necessarily all at the same point.

All *efficient* portfolios are located along the CML; they differ only according to the proportion of the entire portfolio invested in the risk-free asset. It follows that the Sharpe ratios for all efficient portfolios must equal one another (see chapter 5, section 5.4.3). Let (μ_E, σ_E) denote *any* efficient portfolio. From the definition of the Sharpe ratio,

$$\frac{\mu_E - r_0}{\sigma_E} = \frac{\mu_M - r_0}{\sigma_M} \tag{6.2}$$

because the Sharpe ratios are equal for all efficient portfolios. Rearranging (6.2),

$$\mu_E = r_0 + \frac{\sigma_E}{\sigma_M}(\mu_M - r_0) \tag{6.3}$$

The result, (6.3), holds *only* for efficient portfolios. Expression (6.3) can, alternatively, be derived by recognizing that the rates of return on all efficient portfolios are perfectly positively correlated, $\rho_{EM} = +1$, so that $\beta_E = \sigma_E/\sigma_M$ (see equations (6.5) and (6.6)).

The main prediction of the CAPM is expressed by writing equation (6.1) as

$$\frac{\mu_j - r_0}{\beta_j} = \mu_M - r_0 \quad \text{for } j = 1, 2, \ldots, n \tag{6.4}$$

where M represents the market portfolio. (The M subscript in β_{jM} is dropped when the reference portfolio is the market portfolio.) In chapter 5 it was shown that each asset's 'beta-coefficient', β_j, is given by $\beta_j = \sigma_{jM}/\sigma_M^2$. It is helpful, for later interpretation, to recognize that this is the expression – well known in elementary statistics – for the regression coefficient of r_j on r_M.

Equation (6.4) is commonly rearranged as

$$\mu_j = r_0 + (\mu_M - r_0)\beta_j \quad \text{for } j = 1, 2, \ldots, n \tag{6.5}$$

The value of μ_j in (6.5) can be interpreted, alternatively, (a) as a function of r_0 and μ_M for given β_j, or (b) as a function of β_j for given r_0 and μ_M. Both interpretations are relevant in applications of the CAPM.

An asset's beta-coefficient is a measure of the relationship between its rate of return and the market rate of return. Recalling the definition of the correlation coefficient between r_j and r_M, $\rho_{jM} \equiv \sigma_{jM}/(\sigma_j \sigma_M)$, the covariance σ_{jM} can be written as $\sigma_{jM} = \rho_{jM}\sigma_j\sigma_M$, so that

$$\beta_j = \frac{\sigma_{jM}}{\sigma_M^2} = \frac{\rho_{jM}\sigma_j\sigma_M}{\sigma_M^2} = \rho_{jM}\frac{\sigma_j}{\sigma_M} \tag{6.6}$$

The form $\beta_j = \rho_{jM}\sigma_j/\sigma_M$ is handy later on.

6.2.3 Asset prices

The CAPM is a model of asset prices, though it is typically expressed in terms of rates of return rather than prices. To appreciate why the two approaches are equivalent, recall the definition of the rate of return on asset j:

$$r_j \equiv \frac{v_j - p_j}{p_j} \quad j = 1, 2, \ldots, n \tag{6.7}$$

where p_j is the observed price for asset j and v_j is the (uncertain) payoff for asset j.

By taking expectations of (6.7), appendix 6.1 shows that the CAPM prediction (6.5) can be written as

$$p_j = \frac{\mathrm{E}[v_j]}{1 + r_0 + \theta\beta_j} \quad \text{for } j = 1, 2, \ldots, n \tag{6.8}$$

where $\theta \equiv \mu_M - r_0$ denotes the excess expected return on the market portfolio. To make sense of equation (6.8), recall the case of perfect foresight (see chapter 1) for which $p_j = v_j/(1 + r_0)$. This is the simplest net present value relationship – a consequence of the absence of arbitrage opportunities. Passing from this to the CAPM prediction involves two amendments, both of them implications of risk. First, the payoff, v_j, is unknown and is replaced by its expected value $E[v_j]$. This is the only alteration needed if investors are risk-neutral (i.e. in the absence of risk aversion). But, because investors behave according to a mean-variance objective (and, by implication, are risk-averse), it is also necessary to replace the interest factor, $1 + r_0$, with $1 + r_0 + \theta\beta_j$.

If $\theta\beta_j > 0$, investors discount the expected future payoff at a higher rate when they are risk-averse, rather than risk-neutral. The reaction of investors to risk makes asset j less attractive and, consequently, its market price is lower (compared with an equilibrium in which all investors are risk-neutral). If, as seems plausible, $\theta > 0$ (on average the expected excess return on the market portfolio is positive), and if asset j's return is positively correlated with the market return ($\beta_j > 0$), then $\theta\beta_j > 0$. Later – in section 6.5.1 – the extra term in the denominator is discussed further as asset j's risk premium.

The equilibrating process for asset prices in the CAPM can be described as follows. Each investor uses the same information about what determines v_j (and hence r_j) for each asset. Given the mean-variance assumption, this information can be summarized in terms of expectations, variances and covariances of asset returns. On the basis of this information and their attitudes to risk, investors select their portfolios. If the resulting demands for assets do not equal the (exogenously given) supplies, then asset prices change in response to the market disequilibrium. As prices change, investors adjust their portfolios. Only when equilibrium is attained will the set of prices (and hence rates of return) be compatible with the planned portfolios of investors and the stocks of assets.

Strictly, the CAPM asserts nothing about the equilibrating process; it is a theory of asset market equilibrium. The story in the previous paragraph is intended to support intuition, an informal guide, not a theory of dynamics.

6.3 The characteristic line and the market model

The *characteristic line* for each asset treats $\mu_j - r_0$ as a function of $\mu_M - r_0$; see figure 6.2. From equation (6.5) the characteristic line is a graph of the equation $\mu_j - r_0 = (\mu_M - r_0)\beta_j$, with a slope equal to the beta-coefficient, β_j, of asset j.

In practice, some way must be found to calculate each asset's beta-coefficient. The most direct way (though not the only way) is to estimate β_j using regression analysis applied to past data on rates of return. To make sense of this approach, note that μ_j and μ_M are unobserved – they represent purely

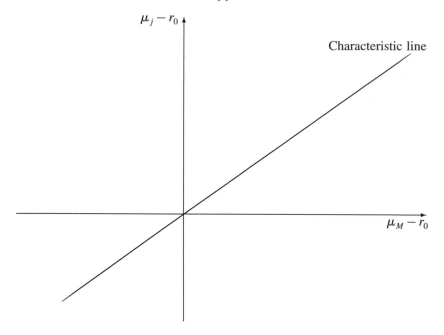

Fig. 6.2. The characteristic line for asset j

The characteristic line treats the CAPM prediction, $\mu_j - r_0 = (\mu_M - r_0)\beta_j$, as a linear relationship between $(\mu_j - r_0)$ and $(\mu_M - r_0)$ with slope equal to β_j. Each asset (including portfolios of assets) has its own characteristic line. They differ according to the value of β_j.

theoretical concepts. If μ_j is replaced by r_j and μ_M by r_M, then it is possible to write

$$r_j = r_0 + (r_M - r_0)\beta_j + \varepsilon_j \qquad j = 1, 2, \ldots, n \qquad (6.9)$$

where ε_j is an unobserved random error. It is assumed that $E[\varepsilon_j | r_M] = 0$; that is, the expected value of the error, conditional upon the rate of return on the market portfolio, is zero. This condition immediately implies that $E[\varepsilon_j] = 0$ and also that $\text{cov}(\varepsilon_j, r_M) = 0$ (recall the law of iterated expectations from chapter 3, page 79). In words: the random error is assumed to be zero on average and uncorrelated with the market rate of return. These conditions enable the estimation of the beta-coefficients using data on rates of return – a subject explored in chapter 9.

In practice, the 'market portfolio' is represented by the portfolio corresponding to a broadly defined stock price index (such as the S&P 500 index for US stocks or the FT-Actuaries All-Share index for shares traded in London). A critical challenge in testing the CAPM arises because these indexes are always approximations to the 'market portfolio', in the sense that they do not coincide exactly with the universe of assets available to investors. For example, many investors have access to other assets, such as real estate, not included in whatever index is assumed to represent the market.

The CAPM is a close relative of another model, the 'market model'. The market model asserts simply that there is a linear relationship between the rate of return on each asset and the rate of return on the market portfolio:

$$r_j = b_{j0} + b_{j1}r_M + \varepsilon_j \quad j = 1, 2, \ldots, n \tag{6.10}$$

where b_{j0} and b_{j1} are parameters. Also, $\mathrm{E}[\varepsilon_j | r_M] = 0$, as for the CAPM.

The CAPM can be considered as a special case of the market model where $b_{j1} = \beta_j$ and $b_{j0} = (1 - \beta_j)r_0$ (compare (6.9) with (6.10)). The market model reappears in the guise of a 'factor model' in chapter 9. Although the market model might be interpreted as a generalization of the CAPM, no argument has been offered – so far, at least – to justify *why* the market model should hold. The CAPM has the advantage that its foundations are explicit and, consequently, that it provides definite predictions, some of which are explored in the following sections.

6.4 The security market line

A central implication of the CAPM is the security market line (SML), depicted in figure 6.3. The SML plots μ_j against β_j. As already remarked, it is another way of interpreting equation (6.5), $\mu_j = r_0 + (\mu_M - r_0)\beta_j$.

Here the intercept equals the risk-free rate, r_0, and the slope equals $\mu_M - r_0$. The CAPM predicts that the expected rates of return and beta-coefficients for *all* assets and portfolios of assets, not just efficient portfolios, lie on the SML.[3] Sometimes the SML is written in terms of the excess of the expected return over the risk-free rate, $(\mu_j - r_0)$; the SML then passes through the origin in the diagram.

A practical application of the CAPM is to plot the observed average rates of return on individual assets, or portfolios of assets, against their estimated beta-coefficients. The CAPM predicts that the resulting graph will trace out the SML – that is, a line with intercept given by the risk-free rate and slope equal to the average return on the market portfolio minus the risk-free rate. It is always necessary to allow for some statistical error, so that the observations will not fall exactly on a line. Statistical analysis provides a systematic way of studying how well the data matches the prediction of the theory (see chapter 9).

---

[3] Why would any investor ever wish to hold an asset with a *negative* beta-coefficient? It is, after all, a risky asset with an expected return *lower* than the risk-free rate. The answer is that such an asset might be included in a *portfolio* of assets because its covariance with the return on other assets enables the investor to control the risk on the portfolio as a whole.

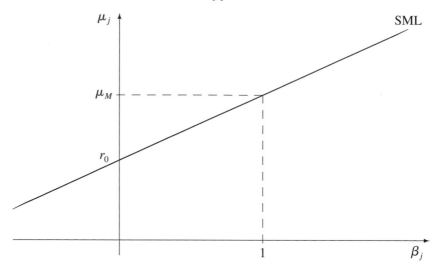

Fig. 6.3. The security market line

The SML views the CAPM prediction $\mu_j = r_0 + (\mu_M - r_0)\beta_j$ as a linear
relationship between μ_j and β_j. The model predicts that the average
rates of return and beta-coefficients for all assets, and all portfolios of
assets, will be located along the SML.

6.4.1 Disequilibrium

How are divergences of average rates of return and beta-coefficients from the
SML to be interpreted? One possibility is that the divergences are simply the
result of statistical variation or mismeasurement; μ_j, μ_M and β_j are, after all,
purely theoretical concepts – unknown parameters that reflect investors' beliefs.

As mentioned above, ways must be found for estimating these parameters in
order to implement the theory. Then, if the theory is to have any practical value,
it must be presumed that there is a correspondence, albeit imperfect, between the
theoretical concepts and their estimated counterparts.

Suppose that some of the estimated μ_j and β_j do not fall on the SML. Consider,
for example, assets A and B in depicted in figure 6.4. Asset A lies above the
SML; it has a mean rate of return higher than that predicted by the CAPM. This
is commonly understood to imply that asset A is *underpriced* (or *undervalued*).
In response, an adherent of the CAPM would wish to purchase asset A, believing
that its price will rise as the market tends towards an equilibrium.

Similar reasoning can be applied to asset B, the mean rate of which is lower
than that predicted by the CAPM. Asset B is *overpriced* (or *overvalued*). The
CAPM predicts that investors will sell B, believing that its price will fall as the

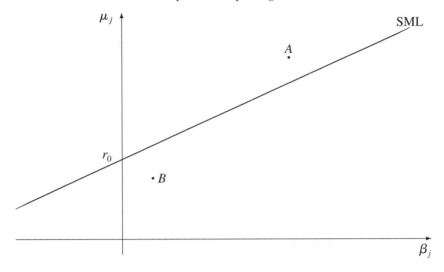

Fig. 6.4. Disequilibrium in the CAPM

The mean rate of return on asset A is greater than predicted by the CAPM given its beta-coefficient: the point A lies above the SML. Hence, A is *underpriced* – conditional on the validity of the CAPM. Point B indicates that the mean return on asset B is lower than predicted by the CAPM given its beta-coefficient. Asset B is *overpriced*, again, conditional on the validity of the CAPM.

market tends towards an equilibrium. In a sense, asset A 'yields more than it should' (where *should* is not normative but refers to the CAPM prediction); and asset B 'yields less than it should'.

These informal stories – they are no more than that – invite the interpretation of asset market disequilibrium when divergences occur such as those depicted by A and B; call this 'CAPM disequilibrium'. Notice that CAPM disequilibrium is different from the notion of disequilibrium as an imbalance of demand and supply. Asset markets could be in equilibrium in the sense that the existing stocks are willingly held at the current market prices (i.e. demand equals supply) but in disequilibrium in the sense depicted in figure 6.4.

A simple way of representing CAPM disequilibrium is to rewrite (6.5) as

$$\mu_j = \alpha_j + r_0 + (\mu_M - r_0)\beta_j \qquad j = 1, 2, \ldots, n$$

The term α_j measures the extent to which asset j is overpriced $(\alpha_j < 0)$ or underpriced $(\alpha_j > 0)$ in comparison with the prediction of the CAPM. Thus, non-zero α_j terms signal the presence of CAPM disequilibrium.

This is not the only interpretation, however. For the observation of non-zero α_j terms could be viewed as evidence against the CAPM itself, rather than evidence that (a) asset prices are determined according to the CAPM and (b) there is CAPM disequilibrium. In other words, evidence that $\alpha_j \neq 0$ might mean that the CAPM should be discarded in favour of an alternative theory. This sort of conclusion deserves to be handled with caution. (What, for instance, is the alternative theory?) Even so, a systematic study of CAPM disequilibrium – the possibility that $\alpha_j \neq 0$ – offers a suitable avenue for testing the CAPM (and is pursued further in chapter 9).

6.5 Risk premia and diversification

6.5.1 Risk premia

The *risk premium* on asset j is commonly defined as the excess of its expected rate of return over the risk-free rate of return – that is, $\mu_j - r_0$. The magnitude of the risk premium will, evidently, depend on its 'risk' – interpreted, so far, as the standard deviation of its rate of return, σ_j. The CAPM, together with most other models of asset prices, implies that the association of σ_j with risk is misleading.

In the case of the CAPM, the excess expected return is (see (6.5))

$$\mu_j - r_0 = (\mu_M - r_0)\beta_j \qquad \text{for } j = 1, 2, \ldots, n \qquad (6.11)$$

This asserts that the risk premium equals the product of the excess expected return on the market portfolio, $(\mu_M - r_0)$, and the asset's beta-coefficient, β_j. The standard deviation, σ_j, does not appear explicitly (though, clearly, it is one of the determinants of $\beta_j = \rho_{jM}\sigma_j/\sigma_M$).

In the context of equation (6.11), the CAPM implies that an asset's risk premium is a function of its beta-coefficient – not its standard deviation. That is (rather imprecisely), the risk premium on any asset corresponds to the correlation between its rate of return and the return on the market portfolio (rather than the variability in the asset's rate of return). To the extent that the CAPM is acceptable, 'risk' should be measured by each asset's beta-coefficient, not its standard deviation of return.

Pushing the intuition further, the larger is β_j, the riskier the asset. An asset with a zero beta-coefficient is uncorrelated with the market and has an expected rate of return equal to the risk-free interest rate. It might seem contradictory to call such an asset 'risk-free', for its return still varies randomly: r_j is not certain and not equal to r_0 (even when $\beta_j = 0$). Instead, for an asset with a zero beta-coefficient, the *expected* return, μ_j, equals r_0.

Assets with negative beta-coefficients (if any such exist) offer a form of insurance against variability in the rate of return on the market portfolio. Hence, the expected rate of return on such an asset is *lower* than the risk-free rate – again, a somewhat paradoxical result. The paradox is resolved by noting that 'risk' in the CAPM is associated with a positive correlation with the market rate of return, so that the absence of risk corresponds not to the certainty associated with r_0 but rather to a negative correlation with the return on the market portfolio.

6.5.2 Diversification

The diversification of a portfolio refers to the choice of a portfolio of assets designed to reduce the variability of the rate of return on the whole portfolio compared with the variability of any of its constituents.[4] Notice the absence of the word 'risk' in the previous sentence; its omission is deliberate, for a reason that should shortly become clear.

From equation (6.9), $r_j = r_0 + (r_M - r_0)\beta_j + \varepsilon_j$, the variability in the return on asset j has two sources: (a) variations in the market rate of return, r_M, and (b) variations in the random error, ε_j. More formally, it can be shown that

$$\sigma_j^2 = \beta_j^2 \sigma_M^2 + \sigma_{\varepsilon_j}^2 \qquad (6.12)$$

where the variance of ε_j is denoted by $\sigma_{\varepsilon_j}^2$.[5] The two terms on the right-hand side of (6.12) are, somewhat misleadingly, associated with market risk and idiosyncratic risk, respectively – misleadingly because risk and variability are distinct in the CAPM, as already argued. (Common synonyms for *market risk* in this context are 'systematic' or 'undiversifiable' risk; and 'unsystematic', 'unique' or 'diversifiable' risk for *idiosyncratic risk*.)

The role of diversification in the CAPM is that portfolios comprising a suitably chosen 'wide array' of assets serve to reduce idiosyncratic risk. To understand how this can be achieved, notice that, because (6.12) holds for an individual asset, it must hold for any portfolio P of assets:

$$\sigma_P^2 = \beta_P^2 \sigma_M^2 + \sigma_{\varepsilon_P}^2$$

where $\sigma_{\varepsilon_P}^2$ is the variance of the portfolio's random error term, ε_P. Note that $\varepsilon_P = \sum_{j=1}^{n} a_j \varepsilon_j$, where a_j is the proportion of asset j in portfolio P.

Now, by a suitable choice of the portfolio proportions, a_j, it is possible to reduce the idiosyncratic risk, $\sigma_{\varepsilon_P}^2$, arbitrarily close to zero. To see how this might be achieved, suppose that P is a 'well-diversified' portfolio constructed to satisfy two criteria: (a) that the number of assets in the portfolio P is N with $a_j \approx 1/N$ (e.g. with $N = 100$ assets, each asset forms approximately 1 per cent

---

[4] In this context, 'variability' can be understood as referring to the variance or standard deviation of assets' returns.

[5] The crucial assumption in obtaining (6.12) is that r_M and ε_j are uncorrelated; otherwise, a covariance term would appear. Unforeseen fluctuations in the risk-free rate, r_0, are ignored throughout.

of the portfolio); and (b) that the ε_j for each asset j in P is uncorrelated with the ε_k for every other asset k in P. This being so, it follows that

$$\sigma_{\varepsilon_P}^2 = \sum_{j=1}^{N} a_j^2 \sigma_{\varepsilon_j}^2 \quad \text{(because the returns on assets are uncorrelated)}$$

$$\approx \sum_{j=1}^{N} \left[\frac{1}{N}\right]^2 \sigma_{\varepsilon_j}^2 \quad \text{(given that } a_j \approx 1/N)$$

$$\sigma_{\varepsilon_P}^2 \approx \frac{1}{N} \left\{ \frac{\sigma_{\varepsilon_1}^2 + \sigma_{\varepsilon_2}^2 + \cdots + \sigma_{\varepsilon_N}^2}{N} \right\} \tag{6.13}$$

Consider the term in braces, { }, in equation (6.13). This is the total idiosyncratic risk associated with all the assets contained in P divided by the number of assets, N, in the portfolio. Both the numerator and denominator of the ratio increase as N is increased. It is plausible to suppose that the ratio remains bounded as N becomes arbitrarily large. This would be true if, for instance, the variances, $\sigma_{\varepsilon_j}^2$, are the same for every asset. But it can also be true under less restrictive conditions.[6]

If the term in large braces remains bounded, then, as N is increased, $\sigma_{\varepsilon_P}^2$ is reduced. In the limit, as $N \to \infty$, the idiosyncratic risk approaches zero. This is the sense in which a well-diversified portfolio can eliminate idiosyncratic risk – or, more precisely, that a well-diversified portfolio can eliminate idiosyncratic variability.

The two requirements of a well-diversified portfolio are, firstly, that it should be 'balanced' so that the proportion held of each asset is approximately equal and, secondly, that the idiosyncratic components should be uncorrelated across assets. If the second condition is not satisfied, then covariance terms will appear in the right-hand-side term of (6.13) (but see footnote 6). There is an awkward incompatibility with the CAPM here in that the second condition cannot strictly hold in a CAPM equilibrium: there must exist non-zero correlations among at least some of the random errors, ε_j (see appendix 6.2).

An interpretation of diversification in the context of the CAPM is to view the universe of assets in the entire market as exceedingly large – larger than the number of assets likely to be held in any portfolio. Each of the component assets in a diversified portfolio is then assumed to satisfy the condition that the idiosyncratic components of return are uncorrelated, at least as an approximation. However, the interpretation rests uncomfortably with the prediction of the CAPM

---

[6] A more elegant way to state the relevant condition is to require that the probability distributions of the random variables, ε_j, satisfy the assumptions of a law of large numbers. (A classic reference is Feller, 1970, chap. 10.) Once this is recognized, it is also apparent that the assumption that ε_j are uncorrelated with one another is more restrictive than necessary – some laws of large numbers permit such correlations.

that the composition of every investor's risky asset portfolio reflects the asset proportions in the market as a whole.

Diversification should not, in any case, be construed as a panacea for attenuating, let alone eliminating, risk. Another way of reducing idiosyncratic variability is for the investor to obtain more information about each asset's issuer – for example, to inquire about the policies of companies the shares of which are candidates for inclusion in a portfolio. The mean-variance model underpinning the CAPM takes the means and variances as given, not as the objects of active research. Some investors may seek, instead, to achieve their goals not by spreading wealth across a broad range of assets but by devoting effort to scrutinize individual companies, and then concentrating their portfolios on assets that they judge to satisfy their needs (either because the assets have low risk, or high expected return, or an acceptable combination of both).

6.6 Extensions

6.6.1 The Black CAPM

Thus far it has been assumed that investors can borrow or lend without restriction. Now remove this opportunity and assume, instead, that *all* assets are risky. All the other assumptions of the CAPM remain in place. This defines what is called here the 'Black CAPM' (see Black, 1972).

Retaining the assumption that investors have homogeneous beliefs, they all face the same portfolio frontier, depicted by *FF* in figure 6.5. It should come as no surprise that the market portfolio is efficient in the sense that it is located on the upward-sloping portion of *FF*. (For a formal justification, see appendix 6.3.)

Let the market portfolio be depicted by the point *M* on *FF*. A line tangent to *M* meets the vertical axis at some point, ω, by construction. The ray from ω passing through *M* is interpreted as the capital market line in the Black model.

All the portfolios (or individual assets) located on the horizontal line starting at *W* have an expected rate of return equal to ω. It can be shown that the beta-coefficients for all the portfolios located on this line are equal to zero: these are the 'zero-beta portfolios' (see chapter 5, appendix 5.2.3). From the definition of the beta-coefficient, it follows that there is a zero-correlation coefficient between the rate of return on the market portfolio and the rate of return on every zero-beta portfolio.

Intuitively (and also formally), ω plays the same role as r_0 when borrowing or lending is permitted at a risk-free rate. Indeed, the resemblance is so intimate that the expected rate of return for any asset (or portfolio) can be written as

$$\mu_j = \omega + (\mu_M - \omega)\beta_j \qquad j = 1, 2, \ldots, n \tag{6.14}$$

which is analogous to equation (6.5) (see appendix 6.3 for the details).

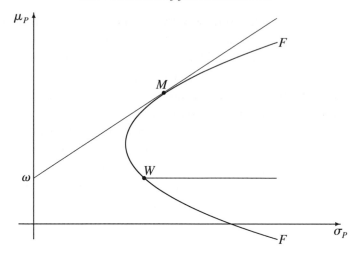

Fig. 6.5. Zero-beta portfolios

In the absence of a risk-free asset, the market portfolio is located at a point such as M on the frontier FF. The tangent to FF at M meets the vertical axis at ω. Feasible portfolios (or individual assets) with an expected rate of return equal to ω are located along the horizontal line starting at W. The rate of return on all these portfolios is uncorrelated with the return on the market portfolio. Hence, all their beta-coefficients are zero.

Thus, even when all assets are risky, a 'characteristic line' for each asset and a 'security market line' can be constructed from (6.14) in the same way as when a risk-free asset is available. The difference is that the risk-free rate of return is replaced by ω, the expected rate of return on a zero-beta portfolio. Otherwise, the analysis is identical with that of previous sections.

Applications of the model are much the same as when a risk-free asset is available, except that now ω must be estimated or calculated separately – say, by constructing a zero-beta portfolio. In this case the predictions of the CAPM are less definite – an additional unknown parameter, ω, is present – but empirical analysis is still feasible, as described in chapter 9.

It is possible to modify the Black CAPM to allow for lending at the risk-free rate but not borrowing, or for lending at a lower rate than the borrowing rate. The details are, of course, more involved but the approach is similar; consequently, these cases are not studied further here.

6.6.2 Other CAPM models

Following the introduction of the CAPM, a host of extensions were proposed – and they continue to be. They all boil down to relaxing one or more of the assumptions listed at the outset, in section 6.1, and result in models that bear a more or less close resemblance to the CAPM according to the alterations that are made. Some of the modifications are routine – for example, allowing for different tax rates on dividend income and capital gains. Others, such as allowing for heterogeneous beliefs (i.e. different values for means and variances across investors), can be expressed only in complicated models.

Possibly the most important class of modifications to the CAPM involves generalizing the underlying single-period mean-variance framework to allow for intertemporal decision making. The resulting models are collectively known either as the intertemporal CAPM (ICAPM) or the consumption-based CAPM (CCAPM). They allow for intertemporal planning by investors who are now assumed to have the opportunity to revise their portfolio decisions and to consume part of their wealth, according to their preferences. In addition, other sources of income (such as from employment) can be introduced. An examination of these issues must await chapter 11.

Another way of obtaining the SML (also discussed in chapter 11) deserves mention at this point. Recall the fundamental valuation relationship from chapter 4. This states that each expected-utility-maximizing investor selects a portfolio such that $E[(1+r_j)H] = 1$ for each asset, j, where H is a random variable that depends on the investor's preferences. In chapter 11 it is shown that the condition needed to obtain the SML – $\mu_j = r_0 + (\mu_M - r_0)\beta_j$ – is that the random variable H is perfectly positively correlated with r_M (i.e. $\rho_{HM} = +1$). It is possible to show that the H for a mean-variance objective function satisfies this condition, though $\rho_{HM} = +1$ holds more generally, as explored in chapter 11.

6.7 Summary

This chapter has examined the assumptions and implications of the conventional, static capital asset pricing model. The main points are these.

1. The CAPM assumes a world in which (a) asset markets are in equilibrium (supply = demand); (b) investors choose portfolios according to a mean-variance objective; and (c) investors behave according to common values of the means and variances of asset returns.
2. The CAPM predicts that all investors hold the same risky asset portfolio (in which the portfolio proportion of each asset equals its proportion in the market as a whole). Not all investors need endure the same risk, because they need not all hold the same proportion of the risk-free asset in their portfolios.
3. The CAPM implies that expected asset returns can be predicted from the *security market line* (figure 6.3). This is the main prediction of the CAPM:

$$\mu_j = r_0 + (\mu_M - r_0)\beta_j \quad \text{for } j = 1, 2, \ldots, n$$

4. The variability of the rate of return on any asset, or portfolio, can be divided into its systematic risk (how its return varies with the return on the market portfolio) and idiosyncratic (or unique) risk. Portfolio diversification seeks to make the idiosyncratic risk negligible. In view of the different sources of variability, the CAPM implies that each asset's beta-coefficient, β_j, is a more appropriate measure of risk than its standard deviation of return, σ_j.

5. The CAPM can be extended in a variety of ways, the most important being: (a) to relax the condition that unlimited borrowing and lending are possible at a risk-free interest rate; and (b) to allow for the intertemporal planning of portfolio allocation and consumption decisions.

Finally, note that, although the CAPM predicts that mean rates of return lie on the SML, the CAPM is not the *only* model from which this prediction can be derived. In particular, it is possible to obtain the same prediction as a special case of the arbitrage pricing theory instead of relying on the mean-variance analysis that underpins the CAPM. The APT is the subject of chapter 8.

Further reading

A rigorous exposition of the CAPM, together with some informative background remarks about its development, can be found in the 'capital asset pricing model' entry in *The New Palgrave Dictionary of Money and Finance* (Newman, Milgate and Eatwell, 1992, Vol. I, pp. 287–92). Perold's (2004) reflections on the fortieth anniversary of the CAPM provide an introduction to the topic that should be attractive for students.

Extended, business-management-oriented expositions appear in many texts, including Grinblatt and Titman (2001, chap. 5) and Sharpe, Alexander and Bailey (1999, chap. 10). An excellent analysis at a level of detail one stage more advanced than that offered here is provided by Elton, Gruber, Brown and Goetzmann (2003, chaps. 13 & 14). A detailed but accessible exposition including several extensions can be found in Fama (1976, chap. 8). The early sections of chapter 5 in Campbell, Lo and MacKinlay (1997) contain a concise review, at an advanced level, of the CAPM analysis.

Appendix 6.1: The CAPM in terms of asset prices

The CAPM can be expressed in terms of asset prices by manipulating equation (6.5), $\mu_j - r_0 = (\mu_M - r_0)\beta_j$, after substituting for the expected rate of return, $\mu_j = (\mathrm{E}[v_j] - p_j)/p_j$, as follows:

$$\mu_j - r_0 = (\mu_M - r_0)\beta_j \qquad j = 1, 2, \ldots, n$$

$$\frac{E[v_j] - p_j}{p_j} - r_0 = \theta\beta_j \quad \text{where } \theta \equiv \mu_M - r_0$$

$$\frac{E[v_j]}{p_j} - 1 - r_0 = \theta\beta_j$$

$$\frac{E[v_j]}{p_j} = 1 + r_0 + \theta\beta_j$$

$$p_j = \frac{E[v_j]}{1 + r_0 + \theta\beta_j}$$

which appears as equation (6.8) (page 148) in section 6.2.3.

An alternative to allowing for risk via an increase in the denominator of the present value relationship is to account for its effect as a *reduction* in the asset's expected payoff – i.e. to subtract a term from the numerator. To do this, first define the *beta-coefficient* for the *payoff* on asset j (instead of its rate of return) as follows:

$$\beta_j^* \equiv \frac{\text{cov}(v_j, v_M)}{\text{var}(v_M)} \quad j = 1, 2, \ldots, n$$

where v_M is the payoff on the market portfolio. Substituting into the definitions of covariances and variances, it follows that $\beta_j = p_M\beta_j^*/p_j$, where p_M is the market price of a unit of the market portfolio. Using this relationship, and rewriting the basic CAPM condition in the same way as before, gives

$$\frac{E[v_j] - p_j}{p_j} - r_0 = \theta\beta_j \quad j = 1, 2, \ldots, n$$

$$\frac{E[v_j]}{p_j} - 1 - r_0 = \frac{\theta p_M\beta_j^*}{p_j}$$

$$\frac{E[v_j]}{p_j} - \frac{\theta p_M\beta_j^*}{p_J} - 1 + r_0$$

$$\frac{E[v_j] - \theta p_M\beta_j^*}{p_j} = 1 + r_0$$

$$p_j = \frac{E[v_j] - \theta p_M\beta_j^*}{1 + r_0} \tag{6.15}$$

Equation (6.15) expresses the price of each asset, j, as a net present value, not by adding a term to $1 + r_0$ but, rather, by subtracting $\theta p_M\beta_j^*$ from the expected payoff, $E[v_j]$. The term $\theta p_M\beta_j^*$ reflects a notional deduction made to take account of the aversion to risk that investors associate with uncertainty about the realization of v_j. The notional amount deducted depends (via β_j^*) on the correlation between the payoff on asset j and the payoff on the market portfolio, v_M. The larger the value of β_j^*, the greater the variability in v_j associated with changes in v_M and, hence, the greater the deduction from expected earnings necessary to 'compensate' for the additional risk.

Appendix 6.2: Linear dependence of ε_j in the CAPM

This appendix demonstrates a property (noted in section 6.5.2) of the random errors in the CAPM. In particular, for the universe of assets in the market as a whole, the ε_j in equation (6.9), $r_j = r_0 + (r_M - r_0)\beta_j + \varepsilon_j$, must be linearly dependent.

To establish the linear dependence, first multiply (6.9) by m_j, the proportion of asset j in the market portfolio, and sum over j:

$$m_j r_j = m_j r_0 + m_j (r_M - r_0)\beta_j + m_j \varepsilon_j \qquad j = 1, 2, \ldots, n$$

$$\sum_{j=1}^{n} m_j r_j = r_0 \sum_{j=1}^{n} m_j + (r_M - r_0) \sum_{j=1}^{n} m_j \beta_j + \sum_{j=1}^{n} m_j \varepsilon_j \tag{6.16}$$

By definition,

$$r_M \equiv \sum_{j=1}^{n} m_j r_j$$

$$\sum_{j=1}^{n} m_j = 1$$

and

$$\sum_{j=1}^{n} m_j \beta_j = \sum_{j=1}^{n} m_j \sigma_{jM} / \sigma_M^2 = \sigma_M^2 / \sigma_M^2 = 1$$

Hence, from (6.16),

$$r_M = r_0 + (r_M - r_0) + \sum_{j=1}^{n} m_j \varepsilon_j$$

from which it follows immediately that $\sum_{j=1}^{n} m_j \varepsilon_j \equiv 0$. The $\varepsilon_1, \varepsilon_2, \ldots, \varepsilon_n$ are, therefore, linearly dependent in the CAPM, as asserted.

Appendix 6.3: The CAPM when all assets are risky

The following paragraphs seek to provide a formal justification for the Black CAPM, as described in section 6.6.1, and, in particular, as depicted in figure 6.5. It is necessary, first, to confirm that the market portfolio is mean-variance efficient.

If the market portfolio lies on the portfolio frontier, then it must be efficient (i.e. on the positively sloped arm of the frontier). The reason for this is that, by definition, the asset proportions in the market portfolio are all positive, $m_j > 0$: no asset can be short-sold in the aggregate. Hence, it is necessary to show only that the market portfolio is indeed on the frontier. That it is on the frontier is an implication of (a) homogeneous beliefs, so that each investor faces the same portfolio frontier, and (b) the first mutual fund theorem, that all frontier portfolios can be constructed as portfolios of two mutual funds (see chapter 5).

Given that all investors face the same portfolio frontier (homogeneous beliefs), each investor can be assumed to choose a portfolio of the same two mutual funds. Investors may differ in their preferences and, hence, hold different portfolios of the two mutual funds. Some investors might even short-sell one of the two mutual funds. All that then needs to be shown is that the market portfolio can be constructed as a portfolio of the two funds.

Let the two mutual funds both be frontier portfolios and label them U and V, with asset proportions $u_1, u_2, \ldots, u_n$ and $v_1, v_2, \ldots, v_n$, respectively. (That is, for example, v_j is the proportion of j in portfolio V.) By construction, $\sum_{j=1}^{n} u_j = 1$ and $\sum_{j=1}^{n} v_j = 1$.

Let θ_i denote the proportion of investor i's total assets, B_i, invested in fund U, so that $1 - \theta_i$ is the proportion invested in V. Thus, investor i effectively has an investment in asset j equal to $u_j \theta_i B_i + v_j (1 - \theta_i) B_i$. Summing over all investors gives the total demand to hold asset j, which, in 'supply = demand' equilibrium, equals its market value, $p_j X_j$:

$$p_j X_j = \sum_{i=1}^{m} (u_j \theta_i B_i + v_j (1 - \theta_i) B_i)$$

$$= u_j \sum_{i=1}^{m} \theta_i B_i + v_j \sum_{i=1}^{m} (1 - \theta_i) B_i \qquad j = 1, 2, \ldots, n \qquad (6.17)$$

where $\sum_{i=1}^{m} \theta_i B_i$ and $\sum_{i=1}^{m} (1 - \theta_i) B_i$ are the total market values of U and V, respectively.

Let $B \equiv \sum_{j=1}^{n} p_j X_j = \sum_{i=1}^{m} B_i > 0$ denote the aggregate market value of all assets, and define

$$m_U \equiv \frac{\sum_{i=1}^{m} \theta_i B_i}{B} \qquad m_V \equiv \frac{\sum_{i=1}^{m} (1 - \theta_i) B_i}{B} \qquad (6.18)$$

Note that, by construction, $m_U + m_V = 1$.

The proportion of asset j in the market portfolio is $m_j = p_j X_j / B > 0$. Dividing through (6.17) by B, and substituting m_U and m_V from (6.18), enables the m_j proportions to be expressed as

$$m_j = u_j m_U + v_j m_V \qquad j = 1, 2, \ldots, n$$

Hence, the market portfolio can be expressed as a portfolio of the mutual funds U and V, with weights m_U and m_V, respectively. The market portfolio is, therefore, on the frontier, as required.

Given that the market portfolio is efficient, it follows that ω can be constructed as depicted in figure 6.5. It remains to derive the equation for the security market line. To obtain the SML, note that market portfolio must satisfy the conditions derived for an efficient portfolio in appendix 5.2 to chapter 5, namely

$$\frac{\mu_j - \omega}{\sigma_{jM}} = \frac{\mu_M - \omega}{\sigma_M^2} \tag{6.19}$$

Rearranging (6.19) and substituting $\beta_j = \sigma_{jM}/\sigma_M^2$ yields equation (6.14) in section 6.6.1, thus completing the derivation.

References

Black, F. (1972), 'Capital market equilibrium with restricted borrowing', *Journal of Business*, 45(3), pp. 444–54.

Campbell, J. Y., A. W. Lo and A. C. MacKinlay (1997), *The Econometrics of Financial Markets*, Princeton, NJ: Princeton University Press.

Elton, E. J., M. J. Gruber, S. J. Brown and W. N. Goetzmann (2003), *Modern Portfolio Theory and Investment Analysis*, New York: John Wiley & Sons, 6th edn.

Fama, E. F. (1976), *Foundations of Finance*, Oxford: Basil Blackwell.

Feller, W. (1970), *An Introduction to Probability Theory and Its Applications*, Vol. I, New York: John Wiley & Sons, 3rd edn.

Grinblatt, M., and S. Titman (2001), *Financial Markets and Corporate Strategy*, New York: McGraw-Hill, 2nd edn.

Newman, P., M. Milgate and J. Eatwell (eds.) (1992), *The New Palgrave Dictionary of Money and Finance*, London: Macmillan (three volumes).

Perold, A. F. (2004), 'The capital asset pricing model', *Journal of Economic Perspectives*, 18(3), pp. 3–24.

Sharpe, W. F., G. J. Alexander and J. V. Bailey (1999), *Investments*, Englewood Cliffs, NJ: Prentice Hall International, 6th edn.

7

Arbitrage

Overview

Arbitrage was introduced in chapter 1, where it was argued that an unintended consequence of the quest for arbitrage profits is to link asset prices together in predictable ways. This short chapter delves more carefully into the precise implications of arbitrage trading. It is rather abstract because the analysis concentrates on exploring fundamental principles. Although, initially, the principles may seem irrelevant for practical applications, they form the building blocks of many models that *are* of immediate relevance in explaining observed patterns of asset prices.

Section 7.1 reflects on the pitfalls commonly encountered in applications of the arbitrage principle (i.e. the assertion that arbitrage opportunities vanish in market equilibrium). Having acknowledged the pitfalls, section 7.2 ignores them and offers a formal statement of the arbitrage principle. Section 7.3 continues the analysis with the statement of two additional and equivalent ways of expressing the arbitrage principle: in terms of the existence of state prices and the risk-neutral valuation relationship (RNVR).

Together, sections 7.2 and 7.3 describe three fundamental propositions that capture the essence of the arbitrage principle. (Appendix 7.1 sketches a proof of the propositions.) Although the propositions have wide relevance, especially in the study of financial derivatives (e.g. options), they are rarely applied directly to calculate asset prices. Instead, the propositions make precise *why* arbitrage plays such a key role in finance.

7.1 Arbitrage in theory and practice

In much of financial analysis, 'arbitrage' is interpreted loosely as the class of investment strategies designed to profit from perceived discrepancies among asset prices, while incurring low (but non-negligible) risks.[1] While this might be a reasonable description of some investors' behaviour, a narrower definition serves to illuminate more clearly the implications of the absence of arbitrage opportunities for asset prices. For this reason, throughout this book arbitrage is confined strictly to investment strategies that entail *zero* risk. The payoff from any such strategy is then the risk-free rate of return on the initial capital outlay – or, more conveniently, a zero payoff from a zero initial outlay.

The advantage of the narrow definition adopted here is that it focuses attention on the arbitrage principle as a generalization of the 'Law of One Price' (LoOP). If the same asset has two different prices, there is an immediate arbitrage opportunity: sell at the higher price and buy at the lower. (See the example in chapter 1, page 16.) That such discrepancies cannot persist seems so natural as to be self-evident.

There are pitfalls, however. Firstly, it may be difficult to determine whether or not an arbitrage opportunity is present. The consequences of the *absence* of such opportunities are then equally difficult to determine.

Secondly, suppose that unexploited arbitrage opportunities are observed. That must be because one or more of the assumptions on which the arbitrage principle rests is violated. The response is then either to refine the assumptions so as to restore the principle or, alternatively, to deny its usefulness. The former would, taken to its limit, render the principle a tautology and rob it of predictive significance. The latter is potentially more damaging in implying that a keystone of modern finance (indeed, of economics more broadly) requires replacement.

Counter-examples to the LoOP – suggesting the existence of unexploited arbitrage opportunities – in financial markets are well documented. A particularly stark illustration is provided by 3Com (a computing equipment and services provider), which, in March 2000, sold 5 per cent of the shares in its wholly owned subsidiary, Palm (a manufacturer of hand-held computers). At the same time, 3Com announced that it intended to dispose of all its remaining Palm shares. Owners of 3Com shares would receive one and a half Palm shares for every 3Com share – i.e. each 3Com share would become a bundle of one 3Com share and one and a half Palm shares. Given that the worst that could have happened was for 3Com to become worthless after the disposal, the LoOP predicts that the value of each existing 3Com share should have been at least one and a half times that of each Palm share. In fact, for a time, the price of 3Com shares fell below Palm shares, blatantly in contradiction of the LoOP prediction.[2]

---

[1] For example, Shleifer (2000, especially chap. 4) presents a model in which *limited* arbitrage is identified with the strategies of specialists who seek to exploit their perceptions of discrepancies among asset prices. In Shleifer's analysis, limited arbitrage is risky and requires a positive commitment of capital.

[2] See Lamont and Thaler (2003b) for a detailed analysis of 3Com's disposal of Palm, as well as several other violations of the LoOP.

Although the discrepancy eventually disappeared, it did so only over a period of several weeks. Moreover, such episodes are not uncommon – they cannot be dismissed as isolated incidents. The question here is: what relevance do such observations have for the arbitrage principle?

Lamont and Thaler (2003b) contend that, while the LoOP was violated in the 3Com–Palm case, the arbitrage principle was not. The reason is that market frictions – in particular, obstacles to short-selling shares – meant that the arbitrage opportunity was apparent rather than real: investors were unable exploit it. Regardless of whether it is appropriate to claim that the arbitrage principle remained intact, the substantive point is that market frictions hindered the effectiveness of attempts that investors might have made to profit from the arbitrage opportunity.[3]

To the extent that market frictions impede the operation of arbitrage, they undermine the capacity of the arbitrage principle accurately to predict links among asset prices, as the evidence from 3Com's spin-off of Palm so clearly shows. Market frictions are never entirely absent. And, the greater they are, the less scope there is for arbitrage to yield useful implications about asset prices. Nonetheless, if market frictions are small, their impact on asset prices should also be small. Pursued to its extreme, the assumption of frictionless markets is an idealization, but one that enables the arbitrage principle to provide a benchmark for determining the links among asset prices. It is in this spirit that the remainder of this chapter explores the implications of the absence of arbitrage opportunities.

7.2 Arbitrage in an uncertain world

The role of arbitrage in an uncertain world is the same as in a world of certainty: it places restrictions on patterns of asset prices that are consistent with market equilibrium. The predictions of arbitrage theory apply quite generally, in the sense that they do not rely on the criteria that investors use to choose their portfolios – other than on the mild requirement that more wealth is preferred to less. There is a penalty for this generality: the arbitrage principle, on its own, cannot determine equilibrium asset prices; it just rules out some as being incompatible with market equilibrium.

Arbitrage is the process by which investors seek to make risk-free gains (positive payoffs) with zero initial outlay. That is, arbitrage refers to all the actions that investors take to secure gains without committing any capital and without bearing any risk.

---

[3] The main thrust of Lamont and Thaler's argument is, however, not about arbitrage but, rather, to highlight the presence of 'investors who are ... irrational, woefully uninformed, endowed with strange preferences, or for some other reason willing to hold overpriced assets' (p. 231). Market frictions serve to identify the existence of such investors, the actions of whom would otherwise not affect asset prices.

An arbitrage portfolio is defined by the following conditions.

1. The portfolio requires *zero initial outlay*: some assets are held in positive amounts, some in negative amounts and, perhaps, some in zero amounts.[4] (Only portfolios that contain a positive or a negative amount of at least one asset are considered – i.e. all portfolios are assumed to be non-vacuous, or non-trivial.)
2. The portfolio is *risk-free*: the payoff on the portfolio in every state must be either positive or zero. It must not be positive in some states and negative in others.

Formally, an **arbitrage portfolio**, $x_1, x_2, \ldots, x_n$, satisfies these conditions.

1. *Zero initial outlay*: $p_1 x_1 + p_1 x_2 + \cdots + p_n x_n = 0$, with not all $x_j = 0$ for $j = 1, 2, \ldots, n$.
2. *Risk-free*: $v_{k1} x_1 + v_{k2} x_2 + \cdots + v_{kn} x_n \geq 0$, for every state $k = 1, 2, \ldots, \ell$,

where x_j denotes the quantity of asset j, p_j is the price of asset j, and v_{kj} is the payoff of asset j in state k. A risk-free asset is allowed but, if present, it is not distinguished by a separate, identifying subscript (i.e. it is included among the n assets). Let **x** denote the portfolio as a whole (i.e. the vector with elements $\{x_1, x_2, \ldots, x_n\}$).

For notational convenience, define the payoff for portfolio **x** in state k as

$$v(\mathbf{x}, k) \equiv v_{k1} x_1 + v_{k2} x_2 + \cdots + v_{kn} x_n$$

Thus, if **x** is an arbitrage portfolio, it involves zero initial outlay and $v(\mathbf{x}, k) \geq 0$ for every state k. Several more definitions are useful in what follows.

Arbitrage opportunity: a set of asset prices such that an arbitrage portfolio exists, *and* $v(\mathbf{x}, k) > 0$ for at least one k. That is, a strictly *positive* payoff occurs in one or more states and a loss in no state.

Arbitrage profit: the amount of the payoff from an arbitrage opportunity. (Note that the amount of the payoff generally varies across states and also differs from one arbitrage portfolio to another.)

Absence of arbitrage opportunities: a set of asset prices for which exactly one of the following two conditions holds.

(a) For every arbitrage portfolio, $v(\mathbf{x}, k) = 0$ in every state.
(b) No arbitrage portfolio exists. That is, for every portfolio requiring zero initial outlay, $v(\mathbf{x}, k) \geq 0$ for some state(s) and $v(\mathbf{x}, k) < 0$ for some state(s).

Arbitrage principle: the arbitrage principle asserts that arbitrage opportunities are absent.

Market equilibrium: a set of asset prices and an allocation of asset holdings across investors such that the demand to hold assets is no greater than the supply

---

[4] Some definitions allow the initial outlay to be negative; that is, the portfolio could generate a surplus of funds at the outset. This would correspond to a situation in which the funds generated from the assets sold short (i.e. held in negative amounts) exceeds the cost of the assets held in positive amounts. The extra generality serves no purpose here.

available. (If every asset price is greater than zero, demand *equals* supply in market equilibrium.)

An alternative way of stating the arbitrage principle is to assert that any *positive* initial outlay is either (a) a risk-free investment that yields the risk-free rate of return (i.e. the rate of return on an asset that has the same payoff in every state) or (b) a risky investment. Let $A > 0$ denote the initial outlay. In this formulation, an arbitrage portfolio, by definition, must satisfy $v(\mathbf{x}, k) \geq (1 + r_0)A$, in every state, k, where r_0 denotes the risk-free interest rate.[5] An arbitrage opportunity now becomes a portfolio with initial outlay A, a payoff $v(\mathbf{x}, k) \geq (1 + r_0)A$ in every state, and $v(\mathbf{x}, k) > (1 + r_0)A$ in at least one. Finally, the absence of arbitrage opportunities is characterized by a set of asset prices such that the rate of return on the initial outlay either (a) equals the risk-free rate in every state, or (b) is greater than the risk-free rate in some states and smaller in others.

The implications of the arbitrage principle are discussed below in the context of three propositions that provide different sets of necessary and sufficient conditions for the absence of arbitrage opportunities. A formal demonstration of each proposition is outlined in appendix 7.1. The mathematical methods employed in the appendix may seem rather daunting and are not necessary to understand the remainder of this section.

The first proposition implies that the arbitrage principle is relevant in a range of circumstances; it places only a mild restriction on investors' behaviour (for instance, individuals need not be mean-variance investors nor need they obey the EUH).

Proposition I. The arbitrage principle holds in frictionless asset markets if, and only if, there exists an investor who prefers more wealth to less and for whom an optimal portfolio can be constructed.

To grasp why proposition I holds, suppose that the arbitrage principle fails in the sense that there exists a portfolio that (a) requires zero initial outlay and (b) yields a non-negative payoff in every state, with a positive payoff in at least one state. Now identify an investor who prefers more wealth to less in each state. The investor must be willing to hold the portfolio in question: it costs nothing, is risk-free and yields a positive payoff in at least one state. But – here is the crucial point – the investor would seek to magnify this portfolio (keeping the asset proportions the same) to an unbounded extent (because more wealth is preferred to less). Formally, the investor has no optimal portfolio. (Infinite wealth, a fantasy that dreams are made on, is just that: a fantasy.)

Hence, by a contradiction, the existence of an investor who prefers more wealth to less, and for whom an optimal portfolio can be found, must imply that the

---

[5] That is: in an arbitrage portfolio with initial outlay A, the rate of return in each state equals $(v(\mathbf{x}, k)/A) - 1$, which is no less than r_0.

arbitrage principle holds true: arbitrage opportunities are absent. The converse – namely that the arbitrage principle implies the existence of an investor satisfying the stated conditions – is also true, but requires more delicate reasoning of the sort described in appendix 7.1.

7.2.1 Implications of the arbitrage principle: an example

That the arbitrage principle has important implications for asset prices is shown in the following example. Suppose that there are two possible states and three assets with the following payoffs and prices:

	Assets		
	A	B	C
State 1	10	8	9
State 2	8	0	12
Price	3	2	$p_C =$?

The absence of arbitrage opportunities implies that the price of asset C, p_C, is not arbitrary. To see this, consider some arbitrary values of p_C and check that risk-free profits can be made (except at the equilibrium value of p_C, of course).

Suppose that $p_C = 1$. Now consider the portfolio: sell one unit of A, buy one unit of B and buy one unit of C – that is: $x_A = -1, x_B = +1, x_C = +1$. This portfolio uses zero capital (the cost of B and C is met from the sale of A) and has a positive payoff in *both* states:

$$10 \times (-1) + 8 \times (+1) + 9 \times (+1) = 7 > 0$$
$$8 \times (-1) + 0 \times (+1) + 12 \times (+1) = 4 > 0$$

Hence, $p_C = 1$ cannot be an equilibrium: a portfolio can be found that costs nothing and yields a positive, risk-free payoff.

Suppose, alternatively, that $p_C = 4$. Now consider the portfolio: buy two units of A, sell one unit of B and sell one unit of C – that is: $x_A = +2, x_B = -1$, $x_C = -1$. This portfolio uses zero capital (the revenue from selling B and C equals the cost of A) and has a positive payoff in *both* states:

$$10 \times (+2) + 8 \times (-1) + 9 \times (-1) = 3 > 0$$
$$8 \times (+2) + 0 \times (-1) + 12 \times (-1) = 4 > 0$$

Hence, $p_C = 4$ cannot be an equilibrium: a portfolio can be found that costs nothing and yields a positive risk-free payoff.[6]

What is the equilibrium value of p_C? Consider any portfolio x_A, x_B, x_C of assets for which the payoff equals zero in each state. It must satisfy

$$10x_A + 8x_B + 9x_C = 0$$

$$8x_A + 0x_B + 12x_C = 0$$

These conditions imply that $x_A/x_C = -\frac{3}{2}$ and $x_B/x_C = \frac{3}{4}$.

In the absence of arbitrage opportunities, portfolios with these ratios must require a zero initial outlay:

$$3x_A + 2x_B + p_C x_C = 0$$

Hence, if $x_C \neq 0$ (there is no point in choosing $x_C = 0$)

$$3(x_A/x_C) + 2(x_B/x_C) + p_C = 0$$

$$3 \times -\tfrac{3}{2} + 2 \times \tfrac{3}{4} \quad + p_C = 0$$

$$p_C = 3$$

The price of C must equal 3. Any other price allows the construction of portfolios that yield positive – and hence unbounded – profits.

Remarks

The example is simple but it illustrates some fundamental points about the operation of arbitrage in an uncertain world.

1. The arbitrage principle is a generalization of the law of one price. Assets A, B and C clearly have different payoffs and have different prices, but there must exist a particular relationship among the prices in order to rule out the opportunity for arbitrage profits.
2. The arbitrage principle does *not* assert that every portfolio with a zero initial outlay has a zero payoff in all states. Most zero-initial-outlay portfolios will be *risky* in the sense that they yield a positive payoff in some states, a negative payoff in others and, possibly, a zero payoff in yet others. These are not arbitrage portfolios.
3. There may exist no arbitrage portfolios at all. The arbitrage principle asserts that those that *do* exist yield a zero payoff in every state. If an arbitrage portfolio exists, there will exist infinitely many – for any arbitrage portfolio, scale all the asset holdings up or down by an arbitrary positive proportion; the result is also an arbitrage portfolio.

---

[6] Notice that there is an infinity of portfolios with a zero initial outlay and for which the payoff is positive in one state and negative in the other. These are not arbitrage portfolios. In this context, they reveal nothing about the pattern of equilibrium prices.

4. If the arbitrage principle is to have predictive power, market frictions must be absent. Conversely, in the presence of transaction costs or institutional constraints on trading, the arbitrage principle implies little, if anything, about the pattern of asset prices (according to the severity of the frictions).

5. The absence of arbitrage opportunities does not itself provide a way of computing asset prices in market equilibrium. More modestly, it identifies *links* among prices.

The usefulness of the arbitrage principle varies among the problems to which it is applied. In the study of derivatives markets, the absence of arbitrage opportunities is often the vital element. Similarly, in corporate finance the Modigliani–Miller theorems rest on the arbitrage principle (see chapter 18, page 457). But in equity markets the applicability of the arbitrage principle is more limited: extra theoretical apparatus (e.g. a factor model) is required; and approximations often need to be made, as in the arbitrage pricing theory, explored in the following chapter.

7.3 State prices and the risk-neutral valuation relationship

The arbitrage principle has two further implications that, although rather abstract, are useful in applications. One of these is the existence of *state prices*. So far, prices have been associated with assets, but it is also possible to make sense of prices that are associated with individual states of the world. Once the existence of state prices has been established, the *risk-neutral valuation relationship* provides a convenient way of expressing any asset price in the absence of arbitrage opportunities.

7.3.1 The existence of state prices

A state price, q_k, is defined to be the price of an asset that has a payoff of one unit of wealth in state k and zero in every other state. In most circumstances these state prices (if they exist) are implicit, in the sense that they are not the prices of any actual assets but, instead, can be inferred from the payoffs of assets that *are* traded. It is conceivable, of course, that securities that have a unit payoff in one state and zero in all others are observed in practice, but the importance of state prices is not dependent on whether they are, or are not.

Proposition II. The arbitrage principle is equivalent to the existence of positive state prices, $q_1, q_2, \ldots, q_\ell$ such that

$$p_j = q_1 v_{1j} + q_2 v_{2j} + \cdots + q_\ell v_{\ell j} \qquad j = 1, 2, \ldots, n \qquad (7.1)$$

This result is often called the *linear pricing rule*. In words: in the absence of arbitrage opportunities the price of each asset must be equal to the sum of its payoff in each state multiplied by a state price corresponding to that state. Appendix 7.1.1 is devoted to demonstating proposition II.

The linear pricing rule is an *equivalence*: if arbitrage opportunities are absent, state prices exist; if state prices exist, arbitrage opportunities are absent. Therefore, if the arbitrage principle holds, it implies that every asset price can be written as a weighted average of its payoffs, the weights being the state prices.

Proposition II makes no claim about the *uniqueness* of state prices. If they exist at all, then there may be many sets of them. State prices are unique if asset markets are *complete* in the sense discussed in chapter 4. (An asset market is complete if there exist sufficiently many assets so that, for every state, it is possible to construct an Arrow security – an asset with a unit payoff in the state in question and a zero payoff in all other states. Construction of an Arrow security involves choosing a portfolio of assets in such a way as to yield the required payoff.)

7.3.2 The risk-neutral valuation relationship

An immediate implication of the linear pricing rule is the *risk-neutral valuation relationship* (sometimes called the 'existence of martingale probabilities', or the 'existence of an equivalent martingale measure' or the 'martingale valuation relationship'). The RNVR states the following.

Proposition III. The linear pricing rule is equivalent to the existence of:

1. *a risk-free rate of return, r_0, with associated discount factor, $\delta \equiv 1/(1 + r_0)$; and*
2. *probabilities,*[7] *$\pi_1, \pi_2, \ldots, \pi_\ell$, one for each state, such that*

$$p_j = \delta E^*[v_j] \qquad j = 1, 2, \ldots, n \tag{7.2}$$

The symbol v_j denotes the list of payoffs, one for each state, for asset j. (In this context, v_j is a 'random variable': a set of outcomes, each with its associated probability.) The expectation, $E^*[v_j]$, is the payoff of asset j in each state weighted by the probability of that state and summed over the states

$$E^*[v_j] \equiv \pi_1 v_{1j} + \pi_2 v_{2j} + \cdots + \pi_\ell v_{\ell j} \tag{7.3}$$

The asterisk (*) superscript appears as a reminder that the probabilities in (7.3) are purely artificial; they are an *implication* of the proposition and need not correspond to any investor's beliefs (see remark 1, below).

Remarks

1. The RNVR states that, in the absence of arbitrage opportunities, each asset's price can be written as the *expected* NPV of its payoff discounted at a risk-free rate of return. A derivation of the RNVR appears in appendix 7.1.2.

---

[7] The probabilities can be interpreted merely as numbers that are non-negative and sum to one. In this application the probabilities are strictly positive.

Be careful not to read too much significance into the RNVR. The probabilities do not necessarily describe the beliefs of any investor who behaves in accordance with some principle – e.g. the EUH, for which probabilities are relevant. Nor are they the objective probabilities of states, whatever meaning might be given to 'objective'. (Recall the discussion in chapter 4 about the interpretation of probabilities.)

2. *Example*: refer to the example above, in section 7.2.1. The discount factor, δ, and the probabilities can be calculated by writing out the statement of the RNVR. With just two states, the probabilities of the states can be denoted by π and $(1-\pi)$, respectively, so that the RNVR appears as

$$p_A = 3 = \delta(10\pi + 8(1-\pi))$$

$$p_B = 2 = \delta(8\pi + 0(1-\pi))$$

$$p_C = 3 = \delta(9\pi + 12(1-\pi))$$

Substitutions between any two of these equations show that $\delta = \frac{5}{16}$ and $\pi = \frac{4}{5}$.[8] Notice that, *in the absence of arbitrage opportunities*, the values derived from any pair of the three equations must satisfy the third. Finally, the implicit state prices q_1 and q_2 can be calculated from $q_1 = \delta\pi$ and $q_2 = \delta(1-\pi)$, so that $q_1 = \frac{5}{16} \times \frac{4}{5} = \frac{1}{4}$ and $q_2 = \frac{5}{16} \times \frac{1}{5} = \frac{1}{16}$.

3. Another way of writing the RNVR condition is

$$E^*[r_j] = r_0 \qquad j = 1, 2, \ldots, n \qquad (7.4)$$

This can be demonstrated by recalling that $r_{kj} = (v_{kj} - p_j)/p_j$, substituting into $p_j = \delta E^*[v_j]$, and rearranging the result. (Remember that r_j and v_j – omitting the k subscript – denote the lists of rates of return and payoffs, respectively, for asset j, with one element in each list corresponding to the state.)

Expressed in this way, the RNVR can be interpreted as the assertion that each asset yields, on average, a rate of return, $E^*[r_j]$, equal to the risk-free rate. Beware: as already emphasized, the probabilities' weights used in calculating the expectation are purely artificial. Hence, the meaning of 'on average' in this context is confined to expectations obtained using these probabilities.

Yet another rearrangement of $p_j = \delta E^*[v_j]$ allows the RNVR to be written as

$$E^*[(1+r_j)\delta] = 1 \qquad j = 1, 2, \ldots, n \qquad (7.5)$$

If (a) δ is replaced by the random variable H, and (b) the probabilities are replaced by those corresponding to individual beliefs, then (7.5) becomes the *fundamental valuation relationship* in portfolio theory. While this is a purely formal reinterpretation, it does hint at points of contact between the RNVR and the FVR.

4. *What is 'risk-neutral' about risk-neutral valuation?* If investors are risk-neutral (see chapter 4) and *if* their beliefs are expressed by the probabilities $\pi_1, \pi_2, \ldots, \pi_\ell$,

---

[8] The implied risk-free interest rate is thus $r_0 = (1/\delta) - 1 = 220\%$. It is rather far-fetched at such a huge value – but this is only a numerical example.

then expressions such as (7.2) or (7.4) or (7.5) express the *fundamental valuation relationship*. (Once again, see chapter 4.)

5. *Why is the RNVR worth studying?* The RNVR is useful in many asset pricing problems because it facilitates the calculation of equilibrium asset prices. This is particularly so for the APT (chapter 8), options pricing theory (e.g. the Black–Scholes model, chapter 19), corporate finance (the Modigliani–Miller theorem, chapter 18, section 18.6) and many other problems involving derivative securities.

Summary

In a world of uncertainty with frictionless asset markets, the following conditions are equivalent.

1. An absence of arbitrage opportunities.
2. The existence of at least one investor who prefers more wealth to less and for whom an optimal portfolio can be constructed.
3. The existence of positive state prices, $q_1, q_2, \ldots, q_\ell$, where q_k is the market price of an asset with a payoff of one unit of wealth in state k and zero in every other state.
4. The risk-neutral valuation relationship: namely, that there exists a risk-free rate of return and state probabilities such that

$$r_0 = \mathrm{E}^*[r_1] = \mathrm{E}^*[r_2] = \cdots = \mathrm{E}^*[r_n]$$

or, equivalently $\quad p_1 = \delta\mathrm{E}^*[v_1] \quad p_2 = \delta\mathrm{E}^*[v_2] \quad \cdots \quad p_n = \delta\mathrm{E}^*[v_n]$

7.4 Summary

In frictionless markets, the absence of arbitrage opportunities corresponds to the existence of links among asset prices. When market frictions (transaction costs or institutional impediments to trading, or both) are non-negligible, observed prices may be influenced more by the frictions than by the quest for arbitrage profits (even though arbitrage opportunities are absent).

This chapter has examined circumstances in which investors, in seeking to obtain arbitrage profits, unwittingly drive asset prices to follow particular patterns. The most important aspects of the analysis are these.

1. By construction, arbitrage portfolios (a) require zero initial outlay and (b) are risk-free. The arbitrage principle asserts that arbitrage portfolios yield a zero payoff in every possible state of the world. Less formally: the return to capital investment is positive only if either (a) a positive amount of capital is committed, or (b) the investment is risky, or both.
2. By invoking the mild assumption that at least one investor prefers more wealth to less, market equilibrium in frictionless markets implies that the arbitrage principle is satisfied.

3. Equivalently, the arbitrage principle implies the existence of state prices – one for each state – for (possibly hypothetical) assets, each of which has a payoff equal to a unit of wealth in exactly one state and zero in every other.

4. Also equivalently, the arbitrage principle implies the RNVR – i.e. the existence of a set of artificial ('risk-neutral' or 'martingale-equivalent') probabilities such that the price of each asset equals the expected payoff (using these probabilities), discounted by a risk-free interest rate. Alternatively, the RNVR states that the expected rate of return on each asset, again using the artificial probabilities, equals the risk-free interest rate.

Further reading

An excellent starting point for the fundamentals of arbitrage is the paper by Varian (1987). Also valuable are the entries on 'arbitrage' and 'arbitrage pricing theory' in *The New Palgrave Dictionary of Money and Finance* (Newman, Milgate and Eatwell, 1992). These short articles are exemplars of conciseness, clarity and rigour. Moreover, they provide a guide to the main contributions on arbitrage analysis. An exploration of arbitrage policies, more broadly construed as practical investment strategies, can be found in Shleifer and Vishny (1997), Shleifer (2000) and Lamont and Thaler (2003a).

Appendix 7.1: Implications of the arbitrage principle

This appendix outlines a proof for each of the three propositions stated in sections 7.2 and 7.3. The demonstration of proposition II requires the most intricate reasoning and this is studied first. Proposition III then follows immediately. Lastly, a proof of proposition I is sketched.

A.7.1.1: The existence of state prices

The proof of proposition II offered here relies on a member of the family of 'theorems of the alternative': purely mathematical results that are well known in the analysis of linear inequalities and that provide a foundation for linear programming.[9] All that needs to be done to prove proposition II is to state the proposition in a suitable form and then make an appeal to the relevant theorem of the alternative. The adoption of matrix notation simplifies some potentially cumbersome algebra.

The first step in the proof involves stating the proposition in terms of matrices and vectors. Matrices (arrays) are denoted by boldface upper-case letters, such as

---

[9] Excellent references are those by Gale (1960, chap. 2) and Mangasarian (1994, chap. 2). Dorfman, Samuelson and Solow (1958, app. B) provide helpful intuition.

V, while vectors (here designated as matrices with a single column) are denoted by boldface lower-case letters, such as **x**. The prime symbol, $'$, denotes *transposition*, so that **x**$'$ is a *row* vector that merely turns **x** from a column into a row. It is important to be clear how inequalities apply to vectors: **x** > 0 states that every element of **x** is positive; **x** $\geqq 0$ states that every element **x** is non-negative but all elements could be zero; **x** ≥ 0 states that every element of **x** is non-negative and at least one element is strictly positive; and **x** $= 0$ states that every element of **x** is zero.

Let **V** denote the matrix of asset payoffs. This matrix has ℓ rows (the number of states) and n columns (the number of assets). A typical element of **V** is v_{kj}, the payoff of asset j in state k. The payoff matrix is assumed to be *non-vacuous* in the sense that not every element is zero.

Let **p** denote the vector of asset prices. This vector has n elements and is assumed to be non-negative and non-vacuous: **p** ≥ 0. A typical element of **p** is p_j, the price of asset j.

Let **x** denote a portfolio. This vector has n elements, with x_j (the number of units of asset j) being a typical element. Each element of **x** could be positive, negative or zero. It is assumed to be non-vacuous. The inner-product between the prices and portfolio quantities, **p**$'$**x**, expresses the total outlay on the portfolio, **x** (i.e. the sum of the price times the quantity of each asset).

An *arbitrage opportunity* is formally defined by a portfolio **x** satisfying

$$\begin{bmatrix} \mathbf{V} \\ -\mathbf{p}' \end{bmatrix} \mathbf{x} \geq 0 \tag{7.6}$$

This statement allows for the existence of an arbitrage portfolio with (a) zero initial outlay, **p**$'$**x** $= 0$, and (b) non-negative payoffs in all states and positive in at least one: **Vx** ≥ 0. But it also allows for a portfolio with a negative initial outlay **p**$'$**x** < 0 and payoffs that might be zero in all states **Vx** $\geqq 0$, though possibly with some, or all, positive. Equation (7.6) thus allows very generally for a portfolio that generates arbitrage profits.

At this point a theorem of the alternative is applied. One of the theorems, sometimes called 'Stiemke's theorem',[10] states that exactly one of the two following results is true: *either* (a) there exists an **x** that satisfies (7.6); *or* (b) there exist a vector **z** and a number θ such that

$$\mathbf{z}'\mathbf{V} + \theta(-\mathbf{p}') = 0 \quad \text{with} \quad \mathbf{z} > 0, \ \theta > 0 \tag{7.7}$$

[10] See Mangasarian (1994, p. 32) or Gale (1960, p. 49, corollary 2). A slightly different approach is adopted in *The New Palgrave Dictionary of Money and Finance* (Newman, Milgate and Eatwell, 1992, Vol. I, pp. 45–6).

It is important to note that, if (7.7) holds, there is no $\mathbf{x}$ that satisfies (7.6); if there exist $\mathbf{z} > 0$ and $\theta > 0$, there is an absence of arbitrage opportunities. Conversely, if (7.6) holds for some $\mathbf{x}$, then it is not possible to find $\mathbf{z}$ and θ that satisfy (7.7); if there is an arbitrage opportunity, then (7.7) does not hold.

The final step is to interpret (7.7) in terms of state prices. Divide through by θ and rearrange (7.7):

$$\mathbf{q}'\mathbf{V} = \mathbf{p}' \quad \text{where } \mathbf{q} \equiv \mathbf{z}/\theta \tag{7.8}$$

The vector $\mathbf{q} > 0$ has n elements, with typical member q_k denoting the state price corresponding to state k. To check that (7.8) is identical with equation (7.1) in the statement of proposition II, write out a typical column, say j:

$$q_1 v_{1j} + q_2 v_{2j} + \cdots + q_\ell v_{\ell j} = p_j \tag{7.9}$$

The proof of proposition II is complete. The theorem of the alternative shows that exactly one of the following is true: (a) arbitrage opportunities are absent and there exists a set of positive state prices; (b) an arbitrage opportunity is present and there does not exist a set of positive state prices. The arbitrage principle is equivalent to the existence of a set of positive state prices – precisely what proposition II claims.

A7.1.2: The risk-neutral valuation relationship

Proposition III merely involves scaling the state prices so that they sum to one and, hence, can be interpreted as probabilities. Let $\sum q_k$ denote the sum of the state prices:

$$\sum q_k = q_1 + q_2 + \cdots + q_\ell$$

Define ℓ numbers, $\pi_k = q_k/\sum q_k$. These numbers have the required properties of probabilities: they are non-negative (in fact, they are all positive) and they sum to one. Hence, they can be interpreted as probabilities.

Now, using the linear pricing rule, (7.9), write the equilibrium asset prices as

$$\begin{aligned}
p_j &= q_1 v_{1j} + q_2 v_{2j} + \cdots + q_\ell v_{\ell j} \quad j = 1, 2, \ldots, n \\
&= \left(\sum q_k \right) \left(\pi_1 v_{1j} + \pi_2 v_{2j} + \cdots + \pi_\ell v_{\ell j} \right) \\
&= \delta E^*[v_j]
\end{aligned} \tag{7.10}$$

where δ is defined to be $\sum q_k$ so that $r_0 = (1/\delta) - 1$, as asserted in proposition III.

Conversely, starting from equation (7.10), define $q_k = \delta \pi_k$ for $k = 1, 2, \ldots, \ell$. Hence, (7.9) can be constructed from (7.10). Thus, the RNVR is equivalent to the existence of state prices – as proposition III asserts.

A7.1.3: The arbitrage principle and the existence of an optimal portfolio

The simpler half of proposition I – that the existence of an optimal portfolio for a wealth-preferring investor implies the absence of arbitrage opportunities – is outlined in section 7.2 and is not repeated here. It is more challenging to prove that the arbitrage principle implies the existence of an optimal portfolio. The following sketch is intended to be suggestive rather than rigorous.

Consider an investor with preferences that can be represented by an objective function of the form (see chapter 4):

$$\mathcal{U} = U(W_1, W_2, \ldots, W_\ell)$$

where W_k is the level of wealth in state k:

$$W_k = v_{k1}x_1 + v_{k2}x_2 + \cdots + v_{kn}x_n \qquad k = 1, 2, \ldots, \ell$$

The investor is assumed to maximize $\mathcal{U}$ subject to the constraint

$$p_1 x_1 + p_2 x_2 + \cdots + p_n x_n = A$$

where A is the initial level of wealth. (Note that A need not be zero: it is not necessary to assume that the investor is trying to exploit an arbitrage opportunity.)

In elementary consumer theory it is shown that, at a maximum of utility, $\partial U/\partial x_j = \phi p_j$ for every x_j and for some number $\phi > 0$. Now take account of the indirect relationship between $\mathcal{U}$ and x_j via W_k, to write $\partial W_k/\partial x_j = v_{kj}$, and hence

$$\frac{\partial U}{\partial x_j} = \frac{\partial U}{\partial W_1}\frac{\partial W_1}{\partial x_j} + \frac{\partial U}{\partial W_2}\frac{\partial W_2}{\partial x_j} + \cdots + \frac{\partial U}{\partial W_\ell}\frac{\partial W_\ell}{\partial x_j}$$

$$= U_1 v_{1j} + U_2 v_{2j} + \cdots + U_\ell v_{\ell j}$$

where $U_k \equiv \partial U/\partial W_k$, the marginal utility of wealth in state k. Therefore, $\partial U/\partial x_j = \phi p_j$ becomes

$$U_1 v_{1j} + U_2 v_{2j} + \cdots + U_\ell v_{\ell j} = \phi p_j$$

$$\frac{U_1}{\phi} v_{1j} + \frac{U_2}{\phi} v_{2j} + \cdots + \frac{U_\ell}{\phi} v_{\ell j} = p_j \qquad (7.11)$$

Equation (7.11) suggests that, if $U_k > 0$, the necessary condition for a utility maximum can be expressed as an equality between a weighted sum of asset payoffs, v_{kj} (with weights U_k/ϕ), and the price of each asset, p_j. Proposition II states that, if these weights are equal to state prices, q_k, then the equality is equivalent to the absence of arbitrage opportunities. Hence, if $U_k/\phi = q_k$ (for $k = 1, 2, \ldots, \ell$) the arbitrage principle implies the existence of an optimal portfolio for an investor who prefers more wealth to less.

The reasoning in the previous paragraph is loose and incomplete. It does suggest, however, how a formal proof could be constructed.[11] Proposition II provides the crucial equivalence between the arbitrage principle and state prices. The state prices can then be interpreted as marginal utilities (suitably scaled by ϕ) in an optimization problem. While equation (7.11) is only a necessary condition for preference optimization, an assumption – standard in consumer theory – that $U(\cdot)$ is a *strictly quasi-concave function* of its arguments renders the necessary condition sufficient as well as necessary. Thus, not only does the existence of an optimal portfolio imply the arbitrage principle (as argued in section 7.2) but also the arbitrage principle implies the existence of an optimal portfolio for an investor who prefers more wealth to less – as proposition I asserts.

[11] A more complete argument, from which that here has been adapted, appears in *The New Palgrave Dictionary of Money and Finance* (Newman, Milgate and Eatwell, 1992, Vol. I, p. 46).

References

Dorfman, R., P. A. Samuelson and R. M. Solow (1958), *Linear Programming and Economic Analysis*, New York: McGraw-Hill.

Gale, D. (1960), *The Theory of Linear Economic Models*, New York: McGraw-Hill.

Lamont, O. A., and R. H. Thaler (2003a), 'Anomalies: the law of one price in financial markets', *Journal of Economic Perspectives*, 17(4), pp. 191–202.

(2003b), 'Can the market add and subtract? Mispricing in tech stock carve-outs', *Journal of Political Economy*, 111(2), pp. 227–68.

Mangasarian, O. L. (1994), *Nonlinear Programming*, Philadelphia: Society for Industrial and Applied Mathematics (reprint of an original published in 1969).

Newman, P., M. Milgate and J. Eatwell (eds.) (1992), *The New Palgrave Dictionary of Money and Finance*, London: Macmillan (three volumes).

Shleifer, A. (2000), *Inefficient Markets*: *An Introduction to Behavioral Finance*, Oxford: Oxford University Press.

Shleifer, A., and R. W. Vishny (1997), 'The limits of arbitrage', *Journal of Finance*, 52(1), pp. 35–55.

Varian, H. R. (1987), 'The arbitrage principle in financial economics', *Journal of Economic Perspectives*, 1(2), pp. 55–72.

8

Factor models and the arbitrage pricing theory

Overview

Arbitrage alone goes far to pin down asset prices, but not far enough. In order to obtain definite predictions, it is necessary to embed the arbitrage principle in a framework that imposes additional conditions on the observable pattern of prices.

Factor models, described in section 8.1, provide one such framework. These models postulate that asset prices – or, equivalently, rates of return – are linear functions of a small number of variables, the so-called 'factors'. As such, factor models can be treated as explanations of asset prices in their own right, without any obligation to appeal to the arbitrage principle. But it will be argued in section 8.1, and also in chapter 9, that factor models are of limited explanatory power on their own. This is where arbitrage becomes useful.

The arbitrage pricing theory, analysed in section 8.2, applies the principles studied in the previous chapter to factor models. Here it is shown how, in an approximate but precise sense, arbitrage portfolios can be constructed when asset returns are assumed to be determined in accordance with a factor model. In the absence of arbitrage opportunities, these portfolios will yield zero payoffs (again, in an approximate but precise sense) in every eventuality. The upshot is a set of restrictions on asset prices (and, hence, rates of return) that are predicted to hold under the stated conditions.

In the broadest terms, the predictions can be interpreted as explanations of assets' risk premia, the analysis of which begins section 8.3. The section goes on to explore an important special case, in which the factors themselves take the form of portfolio rates of return, and concludes with a comparison of the APT with the CAPM.

8.1 Factor models

8.1.1 A single-factor model

Factor models of asset prices postulate that rates of return can be expressed as linear functions of a small number of factors. The simplest, *single*-factor model is written as

$$r_j = b_{j0} + b_{j1}F_1 + \varepsilon_j \qquad j = 1, 2, \ldots, n \qquad (8.1)$$

where r_j is the rate of return on asset (or portfolio) j, F_1 denotes the factor's value, b_{j0} and b_{j1} are parameters and ε_j denotes an unobserved random error. The rate of return on asset j, r_j, could be replaced by the excess return, $r_j - r_0$, over a risk-free rate, r_0, without affecting the analysis in any substantive way. The slope parameter, b_{j1}, is sometimes referred to as the 'factor loading'.

It is assumed that $E[\varepsilon_j | F_1] = 0$; that is, the expected value of the random error, conditional upon the value of the factor, is zero. This implies, immediately, that $E[\varepsilon_j] = 0$ and $\text{cov}(\varepsilon_j, F_1) = 0$ (recall the law of iterated expectations from chapter 3, page 79). In words: the random error is assumed to be zero on average and uncorrelated with the factor.[1]

The model is silent about what the 'factor' represents – more about this later. Whatever it is that the factor expresses, the model asserts merely that there exists a linear relationship between the factor and the rate of return on each asset. The same factor determines all the rates of return but also determines that the values of the parameters b_{j0} and b_{j1} can differ across assets.

The factor model expressed by (8.1) is *approximate* in the presence of the error term, ε_j. The role of ε_j is to allow unexplained forces to affect the rate of return. In *exact* factor models the error is identically zero. Exact factor models are not regarded as very plausible in practice but are useful for expositional purposes. Unless explicitly stated to the contrary, 'factor models' are understood to be approximate in the sense that ε_j is not identically zero.

The single factor model is illustrated in figure 8.1. According to the values taken on by ε_j, the observed values of the factor and rates of return would result in a scatter of points around the line defined by $r_j = b_{j0} + b_{j1}F_1$.

Values of the factor F_1 can, in principle, be observed, and although b_{0j} and b_{1j} are not observed they can be estimated, given the assumptions made about ε_j. Thus, knowledge of F_1 could be used to predict asset returns, albeit not perfectly given the presence of the random error. Moreover, if all asset returns are determined according to the factor model (8.1), then an *approximate* absence of arbitrage opportunities implies links among rates of return – this is the heart of

---

[1] In some treatments of the APT it is assumed also that the covariances of the random errors for all pairs of assets are zero – that is, $\text{cov}(\varepsilon_i, \varepsilon_j) = 0$ for all $i \neq j$. This 'strict' version of factor models is more restrictive than required for many applications and hence is neglected here.

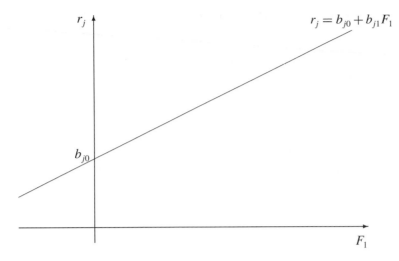

Fig. 8.1. A single-factor model

In a single-factor model, the rate of return on each asset, r_j, is assumed to be a linear function of a factor's value, F_1, with intercept b_{j0} and slope b_{j1}. The intercept and slope parameters may take positive or negative values and generally differ across assets. The existence of a random error means that observed values of r_j are scattered around the line.

the APT. (The absence of arbitrage opportunities is, in a precise sense, *approximate* given the presence of the error, ε_j, in the factor model.) The links among rates of return then allow calculation of a *risk premium* associated with the factor.

8.1.2 Models with multiple factors

For most applications the single-factor model is too restrictive; several factors are allowed to affect the rates of return on assets. The generalization to two factors takes the form

$$r_j = b_{j0} + b_{j1}F_1 + b_{j2}F_2 + \varepsilon_j \qquad j = 1, 2, \ldots, n \qquad (8.2)$$

with factor loadings b_{j1} and b_{j2}. In (8.2) there are two systematic influences on the rate of return from each asset. Apart from this, the interpretation is exactly the same as for the single-factor model.

The single-factor and two-factor models are convenient for expositional purposes because their predictions extend to the *multifactor model*:

$$r_j = b_{j0} + b_{j1}F_1 + b_{j2}F_2 + \cdots + b_{jK}F_K + \varepsilon_j \qquad j = 1, 2, \ldots, n \qquad (8.3)$$

In (8.3) there are K distinct factors. As will be seen later, a restriction must be placed on the number of factors in the APT. In particular, K must not be too large. More precisely, K should be small relative to n, the number of assets: $K \ll n$.

The properties of the random errors are assumed to carry over to the multifactor models – that is, $E[\varepsilon_j|F_1] = 0$, $E[\varepsilon_j|F_2] = 0, \ldots, E[\varepsilon_j|F_K] = 0$ for each asset j.

8.1.3 What are the factors?

An awkward question that is rarely asked, and even more rarely answered, is: 'Where does the factor model come from?' That is, what are the factor model's theoretical foundations? It is not underpinned by any one theory of investor behaviour, at least not in any obvious way. Instead, factor models can be understood as devices to make operational other theories of investors' behaviour, firms' behaviour or other aspects of how the whole economy works. For example, the intertemporal capital asset pricing model (mentioned in chapter 11) could be interpreted as providing a justification for the use of factor models. Alternatively, a straightforward – though not very satisfactory – answer to the question is that any factor model is a simple representation of how the world works. It generates testable hypotheses, a means of exploring the evidence, rather than representing a profound behavioural explanation of financial markets.

Whatever the justification for factor models, criteria are needed to select the factors. Very often this selection is *ad hoc*, the criterion being to choose those variables that are considered most likely to influence asset returns. Thus, the rate of growth of gross national product might be used, or changes in the rate of inflation, or the unemployment rate, or the rate of capital accumulation, or the foreign exchange rate. Some factors will, possibly, be relevant in the determination of some assets' rates of return but irrelevant for others (i.e. some of the b_{ji} parameters may be zero).

One important special case (often found in empirical applications) is where the factors are rates of return on portfolios of assets. For example, the rate of return on the market portfolio could be a factor. Similarly, rates of return on portfolios formed in other ways could also play the role of factors. (It is often convenient, though not essential, for the factors to be expressed as the excess rates of return over a risk-free rate.) While popular in applications, factor models in which all the factors are portfolio returns evade the fundamental issue of specifying the economic forces that determine asset payoffs – they just explain asset returns in terms of themselves. It is as if the capital markets are completely isolated from the rest of the economy – hardly a very plausible assumption.

In chapter 9 it is argued that the freedom offered by the APT in the choice of factors should be interpreted as a weakness of the model, not a strength.

While it is possible in applied work to allow the factors to remain unobserved, such an approach also incurs difficulties of interpretation. These are reviewed in chapter 9.

8.2 APT

8.2.1 Arbitrage: a restatement

In order to keep the notation as simple as possible, it is helpful to write the arbitrage conditions with different symbols. In particular, let y_j denote the outlay on asset j (i.e. $y_j \equiv p_j x_j$) for each asset. Also, rates of return replace payoffs using the definition $r_{kj} \equiv (v_{kj}/p_j) - 1$. Finally, neglect the subscript for the state, so that $r_j \equiv (v_j/p_j) - 1$. With these notational changes, an arbitrage portfolio $y_1, y_2, \ldots, y_n$ satisfies:

1. *zero initial outlay*: $y_1 + y_2 + \cdots + y_n = 0$, with $y_j \neq 0$ for at least two j; and
2. *risk-free*: $r_1 y_1 + r_2 y_2 + \cdots + r_n y_n \geqq 0$, for every state.

For every arbitrage portfolio, the arbitrage principle then asserts that in market equilibrium

$$r_1 y_1 + r_2 y_2 + \cdots + r_n y_n = 0 \quad \text{in each state}$$

It is this condition that is applied (as an approximation) in the APT.

In factor models there are two distinct sources of risk.

1. *Systematic risk*, associated with the variations in factors.
2. *Unsystematic risk*, associated with the random error.

Suppose that a portfolio can be found that requires a zero initial outlay and that eliminates both systematic and unsystematic risk. This is an arbitrage portfolio, and (as a consequence of the arbitrage principle) in market equilibrium must yield a zero rate of return in every state. In such a world the prices of the assets (and, hence, rates of return) are linked. It is precisely this link that constitutes the APT. The awkwardness is that the unsystematic risk can be eliminated only in an approximate sense. Hence, the absence of arbitrage opportunities is only approximate.

8.2.2 The APT in a single-factor world

The APT is most straightforward to comprehend in a single-factor model. The reasoning then extends readily to multifactor models. Write the single-factor model as (see (8.1) on page 184):

$$r_j = b_{j0} + b_{j1} F_1 + \varepsilon_j \qquad j = 1, 2, \ldots, n \tag{8.4}$$

An arbitrage portfolio, $y_1, y_2, \ldots, y_n$, is now constructed for a world in which asset returns are generated according to (8.4). By definition, the portfolio must satisfy the following condition.

APT condition 1. The portfolio requires zero initial outlay:

$$y_1 + y_2 + \cdots + y_n = 0$$

The elimination of systematic risk involves choosing a portfolio such that, whatever the value of the factor, F_1, its effect on the portfolio return is zero. This can be achieved, in the presence of at least two assets, by choosing the portfolio to satisfy the next condition.

APT condition 2. The elimination of systematic risk:

$$y_1 b_{11} + y_2 b_{21} + \cdots + y_n b_{n1} = 0 \tag{8.5}$$

It is trickier to eliminate the unsystematic risk. The portfolio return stemming from the unsystematic component is written as

$$\text{unsystematic return} = y_1 \varepsilon_1 + y_2 \varepsilon_2 + \cdots + y_n \varepsilon_n$$

The condition that $E[\varepsilon_j] = 0$ implies that the expected value of the unsystematic return is zero. This can be understood as stating that 'on average' the unsystematic return is zero. But this is not enough to eliminate risk, because it implies merely that positive values in some states are balanced by negative values in others. The arbitrage principle requires that the unsystematic return is zero in *every* state. Such a stringent requirement cannot be satisfied without error in an *approximate* factor model.

The problem of eliminating unsystematic risk occurs because there are generally too few assets compared with the number of states. There are n assets and – although n could be a large number – there might be an even larger number of states. If the number of states is finite and small enough and if the number of different assets is large enough, then unsystematic risk could be eliminated in the same way as systematic risk. Such a possibility is implausible for most applications. (Note that it is not permissible to generate additional assets merely by taking linear combinations of existing assets. There must be sufficiently many genuinely different assets, in the sense that linear combinations of existing assets are not included in the count.[2])

If unsystematic risk cannot be completely eliminated, resort must be made to approximate elimination. This is achieved by choosing a *well-diversified* portfolio. Under certain conditions – conditions needed to apply the law of large numbers

---

[2] The precise meaning of 'genuinely different' in this context is that the payoffs of the n assets form a linearly independent set.

in probability theory[3] – it can be shown that, if the number of assets, n, is large in a precise sense, then the portfolio can be chosen so that the unsystematic return is arbitrarily close to zero for every possible realization of the errors, $\varepsilon_1, \varepsilon_2, \ldots, \varepsilon_n$. This implies the third condition.

APT condition 3. Unsystematic risk is eliminated approximately:

$$\text{unsystematic return} = y_1\varepsilon_1 + y_2\varepsilon_2 + \cdots + y_n\varepsilon_n \approx 0$$

By applying conditions 1 to 3 to (8.4), it follows that

$$r_1y_1 + r_2y_2 + \cdots + r_ny_n \approx b_{10}y_1 + b_{20}y_2 + \cdots + b_{n0}y_n \qquad (8.6)$$

Expression (8.6) denotes the return that could, almost surely, be obtained on the chosen portfolio. The portfolio is approximately risk-free because all the terms on the right-hand side of (8.6) are given and the same for all states.

From now on – with the sacrifice of precision – the approximation is replaced by an exact equality. If the return on the constructed portfolio is not zero, there is an opportunity for arbitrage profit. Hence, the arbitrage principle that there is a zero return on the arbitrage portfolio ($r_1y_1 + r_2y_2 + \cdots + r_ny_n = 0$), from (8.6), implies the final condition.

APT condition 4. In market equilibrium, the zero return on the arbitrage portfolio requires

$$b_{10}y_1 + b_{20}y_2 + \cdots + b_{n0}y_n = 0$$

8.2.3 The APT: extension to multiple factors

The analysis so far holds for multifactor models, except that condition 2 must be extended to cover each factor separately.

APT condition 2 (multifactor models). The elimination of systematic risk:

$$y_1b_{1i} + y_2b_{2i} + \cdots + y_nb_{ni} = 0 \qquad i = 1, 2, \ldots, K \qquad (8.7)$$

The portfolio, $y_1, y_2, \ldots, y_n$, is guaranteed to exist only if $K < n$; i.e. there are fewer factors than assets. Otherwise, there may exist no portfolio that eliminates the systematic risk.

The four APT conditions collectively imply that assets' rates of return are linked in a particular way in any market equilibrium – otherwise, arbitrage opportunities would exist. Such opportunities would not provide entirely risk-free profits in the presence of the random errors. However, condition 3 ensures that the risk can be

---

[3] It is common to assume a 'strict' factor model (in the sense that the ε_j are independent across assets) when invoking the law of large numbers. See Feller (1970, chap. 10) for a classic treatment. It is possible to relax the assumption of independence and yet still apply some versions of the law of large numbers to eliminate unsystematic risk.

made arbitrarily small. By applying APT conditions 1, 2 and 4 to an exact factor model, appendix 8.1 derives the predictions discussed in the next section. While the appendix provides a formal justification for the APT, it is not essential for an understanding of the rest of the chapter.

8.3 Predictions of the APT

8.3.1 Risk premia in the APT

In a single-factor model, the APT conditions imply the existence of λ_0 and λ_1 such that

$$\mu_j = \lambda_0 + \lambda_1 b_{j1} \qquad j = 1, 2, \ldots, n \tag{8.8}$$

where the values of λ_0 and λ_1 are the same for every asset. Equation (8.8) holds as a strict equality only for an *exact* single-factor model. For approximate single-factor models (when the random error, ε_j, is not identically zero), expression (8.8) should properly be expressed as an approximate equality. The difference between the implications of the two models can be important in applied work, but it is neglected here. (A review of the issues relevant for empirical studies must await chapter 9.)

If a risk-free asset is present, its return, r_0, equals λ_0. (By virtue of being risk-free, $\varepsilon_0 = 0$, in every state, and hence $b_{01} = 0$.) Alternatively, if the factor model is constructed to explain excess returns, $r_j - r_0$, then $\lambda_0 = 0$.

When $\lambda_0 = r_0$, the APT prediction is often expressed as

$$\mu_j - r_0 = \lambda_1 b_{j1} \qquad j = 1, 2, \ldots, n \tag{8.9}$$

The weight λ_1 is interpreted as the *risk premium* associated with the factor – that is, the risk premium corresponds to the source of the systematic risk. Imagine an asset the return on which responds to a single factor with a unit factor loading $(b_{j1} = 1)$, then its risk premium, $\mu_j - r_0$, would equal just λ_1.

In the single-factor model, the APT has a simple graphical representation, shown in figure 8.2. The model predicts that all expected asset returns, μ_j, are located along the straight line with slope λ_1 and intercept r_0. If assets, or arbitrary portfolios of assets, fail to lie on the line, then the APT asserts that it is possible to construct portfolios that yield arbitrage profits (in the approximate sense outlined above).

If there are two factors, $\mu_j - r_0 = \lambda_1 b_{j1}$ is replaced with

$$\mu_j - r_0 = \lambda_1 b_{j1} + \lambda_2 b_{j2} \qquad j = 1, 2, \ldots, n \tag{8.10}$$

where λ_1 and λ_2 are risk premia associated with the factors F_1 and F_2, respectively. Finally, in the multifactor model with K factors

$$\mu_j - r_0 = \lambda_1 b_{j1} + \lambda_2 b_{j2} + \cdots + \lambda_K b_{jK} \qquad j = 1, 2, \ldots, n \tag{8.11}$$

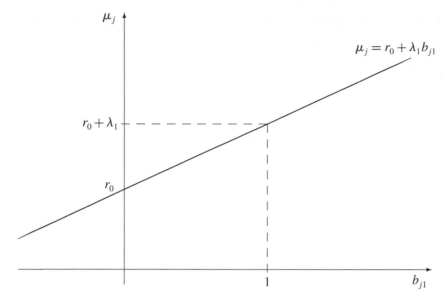

Fig. 8.2. The APT in a single-factor model

The APT with a single-factor model predicts that there is a linear relationship between μ_j and b_{j1} with intercept r_0 and slope λ_1. If $b_{j1} = 1$, the risk premium on asset j, $\mu_j - r_0$, equals λ_1.

Not surprisingly, a graphical representation becomes more difficult with more than one factor. In the two-factor model, expected asset returns are predicted to lie in a two-dimensional plane in μ_j, b_{j1}, b_{j2}, three-dimensional space. With K factors, expected asset returns are predicted to lie in a K-dimensional *hyperplane* in the $K + 1$-dimensional space of $\mu_j, b_{j1}, b_{j2}, \ldots, b_{jK}$.

To gain further understanding of the APT, take the expectations in the single-factor model, $r_j = b_{j0} + b_{j1}F_1 + \varepsilon_j$, to give

$$\mu_j = b_{j0} + b_{j1}\mathrm{E}[F_1]$$

Using the APT prediction, $\mu_j = r_0 + \lambda_1 b_{j1}$, to eliminate μ_j implies that $b_{j0} = r_0 + b_{j1}(\lambda_1 - \mathrm{E}[F_1])$.

Now, substitute for b_{j0} in the factor model, to give

$$r_j - r_0 = b_{j1}(\lambda_1 + F_1 - \mathrm{E}[F_1]) + \varepsilon_j \qquad j = 1, 2, \ldots, n \qquad (8.12)$$

This expression shows how variations in the rate of return (in excess of the risk-free rate) on any asset can be broken down into to the effects of (a) factor variations and (b) idiosyncratic risk (expressed by ε_j). The factor's impact consists of a systematic term, λ_1 (the factor risk premium), and a random term, $F_1 - \mathrm{E}[F_1]$, that is zero, on average. By assumption, the ε_j is also zero on average. Hence, the average asset return in excess of the risk-free rate (its risk premium) is equal to the factor loading, b_{j1}, multiplied by the factor risk premium, λ_1 – exactly as the APT predicts.

The generalization to a multifactor model merely involves the clutter of more notation. Here is the expression for a two-factor model:

$$r_j - r_0 = b_{j1}(\lambda_1 + F_1 - E[F_1]) + b_{j2}(\lambda_2 + F_2 - E[F_2]) + \varepsilon_j \qquad j = 1, 2, \ldots, n$$

The APT can be expressed in terms of asset prices instead of rates of return by using exactly the same reasoning as for the CAPM in chapter 6. Consider, once again, the equilibrium condition for a single-factor model, $\mu_j - r_0 = \lambda_1 b_{j1}$. All that needs to be done is to substitute the definition of the asset's expected rate of return, $\mu_j \equiv (E[v_j] - p_j)/p_j$, and rearrange to obtain

$$p_j = \frac{E[v_j]}{1 + r_0 + \lambda_1 b_{j1}} \qquad j = 1, 2, \ldots, n \qquad (8.13)$$

where $E[v_j]$ is the expected payoff on asset j.[4] In multifactor models the only complication is that the $\lambda_1 b_{j1}$ term in the denominator must be replaced by the sum $\lambda_1 b_{j1} + \lambda_2 b_{j2} + \cdots + \lambda_K b_{jK}$.

8.3.2 The APT when factors are portfolio returns

As already noted (section 8.1.3), it is often assumed that the factors are themselves portfolios of assets. It turns out that this assumption has an interesting implication, which is particularly relevant in applied studies.

Suppose for convenience that: (a) there are just two factors (the extension to K factors involves extra notation, nothing more); (b) asset returns are expressed as rates of return in excess of a risk-free rate; and (c) the value of each factor is equal to the excess rate of return on a portfolio (the portfolio rate of return minus the risk-free rate). The portfolios are not arbitrary; their composition is part of the a priori specification of the model – an issue not addressed here.[5] It is possible that one of the portfolios is the market portfolio of all assets, but this is not obligatory – it depends on the assumptions underlying the construction of the factor model.

Label the portfolios A and B. Formally, the assumptions imply

$$r_j - r_0 = b_{j0} + b_{j1}F_1 + b_{j2}F_2 + \varepsilon_j \qquad j = 1, 2, \ldots, n \qquad (8.14)$$

where $F_1 \equiv r_A - r_0$ and $F_2 \equiv r_B - r_0$.

---

[4] Notice that the expectation appears without an asterisk superscript. This is because the expectation in (8.13) is taken with respect to the probabilities underlying the factor model, not the artificial martingale probabilities.

[5] An application is discussed briefly in chapter 9, section 9.5.

As the factors are themselves portfolios of assets, the factor model also holds for the factors considered as assets. Thus, portfolio A trivially satisfies the factor model:

$$r_A - r_0 = b_{A0} + b_{A1}F_1 + b_{A2}F_2 + \varepsilon_A \tag{8.15}$$

with $b_{A0} = 0$, $b_{A1} = 1$, $b_{A2} = 0$ and $\varepsilon_A \equiv 0$. Similarly, for portfolio B: $b_{B0} = 0$, $b_{B1} = 0$, $b_{B2} = 1$ and $\varepsilon_B \equiv 0$. Each factor satisfies the factor model exactly – exactly but trivially.

It follows immediately from the APT that $\lambda_1 = E[F_1] = \mu_A - r_0$ and $\lambda_2 = E[F_2] = \mu_B - r_0$. Now, for every other asset, take the expectations in the factor model, equation (8.14), and compare the result with the APT prediction:

$$\mu_j - r_0 = b_{j0} + b_{j1}E[F_1] + b_{j2}E[F_2] \text{ (factor model expectation)}$$

$$\mu_j - r_0 = b_{j1}\lambda_1 + b_{j2}\lambda_2 \qquad \text{(APT prediction)}$$

Given that $\lambda_1 = E[F_1]$ and $\lambda_2 = E[F_2]$, it follows that $b_{j0} = 0$ for *every* asset.

In summary, when the factors are expressed as returns on portfolios A and B, asset returns must satisfy

$$r_j - r_0 = b_{j1}(r_A - r_0) + b_{j2}(r_B - r_0) + \varepsilon_j \qquad j = 1, 2, \ldots, n \tag{8.16}$$

The implication that $b_{j0} = 0$ constitutes an important prediction that can be tested in empirical applications.

8.3.3 APT and CAPM

Suppose that (a) the APT holds in a single-factor model, and (b) the factor is the excess rate of return on the market portfolio as defined in the CAPM, so that $F_1 = r_M - r_0$.

From equation (8.16) it follows that

$$r_j - r_0 = b_{j1}(r_M - r_0) + \varepsilon_j \qquad j = 1, 2, \ldots, n \tag{8.17}$$

and hence

$$\mu_j - r_0 = b_{j1}(\mu_M - r_0) \qquad j = 1, 2, \ldots, n \tag{8.18}$$

This is exactly the CAPM prediction if b_{j1} is interpreted as the beta-coefficient. Hence, if asset returns are explained by a single-factor model, where the single factor is the market rate of return, then the prediction of the APT is identical with that of the CAPM.

It is possible for the CAPM and APT to be compatible with one another even if the return on the market portfolio is not one of the factors – indeed, even if the factors are not portfolio returns at all. To establish the compatibility assume that both the CAPM and APT are true. Suppose (again, only to avoid cumbersome notation) that there are just two factors.

Assuming that the APT holds, consider two assets (portfolios, perhaps) labelled P and Q such that: P has a risk premium equal to λ_1; and Q has a risk premium equal to λ_2.[6] That is,

$$\mu_P - r_0 = \lambda_1$$

$$\mu_Q - r_0 = \lambda_2$$

Assuming also that the CAPM holds, its prediction for portfolios P and Q is

$$\mu_P - r_0 = \beta_P(\mu_M - r_0) = \lambda_1 \qquad (8.19)$$

$$\mu_Q - r_0 = \beta_Q(\mu_M - r_0) = \lambda_2 \qquad (8.20)$$

As always, the APT implies

$$\mu_j - r_0 = \lambda_1 b_{j1} + \lambda_2 b_{j2} \qquad j = 1, 2, \ldots, n$$

Substitute for λ_1 and λ_2 from (8.19) and (8.20) to obtain

$$
\begin{aligned}
\mu_j - r_0 &= [\beta_P(\mu_M - r_0)]b_{j1} + [\beta_Q(\mu_M - r_0)]b_{j2} \\
&= [\beta_P b_{j1} + \beta_Q b_{j2}](\mu_M - r_0) \\
&= \beta_j(\mu_M - r_0) \qquad (8.21)
\end{aligned}
$$

where $\beta_j = \beta_P b_{j1} + \beta_Q b_{j2}$, for $j = 1, 2, \ldots, n$.

Equation (8.21) is the CAPM prediction for asset j. This shows that both the APT and CAPM *could* hold in the same capital market – not that they *must*, of course. Both could be consistent with the same set of observations, though they might not be. In a sense, the APT is more general than the CAPM because, if the CAPM is true, the predictions of the two are indistinguishable (observationally equivalent). However, there are circumstances for which the APT predictions could hold when those of the CAPM do not.

8.4 Summary

On its own, the arbitrage principle, being founded on so few assumptions, provides few testable predictions about asset prices. The principle is made empirically relevant when applied to a model of asset prices.

This chapter analyses one such application, the arbitrage pricing theory. The APT comprises two components.

---

[6] P and Q are 'factor-specific' portfolios, chosen such that their rates of return respond only to factors 1 and 2, respectively; and respond with unit coefficients $b_{P1} = 1$, $b_{Q2} = 1$.

1. *Factor models.* These postulate that each asset's rate of return is a linear function of a small number of factors. The models do not themselves involve arbitrage at all. Instead, factor models provide a framework in which the arbitrage principle can be invoked.

2. *Application of the arbitrage principle.* The absence of arbitrage opportunities in the context of a factor model implies a set of restrictions on observable asset prices (or, equivalently, on expected rates of return). In particular, the APT predictions enable a risk premium to be associated with each of the factors. The risk premia differ across factors but are equal across assets. It is this implication that gives predictive force to the APT in empirical applications. Also:

   (a) a special case, useful in applied studies, corresponds to factor models in which the factors are themselves rates of return on portfolios of assets; and

   (b) the APT and CAPM are not incompatible with one another, though the APT is consistent with a broader range of empirical evidence – and consequently is more difficult to reject in econometric studies.

Further reading

All modern finance texts offer expositions of factor models and the APT, though the fundamental requirements for, and implications of, the arbitrage principle often receive only scant attention. Accessible textbook treatments include those by Elton, Gruber, Brown and Goetzmann (2003, chap. 16), Grinblatt and Titman (2001, chap. 6) and Sharpe, Alexander and Bailey (1999, chaps. 11 & 12).

For the APT itself, the seminal reference remains that of Ross (1976), though beginners will find this difficult. Also valuable is the entry on 'arbitrage pricing theory' in *The New Palgrave Dictionary of Money and Finance* (Newman, Milgate and Eatwell, 1992).

Appendix 8.1: The APT in a multifactor model

This appendix explains why the absence of arbitrage opportunities in a multifactor model implies the existence of risk premia, $\lambda_1, \lambda_2, \ldots, \lambda_K$, together with λ_0, as claimed at the start of section 8.3. The reasoning is analogous to that adopted in appendix 7.1.1, in chapter 7: the formal conditions defining an arbitrage opportunity are stated; an appeal is then made to one of the 'theorems of the alternative' (different from but a close relative of the one applied in chapter 7) to establish the existence of the risk premia.

To avoid the limiting arguments needed when appealing to the law of large numbers, the factor model is assumed to be *exact* in the sense that the random

errors are identically zero.[7]   In matrix notation, the multifactor model – see
equation (8.3) – can be written as

$$\mathbf{r} = \mathbf{b_0} + \mathbf{BF} \tag{8.22}$$

where $\mathbf{r}$ is a vector of rates of return, one for each asset, with typical element r_j;
$\mathbf{F}$ is a vector of factor values, with typical element f_i; $\mathbf{b_0}$ is a vector of n intercept
parameters, with typical element b_{j0}; and $\mathbf{B}$ is a matrix with n rows (one for each
asset) and K columns (one for each factor) with typical element b_{ji} (so that b_{ji}
denotes the increment in the rate of return on asset j in response to a unit change
in factor i).

   In this context, the vector $\mathbf{y}$ denotes a portfolio with typical element y_j, the
outlay (price *times* quantity) on asset j.   In section 8.2, the chosen portfolio
has zero total outlay: in matrix notation, $\mathbf{y}'\boldsymbol{\iota} = 0$, where $\boldsymbol{\iota}$ is the vector with n
elements, each taking the value 1, so that $\mathbf{y}'\boldsymbol{\iota}$ equals the total outlay on the portfolio. The portfolio is also chosen to eliminate systematic risk from the factors:
formally, $\mathbf{y}$ is chosen to satisfy $\mathbf{y}'\mathbf{B} = \mathbf{0}$ (where $\mathbf{0}$ is a row vector of K zeros).
Hence, from (8.22), $\mathbf{y}'\mathbf{r} = \mathbf{y}'\mathbf{b_0}$. In words: the overall return on the portfolio
equals the sum of the portfolio proportions multiplied by the intercept parameter
for each asset (because systematic risk has been eliminated and unsystematic risk
was eliminated at the outset by assuming that the random errors are identically
zero).

   In the absence of arbitrage opportunities, $\mathbf{y}'\mathbf{r} = \mathbf{y}'\mathbf{b_0} = 0$ (a risk-free portfolio
with zero outlay yields a zero return).   Hence, an *arbitrage opportunity* can be
expressed by the existence of a portfolio, $\mathbf{y}$, such that $\mathbf{y}'\mathbf{b_0} > 0$. If a positive
arbitrage profit can be made, then (by expanding or contracting the scale of the
portfolio to any degree) it can be fixed at any level.   The profit may as well
(without loss of generality) be set at $\mathbf{y}'\mathbf{b_0} = 1$.

   Summarizing so far, an arbitrage opportunity in the multifactor model can be
expressed by

$$\mathbf{y}'[\boldsymbol{\iota}, \mathbf{B}] = \mathbf{0} \quad \text{and} \quad \mathbf{y}'\mathbf{b_0} = 1 \tag{8.23}$$

where $\mathbf{y}'[\boldsymbol{\iota}, \mathbf{B}] = \mathbf{0}$ is a compact form of $\mathbf{y}'\boldsymbol{\iota} = 0$ and $\mathbf{y}'\mathbf{B} = \mathbf{0}$. (Note the inconsequential abuse of notation: $\mathbf{0}$ has $K + 1$ elements for the product with the
augmented matrix, and K elements for the product of $\mathbf{y}$ with $\mathbf{B}$ alone.)

   A theorem of the alternative can now be applied to (8.23).   In this case, the
relevant theorem – sometimes known as 'Gale's theorem for linear equalities'[8] –
states that exactly one of the two following results is true: *either* (a) there exists a $\mathbf{y}$

---

[7] An analysis that allows for non-zero random errors appears in *The New Palgrave Dictionary of Money and Finance* (Newman, Milgate and Eatwell, 1992) entry on 'arbitrage pricing theory' (Vol. I, pp. 52–6).
[8] See Gale (1960, p. 41 (theorem 2.5)) or Mangasarian (1994, p. 33).

that satisfies (8.23); *or* (b) there exists a vector with elements $(\lambda_0, \theta_1, \theta_2, \ldots, \theta_K)$ such that

$$\mathbf{b_0} = \iota\lambda_0 + \mathbf{B}\boldsymbol{\theta} \qquad (8.24)$$

where $\boldsymbol{\theta}$ denotes the $K \times 1$ column vector with elements $(\theta_1, \theta_2, \ldots, \theta_K)'$. The implication is either: (a) that there exists an arbitrage opportunity, as expressed by (8.23); or (b) that there exist $K + 1$ numbers, $\lambda_0, \boldsymbol{\theta}$ satisfying (8.24), *but not both*.

The derivation of the risk premia now involves merely giving an interpretation to the numbers $(\lambda_0, \theta_1, \theta_2, \ldots, \theta_K)$. To do this, substitute for $\mathbf{b_0}$ in (8.22):

$$\mathbf{r} = \iota\lambda_0 + \mathbf{B}(\boldsymbol{\theta} + \mathbf{F})$$

and take the expectations:

$$\boldsymbol{\mu} = \iota\lambda_0 + \mathbf{B}(\boldsymbol{\theta} + \boldsymbol{\mu}_F) \qquad (8.25)$$

where $\boldsymbol{\mu}$ is a vector of expected rates of return with typical element $\mu_j = \mathrm{E}[r_j]$, and $\boldsymbol{\mu}_F$ is a $K \times 1$ vector of expected factor values with typical element $\mathrm{E}[F_i]$.

Notice that $\boldsymbol{\theta}$ and $\boldsymbol{\mu}_F$ in (8.25) are the same for all assets. Hence, it is possible to define a vector with elements $(\lambda_1, \lambda_2, \ldots, \lambda_K)$ such that $\lambda_i \equiv \theta_i + \mathrm{E}[F_i]$, for $i = 1, 2, \ldots, K$. Now, writing out (8.25) for individual assets gives

$$\mu_j = \lambda_0 + \lambda_1 b_{j1} + \lambda_2 b_{j2} + \lambda_K b_{jK} \qquad j = 1, 2, \ldots, n \qquad (8.26)$$

If a risk-free asset is present, λ_0 can be interpreted as its rate of return. Compare (8.26) with (8.11) on page 190; they are identical. This completes the demonstration; in the absence of arbitrage opportunities in the factor model, there must exist risk premia satisfying (8.26), above.

Appendix 8.2: The APT in an exact single-factor model

Appeal to the risk-neutral valuation relationship (see page 174) provides another way of deriving risk premia in the APT. In what follows, the RNVR is applied to an exact *single*-factor model (generalization to a multifactor model requires only notational changes). The exact single-factor model is expressed as

$$r_j = b_{j0} + b_{j1}F_1 \qquad j = 1, 2, \ldots, n \qquad (8.27)$$

Recall that the RNVR requires that

$$r_0 = \mathrm{E}^*[r_j] \qquad j = 1, 2, \ldots, n$$

Now take the expectation in (8.27) to give

$$r_0 = \mathrm{E}^*[r_j] = b_{j0} + b_{j1}\mathrm{E}^*[F_1] \qquad j = 1, 2, \ldots, n \qquad (8.28)$$

Notice also that

$$\mu_j = b_{j0} + b_{j1}E[F_1] \qquad j = 1, 2, \ldots, n \qquad (8.29)$$

where the expectation is taken with respect to the probabilities underlying the factor model, *not* those implicit in the RNVR.

Define $\lambda_1 \equiv E[F_1] - E^*[F_1]$ and combine (8.28) and (8.29) to eliminate b_{0j}:

$$\mu_j - r_0 = \lambda_1 b_{j1} \qquad j = 1, 2, \ldots, n$$

which is just (8.9) in section 8.3.1, page 190 – as claimed.

References

Elton, E. J., M. J. Gruber, S. J. Brown and W. N. Goetzmann (2003), *Modern Portfolio Theory and Investment Analysis*, New York: John Wiley & Sons, 6th edn.

Feller, W. (1970), *An Introduction to Probability Theory and Its Applications*, Vol. I, New York: John Wiley & Sons, 3rd edn.

Gale, D. (1960), *The Theory of Linear Economic Models*, New York: McGraw-Hill.

Grinblatt, M., and S. Titman (2001), *Financial Markets and Corporate Strategy*, New York: McGraw-Hill, 2nd edn.

Mangasarian, O. L. (1994), *Nonlinear Programming*, Philadelphia: Society for Industrial and Applied Mathematics (reprint of an original published in 1969).

Newman, P., M. Milgate and J. Eatwell (eds.) (1992), *The New Palgrave Dictionary of Money and Finance*, London: Macmillan (three volumes).

Ross, S. A. (1976), 'The arbitrage theory of capital asset pricing', *Journal of Economic Theory*, 13(3), pp. 341–60.

Sharpe, W. F., G. J. Alexander and J. V. Bailey (1999), *Investments*, Englewood Cliffs, NJ: Prentice Hall International, 6th edn.

9

Empirical appraisal of the CAPM and APT

Overview

Empirical work on the CAPM and APT has two main objectives: (i) to test whether or not the theories should be rejected; and (ii) to provide information that can aid financial decisions. The two aims are clearly complementary: only theories that are compatible with the evidence are likely to be helpful in making reliable decisions.

To accomplish objective (i), tests are conducted that could – potentially, at least – reject the model. The model is deemed to pass the test if it is not possible to reject the hypothesis that it is true. Such a methodology imposes a severe standard, for it is invariably possible to find evidence that contradicts the predictions of any testable economic theory. Hence, the methods of statistical inference need to be applied in order to draw sensible conclusions about just how far the data support the model. Definitive judgements are never possible in applied work. This need not be an excuse for despair but should serve as a counsel for cautious scepticism.

Tests are almost never as clear-cut as they at first seem. They are typically tests of *joint* hypotheses, so that care is necessary to recognize what is, or is not, being tested. Also, the relevant *alternative* to the hypothesis being tested often remains vague, or, even more commonly, is ignored. For example, if the CAPM is rejected, which theory is it rejected in comparison with? No simple answer may be available. While these problems are in no way peculiar to financial economics, they are as important here as in any empirical work. The art is to frame meaningful hypotheses and draw justifiable conclusions from the evidence – always a challenging task.

To accomplish objective (ii), above, the empirical work uses the theory as a vehicle for organizing and interpreting data without deliberately seeking ways of rejecting it. An illustration of this approach is found in the area of portfolio

200

decision making, in particular with regard to the selection of which assets to buy or sell. For example, investors may be advised to buy assets that the CAPM predicts are 'underpriced' and to sell those that the CAPM predicts are 'overpriced'. Empirical analysis is needed to provide a guide – it can never do more than that – about which assets fall into the respective categories.

Another illustration appears in the field of corporate finance, where estimated beta-coefficients in the CAPM are sometimes used in assessing the riskiness of different investment projects. It is then possible to calculate 'hurdle rates' that projects must achieve if they are to be undertaken.

This chapter focuses on tests made of the CAPM and APT. The tests are, of course, relevant for other applications of the models, though the emphasis is somewhat different from that needed to aid portfolio selection or corporate financial decisions.

9.1 The CAPM

Begin with the CAPM when a risk-free asset is present – that is, the Sharpe–Lintner (SL) version of the model. Recall that the main prediction of the CAPM (see chapter 6, section 6.2) is

$$\mu_j - r_0 = (\mu_M - r_0)\beta_j \qquad j = 1, 2, \dots, n \qquad (9.1)$$

where $\mu_j \equiv \mathrm{E}[r_j]$ is the expected rate of return on asset j, r_0 is the risk-free interest rate, $\mu_M \equiv \mathrm{E}[r_M]$ is the expected rate of return on the market portfolio and $\beta_j = \sigma_{jM}/\sigma_M^2$ is the *beta-coefficient* for asset j.[1] In assessing empirical studies it is important to remember that one of the implications of the CAPM is that this equation holds not just for individual assets but also for all portfolios of assets (not just efficient portfolios). For reasons discussed below, most applications of the CAPM use portfolios of assets in carrying out the tests. From now on, 'assets' should be understood, without further reminder, to include portfolios of individual assets.

The two main approaches to testing the CAPM differ from one another according to how (9.1) is viewed.

1. *Time series.* These tests use observations on rates of return for a sequence of dates to measure the excess returns $\mu_j - r_0$ and $\mu_M - r_0$ (one pair for each date). The objectives are (a) to estimate β_j for each asset and (b) to investigate how well (9.1) fits the data.

2. *Cross-section.* These tests rely upon average excess returns (i.e. a value of $\mu_j - r_0$ for each asset) and estimates of β_j coefficients. There is one pair, $(\mu_j - r_0, \beta_j)$, for each asset. The objective is to appraise the *security market line* – that is, $\mu_j - r_0$ as a linear function of β_j. Here, the expected excess return on the market portfolio, $\mu_M - r_0$, is interpreted as a parameter to be estimated.

---

[1] A different but equivalent notation for covariances and variances is used in the remainder of this chapter, so that $\beta_j = \mathrm{cov}(r_j, r_M)/\mathrm{var}(r_M) \equiv \sigma_{jM}/\sigma_M^2$.

Sometimes (with journalistic hyperbole) tests of the CAPM are posed in the form of a question: 'is beta dead?' The death of beta simply corresponds to a rejection of the CAPM in the sense that estimated beta-coefficients do not provide an acceptable guide to observed risk premia.

If borrowing or lending at a risk-free rate is not possible, the 'Black CAPM' replaces r_0 with the expected rate of return, ω, on a zero-beta portfolio (see chapter 6, section 6.6). In this case the tests are more complicated, because there is typically no direct way of measuring ω. Even so, tests can be constructed, as explained below.

9.2 Tests of the CAPM: time series

9.2.1 Estimating alpha-and beta-coefficients

One way of allowing for the possibility that the CAPM does *not* hold is to add an intercept, α_j, to (9.1) as follows:

$$\mu_j - r_0 = \alpha_j + (\mu_M - r_0)\beta_j \qquad (9.2)$$

The CAPM predicts that the *alpha-coefficient*, α_j, is zero for every asset. Hence, a test of the CAPM can be constructed by testing the hypothesis that $\alpha_j = 0$ for each asset. Evidence that one or more $\alpha_j \neq 0$ is evidence against the CAPM.

In order to test hypotheses about the CAPM as expressed by (9.2), it is necessary to find observable counterparts for the theoretical values μ_j, r_0 and μ_M. For r_0, it is normally acceptable to use a market interest rate (such as the rate on short-term government debt), here denoted by r_{0t}, the t subscript indicating the date at which the interest rate is observed. Similarly, the measured rate of return on asset j at date t, denoted by r_{jt}, provides an observable counterpart for μ_j.

The choice of an observable counterpart for μ_M is more troublesome. The portfolio for which μ_M is the expected return should, according to the CAPM, be the portfolio of *all* assets, with the weight of each asset equal to its market share (i.e. the asset's capital value in proportion to the total market value of all assets). In practice, the shares underlying a more or less broadly defined index of asset prices is used to represent the market portfolio. Very often one of the published indexes – such as the S&P 500 index, for New York, or the FT-Actuaries All-Share index, for London – is considered to form a reasonable basis for measuring r_M, the empirical counterpart of μ_M. The fact that any one of these indexes is at best an approximation to the price of the market portfolio inspired 'Roll's criticism' of CAPM tests, discussed later (see section 9.4). A way of sidestepping the criticism is to acknowledge that the tests are conditional upon whatever portfolio is chosen to represent the market.

After making the necessary substitutions, $\mu_j - r_0 = \alpha_j + (\mu_M - r_0)\beta_j$, (9.2) becomes

$$r_{jt} - r_{0t} = \alpha_j + (r_{Mt} - r_{0t})\beta_j + \varepsilon_{jt} \qquad j = 1, 2, \ldots, n \quad t = 1, 2, \ldots, T \qquad (9.3)$$

where r_{Mt} denotes the rate of return on the portfolio chosen to represent the market and T is the number of observations in the sample. The unobserved random errors ε_{jt} are introduced to acknowledge that the CAPM does not hold exactly when the theoretical expected values are replaced by their observed counterparts. It is assumed (see chapter 6) that $E[\varepsilon_{jt}|r_{Mt}] = 0$, a condition needed in the interpretation of the statistical results.

In order to make (9.3) easier to comprehend, it is convenient to define new variables: $z_{jt} \equiv r_{jt} - r_{0t}$ and $z_{Mt} \equiv r_{Mt} - r_{0t}$. The z_{jt} and z_{Mt} are *excess* rates of return (i.e. rates of return in excess of the risk-free interest rate). Now (9.3) becomes

$$z_{jt} = \alpha_j + z_{Mt}\beta_j + \varepsilon_{jt} \qquad (9.4)$$

where it is assumed that $E[\varepsilon_{jt}|z_{Mt}] = 0$. For any given asset (i.e. if j is fixed), (9.4) can be interpreted as a regression equation via which estimates of α_j and β_j can be obtained by ordinary least squares (OLS). Let $\widehat{\alpha}_j$ and $\widehat{\beta}_j$, respectively, denote the OLS estimators. Then, from elementary statistics,

$$\text{alpha-coefficient:} \quad \widehat{\alpha}_j = \bar{z}_j - \widehat{\beta}_j \bar{z}_M$$

$$\text{beta-coefficient:} \quad \widehat{\beta}_j = \frac{\text{cov}(z_j, z_M)}{\text{var}(z_M)} \qquad (9.5)$$

where z_j and $\bar{z}_M$ are sample means of the excess returns; $\text{cov}(z_j, z_M)$ is the sample covariance between the excess return on asset j and the market; and $\text{var}(z_M)$ is the sample variance of the return on the market portfolio.[2]

By applying the OLS formulae, (9.5), to time series data, it is possible to obtain a pair of parameter estimates for each asset: $(\widehat{\alpha}_j, \widehat{\beta}_j)$, one pair from each regression. In order to make sense of the results as estimates of the parameters α_j and β_j, it is necessary to make further assumptions about the properties of ε_{jt}. Standard sets of assumptions are readily available in econometrics.[3]

---

[2] The theoretical expression for β_j involves a covariance and variance defined in terms of the rates of return rather than *excess* rates of return. By construction, however, the risk-free interest rate, r_0, is non-random. Hence, the covariance can be defined, equivalently, in terms of the excess rates of return. In the empirical implementation of the SL model it is convenient to work with excess returns throughout. Note that the presence of a risk-free asset does not mean that its rate of return is constant across time – strictly, r_0 should be written as r_{0t}. It is necessary to allow for this variability across time in calculating the sample statistics.

[3] See, for example, Hayashi (2000, chap. 1) or Brooks (2002, pp. 55–6). A standard set of assumptions – the 'classical linear regression model' – requires most importantly that $E[\varepsilon_{jt}|z_{Mt}] = 0$. This implies that the disturbance, ε_{jt}, is uncorrelated with the excess return on the market portfolio, z_{Mt}; i.e. $\text{cov}(\varepsilon_{jt}, z_{Mt}) = 0$ – that the disturbance and market return are *orthogonal*. (Given the non-randomness of the risk-free rate, $z_{Mt} \equiv r_{Mt} - r_{0t}$ and r_{Mt} can be used interchangeably here.)

Many time series studies of the CAPM are based on *portfolios* rather than the shares of *individual* companies. These artificial portfolios are constructed for a variety of reasons, including these: (a) the random influences on individual stocks tend to be large compared with those on suitably constructed portfolios (hence, the α_j and β_j are more accurately estimated for portfolios); and (b) the tests of $\alpha_j = 0$ are somewhat more straightforward to implement for portfolios (because the portfolios can be chosen such that correlations among the $\widehat{\alpha}_j$ are smaller than for the shares of individual companies).

9.2.2 Testing the CAPM

The time series tests of the CAPM focus on the hypothesis that the assets' regression intercepts are jointly equal to zero – i.e. $\alpha_1 = 0, \alpha_2 = 0, \ldots, \alpha_n = 0$. Also, various 'diagnostic tests' are available to provide evidence about how closely the model fits the data and about whether the assumptions on ε_{jt} are compatible with the data. If (a) the tests do not reject the null hypothesis that the regression intercepts are zero, and (b) the diagnostic results support the model's specification, then the evidence favours the CAPM. Otherwise, the evidence casts doubt on the CAPM.

Another way of testing the CAPM is to allow other variables (e.g. the rate of economic growth, the level of unemployment, or whatever) to influence z_{jt} as well as z_{Mt}. The CAPM predicts that variables *other than* z_{Mt} should *not* influence z_{jt}. While test procedures for this sort of hypothesis are readily available, the outcome of the tests may not be very informative; some imagination, combined with a little effort, often suffices to locate other variables that are correlated with z_{jt}. This being so, there is a high probability of rejecting the CAPM even if it is true. Hence, when other variables are found to contribute to the determination of z_{jt} in addition to z_{Mt}, their significance could result merely because they happen to be correlated with z_{Mt} in the given sample of data – a statistical fluke. This does not mean that the CAPM is immune to rejection. Instead, the evidence deserves careful evaluation before the model is condemned.

It is never possible to know for sure what the tests imply about the validity of the CAPM. For example, suppose that there is evidence that $\alpha_j \neq 0$ for some asset(s). This could mean that the CAPM should be abandoned in favour of some other model. Alternatively, it could mean that the CAPM normally holds but that asset markets were in *dis*equilibrium during part or all of the sample period.[4] This sort of ambiguity is inevitable in applied work.

---

[4] It is common in the CAPM to interpret $\alpha_j \neq 0$ as expressing disequilibrium in the sense of temporary divergences of (μ_j, β_j) pairs from the SML (see chapter 6, section 6.4.1).

9.2.3 The Black CAPM

In applied studies it is rarely possible to be confident about whether it is reasonable to assume that investors can borrow and lend unlimited amounts at the risk-free rate. Consequently, it is worthwhile to modify the approach outlined so far, and thereby to test the Black CAPM. Here the CAPM prediction can be written as

$$\mu_j = \omega + (\mu_M - \omega)\beta_j \qquad j = 1, 2, \ldots, n \qquad (9.6)$$

where ω is the expected rate of return on a zero-beta portfolio (see chapter 6, section 6.6.1). An empirical counterpart of (9.6) is obtained by substituting r_{jt} for μ_j and r_{Mt} for μ_M.

If ω is treated as a parameter, then the empirical model becomes

$$r_{jt} = \alpha_j + r_{Mt}\beta_j + \varepsilon_{jt} \qquad j = 1, 2, \ldots, n, \quad t = 1, 2, \ldots, T \qquad (9.7)$$

where the intercept, α_j, is now defined by $\alpha_j \equiv \omega(1 - \beta_j)$

As with the Sharpe–Lintner CAPM, it is routine to construct the OLS estimators, $\widehat{\alpha}_j$ and $\widehat{\beta}_j$:

$$\text{alpha-coefficient:} \widehat{\alpha}_j = \bar{r}_j - \widehat{\beta}_j \bar{r}_M \qquad \text{beta-coefficient:} \widehat{\beta}_j = \frac{\text{cov}(r_j, r_M)}{\text{var}(r_M)}$$

where $\bar{r}_j$ and $\bar{r}_M$ are sample means of the rates of return; $\text{cov}(r_j, r_M)$ is the sample covariance between the rate of return on asset j and the market; and $\text{var}(r_M)$ is the sample variance of the rate of return on the market portfolio. (See appendix 9.1 for the Black CAPM expressed in terms of excess returns.)

Expressed as (9.7), the CAPM predicts that $\alpha_j/(1 - \beta_j)$ – which equals ω, the expected excess return on any zero-beta portfolio – is the same for every asset, $j = 1, 2, \ldots, n$. Thus, for example, the estimated value for asset 5, $\widehat{\alpha}_5/(1 - \widehat{\beta}_5)$, should equal that for asset 9, $\widehat{\alpha}_9/(1 - \widehat{\beta}_9)$ (where '5' and '9' correspond to any pair of assets). In practice, the two estimates always differ as a result of statistical dispersion;[5] they have to be *significantly* different to warrant a rejection of the Black CAPM. Complicated though the hypothesis may appear, it can be tested, albeit less simply than with the test of $\alpha_j = 0$ in the Sharpe–Lintner model.

9.2.4 Summary

A beta-coefficient for each asset can be estimated if data are available for (a) the rate of return on the asset, (b) the rate of return on the market portfolio and (c) the risk-free interest rate. Excess returns on the asset and the market portfolio are calculated by subtracting the risk-free interest rate from each, respectively.

---

[5] Even if the model is correctly specified, the ε_{jt} terms are almost surely non-zero. Hence, estimates of α_j and β_j are almost surely not equal to any 'true' underlying values.

Then the beta-coefficient is estimated as the ratio of the covariance between excess returns on the asset and the market to the variance of the excess return on the market portfolio.

In the presence of unlimited borrowing or lending at a risk-free rate, the CAPM predicts that the alpha-coefficient for each asset is zero. If statistical tests imply that some, or all, alpha-coefficients are non-zero, this constitutes evidence against the CAPM.

In the absence of risk-free borrowing and lending, a beta-coefficient for each asset can be estimated as the ratio of the covariance between the asset's return and the market return to the variance of the market return. Now the alpha-coefficient for each asset is no longer predicted to be zero. Even so, it is possible to test whether the pattern of alpha-coefficients is compatible with the Black CAPM.

9.3 Tests of the CAPM: cross-sections

9.3.1 Estimating the security market line

Like the time series tests, the cross-section tests begin with $\mu_j - r_0 = (\mu_M - r_0)\beta_j$, (9.1), though now the equation is interpreted as a relationship between the expected excess return, $(\mu_j - r_0)$, and the beta-coefficient, β_j, for each asset.

In the cross-section tests – equivalently, tests of the SML – observable counterparts must be found for $(\mu_j - r_0)$ and β_j. One way to proceed is to replace $(\mu_j - r_0)$ with the sample average of the observed excess return on each asset j, the average being calculated over some time period – say, a year or several years. Let $\bar{z}_j \equiv \bar{r}_j - \bar{r}_0$ denote the sample average for asset j. For the beta-coefficients, it is natural to choose as their empirical counterparts the values, $\widehat{\beta}_j$, obtained in the time series estimations described in the previous section.

With these conventions, the empirical counterpart of the SML is written

$$\bar{z}_j = \gamma_0 + \gamma_1 \widehat{\beta}_j + \eta_j \qquad j = 1, 2, \ldots, n \tag{9.8}$$

where γ_0 and γ_1 are parameters and η_j is an unobserved random error, or disturbance, term. In the *cross-section* of asset returns, the n observations come in pairs with one observation per asset: $(\bar{z}_j, \widehat{\beta}_j)$, for $j = 1, 2, \ldots, n$. Contrast this with the *time series* analysis, for which there is a separate regression for each asset, with one observation per time period: (z_{jt}, z_{Mt}), for $t = 1, 2, \ldots, T$.

The CAPM predicts that (a) $\gamma_0 = 0$ and (b) γ_1 equals the expected excess return on the market portfolio, $\mu_M - r_0$, which can be estimated by $(\bar{r}_M - \bar{r}_0)$. Alternatively, the CAPM predicts that $\gamma_1 > 0$ – a weaker hypothesis that may be more appropriate because the value $(\bar{r}_M - \bar{r}_0)$ is itself obtained from sample observations. Hence, comparing estimates of γ_0 and γ_1 with these predictions enables inferences to be drawn about the compatibility of the CAPM with observed patterns of asset market returns.

The cross-section in the Black CAPM

For the Black CAPM, the empirical counterpart of the SML, $\mu_j = \omega + (\mu_M - \omega)\beta_j$, (9.6) above, can be written as

$$\bar{r}_j = \gamma_0 + \gamma_1 \widehat{\beta}_j + \eta_j \qquad j = 1, 2, \ldots, n \qquad (9.9)$$

Here γ_0 is interpreted as the expected rate of return on any zero-beta portfolio (they all have the same expected return, by construction) and γ_1 is the excess of the expected rate of return on the market over the expected return on a zero-beta portfolio.

Alternatively, the Black CAPM can be expressed in terms of excess returns – i.e. returns in excess of an asset with rate of return r_0. Equation (9.8) still applies but the interpretation of the parameters differs. Now γ_0 is the expected excess return on a zero-beta portfolio, $\gamma_0 = \omega - r_0$, and γ_1 equals the difference between the expected rates of return on the market and a zero-beta portfolio, $\gamma_1 = \mu_M - \omega$. (A derivation appears in appendix 9.1.)

9.3.2 The CAPM with a single cross-section

In their study – a minor classic in finance – Black, Jensen and Scholes (1972) use monthly data on stocks traded on the New York Stock Exchange. The results listed in table 9.1 group the individual stocks into ten portfolios (the intention being to generate a range of beta-coefficients as well as to attenuate estimation errors). The column headed 'Excess return' lists the average excess return over the years 1931 to 1965; the column headed 'Beta-coefficient' lists the $\widehat{\beta}_1, \widehat{\beta}_2, \ldots, \widehat{\beta}_{10}$ estimated over the same period.

The values in table 1 are plotted in figure 9.1, together with the ordinary least squares fitted line. In this illustration, the fitted line has intercept 0.0036 and slope 0.0108, so that

average excess return $= 0.0036 + 0.0108 \times$ estimated beta-coefficient

(more compactly, $\bar{z}_j = 0.0036 + 0.0108\widehat{\beta}_j$)

As already indicated, the intercept and slope in this regression can be interpreted as estimates of γ_0 and γ_1, respectively, in $\bar{z}_j = \gamma_0 + \gamma_1\widehat{\beta}_j + \eta_j$, (9.8) above.

The CAPM predicts that $\gamma_0 = 0$. Although 0.0036 may look small, it is significantly different from zero according to conventional statistical criteria. Hence, this is evidence *against* the CAPM.

208

The economics of financial markets

Table 9.1. *Estimates from Black, Jensen and Scholes (1972)*

	Excess return (%)	Beta-coefficient
Portfolio 1	0.021	1.561
Portfolio 2	0.018	1.384
Portfolio 3	0.017	1.248
Portfolio 4	0.016	1.163
Portfolio 5	0.015	1.057
Portfolio 6	0.014	0.923
Portfolio 7	0.013	0.853
Portfolio 8	0.012	0.753
Portfolio 9	0.011	0.629
Portfolio 10	0.009	0.499

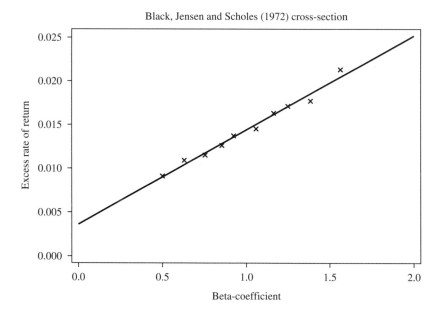

Fig. 9.1. A test of the CAPM

Each point in the figure plots an excess return and beta-coefficient from the list in table 9.1. The straight line depicts the ordinary least squares estimate of the security market line. The observed points lie close to the line – but are they close enough to support the CAPM?

Also, the CAPM predicts that γ_1 equals the expected excess return on the market portfolio, $\bar{r}_M - \bar{r}_0$. The measured value for $\bar{r}_M - \bar{r}_0$ in the Black–Jensen–Scholes sample was 0.0142, somewhat higher than the estimate, 0.0108.[6]

In the many empirical studies of the CAPM a wide variety of results have been reported. However, it is not unusual for tests similar to those reported here to provide evidence against the CAPM (namely, too large an intercept and too small a slope compared with what is predicted by the model).

A common, often revealing, practice in empirical work is to carry out the statistical analysis for subsamples of the whole data set. This provides evidence of whether the estimated parameters are 'stable' (i.e. differ only insignificantly across the whole sample), and hence whether the model's predictions are robust to sampling variation. For instance, Black, Jensen and Scholes (1972) find evidence of non-constant expected rates of return on zero-beta portfolios in the Black CAPM – i.e. the parameters γ_0 and γ_1 appear to differ across time periods (subsamples), providing further reason to doubt the empirical validity of the CAPM.

Caution is necessary in interpreting the estimates of the SML reported so far. One reason is that the beta-coefficients in the cross-section test are *estimates*. Inevitably, errors of estimation creep in. Hence, conventional statistical tests need modification to take these errors into account.

More troublesome is the fact that the use of estimated beta-coefficients can bias the estimates. In particular, it can be shown that the estimated SML is flatter than the 'true' line.[7] Methods are available to correct for the bias and to provide tests that take into account the first-stage estimation of the beta-coefficients. Indeed, one of the reasons why Black, Jensen and Scholes (1972) group assets into the ten portfolios is to circumvent this problem. Despite such efforts, caution should remain in the interpretation of the results.

9.3.3 The CAPM with multiple cross-sections

In the cross-section analysis, so far, the sample average excess return, $\bar{r}_j$, represents the empirical counterpart of the expected excess return, $\mu_j - r_0$, for asset j. But this is not the only candidate for measuring $\mu_j - r_0$. The observed excess return, z_{it}, for *any* time period, t, could form the dependent variable in a cross-section regression.

---

[6] But is the estimate significantly different from 0.0142? The standard error of the estimated coefficient turns out to be approximately 0.0005. The difference, $0.0142 - 0.0108 = 0.0034$, is more than twice the standard error, suggesting in a rough-and-ready way that the evidence supports the interpretation of a significant difference.

[7] This is an example of the well-known 'errors-in-variables' problem in econometrics. See, for example, Hayashi (2000, pp. 194–6) or Johnston and DiNardo (1997, pp. 153–5). In CAPM cross-sections the variable measured with error is $\widehat{\beta}_j$.

In this context it is possible to obtain estimates of γ_0 and γ_1 for every time period – i.e. as many cross-section regressions as there are time periods. These are the so-called 'Fama–MacBeth (FM) regressions', named for the innovative contribution of Fama and MacBeth (1973). Each of the cross-sections $t = 1, 2, \ldots, T$ yields a separate (generally different) pair of estimates for (γ_0, γ_1). These estimates can then be averaged to provide a summary estimate for each of γ_0 and γ_1.

Formally, the cross-section regression for each t is given by

$$z_{jt} = \gamma_{0t} + \gamma_{1t}\widehat{\beta}_j + \eta_{jt} \qquad j = 1, 2, \ldots, n \qquad (9.10)$$

Notice the t subscript that now appears on the $(\gamma_{0t}, \gamma_{1t})$ parameters, and on the disturbance, η_{jt}. Ordinary least squares can be applied to obtain estimates $(\widehat{\gamma}_{0t}, \widehat{\gamma}_{1t})$ for each t.[8] These can then be averaged to obtain the FM estimates:

$$\overline{\widehat{\gamma}}_0 = \frac{1}{T} \sum_{t=1}^{T} \widehat{\gamma}_{0t}$$

$$\overline{\widehat{\gamma}}_1 = \frac{1}{T} \sum_{t=1}^{T} \widehat{\gamma}_{1t}$$

How do the FM estimates, $(\overline{\widehat{\gamma}}_0, \overline{\widehat{\gamma}}_1)$, compare with those obtained in the single regression for the average excess return, $\overline{z}_j$? The answer is: they are *identical* if the explanatory variables in the regression – in this case just the $\widehat{\beta}_j$ – are constant across time (i.e. the same for each time period).[9]

If the parameter estimates are identical, then why bother with the Fama–MacBeth regressions? There are two reasons. First, depending on the assumptions made about the correlations among the disturbances η_{jt} (both across assets, j, and time, t), the diagnostic statistics, such as standard errors, will be affected. If the diagnostic statistics are affected then so may be the inferences about whether the CAPM provides an acceptable explanation of asset returns.

Second – and more importantly – the FM regressions can accommodate explanatory variables that differ across time (valuable information may be lost if such variables are averaged over the sample). For example, in Fama and MacBeth (1973) the beta-coefficients are estimated for a sequence of time periods (months) *preceding* the cross-section date (not for the whole sample of dates). Thus, each cross-section of returns depends only on information that is, in principle, available

---

[8] As always, the inferences from the estimates depend on the assumptions made about the disturbances, η_{jt}. Here, the crucial assumption is that the disturbances are uncorrelated with the beta-coefficients.

[9] For a proof of this result and a thorough analysis of Fama–MacBeth approach, see Cochrane (2001, pp. 244–50). Notice that the result holds even if additional explanatory variables are included in the FM regressions, so long as these variables are constant across time. Also, note that it is straightforward to express the Black CAPM in terms of FM regressions.

before the returns are observed – and hence relevant for tests of hypotheses about asset market efficiency.

Once the FM estimates, $(\overline{\overline{\gamma}}_0, \overline{\overline{\gamma}}_1)$, and the associated diagnostic statistics (such as standard errors) have been obtained, the results can be analysed in the same way as for the single cross-section described above. Some examples are discussed below. Notice that, in the absence of a risk-free asset, the only modification needed is to replace the excess return, z_{jt}, for each asset with its rate of return r_{jt}, throughout, and reinterpret the parameter estimates in exactly the same way as for the Black CAPM in the single cross-section.

9.3.4 The relevance of irrelevant variables

Among the many cross-section tests of the CAPM, the most popular is to investigate whether *other variables*, as well as the beta-coefficient, influence the average rates of return on assets; i.e. are there other determinants of $\mu_j - r_0$?

A procedure designed to address this question is as follows: include additional variables in the cross-section estimations and test whether their influence is statistically significant. If the estimated coefficients on the additional variables are *not* statistically significant this is evidence favouring the CAPM. Conversely, if the impact of the additional variables on asset returns is significant, the evidence points against the CAPM – because the CAPM predicts that beta-coefficients alone are sufficient to explain the cross-section of returns.

This is not the inference that is always made, however. Sometimes the results are interpreted to favour some extension or modification of the CAPM. Such an inference should not be accepted uncritically. For, by experimenting with many different combinations of variables in the cross-section regressions, it will almost surely be possible to find *some* variables that are statistically significant. Until a priori theoretical support is offered for one set of explanatory variables rather than another, any such empirical specification is, at best, a tentative replacement for the CAPM. The tests may provide evidence *against* the CAPM but are of limited value unless the results can be interpreted as supporting an alternative theory of asset returns.

In their study of asset returns, Fama and MacBeth (1973) construct two new cross-section variables: $\widehat{\beta}_j^2$, the square of asset j's estimated beta-coefficient; and s_{e_j}, the standard deviation of the residual in the time series regression for asset j. The former, $\widehat{\beta}_j^2$, is intended to test the *linearity* of the relationship between beta-coefficients and asset returns. The presence of s_{e_j} can be understood as a way of trying to capture the impact of time series variability in asset returns other than the return on the whole market (which is what the beta-coefficients are assumed to pick up) – i.e. s_{e_j} should reflect the idiosyncratic components of risk.

Formally, the cross-section regression becomes

$$r_j = \gamma_0 + \gamma_1\widehat{\beta}_j + \gamma_2\widehat{\beta}_j^2 + \gamma_3 s_{e_j} + \eta_j \qquad j = 1, 2, \ldots, n$$

where the time subscripts in the FM regression have been omitted for simplicity, and the dependent variable is the level of asset returns (rather than the excess over a risk-free rate).

Using monthly data on portfolios constructed for shares traded on the NYSE, Fama and MacBeth (1973) obtain the following results for the time period 1935 to 1968:

$$\text{average return} = 0.0020 + 0.0114\widehat{\beta}_j - 0.0026\widehat{\beta}_j^2 + 0.0516 s_{e_j} + \text{residual error}$$

What matters in testing the CAPM is whether the parameter estimates are significantly different from zero. In a battery of statistical tests, Fama and MacBeth cautiously conclude that the coefficient estimate on $\widehat{\beta}_j$ is statistically significant – supporting the CAPM – while those on $\widehat{\beta}_j^2$ and s_{e_j} are not – again, supporting the CAPM.[10] Their results, however, offer only equivocal evidence favouring the CAPM, leaving ample scope for doubt.

Enormous efforts have been devoted to identifying the determinants of cross-sections in asset returns. Variables that have been found to be statistically significant include: (a) the earnings/price ratio, E/P – profits as a proportion of the share price; (b) the debt/equity ratio – an index of the company's leverage; (c) the size of the company, as measured, for example, by the market value of its equity, ME; (d) the ratio of the book value of the firm's equity, BE, to its market value, ME – i.e. BE/ME.

In a paper that attracted intense scrutiny when it was published, Fama and French (1992) focus on the impact of ME and BE/ME on monthly cross-sections of individual company returns for over 2000 US non-financial firms. Fama and French (FF) conclude provocatively (p. 445) that

... market β seems to have no role in explaining the average returns on [United States] stocks for 1963–1990, while size [ME] and book-to-market equity [BE/ME] capture the cross-sectional variation in average stock returns that is related to leverage and E/P.

An illustration of the results from their FM regressions is

$$\text{average return} = 2.07 - 0.17\widehat{\beta}_j - 0.12\ln(\text{ME}) + 0.33\ln(\text{BE/ME})$$

$$+ \text{ residual error}$$

---

[10] The t-ratios for the three slope coefficients are 1.85, −0.086 and 1.11, respectively (Fama and MacBeth, 1973, p. 623). While 1.85 is low relative to the conventional critical value, 2.00, Fama and MacBeth argue that this provides adequate evidence that the coefficient on $\widehat{\beta}_j$ is non-zero, while the estimated coefficients on $\widehat{\beta}_j^2$ and s_{e_j} are not significantly different from zero.

where $\ln(\cdot)$ denotes the natural logarithm operator. Notice that here the average return responds *negatively* to the beta-coefficient, implying that more risky assets yield a *lower* risk premium (after controlling for the effects of ME and BE/ME) – directly contrary to the CAPM. Once again, it is the statistical significance of the estimates that is most important: Fama and French report that the coefficient on $\widehat{\beta}_j$ is insignificantly different from zero, while the coefficients on ME and BE/ME are both significant – hence their conclusion quoted above.[11]

The FF results have been challenged in a variety of ways, most commonly in critiques of their statistical analysis (e.g. by Kothari, Shanken and Sloan, 1995). While there has been a limited measure of success in resuscitating a role for beta-coefficients, there has been less success in providing convincing theoretical explanations for the presence of the other influences on average returns. The evidence inflicts serious damage on the CAPM, but – in the absence of widespread support for an alternative – the damage has not proven fatal.

Jagannathan and Wang (1996) offer an alternative explanation in which the beta-coefficients are allowed to vary across time. Evidence that the beta-coefficients differ across time has already been noted. The CAPM itself does not require that the β_j parameters remain constant; investors presumably base their decisions on whatever information is available, and hence may alter their views about the values of the beta-coefficients. If the beta-coefficients are allowed to change across time, Jagannathan and Wang show that more acceptable estimates of the security market line can be obtained – and, in addition, their empirical model has the advantage of theoretical support.

More recently, Campbell and Vuolteenaho (2003) present a model with two beta-coefficients, one to express the impact on risk premia of firms' expected future earnings ('bad beta'), the second to express the effect of the market interest rate at which future returns are discounted ('good beta'). A theoretical rationale for their model – the intertemporal CAPM – is mentioned later, in chapter 11. Their empirical results help to rectify the previous weaknesses of the CAPM and imply that companies can be separated into groups, according to the values of the two beta-coefficients. This will surely not be the last contribution in an active research area.

9.3.5 Summary

Cross-section tests of the CAPM seek answers to two questions. (a) Are average excess returns on assets correlated with their beta-coefficients? (b) Are other variables important in determining average excess returns on assets?

---

[11] The t-ratios for the three coefficients are -0.62, -2.52 and 4.80, respectively (Fama and French, 1992, p. 448). Thus, using 2.00 as the conventional rough critical value, $\widehat{\beta}_j$ has no significant influence on average returns but ME and BE/ME do.

The answer to question (a) is an equivocal 'maybe'. To some extent, the answer depends on *which* other variables are included in the explanation along with the beta-coefficients. On the whole, estimates of the SML find that it appears to be rather 'flat' (i.e. the slope coefficient with respect to the beta-coefficients is small) even though the influence is sometimes statistically significant (i.e. significantly different from zero).

The answer to question (b) is almost always an emphatic 'yes'. But the justification for any particular explanation over its rivals is rarely compelling and typically less than persuasive.

9.4 Sharpe ratios and Roll's criticism

Recall the definition of the Sharpe ratio (see chapter 5, section 5.4.3) for asset j: $s_j = (\mu_j - r_0)/\sigma_j$. An observable counterpart of the Sharpe ratio is

$$\widehat{s}_j = \frac{\overline{r}_j - \overline{r}_0}{\widehat{\sigma}_j}$$

where $\widehat{\sigma}_j$ is the sample standard deviation of the return on asset j. Replacing j with M defines the observed Sharpe ratio for the market portfolio, $\widehat{s}_M$.

The capital market line (see chapter 6, section 6.2.2) in the CAPM implies that $s_j \leqq s_M$ for every asset. Hence, a comparison of $\widehat{s}_j$ with $\widehat{s}_M$ provides a test of the CAPM. If $\widehat{s}_j$ exceeds $\widehat{s}_M$ for any asset(s), this is evidence *against* the CAPM. From portfolio analysis, $\widehat{s}_j > \widehat{s}_M$ suggests that the market portfolio is not efficient in a mean-variance sense.

According to the CAPM, the market portfolio must, at least, be mean-variance efficient. Hence, any finding that $\widehat{s}_j > \widehat{s}_M$ constitutes evidence against the CAPM. Tests using Sharpe ratios essentially test the same hypothesis as $\alpha_j = 0$ though in a rather less sophisticated way than outlined above, in section 9.2.

This insight is relevant because *Roll's criticism* asserts that every test of the CAPM is *nothing more* than a test of whether the portfolio that represents M is mean-variance efficient. (The assertion is true also for the tests outlined in previous sections.) Roll (1977) presents his criticism rather more forcefully. While acknowledging that the CAPM is testable '*in principle*', Roll argues with unrelenting tenacity (pp. 129–30) that '(a) no correct and unambiguous test of the theory has appeared in the literature, and (b) there is practically no possibility that such a test can be accomplished in the future'.

Roll's pessimistic conclusion seems to hint that a test of the CAPM would be possible with enough ingenuity and effort. To satisfy Roll it would be necessary to obtain data for the rate of return on the 'true' market portfolio. No approximations are allowed. But the market portfolio is, by its nature, a purely theoretical concept.

Compromises and approximations always have to be made to construct relevant empirical counterparts in any theory. For a purist, the 'true' market portfolio could never be observed. Even so, in deference to Roll it should be acknowledged that most empirical representations of the market portfolio are blatantly crude and inadequate approximations to the universe of assets available to investors.

Three possible responses to Roll's criticism are as follows.

1. Accept that 'there is practically no possibility' of testing the CAPM.
2. Always try to construct the empirical market portfolio to correspond as faithfully as possible with the theoretical market portfolio.
3. Acknowledge that every test of the CAPM is a test of a *joint* hypothesis (namely, a model of assets' rates of return jointly with the choice of a market portfolio). In other words: every test of the CAPM is conditional upon the portfolio chosen to represent the market.

The second and third responses are compatible with one another and, not surprisingly, dominate empirical evaluation of the CAPM.

9.5 Multiple-factor models and the APT

Empirical work on multiple-factor models (multifactor models) and the APT bears a close resemblance to that on the CAPM, though from a different theoretical perspective. Both time series and cross-section studies of rates of return make an appearance in much the same way as for the CAPM.

Time series studies are often made of the multifactor models introduced in chapter 8. Statistically at least, they take a form very similar to the regression model outlined above, in section 9.2. The main difference is that other explanatory variables are introduced in addition to, or instead of, the market rate of return. The cross-section tests involve similar methods as in section 9.3, above, except that now the interpretation is based on the arbitrage principle and the explanatory variables are the parameter estimates from the time series regressions (instead of estimated beta-coefficients together, possibly, with other variables).

9.5.1 Multifactor models

Consider, for simplicity, the two-factor model:

$$r_{jt} = b_{j0} + b_{j1}F_{1t} + b_{j2}F_{2t} + \varepsilon_{jt} \qquad j = 1, 2, \ldots, n \quad t = 1, 2, \ldots, T \quad (9.11)$$

where F_{1t} and F_{2t} are the values of the two factors at date t; b_{j0}, b_{j1} and b_{j2} are parameters; and ε_{jt} is an unobserved random error. In some studies, asset returns in excess of a risk-free rate are used instead of r_{jt} – the empirical methods are the same, only the interpretation of the results is affected.

Just as with the CAPM, the parameter values generally differ across assets so that there is a separate time series regression for each asset. Unlike the CAPM, the return on the market portfolio need not be one of the factors. With time series of observations on rates of return and the factors it is a routine matter to obtain estimates $\widehat{b}_{j0}$, $\widehat{b}_{j1}$ and $\widehat{b}_{j2}$ for the three parameters, b_{j0}, b_{j1} and b_{j2}.

In some specifications the factors are chosen from among financial indicators (e.g. interest rate differentials between long-term and short-term government bonds) or macroeconomic variables (e.g. forecast errors for the growth of national income). In others the factors are themselves the rates of return on specially constructed portfolios of assets (one of which might be the market rate of return). It is even possible to dispense entirely with the selection of variables to represent the factors; the factors can be allowed to remain implicit in the data on assets' rates of return.

Fama applauds the multifactor models, but with a hint of irony (for his applause soon becomes muted: Fama, 1991, p. 1594).

The multifactor models are an empiricist's dream. They are off-the-shelf theories that can accommodate tests for cross-sectional relations between expected returns and the loadings of security returns on any set of factors that are correlated with returns.

9.5.2 The APT

By applying the arbitrage principle to the multifactor model (9.11), the APT predicts a cross-section relationship (see chapter 8, section 8.3):

$$\mu_j = \lambda_0 + \lambda_1 b_{j1} + \lambda_2 b_{j2} \qquad j = 1, 2, \dots, n \qquad (9.12)$$

where λ_0, λ_1, and λ_2 are parameters to be estimated. (The adjustments to allow for the presence of a risk-free interest rate are not pursued in this section. A risk-free interest rate could be introduced, as in chapter 8, without affecting the methods in any substantial way.)

By analogy with the CAPM, the cross-section regression could be expressed as

$$\bar{r}_j = \lambda_0 + \lambda_1 \widehat{b}_{j1} + \lambda_2 \widehat{b}_{j2} + \nu_j \qquad j = 1, 2, \dots, n \qquad (9.13)$$

where $\widehat{b}_{j1}$ and $\widehat{b}_{j2}$ are estimates from the time series regression for asset j, $\bar{r}_j$ is the sample average return on asset j and ν_j is an unobserved random error. Now the λ_0, λ_1, and λ_2 parameters are estimated and analysed in the same way as the cross-section coefficients in the CAPM.

Extending the cross-section tests of the CAPM to the APT is, however, more delicate than it might first seem. For, even if b_{j1} and b_{j2} were known without error, the APT implies that (9.12) is an *approximation*. The addition of a random error to (9.12) would be a rough-and-ready way to allow for the approximation.

This random error can then be absorbed into the error in (9.13). Thus, ν_j is now interpreted as a combination of the error of approximation and the disturbance in the cross-section regression. The problem with this approach is that it adds to the difficulty of testing the APT: the two sources of error are awkward to disentangle. Nonetheless, investigations based on (9.13) are the most straightforward to implement even if the results are tricky to interpret.

An alternative approach is to treat the APT predictions, (9.12), as restrictions imposed on the time series estimations of the multifactor model. A test of the APT can then be made by comparing the restricted estimates that force (9.12) to hold as against the unrestricted estimates of (9.11). If the two sets of estimates are close, this is evidence in support of the APT; otherwise, it is evidence against the APT.[12] Notice, however, that this approach makes sense only if there is an underlying *exact* multifactor model; otherwise, the restrictions expressed as (9.12) should be understood as approximations, not equalities. In this interpretation the addition of a random error, ε_{jt}, in (9.11) is justified because some factors that should be included have been omitted from an exact multifactor model – not because an approximate multifactor model is assumed at the outset. In practice, it is difficult to distinguish between an exact model for which some factors have been omitted and an approximate model for which all the factors are present.

In another of their influential contributions, Fama and French (1993) explore the implications of a factor model relevant for both equities and bonds. They propose five factors, all of which can be interpreted as excess returns on particular portfolios. Three of the factors are chosen to represent the stock market: (i) the excess return on a market portfolio; (ii) the difference in the rates of return between small companies and large companies, ranked according to their aggregate equity values; and (iii) the difference in the rates of return of companies ranked according to their BE/ME ratio (the book value of equity as a proportion of the market value of equity). The two remaining factors represent the bond market: (iv) the difference between long term and short-term interest rates; and (v) the difference between the yield on corporate (high risk) bonds and government (low-risk) bonds.

The focus of Fama and French's paper is on *time series* analysis of the degree to which the five factors can account for US equity and bond returns over the period 1963 to 1991. They find that the five factors are able to explain asset returns satisfactorily, the three stock market factors being particularly relevant for equity returns and the two interest rate factors for bonds.

---

[12] The details are too messy to merit inclusion here. A comprehensive treatment appears in the advanced literature – for instance, Campbell, Lo and MacKinlay (1997, chap. 6, pp. 226–8) outline statistical procedures designed to test the hypothesis that the restrictions are satisfied.

In addition, Fama and French test the APT prediction that the intercepts in the regressions should be zero.[13] The test results they report are on the margin of statistical significance (not decisively rejecting the null hypothesis that the intercepts are jointly zero). They argue, however, that the *magnitudes* of the intercepts are sufficiently small to render them economically (if not statistically) insignificant. Of broader importance is their reflection (1993, p. 53) that 'the choice of factors, especially the size and book-to-market factors, is motivated by empirical experience. Without a theory that specifies the exact form of the state variables or common factors in returns, the choice of any particular version of the factors is somewhat arbitrary.'

Despite this reservation, it is possible (as already mentioned) to construct multi-factor models – and, by implication, the APT – without designating observable variables to represent the factors. Instead, statistical methods are applied to infer the presence of factors from patterns in the time series data on assets' rates of return. The specialized tools of 'factor analysis' and 'principal components analysis' are employed in these investigations. The results, however, demand care-ful interpretation, largely because it is a matter of judgement about the number of factors that are permitted. While the freedom of the data to detect the implied factors is a strength of the approach, its weakness is that the results do not provide any guidance about the underlying economic forces that the factors reflect.

Despite the technical sophistication of the tools for studying multifactor models and the APT, a fundamental problem remains: how to select the factors. In an age of powerful computers and abundant data, the temptation is to keep trying different sets of factors until one is found that fits the data well. This process of 'data mining' or 'data snooping' often results in empirical estimations that appear highly satisfactory. But they should be regarded with the greatest suspicion, for conventional statistical criteria are not valid when results are reported only after the data have been searched for the best-fitting specification. (Unless adjustments are made, the criteria fail to take into account the steps by which the final results are obtained.)

There are at least two possible ways to circumvent the problem of factor selec-tion. One is to use the estimated parameters to make out-of-sample forecasts – that is, to forecast observations that were not included in estimating the param-eters used to make the forecast. This can be a handy method of eliminating bad models, but it provides little guidance about how to find good ones. The second method is to build multifactor models that correspond more closely to the predictions of economic theory. Ultimately, empirical specifications are likely to survive only if they have theoretical support (though, admittedly, theories are

---

[13] See chapter 8, section 8.3.2. Fama and French (1993, pp. 31–2) point out that the hypothesis can be derived from theoretical considerations other than the APT.

often built *post hoc* to explain regularities that have been observed in the data). An obstacle here is that theory tends to be unhelpful in recommending variables for selection as factors.

9.5.3 Summary

From a statistical viewpoint, multifactor models and the APT can be interpreted as generalizations of the CAPM, in the sense that asset returns are allowed to depend on several different factors instead of the market return alone. Many investigations have been undertaken. Most find empirical support for their chosen multifactor model and some also support the APT. However, they are weakened by the lack of reliable criteria for selecting among the candidate factors. Once again, Fama makes the relevant point most clearly (1991, p. 1595).

Since multifactor models offer at best vague predictions about the variables that are important in returns and expected returns, there is the danger that measured relations between returns and economic factors are spurious, the result of special features of a particular sample (factor dredging).

The 'empiricists' dream' has become a nightmare.

9.6 Summary

1. Tests of the CAPM focus on *time series* and *cross-section* studies. Time series studies are employed to obtain estimates of the beta-coefficients for assets or portfolio of assets. Cross-section studies investigate how well the rates of return among different assets are correlated with their beta-coefficients.
2. The cross-sectional evidence for a correlation between assets' rates of return and their beta-coefficients is mixed. Some studies find a positively sloped SML. Others cannot reject the hypothesis that the SML is flat (i.e. that there is no association between expected rates of return and beta-coefficients).
3. Most studies find that variables other than beta-coefficients are correlated with cross-sections of average rates of return. The challenge remains to construct acceptable theories that predict which variables should affect assets' rates of return.
4. Tests of multifactor models and the APT are constructed in a similar way to those for the CAPM. Although there is freedom to choose variables to represent the factors, the challenge is the same as for the CAPM: to develop a reliable way to select the factors.

Further reading

Most finance texts review applied work on the CAPM, multifactor models and the APT, although not always with the care that the topics merit. A clear treatment is given by Elton, Gruber, Brown and Goetzmann (2003, chaps. 15 & 16).

An excellent students' guide for empirical work on the CAPM is by Jagannathan and McGrattan (1995). Fama and French (1992, 1993) stimulated much of the applied research that has taken place since the early 1990s. For a perceptive commentary on the empirical weaknesses of the CAPM revealed over its first forty years, see Fama and French (2004). Research in the area remains active, with successive issues of the *Journal of Finance* and the *Journal of Financial Economics* containing many influential contributions to the field.

Brooks (2002) provides an accessible introduction to the econometric methods used in finance. At a more advanced level, Campbell, Lo and MacKinlay (1997, especially chaps. 5 & 6) and Cochrane (2001, chaps. 10–15) provide comprehensive integrated surveys of the modern literature.

Appendix 9.1: The Black CAPM in terms of excess returns

The Black CAPM can be written in terms of excess returns simply by subtracting r_0 from μ_j, ω and μ_M in $\mu_j = \omega + (\mu_M - \omega)\beta_j$, equation (9.6) on page 205:

$$\mu_j - r_0 = \omega - r_0 + (\mu_M - r_0 - (\omega - r_0))\beta_j \qquad j = 1, 2, \ldots, n \qquad (9.14)$$

Now rearrange (9.14) as

$$\mu_j - r_0 = (\omega - r_0)(1 - \beta_j) + (\mu_M - r_0)\beta_j \qquad j = 1, 2, \ldots, n \qquad (9.15)$$

where excess returns have been introduced by subtracting r_0 as needed.[14] The empirical counterpart of (9.15) is then

$$z_{jt} = z_{\omega t}(1 - \beta_j) + z_{Mt}\beta_j + \varepsilon_{jt} \qquad j = 1, 2, \ldots, n \quad t = 1, 2, \ldots, T \qquad (9.16)$$

where $z_{\omega t} \equiv r_{\omega t} - r_{0t}$ is the excess rate of return on a zero-beta portfolio, with $r_{\omega t}$ denoting the random rate of return on a zero-beta portfolio. This is sometimes known as the *two-factor* form of the CAPM, with z_{Mt} and $z_{\omega t}$ as the two factors. The problem with (9.16) is that, although in principle it should be possible to observe $z_{\omega t}$, in practice it is not. Typically, the same regression, (9.4), as for the SL model is calculated. The difference is one of interpretation: α_j is now interpreted as $\alpha_j = (\omega - r_0)(1 - \beta_j)$. This specification of the model is more complicated to test because β_j is now absorbed into α_j, only the term $(\omega - r_0)$ being predicted to be identical for all assets.

---

[14] The use of excess returns in the context of the Black CAPM might seem rather contradictory: the Black CAPM is relevant precisely when borrowing or lending at a risk-free rate is *not* possible. But here r_0 is intended to identify a low-risk interest rate, such as the treasury bill rate, irrespective of whether investors can borrow or lend at the rate. The construction of excess returns is then just a device to make more transparent comparisons with the Sharpe–Lintner model.

References

Black, F., M. C. Jensen and M. Scholes (1972), 'The capital asset pricing model: some empirical tests', in M. C. Jensen (ed.), *Studies in the Theory of Capital Markets*, New York: Praeger, pp. 79–121.

Brooks, C. (2002), *Introductory Econometrics for Finance*, Cambridge: Cambridge University Press.

Campbell, J. Y., A. W. Lo and A. C. MacKinlay (1997), *The Econometrics of Financial Markets*, Princeton, NJ: Princeton University Press.

Campbell, J. Y., and T. Vuolteenaho (2003), *Bad Beta, Good Beta*, unpublished manuscript, Department of Economics, Harvard University.

Cochrane, J. H. (2001), *Asset Pricing*, Princeton, NJ: Princeton University Press.

Elton, E. J., M. J. Gruber, S. J. Brown and W. N. Goetzmann (2003), *Modern Portfolio Theory and Investment Analysis*, New York: John Wiley & Sons, 6th edn.

Fama, E. F. (1991), 'Efficient capital markets II', *Journal of Finance*, 46(5), pp. 1575–1617.

Fama, E. F., and K. R. French (1992), 'The cross-section of expected stock returns', *Journal of Finance*, 47(2), pp. 427–65.

(1993), 'Common risk factors in the returns on stocks and bonds', *Journal of Financial Economics*, 33(1), pp. 3–56.

(2004), 'The capital asset pricing model: theory and evidence', *Journal of Economic Perspectives*, 18(3), pp. 25–46.

Fama, E. F., and J. MacBeth (1973), 'Risk, return and equilibrium: empirical tests', *Journal of Political Economy*, 81(3), pp. 607–36.

Hayashi, F. (2000), *Econometrics*, Princeton, NJ, and Oxford: Princeton University Press.

Jagannathan, R., and E. R. McGrattan (1995), 'The CAPM debate', *Federal Reserve Bank of Minneapolis, Quarterly Review*, 19(4), pp. 2–17.

Jagannathan, R., and Z. Wang (1996), 'The conditional CAPM and the cross-section of expected returns', *Journal of Finance*, 51(1), pp. 3–53.

Johnston, J., and J. DiNardo (1997), *Econometric Methods*, New York: McGraw-Hill, 4th edn.

Kothari, S. P., J. Shanken and R. G. Sloan (1995), 'Another look at the cross-section of expected stock returns', *Journal of Finance*, 50(1), pp. 185–224.

Roll, R. (1977), 'A critique of the asset pricing theory's tests, part 1: on past and potential testability of the theory', *Journal of Financial Economics*, 4(2), pp. 129–76.

10

Present value relationships and price variability

Overview

Perhaps the commonest equation in the whole of finance is the one that sets the value of an asset equal to the net present value (or 'present discounted value') of a sequence of its payoffs. The equation plays a central role in corporate finance, where NPV criteria constitute the basis for the selection of investment projects. In particular, the NPV rule is applied to value assets (projects) the market prices of which may not be readily observed.

This chapter's objective is somewhat different from, though consistent with, that of corporate finance. Here the NPV relationship appears as a *market equilibrium condition* that has testable implications for observed asset prices.

In its simplest and most broadly applicable form, studied in section 10.1, the NPV relationship is a consequence of the arbitrage principle. In this sense it is nothing more than the extension of the results of chapter 7 to a multiperiod framework.

While central to financial theory, arbitrage ideas on their own tend to yield few predictions. Stronger assumptions – in particular about investors' expectations – permit predictions about asset price volatility to be derived. Section 10.2 reviews these assumptions and discusses the degree to which empirical evidence casts doubt on the validity of a theory commonly interpreted as expressing rational investor behaviour. By implication, doubt is also cast on asset market efficiency.

Section 10.3 explores other models, also motivated by the NPV, that seek to provide more empirically acceptable explanations of asset price volatility. These models incorporate facets of 'noise trading' to represent behaviour that could be interpreted as capricious or perhaps even irrational.

Asset markets are notorious for experiencing occasional bouts of optimism followed by pessimism, leading to sharp rises, and subsequent crashes, in prices. Episodes of extreme price fluctuations, sometimes known as 'bubbles', are well documented in the historical record. Their compatibility with the NPV relationship is examined in section 10.4, which reviews several of the more famous examples of asset price bubbles. The section concludes with comments on Ponzi investment schemes – enterprises commonly found during asset market frenzies and from which accusations of fraud invariably emerge.

10.1 Net present value

The purpose of this section is to construct the NPV relationship. Familiar though it is, the NPV equation is open to misinterpretation. However, if constructed carefully the NPV relationship provides several insights into the determination of asset prices, as well as revealing some awkward complications. A provisional assumption is that the future returns are deterministic – that is, known with certainty. Unrealistic though it may be, the assumption of deterministic returns is at the core of many studies of present values. A relaxation of the assumption, to allow for uncertainty, is outlined in section 10.1.2, though a thorough exploration of the topic must await chapter 11.

10.1.1 Certainty

Recall from chapter 1 the relationship between an asset's rate of return and its payoff:

$$\text{rate of return on the asset} \equiv \frac{v - p}{p}$$

where p is the price of the asset today and v is the asset's payoff. Timing is important in what follows, dates being denoted by time subscripts. The present date, 'today', is identified with a t subscript so that p_t is the current price and p_{t+i} is the price i periods into the future. It is assumed that the pay-off is received one time period from the present, so that the asset's rate of return equals $(v_{t+1} - p_t)/p_t$.

In constructing the NPV relationship, it is assumed that: (a) the payoff, expressed by v, is known with certainty; and (b) the interest rate, r, at which funds can be borrowed or loaned in unlimited amounts is known with certainty and is constant across time. Each of these assumptions is relaxed as the analysis progresses.

Here, as elsewhere in these chapters, time is divided into unit intervals, with prices being observed and investors' decisions being made only at t, $t+1$, $t+2$, etc.

Time passes in discrete intervals.[1] Appendix 10.1 studies the NPV when time is treated as a continuous variable rather than as a sequence of discrete unit intervals.

The asset's payoff at each date, v_t, can be split into two components: a 'dividend', or 'coupon', paid by the issuer to the holder, denoted here by d_t; and the market price of a unit of the asset, denoted by p_t. Thus, $v_{t+1} = d_{t+1} + p_{t+1}$. The absence of arbitrage opportunities (see chapter 1) implies that the payoff in the coming period as a proportion of the initial asset price must equal the interest rate:

$$r = \frac{v_{t+1} - p_t}{p_t} = \frac{d_{t+1}}{p_t} + \frac{p_{t+1} - p_t}{p_t} \qquad (10.1)$$

Implicit in this expression is a timing convention that asset prices are quoted *ex-dividend*; that is, p_{t+1} measures the price after, and hence excludes, the dividend paid at that date, d_{t+1}.

Rearranging (10.1) provides an expression for the current price:

$$p_t = \frac{1}{1+r}(d_{t+1} + p_{t+1}) \qquad (10.2)$$

Given that r is assumed constant across time, for any date, $t + i$, $i \geq 0$:

$$r = \frac{d_{t+i+1}}{p_{t+i}} + \frac{p_{t+i+1} - p_{t+i}}{p_{t+i}} \qquad (10.3)$$

or, rearranging,

$$p_{t+i} = \frac{1}{1+r}(d_{t+i+1} + p_{t+i+1}) \qquad (10.4)$$

Equation (10.4) is central to all present value expressions because it is possible to extend the timing forward by substituting out future prices one period at a time. For instance, eliminating p_{t+1} from (10.1) gives

$$p_t = \frac{1}{1+r}\left(d_{t+1} + \frac{1}{1+r}(d_{t+2} + p_{t+2})\right)$$
$$= \frac{d_{t+1}}{(1+r)} + \frac{d_{t+2} + p_{t+2}}{(1+r)^2} \qquad (10.5)$$

Now p_{t+2} can be eliminated, then p_{t+3}, and so on. Thus, from (10.5), the price today can be written as the familiar NPV form:

$$p_t = \frac{d_{t+1}}{(1+r)} + \frac{d_{t+2}}{(1+r)^2} + \frac{d_{t+3}}{(1+r)^3} + \cdots + \frac{d_{t+N} + p_{t+N}}{(1+r)^N} \qquad (10.6)$$

---

[1] For the purposes of the theory discussed here the length of the unit interval is unspecified. It could be, for example, a day, week, month or year. Of course, in empirical applications the choice of a unit interval is likely to be a vital consideration.

The right-hand side of (10.6) is the sum of each dividend d_{t+i} discounted back to the present by multiplication with a *discount factor*, $1/(1+r)^i$. Typically, the last period, $t+N$, denotes the end of the asset's life of N periods, so that p_{t+N} would be a specified value, possibly zero – such as the scrap value for a physical asset or the maturity value if the asset is a bond. Perhaps the asset has no determinate life (as for a company's ordinary shares), so that p_{t+N} could be eliminated by repeated substitution for ever larger N. This important special case is explored shortly.

Recall the underlying justification for expression (10.6): the absence of arbitrage opportunities. If (10.6) does not hold, it would be possible for investors to make unbounded (arbitrage) profits by borrowing at the risk-free rate and buying the asset (if the asset's price is less than the discounted present value of its future returns), or by short-selling the asset and lending the proceeds at the risk-free rate (if the asset's price exceeds the discounted present value of its future returns).[2] Sometimes the NPV relationship is presented as a *definition* of the value of an asset or as a definition of its 'internal rate of return' (i.e. the rate, r, that results in the equality (10.6)). This is not the sense used here; (10.6) is an *equilibrium condition*, not a definition (of the value of an asset, its internal rate of return, or anything else).

It is convenient to write the NPV formula in a slightly different way to aid generalization. The modification involves defining δ_{t+i} to be the discount factor between date t and $t+i$. Thus, in (10.6), $\delta_{t+i} = 1/(1+r)^i$. This done, it is possible to generalize the NPV to allow for a risk-free rate of return that varies from date to date in a known way (note that the assumption of certainty is not yet relaxed). Let r_{t+1} denote the risk-free rate of return between dates t and $t+1$. Then the same reasoning that led from equation (10.3) to (10.6) shows that

$$\delta_{t+i} = \frac{1}{(1+r_{t+1})(1+r_{t+2})\cdots(1+r_{t+i})} \qquad i \geq 1$$

with the NPV condition written as

$$p_t = \delta_{t+1}d_{t+1} + \delta_{t+2}d_{t+2} + \delta_{t+3}d_{t+3} + \cdots + \delta_{t+N}d_{t+N} + \delta_{t+N}p_{t+N}$$

$$= \sum_{i=1}^{N} \delta_{t+i}d_{t+i} + \delta_{t+N}p_{t+N} \qquad (10.7)$$

where (10.7) introduces more compact notation.

---

[2] Clearly, (10.6) holds only if asset markets are frictionless in the sense used in chapters 1 and 7.

While this form of the NPV condition has many applications, it is important also to study indefinitely lived assets – i.e. to examine what happens when $N \to \infty$. It is tempting to replace (10.7) with

$$p_t = \delta_{t+1} d_{t+1} + \delta_{t+2} d_{t+2} + \cdots + \delta_{t+i} d_{t+i} + \cdots$$

$$= \sum_{i=1}^{\infty} \delta_{t+i} d_{t+i} \tag{10.8}$$

that is, the NPV of an infinitely long sequence of dividends is just the sum of the sequence of discounted dividends. Caution should be exercised, however, before too hasty acceptance of the formula.

Firstly, infinite series do not necessarily converge. A natural requirement to impose is that $\delta_{t+N} d_{t+N}$ becomes arbitrarily small as N becomes large – formally, $\lim_{N \to \infty} \delta_{t+N} d_{t+N} = 0$. While necessary for convergence, this condition is not sufficient. Rather than attempt to write down a general condition to ensure that (10.8) is well defined, it is assumed here that the sum converges to a finite value; individual cases will be checked for convergence where necessary.

Secondly, notice that the term $\delta_{t+N} p_{t+N}$ is neglected as $N \to \infty$ (it is assumed to converge to zero). While this neglect does not mean that (10.8) is wrong, it does hint that the equilibrium p_t may not be unique. That there is, indeed, a multiplicity of solutions follows by noting that the NPV relationship is nothing more nor less than a solution of the difference equation (10.3), allowing $N \to \infty$. When the life of the asset is finite – so that p_{t+N} is exogenously determined – its value ensures a unique solution. Otherwise, allowing an unbounded life for the asset, the solution to equation (10.3) is not unique, unless some other condition is imposed. Equation (10.8) provides one solution, but there exists an infinity of others. The sense in which the solution expressed as (10.8) should be the focus of attention, to the exclusion of all other solutions, is discussed in section 10.4. Until that point, solutions other than (10.8) are ignored.

A special case of infinitely lived assets is that for which (a) the interest rate is constant $r_{t+i} = r$, so that $\delta_{t+i} = 1/(1+r)^i$, and (b) the dividend, d_t, grows at a constant rate, g (possibly zero), so that $d_{t+1} = (1+g)d_t, d_{t+2} = (1+g)^2 d_t, \ldots$ Given these assumptions, appendix 10.2 shows that

$$p_t = \frac{d_{t+1}}{(r-g)} \qquad \text{if } r > g \tag{10.9}$$

If $r \leqq g$, the NPV is undefined: here the growth rate of dividends is so high that, even when discounted, the contribution of each return far into the future becomes unbounded. Therefore, their sum is also unbounded and thus undefined.

Special though it is, models deriving from (10.9) play a very important role in applied finance. These 'dividend growth models' seek to forecast equity prices on the basis of assumptions about the future growth of dividends for given current dividends and interest rates.

An even more special case of (10.9) occurs when $d_{t+i} = c$, a constant for every $t + i$ so that $g = 0$ and $p_t = c/r$. This is the NPV relationship for a *perpetuity*, such as a bond each unit of which pays a coupon c per period indefinitely into the future. (See chapter 12, especially page 284.)

10.1.2 Uncertainty

If uncertainty replaces the assumption of deterministic future returns, it is tempting to insert the *expected value* of each return in the NPV relationship:

$$p_t = \delta_{t+1} E_t d_{t+1} + \delta_{t+2} E_t d_{t+2} + \cdots + \delta_{t+i} E_t d_{t+i} + \cdots$$

$$= \sum_{i=1}^{\infty} \delta_{t+i} E_t d_{t+i} \tag{10.10}$$

where $E_t d_{t+i}$ denotes the expectation, conditional on information available today, date t, of the return to be received i periods in the future.[3] Expressions such as (10.10) are often encountered in finance, one example being the dividend growth models of share prices.

The problem is: what sense can be made of the expectations in $p_t = \sum \delta_{t+i} E_t d_{t+i}$? Trivially, their presence must imply that the returns, $d_{t+1}, d_{t+2}, \ldots, d_{t+i}, \ldots$, are generated by a random process. In financial theory, random processes together with their expectations usually express investors' beliefs – beliefs that are subjective and, thus, that generally differ among individual investors. The expectations in (10.10) are not indexed by individual and, hence, there is an implicit assumption that investors are unanimous in their beliefs. Typically in the literature on this topic it is assumed, implicitly or explicitly, that there is some exogenous 'true' process generating the returns and that the process is known to all investors. Even if the plausibility of this is accepted, a behavioural mechanism is required to justify *why* the NPV should take the form given by $p_t = \sum \delta_{t+i} E_t d_{t+i}$.

In the simplest case of deterministic returns, the absence of arbitrage opportunities implies the NPV relationship. Analogous reasoning can be used in the presence of uncertainty, and the result is an equality very similar in appearance to (10.10). (See appendix 10.3 for the details.) The appearance is somewhat

---

[3] The expression $E_t d_{t+i}$ can be read as shorthand for $E[d_{t+i}|\Omega_t]$, where Ω_t represents the set of information available at date t. Uncertainty about the discount factors, δ_{t+i}, is ignored in (10.10) – a common, if not entirely satisfactory, practice. Nothing of substance is lost, or gained, by focusing on infinitely lived assets as in (10.10) from now on.

deceptive, however. For appeal to the arbitrage principle implies that the probabilities underlying the expectations in the NPV relationship are the artificial
'martingale probabilities' that emerge as part of the derivation itself; they do not
necessarily correspond to any investor's beliefs. Moreover, the martingale probabilities are unique only under very special circumstances, namely when markets
are complete (in the sense defined in chapter 4, section 4.1.1).

Another way of justifying $p_t = \sum \delta_{t+i} \mathrm{E}_t d_{t+i}$, (10.10), is to assume that investors
are *risk-neutral* as well as being unanimous in their beliefs about the probabilities
underlying the expectations. In these circumstances, market equilibrium requires
that every asset yields a rate of return equal to the risk-free rate; otherwise,
investors would seek to buy those assets with an expected rate of return in excess
of the risk-free rate and sell those with an expected return less than the risk-free
rate. It follows that an NPV relationship of the form (10.10) must hold for each
asset.

Once the assumption of risk neutrality is relaxed in favour of risk aversion,
equation (10.10) is no longer appropriate to characterize market equilibrium.
When the assumption of risk neutrality is abandoned, allowance needs to be made
for a risk premium; otherwise, some other replacement for the NPV condition
must be found. This was done in a single-period context for the CAPM and APT
by amending the discount factor to include an additional term, the risk premium
(see chapters 6 and 8). In the multiperiod context a theory of intertemporal
optimization can be applied to construct an asset pricing formula in the presence
of risk aversion. This topic is studied in chapter 11.

Why should it matter to construct theoretical justification for $p_t = \sum \delta_{t+i} \mathrm{E}_t d_{t+i}$?
Because the justification aids the interpretation of empirical evidence about asset
price fluctuations. From one perspective, the NPV relationship is studied as a
normative guide, prescribing how asset prices should be determined if investors
behave according to criteria that are considered to be 'rational'. From another
(positive) perspective, no special significance is bestowed on the NPV relationship; it is treated as just another hypothesis that may, or may not, find support
in the evidence. If, as the next section shows, much of the evidence casts doubt
on the reliability of NPV equalities such as $p_t = \sum \delta_{t+i} \mathrm{E}_t d_{t+i}$, there is plenty of
scope for either criticizing the performance of asset markets or constructing better
models of asset prices – or both.

10.2 Asset price volatility

Empirical tests of the NPV relationship take a variety of forms. One approach,
which became popular in the 1980s, focuses on the volatility (observed variability) in asset prices. A claim, commonly heard among critics of financial

markets, is that asset prices are 'too volatile'. The tests described below provide a systematic way to examine this claim, given the assumption that a particular form of the NPV relationship is appropriate as a benchmark against which to judge volatility.

In this section the discount factors applied to future returns are assumed to be based on a constant interest rate, r. Hence, the NPV relationship, $p_t = \sum \delta_{t+i} E_t d_{t+i}$, becomes

$$p_t = \frac{E_t d_{t+1}}{(1+r)} + \frac{E_t d_{t+2}}{(1+r)^2} + \frac{E_t d_{t+3}}{(1+r)^3} + \cdots = \sum_{i=1}^{\infty} \frac{E_t d_{t+i}}{(1+r)^i}$$

This representation of the NPV relationship is interpreted in what follows as the net present value of a dividend stream, $d_{t+1}, d_{t+2}, \ldots$, paid on a company's ordinary shares.

A pioneering analysis of asset price volatility was made by Robert Shiller. It is his approach that is described here.[4] Shiller defines the *ex post rational* asset price p_t^* at date t as

$$p_t^* = \frac{d_{t+1}}{(1+r)} + \frac{d_{t+2}}{(1+r)^2} + \frac{d_{t+3}}{(1+r)^3} + \cdots = \sum_{i=1}^{\infty} \frac{d_{t+i}}{(1+r)^i} \qquad (10.11)$$

The *ex post* rational price can be understood as an idealization, a sort of equilibrium: it is the price predicted by the NPV relationship if investors have *perfect foresight* about future dividends – that is, if their expectations about future dividends are fulfilled. Note for later reference that the *ex post* rational price at date t can also be written in the form (recall equation (10.2) above)

$$p_t^* = \frac{1}{1+r}(d_{t+1} + p_{t+1}^*) \qquad (10.12)$$

Being dependent on the stream $d_{t+1}, d_{t+2}, d_{t+3}, \ldots$, unobserved as of date t, the *ex post* rational price is also unobserved at date t. The relationship between p_t^* and the observed market price, p_t, is obtained by writing

$$d_{t+i} = E_t d_{t+i} + \varepsilon_{t+i} \qquad (10.13)$$

where $E_t d_{t+i} \equiv E[d_{t+i}|\Omega_t]$ is the expectation of d_{t+i} conditional upon information available at date t, Ω_t, and ε_{t+i} is an unobserved forecast error such that

---

[4] For a collection of his papers, see Shiller (1989). Another early contribution, made independently of Shiller's, is that of LeRoy and Porter (1981).

$E[\varepsilon_{t+i}|\Omega_t] = 0.$[5] Substituting from (10.13) into (10.11), the *ex post* rational price can be broken into two components:

$$p_t^* = \frac{E_t d_{t+1} + \varepsilon_{t+1}}{(1+r)} + \frac{E_t d_{t+2} + \varepsilon_{t+2}}{(1+r)^2} + \frac{E_t d_{t+3} + \varepsilon_{t+3}}{(1+r)^3} + \cdots$$

$$= \frac{E_t d_{t+1}}{(1+r)} + \frac{E_t d_{t+2}}{(1+r)^2} + \frac{E_t d_{t+3}}{(1+r)^3} + \cdots \qquad (10.14)$$

$$+ \frac{\varepsilon_{t+1}}{(1+r)} + \frac{\varepsilon_{t+2}}{(1+r)^2} + \frac{\varepsilon_{t+3}}{(1+r)^3} + \cdots$$

Define u_t as the NPV of forecast errors:

$$u_t = \frac{\varepsilon_{t+1}}{(1+r)} + \frac{\varepsilon_{t+2}}{(1+r)^2} + \frac{\varepsilon_{t+3}}{(1+r)^3} + \cdots$$

thus enabling (10.14) to be written compactly as

$$p_t^* = p_t + u_t \qquad (10.15)$$

In words: the *ex post* rational price equals the observed market price plus a forecast error. The market price can be interpreted as the 'market's forecast' of the *ex post* rational price; in this model, p_t plays the role of a forecast of p_t^*.

The forecast error, u_t, is a weighted average of all the future forecast errors of asset returns. It follows from the assumption on ε_{t+i} that $E[u_t|\Omega_t] = 0$ and $E[u_t] = 0$. Hence, $E[p_t^*|\Omega_t] = p_t$. Also, $E[u_t|p_t] = 0$, because $p_t \in \Omega_t$. Consequently, $\text{cov}(p_t, u_t) = 0$: observed asset prices are uncorrelated with the forecast errors. This result is sometimes known as an *orthogonality* condition.

In order to render (10.15) testable, it is necessary to construct a measure of p_t^* and, hence, u_t. The measurement of p_t^* will be discussed shortly but suppose, provisionally, that an estimate has been obtained. Given the estimate of p_t^* (and conditional upon its accuracy), one approach to testing the hypothesis expressed by (10.15) is to examine whether the estimated forecast errors, u_t, are correlated with any members of the information set Ω_t. The hypothesis asserts that all such information is reflected in p_t and, this being so, the correlations should be zero: hence the title of *orthogonality tests* given to this approach. (See chapter 3, section 3.1.)

An alternative, *variance bounds*, approach follows by writing down the variance for p_t^* in (10.15):

$$\text{var}(p_t^*) = \text{var}(p_t) + \text{var}(u_t) + 2\text{cov}(p_t, u_t)$$

$$= \text{var}(p_t) + \text{var}(u_t) \qquad (10.16)$$

---

[5] The information set, Ω_t, is assumed to include p_t, $p_t \in \Omega_t$, but could encompass much else besides. Here the scope of Ω_t remains unspecified, subject to the caveat that only information available at date t is eligible for inclusion.

where (10.16) follows directly from the orthogonality condition, $\mathrm{cov}(p_t, u_t) = 0$. Given that $\mathrm{var}(u_t) > 0$, (10.16) implies immediately that var $(p_t) < \mathrm{var}(p_t^*)$, or, equivalently, that the standard deviation of observed price is less than the standard deviation of the *ex post* rational price: $\mathrm{s.d.}(p_t) < \mathrm{s.d.}(p_t^*)$. This inequality asserts formally that the variability (volatility) of a forecast, p_t, must be less than that of its target, p_t^*, so long as the error, u_t, is uncorrelated with the forecast itself. An upper bound, $\mathrm{s.d.}(p_t^*)$, is placed on the volatility of observed market prices, thus providing a precise statement of what is meant by claims of the sort that asset prices are 'too volatile'. Asset prices are regarded as too volatile if the variability of p_t equals or exceeds that of p_t^*: $\mathrm{s.d.}(p_t) \geq \mathrm{s.d.}(p_t^*)$. But notice that this inference is conditional upon the benchmark rule used to define p_t^*, and also on the method used to estimate it.

In several empirical studies Shiller applies expression (10.12) to construct estimates of *ex post* rational prices (see, for example, Shiller, 1989, chap. 4). A terminal year is chosen – say, 2003 – for which a value of p_{2003}^* is assumed.[6] By working backwards through earlier years, successively adding the discounted values of observed dividends, it is possible to estimate *ex post* rational prices:

$$p_{2002}^* = \frac{1}{(1+r)}(d_{2003} + p_{2003}^*)$$

$$p_{2001}^* = \frac{1}{(1+r)}(d_{2002} + p_{2002}^*) \qquad (10.17)$$

$$p_{2000}^* = \frac{1}{(1+r)}(d_{2001} + p_{2001}^*)$$

$$\vdots \quad \vdots$$

As his source for price and dividend observations, Shiller (2003) uses data from 1871 for Standard and Poor's Composite Index of US stock prices measured in real terms (i.e. the observed price series divided by a price index for economy-wide prices of goods and services).

In order to estimate p_t^*, a value for r – the real interest rate at which the dividends are discounted – must also be assumed. One candidate measure for r is an average of observed real rates of return on the index for the sample period. Another candidate is to allow r to vary from year to year with market interest rates, rather than being constant, as assumed in (10.17).[7]

---

[6] Shiller (2003) obtains p_{2003}^* as the net present value of dividends projected forward at a constant growth rate from 2002, discounted at a constant real interest rate. The rates chosen were the historical averages over Shiller's sample, 1871 to 2003.

[7] Shiller (2003) uses a geometric average equal to 6.67 per cent for the first candidate. For the second, he uses a market rate of interest (adjusted for inflation) plus a risk premium (measured by the average excess return on the index minus the average market interest rate). Shiller's calculations embody a small timing difference from the process defined here: he uses $p_t^* = d_t + p_{t+1}^*/(1+r)$ rather than $p_t^* = (d_{t+1} + p_{t+1}^*)/(1+r)$.

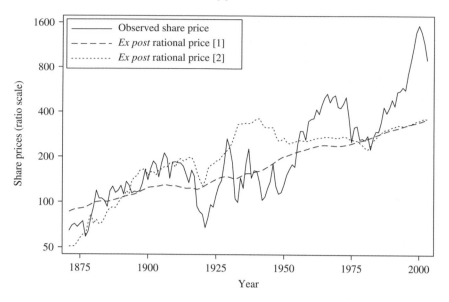

Fig. 10.1. Observed US stock prices, $\widetilde{p}_t$, and *ex post* rational prices, $\widetilde{p}_t^*$

The figure plots Standard and Poor's Composite Index of US stock prices, adjusted for inflation, p_t, together with ex post rational prices, p_t^*, estimated as net present values of future dividends discounted by [1] a constant real rate of return and [2] a time-varying observed real market interest rate. The observed price index shows more variation than either measure of the p_t^*, directly contrary to the hypothesis that p_t^* is an optimal forecast of p_t.

Source: Shiller (2003). The data are available from Shiller's Yale Website: www.econ.yale.edu/~shiller.

Figure 10.1 plots the results of Shiller's calculations. Notice that the *ex post* rational price based on a constant real interest rate (line [1]) shows little variation around a shallow trend. The *ex post* rational price based on market interest rates shows rather more variation, but still much less than for observed prices.

Contrary to being more variable than observed prices, the *ex post* rational price series are both much *less* variable: stock prices are *too volatile*. The sample standard deviation of p_t is approximately 264.23, in comparison with 76.46 and 88.93, respectively, for the two measures of p_t^*. In both cases, the model's prediction is rejected by a wide margin.[8]

---

[8] Caution should be exercised in applying standard statistical criteria when comparing the standard deviations. The strong evidence of a time trend (non-stationarity) in each of the price series implies that the conventional statistical tests procedures are inappropriate. See, for example, Hayashi (2000, chaps. 9 & 10).

How sensitive is this conclusion to (a) the rule for calculating p_t^*, (b) the sample period and (c) the data set? While almost any outcome could be obtained by manipulating the rule for estimating p_t^*, alternatives constructed in the spirit of equation (10.11) tend to contradict the prediction. The result has also been robust to the choice of sample period and data set. Although it would be rash to draw definitive conclusions in this sort of work, it is an understatement to suggest that the evidence raises serious doubts about the empirical plausibility of the NPV model underlying p_t^*.

Shiller draws a strong conclusion from the evidence: *stock prices are too volatile for compatibility with asset market efficiency.*[9] Not surprisingly, such a startling claim has been the subject of detailed scrutiny and criticism. The criticisms fall into three groups: (a) *technical*, involving the statistical procedures employed; (b) *substantive*, challenging the rule for calculating p_t^*; and (c) *interpretational* – i.e. what the results imply for the determination of asset prices.

The *technical* criticisms centre on whether the unobserved 'true' (or 'population') standard deviations are accurately estimated by their observed sample counterparts. Particular attention has been devoted to three issues.

1. The two price series, p_t and p_t^*, should be stationary (that is, essentially trend-free) in order for conventional statistical criteria to apply. Without transformation of some sort, the evidence implies unambiguously that the data are *non*-stationary.
2. Successive values of p_t^* are not independent of one another (they are serially correlated), and this needs to be taken into account.
3. The sample size may be too small to draw valid inferences. Attention here centres on the presence of the price observed at the end of the sample in the calculation of p_t^*. (See equation (10.17), where the terminal price in question is p_{2003}^*.) Although the discounted value of the terminal price in the formula becomes negligible in a sufficiently large sample, its inclusion could have an impact on the inferences made from a finite sample of data.

These and other statistical matters have been the subject of intensive research, but without implications that decisively overturn the results described so far.

The second, *substantive*, group of criticisms focuses on the definition of the *ex post* rational price, p_t^*, itself. Perhaps the most important issue here is the choice of the most appropriate rate, or rates, at which to discount the future dividend stream: the more variable the discount rate, the more variable the

---

[9] Shiller (2000, pp. 185–6) justifies the conclusion as follows. 'If the dividend present value moved up and down massively over time, and if the actual stock price appeared to move with these movements as if it were successfully forecasting the changes in the dividend present value, then we could say that there was evidence that stock prices were behaving in accordance with the tenets of efficient markets theory. But we see no such tendency of the stock price to forecast the dividend present value: the dividend present value is not doing anything especially dramatic, whereas the price is jumping around a great deal.'

estimate of p_t^*. Shiller argues strongly, however, that allowing for reasonable variability in the discount factor will not upset the result. (See the entry on 'volatility' in *The New Palgrave Dictionary of Money and Finance* (Newman, Milgate and Eatwell, 1992, Vol. III, pp. 762–6).)

More fundamentally, doubts can be expressed about the appropriateness of the NPV relationship in the presence of uncertainty about future dividends. The justification of the NPV formula in such circumstances rests on assumptions (e.g. risk neutrality and the unanimity of beliefs) the appropriateness of which are, to say the least, debatable. Hence, it can be argued that modification or replacement of the NPV relationship is required in order to be compatible with plausible assumptions about the behaviour of investors. Various alternatives have been proposed. One such approach – originating in behavioural finance – is outlined in the next section; another – derived from intertemporal optimization – is explored in chapter 11.

The third group of criticisms, those of *interpretation*, challenges the economic significance of the statistical results even if they are accepted at face value. As already indicated, the model underpinning the construction of the *ex post* rational price relies on stringent assumptions. If the assumptions are intended to express normative criteria for asset market efficiency (with its implicit notion of individual rationality), the conditions may be unduly restrictive. Less restrictive assumptions about investor behaviour – involving, for instance, risk aversion and intertemporal consumption planning – need hardly be regarded as irrational but could lead to different predictions.[10] In summary: even if Shiller's specification accords well with the notion of asset market efficiency, rejection of the hypothesis may provide few insights about how well asset markets function.

Alternatively, suppose that the *normative* aspects of the model are disregarded. The tests are then interpreted, instead, in a *positive* way. That is, they provide evidence about how closely a fairly simple, but widely accepted, benchmark model fits the data. Viewed in this way, it is clear that observed asset prices display excess volatility in comparison with the predictions of the model described above – in other words, the model underpredicts *observed* volatility.

A popular class of alternative explanations seeks to explain how expectations are formed about the stream of future asset returns, $d_{t+1}, d_{t+2}, \ldots$ Notice how the motivation changes from studying the pattern of prices that *should* evolve in conformity with certain criteria (normative) to exploring which models can best explain *observed* prices (positive). Many of the tests find that some excess volatility remains, though now the conclusion is weaker: the evidence undermines support for the model as an explanation of observed asset prices. The tests are

---

[10] Caution is in order here, because the results reported in chapter 11 for a more general intertemporal planning framework raise similar concerns about the empirical viability of the models.

relevant for asset market efficiency only to the extent that the model is allowed to prescribe the criteria for efficiency.

10.3 Behavioural finance, noise trading and models of dividend growth

The quest for ways to account for asset price volatility has pursued a variety of routes, most of which now shelter under the umbrella of behavioural finance. A representative example, mentioned in chapter 1, is the *noise trading* model.

The noise trading framework distinguishes between two groups of investors: *rational investors* (sometimes called *smart-money traders*) and *noise traders*. Rational investors are assumed to make decisions according to 'fundamental information' (presumably, the stream of asset returns). Noise traders, by contrast, act according to whim, fad or fancy, their decisions being made without due regard for commonly accepted investment criteria.[11]

A consequence is that asset prices tend to reflect the capricious actions of noise traders. Expectations of share price increases (or decreases), whether well founded or not, become self-fulfilling. It is as if a positive feedback mechanism governs asset prices: price rises stimulate further increases, and conversely. Although rational investors are still present in the market, their actions may be swamped by those of noise traders.

Although attractive at first sight, the distinction between noise traders and rational investors should be treated with caution. For, to the extent that the actions of noise traders affect asset prices, rational investors would be sensible to take these actions into account when making their own decisions. Even if it is feasible to partition information into 'fundamental' and 'non-fundamental', rational investors would not ignore the supposedly irrational activities of noise traders deriving from non-fundamental information. Thus, rational investors might not appear so rational after all. However, despite this reservation, the noise trader approach does succeed in accounting for the impact of investors' beliefs and actions that appear from some external, objective standpoint to be misguided or, at least, neglectful of relevant information.

Barsky and De Long (1993) present an explicit model that captures the role of noise traders.[12] Their model can be expressed in the simple form

$$p_t = \frac{d_t}{(r - g_t)} \tag{10.18}$$

---

[11] Sometimes noise traders are assumed to include investors who trade for *liquidity purposes* (for instance, when assets are sold to provide cash for consumption or when assets are purchased as a consequence of income in excess of consumption). The liquidity motive is, of course, not necessarily to be construed as irrational.

[12] Another important contribution following a similar approach is that of Campbell and Shiller (1989), which focuses on expectations about the ratio of dividends to prices.

where g_t is what Barsky and De Long call the 'permanent' growth rate in dividends as of date t – essentially, the average dividend growth rate expected from date t onwards. Notice the close resemblance between (10.18), $p_t = d_t/(r - g_t)$, and (10.9), $p_t = d_{t+1}/(r - g)$. Apart from a minor technical difference concerning the timing of dividends, the two are identical if there is a fixed dividend growth rate into the infinite future. Although g_t is constant as of date t (i.e. the same for all future time), it is not fixed; investors revise their estimates of dividend growth at each date (presumably as a consequence of the arrival of new information).

Barsky and De Long postulate that d_t and g_t are positively correlated: when dividends change, investors extrapolate the change into the future so that the dividend growth rate changes in the same direction. Thus, an increase in the dividend, d_t, has a direct effect – via the numerator of $p_t = d_t/(r - g_t)$ – and an indirect effect – via the growth rate, g_t – on the asset price, p_t.

Given that g_t responds positively to d_t, the share price increases more than proportionately with the increase in dividend. Hence, the model accounts for the commonly reported responsiveness (*overreaction*) of the share price to dividends.

Barsky and De Long present evidence that supports their model when applied to US data. They interpret the evidence as conforming with a rational expectations approach: investors are assumed to act as if information about the past growth of dividends is used to construct forecasts for the future. The forecasts are not '*ex post* rational' in the sense of the previous section, but neither are they irrational expressions of fads or fancies.

Closely allied with noise trading is the notion of 'style investing' (Barberis and Shleifer, 2003). Here, a substantial proportion of investors are supposed to favour particular 'styles' – groups of companies – for reasons that have little to do with the prospects of the companies paying dividends in the future. An example of a style might be the 'dot.coms' in the late twentieth century.

When a style is in fashion, the market values of its companies tend to increase by amounts that appear excessively optimistic. This is despite the presence of investors who base their decisions on plausible forecasts of future profits. But fashions come and go, so that, over the longer term, average returns tend to be mean-reverting: companies that are in style at one time eventually become inordinately 'out of style' – i.e. unfashionable.

A substantial body of evidence suggests that the mechanisms driving aggregate market indexes (e.g. the S&P 500) are different from those for individual companies' shares. The prices of individual shares tend to fluctuate in ways more compatible with the NPV relationship than do market indexes.[13]

---

[13] This difference has come to be known as 'Samuelson's dictum' of 'micro efficiency and macro inefficiency' (see Samuelson, 1998). Recent evidence is reported by Vuolteenaho (2002) and Jung and Shiller (2002).

For both individual shares and market indexes, price fluctuations may be unpredictable over short periods – but for different reasons. The evidence tends to be consistent with companies' profitability, prospects, etc., dominating fluctuations in individual share prices, with aggregate indexes being more susceptible to the inexplicable vicissitudes of investor sentiment. Shiller sums up forcefully (1989, p. 8).

Returns on speculative assets are nearly unforecastable; this fact is the basis of the most important argument in the oral tradition against a role for mass psychology in speculative markets. One form of this argument claims that because real returns are nearly unforecastable, the real price of stocks is close to the intrinsic value, that is, the present value with constant discount rate optimally forecasted future real dividends. This argument for the efficient markets hypothesis represents one of the most remarkable errors in the history of economic thought.

While this view is widely held, not all would agree with Shiller's claim that 'mass psychology may well be the dominant cause of movements in the aggregate stock market' (1989, p. 8). The next section reviews the role of mass psychology as a cause of extreme asset price fluctuations.

10.4 Extreme asset price fluctuations

Asset price volatility sometimes takes the form of spectacular increases in prices followed by equally spectacular collapses. Many such historical episodes have been documented, each with its own unique characteristics, some more extraordinary than others. Typically they include: (a) a period of manic optimism or frenzy (in which the majority of investors convince themselves that increasing asset prices really are justified by 'fundamentals'); (b) a crisis of confidence (at the juncture of price increases and declines); (c) blatant fraud (which may instigate the crisis of confidence, or which is blamed, *ex post*, for the crisis); and (d) intense pessimism accompanied by economic distress (during which the majority opinion is that low prices are justified by 'fundamentals' – and, by implication, that the earlier optimism was misplaced).

From at least the seventeenth century these phenomena have commonly been called 'bubbles', though in the modern literature the word is used in a very specific sense, discussed further below. Closely related phenomena emerge from 'Ponzi schemes', also considered separately below. Yet other incidents are associated with speculative manias or wild bouts of optimism and pessimism in a single market, or a closely aligned set of markets. Rather than attempting to construct a taxonomy of all these events, there follows an overview of some of the most notorious historical examples.

10.4.1 Some examples from history

Tulipmania, 1636–7

One of the first recorded speculative manias is that for tulip flower bulbs in the Netherlands in the 1630s. Although data are sparse by modern standards, it appears that there was a rapid rise in bulb prices from late 1636 and then a steep decline after February 1637. The magnitude of the rise and subsequent decline remains controversial, because several varieties of tulip bulbs were traded. For the commonest varieties of bulbs, the early months of 1637 saw both a frenzied rise and an equally precipitate decline of prices. The prices of more unusual, exotic varieties increased somewhat less rapidly over several months and then declined, again somewhat less rapidly and over a longer period of time.

To the extent that the evidence can be relied upon, it seems that prices for the more exotic bulbs may have responded to a genuine shortage of supply relative to the demand from those who sought to grow the flowers. The price fluctuations for common varieties were probably stimulated more by speculative motives – that is, the desire to profit from subsequent price changes.[14]

The Mississippi and South Sea Bubbles, 1719–20

Two distinct but closely related sequences of extreme price fluctuations in the years up to 1720 provide early examples of speculative booms and busts in the market for shares in joint-stock companies. Both involve public share offerings by companies (the Mississippi Company in Paris and the South Sea Company in London), and both involve companies that procured monopoly privileges (from the French and British governments, respectively) in return for taking the responsibility to service government debts.

The Mississippi bubble preceded that in London and was the culmination of a number of financial experiments promoted by John Law, a famous – or infamous – Scotsman who was a prominent financier in France until he fell into disgrace shortly after the bubble burst. John Law established or acquired several companies, of which the Mississippi Company was one. Subsequently they merged into a conglomerate, the Compagnie des Indes. Much of the stock of these companies was issued in exchange for government debt (the obligations on which were then renegotiated with the government). Also, the companies initiated various commercial and financial ventures. The prospects for quick, high profits made the shares popular, the rising prices reflecting their popularity at the same time as embodying the potential gains that made them so attractive in the first place. Early in 1720 this self-fulfilling spiral ended suddenly, when some shareholders sought to realize their gains. The collapse in prices was rapid

---

[14] See Garber (1990) for a modern analysis that also discusses the role of futures markets in the tulipmania.

and sustained despite Law's claims that the ventures would lead ultimately to a stream of future returns.

The sequence of events in London mirrored that in Paris. The South Sea Company acquired responsibility for significant amounts of government debt on terms that were perceived to be highly favourable for the company's shareholders. An approximately sevenfold increase in the company's share price occurred during the six months prior to its peak in mid-1720, after which the price fell at an accelerating rate to leave it, in October, roughly where it had started the year. Precisely why the price increase was so rapid and why it peaked when it did are matters of debate. That the episode took place at all is testimony to the capacity of financial markets to undergo manic bouts of optimism and pessimism accompanied by enormous short-term gains and losses.

The Wall Street Crash, 1929

In the week following 23 October 1929 the main share price indexes in New York fell by nearly 30 per cent. While dramatic enough in itself, even more noteworthy is the fact that the crash marked the beginning of a prolonged decline in prices (of practically all goods and services, not just assets) that lasted for several years. Accompanying the price declines were widespread bank failures in the United States and the onset of the Great Depression, a slump that persisted throughout the 1930s in much of the developed world.

The causes and consequences of the Wall Street Crash remain the subject of lively debate among economic historians. The controversy is largely about what linked the crash with the subsequent depression, but there is also a debate about whether the crash was in any sense 'justified' in response to the price increases that preceded it. Some commentators interpret the crash as a natural outcome of a speculative mania in 1928 and early 1929. Others claim that share prices were not 'too high', and were forced down by the monetary authorities and the US government as a deliberate act of policy. Whether or not prices were 'too high' and the crash 'justified' depends, of course, on an underlying model of share price determination. While some models are undoubtedly more plausible than others, the available evidence does not favour any one cause of the crash to the exclusion of others. Almost certainly it never will.

The stock market crash, 1987

The most startling feature of the 1987 crash was the fall in share prices of over 20 per cent in New York on a single day, Monday 19 October. Repercussions were felt in all the major stock markets around the world, and prices had fallen by nearly a third towards the end of 1987. Thereafter share prices stabilized and began to rise, albeit unsteadily. Share prices had increased rapidly for about a year before the October crash, so that, with hindsight, the events of 1987 appear as a short-lived boom and bust.

From the early 1970s an expansion in the trading of financial derivatives (options and futures) had gathered momentum. By 1987 the increasing sophistication of these instruments and the prevalence of associated investment strategies (in particular 'programme trading') led some observers to blame the crash on their use. Other commentators disputed this, placing more emphasis on US trade and budget deficits, and on proposed tax legislation under consideration in the US Congress. Although the range of contending causes for the 1987 crash differs from that for 1929, again the evidence does not point unambiguously to any simple explanation of the timing and magnitude of the price fluctuations. What is notable is that, by contrast with 1929, the crash of 1987 is not associated with a subsequent recession. The financial system continued to function – there was no collapse.

The stock market bubble, 1999–2000

In the late 1990s the stock prices of companies promoting new information technologies – especially the *dot.com* Internet companies quoted on NASDAQ[15] – began their rapid ascent, even though many had never reported any profits. The prices of other shares, especially in New York, had begun their swift ascent several years earlier, in the mid-1990s, marking the onset of 'irrational exuberance'. (The oft-quoted phrase is attributed to Alan Greenspan, chairman of the US Federal Reserve Board, in a speech on 5 December 1996.)

Despite the misgivings of cautious but perceptive analysts (e.g. Shiller, 2000), asset prices continued to increase. Then, in March 2000, the prices of the Internet stocks fell precipitately. By mid-2001 the steep descent of share prices had become widespread, and it continued as the US economy slowed towards recession.

While stock markets recovered swiftly in the immediate aftermath of the terrorist attacks on 11 September 2001, '9/11', a more sustained collapse of share prices began in mid-2002. Labelled 'the Great Telecoms Crash' in *The Economist* (20 July 2002), the price falls were precipitated by the financial distress that had become apparent among telecommunications companies. Many of these companies had accumulated heavy burdens of debt during their boom years. Moreover, corporate scandals emerged from the discovery of widespread accounting practices that allowed the overstatement of profits. Bankruptcies followed (e.g. WorldCom, a large American telecoms firm), together with an atmosphere

---

[15] NASDAQ is an abbreviation for the National Association of Securities Dealers Automated Quotation system, in New York. NASDAQ was introduced in 1971 as a development in the operation of the over-the-counter securities market.

of distrust, especially following the collapse of Enron, the huge American energy trading corporation.

10.4.2 Bubbles

The concept of a financial bubble has been given a more formal interpretation in economic research than in the rather imprecise senses used so far. This interpretation stems from a recognition that the NPV relationship, $p_t = \sum_{i=1}^{\infty} \delta_{t+i} d_{t+i}$ (10.8), is only one of the solutions to the condition linking prices across time, namely $p_t = (d_{t+1} + p_{t+1})/(1+r)$ (10.2).[16] To construct other solutions, suppose that $b_t, b_{t+1}, \ldots b_{t+i}, \ldots$ is any sequence of numbers satisfying $b_{t+1} = (1+r)b_t$. Now rewrite the NPV relationship as

$$p_t = \sum_{i=1}^{\infty} \delta_{t+i} d_{t+i} + b_t \qquad (10.19)$$

It can also be checked that (10.19) satisfies $p_t = (d_{t+1} + p_{t+1})/(1+r)$. Hence, because b_t is arbitrary, the NPV relationship is not unique.

Furthermore, it is possible to allow for uncertainty in the usual way, by replacing variables with their expectations, so that equation (10.10) becomes

$$p_t = \sum_{i=1}^{\infty} \delta_{t+i} E_t d_{t+i} + b_t \qquad (10.20)$$

The sequence $b_t, b_{t+1}, \ldots, b_{t+i}, \ldots$ is assumed to satisfy $E_t b_{t+1} = (1+r)b_t$, $E_t b_{t+2} = (1+r)^2 b_t, \ldots, E_t b_{t+i} = (1+r)^i b_t, \ldots$

In these extensions of the NPV relationship, the b_t term is called the 'bubble'. The discounted value of the dividend stream is called the 'fundamental' value of the asset. Viewed in this way, asset prices need not equal the NPV of future payoffs but can become any one of an infinite number of values according to the size of the bubble. The 'bubble' term captures all the speculative and self-fulfilling aspects of potentially wild asset price changes. If, as in most circumstances, asset prices are non-negative ($p_t \geq 0$), then negative bubbles can be ruled out (otherwise, at some finite date, τ, $p_\tau < 0$). Apart from this restriction, any positive value for the bubble at any date is sufficient to instigate the explosive process.

The bubbles, as expressed by (10.19) or (10.20), never burst. The sequence of price changes goes on for ever. This implausible feature can be eliminated by assuming that at each date there is a non-zero probability, say π, that the bubble continues and a probability $1 - \pi$ that it bursts (all subsequent values of the bubble becoming zero, thereafter).

[16] It is assumed for simplicity, and without loss of generality, that the interest rate is constant.

Much research has been devoted to theoretical and empirical aspects of bubbles. In the theoretical vein the research tends to focus on the circumstances in which bubbles will not occur. That is, it seeks to answer the question: what assumptions are sufficient to ensure that all the b_{t+i} values are zero? The required assumptions typically involve investors who optimize over an infinite horizon with perfect foresight (or, at least, know the random process governing the bubble). But the conditions for ruling out bubbles are model-sensitive, without generally applicable conclusions. Given the evidence that bubbles, although dramatic when they occur, are isolated incidents, it is a weakness of the approach expressed by (10.19) or (10.20) that it leaves unanswered the question of when the bubble terms are likely to be non-zero.

Although, in a sense, the size of a bubble is arbitrary (it can start from any positive value), its trajectory, once initiated, is not. Empirical work thus concentrates on examining the evidence that time series of prices follow the predicted pattern. Because future dividend streams are unobserved, such exercises are fraught with difficulties. Careful studies of the data suggest that many phenomena that appear, on first inspection, to be bubbles can be explained by the 'fundamentals' term. This result can be interpreted in two ways: (a) that bubbles are rare; or, (b) that a more comprehensive theory of bubbles than is expressed by (10.20) is needed to explain the evidence.

10.4.3 Ponzi schemes

Ponzi schemes are named after one Charles Ponzi (of Boston, Massachusetts), who persuaded investors to participate in the exploitation of foreign exchange rate fluctuations during the unstable period following the First World War. Ponzi's venture ostensibly sought to earn arbitrage profits by trading in international postal coupons. Whatever the exact nature of Ponzi's motives and strategy, the scheme collapsed and Ponzi earned a prison sentence for his ingenuity.

The Oxford English Dictionary (vol. XII, p. 101) defines a Ponzi scheme as 'a form of fraud in which belief in the success of a fictive enterprise is fostered by payment of quick returns to first investors from money invested by others'. The crucial aspect of Ponzi schemes (also known as 'pyramid schemes' or 'chain letters') in economics is the way in which investors' gains accumulate from the subsequent contributions of later participants. The funds remitted by later investors are used to pay off those who invested earlier.

The investment may or may not pay a positive stream of dividends, but, if it does, the nature of Ponzi schemes require the dividends to be paid out of the flow of funds from new investors. Ponzi schemes are much like bubbles and can be analysed using expressions such as (10.20), the distinguishing feature being the continuous arrival of new investors prepared to participate in the schemes.

Pay-as-you-go pension plans organized by governments resemble Ponzi schemes. By taxing the younger, working generations, governments offer to pay an increasing flow of pensions to older, retired generations. Given (a) the confidence that governments will always have access to the requisite tax-raising powers, (b) the arrival (birth) of successive new generations and (c) a sufficiently strong rate of economic growth, then pay-as-you-go schemes could satisfy everyone concerned – for ever.

Non-government (private) Ponzi schemes have invariably – to date, at least – ended in collapse, typically in a blaze of recriminations accompanied by the disappearance, castigation or imprisonment of the scheme's promotor. All that is needed for a scheme to fail is a slow down (not even a *decline* is required) in the arrival rate of new funds. As soon as this happens, existing investors, failing to receive their promised returns, take fright, and try to liquidate their assets. By design and of necessity, there will be insufficient funds to meet the promised payoffs.

Despite the inherent fragility of Ponzi schemes, they are commonplace, especially in newly emerging financial systems. Witness the popularity of several such schemes following the retreat of communism in the Soviet Union and eastern Europe in the early 1990s. Examples include the Caritas scheme in Romania (1992/93), the MMM company in Russia (1995/96), several schemes in Albania (1996) and the 'Banyumas Mulia Abadi' company in Indonesia (1999). In most cases the promoters advertise their companies as investing in assets purporting yield a genuine stream of returns. The veracity, or otherwise, of their claims is revealed as soon the inflow of funds slows down. Even more blatant (in the sense of exploiting pure greed) are the Internet pyramid schemes inviting email subscribers to make a number of small payments in anticipation of massive returns.

10.5 Summary

1. The NPV relationship is pervasive in finance.

   (a) It expresses the current price of an asset as the discounted value of its stream of future returns, the discount factors being based on interest rates at which funds can be borrowed or lent.

   (b) If the stream of returns is deterministic (known with certainty), the NPV relationship can be obtained as a consequence of the absence of arbitrage opportunities.

(c) If the stream of returns is uncertain, the validity of the NPV is more fragile and relies on either: (a) expectations based on artificial martingale probabilities (implied by the absence of arbitrage opportunities); or (b) risk-neutral preferences of investors, together with unanimous beliefs about the occurrence of future states of the world.

2. A substantial body of empirical evidence suggests that asset prices are more volatile than predicted by the NPV relationship, when investors base their decisions on accurate forecasts of future dividends.

3. More successful attempts to model asset price volatility are founded on (a) the existence of 'noise traders' – investors who respond to fads and fashions; or (b) imperfect, though not necessarily irrational, forecasts of future dividends.

4. Extreme fluctuations in asset prices may be compatible with the NPV relationship, although the usefulness of the relationship in such circumstances (i.e. in studying 'bubbles') is debatable, because the necessary modifications to the relationship are difficult to construct.

Further reading

The NPV relationship is ubiquitous in finance texts, often being taken for granted. Its close relatives, the so-called 'dividend growth models' (or 'dividend discount models') of share prices, are also commonplace in the literature. See, for example, Sharpe, Alexander and Bailey (1999, chap. 18). LeRoy (1989) surveys the literature on asset price volatility, a subject treated thoroughly by Shiller in his collection of essays on *Market Volatility* (1989). Much of the more recent applied work is reviewed carefully by Campbell, Lo and MacKinlay (1997, chap. 7). The noise trader approach received early stimulus from Black (1986); an overview is provided by Shleifer and Summers (1990) and a detailed analysis by Shleifer (2000).

The literature on extreme asset price fluctuations is large and varied. Taking a historical viewpoint, Kindleberger's *Manias, Panics and Crashes* (1978) provides an entertaining and perceptive account. Less reliable, but equally entertaining, is McKay (1980). More seriously, Garber (1990) offers some important insights.[17] Several entries in *The New Palgrave Dictionary of Money and Finance* (Newman, Milgate and Eatwell, 1992) provide admirably concise surveys from an analytical perspective. Of particular interest are the entries on: asset price bubbles; crashes; Ponzi games; rational bubbles; the South Sea Bubble; speculation; the stock market crash of October 1929; and the stock market crash of October 1987. Shiller (2000) provides one of the most carefully researched accounts of the Wall Street boom of the late 1990s. Shiller (2002) and LeRoy (2004) explore the determinants of bubbles in modern financial markets.

---

[17] For a more detailed study, with the same conclusions, see Garber (2000).

Appendix 10.1: Present values in continuous time

If time is measured continuously rather than in discrete unit intervals, the substance of NPV relationships is the same even though appearances differ. The rate of return on an asset is now defined as the proportional rate of change in its value at each instant of time – that is, the ratio of its payoff to its market value, $v(t)/p(t)$. Given that the payoff is the sum of the asset's dividend and its capital gain or loss, the instantaneous rate of return, $\rho(t)$, at time t (sometimes called the *force of interest*) is given by

$$\rho(t) = \frac{d(t) + \dot{p}(t)}{p(t)} \qquad (10.21)$$

where $v(t) = d(t) + \dot{p}(t)$, and $\dot{p}(t)$ denotes the rate of change of the asset's price with respect to time – i.e. its time derivative. Equation (10.21) can be rearranged as a linear ordinary differential equation:

$$\dot{p}(t) = \rho(t)p(t) - d(t) \qquad (10.22)$$

For the mathematical background and method of solution for this sort of equation, see, for example, Sydsæter and Hammond (1995, chap. 21).

Suppose, provisionally, that $\rho(t) = \rho$ is constant across time. This could be so because the rate of interest is constant and, in the absence of arbitrage opportunities, equal to the rate of return on the asset. With $\rho(t)$ constant, the solution of (10.22) can be written

$$p(t) = \int_{t}^{T} e^{-\rho(\tau - t)} d(\tau)d\tau + \overline{p}\,e^{-\rho(T - t)} \qquad (10.23)$$

where $\overline{p}$ denotes the value of the asset at the end of its life, time T. The integral replaces the summation operator in discrete time and $e^{-\rho(\tau - t)}$ is the discount factor between today, t, and time τ. Note carefully the distinction between $d(\tau)$, the flow of dividends at time τ, and $d\tau$, the differential operator defined in conjunction with integration.

More generally, if $\rho(t)$ is allowed to vary across time, the solution, (10.23), is replaced with

$$p(t) = \int_{t}^{T} e^{-\int_{t}^{\tau} \rho(\varepsilon)d\varepsilon} d(\tau)d\tau + \overline{p}\,e^{-\int_{t}^{T} \rho(\varepsilon)d\varepsilon} \qquad (10.24)$$

where the discount factor, $e^{-\int_{t}^{\tau} \rho(\varepsilon)d\varepsilon}$, is analogous to the reciprocal of the product of the 'one plus the interest rate' terms that appear in the discrete time version of the NPV. Samuelson (1936–37) merits careful reading for details of this analysis.

If the asset is infinitely lived, $T \to \infty$, then (10.24) is typically replaced by the so-called 'improper' integral:

$$p(t) = \int_t^\infty e^{-\int_t^\tau \rho(\varepsilon)d\varepsilon} d(\tau)d\tau$$

or

$$p(t) = \int_t^\infty e^{-\rho(\tau - t)} d(\tau)d\tau \quad \text{if } \rho \text{ is constant} \tag{10.25}$$

In order for (10.25) to hold, notice that (a) the limit of the integral as $T \to \infty$ must be well defined (i.e. conditions must be placed on the convergence of the present value of the dividend stream), and (b) the solution for $p(t)$ is not unique unless some condition is imposed to rule out the presence of bubbles.

In a further generalization, much of modern financial analysis is conducted in continuous time, allowing for random dividends and interest rates. This advanced topic is not explored here.

Appendix 10.2: Infinitely lived assets: constant growth

If the dividend stream grows at a constant rate, g, the NPV relationship for an infinitely lived asset takes the form

$$
\begin{aligned}
p_t &= \frac{d_{t+1}}{(1+r)} + \frac{(1+g)d_{t+1}}{(1+r)^2} + \frac{(1+g)^2 d_{t+1}}{(1+r)^3} + \cdots \\[2mm]
&= \frac{d_{t+1}}{(1+r)}\left(1 + \left(\frac{1+g}{1+r}\right) + \left(\frac{1+g}{1+r}\right)^2 + \cdots\right) \\[2mm]
&= \frac{d_{t+1}}{(1+r)}\left(\frac{1}{1 - \dfrac{1+g}{1+r}}\right) \\[2mm]
&= \frac{d_{t+1}}{(r-g)} \quad \text{if } r > g
\end{aligned}
\tag{10.26}
$$

If $r \le g$, p_t is unbounded – i.e. formally undefined.

Appendix 10.3: The RNVR with multiple time periods

In chapter 7 it was shown that the absence of arbitrage opportunities is equivalent to the *risk-neutral valuation relationship*. Applying the notation of this chapter, the RNVR can be summarized as $p_t = E_t^*[v_{t+1}]/(1+r_{t+1})$, which repeats the relevant expression in chapter 7 with the addition of subscripts to denote the time dimension implicit in the earlier discussion. Recall that the * superscript appears as a reminder that the probabilities underlying the expectation emerge as a consequence of the absence of arbitrage opportunities (and need not correspond to any investor's beliefs). Substituting the definition of the payoff, $v_{t+1} = d_{t+1} + p_{t+1}$,

$$p_t = \frac{E_t^*[d_{t+1} + p_{t+1}]}{(1 + r_{t+1})} \tag{10.27}$$

Note that $E_t^*[\cdot]$ has a time subscript: the state probabilities depend on the date at which they are evaluated. Equation (10.27) holds for any date, $t + s$, in the future and hence can be written

$$p_{t+s} = \frac{E_{t+s}^*[d_{t+s+1} + p_{t+s+1}]}{(1 + r_{t+s+1})} \qquad \text{for } s \geq 0 \tag{10.28}$$

By letting s take on the values $s = 1, 2, \ldots$, successive values for p_{t+s} from (10.28) can be substituted into (10.27). Repeated application of the law of iterated expectations shows also that $E_t[E_{t+s}[\cdot]] = E_t[\cdot]$ (see chapter 3, page 79).

After making the substitutions using (10.28), and assuming the convergence of the sum of expected discounted returns, (10.27) becomes

$$p_t = E_t^*[\delta_{t+1} d_{t+1} + \delta_{t+2} d_{t+2} + \cdots + \delta_{t+s} d_{t+s} + \cdots] \tag{10.29}$$

where $\delta_{t+s} = [(1 + r_{t+1})(1 + r_{t+2}) \cdots (1 + r_{t+s})]^{-1}$, for $s \geq 1$, so that δ_{t+s} denotes the discount factor for the time period t to date $t + s$. Note that, if the individual discount factors are all equal, then $\delta_{t+s} = (1 + r)^{-s}$ – that is, the common discount factor expressed in terms of a constant interest rate.

If a behavioural interpretation is given to the condition (10.29), the probabilities underlying the expectation correspond to investors' (unanimous) beliefs and the * superscript can be omitted. It is necessary to remember, however, that, to make sense of the result, an additional assumption about individual behaviour – typically, risk neutrality – must be invoked. Furthermore, in the NPV as expressed by equation (10.10), $p_t = \sum_{i=1}^{\infty} \delta_{t+i} E_t d_{t+i}$, the expectations operator is applied on the assumption that the discount factors are non-random – i.e. the risk-free interest rates, though not necessarily constant across time, are known with certainty at date t.

References

Barberis, N., and A. Shleifer (2003), 'Style investing', *Journal of Financial Economics*, 68(2), pp. 161–99.

Barsky, R. B., and J. B. De Long (1993), 'Why does the stock market fluctuate?', *Quarterly Journal of Economics*, 108(2), pp. 291–311.

Black, F. (1986), 'Noise', *Journal of Finance*, 41, pp. 529–43.

Campbell, J. Y., A. W. Lo and A. C. MacKinlay (1997), *The Econometrics of Financial Markets*, Princeton, NJ: Princeton University Press.

Campbell, J. Y., and R. J. Shiller (1989), 'The dividend-price ratio and expectations of future dividends and discount factors', *Review of Financial Studies*, 1(3), pp. 195–228.

Garber, P. M. (1990), 'Famous first bubbles', *Journal of Economic Perspectives*, 4(2), pp. 35–54.

(2000), *Famous First Bubbles: The Fundamentals of Early Manias*, Cambridge, MA: MIT Press.

Hayashi, F. (2000), *Econometrics*, Princeton, NJ, and Oxford: Princeton University Press.

Jung, J., and R. J. Shiller (2002), *One Simple Test of Samuelson's Dictum for the Stock Market*, Discussion Paper no. 1386, Cowles Foundation, Yale University.

Kindleberger, C. P. (1978), *Manias, Panics and Crashes: A History of Financial Crises*, London: Macmillan.

LeRoy, S. F. (1989), 'Efficient capital markets and martingales', *Journal of Economic Literature*, 27(4), pp. 1583–1621.

(2004), 'Rational exuberance', *Journal of Economic Literature*, 47(3), pp. 783–804.

LeRoy, S. F., and R. D. Porter (1981), 'The present-value relation: tests based on implicit variance bounds', *Econometrica*, 49(3), pp. 555–74.

McKay, C. (1980), *Extraordinary Popular Delusions and the Madness of Crowds*, New York: Harmony Books (reprint of an original published in 1841).

Newman, P., M. Milgate and J. Eatwell (eds.) (1992), *The New Palgrave Dictionary of Money and Finance*, London: Macmillan (three volumes).

Samuelson, P. A. (1936–37), 'Some aspects of the pure theory of capital', *Quarterly Journal of Economics*, 51(3), pp. 469–96 (reprinted as chapter 17 in Stiglitz, 1966).

(1998), 'Summing up on business cycles: opening address', in J. C. Fuhrer and S. Schuh (eds.), *Beyond Shocks: What Causes Business Cycles*, Boston: Federal Reserve Bank of Boston, pp. 33–6.

Sharpe, W. F., G. J. Alexander and J. V. Bailey (1999), *Investments*, Englewood Cliffs, NJ: Prentice Hall International, 6th edn.

Shiller, R. J. (1989), *Market Volatility*, Cambridge, MA: MIT Press.

    (2000), *Irrational Exuberance*, Princeton, NJ, and Oxford: Princeton University Press.

    (2002), 'Bubbles, human judgment and expert opinion', *Financial Analysts Journal*, 58(3), pp. 18–26.

    (2003), 'From efficient markets to behavioral finance', *Journal of Economic Perspectives*, 17(1), pp. 83–104.

Shleifer, A. (2000), *Inefficient Markets: An Introduction to Behavioral Finance*, Oxford: Oxford University Press.

Shleifer, A., and L. H. Summers (1990), 'The noise trader approach to finance', *Journal of Economic Perspectives*, 4(2), pp. 19–33.

Stiglitz, J. E. (ed.) (1966), *The Collected Scientific Papers of Paul A. Samuelsonw*, Vol. I, Cambridge, MA: MIT Press.

Sydsæter, K., and P. J. Hammond (1995), *Mathematics for Economic Analysis*, Englewood Cliffs, NJ: Prentice Hall International.

Vuolteenaho, T. (2002), 'What drives firm-level stock returns?', *Journal of Finance*, 57(1), pp. 233–64.

11

Intertemporal choice and the equity premium puzzle

Overview

While all financial decisions involve the future, in earlier chapters individual decision making has been limited to a single date. In chapter 10 several intertemporal aspects of asset price determination were studied, but individual maximizing decisions were neglected. In this chapter the optimizing choices of investors return to the foreground. As a consequence, it is possible to address questions about how investors' portfolios are affected by the opportunity to change their asset holdings in the future, or to consume some of their wealth, or to add to their investments from a flow of saving.

Although the analysis of investment decisions becomes more complicated in a multiperiod setting, the fundamental valuation relationship plays a central role throughout. Recall that the FVR, introduced in chapter 4, takes the form

$$\mathrm{E}[(1+r_j)H] = 1 \tag{11.1}$$

where $\mathrm{E}[\cdot]$ is an expectations operator reflecting the beliefs of the investor, r_j is the rate of return on asset j ($j = 1, 2, \ldots, n$), and H is a random variable that depends on each investor's risk preferences. The FVR remains the focus of attention in portfolio selection, and the inclusion of time subscripts makes explicit the role of the dates at which decisions are made or information becomes available. Most importantly, in the multiperiod choice setting, H can be given a particular and precise interpretation as a *stochastic discount factor*.

Several new dimensions are added to the analysis when individual choice is extended to intertemporal planning. One is to treat the investor as a consumer whose decisions are ultimately made to optimize the allocation of consumption among different goods and across time. Here, the accumulation of wealth is an intermediate objective, a stepping stone towards the consumption of goods and services; the optimal choice of consumption according to preferences is assumed

250

to be the ultimate aim of individual decisions. Section 11.1 begins with a review of a two-period world for which the future is certain. Simplistic though this must seem, the principles generalize readily to a world with uncertainty, many assets and long time horizons; the extensions are made in section 11.2.

The remainder of the chapter applies the ideas developed in sections 11.1 and 11.2. Section 11.3 studies the life cycle portfolio decisions of investors. The famous equity premium puzzle is explored in section 11.4, while section 11.5 shows how the capital asset pricing model can be extended to allow for investors' intertemporal planning.

11.1 Consumption and investment in a two-period world with certainty

The allocation of consumption over time introduces, by implication, a saving decision – a second way in which wealth can be accumulated or depleted (the first way being via the return on assets). Each individual's decisions can, in principle, be extended to include labour supply and, consequently, a new source of income (remuneration for employment) in addition to the return on assets. The analysis is already complicated enough, however, and this chapter neglects labour/leisure choices. Also, sources of income other than the return on assets are ignored in this section. Finally, it is assumed that goods at each date can be aggregated into a single 'consumption' good each unit of which has a price equal to one unit of account (so that changes in the general price level are neglected). Each of these assumptions can be relaxed without sacrificing the fundamental insights of the analysis.

In elementary microeconomics the intertemporal consumption decision is modelled by assuming that the individual chooses consumption C_t in the present period and consumption C_{t+1} one period into the future. The individual is assumed to be 'endowed' with a given quantity of goods in each of the two periods, and, inasmuch as C_t and C_{t+1} differ from the endowments in t and $t+1$, the individual saves or borrows between the present, t, and the future, $t+1$. Here it is assumed that the endowment takes the form of wealth, W_t, available at the present, date t. (Presumably, W_t was accumulated in the past – i.e. dates prior to t.) The difference between wealth and current consumption, $W_t - C_t$, represents saving (if positive) or borrowing (if negative).[1]

It is assumed provisionally that wealth is transferred between t and $t+1$ at a given, certain interest rate, r_{t+1}. Hence, wealth at the start of the next period,

---

[1] Commonly, saving is defined as the excess of current *income* over current consumption. Here flows of income other than returns on assets are assumed to be zero, so that 'saving' is used in an unconventional way to refer to wealth net of current consumption.

date $t+1$, equals $W_{t+1} = (1+r_{t+1})(W_t - C_t)$. Given that all wealth is consumed at $t+1$, the individual's budget constraint is simply

$$C_{t+1} = (1+r_{t+1})(W_t - C_t) \qquad (11.2)$$

In this framework each 'date', t, denotes the start of the time period, and consumption in period t takes place between date t and date $t+1$. Also, the rate of return, r_{t+1}, corresponds to wealth accumulated in the period immediately preceding date $t+1$. These timing conventions are maintained throughout.

The individual's preferences are assumed to be defined over the planned consumption bundle, C_t, C_{t+1}, with preferences represented by a utility function $U(C_t, C_{t+1})$. For little reason other than tractability and ease of interpretation, it is assumed that the utility function takes the form

$$U(C_t, C_{t+1}) = u(C_t) + \delta u(C_{t+1}) \qquad (11.3)$$

where $\delta \leq 1$ denotes a subjective discount factor, which reflects the rate at which the individual weights future consumption relative to the present.[2] Sometimes the subjective trade-off between the present and the future is expressed by the 'rate of time preference', defined as $(1/\delta) - 1$.

The function $u(\cdot)$ applies to consumption in just one time period and is sometimes called the 'felicity function' to distinguish it from $U(\cdot, \cdot)$.[3] It is assumed to be the same for every time period, thus reinforcing the interpretation of δ as encapsulating a preference for consumption in the present compared with the future. Marginal utility is assumed to be positive but diminishing: $u'(\cdot) > 0$, $u''(\cdot) < 0$, at each level of consumption.

Figure 11.1 depicts an optimum, at E, for the consumer. Just as in elementary consumer theory, E denotes a tangency between the budget constraint (the line joining W_t and $(1+r_{t+1})W_t$) and an indifference curve – the highest that can be attained subject to the budget constraint.

For the purposes of this chapter the relevant implication of figure 11.1 is the condition that defines the tangency – i.e. the necessary, or first-order, condition for an interior maximum of utility.[4] The condition plays such an important role that it deserves explaining in words.

Suppose that the individual transfers one 'small' unit of wealth from the present period to the next. This results in a loss of utility, equal to the marginal utility of forgone consumption, in the present. By the next date wealth will have grown in

---

[2] The δ parameter should not be confused with discount factors derived from market interest rates. Here δ reflects an aspect of *preferences*, and only in rather special equilibria will δ equal a *market* discount factor.

[3] The distinction between the utility function and the felicity function is neglected except where ambiguity may result.

[4] By definition, an *interior* maximum excludes a corner solution at which one of the chosen consumption levels is zero.

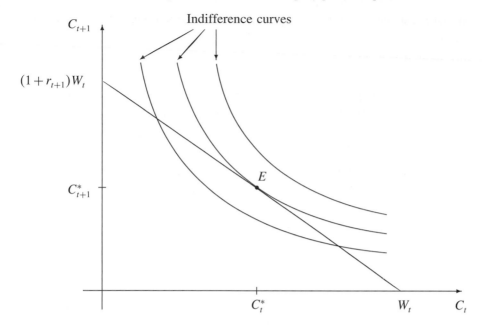

Fig. 11.1. Two-period consumption plans

The investor chooses between consumption 'today', C_t, and consumption 'tomorrow', C_{t+1}. The choice is made to maximize utility subject to a wealth constraint. Each indifference curve is drawn for a given level of utility. The line joining W_t and $(1+r_{t+1})W_t$ represents the wealth constraint. Point E depicts the point of maximum utility, such that consumption is allocated to reach the highest possible indifference curve without violating the wealth constraint. The tangency at E defines the necessary, or first-order, condition for a maximum of utility.

proportion to the interest rate. The increment to wealth yields a gain in utility – viewed from the present – equal to one plus the interest rate *times* the discount factor *times* the marginal utility next period. Unless the gain of utility (in the future) equals the loss (in the present), utility cannot be at a maximum.

More formally, a *necessary* condition for an interior optimum is that

$$(1+r_{t+1}) \times \delta \times u'(C_{t+1}) = u'(C_t)$$

$$(1+r_{t+1})\delta\frac{u'(C_{t+1})}{u'(C_t)} = 1 \qquad (11.4)$$

The solution of (11.4) together with the budget constraint, (11.2), yields the utility maximizing values, C_t^*, C_{t+1}^*, for consumption, depicted by point E in figure 11.1.

(The asterisk, *, superscript is normally omitted to keep the notation as uncluttered as possible.)

Simple though it is, equation (11.4) provides a foundation for the analysis in the remainder of this chapter. It is really nothing more than the FVR – equation (11.1) in this very special setting. The next section extends the analysis to allow for (a) uncertainty, (b) multiple assets and (c) long time horizons.

11.2 Uncertainty, multiple assets and long time horizons

11.2.1 Uncertainty

Uncertainty is typically introduced by assuming that at each date the individual acts to maximize the *expected* value of utility; i.e. the axioms of the expected utility hypothesis are assumed to be satisfied. Whether it is appropriate simply to introduce uncertainty by assuming that individuals maximize the *expected* value of the same objective function as under conditions of certainty is a debatable matter. It is not a debate pursued here. Instead, the standard practice is followed, namely to assume that the individual maximizes the expected value of $U(C_t, C_{t+1})$.

If the EUH holds, the necessary condition (11.4) becomes

$$\delta \mathrm{E}_t \left[(1 + r_{t+1}) \frac{u'(C_{t+1})}{u'(C_t)} \right] = 1 \qquad (11.5)$$

where the expression $\mathrm{E}_t[\cdot]$ denotes the expectation conditional upon whatever information the individual has at date t – that is, $\mathrm{E}_t[\cdot] \equiv \mathrm{E}[\cdot \,|\, \Omega_t]$, where Ω_t denotes the information set at date t.

Condition (11.5) is the FVR for the individual's decision problem under uncertainty.[5] Compare (11.5) with (11.1) to see that, in this case, $H = \delta u'(C_{t+1})/u'(C_t)$. Admittedly, a single asset only is present here, and no formal justification has been given for equation (11.5). Next, multiple assets are introduced and the FVR is derived rather than merely asserted.

11.2.2 Multiple assets

In the presence of multiple assets the notation for the rate of return must distinguish among assets. Thus, r_{t+1} is replaced with $r_{j,t+1}$ where the subscript 'j' labels the asset and $j = 1, 2, \ldots, n$, for the n available assets. In the FVR all that needs to be done is (a) to replace r_{t+1} with $r_{j,t+1}$ and (b) to recognize that, at a portfolio

---

[5] In view of the law of iterated expectations, it is permissible to take the 'expectation of the expectation conditional on information at date t' and to write the FVR omitting the t subscript on the expectations operator. Thus, the FVR holds regardless of whether the information available at t affects the investor's decision. This does not imply that the *solution* of the FVR is unaffected by the information, rather that the algorithm, applied to whatever information is available, remains the same.

optimum, the equation must hold for every asset, $j = 1, 2, \ldots, n$. The reasoning that justifies the FVR in this framework is as follows.

The FVR is a *necessary* (or first-order) condition for the maximization of expected utility. Hence, it is appropriate to start at an optimum – i.e. a consumption and portfolio plan that maximizes expected utility. Now suppose that a small amount of wealth becomes available for investment in any of the assets.[6] The return on the additional investment generates some extra wealth for consumption in the next period (at date $t + 1$).

The increment to the expected utility of consumption next period must be the same the holding of whichever asset is increased – otherwise, the investor could not have started at an optimum. If the additional wealth at date t is invested in asset j, then wealth at $t + 1$ increases by $(1 + r_{j,t+1})$. Expected utility increases by $\delta E_t[(1 + r_{j,t+1})u'(C_{t+1})]$. (Notice that δ appears because the investor evaluates the *present value*, at t, of expected utility at $t + 1$.)

This increment in expected utility must be the same for all assets:

$$\delta E_t[(1 + r_{j,t+1})u'(C_{t+1})] = \lambda_t \quad j = 1, 2, \ldots, n \tag{11.6}$$

where λ_t is not yet determined but does *not* have a j subscript – it is the same for all assets.[7]

The next step is to eliminate λ_t. Suppose that, starting again from an optimum, the investor shifts a small amount of consumption from date t to $t + 1$. Given that the starting point is an optimum, it follows that the present value of the gain in expected utility at $t + 1$ equals the loss of utility at t.[8] Formally,

$$\delta E_t[(1 + r_{j,t+1})u'(C_{t+1})] = u'(C_t) \tag{11.7}$$

where the left-hand side is the present value of the increment in expected utility at $t + 1$ and the right-hand side is the loss of utility at t. Any asset j can be used to evaluate the left-hand-side term. Thus, $\lambda_t = u'(C_t)$.

Now replace λ_t in (11.6) with $u'(C_t)$, and rearrange to obtain the FVR, in this context sometimes called an *Euler condition*:

$$\delta E_t[(1 + r_{j,t+1})u'(C_{t+1})] = u'(C_t)$$

$$E_t\left[(1 + r_{j,t+1})\delta\frac{u'(C_{t+1})}{u'(C_t)}\right] = 1 \quad j = 1, 2, \ldots, n \tag{11.8}$$

---

[6] The 'small amount' may seem vague but can be made precise: it is the limiting value obtained in differential calculus needed to make sense of marginal concepts.

[7] The expression is an equality because corner solutions, with a zero holding of one or more assets, are ignored.

[8] Notice that, from (11.6), it does not matter which asset is used to transfer the wealth from t to $t + 1$, because at an optimum all assets yield the same increment in expected utility.

Normally, a shorthand symbol, H_{t+1}, is defined: $H_{t+1} \equiv \delta u'(C_{t+1})/u'(C_t)$. In words: H_{t+1} denotes the discounted value of the marginal rate of substitution between consumption at $t+1$ and t. As previously mentioned, the random variable, H_{t+1}, is often called the *stochastic discount factor*. Sometimes it is called the *intertemporal marginal rate of substitution*, or the *pricing kernel*.

In principle, though rarely in practice, the equations in defining the investor's optimum can be solved for assets' portfolio proportions and for the investor's consumption plan. More relevant than obtaining an explicit solution to (11.8) in the following sections is to explore the implications of the FVR for investors' decisions.

Just as for the EUH applied to the single-period portfolio selection problem studied in chapter 5, few implications can be obtained without specifying the form of the utility function, $u(\cdot)$. A common assumption is that the utility function is iso-elastic – i.e. has constant relative risk aversion, defined by the parameter γ (see page 94).[9]

Formally, the *iso-elastic* utility function can be expressed as

$$u(C) = \begin{cases} C^{1-\gamma}/(1-\gamma) & \text{for } \gamma \neq 1 \\ \ln\ C & \text{for } \gamma = 1 \end{cases} \qquad (11.9)$$

where γ, a constant, is the coefficient of relative risk aversion. (The time subscript on C, consumption, has been omitted to simplify the notation.) From (11.9) it follows that $u'(C) = C^{-\gamma}$; the marginal utility of consumption, $u'(C)$, has constant elasticity, equal to $-\gamma$, the negative of the coefficient of relative risk aversion. Thus, γ is a measure of how rapidly marginal utility declines when consumption is increased. The larger is γ the more sensitive the investor's utility is to fluctuations in consumption, which are a consequence of fluctuations in wealth that occur in response to random changes in assets' returns.

The assumption of iso-elastic utility implies some important predictions about investor behaviour.[10]

1. Consumption, C_t, at each date is proportional to wealth, W_t, although the factor of proportionality generally differs from one date to another. For logarithmic utility, $\gamma = 1$, the factor of proportionality equals δ^{-1} at each date.

---

[9] In chapter 4, utility is expressed as a function of terminal wealth rather than consumption, because in that setting it is as if the investor consumes the entire accumulated wealth once the assets' pay-offs become known. Chapter 4 ignores the investors' decision to allocate consumption across time.

[10] For proofs, see Samuelson (1969), the methods of which are outlined in appendix 11.1.

2. The *proportion* of wealth invested in each asset is independent of the *level* of wealth. The portfolio proportions generally differ across time but do not depend on the level of wealth. Thus, given the CRRA assumption, if an individual invests 10 per cent of his/her wealth in a particular asset when wealth equals $5000, then 10 per cent will be invested in the asset if the individual's wealth is $2000, or $500,000, or whatever.

These restrictions enable calculations to be made that would otherwise be difficult or impossible. For that reason – not because there is any compelling reason investors should behave according to CRRA utility – the iso-elastic form is widely used.

11.2.3 Long time horizons

So far only two dates, t and $t + 1$, have been considered. However, the reasoning that resulted in the FVR (11.8) above is the same no matter the length of the investor's horizon. Hence, no changes are needed in (11.8); it holds for all adjacent dates between which the investor allocates wealth.

If the investor's horizon is T time periods (say, 'years') from the present, t, then a function $U(C_t, C_{t+1}, \ldots, C_T)$ is assumed to represent the investor's preferences – i.e. 'life-time utility'. Moreover, the function is typically assumed to take the special form

$$U(C_t, C_{t+1}, \ldots, C_T) = u(C_t) + \delta u(C_{t+1}) + \delta^2 u(C_{t+2}) + \cdots + \delta^{T-t} u(C_T)$$
(11.10)

The investor is then assumed to choose a consumption and portfolio plan that maximizes the expected value of lifetime utility – i.e. to maximize $E_t[U(\cdot)]$ – where the t subscript is a reminder that the expectation is made on the basis of beliefs at the current date, t. The investor implements the consumption and portfolio plan for the current date. Then, as time moves forward to date $t + 1$, the investor re-optimizes on the basis of new information, looking forward from $t + 1$ to T, implements the plan for $t + 1$, and so on.

In some formulations of the intertemporal optimization problem, the investor's preferences are modified to allow for bequests – i.e. passing wealth on to the investor's heirs. This is achieved by writing utility as

$$U(C_t, C_{t+1}, \ldots, C_T) = u(C_t) + \delta u(C_{t+1}) + \delta^2 u(C_{t+2}) + \cdots$$
$$+ \delta^{T-t} u(C_T) + \delta^{T-t+1} B(W_{T+1})$$

where $B(\cdot)$ denotes a *bequest function* that depends on the amount of wealth bequeathed at the end of the investor's life.

Even allowing for bequests in this way, the additive form for lifetime utility neglects many potentially important aspects of human nature. For example, an investor's behaviour may be influenced by consumption in previous periods, resulting in *habit persistence*. Also, quite apart from habit, preferences may depend differently on consumption at different points in the life cycle (e.g. depending on whether there are children in the household).

Yet another complication is to allow for the investor to plan over the indefinite future, so that $T \longrightarrow \infty$. A complication – not studied here – is that, in this case, the value of expected utility may be unbounded. Hence, additional assumptions are required to ensure that the investor's planning decisions are well defined (i.e. that there exists a solution to the optimization problem).

Summary

The most important result of this section is that, in the presence of uncertainty, multiple assets and a long time horizon, the FVR is expressed as (11.8), above. A less informal treatment of intertemporal investment decision making appears in appendix 11.1, which provides a derivation of the FVR.

11.3 Lifetime portfolio selection

While the previous section outlined the principles of intertemporal decision making based on the EUH, it obtained no definite predictions about individual behaviour. This section applies the principles to explore a particular issue, namely how an investor's portfolio composition changes with the passage of time through the life cycle.

Suppose for simplicity that investors choose between just two assets, one risky – say, a bundle of equities – and the other risk-free – say, a bond or other fixed-interest security. Should a young investor (with a long time horizon) hold a higher proportion of equities than an old investor (with a short time horizon)? The *conventional recommendation* in financial wisdom replies with a confident 'yes'. Why?

It is generally accepted that the average return on equity is higher than that on bonds. Although equities are riskier than bonds, it is argued that over long periods (say, twenty years or more) the ups and downs of the stock market tend to 'even out' the risks. Thus, young investors – facing long horizons – are advised to hold a high proportion of equities in their portfolios, because ultimately the payoff is higher than that from bonds in return for bearing little, if any, extra risk. Older investors – facing shorter expected lifespans – are advised to hold a higher proportion of bonds in order to avoid equities' inherent risks.

Plausible though the recommendation seems, probing its underlying assumptions uncovers challenges to its validity. The challenges raise several questions (addressed below). (a) Is it reasonable to suppose that equity returns become less variable over long horizons? (Section 11.3.1.) (b) Even if equities do have this property, how sensitive is the portfolio decision to alternative investor objectives, in particular to different risk preferences? (Section 11.3.2.) (c) How important are transaction costs – i.e. the costs of buying or selling assets? (Section 11.3.3.) (d) How does the existence of other sources of income, especially from employment, affect the composition of an investor's optimal portfolio? (Section 11.3.4.)

11.3.1 Asset return distributions

The total rate of return over a period of, say, twenty years is approximately the sum of the annual rates for each of the component years. If the annual rates of return are identically and independently distributed (i.i.d.), then the expected total return increases in proportion to the period's length, while the standard deviation of total return increases more slowly, in proportion to the square root of the period's length. This is the sense in which the average return on equities becomes less variable as the horizon becomes longer.

If annual returns are *not* i.i.d., however, this result may no longer hold. For example, suppose that equity returns are *mean-reverting*; i.e. sequences of above-average returns are followed by sequences of below-average returns and *vice versa* – a phenomenon for which there is some evidence. In this case, the payoff on a portfolio could be enhanced by switching into equities before a spell of above-average returns and into bonds immediately before a spell of below-average returns. Such a strategy obviously requires foresight about *when* returns will be above or below average – not merely that they do fluctuate in this way – and a model that enables prediction of future returns conditional upon current information (see below, section 11.4.4, for comments on the role of conditioning information in forecasting equity returns).

Adapting portfolio strategies to exploit asset returns that are not i.i.d. may, thus, introduce additional hazards, because the strategies depend upon knowledge of a sort that is likely to be difficult to acquire and to use with any confidence. Despite evidence for the fragility of the assumption that asset returns are i.i.d., no specific alternative commands widespread support. For this reason, the i.i.d. assumption is retained in what follows.

11.3.2 Investors' objectives

Investors' objectives express their preferences for bearing risks that follow from their actions (i.e. portfolio choices). If the assumptions underlying the EUH are deemed plausible, then the preferences are expressed in terms of each investor's von Neumann–Morgenstern utility function.[11]   Even with the EUH, additional assumptions about the utility function are needed to obtain definite predictions about behaviour. The most common assumption was introduced above, namely that the coefficient of relative risk aversion, γ, is constant (CRRA utility), implying that the proportion of wealth invested in each asset is constant for different levels of wealth – the higher is γ the lower the proportion of wealth invested in risky assets. This proportion does not, however, depend on the level of wealth.

Consequently, as wealth changes with age, investors with CRRA utility functions do not change the share of their portfolios invested in risky equity relative to safe bonds. (This result also requires the i.i.d. assumption on asset returns.) Hence, the conventional recommendation outlined above is *not* implied in this case; CRRA investors should not change the composition of their portfolios across the life cycle.

Of course, investors could behave according to the EUH but need not have CRRA utility functions. A utility function could be found that justifies almost any relationship between wealth and portfolio shares. Thus, as noted above, the EUH on its own does not allow definite predictions about portfolio composition over the life cycle.

If the EUH is abandoned, an even greater range of patterns of behaviour can be rationalized. The commonly encountered alternatives include the following.

1. *Target wealth.*   The investor may seek to accumulate a target level of wealth at a particular age – say, just before retirement. If the young investor believes that the target can be achieved by investing in low-risk bonds, then an optimal portfolio strategy would be to hold a high proportion of bonds early in life. Once the target is attained, the investor can afford to take risks and place surplus wealth in equities. Note that this is directly contrary to the conventional recommendation; in this scenario the share of equities would increase, not decrease, with age. If – as perhaps seems more likely – the rate of return on low-risk investments is not sufficient to reach the target wealth level, then, once again, there are no clear predictions about how portfolio shares should change over the life cycle.

2. *Minimizing the risk of loss.* The argument here highlights the ambiguities in the notion of 'risk'. The EUH provides just one way for investors to weigh up the alternative outcomes.

   But perhaps investors instead focus on some particular aspect of the asset return distribution – for example, on the probability of making any loss at all. In this case, if equity returns are i.i.d. then the longer the time horizon the smaller the probability of loss, justifying a high share of equity investment when young – the conventional recommendation, again. However, if 'risk' refers to the *magnitude* of any loss, a high

---

[11] See chapter 4, especially section 4.2. With the investor consuming some part of wealth throughout the life cycle, the von Neumann–Morgenstern utility function is assumed to depend on consumption at each date, rather than terminal wealth.

share of equities could result in the loss of a high proportion of the portfolio. The result is now an investment strategy directly contrary to the conventional recommendation.

The rather trivial conclusion is that ambiguities in the meaning of risk imply ambiguities about which portfolio policy to adopt.[12]

3. *Behavioural alternatives*. Doubts about the meaning of risk can be broadened to encompass the concerns raised in the behavioural alternatives that focus on investor psychology. The issues outlined in chapter 4, section 4.3, are relevant here. Adding the time horizon to the agenda provides yet another opportunity for the complexities of investor psychology to have an impact on decisions.

11.3.3 Transaction costs

So far in this section it has been assumed that the portfolio composition can be changed, without cost, as many times as necessary over the horizon. The presence of transaction costs implies that investors may choose to make changes in the portfolio only infrequently, perhaps only once every several years.

Given infrequent changes in the portfolio and the perceived high returns on equities over long periods, it might seem plausible that, the longer the horizon, the higher the share of equities held in the portfolio. However, while equities offer the prospect of high returns over long periods, they also bring the possibility of high losses. Once again, the investor's decision will depend on how risk is assessed. More risk-averse investors are likely to hold a smaller proportion of equities regardless of whether the portfolio's composition is changed infrequently as a result of transaction costs (or for other reasons).

11.3.4 The role of human capital

The most obvious source of income for an investor, other than from investments, is from employment – i.e. labour income (wages or a salary). The net present value of future labour income – human capital – can be interpreted as a component of the investor's total wealth, along with financial wealth (and other forms of wealth such as real estate, an automobile or other consumer durable goods). Viewed in this light, the composition of the financial wealth portfolio (the share of equities relative to bonds) could depend upon other aspects of each investor's wealth-holding.

Whether or not financial portfolio composition is affected by an investor's human capital depends on the random pattern of returns from human capital. If labour income is risky (perhaps because of the prospect of unemployment), this could affect the investor's willingness to bear financial risks, and consequently the

---

[12] Kritzman and Rich (2002) explore the importance of risks associated with fluctuations in asset values throughout the period of investment, not just at the investor's horizon.

proportion of equity could be lower than for an investor in a secure occupation. Pursuing this reasoning, a young person in a secure job has high human wealth and would tend to invest a high proportion of financial wealth in equities. An older person, with little if any time remaining in employment, would have low human wealth and tend to hold a higher share of financial wealth in low-risk bonds.

Potentially more important, however, is the *correlation* between the rate of return on financial assets and labour income. The higher the correlation between labour income and equity returns, the lower the proportion of equity that a risk-averse young investor would tend to hold. As the investor becomes older, human capital declines (fewer years of employment remain), the importance of the correlation between labour income and equity returns declines, and the individual would tend to hold a higher share of equities relative to bonds.

The magnitude and sign of the correlation between returns on equities and human capital depends on the investor's occupation. For some individuals it could have an important impact on financial investments; for others it would be irrelevant.

11.3.5 Summary

The conclusion of this section is negative: no generally applicable recommendation is available for how the composition of an investor's portfolio should change over his or her life cycle. The analysis does, however, point to the factors relevant in formulating a recommendation, which are, most importantly, (a) the distribution across time of the returns on risky investments, (b) the investor's attitude to risk and (c) the correlation among risky asset streams, particularly between labour income and the return on equities.

11.4 The equity premium puzzle and the risk-free rate puzzle

11.4.1 The puzzles

The equity premium puzzle (EPP), proposed by Mehra and Prescott (1985), stems from an incompatibility between the model outlined in section 11.2 and observed differences between the rates of return on equity and low-risk assets. The puzzle is commonly stated by asserting that the equity premium – the excess of the average return on equity above a low-risk rate – is too large to be explained by the intertemporal optimization model of section 11.2. The EPP is a *quantitative* puzzle, in that the model predicts a positive premium but smaller than commonly observed.

Accepting that the measurements are accurate, it is surely the model that is at fault (because it predicts too low an equity premium), not financial markets for generating the wrong observations. Table 11.1 summarizes the evidence.

Table 11.1. *Estimates of the equity premium*

Country	Time period	Equity return(%)	Low-risk return(%)	Equity premium(%)
United States	1802–1998	7.0	2.9	4.1
United States	1889–2000	7.9	1.0	6.9
United States	1926–2000	8.7	0.7	8.0
United States	1947–2000	8.4	0.6	7.8
United Kingdom	1947–1999	5.7	1.1	4.6
Japan	1970–1999	4.7	1.4	3.3
Germany	1978–1997	9.8	3.2	6.6
France	1973–1998	9.0	2.7	6.3

Source: Mehra (2003). The reported measures are compound, or geometric, annual percentage rates of return over the given time periods. The equity return is an estimate of the overall market rate. The low-risk rate is the return on bonds or bills, intended to approximate a 'risk-free' rate. The rates have been corrected for inflation and, hence, should be interpreted as 'real'.

For the United States at least, average returns on stocks (equity) have averaged over 7 per cent for long intervals since the early 1800s. What seems to have made the US equity premium high since the 1920s is a low, risk-free real rate of return (less than 3 per cent, and by some measures less than 1 per cent). The equity premium in other countries is not so consistently high as in the United States but is nonetheless still of a magnitude that merits investigation.

A second puzzle, the *risk-free rate puzzle* (RFRP), follows immediately from the evidence in table 11.1. According to the RFRP, the reported risk-free rate is too low to be compatible with the model given the observed rate of growth in consumption, C_t. The model predicts that, with such a low risk-free rate, consumers should have saved less and consumption should have grown more rapidly. Given that both the EPP and RFRP are so closely related, they are studied together.

11.4.2 EPP: theory and evidence

Three specific assumptions are typically invoked in studies of the EPP.

1. *Beliefs and preferences.* Every investor is assumed to have preferences of the form assumed in section 11.2, with an iso-elastic utility function, $u(C) = C^{1-\gamma}/(1-\gamma)$. Differentiation and substitution into $H = \delta u'(C_{t+1})/u'(C_t)$ results in $H = \delta(C_{t+1}/C_t)^{-\gamma}$ (where, again, the time subscript on H is omitted for simplicity).

Although all investors may act as if they have iso-elastic utility, this does not in itself imply that H is the same for everyone, for there may exist differences across investors in wealth and other sources of income as well as the parameter γ.[13] A multiplicity of H values would make the theory difficult to apply. Consequently, some way of justifying a common, unique H is needed. One approach is to assume that investors are identical in every respect so that the analysis applies to a 'representative individual'. This very restrictive condition can be relaxed by assuming instead that markets are 'complete', as follows.

2. *Complete markets.* Markets are *complete* in the sense introduced in chapter 4, when it is as if, for each state, there exists an asset with a payoff of one unit of wealth if that state occurs and zero if any other state occurs.[14] This does not mean that uncertainty has evaporated, but can be interpreted as asserting that every risk can be insured: every state of nature has its price. Armed with this assumption it is possible to demonstrate that the stochastic discount factor is the same for all investors – i.e. H is unique. (Chapter 4, appendix 4.2, contains a proof.)

The assumption of complete markets may seem too far-fetched to make sense, though this is a matter of debate among researchers. In any case, it plays a role by identifying a benchmark for which H is unique, without requiring the arguably more unrealistic assumption that investors are identical.

3. *Frictionless markets.* This assumption – that transaction costs are zero and that there are no institutional constraints on asset trades – is implicit in all the analysis. It is made explicit now in order to highlight it as a potential culprit for the failure of the model to predict the observed equity premium.

The EPP can be exposed by manipulating the FVR, (11.1):

$$\mathrm{E}\left[(1+r_j)H\right] = 1 \tag{11.11}$$

Choose two assets, equity, with rate of return r_e and bonds[15] with rate of return, r_b. Hence

$$\mathrm{E}[(1+r_e)H] = 1$$
$$\mathrm{E}[(1+r_b)H] = 1 \tag{11.12}$$
$$\mathrm{E}[(r_e-r_b)H] = 0 \tag{11.13}$$

---

[13] Another potential source of diversity across investors is differences in beliefs. This can be avoided either by assuming unanimity of beliefs or by assuming that the formal expectations operations that appear in the derivations are taken over all investors' beliefs, not merely over one, unanimously believed, set of probabilities.

[14] These so-called *Arrow securities* do not actually have to be traded. All that is needed is to assume that investors could, in principle, create them by holding the appropriate portfolios of assets that do exist.

[15] Although bonds are not normally entirely risk-free, their rates of return are used in calculating the equity premium. In any case, as the derivation shows, it is not necessary to assume that the rate of return on bonds is entirely risk-free. Invariably, the equity premium is measured and interpreted in 'real' terms, either by adjusting both equity and bond returns for inflation or as the difference between two nominal rates (so that the impact of inflation cancels out).

Now, under the assumption of iso-elastic utility in the intertemporal consumption and portfolio selection model, (11.13) becomes

$$E[(r_e - r_b)(1+c)^{-\gamma}] = 0 \qquad (11.14)$$

where $c \equiv (C_{t+1}/C_t) - 1$ denotes the rate of growth of consumption. Similarly, (11.12) can be written

$$\delta E[(1+r_b)(1+c)^{-\gamma}] = 1 \qquad (11.15)$$

Notice that δ can be factored out of the expectation and eliminated from (11.14) but not from (11.15).

The EPP asserts that *the value of γ needed to satisfy (11.14) in the data is much larger than values of γ estimated in other contexts* (which focus on measuring γ as an index of risk aversion). While there is no consensus about the exact magnitude of γ obtained in these other models, many studies favour a value less than three. This is much lower than estimates obtained from using sample averages to represent expected returns, and the average rate of growth per capita consumption for c, in (11.14). Kocherlakota (1996), for example, finds that a γ of at least 8.5 is needed to satisfy the sample variant of (11.14).[16]

A second way of expressing the EPP is in terms of the covariance between equity returns and the rate of growth of per capita consumption. Appendix 11.2 shows that the equity premium can be approximated as

$$E[r_e] - r_0 = \frac{\gamma \text{cov}(r_e, c)}{1 - \gamma E[c]} \qquad (11.16)$$

where the risk-free rate, r_0, replaces r_b – the difference is cosmetic because a bond rate of return is almost always used to represent the risk-free rate.[17]

From this perspective, the EPP asserts that the covariance between the equity returns and consumption growth for acceptable values of γ is too high. Alternatively, for observed equity premia and acceptable values of γ, the observed covariance between equity returns and consumption growth is too low. It should not be forgotten that these assertions follow from the assumptions enumerated above. If these assumptions are called into doubt, then so also are the assertions.

The RFRP is expressed via (11.15): $\delta E[(1+r_b)(1+c)^{-\gamma}] = 1$. Here the value of δ is relevant as well as γ. It is typically assumed that $\delta < 1$: individuals tend to value present consumption more highly than consumption in the future. In other

---

[16] Kocherlakota (1996) uses data for the United States over the period 1889 to 1978. Over these years the average annual, inflation-adjusted rate of return on equity was approximately 7 per cent, the average rate of return on risk-free bonds was about 1 per cent and the average rate of growth of per capita consumption was about 1.8 per cent.

[17] A close relative of (11.16) is the 'Hansen–Jagannathan lower bound' for H, which appears in appendix 11.2, (11.35), on page 277.

words, it is commonly supposed that any consumer who faces a constant stream of consumption over time would prefer to shift some of it from the future to the present. Whether this is a plausible assumption is open to debate. However, as Kocherlakota (1996) shows, the values of δ and γ estimated to satisfy both (11.14) and (11.15) imply that $\delta = 1.08$, at least for his sample.

11.4.3 Assessing the evidence

In summary, the evidence supports:

(a) the *equity premium puzzle*: that investors tend to hold too high a proportion of low-risk bonds relative to equities for plausible values of γ; and
(b) the *risk-free rate puzzle*: that, given a high value of γ, investors tend to transfer too much wealth from the present to the future for plausible values of δ.

Another, less dramatic, interpretation is that the evidence obtained by applying (11.14) and (11.15) favours estimates of γ and δ higher than conventional wisdom allows (i.e. higher than found in other studies). Yet another interpretation is that (11.14) and (11.15) represent a flawed model; that is, the assumptions underlying the model are open to doubt, at least in some respects.

How can the EPP and RFRP be resolved? Here are several possibilities.

1. *Mismeasurement.* The estimates of γ and δ could be spurious in the sense that they are the result of incorrect inferences from the data.
   Incorrect inferences can arise for a variety of technical reasons, but the most important is perhaps that the estimates rely on one historical sample of data, essentially from the late nineteenth century to the present. While this may seem a long period and while empirical studies have been made for several countries, doubts have been raised about whether reliable estimates of the parameters are obtained. (See below, section 11.4.4, for additional remarks about measurement issues.)
2. *Inappropriate comparisons.* Suppose that the estimates of γ and δ from (11.14) and (11.15) *are* reasonably accurate. It could be that the values obtained from other, non-financial applications are misleading. From this perspective, it is argued that the estimates of δ and γ – often obtained informally – are too low. While this is possible, doubts about the reliability of parameter estimates in EPP and RFRP studies suggest that it would probably be rash to resolve the puzzles simply by dismissing estimates from other applications.
3. *Faulty model.* If the model's assumptions are flawed, then its predictions are likely to be inconsistent with the evidence, given values of γ and δ that are considered reasonable. For example, in the framework outlined above, the γ parameter plays a dual role: it represents preferences with respect to both risk aversion *and* the intertemporal substitution of consumption. Relaxing the rigid link between the two

would make the model compatible with a broader range of behaviour and thus offer some prospect of resolving the puzzles.

Intensive research efforts have been devoted to exploring different specifications of the model outlined above. Each of the three main assumptions – preferences, complete markets and frictionless markets – has been scrutinized to see whether it can be held responsible for the puzzles. While many studies claim to resolve, at least partially, the EPP and RFRP, a consensus view has yet to emerge. (See Kocherlakota, 1996, for a survey of results obtained by modifying the model's assumptions.)

4. *Flawed individual behaviour.* Investors do not behave as they are supposed to. It is tempting, from the literature on the puzzles, to form the view that individuals' preferences or beliefs – and hence their decisions – are at fault, not the model. Such an interpretation may be naïve, though it is not unusual to associate the model of sections 11.2 and 11.5 as representing one variety of 'market efficiency'. Hence, the evidence could be understood to imply that investors are irrational or misbehave in some way. Such a conclusion should be treated with caution. For the model relies on assumptions that, even when relaxed in the ways outlined above, may be too restrictive to encompass rational behaviour.

11.4.4 Forecasting the equity premium

The discussion of the EPP so far has explored why the observed equity premium appears to be incompatible with the intertemporal optimizing model of investor behaviour. In this context, the model generates predictions about the magnitude of the *unconditional* expectation of the equity premium. Averages of realized asset returns are then constructed to estimate the unconditional expectation, with the results described above.

A different approach focuses on estimating the *conditional* equity premium – i.e. the equity premium conditional upon information available to investors when the expectation is formed. Such estimates tend to be 'forward-looking' and hence are sometimes referred to as '*ex ante*' measures or forecasts. From this perspective, estimates of the unconditional equity premium are '*ex post*' measures – although both estimates are typically computed using the same historical data.

In order to construct conditional estimates, it is necessary to postulate a model from which the relationship between the expected premium and available information can be derived. For this purpose, consider the simplest variant of the 'dividend growth models' (see chapter 10, pages 227 and 235):

$$r_e = \frac{d}{p} + g \tag{11.17}$$

where, rather imprecisely, r_e denotes the future rate of return on equity, d/p is the current ratio of the dividend to the equity price and g denotes the future growth rate of dividends. Here, the 'future' could refer to a year or several years beyond the present.

The equity premium, $r_e - r_0$, can now be forecast as the sum of the forecasts of d/p and g, minus the risk-free rate, r_0.[18] If forecasts are made for the immediate future, r_0 is typically approximated with an index of currently observed interest rates (e.g. a short-term government bond or bill rate). The dividend/price ratio, d/p, is commonly assumed to be stationary, even though its components, d and p, may well exhibit non-stationarity in the form of time trends. Hence, forecasts of d/p can be set equal to averages of values observed immediately prior to the forecast period. Similarly, forecasts of the growth rate, g, are often set equal to averages of recently observed dividend growth rates, although other indexes, such as the rate of growth of corporate earnings, are sometimes used instead.

All these assumptions can be problematical in practice, for the future has an irritating propensity to diverge from extrapolations of the present. It is precisely when fluctuations (in stock prices or whatever) are imminent that the present is likely to be an unreliable guide to the future. Even so, crude estimates of the *ex ante* or conditional equity premium constructed in this way deserve comparison with measures of its *ex post* counterpart. For example, when a stock market boom nears its peak, as it did in early 2000, p will have increased significantly – the *ex post* equity premium is high. But, if (as is common) dividends have increased less rapidly, d/p will be low and forecasts of dividend growth may be more modest than recently observed appreciations in stock prices. Consequently, the *ex ante* equity premium is lower than the *ex post* premium. Conversely, after prolonged falls in equity prices, d/p may be relatively high and g may remain stable, such that the *ex ante* equity premium exceeds its *ex post* counterpart.

Comparisons between *ex ante* and *ex post* measures of the equity premium are fragile in the sense that *ex ante* values necessarily depend on – and may be sensitive to – the assumptions of the model from which the forecasts are generated. Although perhaps less problematical, the estimation of the *ex post* or unconditional equity premium using a sample average of historical data may not withstand close scrutiny. It may, for instance, be reasonable to assume that models of the unconditional equity premium should permit changes in expected returns on equity, for example as a consequence of technological advance, or a discrete 'regime shift', in which 'true' (i.e. model-based predictions of) equity returns change over time. In such circumstances, the sample averages of the

---

[18] As remarked in footnote 15, above, adjustments are made to remove the effect of economy-wide inflation. It is also worth noting that an estimate of the *ex post* equity premium can be obtained by replacing g with the realized rate of change in equity prices during the sample period.

realized equity premium require adjustment to allow for changes in the underlying expected equity return over the sample period.

Clearly, there is ample scope for controversy about the size of the equity premium – and hence about whether the EPP is a genuine puzzle. For example, it can be (and has been) argued that realized equity premia in the second half of the twentieth century (see table 11.1) are greater than estimates of *ex ante* premia obtained from data on dividends or earnings. One possible inference is that the *ex post* equity premium has been overestimated. Another is that the *ex ante* estimates are unreliable, perhaps because the forecasting models on which they rest are at fault. A third is that both estimates are accurate but investors' forecasts were systematically in error throughout the sample period. There is no consensus about which inference is correct, although the third – persistent expectational errors – perhaps warrants least respect.

Why should these potentially conflicting inferences command attention? Partly because they are relevant for the EPP. But, while the EPP may appear to be merely an academic exercise, its resolution has implications for the optimal allocation of investments between equities and bonds. If the equity premium is, say, 2 per cent rather than 6 per cent, this could have a significant impact on the composition of investors' portfolios.

11.5 Intertemporal capital asset pricing models

While the intertemporal consumption and portfolio selection model can be used to study problems such as the equity premium puzzle, it can also be deployed to build asset pricing models of the sort studied in chapters 6 and 8. The CAPM discussed in those chapters involved a theory of investor behaviour (the mean-variance model), together with assumptions about financial markets (homogeneous beliefs about future returns, and an equilibrium of supply and demand for each asset)

The purpose of this section is much the same as chapters 6 and 8, but it uses the multiperiod framework outlined in section 11.2 as the model of investor behaviour. What emerges is the *consumption* capital asset pricing model. There are, in fact, several varieties of the CCAPM, and, in addition, other sorts of intertemporal capital asset pricing models as well. Two of these deserve mention.

1. The CAPM when each investor has a terminal wealth objective. In this model investors choose portfolios to maximize a mean-variance objective at the horizon date, T – i.e. allowing portfolios to be revised at each date t to $T - 1$, but not allowing any of the accumulated wealth to be consumed along the way. Now it is possible to ask whether the static CAPM (see chapter 6) still holds for each separate period.

The answer is a cautious, rather equivocal, 'yes' – it does hold but only under restrictive conditions. In particular, if (a) each investor has a mean-variance objective (quadratic terminal preferences) and (b) rates of return are distributed independently across time, then the CAPM continues to hold – even though investors may have different time horizons. The CAPM also holds if returns are Normally distributed and, once again, distributed independently across time.[19]

2. The *intertemporal* CAPM. In this approach it is assumed that there exists a limited number of 'state variables' (e.g. technology, employment income, the weather) that are correlated with assets' rates of return. Then, using a framework similar in spirit to that of the previous section, it is possible to derive predictions similar to those of the multifactor models introduced in chapter 8.

   The ICAPM is typically constructed under the assumption that portfolio and consumption decisions are made in continuous time. This being so, it can be shown that the CCAPM emerges as a special case of the ICAPM. The mathematics of continuous time stochastic processes are too advanced to be presented here, and, instead, the CCAPM is introduced in terms of the simpler model of investor behaviour in discrete time.

Following tedious algebraic manipulations, the FVR, $E[(1+r_j)H]=1$, can be written in the form

$$\mu_j - \mu_0 = \theta_H \beta_{jH} \quad j = 1, 2, \ldots, n \qquad (11.18)$$

an expression that bears a striking resemblance to the static, one-period CAPM, prediction, $\mu_j - r_0 = (\mu_M - r_0)\beta_j$. (See appendix 11.3 for the derivation of (11.18), and chapter 6 for the static CAPM.) In (11.18) the symbols are interpreted as follows:

$\mu_j =$ the expected rate of return on asset j, $E[r_j]$;

$\beta_{jH} \equiv \text{cov}(r_j, H)/\text{var}(H)$: the *beta-coefficient* between j and H;

$\mu_0 =$ the expected return on an asset with zero beta-coefficient with H – i.e. $\beta_{0H} = 0$; and

$\theta_H =$ a number, the same for all assets.

Equation (11.18) can be interpreted similarly to that for the CAPM. It states that the 'excess return' on each asset is proportional to its beta-coefficient (where the beta-coefficient is now defined for the asset's rate of return and the stochastic discount factor, H). Its distinctive features are these.

1. The excess expected return, $\mu_j - \mu_0$, is defined in terms of the expected rate of return on a zero-beta asset, or portfolio. This asset plays the same role as the zero-beta portfolio in the 'Black CAPM'. In the CCAPM, however, the 'zero-beta' corresponds

---

[19] Levy and Samuelson (1992) present a formal justification for these conclusions, together with an analysis of other conditions that result in the CAPM when investors plan over long horizons.

to H, rather than the rate of return on the market portfolio. That is, suppose that the rate of return on the asset in question is r_0, then $\beta_{0H} \equiv \text{cov}(r_0, H)/\text{var}(H) = 0$ is equivalent to $\text{cov}(r_0, H) = 0$ – the rate of return r_0 is uncorrelated with H. The symbol r_0 – normally reserved for the risk-free asset – has been chosen deliberately because, if a risk-free asset exists, it would certainly have a zero beta-coefficient (with respect to H, or anything else).

2. In the CCAPM, θ_H replaces $(\mu_M - \mu_0)$, the excess expected return on the market portfolio. The actual value of θ_H is not especially interesting (it is derived in appendix 11.3). But θ_H is not the same as in the CAPM, because H need not be the rate of return on any portfolio. It can be shown that, if there exists an asset (such as the market portfolio) the rate of return on which has a correlation coefficient of $+1$ with H, then (11.18) can be written in the CAPM form.[20] In this sense, the CCAPM is a generalization of the CAPM. Whether it is a very helpful generalization is another matter.

Given the definition of β_{jH}, it is possible to construct – just as with the CAPM – a regression model for each r_j and H:

$$r_j = \alpha_{jH} + \beta_{jH}H + \varepsilon_j \quad j = 1, 2, \ldots, n \tag{11.19}$$

where $\alpha_{jH} = \mu_j - \beta_{jH}E[H]$ and ε_j is an unobserved random variable with standard properties: $E[\varepsilon_j] = 0$, $E[\varepsilon_j|H] = 0$.[21] By construction of the regression model, $\beta_{jH} = \text{cov}(r_j, H)/\text{var}(H)$, as required.

The main limitation of the CCAPM as expressed by (11.18) is immediately apparent: H, the stochastic discount factor, is a purely subjective reflection of preferences and can differ from one investor to another. Without additional restrictions on H, the model is simply *too general*.

The commonest refinement of the CCAPM is to replace H with the (proportional) rate of growth of aggregate (economy-wide) consumption. Indeed, the model is sometimes *defined* this way. This specialization comes about by recognizing that H depends on consumption – here, at last, the intertemporal model of section 11.2 appears – and by approximating H with $H \approx 1 - \gamma c$, where c is the rate of growth of consumption and γ, is the (constant) coefficient of relative risk aversion (see equation (11.9) on page 256). Appendix 11.3 provides a formal explanation of why the approximation makes sense.

---

[20] This assertion is not hard to prove because, if H has a correlation coefficient equal to $+1$ with any random variable x, then H can be written as a linear function of x. Substitution in the definitions underlying (11.18) then proves the result.

[21] It is worth noting that the regression model would take the same form if r_j were replaced by the excess return, $r_j - r_0$. The β_{jH} coefficient is unchanged because, by construction, being risk-free, r_0 is uncorrelated with H.

As already noted, H may differ across investors. Thus, in general, the model does not apply to c as defined because the rate of growth of consumption may differ across investors. Conditions implying that H is unique – i.e. the same for all investors – were outlined above in the context of the equity premium puzzle (section 11.4). These conditions are assumed to hold here also.

If H is replaced with c, it is possible to rewrite the CCAPM equation, $\mu_j - \mu_0 = \theta_H \beta_{jH}$, as

$$\mu_j - \mu_0 = \theta_c \beta_{jc} \quad j = 1, 2, \ldots, n \tag{11.20}$$

where $\beta_{jc} = \text{cov}(r_j, c)/\text{var}(c)$ and θ_c, as before, is a number that is the same for all assets. With identical reasoning as for H, a regression model for r_j and c can be constructed:

$$r_j = \alpha_{jc} + \beta_{jc} c + \varepsilon_j \quad j = 1, 2, \ldots, n \tag{11.21}$$

where $\alpha_{jc} = \mu_j - \beta_{jc} E[c]$ and ε_j is assumed to have the same properties as in (11.18).

Equations (11.20) and (11.21) are at the heart of the CCAPM. They show that the CCAPM can be interpreted much like the static CAPM but with the rate of growth of consumption, c, replacing the rate of return on the market portfolio, r_M. Alternatively, (11.21) can be viewed as a factor model with c as one of the factors. The two interpretations are complementary, not incompatible. Furthermore, as already hinted, the CCAPM can be placed within the context of the ICAPM; the latter includes a wider range of factors along with c in (11.21).

Empirical tests of the CCAPM can be formulated in the same way as for the CAPM, with observations on c replacing those on r_M. Similarly, the ICAPM can justify the introduction of additional factors in the context of multifactor models (see chapter 9).

Much as for the static CAPM, the evidence on the CCAPM is equivocal and certainly not entirely supportive. In particular, the covariance between rates of return and the rate of growth in consumption (reflected in estimates of β_{jc}) tend to be lower than predicted. This result is just another way of expressing the observations at the core of the equity premium puzzle.

Summary

The multiperiod consumption and portfolio planning model of individual behaviour is used as a building block for several models of asset prices. Most generally, the models imply a linear relationship between (a) the expected rate of return on each asset in excess of the expected return on a zero-beta asset and (b) the asset's beta-coefficient (defined using the stochastic discount factor, not the rate of return on the market portfolio). Given that the stochastic discount factor, H, is unobserved, it is usually replaced by the rate of growth of aggregate consumption, though, in principle, it could be replaced by any variable with which H has a perfect positive correlation.

11.6 Summary

This chapter has shown how the FVR condition for optimal portfolio selection can be interpreted when investors make consumption and investment decisions in an intertemporal setting. The main implications are as follows.

1. Under restrictive but commonly made assumptions about intertemporal preferences, it is possible to reduce multiperiod planning to a sequence of one-period decision problems.
2. When investors plan to consume during each period of time, the FVR implies the existence of a stochastic discount factor that depends on the investor's level of consumption at adjacent dates.
3. The conventional financial wisdom – that young investors should hold a higher proportion of their wealth in (risky) equities relative to (safe) bonds than older investors – should be treated with caution. While not necessarily wrong, the basis of the advice is less secure than initially appears.
4. The equity premium puzzle and the risk-free rate puzzle highlight evidence incompatible with the intertemporal optimizing model. Attempts to resolve the puzzles by modifying the assumptions underlying the model have been only partially successful.
5. The consumption CAPM is derived from the intertemporal consumption and portfolio selection model. In the CCAPM, the rate of growth of consumption plays a role analogous to the rate of return on the market portfolio in the static CAPM.

Further reading

Important though they are, the topics studied in this chapter have received extensive textbook treatment only at an advanced level. Access to the subject matter is probably most easily motivated via the equity premium puzzle, for which Kocherlakota (1996) and Siegel and Thaler (1997) provide illuminating entry points. The more recent controversies are well covered by Jagannathan, McGrattan and Scherbina (2000), Constantinides (2002), Fama and French (2002) and Mehra (2003). Also worth consulting is the summary in Lengwiler (2004, sect. 7.2). Mehra and Prescott (2003) offer a comprehensive survey of all the major contributions.

Multiperiod portfolio decisions are studied by Markowitz (1987, chap. 3). Formidable and dated though it may appear, the paper by Samuelson (1969) remains among the more accessible expositions that integrate multiperiod portfolio and consumption decisions; it contains many useful insights, and repays careful study. A thorough investigation of long-term portfolio decisions is presented by Campbell and Viceira (2002).

Cochrane's advanced text, *Asset Pricing* (2001), develops the entire theory of finance based on the stochastic discount factor, together with empirical applications. Chapter 21 focuses explicitly on the equity premium puzzle. At a similarly advanced level, Campbell, Lo and MacKinlay (1997, chap. 8) present a concise survey of the literature written from the perspective of applied econometrics.

Appendix 11.1: Intertemporal consumption and portfolio selection

This appendix studies the intertemporal planning of consumption and portfolio selection, following the approach introduced in Samuelson (1969). The analysis relies on the standard dynamic programming device of reducing the intertemporal optimization problem to a sequence of single-period problems.

The investor is assumed to choose a consumption and portfolio plan to maximize the expected value of a von Neumann–Morgenstern utility function of the form given in expression (11.10), on page 257, with horizon at date T. At each date the investor looks forward exactly one period, starting from the penultimate date $T - 1$, the solution for which enables optimization at $T - 2$, and so on back to the present, date t.

At date $T - 1$ there is one period remaining and the investor solves the following problem:

choose C_{T-1} and a_{T-1} to

maximize $u(C_{T-1}) + \mathrm{E}_{T-1}[u(W_T)]$

where $W_T = (W_{T-1} - C_{T-1})(1 + r_{P,T})$

$r_{P,T-1} = \sum_j a_{j,T-1} r_{j,T}$ and $\sum_j a_{j,T-1} = 1$

Note that a_{T-1} is the vector shorthand for the list of asset proportions, $a_{j,T-1}$, chosen at date $T - 1$. The range of j is $j = 1, 2, \ldots, n$ if all assets are risky, and $j = 0, 1, 2, \ldots, n$ if a risk-free asset, 0, is available.

The maximized value of lifetime utility as of date $T - 1$ is given by

$$J_{T-1}(W_{T-1}) \equiv \max_{C_{T-1}, a_{T-1}} \{u(C_{T-1}) + \delta \mathrm{E}_{T-1}[u(W_T)]\} \qquad (11.22)$$

remembering that $W_T = (W_{T-1} - C_{T-1})(1 + r_{P,T})$. Using the same reasoning that yields (11.22), the maximized value of utility viewed from any date $t+i$ can be written

$$J_{t+i}(W_{t+i}) \equiv \max_{C_{t+i}, a_{t+i}} \{u(C_{t+i}) + \delta E_{t+i}[J_{t+i+1}(W_{t+i+1})]\} \qquad (11.23)$$

for $i = 0, 1, 2, \ldots, T - t - 1$, with $W_{t+i+1} = (W_{t+i} - C_{t+i})(1 + r_{P,t+i+1})$.

For notational simplicity, consider the optimization problem for the current date, t:

choose C_t and a_t to

maximize $u(C_t) + E_t[J_{t+1}(W_{t+1})]$

where $W_{t+1} = (W_t - C_t)(1 + r_{P,t+1})$

$r_{P,t+1} = \sum_j a_{jt} r_{j,t+1}$ and $\sum_j a_{jt} = 1$

This problem can be studied by constructing the Lagrangian:

$$\mathcal{L} = u(C_t) + \delta E_t[J_{t+1}((W_t - C_t)\sum_j a_{jt}(1 + r_{j,t+1}))] + \xi_t(1 - \sum_j a_{jt}) \quad (11.24)$$

where ξ_t is a Lagrange multiplier.

At a maximum, the partial derivative of $\mathcal{L}$ with respect to any asset proportion must be zero at an interior optimum:

$$\frac{\partial \mathcal{L}}{\partial a_{jt}} = \delta(W_t - C_t)E_t[J'_{t+1}(W_{t+1})(1 + r_{j,t+1})] - \xi_t = 0$$

$$\delta E_t[J'_{t+1}(W_{t+1})(1 + r_{j,t+1})] - \lambda_t = 0 \quad \text{for } W_t \neq C_t \quad (11.25)$$

where $\lambda_t = \xi_t/(W_t - C_t)$. Multiplying (11.25) by a_{jt} and summing over j yields

$$\delta E_t[J'_{t+1}(W_{t+1})(1 + r_{P,t+1})] - \lambda_t = 0 \qquad (11.26)$$

bearing in mind that $\sum_j a_{jt} = 1$.

Also, at a maximum, the partial derivative of $\mathcal{L}$ with respect to consumption at date t must be zero at an interior optimum:

$$\frac{\partial \mathcal{L}}{\partial C_t} = u'(C_t) - \delta E_t[J'_{t+1}(W_{t+1})(1 + r_{P,t+1})] = 0 \qquad (11.27)$$

Therefore, combining (11.25), (11.26) and (11.27),

$$\delta E_t[J'_{t+1}(W_{t+1})(1 + r_{j,t+1})] = u'(C_t) \quad j = 1, 2, \ldots, n \qquad (11.28)$$

In order to obtain the FVR, (11.8), it remains to establish that $J'_{t+1}(W_{t+1}) = u'(C_{t+1})$. This is an implication of the envelope theorem applied to (11.23) for $i = 1$. In words: the increment to maximized utility at any date obtained from an increment of wealth must equal the marginal utility of consumption at that date. Why? Because the increment in wealth could be immediately consumed, providing an increment to maximized utility equal to the marginal utility of consumption. This increment also equals the present value of the increment to utility obtained from investing the increment in wealth (and thereby delaying consumption to a later date); otherwise, the individual could not have been at a utility maximum, as required by the definition of $J_{t+i}(W_{t+i})$.

Appendix 11.2: Simplifying the FVR

This appendix presents derivations that simplify the FVR, especially in the context of the equity premium puzzle. It also obtains a linear approximation for H in terms of the rate of growth of consumption.

First, note that the following identities hold for any two random variables, X and Y:

$$\text{cov}(X, Y) \equiv \text{E}[(X - \text{E}[X])(Y - \text{E}[Y])]$$

$$= \text{E}[XY] - \text{E}[X]\,\text{E}[Y]$$

$$\text{E}[XY] = \text{cov}(X, Y) + \text{E}[X]\,\text{E}[Y] \tag{11.29}$$

Recall the FVR, $\text{E}[(1 + r_j)H] = 1$ – a condition that holds for every asset in the investor's portfolio.[22] Hence, for any two assets j and 0,

$$\text{E}[(1 + r_j)H] = 1$$

$$\text{E}[(1 + r_0)H] = 1 \tag{11.30}$$

$$\text{E}[(r_j - r_0)H] = 0 \tag{11.31}$$

Now apply (11.29) to (11.31) with $X = (r_j - r_0)$ and $Y = H$, to obtain

$$0 = \text{cov}(r_j - r_0, H) + \text{E}[r_j - r_0]\text{E}[H] \tag{11.32}$$

In this book, r_0 typically denotes the non-random rate of return on a risk-free asset. By implication, r_0 is uncorrelated with any random variable, and hence $\text{cov}(r_0, H) = 0$. But the zero-covariance property holds more generally – that is, for any risky asset with a rate of return uncorrelated with H.[23] Consequently,

---

[22] The expectations, variances and covariances in what follow could (indeed, should) be conditioned on information available at date t, at which investment decisions are taken. However, the expressions derived for the conditional moments hold also for their unconditional counterparts. Therefore, because the issue of timing is not the focus of attention here, and in order to avoid inessential notation, only the unconditional operators appear in what follows.

[23] Such an asset is often termed a *zero-beta* asset (or portfolio). Here, the 'beta-coefficient' is defined as $\beta_{0H} \equiv \text{cov}(r_0, H)/\text{var}(H)$. The rationale for this definition becomes clearer in the context of the consumption CAPM.

$cov(r_j - r_0, H) = cov(r_j, H)$. Notice also, from (11.30), that $E[H] = 1/(1 + E[r_0])$, or $(1 + E[r_0]) = 1/E[H]$.

Applying the zero-covariance property to (11.32) and rearranging gives

$$E[r_j] - E[r_0] = -\frac{cov(r_j, H)}{E[H]} \tag{11.33}$$

an expression that suggests an interpretation of the risk premium on an asset in terms of the covariance of its rate of return with the stochastic discount factor, H.

Equation (11.33) is central to the analysis of asset price fluctuations from the perspective of intertemporal choice models. One well-known variant of (11.33) is the 'Hansen–Jagannathan lower bound'[24] for H, obtained as follows. Let ρ_{jH} denote the correlation coefficient between r_j and H. By definition, $\rho_{jH}\sigma(r_j)\sigma(H) = cov(r_j, H)$, where $\sigma(\cdot)$ denotes the standard deviation of its argument. Now eliminate $cov(r_j, H)$ from (11.33) and rearrange to give

$$\frac{E[r_j] - E[r_0]}{\sigma(r_j)} = -\frac{\rho_{jH}\sigma(H)}{E[H]} \tag{11.34}$$

Now, because $-1 \leq \rho_{jH} \leq +1$,

$$\left| \frac{E[r_j] - E[r_0]}{\sigma(r_j)} \right| \leq \frac{\sigma(H)}{E[H]} \quad \text{(Hansen–Jagannathan lower bound on } H) \tag{11.35}$$

The left-hand side of (11.35) is the Sharpe ratio for asset j (or any portfolio, such as that comprising all equities). Depending on the definition of H, it may be possible to estimate the right-hand side, $\sigma(H)/E[H]$, and hence test an implication of the model.

Nothing in the derivation so far requires H to take any particular form. Equations (11.31) and (11.33), for instance, hold for any FVR. In order to obtain a simpler interpretation for the risk premium, it is helpful to assume that $H = \delta(C_{t+1}/C_t)^{-\gamma}$, as implied for the iso-elastic utility function (for which $u'(C) = C^{-\gamma}$).

A further simplification is achieved by noting that the non-random δ parameter can be factored out of the expectations involving H. As a consequence, δ can be cancelled from the expressions that follow. To save making the cancellation explicitly at each step, H is written as $H = (C_{t+1}/C_t)^{-\gamma}$ in this appendix from now on.

Define $x \equiv C_{t+1}/C_t$, and write $H = f(x)$ where $f(x) \equiv x^{-\gamma}$. Also, note that $f'(x) = -\gamma x^{-\gamma-1}$. Now a Taylor series expansion about the point $x = 1$ is applied to obtain a linear approximation for H as a function of $c \equiv (C_{t+1}/C_t) - 1$, the

---

[24] Named after the authors' pioneering paper: Hansen and Jagannathan (1991).

rate of growth of consumption.[25] Retaining only the first two terms in the Taylor series implies

$$H = f(x)$$

$$\approx f(1) + f'(1)(x - 1)$$

$$\approx 1 + (-\gamma)1^{-\gamma-1}(x - 1)$$

$$\approx 1 - \gamma \left(\frac{C_{t+1}}{C_t} - 1 \right)$$

$$\approx 1 - \gamma c \tag{11.36}$$

Now, allowing the approximation to become a genuine equality, $\mathrm{cov}(r_j, H) = -\gamma\mathrm{cov}(r_j, c)$, and the risk premium

$$\mathrm{E}[r_j] - \mathrm{E}[r_0] = -\frac{\mathrm{cov}(r_j, H)}{\mathrm{E}[H]} = \frac{\gamma\mathrm{cov}(r_j, c)}{1 - \gamma\mathrm{E}[c]} \tag{11.37}$$

In equation (11.16), on page 265, r_j is replaced by the rate of return on equity and $\mathrm{E}[r_0]$ is replaced by the risk-free rate of return, r_0 (instead of the slightly more general rate of return that satisfies the zero covariance condition outlined above).

Appendix 11.3: The consumption CAPM

The fundamental CCAPM predictions, $\mu_j - \mu_0 = \theta_H \beta_{jH}$ and $\mu_j - \mu_0 = \theta_c \beta_{jc}$, follow immediately from the derivations in appendix 11.2.

Rearranging equation (11.33) gives

$$\frac{\mathrm{E}[r_j - r_0]}{\mathrm{cov}(r_j, H)} = \frac{-1}{\mathrm{E}[H]}$$

$$\frac{\mathrm{E}[r_j - r_0]}{\mathrm{cov}(r_j, H)/\mathrm{var}(H)} = \frac{-\mathrm{var}(H)}{\mathrm{E}[H]}$$

$$\frac{\mathrm{E}[r_j - r_0]}{\beta_{jH}} = \frac{-\mathrm{var}(H)}{\mathrm{E}[H]}$$

$$\mathrm{E}[r_j] - \mathrm{E}[r_0] = \theta_H \beta_{jH}$$

$$\mu_j - \mu_0 = \theta_H \beta_{jH} \tag{11.38}$$

where $\theta_H \equiv -\mathrm{var}(H)/\mathrm{E}[H]$, $\mu_j \equiv \mathrm{E}[r_j]$ and $\mu_0 \equiv \mathrm{E}[r_0]$. This establishes the CCAPM as expressed by (11.18).

---

[25] The time subscript, $t+1$, is omitted from c_{t+1} to avoid excessive notation.

To obtain the CCAPM in terms of c, recall the approximation, (11.37), and treat the approximation as an equality[26]: $H = 1 - \gamma c$, so that $E[H] = 1 - \gamma E[c]$, $\mathrm{cov}(r_j, H) = -\gamma \mathrm{cov}(r_j, c)$ and $\mathrm{var}(H) = \gamma^2 \mathrm{var}(c)$. Hence, $\beta_{jH} = -\mathrm{cov}(r_j, c)/(\gamma \mathrm{var}(H))$. Substituting into (11.39), above, yields

$$\mu_j - \mu_0 = \theta_H \beta_{jH}$$

$$= \left(\frac{-\mathrm{var}(H)}{E[H]} \right) \left(\frac{\mathrm{cov}(r_j, H)}{\mathrm{var}(H)} \right)$$

$$= \left(\frac{-\gamma^2 \mathrm{var}(c)}{1 - \gamma E[c]} \right) \left(\frac{-\gamma \mathrm{cov}(r_j, c)}{\gamma^2 \mathrm{var}(c)} \right)$$

$$= \frac{\gamma \mathrm{var}(c)}{1 - \gamma E[c]} \frac{\mathrm{cov}(r_j, c)}{\mathrm{var}(c)}$$

$$= \theta_c \beta_{jc} \qquad (11.39)$$

where $\theta_c = \gamma \mathrm{var}(c)/(1 - \gamma E[c])$. This concludes the derivation of equation (11.20).

---

[26] The δ parameter has been omitted throughout because it cancels from the following derivations.

References

Campbell, J. Y., A. W. Lo and A. C. MacKinlay (1997), *The Econometrics of Financial Markets*, Princeton, NJ: Princeton University Press.

Campbell, J. Y., and L. M. Viceira (2002), *Strategic Asset Allocation: Portfolio Choice for Long-Term Investors*, Oxford: Oxford University Press.

Cochrane, J. H. (2001), *Asset Pricing*, Princeton, NJ: Princeton University Press.

Constantinides, G. M. (2002), 'Rational asset pricing', *Journal of Finance*, 57(4), pp. 1567–91.

Fama, E. F., and K. R. French (2002), 'The equity premium', *Journal of Finance*, 57(2), pp. 637–59.

Hansen, L. P., and R. Jagannathan (1991), 'Implications of security market data for models of dynamic economies', *Journal of Political Economy*, 99(2), pp. 225–62.

Jagannathan, R., E. R. McGrattan and A. Scherbina (2000), 'The declining U.S. equity premium', *Federal Reserve Bank of Minneapolis, Quarterly Review*, 24(4), pp. 3–19.

Kocherlakota, N. R. (1996), 'The equity premium: it's still a puzzle', *Journal of Economic Literature*, 34(1), pp. 42–71.

Kritzman, M., and D. Rich (2002), 'The mismeasurement of risk', *Financial Analysts Journal*, 58(3), pp. 91–9.

Lengwiler, Y. (2004), *Microfoundations of Financial Economics*, Princeton Series in Finance, Princeton, NJ and Woodstock, UK: Princeton University Press.

Levy, H., and P. A. Samuelson (1992), 'The capital asset pricing model with diverse holding periods', *Management Science*, 38(11), pp. 1529–42.

Markowitz, H. M. (1987), *Mean-Variance Analysis in Portfolio Choice and Capital Markets*, Oxford: Blackwell.

Mehra, R. (2003), 'The equity premium: why is it a puzzle', *Financial Analysts Journal*, 59(1), pp. 54–69.

Mehra, R., and E. C. Prescott (1985), 'The equity premium: a puzzle', *Journal of Monetary Economics*, 15(2), pp. 145–61.

  (2003), 'The equity premium in retrospect', in G. M. Constantinides, M. Harris and R. Stulz (eds.), *Handbook of the Economics of Finance*, Amsterdam: North-Holland, Vol. IB, chap. 14, pp. 889–938.

Merton, R. C. (ed.) (1972), *The Collected Scientific Papers of Paul A. Samuelson*, Vol. III, Cambridge, MA: MIT Press.

Samuelson, P. A. (1969), 'Lifetime portfolio selection by dynamic stochastic programming', *Review of Economics and Statistics*, 51(3), pp. 239–46 (reprinted as chapter 204 in Merton, 1972).

Siegel, J. J., and R. H. Thaler (1997), 'Anomalies: the equity premium puzzle', *Journal of Economic Perspectives*, 11(1), pp. 191–200.

12

Bond markets and fixed-interest securities

Overview

Among all the assets available to investors, bonds are accorded a special status. Their distinctive characteristic is that bonds are low-risk assets. In some circumstances the risks can be ignored altogether. In others the risks can be quantified with a precision that is not available for most other assets, especially stocks and shares.

Consequently, the concept of the 'yield' on a bond can be more predictable, less uncertain than for other assets. Also, bonds share characteristics that enable them to be classified according to just a few dimensions, most importantly the time to maturity and the sequence of payments (typically fixed in advance) made in fulfilment of the bond contract.

Section 12.1 describes the main characteristics of bond contracts and outlines some examples of the bonds commonly found in practice. Although *zero-coupon* bonds are not among the commonest, they are key to an understanding of the links among all bonds. Their properties are studied in section 12.2. The properties of the more familiar *coupon-paying* bonds are studied in section 12.3, which also introduces an index of the responsiveness of a bond's price to its yield: the Macaulay duration.

Only for those bonds that are openly traded will market prices be readily observable. For others, including bonds that are traded infrequently (illiquid bonds), ways need to be devised for ascribing notional market values. One such method, suggested by the arbitrage principle, is discussed in section 12.4.

Although bonds are low-risk investments, typically some risks remain. Section 12.5 outlines the various sorts of risk. Section 12.6 goes on to show how the Macaulay duration can be applied to control the exposure of bond portfolios to one sort of risk, namely the risk of bond price changes that occur as a consequence of unforeseen yield fluctuations.

Most of this chapter treats bond prices (and hence rates of return) as the outcome of open market trading – i.e. of the balance between demand and supply. Another approach is to view the theory as providing a method of valuing bonds that may or may not be traded in open markets. In over-the-counter (OTC) markets it is often the case that some bonds are not actively traded – their markets are 'illiquid'; hence, the need for a method of valuation if a reliable market price is not available. This is the subject of section 12.4.

The unit time period

While rates of return are conventionally measured at an *annual* rate, other relevant time intervals need not coincide with a calendar year. (Recall chapter 1, section 1.6.) In particular, returns may be compounded more or less frequently than once per year, investors may have planning horizons longer or shorter than a year, and they may take the opportunity to revise their decisions many or a few times each year. For most of this chapter these distinctions are neglected. Unless explicitly noted, it should be assumed that the unit time interval corresponds to 'one year'. The complications that occur when it is necessary to consider intervals of different length will be addressed as they arise.

12.1 What defines a bond?

The prototypical bond is a contract that commits the issuer to make a definite sequence of payments until a specified terminal date. For example, the issuer might promise to pay $100 per annum from the present until 30 June 2025, at which time the contract will terminate with a lump sum payment of $1000.

An important characteristic of many bonds is that they are commonly bought and sold in secondary markets. In this context, bonds are a special form of loan, which is commonly an agreement between two parties (borrower and lender) that is typically not traded with anyone else. Also, bonds are often long-lived; e.g. twenty or more years from the date of issue is not uncommon.

While, in principle, bonds can be issued by anyone, in practice they are issued by governments, their agencies (including supranational bodies, such as the World Bank) and incorporated companies. For companies, bonds provide a way of acquiring capital at a known cost, without sacrificing rights of control over the company if the terms of the contract are fulfilled.

In the example above, 30 June 2025 is called the *maturity date*, the lump sum of $1000 is called the *face value* (or 'maturity value', or 'principal') and the sequence of $100 payments are known as *coupons*. Sometimes the bond would be referred to as a '10% bond', because $100 is 10 per cent of $1000. But, note carefully, there is no particular reason to suppose that the rate of return on the bond – however measured – equals 10 per cent. Various ways of defining the rate of return are described in the following sections. The remainder of this section outlines some of the important characteristics that serve to differentiate one bond from another.

Bonds can be, and often are, quite complex financial instruments, with all sorts of provisions written into the formal contract – known as the bond's *indenture*.[1] Three important attributes have already been mentioned: the *maturity date*; the *face value*; and the *coupons*. A fourth attribute, the rights conferred on bond-holders in the event of the issuer's *default*, may be omitted from the indenture and resolved by litigation if a dispute arises. Alternatively, the rights may be – partially, at least – specified in the contract.

About the face value there is little more to add, except to note that it can be set equal to any convenient value (e.g. $100 or $1) so long as the bond's coupons and its price are scaled accordingly; i.e. the face value effectively defines the unit of measurement for a bond.

The remaining three attributes of a bond deserve further elaboration.

12.1.1 Maturity (redemption) date

Let T denote the maturity date and let t denote the present date, 'today'. Then the 'life' or *time to maturity* of the bond, n, is simply $n = T - t$. The maturity date may be fixed and finite, though it need not be. Other possibilities include the following.

1. *Callable* bonds, which include provisions specifying conditions in which the *issuer* can terminate the contract before T, typically by paying the face value of each bond to its current owner. Rates of return on callable bonds can be analysed with the aid of option price theory, for a callable bond is effectively a package of (a) a bond without such a provision and (b) a call option held by the issuer, who has the right pay a stated sum to terminate the contract according to the conditions stated in the bond's indenture (see chapter 18).

2. *Convertible* bonds, which allow *holders* to exchange the bond for another asset. For example, a convertible bond indenture might specify that it is to be redeemed either (a) in cash at face value or (b) with a unit of the issuer's ordinary shares, at the discretion of the holder. Alternatively, the indenture might stipulate that the holder can convert the bond into shares over a specified period during the bond's life.

   Just as for a callable bond, a convertible bond can be interpreted as a bundle comprising an *in*convertible bond (i.e. without the conversion facility) and an option.

---

[1] Originally, bond contracts were inscribed as documents that were torn in two, one piece held by the owner, the other by the issuer. When the time arrived for an obligation on the bond to be met (e.g. repayment), the issuer could confirm the legitimacy of the claim by matching the indents on the two halves of the document. If they tallied, the claim was probably genuine.

In this case, the bondholder owns the option – i.e. the discretion to act (make the conversion).

3. *Perpetuities,* for which $T \to \infty$. A perpetuity is a promise to make a coupon payment every time period, indefinitely into the future. It is a special sort of *annuity*[2] – one with no specified termination date.

   The British government *consol*[3] is commonly treated as a perpetuity. This is not strictly correct, because the government can redeem the bond (or convert it to another security) at its discretion. Given that the coupon on most consols is £2.50 per £100 of face value, only if the interest rate falls below 2.50 per cent is redemption likely to be contemplated. Redemptions – more accurately, conversions to lower-coupon stock – have, in fact, occurred in times of exceptionally low interest rates.[4]

4. *Sinking funds,* which oblige the issuer to redeem existing bonds over an extended period of time, typically by the purchase of outstanding bonds at current market prices.

12.1.2 Coupons

Denote the sequence of coupons by $c_{t+1}, c_{t+2}, \ldots, c_T$ per unit of the bond.[5] Normally, the bond also repays its face value, m, at date T. Bonds that pay a sequence of coupons together with the face value at maturity are sometimes called 'balloons'.

The simplest, and most commonly encountered, bond is one for which the coupons are constant: $c, c, \ldots, c$. As already noted, c is usually expressed as a percentage of the face value, so that, for example, '$2^{1}/_{2}$% consols' pay £2.50 per annum, for each £100 face value.

Timing of coupon payments

Although coupons are almost always expressed at annual rates, their payment is commonly split into instalments, typically made at six-monthly intervals. For example, a 5 per cent coupon means that five units of account (dollars, euros or whatever) are promised each year on a bond with face value of 100 units. With six-monthly instalments, $2^{1}/_{2}$ per cent of the face value is paid twice per year. Between the dates at which coupons are paid, the price at which a bond is traded is 'dirty', in the sense that the price reflects an element of accrued interest. It is

---

[2] An annuity is a coupon-paying bond with face value equal to zero (i.e. $m = 0$); it provides a sequence of payments, c, that terminates at a specified date (or when a specified event, such as the death of the annuitant, occurs).

[3] The label 'consol' is an abbreviation of 'Consolidated Fund Stock', first issued in the early 1750s.

[4] Readers with long memories will recall the Goschen conversion of 1888, when British government stock with a coupon rate of 3 per cent was reduced to $2^{1}/_{2}$% – see *Palgrave's Dictionary of Political Economy* (Higgs, 1894, Vol. I, pp. 404–5). Another conversion was made in the early 1930s.

[5] Coupons acquired their name from the practice of issuing bonds with attached tickets – 'coupons' – that holders would clip off on each stipulated date and present to the issuer in return for the amount due.

possible to estimate the implied value of accrued interest and to subtract it from the dirty price to obtain a *clean* price. In this chapter, all bond prices are assumed clean – i.e. a correction has been made to eliminate the effect of interest accrued since the last coupon payment.

Zero-coupon bonds

Also called 'pure discount bonds' or 'bullet bonds', zero-coupon bonds are those for which $c = 0$. They pay a lump sum, the bond's face value, at maturity. Zero-coupon bonds play an important role in financial analysis, for reasons shortly to be explained.

While zero-coupon bonds do exist (e.g. treasury bills, very short-term government debt), they are less commonly issued than theory might suggest. Given their importance in financial analysis, zero-coupon bonds are often created synthetically as *stripped bonds*, or 'strips'. To create a stripped bond, a financial intermediary purchases a coupon-paying bond and 'repackages' it in the form of a sequence of zero-coupon bonds, one for each coupon (each coupon of the underlying bond becomes the face value of one of the stripped bonds) and one for the face value paid at maturity. The trading of stripped government bonds has become active, with official sanction and support, in several markets since the 1980s.

A coupon-paying bond can be viewed as a portfolio of zero-coupon bonds. For example, a three-year bond, with face value $1000, promising to pay a coupon of $40 every six months, can be treated as a portfolio of five zero-coupon bonds each with face value $40, each maturing separately at six-month intervals, and one three-year zero-coupon bond with face value $1040. Viewing coupon-paying bonds from this perspective simplifies the analysis, which can otherwise prove intractable.

Variable coupons

Rather than the promise of a constant coupon, the bond indenture might contain a rule for calculating regular payments over the life of the bond. Examples include: (a) *floating-rate* bonds, for which the coupon is linked to an observed interest rate that varies across time; and (b) *index-linked* bonds, for which the coupon is linked to a specified index of prices, such as the retail price index in Britain (see chapter 13, section 13.2).

12.1.3 Default

In the event that the issuer defaults on any clause of the contract (e.g. by failing to make a coupon payment), it is at the discretion of the bondholders to make a legal claim on the issuer's assets. Bond indentures sometimes include clauses that place restrictions on, or provide privileges for, parties to the contract.[6] Here are two examples.

1. The contract could give priority to some bonds over others with respect to their claims on the issuer's assets. For instance, *senior* debt contracts include provisions to the effect that the issuer pledges not to take on other debt obligations that have a prior claim on the issuer's assets in the event of default. A hierarchy of debt can be built up, with an array of *subordinated* bonds, the holders of which have no claim on the issuer's assets until the obligations to other nominated bondholders are met. The courts of law are, of course, the arbiters for the dispersal of assets in the event of default, but, subject to the ultimate judicial prerogative, there may be opportunities for a bond issuer to designate priorities for some creditors relative to others.

2. A specific asset, or group of assets, may be identified as *collateral* for the bond. In the case of *collateralized bonds*, the specified assets alone constitute security for the bond (i.e. the holders have no other claim on the assets of the issuer).

   In some cases, by specifying particular assets as collateral, an issuer may make loans more marketable (transferable from one holder to another). This process can lead to the *securitization* of loans. For instance, loans on real estate can be packaged together and traded as bonds backed by the property that was mortgaged to obtain the loan.

Bond rating agencies (e.g. Moody's or Standard & Poor's) make a living out of appraising the prospects for bonds' default. However, this important topic is not pursued here; in the remainder of this chapter, except where explicitly noted, it is assumed that default does not occur in any state of the world. In this sense, at least, bonds are risk-free. Even in the absence of default, bonds are not entirely free of risk, as explained below.

12.2 Zero-coupon bonds

12.2.1 Nominal zero-coupon bonds

Zero-coupon (pure discount) bonds play a pivotal role in bond market analysis. The reason is simple: zero-coupon (ZC) bonds are much easier to analyse than coupon-paying bonds. Any ZC bond can be specified with just two parameters: its face value, m, and the date, T, at which the issuer pays m to the bond's holder. Unless explicitly indicated otherwise, ZC bonds are assumed to be *nominal* in the sense that the redemption value is fixed in units of account – e.g. $m = \$100$.

---

[6] A bond *covenant*, appended to the indenture, might specify how conflicts between issuer and holder should be resolved in the event of dispute, possibly by passing rights of corporate control to the bondholders. The label '*debentures*' encompasses a class of securities that include clauses allowing holders to obtain a stake in the issuing company under certain conditions. For an entertaining discussion of the differences between British and American usage in this and other respects, see *The New Palgrave Dictionary of Money and Finance* (Newman, Milgate and Eatwell, 1992, Vol. II, pp. 102–3).

It is usual to express the second parameter as the *time to maturity*, $n \equiv T - t$, where t denotes the present date. Thus, as of $t = 2006$, a ZC maturing in $T = 2020$ is a 'fourteen-year' ($n = 14$) bond. In 2007 it becomes a thirteen-year bond, and so on.

In fact, only one parameter – the time to maturity – is needed to define a ZC bond, because its price (market value) can be expressed as a proportion of m, which is typically set at a factor of 100 (e.g. $1000 or $100,000). For this reason, ZC bonds are described only as bonds with a given number of years to maturity (e.g. 'fourteen-year' bonds). In what follows, however, a separate symbol, m, is retained to denote the face value.

Let p_n denote the market price today of an n-period ZC bond. Then the yield to maturity, or *spot yield*, on this n-period ZC bond is defined as the constant annual rate of return, y_n, that would be received if the bond is held until maturity:

$$y_n = \left(\frac{m}{p_n}\right)^{1/n} - 1 \qquad (12.1)$$

Thus, a bond with face value $m = 100$, four years to maturity, $n = 4$, and with price $p_4 = 83$ has a spot yield of approximately $4.77\% \approx \left(\frac{100}{83}\right)^{(1/4)} - 1$ per annum (the return being compounded once per year).

Equivalently, y_n can be defined to satisfy

$$p_n = \frac{m}{(1 + y_n)^n} \qquad (12.2)$$

In words: the spot yield on a ZC bond is the rate of return that equates its market price to the net present value of its face value. (Appendix 12.1.3 outlines the analogous expressions for continuously compounded yields.)

At each date there exists a sequence of spot yields $y_1, y_2, \ldots, y_n, \ldots$, one for each maturity. The spot yields are not necessarily equal. Indeed, analysis of the relationship among them forms the subject matter of the term structure of interest rates (see chapter 13).

Also, the prices (or yields) fluctuate over time. Strictly, the notation should reflect this. However, except where ambiguity would ensue, additional notation for the date is omitted in what follows.

The spot yield, y_n, is the rate of return on the bond only if it is held to maturity. If the investor's holding period differs from n, the bond is risky because either: (a) for a holding period less than n, the bond will be sold before maturity; or (b) for a holding period greater than n, m will be reinvested at date T (when the bond matures) for a subsequent return that is not known until T, or later.

Consider, for example, the holding period yield on an n-year bond over the coming year. Let $p_{n,t}$ denote the price of an n-year bond today (date t) and

$p_{n-1,t+1}$ denote its price at $t+1$ (by which time the bond will have $n-1$ years remaining to maturity). Then the one-year holding period yield is defined as $\dfrac{p_{n-1,t+1}}{p_{n,t}} - 1$ (i.e. the capital gain, or loss, on the bond over the period in question).

Except for bonds about to mature (i.e. such that $p_{0,t+1} \equiv m$) the future value of the bond is uncertain: $p_{n-1,t+1}$, for $n > 1$, depends on market conditions at date $t+1$ in the future. Hence, holding period yields tend to be uncertain. In this context, bonds are just like any other asset the future value of which is unknown.

The relationship between a ZC bond's price and its spot yield is shown in figure 12.1. (The subscripts have been omitted for simplicity; i.e. the curve depicts the relationship between price and yield for a particular bond at a given date.) Two properties of the relationship hold for all bonds: (a) the curve is negatively sloped; and (b) it is convex from below. That is, (a) the higher the yield, the lower the bond price, and (b) for successive increases in the yield, the smaller are the reductions in price.[7] Somewhat imprecisely, the convex relationship between p and y is often called simply the bond's 'convexity'.

The motivation for studying a bond's price as a function of its yield stems from the recognition that bond yields are intimately related to one another and to the risk-free interest rate (which can here be interpreted as the yield on a one-year bond, y_1). Suppose then – as is common – that central bank monetary policy controls the risk-free rate. The policy-determined risk-free rate then impacts upon bond yields and, hence, their prices. In the simplest (and unrealistic) case, if the yields on all bonds equal the risk-free interest rate, then monetary policy directly determines all bond prices. Realistic scenarios are more complex. Even so, the impact is broadly similar: restrictive monetary policy (higher interest rates) is associated with a fall in bond prices.

12.2.2 Real zero-coupon bonds

Consider a ZC bond the face value of which is protected against changes in the price level of goods and services between its date of issue – say, t – and maturity, T. The payoff at maturity of this *real bond* is then equal to $m \times z_T/z_t$, where z_t is an index of the price level when the bond is issued and z_T is the index value when the bond matures at T. For example, suppose that $m = \$100$, $z_t = 180$ and $z_T = 270$. The price level increases by one-half, $(270 - 180)/180$, over the life of the bond; consequently, the payoff at maturity is $\$150$.

---

[7] These results can be demonstrated by differentiating expression (12.2) with respect to y (omitting the n subscripts): $dp/dy = -nm/(1+y)^{n+1} < 0$, and $d^2p/dy^2 = n(n+1)m/(1+y)^{n+2} > 0$.

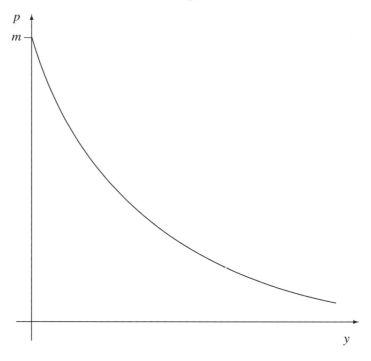

Fig. 12.1. A zero-coupon bond's price, p, as a function of its yield, y

A ZC bond's price, p, is related to its yield via $p = m/(1+y)^n$ (omitting the n subscript on price and yield, for simplicity). The curve has a negative slope because a higher value of y implies that the future payoff on the bond, m, is discounted at a higher rate, thus resulting in a lower value for its net present value (which, by definition, is equal to the bond's price). Note that different values for n and m shift the curve: there is a separate relationship for each bond.

In order to explore the relationship between nominal and real yields, let $\tilde{p}_n$ denote the price of an n-year real ZC bond. Its *nominal* spot yield, $\tilde{y}_n$, is defined by the solution to

$$\tilde{p}_n = \frac{m \times z_T / z_t}{(1 + \tilde{y}_n)^n} = \frac{m(1 + \pi_n)^n}{(1 + \tilde{y}_n)^n} \tag{12.3}$$

where π_n denotes the annual inflation rate for the n years between t and T – i.e. $\pi_n = (z_T / z_t)^{1/n} - 1$. Notice that z_T is unknown at any time before T. Hence, the nominal spot yield on a real ZC bond is uncertain until its maturity date.

Let $\tilde{y}_n^*$ denote the *real* spot yield on the real n-year ZC bond. This yield can be defined analogously with the (nominal) spot yield on the nominal bond, to satisfy

$$\tilde{p}_n = \frac{m}{(1 + \tilde{y}_n^*)^n} \tag{12.4}$$

Notice that the real spot yield on a real ZC bond can be calculated (from p_n and m) at any date prior to maturity: $\tilde{y}_n^*$ is not uncertain.

Combining (12.3) and (12.4) to eliminate $\tilde{p}_n$ and m gives

$$(1+\tilde{y}_n) = (1+\tilde{y}_n^*)(1+\pi_n) \quad \text{or} \quad \tilde{y}_n \approx \tilde{y}_n^* + \pi_n \tag{12.5}$$

where the approximation becomes a strict equality if rates are continuously compounded. In words: (12.5) expresses the familiar decomposition of a nominal rate into a real rate plus an inflation rate; the nominal spot yield equals the real spot yield plus the rate of inflation.

Given that the price level at date T, z_T, and hence the rate of inflation, π_n, is not observed until the bond matures, it is not possible to determine the *nominal* spot yield for $t < T$ with certainty. As already noted, however, its *real* spot yield can be measured with certainty, from (12.4).

Symmetrically, for a nominal ZC bond it is possible to measure its *nominal* spot yield with certainty, but its *real* spot yield is uncertain at any date prior to maturity.[8] The following table summarizes the various yield measures.

	Spot yields	
	Nominal	Real
Nominal ZC bond	y_n, certain	y_n^*, uncertain
Real ZC bond	$\tilde{y}_n$, uncertain	$\tilde{y}_n^*$, certain

It might seem natural to argue that competition among investors in the markets for nominal and real bonds will ensure that their expected nominal spot yields are equal, $y_n = \tilde{y}_n$ – or, alternatively, that their expected real yields are equal, $y_n^* = \tilde{y}_n^*$. If that were so – it is a big 'if' – then it would be possible to infer the expected rate of inflation between dates t and T (or, more precisely, the expected annual average rate of inflation between the two dates). More formally, given that y_n and $\tilde{y}_n^*$ can both be calculated at any date, it is tempting to replace $\tilde{y}_n$ with y_n in $\tilde{y}_n \approx \tilde{y}_n^* + \pi_n$, enabling the calculation of π_n as $\pi_n \approx y_n - \tilde{y}_n^*$ (with continuous compounding the approximation becomes an exact equality, as usual).

The reason why such calculations should be interpreted with caution is that the returns on both nominal and real bonds are uncertain (because the future price

---

[8] The *real* spot yield on a nominal n-year ZC bond, y_n^*, is defined to satisfy $p_n = \dfrac{m \times z_t/z_T}{(1+y_n^*)^n}$, implying that $(1+y_n) = (1+y_n^*)(1+\pi_n)$ or $y_n \approx y_n^* + \pi_n$. Notice that the price levels, z_t and z_T, are interchanged compared with (12.3). For both nominal and real ZC bonds, m is set in units of account (e.g. dollars). But, for real bonds, m is adjusted for inflation while for nominal bonds it is not. The real value of a fixed nominal payoff diminishes if the price level increases between t and T, while a fixed real payoff does not, because m is scaled up by the requisite amount.

level is unknown). The *real* return on nominal bonds is uncertain just as the *nominal* return on real bonds is uncertain. More formally, y_n^* (the real yield on a nominal ZC bond) and $\tilde{y}_n$ (the nominal yield on a real ZC bond) are unknown at all dates $t < T$. Consequently, the expressions in the previous paragraph should be replaced with $y_n = E_t[\tilde{y}_n]$ (equality of nominal yields) and $E_t[y_n^*] = \tilde{y}_n^*$ (equality of real yields), where $E_t[\cdot]$ denotes the operator for expectations conditional upon information at date t. Thus, for example, $E_t[\pi_n] \approx E_t[\tilde{y}_n] - \tilde{y}_n^*$.

Only if unknown future values are replaced with their expected values (typically rationalized on an assumption of investors' risk neutrality) is it legitimate to predict that the nominal, or real, yields on both sorts of bonds will be equal. Apart from such extreme circumstances, risk premia create a wedge between the (nominal or real) yields on nominal and real bonds.

Example

Suppose that the price of a ten-year nominal ZC bond with face value $100 is currently $p_{10} = \$52$, while the price for a real ZC bond is $\tilde{p}_n = \$78$. The *nominal* spot yield on the nominal bond, y_{10}, is (approximately) 6.8 per cent, while the *real* yield on the real bond, $\tilde{y}_{10}^*$, is (approximately) 2.5 per cent.[9] Thus, the expected annual inflation rate over the ensuing ten years might be measured by $y_{10} - \tilde{y}_{10}^*$; i.e. $6.8 - 2.5 = 4.3\%$. But, as argued, this ignores risk aversion on the part of investors who are uncertain about future inflation rates.

12.3 Coupon-paying bonds

In practice, the number and volume of coupon-paying bonds dominate bond markets. The existence of coupons complicates the analysis, partly because a bond's yield will depend on the amount of its coupon but also because the definition of 'yield' is itself more problematical.

Consider a bond that promises to pay to its holder a coupon of c per year for n years plus the face value, m, when the bond terminates at maturity. If the current market price of the bond is p, then its *yield to maturity*, y, is defined as the solution to

$$p = \frac{c}{(1+y)} + \frac{c}{(1+y)^2} + \frac{c}{(1+y)^3} + \cdots + \frac{c+m}{(1+y)^n} \qquad (12.6)$$

The yield to maturity can be understood as the *internal rate of return* on the bond. Notice that both p and y depend upon: (i) the time to maturity, n; (ii) the coupon, c; and (iii) the face value of the bond, m. This dependence has been suppressed

---

[9] Formally, $y_{10} = \left(\dfrac{100}{52}\right)^{1/10} - 1 \approx 0.068$, and $\tilde{y}_{10}^* = \left(\dfrac{100}{78}\right)^{1/10} - 1 \approx 0.025$.

in the notation to avoid clutter.[10] But it should be emphasized that the prices (and yields) of bonds with different n, c and m will almost certainly differ among one another. While this is not explicit in the notation, it should be clear from the context.

It is sometimes convenient to simplify (12.6) as

$$p = \frac{c}{y}\left(1 - \frac{1}{(1+y)^n}\right) + \frac{m}{(1+y)^n} \tag{12.7}$$

(See appendix 12.1.1 for the derivation of (12.7).) For coupon-paying bonds – unlike those with $c = 0$ – an explicit algebraic formula for y is unavailable except for special cases (in particular, when $n < 5$). But, if all coupons are non-negative, a unique solution exists and can be found by numerical methods.

The yield to maturity on a coupon-paying bond does not have the same interpretation as the spot yield on a ZC bond. In particular, it need *not* be the case that the rate of return from holding a coupon-paying bond from the present until maturity equals the value of y that satisfies (12.6). Why not? Because the stream of coupons received between the date of purchase and maturity may, of necessity, be reinvested at rates different from y. Indeed, the coupons might not be reinvested at all. Only if every coupon is reinvested (from the date of its receipt until maturity) at rate y will the rate of return from holding the bond until it matures equal the yield to maturity, y, as calculated from (12.6).

For coupon-paying bonds, the value of y is, at best, an approximation to the rate of return from holding the bond from the present until it matures. Unless forward contracts are available to guarantee the rates at which future coupons can be reinvested, then the rate of return on a coupon-paying bond is inherently uncertain. The risk associated with the rates at which coupons can be reinvested is referred to as *reinvestment risk*.

Two other concepts of yield are occasionally useful for coupon-paying bonds. First, if the price of the bond equals its face value ($p = m$ in (12.7)), then the resulting y is termed its *par yield*. The par yield equals the coupon as a proportion of the bond's face value – i.e. c/m. Thus, for example, if a bond with face value $m = \$100$ pays a coupon of \$10 and has a market price of \$100, then its par yield (and also, with $p = 100$, its yield to maturity) equals $c/m = 10\%$. To show that $p = m$ implies that $y = c/m$, substitute for p in (12.7) and rearrange the expression.

Second, a bond's *flat* (or *current*) yield is defined as c/p. The flat yield is a misleading measure of the return on a bond except for perpetuities –

---

[10] A complication neglected here – again, to avoid notational clutter – is that coupons are expressed at an annual rate but commonly paid twice a year; i. $c/2$ is paid every six months. While the complication is of practical relevance, it raises no new issue of principle.

coupon-paying bonds for which $n \rightarrow \infty$. For these bonds, c/p is the annual yield on the bond, when purchased at price p if it is held indefinitely. To show this, let n tend to infinity in (12.7).

For example, if $c = \$10$ and $p = \$200$, the flat yield equals $c/p = 10/200 = 5\%$. An investor would obtain a return of 5 per cent per annum indefinitely. But, if the bond is disposed of at some date in the future (as it surely will be), the rate of return between purchase and disposal differs from 5 per cent if the selling price is other than $200, its purchase price. Even so, the flat yield is a handy approximation for the rate of return on a perpetuity (or a bond with a long time to maturity) if it is held for many years.[11]

Many of the topics studied in the context of ZC bonds carry over to coupon-paying bonds, albeit with complications. Thus, holding period yields are uncertain, partly because of the prospect of capital gains and losses but also as a consequence of reinvestment risk. Also, as for ZC bonds, the price of a bond is a negative and convex function of its yield to maturity – a result that should not be surprising given that the coupon-paying bond can be construed as a portfolio of ZC bonds.

Macaulay duration

Probably because of their dominance in bond markets, much attention is devoted in bond analysis to the relationship between yields to maturity and the prices of coupon-paying bonds. Formal analysis focuses on the responsiveness of p to y. One possible measure is $\partial p/\partial y$, the rate of change of price with respect to yield. (The partial derivative notation is used as a reminder that n, c and m are held constant in calculating the rate of change.)

The partial derivative is unsatisfactory, in the sense that its value depends on the units in which the bond is measured (e.g. doubling c and m doubles $|\partial p/\partial y|$).

The Macaulay duration, named after its inventor, Frederick Macaulay, provides a more robust measure for the responsiveness of p to y. (See Macaulay (1938, pp. 48–9) for the original definition and analysis.) The Macaulay duration, D, is defined as

$$D = \frac{1}{p} \left(\frac{1 \cdot c}{(1+y)} + \frac{2 \cdot c}{(1+y)^2} + \frac{3 \cdot c}{(1+y)^3} + \cdots + \frac{n \cdot (c+m)}{(1+y)^n} \right) \qquad (12.8)$$

---

[11] But remember that some bonds – e.g. *consols* – that are commonly treated as perpetuities can, according to their terms of issue, be redeemed at the issuer's discretion. In this case, holders face the contingency that, if market interest rates fall low enough (such that $p > m$), the issuer may choose to redeem the bonds at face value. The prospect of a capital loss from such a 'conversion' (refinancing one bond with another) may limit investors' demand for the bonds; consequently, their market prices would be lower than otherwise. (See above, page 284, for the conversion of British government consols.)

(A formal derivation of D appears in appendix 12.1.2.) For example, suppose that a bond with face value $m = \$100$ pays a coupon $c = \$20$ for two years, $n = 2$. If $y = 10\%$, then the bond price is

$$p = \frac{20}{(1+0.10)} + \frac{20+100}{(1+0.10)^2} \approx 117.36 \qquad (12.9)$$

and the Macaulay duration is

$$D = \frac{1}{117.36}\left(\frac{1 \times 20}{(1+0.10)} + \frac{2 \times (20+100)}{(1+0.10)^2}\right) \approx 1.85 \qquad (12.10)$$

It should be remembered that the value of D depends upon n, c and m. Indeed, the main purpose of constructing D is to obtain a single number to measure the responsiveness of p to y, allowing for differences in c and n among bonds.[12]

An important aspect of D is its time dimension. In the example above, the time to maturity is $n = 2$ years, while $D \approx 1.85 < 2$. For a coupon-paying bond, $D < n$, always. Intuitively this is because a portion of the payoff on the bond – the coupon of \$20 at date 1 – is received *before* the bond matures at date 2. It is *as if* the bond will mature shortly before date 2: the Macaulay duration captures the precise sense of this notion.

Apparently unaware of the Macaulay duration, Hicks (1939, p. 186) independently expresses the same concept as the *average period*. 'It is the *average length of time for which the various payments are deferred from the present, when the times of deferment are weighted by the discounted values of the payments.*'

The payoff on a *zero-coupon* bond occurs entirely at maturity. Consequently, $D = n$ for zero-coupon bonds. To show this, substitute $c = 0$ into the definition of D, (12.8).

For coupon-paying bonds with the same time to maturity and with the same yield, the one with the *higher* coupon has the *smaller* D – that is, $\partial D / \partial c < 0$. In words: higher coupons mean that a higher proportion of the bond's payoff occurs before maturity and, hence, its 'average period' is smaller.

Similarly, for bonds with the same coupon and the same yield, the longer the time to maturity the greater is D; that is, $\partial D / \partial n > 0$ – the higher the value of n, the longer bondholders must wait for the bond's payoff.

The relationship between D and $\partial p / \partial y$ is given by

$$\frac{\partial p}{\partial y}\frac{1}{p} = -\frac{D}{(1+y)} \qquad (12.11)$$

---

[12] A second, alternative, definition of duration replaces y in the definition of D with the spot yield on a ZC bond with the same term to maturity as the relevant payment. For example, the discount factor applied to a coupon payment due in two years' time becomes $1/(1+y_2)^2$ rather than $1/(1+y)^2$, where y_2 is the spot yield on a two-year ZC bond and y is the yield to maturity on the coupon-paying bond. A sequence of spot yields (one for each payment date) is required for this calculation. The justification for this procedure should be inferred from the discussion in section 12.4.

which can be obtained by calculating $\partial p / \partial y$, (12.6) – i.e by partially differentiating p in (12.6) with respect to y, and then dividing by p.

The larger is D the greater the responsiveness of the bond's price to a change in its yield. Sometimes (12.11) is referred to as the *modified duration*. It measures the proportionate change in the bond price in response to a change in the bond's yield. (Notice the *minus* sign: an increase in the yield is associated with a fall in price.)

Finally, note that (12.11) represents the proportionate rate of change as a linear approximation. That is, treating D as a constant (for given values of y, c, n and m) provides an accurate measure of responsiveness only for 'small' changes in y – changes such that the *convexity* of the relationship between p and y can be neglected. If closer approximations are needed (for 'large' interest rate changes), then the second derivative, $\partial^2 p / \partial y^2$ (an index of convexity), becomes relevant.[13]

12.4 Bond valuation

The analysis in the previous section is appropriate for bonds the prices of which are observed as the outcome of open market trading.[14] Fortunately, the analysis can be adapted to prescribe a rule for valuing bonds that are not traded or are traded only infrequently (i.e. traded in 'thin' markets). The rule is designed to provide a method for computing bond values as functions of observed prices for other bonds that are actively traded. The arbitrage principle provides the necessary link between the bond valuation and observed prices.

Consider, for example, a zero-coupon bond that pays \$100 one year from the present. Also, suppose that the risk-free rate of interest is 25 per cent. In a frictionless market, the absence of arbitrage opportunities ensures that the bond will be traded for \$80. Why? Because only at this price is the rate of return on the bond, $(100/80) - 1$, equal to the interest rate, 25 per cent. At any other price, arbitrage profits can be made: if the bond's price is lower than \$80, funds would be borrowed to buy the bond; if the bond's price exceeds \$80, it would be sold short, the proceeds being lent at interest.

To generalize the analysis, first note that the spot yield on the bond, y_1, equals $(m/p) - 1$. (See equation (12.1) on page 287, with $n = 1$.) In words: the arbitrage principle implies that the spot yield on a one-period ZC bond equals the risk-free interest rate.

---

[13] In the context of bond prices, convexity is conventionally expressed as $\dfrac{1}{p}\dfrac{\partial^2 p}{\partial y^2}$; i.e. the rate of change of price in response to yield, as a proportion of price. For details, see de La Grandville (2001, chap. 7).

[14] The assumption is that secondary markets for these bonds as sufficiently active that realized market prices are reliable indicators of the prices at which investors can buy or sell the bonds.

Thus, a rule for valuing one-period ZC bonds is: the bond's value equals the net present value, discounting at the risk-free interest rate. In the example, the discount factor equals $1/(1+0.025)$ and the bond's valuation is $\$80 = \$100 \times 1/(1+0.25)$.

The trivial reasoning in this example can be applied to more realistic bond contracts. Consider, for instance, a bond contract that promises to pay a coupon c for the next n years, together with an amount m at maturity. Label this bond as 'B'.

Bond B can be regarded as equivalent to n ZC bonds, the first paying c after one year, the second paying c after two years, and so on to the one that pays $c+m$ after n years. In the absence of arbitrage opportunities, the value of B equals the sum of its stream $c, c, \ldots, c+m$ weighted by the ZC bond prices:

$$\text{value of } B = p_1 c + p_2 c + p_3 c + \cdots + p_n(c+m) \tag{12.12}$$

where p_j denotes the price of a ZC bond paying one unit of account (say, $1) after j years. If bond B could be purchased or sold for a value different from that given by (12.12), then an investment strategy (involving bond B and the zero-coupon bonds) could be devised that would guarantee arbitrage profits.

Expression (12.12) can, equivalently, be written as

$$\text{value of } B = \frac{c}{(1+y_1)} + \frac{c}{(1+y_2)^2} + \frac{c}{(1+y_3)^3} + \cdots + \frac{c+m}{(1+y_n)^n} \tag{12.13}$$

where $p_j = 1/(1+y_j)^j$ (see equation (12.2) on page 287, with $m=1$). Note carefully that (12.13) is *not* the same as equation (12.6) on page 291. Compare the two. Equation (12.6) defines a yield to maturity, y, for a bond with observed market price p. Expression (12.13) values the bond for a given sequence of spot yields, $y_1, y_2, y_3, \ldots, y_n$, on ZC bonds. In the absence of arbitrage opportunities, the value of B equals p. But note the difference. In (12.6) it is assumed that the bond price, p, is known (observed in the market) and y is calculated to satisfy the condition. In (12.13) it is assumed that realized ZC bond prices are used to value a bond, B, the market price for which may not be observed.

In summary, it is often possible to derive a rule, such as (12.13), to value a bond as a function of the realized prices (or spot yields) of other bonds. The result is commonly called the 'fair' value of the bond. (The adjective 'fair' in this context has no ethical connotation; it merely refers to the absence of arbitrage opportunities in frictionless markets.)

But there is a catch. Spot yields are calculated from the prices of ZC bonds. While such bonds do exist, they may be traded for only a restricted range of maturities; a spot yield may not be observed for every maturity. Indeed, the practice of creating stripped bonds effectively creates ZC bonds artificially from coupon-paying bonds (see above, page 285).

Possibly the most important reason why it is necessary to make bond valuations (whether for ZC bonds or bonds with complicated indentures) is the presence of market frictions. Market frictions may restrict the range of bonds that are traded. But recall that the arbitrage principle (invoked in the rule described above) relies for its validity on the *absence* of frictions.

The upshot is that the bond valuation rules are justified on the basis of an assumption – frictionless markets – that is, at best, an idealization. Just as with the application of any theory, in practice the rules require approximations in the form of assumptions that should signal the need for caution, even scepticism, about their applicability.

12.5 Risks in bond portfolios

While bonds are normally less risky than many other assets, such as equities, bond portfolios are rarely risk-free. The risks associated with holding bonds can be divided into two broad categories: (a) *interest rate* risk; and (b) *basis* risk.

Interest rate risk reflects the impact of market-wide credit conditions on bond prices. If, as is commonly observed, bond yields tend to move broadly together, then a general rise in the cost of borrowing (e.g. as a consequence of restrictive monetary policy) raises bond yields, thus reducing bond prices and the market value of portfolios containing bonds. The Macaulay duration serves to measure the responsiveness of bond prices to their yields, and hence provides an index of the magnitude of interest rate risk.

Basis risk encompasses all sources of risk except interest rate risk, including the following.[15]

1. *Credit risk* reflects the possibility of default, ignored in much of this chapter. *Event risk* forms a subset of credit risk associated with specific incidents (e.g. an earthquake, environmental catastrophe or terrorist attack) that could precipitate default.
2. *Reinvestment risk* : reflects unforeseen changes in future interest rates at which the coupon receipts from a bond can be reinvested (see page 292).
3. *Timing risk* reflects the contingency that the cash flow of a bond is altered during its lifetime. For example, the issuer of a callable bond might exercise the option to terminate the contract prior to the bond's maturity date. At any date prior to maturity, it is uncertain whether the option will be exercised

---

[15] See *The New Palgrave Dictionary of Money and Finance* (Newman, Milgate and Eatwell, 1992, Vol. I, pp. 218–19).

4. *Exchange rate risk* reflects unforeseen fluctuations in the exchange rates among currencies. For example, a Japanese investor who holds bonds denominated in US dollars faces exchange rate risk if the investor's portfolio is valued in terms of Japanese yen.
5. *Purchasing power risk* reflects unanticipated changes in the future value of money and, hence, the real value of bond returns. Real bonds and other index-linked securities, for which the payoffs are adjusted in accordance with price changes, protect the holder against this contingency.

12.6 Immunization of bond portfolios

Immunization strategies (also known as *neutral hedge* strategies) are designed to eliminate (or, at least, manage) changes in the market value of bond portfolio as a consequence of yield fluctuations; i.e. they seek to 'immunize' against interest rate risk. The fundamental principle of immunization in this context is that bond portfolios should be selected such that, when yields change, individual bond values also change so as to offset one another. This being so, the Macaulay duration of each bond plays a key role in guiding decisions about the bond's proportion in the portfolio.

Immunization strategies tend to be adopted by organizations that have predictable liabilities (e.g. to make future payments) and that seek to ensure that their assets are adequate to fulfil these obligations.[16] Portfolio selection policies can then be devised to match their assets and liabilities so as to minimize, or even eliminate, interest rate risk. The principle is: choose a portfolio of assets and liabilities such that the overall Macaulay duration of the assets equals the overall Macaulay duration of the liabilities.

For example, if a company has a liability falling due after eight years, it can immunize against interest rate risk by choosing an asset portfolio with an overall duration equal to eight years. In this context, 'overall' refers to a weighted average of individual bonds' Macaulay durations, as explained below.

A typical portfolio immunization problem is: for a given liability stream (say, a flow of payments on a bond that has been *issued*) choose a portfolio of bonds that has the same Macaulay duration as the liability stream. Then, changes in interest rates should lead to changes in assets and liabilities that exactly offset one another.

To understand the immunization rule, begin by assuming that the yields to maturity on all bonds are equal to one another at a level denoted by y. This implausible condition is relaxed later.

---

[16] Insurance companies and pension funds once tended to favour bond portfolio immunization, but, in the closing decades of the twentieth century, many became attracted by the higher returns on equities. They subsequently learned that the risks of equities are not so readily controlled as those of bonds.

Suppose that the investor has a *liability* with a current market value of $z(y)$. A portfolio comprising two bonds with market prices $p_1(y)$ and $p_2(y)$, respectively, is chosen such that

$$x_1 p_1(y) + x_2 p_2(y) = z(y) \tag{12.14}$$

where x_1, x_2 denote the number of units of the two bonds in the portfolio. (It is straightforward to extend the analysis to allow for more bonds in the portfolio.)

The condition required for immunization is that any variation in y should be associated with a change in the value of assets by the same aggregate amount as the change in the value of liabilities. Formally, from (12.14), with 'small' changes in y

$$x_1 \frac{\partial p_1}{\partial y} + x_2 \frac{\partial p_2}{\partial y} = \frac{\partial z}{\partial y} \tag{12.15}$$

where $\partial p_j / \partial y$, for $j = 1, 2$, denotes the rate of change of p_j in response to the change in y. Similarly, $\partial z / \partial y$ is the change of z in response to the change in y. Expression (12.15) can be written as

$$\frac{x_1 p_1}{z} \left(-(1+y) \frac{\partial p_1}{\partial y} \frac{1}{p_1} \right) + \frac{x_2 p_2}{z} \left(-(1+y) \frac{\partial p_2}{\partial y} \frac{1}{p_2} \right) = -(1+y) \frac{\partial z}{\partial y} \frac{1}{z} \tag{12.16}$$

(To obtain (12.16), divide (12.15) by z, multiply by $-(1+y)$, then multiply and divide the terms on the left-hand side by p_1 and p_2, respectively.)

Finally, rewrite (12.14) and (12.16) as

$$a_1 + a_2 = 1 \tag{12.17}$$

$$a_1 D_1 + a_2 D_2 = D_z \tag{12.18}$$

where $a_j = x_j p_j / z$ is the portfolio proportion of bond $j = 1, 2$, D_j is the Macaulay duration of bond j and D_z is the Macaulay duration of the liability stream.

Choosing portfolio proportions a_1 and a_2 to satisfy (12.17) and (12.18) achieves immunization. With these choices, small fluctuations in y result in changes in the value of assets $p_1 x_1 + p_2 x_2$ that equal the changes in liabilities z. The portfolio has been immunized.

Complications

1. *Unequal yields.* It has been assumed so far that the yields of all assets and liabilities equal y. While this is normally a poor approximation for observed yields, what matters is whether *changes* in yields are equal. If all yields move up or down together by roughly equal amounts, then the conclusion still holds (because the Macaulay duration is a measure of the impact of small changes in y).

   Yield differences among bonds are the consequence of a variety of factors, with the time to maturity, n, being given most prominence. The relationships between bond yields and n, known as *yield curves*, are the centre of attention in theories of the *term structure of interest rates*, which are explored in chapter 13.

Essentially, what has been assumed so far in this section is that yield curve shifts are *parallel* – i.e. that yields on bonds with differing maturities change by the same amount. If yield curve shifts are *non-parallel*, then immunization against interest rate risk is more complicated. In particular, it is necessary to predict how the yields on bonds respond to changes in monetary policy, the stocks of bonds (e.g. as a consequence of government debt management policies) or any other determinant of the supply of, and demand to hold, bonds.

An additional complication is that yields are not a function of time to maturity alone; they depend also coupon rates c/m – rates that commonly differ across bonds. Yield curves are constructed for bonds with differing maturities but with the same coupon rate (normally, zero – i.e. zero-coupon bonds), thus resulting in the need for adjustments to allow for coupon rates that differ across bonds.

2. *Multiple solutions.* When many bonds (with different maturities, coupons, etc.) are available, there may exist more opportunities to achieve immunization. For example, a portfolio manager could seek to match the terms to maturity of individual assets closely to those of individual liabilities (resulting in so-called 'bullet', or 'focused', portfolios).

3. *Rebalancing.* The above analysis holds only for 'small' changes in interest rates – small to the extent that linear approximations of the relationship between bond prices and yields are tolerable. When yield changes are large, the non-linear relationship between p and y renders the linear approximation inaccurate: the resulting errors can become significant. Here is where the *convexity* of the relationship between p and y becomes important. It is possible to improve the accuracy of the linear approximation implicit in (12.11) by adding a quadratic term (essentially, the second term in a Taylor series expansion of the non-linear relationship between bond price and yield to maturity). More importantly, immunization in response to large yield changes requires adjustments – 'rebalancing' – of the bond portfolio to preserve the effectiveness of the strategy. Such adjustments can be of practical significance, because rebalancing, by definition, involves trading bonds. Hence, if trading is frequent, transaction costs may outweigh the benefits of immunization.

4. *Basis risk.* Other sources of risk (e.g. credit risk) may, at times, have a greater impact on bond prices than interest rate risk. Insofar as immunization is effective at all, it is with respect to interest rate risk. Immunization does not confer immunity to basis risk.

12.7 Summary

1. Among all classes of assets, bonds are special because they promise to pay specified amounts of money at designated dates in the future. This makes the risks of holding them easier to control than for most other assets.

2. Two key parameters that distinguish bonds from one another are (a) the date of maturity, at which the obligations on the bond terminate, and (b) the coupons (if any)

paid to bondholders. The face value of a bond (typically paid to holders at maturity) effectively defines the units in which it is measured. Though bonds also differ in the likelihood that the issuer will default on the obligations stipulated in the bond's indenture, the prospect of default has been ignored in this chapter.

3. Zero-coupon bonds are central to financial theory. As the name suggests, these bonds oblige their issuers to make a single payment on maturity. A coupon-paying bond can be analysed as a *portfolio* of ZC bonds, each corresponding to one of the scheduled payments on the coupon-paying bond. The payoff of most ZC bonds is fixed in nominal terms – i.e. units of money. The payoff on *real* ZC bonds is adjusted to allow for changes in the price level from the bond's date of issue until it matures.

4. The spot yield on a ZC bond is the rate of return that would accrue to an investor who holds the bond from the date of purchase until it matures; the spot yield on a ZC bond is its yield to maturity. The yield to maturity on a coupon-paying bond is its internal rate of return, the rate such that the net present value of the bond equals its market price. An index of the responsiveness of a bond's price to its yield to maturity is provided by the Macaulay duration. It has a time dimension: for ZC bonds the Macaulay duration equals the time to maturity, while for coupon-paying bonds it is smaller than the time to maturity (reflecting the fact that bondholders receive part of the bond's payoff *before* it matures).

5. The risks associated with holding bonds are divided into two groups: *interest rate risk*, and *basis risk*. Interest rate risk results from the impact of general interest rate fluctuations on bond prices. Basis risk refers to all the other contingencies that affect bonds' rates of return.

6. Immunization strategies are, by construction, designed to protect the value of bond portfolios against interest rate risk. Portfolios can be immunized against interest rate risk with varying degrees of success, according to the range of available bonds, fluctuations in the term structure of interest rates and the magnitude of interest rate fluctuations.

Further reading

All finance texts devote some attention to bond markets, such as those by Elton, Gruber, Brown and Goetzmann (2003, chaps. 20–21) and Luenberger (1998, chap. 3). For concise expositions, see the entries on 'bond markets' and 'duration and immunization' in *The New Palgrave Dictionary of Money and Finance* (Newman, Milgate and Eatwell, 1992). Modern specialist texts dedicated to fixed-interest securities include those by de La Grandville (2001) and Jarrow (2002). See also Cvitanić and Zapatero (2004, chaps. 2 & 10) for a modern treatment of the markets in fixed-interest securities.

The three volumes of Ross (2000) incorporate a comprehensive collection of classic contributions to the economics of bond markets. Most of the articles found in these volumes are at an advanced level, being at the frontier of research when they were written. From an applied (econometric) perspective, chapter 10 of Campbell, Lo and MacKinlay (1997) offers a concise overview of the literature.

Appendix 12.1: Some algebra of bond yields

This appendix derives the summation formula for coupon-paying bonds, (12.7), the Macaulay duration, (12.8), and expressions for yields when rates are continuously compounded.

A12.1.1: Yield to maturity on coupon-paying bonds

In order to obtain equation (12.7), first rearrange (12.6) as

$$p = c \left\{ \frac{1}{(1+y)} + \frac{1}{(1+y)^2} + \frac{1}{(1+y)^3} + \cdots + \frac{1}{(1+y)^n} \right\} + \frac{m}{(1+y)^n} \qquad (12.19)$$

The expression in large braces, $\{\cdot\}$, is a geometric series. Let S_n denote the sum in $\{\cdot\}$. It follows that S_{n+1} can be written in two different ways:

$$S_{n+1} = S_n + \frac{1}{(1+y)^{n+1}} \qquad \text{or} \qquad S_{n+1} = \frac{S_n}{1+y} + \frac{1}{1+y}$$

Equating the expressions for S_{n+1} and simplifying,

$$S_n + \frac{1}{(1+y)^{n+1}} = \frac{S_n}{1+y} + \frac{1}{1+y}$$

$$(1+y)S_n + \frac{1}{(1+y)^n} = S_n + 1$$

$$(1+y)S_n - S_n = 1 - \frac{1}{(1+y)^n}$$

$$S_n = \frac{1}{y} \left(1 - \frac{1}{(1+y)^n} \right) \qquad (12.20)$$

Now substitute (12.20) for the expression (i.e. S_n) in braces in (12.19), to give

$$p = c \cdot \frac{1}{y} \left(1 - \frac{1}{(1+y)^n} \right) + \frac{m}{(1+y)^n}$$

which is just (12.7), as required.

A12.1.2: Macaulay duration

In order to obtain the formula for the Macaulay duration, D, equation (12.8) begin by differentiating p with respect to y in

$$p = \frac{c}{(1+y)} + \frac{c}{(1+y)^2} + \frac{c}{(1+y)^3} + \cdots + \frac{c+m}{(1+y)^n}$$

to give

$$\frac{\partial p}{\partial y} = \frac{-1 \cdot c}{(1+y)^2} + \frac{-2 \cdot c}{(1+y)^3} + \frac{-3 \cdot c}{(1+y)^4} + \cdots + \frac{-n \cdot (c+m)}{(1+y)^{n+1}}$$

$$= \frac{-1}{(1+y)} \left(\frac{1 \cdot c}{(1+y)} + \frac{2 \cdot c}{(1+y)^2} + \frac{3 \cdot c}{(1+y)^3} + \cdots + \frac{n \cdot (c+m)}{(1+y)^n} \right)$$

$$-\frac{(1+y)}{p} \frac{\partial p}{\partial y} = \frac{1}{p} \left(\frac{1 \cdot c}{(1+y)} + \frac{2 \cdot c}{(1+y)^2} + \frac{3 \cdot c}{(1+y)^3} + \cdots + \frac{n \cdot (c+m)}{(1+y)^n} \right) \quad (12.21)$$

The right-hand side of (12.21) is the Macaulay duration, D – compare also with equation (12.11).

A12.1.3: Continuous compounding

Throughout chapter 12 it is assumed that yields are measured as rates compounded once per unit time period – i.e. once per year. Assume, instead, that yields are measured at continuously compounded rates, as described in chapter 1, appendix 1.3. Then the spot yield, y_n, on an n-year zero-coupon bond with face value m trading at price p_n is defined as

$$y_n = \frac{\ln(m) - \ln(p_n)}{n} \quad (12.22)$$

or, equivalently, as the value of y_n that satisfies $p_n = me^{-ny_n}$. Beware: to conserve notation, the same symbol, y_n, is used for the continuously compounded yield as for the annually compounded yield. The *value* of y_n will depend on the frequency of compounding. For example, if $n = 2$, $m = 100$ and $p_n = 80$, then the yield with annual compounding is $\left(\frac{100}{80} \right)^{1/2} - 1 \approx 11.80\%$, while, with continuous compounding, it is $\frac{\ln(100) - \ln(80)}{2} \approx 11.16\%$.

For a real ZC bond, the nominal spot yield (again using the same notation as in section 12.2) is the value of $\tilde{y}_n$ that satisfies

$$p_n = m(z_T/z_t)e^{-n\tilde{y}_n}$$

that is

$$\tilde{y}_n = \frac{\ln(m) - \ln(p_n)}{n} + \frac{\ln(z_T) - \ln(z_t)}{n} = \tilde{y}_n^* + \pi_n$$

In words: the nominal interest rate (spot yield) equals the real interest rate (spot yield) plus the rate of inflation.

For a (nominal) coupon-paying bond, the continuously compounded yield to maturity is defined as the value of y that satisfies

$$p = c \cdot e^{-1y} + c \cdot e^{-2y} + \cdots + c \cdot e^{-(n-1)y} + (c+m) \cdot e^{-ny} \qquad (12.23)$$

where a coupon of c is paid at discrete dates '1', '2', ..., 'n' (separated by yearly or half-yearly intervals) from the present. Compare (12.23) with (12.6). No explicit formula for y is available for coupon-paying bonds (just as is the case with annual compounding).

If it can be imagined, as an approximation, that coupons are paid in a continuous stream between dates t and T, then (12.23) becomes

$$p = \int_0^n c e^{-y\tau} \, d\tau + m e^{-ny} = \frac{c}{y}(1 - e^{-ny}) + m e^{-ny}$$

where $n = T - t$, the life of the bond.

References

Campbell, J. Y., A. W. Lo and A. C. MacKinlay (1997), *The Econometrics of Financial Markets*, Princeton, NJ: Princeton University Press.

Cvitanić, J., and F. Zapatero (2004), *Introduction to the Economics and Mathematics of Financial Markets*, Cambridge, MA, and London: MIT Press.

de La Grandville, O. (2001), *Bond Pricing and Portfolio Analysis*, Cambridge, MA, and London: MIT Press.

Elton, E. J., M. J. Gruber, S. J. Brown and W. N. Goetzmann (2003), *Modern Portfolio Theory and Investment Analysis*, New York: John Wiley & Sons, 6th edn.

Hicks, J. R. (1939), *Value and Capital*, Oxford: Oxford University Press.

Higgs, H. (ed.) (1894), *Palgrave's Dictionary of Political Economy*, London, Macmillan (three volumes).

Jarrow, R. A. (2002), *Modeling Fixed-Income Securities and Interest Rate Options*, Stanford, CA: Stanford University Press, 2nd edn.

Luenberger, D. G. (1998), *Investment Science*, New York and Oxford: Oxford University Press.

Macaulay, F. R. (1938), *Some Theoretical Problems Suggested by the Movements of Interest Rates, Bond Yields and Stock Prices in the United States since 1856*, New York: National Bureau of Economic Research.

Newman, P., M. Milgate and J. Eatwell (eds.) (1992), *The New Palgrave Dictionary of Money and Finance*, London: Macmillan (three volumes).

Ross, S. A. (ed.) (2000), *The Debt Market*, The International Library of Critical Writings in Financial Economics, Cheltenham: Edward Elgar (three volumes).

13

Term structure of interest rates

Overview

Bonds share attributes – described in the previous chapter – that make them suitable for treatment as a class separate from, for instance, equities. While they may constitute a separate class, bonds are not homogeneous. Of the dimensions relevant for distinguishing among bonds, the time to maturity is one of the most important. It is on the relationship between each bond's time to maturity and its rate of return that analysis of the term structure of interest rates focuses.

A common way of representing the term structure is as a yield curve that depicts the yields on different bonds as a function of the number of years to maturity. Section 13.1 studies the construction of yield curves for nominal bonds – those with payoffs fixed in units of money – illustrated with a yield curve for British government bonds. The illustration is pursued further in section 13.2, which presents a yield curve for index-linked bonds – those with payoffs adjusted to protect against inflation. Section 13.2 also reviews how estimates of expected future inflation rates can be obtained by comparing the yield curves for nominal and index-linked bonds.

Another way of expressing the term structure of interest rates is via a set of 'implicit forward rates' – interest rates that are implicit in, and can be inferred from, the prices of bonds with different maturities. Section 13.3 studies the role and interpretation of implicit forward rates.

The remainder of the chapter explores the determinants of the term structure, beginning in section 13.4 with the 'expectations hypothesis', a theory central to all explanations of the yield curve's shape. Central though it is, the expectations hypothesis is open to attack on several fronts, particularly for neglecting the impact of risk aversion on the decisions of bondholders and issuers. Section 13.5 discusses the implications for the term structure of allowing for risk aversion. Finally, section 13.6 comments on the role of the arbitrage principle in the theory of the term structure and its applications.

13.1 Yield curves

13.1.1 Yield curves in principle

A bond's time to maturity is one of its distinguishing characteristics, but not the only one. As chapter 12 has showed, bond contracts differ across several dimensions. The diversity can be narrowed substantially, however, because yield curves are almost always constructed for government bonds. For these, the risk of default is negligible and can be ignored. Also, government bonds tend to be standardized such that their differences reduce to just two dimensions: time to maturity, n, and the coupon rate, c/m.[1]

Given that yield curves are drawn with the yield to maturity, y, as a function of n, a way must be found for controlling for coupons. This is most straightforwardly achieved by assuming that all coupons are zero; i.e. the yield curve is constructed for *zero-coupon* bonds, the spot yield (yield to maturity on ZC bonds) being plotted against the time to maturity. Recalling that *coupon-paying* bonds can be treated as portfolios of ZC bonds, this assumption is not as restrictive as it might first appear. (See chapter 12, page 285.)

Panel (a) in figure 13.1 depicts an upward-sloping yield curve. This is the conventional and most commonly observed shape, with bonds of longer maturities attracting higher yields. Intuitively, the rationale is that bonds with many years to redemption (long-term bonds) are riskier – because future interest rate fluctuations will have a greater impact on their prices – than bonds nearing maturity (short-term bonds). Hence, long-term bonds command premia, as reflected in higher yields, relative to short-term bonds. Consequently, the yield curve is positively sloped. This argument receives scrutiny later, in section 13.5.

Yield curves are not necessarily positively sloped, however. They are, on occasion, observed to slope downwards, with short term bond yields exceeding those of long-term bonds. A convenient assumption in theory – and sometimes a close approximation, in fact – is that the yield curve is *flat* – i.e. y is the same for all maturities, n. (See, for instance, the analysis of immunization in chapter 12, section 12.6.)

But there is no reason, in principle, why yield curves should be monotonic (positively sloped, negatively sloped, or flat) throughout. For example, it is possible that the yield curve is negatively sloped for some maturities and positively sloped for others, as depicted in panel (b) of figure 13.1. Such shapes, while perhaps uncommon, are by no means pathological. When observed, they are usually attributed to specific or peculiar events in bond markets, often following an abrupt reversal or intensification of monetary policy.

---

[1] It is not necessary to treat the face value, m, and the coupon, c, separately. As pointed out in chapter 12, m can be treated as the unit of measurement for defining bonds, and is typically a factor of 100 – e.g. $1,000,000.

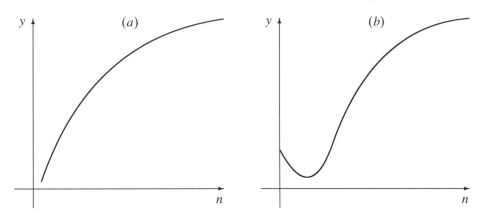

Fig. 13.1. Yield curves

Each point on the *yield curve* plots the spot yield on a ZC bond as a
function of its time to maturity. A typical, positively sloped yield curve
is shown in panel (a). Alternatively, yield curves may be negatively
sloped or constant across maturities (*flat* yield curve). Also, it is
possible for yield curves to be positively sloped over some maturities
and negatively sloped over others, as panel (b) shows.

13.1.2 Yield curves in practice

As already hinted, a stumbling block in the practical construction of yield curves
is that bond markets are populated largely with *coupon-paying* bonds rather
than ZC bonds, the prices of which are required for the calculation of spot
yields. Recognizing, once again, that coupon-paying bonds can be interpreted as
portfolios of ZC bonds, it is possible to disentangle spot yields on hypothetical ZC
bonds, with various maturities, from the realized prices of coupon-paying bonds.

Even so, in practice, the range of realized bond maturities rarely spreads
uniformly across the maturity spectrum. There may, for example, be no bonds to
be redeemed thirteen or fourteen years from the present, while several bond issues
with a maturity of either eleven or fifteen years happen to exist. In particular
(in Britain, at least), few government bonds ('gilts'), with less than two years to
maturity, are traded. Consequently, methods need to be found that 'fill in' the
gaps, using the available data to estimate yield curves that are robust to transient
quirks that would otherwise distort the outcome.

The Bank of England publishes daily yield curves for British government debt,
estimated from realized bond prices and 'repo' rates (see chapter 14, section 14.5)
for maturities less than two years.[2] Panel (a) of figure 13.2 depicts the estimated

---

[2] See Anderson and Sleath (1999, 2001) for details of how the yield curves are estimated. The data needed
to construct the yield curves are available from the Bank of England's Website.

(a) United Kingdom yield curve, 29 March 2004

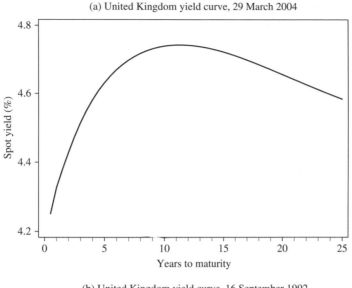

(b) United Kingdom yield curve, 16 September 1992

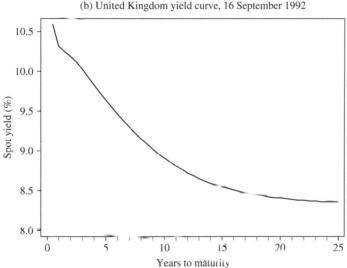

Fig. 13.2. Estimated yield curves

Estimated yield curves for British government bonds are drawn for two different dates. Both depict the spot yield to maturity on nominal ZC bonds (i.e. bonds that promise to make a single specified money payment after the number of years to maturity shown in the figure). Panel (a) shows a commonly observed yield: a positively sloped curve, albeit with slightly lower yields for high-maturity bonds. Panel (b) shows the yield curve on 'Black Wednesday' in 1992, when restrictive monetary policy raised short-term interest rates in an attempt to stave off a speculative attack against sterling.

yield curve for late March 2004. It has broadly the conventional shape, being positively sloped, though perhaps with a tendency to decline at longer maturities. But don't be deceived: notice from the vertical axis that the yields for all maturities lie within a narrow band of less than one percentage point. The yield curve in figure 13.2 (a) is almost flat.

By way of contrast, figure 13.2 (b) shows the dramatically downward-sloping yield curve for 'Black Wednesday', 16 September 1992, when the British government was obliged to concede that it could no longer fulfil its obligations under the European Exchange Rate Mechanism (ERM). Immediately before this date, monetary policy had been intensified to raise short-term interest rates in a futile attempt to keep the sterling exchange rate within the narrow band required for membership of the ERM. The policy failed to stem massive sales of sterling as speculators anticipated the capital gains that would accrue if sterling depreciated upon exit from the ERM – which it did. While the restrictive monetary policy may have raised the yields on bonds of all maturities (relative to what they would otherwise have been), it raised short-term interest rates much more than long-term rates. Invoking the theories studied later, in sections 13.4 and 13.5, the negatively sloped yield curve may have been the consequence of investors acting on beliefs that interest rates would not remain high for very long – probably because they anticipated (correctly) that sterling's membership of the ERM was doomed.

13.2 Index-linked bonds

Thus far, attention has centred on yield curves for nominal (or 'conventional') ZC bonds, the maturity values of which are specified in money terms. While nominal yield curves are by far the most commonly encountered, it is possible to construct yield curves for other sorts of bonds, in particular *real* ZC bonds – i.e. bonds for which the maturity values are adjusted to protect against changes in the price level.[3]

Yield curves for real bonds receive particular attention because they facilitate estimates of expected future inflation rates, as described in chapter 12, section 12.2.2, and below. No new issues of principle arise in the construction of yield curves for real bonds. Strictly, however, actual instances of *real* bonds are not observed. Instead, they are approximated by *index-linked* (IL) bonds.

The main distinction between real and IL bonds is that, for IL bonds, the issuer's payments are not adjusted for the change in the price level from the bond's issue

---

[3] In practice, the adjustments are always for *increases* in the price level – i.e. as a consequence of inflation. Although decreases in the price level can – and do – sometimes occur, securities that approximate real bonds have always been issued to counteract the effect of increases in the price level.

to the date at which the payment is due but, rather, to a stipulated date that *precedes* the payment date. For instance, the payments on British government IL bonds ('IL gilts') are adjusted for increases in the retail price index (RPI) to that prevailing eight months prior to the payment date.[4] After allowing for the complications of timing, it is possible to estimate real yield curves using the methods outlined above for nominal bonds.[5]

Figure 13.3 depicts estimated real yield curves corresponding to the same dates as the nominal yield curves of figure 13.2. The values shown in the graphs can be interpreted as the annual average rates of return over the indicated times to maturity, *after allowing for inflation*. For example, as of late March 2004 the average real interest rate for the ensuing ten years was approximately 1.83 per cent per annum. In September 1992 the real interest rate for 1992 to 2002 was approximately 5.09 per cent per annum.

The values shown in figure 13.3 are estimates obtained from market yields. Hence, they may be compared directly with the nominal yields of figure 13.2, so as to estimate the expected rates of inflation implied by market bond prices (the expectations prevailing on the dates for which the yield curves are drawn). For example, as of late March 2004 the average expected inflation rate over the ensuing ten years was 2.91 per cent per annum – i.e. a nominal yield of 4.74 per cent minus a real yield of 1.83 per cent. Similarly, as of September 1992 the expected annual inflation rate for 1992 to 2002 was 3.82 per cent $(= 8.91 - 5.09)$.

Setting aside measurement errors in constructing the estimates, inspection of the graphs shows that the expected inflation rates differed little across time periods into the future (i.e. across maturities), though they did differ markedly between 1992 and 2004. This is not uncommon: although investors change their perceptions of inflation as time passes, at any one date they appear to expect that roughly the same annual inflation rate will be observed for several years.

For the reason outlined in chapter 12, section 12.2.2, caution should be exercised when interpreting the differences between realized nominal and real yields as expected inflation rates. For nominal and real bonds are both risky, each in their own way. Because future inflation is uncertain, the real return on nominal bonds is unknown. Similarly, the nominal return on real bonds is unknown. Hence, interpreting the difference between nominal yields on nominal bonds and real

---

[4] That is, formally, the amount paid equals $m \times (RPI_{T-\ell}/RPI_t)$, where m is the amount in money (e.g. £100) promised at the date of issue; t is the date of issue; T is the date at which the payment falls due; and ℓ, the 'indexation lag', equals eight months for British IL gilts. Once again, coupon-paying bonds are treated as portfolios of ZC bonds, so that each coupon can be interpreted as the face value of a ZC bond with the relevant maturity.

[5] For details, see Anderson and Sleath (2001). In addition to the eight-month indexation lag, the estimation process allows for two additional complications, namely that (a) calendar months differ in the number of days they comprise, and (b) the RPI is observed only two weeks after the date to which it applies.

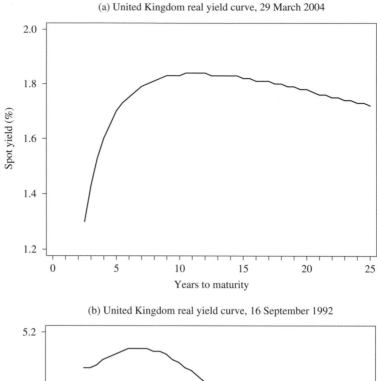

Fig. 13.3. Estimated real yield curves

Real yield curves are obtained from the prices of IL bonds, which promise returns adjusted for increases in the retail price index (intended to counteract the effect of inflation on the value of the bonds' payoffs). Estimated real yield curves are shown for the same two dates as in figure 13.2.   Subtraction of the real yield from the corresponding nominal yield enables the estimation of expected inflation rates (average annual rates corresponding to selected time intervals into the future).

yields on real bonds as the expected rate of inflation is appropriate only if the *expected* real yield on nominal bonds equals the realized real yield on real bonds – or, equivalently, that the *expected* nominal yield on real bonds equals the realized nominal yield on nominal bonds. Estimates of expected inflation measured as the difference between nominal and real yields will be inaccurate to the extent that the realized yields reflect investors' risk aversion about future inflation rates.[6]

13.3 Implicit forward rates

13.3.1 Definitions

Implicit forward rates are indicators of future interest rates inferred from – and thus *implicit* in – observed bond prices. They provide a way of characterizing the term structure of interest rates that is equivalent to the yield curve: for each sequence of spot yields (one for each maturity) there exists a unique sequence of implicit forward rates, and vice versa. *Explicit* forward rates are interest rates relevant for agreements made today on loans that begin and end at stipulated future dates. Implicit forward rates can be understood, instead, as *forecasts* of interest rates on loans that will begin and end in the future. Being forecasts, there is no guarantee that the implicit forward rates will be realized when the future arrives. However, as shown below, there is reason to assert that implicit forward rates will equal explicit forward rates, *where forward markets for loans exist*. It should be emphasized that, throughout the remainder of this section (as for the whole of the chapter), markets are assumed to be frictionless.

In order to define an implicit forward rate, consider the investment of $1 in a zero-coupon bond that matures five years from the present. Alternatively, suppose that $1 is invested in a four-year ZC bond, followed by an investment of the proceeds (i.e. the bond's face value at redemption) in a one-year bond. The one-year rate that results in the same payoff after five years for both strategies is the implicit forward rate between years 4 and 5.

More formally, consider the investment of $1 in a ZC bond that matures n years from the present. After n years, when the bond matures, the investment will be worth $(1 + y_n)^n$, where y_n is the spot yield on an n-period bond purchased today. Similarly, $1 invested in a ZC bond that matures $n - 1$ years from today will accumulate to $(1 + y_{n-1})^{n-1}$, after $n - 1$ years. The implicit forward rate between $n - 1$ and n years in the future is the interest rate that equates the payoffs from the two strategies.

---

[6] Evans (1998) reports evidence for the presence of risk premia implied by investors' risk aversion with regard to uncertainty about future inflation.

In other words, the implicit forward rate is the rate of return that would be received from investing the proceeds of the $(n-1)$-year ZC bond, at maturity, for one more year if the rate of return over $n = (n-1) + 1$ years exactly equals the yield from holding an n-year ZC bond to maturity. In symbols, the implicit one-year interest rate beginning $n-1$ years from today, $_{n-1}f_n$, is defined to satisfy

$$(1+y_n)^n = (1+y_{n-1})^{n-1}(1+\,_{n-1}f_n) \tag{13.1}$$

For example, consider one-year and two-year ZC bonds; then $_1f_2$ satisfies

$$(1+y_2)^2 = (1+y_1)(1+\,_1f_2) \tag{13.2}$$

The implicit forward rate, $_1f_2$, is the interest rate on a one-year investment between dates 1 and 2 if the yield from holding a one-year bond from today followed by a second one-year bond (commencing one year from today) equals today's yield on a two-year ZC bond.

Rearranging (13.1), the implicit forward rate, $_{n-1}f_n$, can be written explicitly as

$$_{n-1}f_n = \frac{(1+y_n)^n}{(1+y_{n-1})^{n-1}} - 1 = \frac{p_{n-1}}{p_n} - 1 \tag{13.3}$$

This expression shows how the implicit forward rate can be calculated from the prices of ZC bonds with the two relevant maturities.[7]

Example

Suppose that $p_5 = 60$ and $p_4 = 66$ for two ZC bonds each with a face value of $100. The implicit forward rate on a one-year bond beginning four years from the present is $_4f_5 = (66/60) - 1 = 10\%$. An investor who expects the one-year interest rate four years from now to exceed 10 per cent could make a speculative profit by selling (i.e. effectively by *issuing*) five-year bonds, and investing the funds in four-year bonds. After four years (when the four-year bonds mature) the payoff would be invested at the one-year interest rate. If the investor's expectation turns out to be correct, a profit would be made after five years (beginning today) following redemption of the five-year bonds (i.e. payment of the face value of the bonds sold, or issued, today). This investment strategy is *risky*: there is no guarantee that the investor's expectation of the interest rate between years 4 and 5 will be realized.

[7] Don't confuse the implicit forward rate defined in (13.3) with the rate of return – holding period yield – obtained from buying an n-year bond today and selling it, as an $(n-1)$-year bond, next year. The holding period yield is the unknown (as of the present) rate of return on a particular bond over the ensuing time period. The implicit forward rate is known at the present, being obtained from the currently observed prices of two different bonds.

The example shows why implicit forward rates may be important for an investor. They enable inferences about interest rates applicable for loans over intervals in the future. This information is relevant for determining which bonds should be sold or purchased, depending on the investor's expectations or future commitments.

13.3.2 Remarks on implicit forward rates

1. The definition of implicit forward rates can be extended readily to cover time-spans different from the unit period of a year. Thus, for example, $_{12}f_{15}$ – defined to satisfy $(1+y_{12})^{12}(1+_{12}f_{15})^3 = (1+y_{15})^{15}$ – is the implicit forward rate on a three-year ZC bond commencing twelve years from the present.

2. If ZC bonds exist for all maturities from the present to n years from today, then successive substitution into (13.1) for ZC bonds of ever-shorter duration results in

$$(1+y_n)^n = (1+y_1)(1+_1f_2)(1+_2f_3)\cdots(1+_{n-2}f_{n-1})(1+_{n-1}f_n) \qquad (13.4)$$

$$(1+y_{n-1})^{n-1} = (1+y_1)(1+_1f_2)(1+_2f_3)\cdots(1+_{n-2}f_{n-1}) \qquad (13.5)$$

$$\vdots$$

$$(1+y_3)^3 = (1+y_1)(1+_1f_2)(1+_2f_3) \qquad (13.6)$$

$$(1+y_2)^2 = (1+y_1)(1+_1f_2) \qquad (13.7)$$

These expressions would look neater if y_1 were replaced by $_0f_1$. But $y_1 \equiv {}_0f_1$: a one-year bond commencing today is trivially identical to a forward agreement commencing zero years from the present (i.e. today). Forward agreements merit separate attention only when they take effect in the future.

Expressions (13.4) to (13.7) show how to recover spot yields from forward rates. They also suggest that the yield on any bond can be interpreted as being dependent on future one-year interest rates – roughly, that bond yields are averages of implicit forward rates on one-year loans. While suggestive, the formula has no predictive force, however, because it does not specify values for the implicit forward rates. For this, a theory of the term structure is required.

3. Time subscripts have been omitted from the definitions of implicit forward rates. This omission is purely to avoid clutter: there is no reason to suppose that the rates will remain constant over time. To denote explicitly the date, t, at which the rate is measured, append a t subscript, so that $_{n-1}f_{n,t}$ denotes the implicit forward rate *as of date t* on a one-year bond issued at date $t+n-1$ for redemption at $t+n$.

4. Spot yields on ZC bonds constitute the data needed for calculating implicit forward rates. Yields to maturity on coupon-paying bonds are unsuitable for the purpose because there should be no presumption that the coupons will be reinvested at the calculated yield (and, hence, no guarantee that the measured yield to maturity will turn out to equal the rate of return on the bond even if held to maturity).

13.3.3 Forward markets for bonds

Suppose that a market exists for loans that commence in the future – i.e. for bonds to be bought and sold (or issued) in the future, not just at the present. For example, a contract signed today (date $t = 0$) might specify that a bond with face value \$100 is to be issued four years from the present, $t = 4$, and redeemed one year later. If the bond's price today (but paid at $t = 4$) equals \$88, then its spot yield equals $(100/88) - 1 \approx 13.64\%$. This rate of return is an observed – *explicit, not implicit* – forward rate.

Given the existence of such forward markets for bonds, the *definition*, equation (13.1), now becomes an *equilibrium condition* if $_{n-1}f_n$ now denotes the observed, rather than the implicit, forward rate. (In effect, market equilibrium requires that the observed forward rate equals the implicit forward rate.) If the observed forward rate differs from the implicit forward rate, then – in the absence of market frictions – there exists an arbitrage opportunity.

Continuing the earlier example, for which the implicit forward rate is $_4f_5 = (66/60) - 1 = 10\%$, suppose that the investor has access to a forward market in bonds. Suppose also that the market price of a bond commencing four years from today that promises to pay \$100 after one year is currently trading for \$88 – i.e. its spot yield exceeds the implicit forward rate, $13.64\% > 10\%$. Notice that, while the *agreement* is made today, the \$88 is paid, or received, not today but in four years' time, when the bond commences. Consider the following strategy: sell eleven five-year bonds for \$660 ($= 11 \times 60$) and use the proceeds to buy ten four-year bonds.[8] Also, in the forward market, buy eleven one-year bonds commencing four years from today: this is a commitment to pay \$968 ($= 11 \times 88$) four years from today in return for \$1100 five years from today (one year after the acquisition of the bonds). Four years from today, \$1000 is received upon the maturity of the ten four-year bonds. Of this, \$968 is used to pay for the eleven one-year bonds (as committed in the forward market contract). One year later (five years from today), the eleven one-year bonds mature with a payoff of \$1100 – exactly enough to redeem the eleven five-year bonds sold at the outset. The payoff from the strategy is an arbitrage profit of \$32 ($= 1000 - 968$) four years from today – an outcome incompatible with market equilibrium in frictionless markets.[9]

---

[8] The number, eleven, of five-year bonds sold is immaterial to the argument and is chosen to keep the arithmetic simple. Any positive number could be chosen. As for every arbitrage opportunity, the scale of the portfolio affects the *magnitude* of the gain, not the result that the payoff is always risk-free.

[9] Even with frictionless markets, it is conceivable that the investor will default on the promise to buy bonds four years into the future or to redeem the five-year bonds at maturity, or both. Chapter 1 describes how good-faith deposits paid into a margin account can eliminate this *performance* risk (or, at least, control it within tolerable bounds).

In the absence of arbitrage opportunities, $_{n-1}f_n$ equals the market rate of return, observed today, for bonds issued $n-1$ years from the present and redeemed after n years. Chapter 14 explores in greater depth how forward markets serve to link the prices of assets traded today for future delivery.

13.4 The expectations hypothesis of the term structure

The expectations hypothesis provides a starting point for all explanations of the term structure. It asserts that expectations about future bond yields determine the shape of the yield curve. Credit for devising the theory is normally accorded to Friedrich Lutz (1940), though others, particularly Sir John Hicks (1939), were pursuing similar lines of enquiry.

At the outset it should be emphasized that the 'expectations hypothesis' is open to a variety of interpretations. Here a fairly strict interpretation – sometimes known as the *pure* expectations hypothesis – is adopted. Some versions tend to make particular assumptions about the expectations formation mechanism or investors' decision-making behaviour.[10] Others concede a loose interpretation of the theory, asserting little more than that expectations of future interest rates influence bond prices.

An informal argument captures the essence of the expectations hypothesis. Consider a world in which one-year ('short-term') and two-year ('long-term') ZC bonds are traded. Suppose initially that the yields on both bonds happen to be equal. If the yield on one-year bonds is expected to rise in the future, investors may prefer to hold one-year bonds so that, when they mature, the proceeds can be reinvested in one-year bonds commencing next year, thus benefiting from the higher expected yield in the future. This preference would be expressed by investors selling two-year bonds and buying one-year bonds, hence leading to an equilibrium in which the price of two-year bonds is lower, and the price of one-year bonds is higher, than otherwise. Given the inverse relationship between yields and prices, the equilibrium yield on two-year bonds becomes higher than the yield on one-year bonds. Hence, the theory predicts that the yield curve has a positive slope if investors expect interest rates to rise.

Conversely, if the one-year bond yield is expected to *fall* in the future, the expectations hypothesis predicts that the yield curve will be negatively sloped. It is predicted to be flat if the one-year yield is expected to remain at its current level. More complicated shapes are consistent with the theory for more complicated patterns of expected future bond prices.

---

[10] Throughout the remainder of this chapter it is assumed that the intervals at which investors review their decisions correspond to the unit period for reporting interest rates – i.e. one year. Allowing investors to revise their portfolios more or less frequently would not materially affect the exposition. But it would surely make it more tortuous.

In order to make the informal reasoning more precise, it is necessary to adapt the notation of previous sections to make explicit the *dates* at which various bond prices (yields) apply. Let $p_{n,t}$ denote the price today, date t, of a ZC bond with n years to maturity. Let $y_{n,t}$ denote its spot yield. (It is harmless to assume that all bonds have the same face value, m – say, \$100.)

After one year, at $t+1$, the same bond will have $n-1$ years to maturity. Its price and spot yield are then written as $p_{n-1,t+1}$ and $y_{n-1,t+1}$, respectively; similarly, for different terms to maturity and different dates – e.g. $p_{4,t+2}$ and $y_{4,t+2}$ denote the price and yield two years from the present for a ZC bond that will then have four years to maturity. The first subscript denotes the *time to maturity*. The second subscript denotes the *date* for which the price (or yield) applies.

Assume, temporarily (and heroically), that bond prices on all future dates are treated as known, or are expected with certainty, as of today, date t. More precisely, investors act as if they know for sure what bond prices will be – they have 'point expectations'. Also, they all agree on these point expectations.[11] (Whether the expectations are realized is another matter. The expectations hypothesis is silent about this, though it would seem to require that realized prices do not systematically deviate from expectations made about them. Otherwise, the theory would hardly merit attention.)

Now compare ZC bonds with one year and two years to maturity. There are three bonds: (i) one-year bonds available today, yielding, $y_{1,t}$; (ii) one-year bonds issued at $t+1$, yielding $y_{1,t+1}$; and (iii) two-year bonds available today, yielding $y_{2,t}$. By assumption, all three rates are known today, date t. Hence, it seems reasonable to claim that in market equilibrium the payoff from investing \$1 in a two-year bond must equal that from investing \$1 in a one-year bond and then reinvesting the proceeds in another one-year bond for the second year:

$$(1+y_{2,t})^2 = (1+y_{1,t})(1+y_{1,t+1}) \tag{13.8}$$

If this equality does not hold, then investors have an incentive either to issue two-year bonds and invest the proceeds in two successive one-year bonds, or to issue two successive one-year bonds and invest the proceeds in two-year bonds. Consequently, for example, if the one-year yield is expected to increase from 5 per cent to 8 per cent next year, today's yield on two-year bonds will equal approximately 6.5 per cent, for $(1+0.065)^2 \approx (1+0.05)(1+0.08)$. Interest rates are expected to rise, and the yield curve is positively sloped, 6.5% > 5.0%.

---

[11] Formally, point expectations can be understood as the extreme circumstance in which the entire probability mass collapses on exactly one outcome (state of the world) – an event with probability 1. Explicit uncertainty (a consequence of relaxing this assumption) allows for many outcomes, each with a non-negative probability. Expectations are then defined in the conventional way, as the sum of probabilities multiplied by the value of the relevant random variable (bond price or yield).

Another way of writing (13.8) exploits the relationship between bond prices and yields:

$$y_{1,t} = \frac{p_{1,t+1}}{p_{2,t}} - 1 \qquad (13.9)$$

In words: the yield on a one-year bond equals the expected payoff on a two-year ZC bond purchased today and sold after one year.

It is tempting to interpret the reasoning underlying this result as an illustration of arbitrage: if the equality does not hold, there is an arbitrage opportunity. Such reasoning is ill-conceived, because $p_{1,t+1}$ and, hence, $y_{1,t+1}$ are *expectations*, albeit expectations held with certainty, about future prices (yields). Strictly, the arbitrage principle applies only if investors can trade at prices such as $p_{1,t+1}$, rather than *expect* to be able to trade at $p_{1,t+1}$ when date $t+1$ arrives. If forward contracts are available, it may indeed be possible for investors to enter into agreements to buy or sell bonds in the future for prices known today. The expectations hypothesis maintains, however, that expectations of future bond yields determine the relationships among currently observed yields, irrespective of the existence of forward markets.

Although the analysis so far involves only one-year and two-year bonds, it holds for bonds of any maturity. For example, suppose that investors have access to trading in one-year bonds and n-year ZC bonds (where $n \geq 2$). Then, reasoning exactly as before, in market equilibrium the yield on one-year bonds equals the expected return on n-year bonds held for one year:

$$y_{1,t} = \frac{p_{n-1,t+1}}{p_{n,t}} - 1 = \frac{(1+y_{n,t})^n}{(1+y_{n-1,t+1})^{n-1}} - 1 \qquad (13.10)$$

The expectations hypothesis of the term structure can be written in at least four ways, all of which are equivalent, assuming point expectations. The variants can be expressed as follows.

1. *Local expectations hypothesis* (LEH): the expected one-year rates of return on all bonds are equal to the spot yield observed on one-year bonds. The LEH is expressed in (13.10), above. In other words: the LEH asserts the equality of the one-year holding period yields on all bonds.
2. *Return to maturity* (RM-EH): the expected return to \$1 invested for n years is the same irrespective of the combination of bonds in which the funds are invested. In the example with one-year and two-year bonds, this form of the hypothesis is expressed as (13.8), above, or for $n > 2$ as

$$(1+y_{n,t})^n = (1+y_{1,t})(1+y_{1,t+1})(1+y_{1,t+2})\cdots(1+y_{1,t+n-1}) \qquad (13.11)$$

In words: the expected payoff on an n-year bond equals the return from investing \$1 in a sequence of one-year bonds, the payoff on each being invested in another one-year bond for the next period. More generally, the sequence of investments need not be in one-year bonds, but in any combination of maturities covering the n years.

To understand the equivalence between the LEH and RM-EH, notice that the assumption of known future bond prices (yields) implies not just that the LEH holds between today and next year (t and $t+1$) but between *every* pair of dates in the future – e.g. $t+5$ and $t+6$, so that $(1+y_{n-5,t+5})^{n-5} = (1+y_{1,t+5})(1+y_{n-6,t+6})^{n-6}$. Tedious algebraic substitutions – either into (13.10) to obtain (13.11), or into (13.11) to obtain (13.10) – demonstrate that the LEH and RM-EH are equivalent.

3. *Yield to maturity*: the yield to maturity on \$1 invested for n years is the same irrespective of the combination of bonds in which the funds are invested. This form of the expectations hypothesis differs only trivially in appearance from the RM-EH. For the two-year bond, (13.8) is replaced with

$$y_{2,t} = \{(1+y_{1,t})(1+y_{1,t+1})\}^{1/2} - 1 \tag{13.12}$$

or, more generally, for n-year bonds with

$$y_{n,t} = \{(1+y_{1,t})(1+y_{1,t+1})(1+y_{1,t+2})\cdots(1+y_{1,t+n-1})\}^{1/n} - 1 \tag{13.13}$$

4. *Unbiased expectations* (UB-EH): implicit forward rates equal expected yields. More concretely, in the example above, this form of the expectations hypothesis asserts that $_1f_2 = y_{1,t+1}$. Now compare expression (13.2) with (13.8):

$$(1+y_2)^2 = (1+y_1)(1+{}_1f_2)$$
$$(1+y_{2,t})^2 = (1+y_{1,t})(1+y_{1,t+1})$$

The are identical, apart from the inessential t subscripts on $y_{1,t}$ and $y_{2,t}$ in (13.8). Looking beyond two years, more generally, the implicit forward rates become

$$\cdots {}_{n-1}f_n = y_{1,t+n-1};\ {}_{n-2}f_{n-1} = y_{1,t+n-2};\ \cdots {}_2f_3 = y_{1,t+2};\ {}_1f_2 = y_{1,t+1} \tag{13.14}$$

Beware: the UB-EH does *not* assert that all implicit forward rates are equal to one another; instead, that each equals the expected one-year rate corresponding to the future year for which the forward rate applies.

Substitution from (13.14) into (13.11) or (13.4) suffices to show the equivalence between the UB-EH and RM-EH (and hence also equivalence with the other variants).

Although the LEH has been defined for a one-year holding period, comparison with the RM-EH suggests that it can be extended to any holding period. That is, the expectations hypothesis implies that the expected rate of return over any time interval – say, seven years – starting today is equal to today's spot yield on seven-year bonds. Notice that the expectations hypothesis does *not* assert that expected rates of return are the same for different holding periods; rather, that they are equal across bonds for any *given* holding period.

More formally, but at the cost of yet more notation, let $r_{n,t+1}$ denote the one-year (i.e. t to $t+1$) holding period yield on an n-year bond – i.e. the rate of return on an n-year bond held over the coming year. By definition, $r_{n,t+1} = (p_{n-1,t+1}/p_{n,t}) - 1$ (see (13.10)). The LEH can now be written as

$$\cdots = r_{n+1,t+1} = r_{n,t+1} = r_{n-1,t+1} = \cdots = r_{2,t+1} = r_{1,t+1} \qquad (13.15)$$

where $r_{1,t+1} \equiv y_{1,t}$ is the spot yield on one-year bonds – i.e. 'the rate of interest'.

As noted above, the expectations hypothesis holds also for other holding periods: '$t+1$' can be replaced with, say, '$t+5$' for a five-year holding period, with the consequence that, for all bonds, holding period yields equal the spot yield on five-year bonds. In symbols: $r_{n,t+5} = y_{5,t}$ for any $n \geq 5$.[12] But the expectations hypothesis does *not* assert the equality of holding period yields across different holding periods; thus, for example, $r_{8,t+1}$ is not predicted to be equal to $r_{8,t+5}$, or $r_{8,t+6}$, or even the spot yield today on eight-year bonds, $y_{8,t}$.

The analysis so far has generated definite predictions about the equality of holding period yields, but it is based on a highly implausible assumption: namely, that investors act as if all future bond prices (yields) are known with certainty. When this assumption is abandoned, it may seem reasonable to replace unknown values with their *expectations*. Thus, for example, condition (13.15) becomes

$$\cdots E_t[r_{n+1,t+1}] = E_t[r_{n,t+1}] = E_t[r_{n-1,t+1}] = \cdots = E_t[r_{2,t+1}] = r_{1,t+1} \quad (13.16)$$

where $E_t[\cdot]$ denotes an expectation conditional upon information available today, t.

While the replacement of unknown future values with their mathematical expectations appears to be a natural way of allowing explicitly for uncertainty, there are awkward implications.

1. The various forms of the expectations hypothesis described above are no longer equivalent. If one holds, the others do not. (See appendix 13.1 for a demonstration.) By implication, if the LEH holds for a one-year holding period, it will not do so for any other holding period – six months, two years, five years or whatever. Thus, to make the theory operational it is necessary to stipulate, *in advance*, which version is assumed. The trouble is that nothing in the analysis so far suggests that any one variant is to be preferred over the others.

2. What justification, grounded on economic principles, can be provided for replacing unknown rates of return with their expectations? This is precisely the question that arose in chapter 10 in going from certain to uncertain future dividend streams. And the answer is the same. Rather than repeat the arguments of chapters 10 and 11, it suffices to note here that bonds can be treated just as other assets and analysed using the same tools. (Appendix 13.2 outlines how this may be achieved.) Except

---

[12] Roll-over strategies are required for bonds with less than five years to maturity – e.g. a three-year bond followed by a two-year bond, or two one-year bonds followed by a three-year bond, and so forth.

in unusual circumstances (e.g. risk-neutral preferences), it is not acceptable merely to replace unknown future returns by their expectations.[13]

Together with a model that explains what determines the relevant expectations, each version of the expectations hypothesis generates testable predictions. The theory is not empirically vacuous. In view of the reservations outlined above, however, theories of the term structure that allow for risk-averse decision makers are, at the very least, worthy of consideration. These are the subject of the next section.

13.5 Allowing for risk preferences in the term structure

13.5.1 The liquidity preference theory of the term structure

One of the first, and most influential, modifications of the expectations hypothesis was proposed by Hicks, and is known variously as the *liquidity preference*, *liquidity premium* or *risk premium* theory.[14] Although not directly motivated by the criticisms raised in the previous section, Hicks's contribution foreshadowed later developments by allowing investors' risk preferences to affect the pattern of bond prices, and hence the term structure.

The theory asserts that, while investors are influenced by expectations of future rates of return, they are *risk-averse* when making decisions about which bonds to hold (or to issue). For example, risk aversion may imply that investors prefer to hold short-term, 'liquid', assets unless a *premium* is included in the return expected from long-term assets: bonds nearing maturity would be preferred to bonds for which maturity is far off. Consequently, long-term bonds would be held only if the expected payoff from holding them exceeds that on short-term bonds. The pattern of bond prices thus reflects the premia demanded by investors if the aggregate demand to hold bonds with different maturities is to match the supply. In the context of the term structure of interest rates, the premia are referred to as *risk, liquidity* or *term* premia. For the purpose of this section, these labels can be treated as synonyms.

Acknowledging (as contended in the previous section) that the expectations hypothesis takes several distinct forms, so also does its modification allowing for risk aversion. Two characterizations of term premia deserve mention here. The first – probably the more common in the literature – is to define the premia

---

[13] Cox, Ingersoll and Ross (1981) show that even risk neutrality is not in itself sufficient (or necessary) to justify the replacement of unknown rates of return with their expectations: it depends on the general equilibrium model within which assumptions about risk preferences are embedded. The sort of risk neutrality implied by the absence of arbitrage opportunities is considered later, in section 13.6.

[14] See Hicks (1939, chaps. 11–13). Although, as befits a classic, this book is neglected now, it remains one of the most influential contributions to economic theory in the twentieth century. Sir John won the Nobel Memorial Prize in 1972, jointly with Kenneth Arrow. Together they represent two of the most original economists in their respective generations.

as differences between implicit forward rates and the relevant expected future interest rate. Formally, using the notation developed in previous sections, let λ_2 denote the term premium for one-year bonds maturing two years from today, date t. This is defined as $\lambda_2 = {}_1f_2 - E_t[y_{1,t+1}]$. In words: the term premium equals the implicit forward rate between one and two years in the future *minus* the expected spot yield on a one-year bond maturing two years from the present. More generally, $\lambda_n = {}_{n-1}f_n - E_t[y_{1,t+n-1}]$ defines the term premium relevant for one-year bonds maturing n years in the future.[15]

A second definition of the term premium focuses on holding yields. Consider a one-year holding period. Let ℓ_2 denote the term premium on a two-year bond, defined as $\ell_2 = E_t[r_{2,t+1}] - r_{1,t+1}$. That is: the term premium on a two-year bond equals the expected return on the bond, if held for one year beginning today – i.e. $E_t[r_{2,t+1}]$, minus the interest rate (today's yield on one-year bond, $r_{1,t+1}$, or, equivalently, $y_{1,t}$). More generally, the term premium on an n-year bond is defined as $\ell_n = E_t[r_{n,t+1}] - r_{1,t+1}$.[16]

Now the term structure can be expressed as

$$E_t[r_{n,t+1}] - \ell_n = E_t[r_{n-1,t+1}] - \ell_{n-1} = \cdots = E_t[r_{2,t+1}] - \ell_2 = r_{1,t+1} \quad (13.17)$$

Compare (13.17) with the prediction of the expectations hypothesis, (13.16).[17] To understand the result, compare (for example) a five-year bond with a one-year bond. Hicks argues that the five-year bond, being riskier than the one-year bond over the ensuing year, has a higher expected holding period yield (positive term premium):

$$E_t[r_{5,t+1}] > r_{1,t+1}$$

the difference being the term premium, ℓ_5.

It is, of course, possible to *define* the term premia such that the equalities in (13.17) *always* hold. If so, as a theory of the term structure, (13.17) is vacuous: it predicts nothing. A testable theory requires that a priori restrictions are imposed on the pattern of term premia. For example, the expectations hypothesis asserts that $\ell_n = \ell_{n-1} = \ldots = \ell_2 = 0$. Loosely specified forms of the expectations hypothesis might allow the term premia to be non-zero but constant across time, or, perhaps, equal to one another.

---

[15] Full generality would require extending the notation to distinguish not only the time interval for which the term premium applies ($n-1$ to n years from today, as described here) but also the date at which the expectation is formed (today, t, here).

[16] Again, full generality requires extending the notation to distinguish not only the bond for which the term premium applies and the holding period but also the date at which the expectation is formed. The extra clutter would add nothing but fatigue to a grasp of this section.

[17] Notice that the equalities (13.17) define term premia for a one-year holding period. They could be defined for other holding periods. There is no reason to presume that, for example, the term premium on an eight-year bond over a three-year holding period equals its premium for a five-year (or any other) holding period.

Hicks's theory predicts that term premia have a positive relationship with time to maturity: the expected holding period yield on a long-term bond includes a higher premium than that on a medium-term bond, which includes a higher premium than on a short-term bond. Formally: $\ell_n > \ell_{n-1} > \ldots > \ell_2 > 0$. (The theory allows some of the strict inequalities to be replaced with weak inequalities.)

In this theory there is an asymmetry between the preferences of lenders and borrowers: lenders prefer to hold short-term bonds, while borrowers prefer to issue long-term bonds. Here is how Hicks expresses it (1939, pp. 146–7 (emphasis added)):

[Bond markets] may be expected to have a *constitutional weakness on one side*, a weakness which offers an opportunity for speculation. If no extra return is offered for long lending, most people (and institutions) would prefer to lend short ... But this situation would leave a large excess of demands to borrow long which would not be met. Borrowers would thus tend to offer better terms in order to persuade lenders to switch over into the long market ...

Speculation thus equilibrates the bonds markets. If long-term bonds are in excess supply, their prices tend to fall, thus providing incentives for speculators to hold the bonds in the expectation of returns in excess of the returns from holding short-term bonds.[18] Consequently, bond prices (and yields) reflect the asymmetry between lenders' and borrowers' preferences – the 'constitutional weakness on one side' of the market.

An implication of the liquidity preference theory is that yield curves are positively sloped if interest rates (i.e. short-period bond yields) are expected to remain constant or to increase in the future. Only if a fall in interest rates, sufficient to outweigh the term premia, is expected would the yield curve display a negative slope.

Plausible though it may seem, and pioneering though it was, Hicks's assertion that most lenders seek to lend short and most borrows seek to borrow long is somewhat arbitrary. An alternative approach, more securely located in the theory of individual behaviour, is to assume that investors behave according to the principles of choice under uncertainty, as studied in chapter 4. Bonds can be treated just like other assets, each investor's decisions being expressed in terms of the fundamental valuation relationship, in portfolio theory. (A sketch of such a theory appears in appendix 13.2.)

The theory of portfolio selection is typically constructed so that the one-period interest rate is identified with 'the' risk-free rate (i.e. the 'r_0' of chapter 4 becomes

---

[18] There is no need to designate speculators as a class apart from borrowers and lenders; the pattern of bond prices may tempt lenders to speculate by holding long-term bonds and borrowers to speculate by issuing short-term bonds. Hicks's theory appears again in the guise of the 'normal backwardation' of commodity prices in futures markets (see chapter 15).

$r_{1,t+1}$, or, equivalently, $y_{1,t}$ in the above notation). This approach makes sense for many applications, in which only a single future date is considered or in which all investment decisions are reviewed every 'period' – i.e. frequently.

However, Hicks's theory implies (a) that investors, including bond issuers, have diverse risk preferences with regard to consumption at different future dates; (b) that they select bond portfolios according to these preferences; and (c) that the pattern of bond prices adjusts to balance portfolio demands with supplies in the aggregate. These considerations provide the stimulus for the *preferred habitat* theory, outlined next.

13.5.2 *The preferred habitat theory of the term structure*

The *preferred habitat* or *hedging pressure* theory of the term structure refines the liquidity preference theory to allow for differing preferences among lenders and borrowers with respect to the maturity of the bonds they hold or issue.[19] As described above, some investors prefer to hold, or issue, short-term bonds, while others prefer to hold, or issue, long-term bonds.

The main implication of this theory is that expectations of future interest rates are not exclusively responsible for the pattern of current bond yields: the stocks of bonds, and investors' demands to hold them, also influence the term structure. If the differentials in bond prices are large enough then investors may choose maturities different from those that they most prefer, but they have to be offered an incentive to do so. The dispersion of risk preferences and stocks of bonds with different maturities can, therefore, exert an impact on the term structure.

An extreme version of the theory – the *segmented markets hypothesis* – asserts that bonds with different times to maturity can be grouped together, such that the prices of bonds within each group are related to one another but not to the prices of bonds belonging to other groups. For instance, it might be that bonds with zero to five years to maturity form one group, six to twelve years another, and thirteen to thirty years a third. If this were so, then the determinants of prices in one group would be irrelevant for the others. Thus, for example, monetary policy (acting on short-term interest rates) might impact upon bond prices in the first group only. Similarly, the actions of pension funds (which, say, hold mainly long-term bonds) might impact upon bonds with thirteen to thirty years to maturity but not upon those with shorter maturities.

Expressed in this extreme way (that markets for bonds with different maturities are completely unrelated), the segmented markets hypothesis has few adherents.

---

[19] The preferred habitat theory was proposed by Modigliani and Sutch (1966), and further developed by Modigliani and Shiller (1973). The late, great Franco Modigliani, in collaboration with his numerous co-workers, made many contributions to modern economics and finance. He was awarded the Nobel Memorial Prize for economics in 1985.

The evidence that bond yields tend to move together, at least in some degree, suggests that there are common influences that affect all bond markets. A less extreme variant of the hypothesis – that markets for bonds with different maturities largely respond to different forces – is less objectionable but is vague (how much is 'largely'?), and differs from the preferred habitat theory only in emphasis.[20]

13.6 Arbitrage and the term structure

While the theories of the term structure reviewed above can make some claim for their empirical relevance, none of them furnishes a satisfying general explanation. They propose illustrations rather than a coherent theoretical framework. Modern attempts to provide such a framework focus on (a) the arbitrage principle or (b) theories of investor behaviour (sometimes embedded within models of general equilibrium). The two need not be incompatible, of course: theories of investor behaviour can serve to give substance to the arbitrage principle, and reinforce its implications.

As a starting point, recall the *risk-neutral valuation relationship* outlined in chapter 7 (see page 173). The RNVR states that, in the absence of arbitrage opportunities, there exists a set of artificial probabilities (the 'equivalent martingale measure') such that the price of any asset equals its expected payoff discounted at a risk-free interest rate. Equivalently, the expected rate of return on each asset (calculated using the equivalent martingale measure) equals the risk-free interest rate.

In the context of bond markets, the relevant rates of return are one-year holding period yields.[21] Hence, in the absence of arbitrage opportunities,

$$\cdots = \mathrm{E}^*[r_{n+1,t+1}] = \mathrm{E}^*[r_{n,t+1}] = \mathrm{E}^*[r_{n-1,t+1}] = \cdots = \mathrm{E}^*[r_{2,t+1}] = r_{1,t+1}$$

(13.18)

where, once again, $r_{1,t+1} \equiv y_{1,t}$ is the spot yield on one-year bonds and $r_{n,t+1}$ is the holding period yield on an n-year bond between dates t (today) and $t+1$. The asterisk, *, appended to the expectations operator, $\mathrm{E}^*[\cdot]$, serves as a reminder that the probabilities are those implied by the arbitrage principle, not (necessarily) those corresponding to the beliefs of any investor. (Formally, the expectations

---

[20] The segmented markets hypothesis is often associated with Culbertson (1957). Culbertson advocates one of the less extreme versions of the hypothesis, which is, perhaps, sensibly understood as a precursor of the preferred habitat theory.

[21] Cox, Ingersoll and Ross (1981) show, in the context of a continuous-time model, that only this form of the expectations hypothesis (i.e. the LEH) is compatible with the absence of arbitrage opportunities when bond returns are random.

operator should be accompanied by a t subscript to indicate that the expectation is taken conditional on information available at date t, but this is omitted for simplicity.)

The result, (13.18), bears a striking resemblance to (13.16). But there is a crucial difference, namely that (13.18) relies only on the weakest assumption about investors' behaviour (that they prefer more wealth to less) and, thus, applies very generally. The shortcoming of such generality is, as usual, that additional assumptions must be made before predictions about the pattern of bond prices (and hence the term structure of interest rates) can be derived.

A common assumption is that bond returns are determined according to a factor model, just as described in chapter 8 – i.e. applying the APT to bonds. The factors could be expressed as observable 'state variables' that characterize the impact of economy-wide forces on the bond market; i.e. variables that emerge from intertemporal optimizing models in much the same way as analysis of the stochastic discount factor informed construction of the CCAPM in chapter 11. In some applications the factors are themselves rates of return on a representative subset of bonds – for example, a short-term bond and a long-term bond. Alternatively, the state variables could be treated as unobservable forces, the impact of which has to be inferred statistically from bond prices observed in the past.

The latter approach appears most often in financial analysis, usually couched in the mathematics of continuous-time stochastic processes. The most basic set-up is the so-called 'one-factor' model, in which the risk-free interest rate is assumed to evolve according to some postulated random process. The arbitrage principle is then invoked to link all other bond prices to one another, and thence to the process assumed for the risk-free rate. Models with multiple factors are analysed slightly differently, each bond price being assumed to respond in its own way to the same set of factors. The arbitrage principle then places restrictions on the pattern of responses, thus linking the bond prices (yields) to provide a model of the term structure.

While these models could be tested in the same ways as other economic models, the emphasis typically focuses on applying them to 'value' bonds or other assets ('derivatives'), the payoffs on which have a determinate relationship to bond returns.[22] In this context, the goal is to obtain a numerical representation of the term structure that enables prediction of any bond price and allied derivatives' prices. These predictions – often called 'fair' values – are notional prices that would be realized (a) in frictionless markets with the absence of arbitrage

---

[22] This approach is sometimes called the 'derivatives approach to pricing' because of its similarity to the methods used in determining option prices. See the introduction to volume I of Ross (2000) and the references cited there.

opportunities, and (b) if the model of the term structure were correct (i.e. an acceptably close approximation to the actual evolution of bond prices).

The predictions can then be compared with realized bond prices in order to inform investment strategies (i.e. to provide signals about which bonds to buy or sell) or to provide price quotations in negotiations about OTC contracts. Alternatively, from a more disinterested academic perspective, the predictions can be tested using methods similar to those described in chapter 9. Here the goal is to identify which theories of economic behaviour are more (or less) consistent with the observed patterns of bond prices and their rates of return.

13.7 Summary

1. Studies of the term structure of interest rates seek to reveal the relationship among the yields on bonds with different times to maturity. Commonly, the term structure is expressed by a yield curve, which plots yields as a function of the number of years remaining before redemption of the bonds.

2. Because the time to maturity is not the only dimension across which bonds differ, it is necessary to control for other characteristics of bonds, in particular their coupon payments. The most straightforward approach is to construct yield curves for zero-coupon bonds (bonds that promise to make a single payment at maturity).

3. Another attribute of some bonds is that the promised payments are adjusted for changes in the price level. From the observed prices (yields) of these index-linked bonds, it is possible to estimate *real* yield curves that express yields to maturity adjusted for future price level changes as a function of time to maturity. It then becomes possible to extract estimates of expected inflation rates, for various periods in the future, from market prices (yields) for real and nominal bonds.

4. Implicit forward rates provide an alternative, and equivalent, way of expressing the term structure of interest rates. Implicit forward rates are interest rates that currently observed bond prices imply would occur for various periods in the future if forward loan contracts could be negotiated in the present. In the event that such forward markets do exist, the arbitrage principle would serve to link the prices of bonds with rates on forward loan contracts.

5. Theories of the term structure attempt to explain the shape of the yield curve (or, equivalently, the pattern of implicit forward rates). The cornerstone of term structure theories is the expectations hypothesis, which asserts that expectations of bond prices (yields) determine observed bond prices (yields). Despite its prominence, the expectations hypothesis (which appears in several guises, some of them equivalent) has weaknesses, both theoretical and empirical.

6. Many early adaptations of the expectations hypothesis stress the relevance of risk aversion on the part of the holders and issuers of bonds. The liquidity preference theory predicts that term, or risk, premia are higher the longer the time to maturity, while the preferred habitat theory argues that term premia depend on the distribution

of investors' risk preferences across the maturity spectrum (i.e. that term premia do not necessarily increase with time to maturity). The most extreme version of the theory, the segmented markets hypothesis, suggests that bonds with different maturities are essentially different from one another, the forces that impact on one market having little influence on the others.

7. Modern analyses of the term structure tend to apply the arbitrage principle in the context of the expectations hypothesis, with factor models representing the underlying forces that drive bond prices.

Further reading

Concise expositions of term structure analysis, including helpful references to the early literature, appear in *The New Palgrave Dictionary of Money and Finance* (Newman, Milgate and Eatwell, 1992) entries on 'term structure of interest rates' and 'yield curve'.

Modern studies of the term structure invariably focus on the formal modelling of relationships among bond prices (yields). They are strong on mathematical technique and weak on economic hypotheses, for which they have little need. Among the more accessible expositions are those by de La Grandville (2001, especially chap. 9), Jarrow (2002), Cairns (2004) and Luenberger (1998, chap. 4). For clear, concise surveys of term structure models and empirical studies, see Yan (2001) and Chapman and Pearson (2001).

Ross (2000) presents a comprehensive collection of the most influential contributions to the theory and applications of the term structure. A more recent survey, elegant though technically challenging, appears in Dai and Singleton (2003). Also at an advanced level, Campbell, Lo and MacKinlay (1997, chap. 11) survey the empirical literature with an emphasis on the application of economic models.

Appendix 13.1: The expectations hypothesis with explicit uncertainty

The equivalence of the four versions of the expectations hypothesis with known future bond prices does not survive the introduction of explicit uncertainty. Fundamentally, this follows from a property of the expectations operator $E[\cdot]$: in particular, that the expectation of a non-linear function of a random variable is not equal to the same function of the expectation of the random variable.[23]

The significance of this result for the expectations hypothesis can be understood by comparing the LEH and the return to maturity forms of the hypothesis, with

---

[23] In this appendix, expectations are not conditioned on information available at date t; i.e. the expectations operator appears as $E[\cdot]$ rather than $E_t[\cdot]$. The notation is simpler and nothing of substance is affected.

just one-year and two-year bonds. Consider first the LEH. Allowing for explicit uncertainty, the LEH asserts that $1 invested in a one-year bond for one year equals the expected payoff on a two-year bond held for one year; that is,

$$(1+y_{1,t}) = \mathrm{E}\left[\frac{(1+y_{2,t})^2}{(1+y_{1,t+1})}\right] \tag{13.19}$$

Compare (13.19) with equation (13.10). Because $(1+y_{2,t})^2$ is known today (it is just the return to maturity on the two-year bond), the LEH can be written as

$$(1+y_{1,t}) = (1+y_{2,t})^2\mathrm{E}\left[(1+y_{1,t+1})^{-1}\right] \tag{13.20}$$

Now consider the RM-EH version, which asserts that

$$(1+y_{2,t})^2 = \mathrm{E}\left[(1+y_{1,t})(1+y_{1,t+1})\right] \tag{13.21}$$

Compare (13.21) with equation (13.11). Because $(1+y_{1,t})$ is known today, (13.21) can be written as

$$(1+y_{2,t})^2 = (1+y_{1,t})\mathrm{E}\left[(1+y_{1,t+1})\right] \tag{13.22}$$

Rearranging (13.22):

$$(1+y_{1,t}) = (1+y_{2,t})^2\{\mathrm{E}\left[(1+y_{1,t+1})\right]\}^{-1} \tag{13.23}$$

Now compare (13.20) with (13.23). The LEH and RM-EH versions express *different* hypotheses, because

$$\mathrm{E}[(1+y_{1,t+1})^{-1}] > \{\mathrm{E}\left[(1+y_{1,t+1})\right]\}^{-1} \tag{13.24}$$

Inequality (13.24) follows from a proposition known as *Jensen's inequality*, which states that, *for any strictly convex function, $F(\cdot)$,*

$$\mathrm{E}[F(X)] > F(\mathrm{E}[X]) \tag{13.25}$$

(A strictly convex function is such that $F''(\cdot) > 0$ – so long as the second derivative is well defined, of course.) In the context of (13.24), $X \equiv (1+y_{1,t+1})$ and $F(X) \equiv X^{-1}$, which is a strictly convex function for $X > 0$.

Reasoning analogous to that above shows that each version of the expectations hypothesis is incompatible with the others. Also, if the LEH holds for a particular holding period, it will not hold for any other. The upshot is that any application of the expectations hypothesis of the term structure, for the interpretation described here, must stipulate which of the versions is assumed. Different versions imply different predictions and, hence, potentially different empirical inferences.

Appendix 13.2: Risk aversion and bond portfolios

An investor's bond portfolio choices can, in principle, be analysed in the same way as the selection of a portfolio comprising any assets. If the investor behaves according to an expected utility criterion, then the optimal portfolio must satisfy the fundamental valuation relationship:

$$E[(1+r_j)H] = 1 \qquad j = 1, 2, \ldots, n \qquad (13.26)$$

where r_j is the rate of return on asset j (e.g. a bond) and H is the *stochastic discount factor*, a random variable dependent on the investor's risk and time preferences. (See chapters 4 and 11.)

In order to gain insights into bond portfolio selection, it is necessary to provide a more definite interpretation of H and r_j in the FVR. Assume that investors make their decisions to maximize the expected value of a multiperiod utility function, $U = U(C_t, C_{t+1}, \ldots, C_T)$. The stochastic discount factor for choices between consumption at dates t and $t+1$ can then be written as $H_{t+1} = U_{t+1}/U_t$, where subscripts denote partial differentiation (i.e. $U_{t+j} \equiv \partial U/\partial C_{t+j}$). If the utility function takes the familiar additively separable form, then $H_{t+1} = \delta u'(C_{t+1})/u'(C_t)$ (see chapter 11).

Notice that H_{t+1} is relevant for a unit period – i.e. one 'year' – holding period. Restricting attention to zero-coupon bonds, the one-year holding period rate of return on a bond with j years to maturity is given by $r_{j,t+1} = (p_{j-1,t+1}/p_{j,t}) - 1$ (for $j = 1$, $p_{0,t+1} \equiv m$, the redemption value of the bond). Thus, the FVR becomes

$$E_t[(1+r_{j,t+1})H_{t+1}] = 1$$

or

$$E_t\left[\frac{p_{j-1,t+1}}{p_{j,t}}H_{t+1}\right] = 1 \qquad j = 1, 2, \ldots, n \qquad (13.27)$$

(The distinction between nominal and real bonds is neglected in this appendix.) For the one-year holding period, $r_{1,t+1} = (m/p_{1,t}) - 1$ is risk-free, so that

$$(1+r_{1,t+1})E_t[H_{t+1}] = 1 \qquad (13.28)$$

Also, the FVR can, as usual, be expressed for rates of return in excess of the risk-free rate:

$$E_t[(r_{j,t+1} - r_{1,t+1})H_{t+1}] = 0 \qquad j = 2, \ldots, n \qquad (13.29)$$

Suppose that the investor is risk-neutral, so that $H_{t+1} = c$, a constant (for all states). Then H_{t+1} can be factored out of the expectation in (13.29), and, as a consequence,

$$E_t[r_{n,t+1}] = E_t[r_{n-1,t+1}] = \cdots = E_t[r_{2,t+1}] = r_{1,t+1} \qquad (13.30)$$

These equalities involve bond prices (from which rates of return are calculated) and investors' beliefs (the probabilities underlying the expectations), but not preferences. Hence, if investors are unanimous in their beliefs, the equalities (13.30) characterize market equilibrium for the bond market (not merely necessary conditions for an investor's optimal bond portfolio).

The implication is that, if risk neutrality is regarded as a plausible approximation for individual preferences, then the FVR predicts that expected returns will be equated for a one-year holding period. Thus, risk neutrality can be used to rationalize the LEH variant of the expectations hypothesis (see (13.16)).

Consider, instead, a holding period of s years. For example, a five-year holding period ($s = 5$) would be relevant for an individual who, for whatever reason, wishes to consume the payoff of an investment after five years (but not before or after). The relevant FVR becomes

$$E_t[(1+\widehat{r}_{j,t+s})H_{t+s}] = 1 \qquad j = 1, 2, \ldots, n \qquad (13.31)$$

where H_{t+s} is the stochastic discount factor relevant for choices between t and $t + s$, $H_{t+s} = U_{t+s}/U_t$ and $\widehat{r}_{j,t+s}$ is the s-year holding period return on a bond with j years to maturity. The circumflex, $\widehat{}$, notation is used to signal that the time interval over which the return is measured is s years, not one year. Thus, $\widehat{r}_{j,t+s} = (p_{j-s,t+s}/p_{j,t}) - 1$, rather than $r_{j,t+s} = (p_{j-s,t+s}/p_{j,t})^{1/s} - 1$, the definition appropriate for 'annual' rates of return.[24]

For an s-year holding period, the risk-free asset is an s-year bond, with $(1 + \widehat{r}_{s,t+s}) = m/p_{s,t}$. Substituting into (13.31) provides

$$(1+\widehat{r}_{s,t+s})E_t[H_{t+s}] = 1 \qquad (13.32)$$

Thus, for example, a five-year ZC bond is risk-free for an investor with a five-year holding period.

Applying exactly the same reasoning as in appendix 11.2 of chapter 11, the FVR can be written as

$$E[(\widehat{r}_{j,t+s} - \widehat{r}_{s,t+s})H_{t+s}] = 0$$
$$\text{cov}(\widehat{r}_{j,t+s}, H_{t+s}) + (E[\widehat{r}_{j,t+s}] - \widehat{r}_{s,t+s})E[H_{t+s}] = 0 \qquad (13.33)$$

---

[24] The definition given here is appropriate for bonds that mature after the end of the holding period – i.e. for $j > s$. For $j < s$, $\widehat{r}_{j,t+s}$ could be constructed as the return from a sequence of bonds in which an investment in j-year bonds is rolled over into other bonds for the remainder of the holding period. While the return on the j-year bond is certain if $j < s$, the returns on the bonds into which its redemption value is invested are not.

where (for convenience) unconditional expectations are used rather than expectations conditional on present information (i.e. the t subscript to the expectations operator is omitted). Rearranging (13.33) gives

$$\mathrm{E}[\widehat{r}_{j,t+s}] - \widehat{r}_{s,t+s} = -\frac{\mathrm{cov}(\widehat{r}_{j,t+s}, H_{t+s})}{\mathrm{E}[H_{t+s}]} \qquad j = 1, 2, \ldots, n \qquad (13.34)$$

This result aids the interpretation of the preferred habitat theory. Suppose, for the sake of example, that all investors have an s-year holding period. Then (13.34) shows that the risk premium on any bond, $\mathrm{E}[\widehat{r}_{j,t+s}] - \widehat{r}_{s,t+s}$, is proportional to the covariance of its rate of return with the stochastic discount factor. In this context, 'risky' assets are bonds the rates of return on which are highly correlated with the marginal utility of consumption at the holding period, $t+s$, for it is this marginal utility that determines H_{t+s}. Bonds with maturities close to s would tend to have small risk premia relative to bonds with longer or shorter maturities.[25]

It is, of course, implausible to assume that the holding period is the same for all investors. Allowing for heterogeneous preferences would greatly complicate the analysis. Even so, this approach shows how it is possible to study the impact of investors' risk preferences on the term structure of interest rates. (A pioneering contribution on similar lines to that sketched here appears in Stiglitz, 1970.)

---

[25] In the context of their model, Cox, Ingersoll and Ross (1981) demonstrate that the behaviour of investors with long holding periods is more subtle than this analysis might suggest. In some circumstances, such investors may choose to bear the risk associated with holding a sequence of short-term bonds even though the expected return over the holding period is no greater than that on a bond with a maturity equal to the holding period – i.e. a bond that is 'risk-free' in the terminology used here.

References

Abel, A. (ed.) (1980), *The Collected Papers of Franco Modigliani*, Cambridge, MA: MIT Press (three volumes).

Anderson, N., and J. Sleath (1999), 'New estimates of the UK real and nominal yield curves', *Bank of England Quarterly Bulletin*, 39(4), pp. 384–92.

——— (2001), *New Estimates of the UK Real and Nominal Yield Curves*, Working Paper no. 126, Bank of England.

Cairns, A. J. G. (2004), *Interest Rate Models: An Introduction*, Princeton, NJ, and Oxford: Princeton University Press.

Campbell, J. Y., A. W. Lo and A. C. MacKinlay (1997), *The Econometrics of Financial Markets*, Princeton, NJ: Princeton University Press.

Chapman, D. A., and N. D. Pearson (2001), 'Recent advances in estimating term-structure models', *Financial Analysts Journal*, 57(4), pp. 77–95.

Cox, J. C., J. E. Ingersoll, Jr., and S. A. Ross (1981), 'A re-examination of traditional hypotheses about the term structure of interest rates', *Journal of Finance*, 36(4), pp. 769–99.

Culbertson, J. M. (1957), 'The term structure of interest rates', *Quarterly Journal of Economics*, 71(4), pp. 485–517.

Dai, Q., and K. J. Singleton (2003), 'Fixed-income pricing', in G. M. Constantinides, M. Harris and R. Stulz (eds.), *Handbook of the Economics of Finance*, Amsterdam: North-Holland, Vol. IB, chap. 20, pp. 1207–46.

de La Grandville, O. (2001), *Bond Pricing and Portfolio Analysis*, Cambridge, MA, and London: MIT Press.

Evans, M. D. D. (1998), 'Real rates, expected inflation, and inflation risk premia', *Journal of Finance*, 53(1), pp. 187–218.

Hicks, J. R. (1939), *Value and Capital*, Oxford: Oxford University Press.

Jarrow, R. A. (2002), *Modeling Fixed-Income Securities and Interest Rate Options*, Stanford, CA: Stanford University Press, 2nd edn.

Luenberger, D. G. (1998), *Investment Science*, New York and Oxford: Oxford University Press.

Lutz, F. A. (1940), 'The structure of interest rates', *Quarterly Journal of Economics*, 55(1), pp. 36–63.

Modigliani, F., and R. J. Shiller (1973), 'Inflation, rational expectations, and the term structure of interest rates', *Economica*, 40, pp. 12–43 (reprinted as chapter 11 in Abel (1980, Vol. I)).

Modigliani, F., and R. R. Sutch (1966), 'Innovations in interest rate policy', *American Economic Review, Papers and Proceedings*, 56(1–2), pp. 178–97 (reprinted as chapter 9 in Abel (1980, Vol. I)).

Newman, P., M. Milgate and J. Eatwell (eds.) (1992), *The New Palgrave Dictionary of Money and Finance*, London: Macmillan (three volumes).

Ross, S. A. (ed.) (2000), *The Debt Market*, The International Library of Critical Writings in Financial Economics, Cheltenham: Edward Elgar (three volumes).

Stiglitz, J. E. (1970), 'A consumption-oriented theory of the demand of financial assets and the term structure of interest rates', *Review of Economic Studies*, 37(3), pp. 321–51.

Yan, H. (2001), 'Dynamic models of the term structure', *Financial Analysts Journal*, 57(4), pp. 60–76.

14

Futures markets I: fundamentals

Overview

Futures contracts and the markets in which they are traded represent one of the most important classes of financial derivatives. A crucial feature of futures contracts is that certain actions, such as the delivery of some asset or commodity, are *deferred* from the present to a determinate date in the future, though many aspects of the actions to be executed are agreed at the outset. But at least as important as this is the fact that futures contracts are themselves traded. Thus, it is necessary to distinguish between the promise to deliver (the futures contract) and whatever object it is that is to be delivered (the underlying asset).

It may seem puzzling that the promises to deliver may, and very often do, vastly exceed the total amount of the commodity that could conceivably be delivered. This chapter, and the following two, seek to demystify what at first sight may appear to be the magical operation of futures markets. Once the specialized jargon and administrative complexity are stripped away, the principles of futures trading become much less puzzling, and, indeed, can be understood by applying conventional economic reasoning.

Futures contracts evolved from a simpler sort of agreement, the forward contract. Section 14.1 begins by describing forward contracts, the features of which serve to highlight the distinctive aspects of futures markets. Having described the main characteristics of futures, section 14.2 outlines how futures exchanges operate in practice. Section 14.3 shows how the arbitrage principle links the forward prices and the current, spot prices of assets underlying forward contracts. Also, a link is established between forward and futures prices for the same underlying asset. The remaining two sections illustrate the application of arbitrage reasoning in foreign exchange markets (section 14.4) and repo markets for the sale and repurchase of bonds (section 14.5).

14.1 Forward contracts and futures contracts

14.1.1 Forward contracts

In a *forward contract*, two parties agree to take a specified action on a specified date in the future. The typical forward contract is an agreement between a buyer and a seller in which the seller agrees to deliver a certain amount of a particular 'good' on a date and place at a price determined at the outset (i.e. when the agreement is made, not when the good is delivered). The 'good' in this context could be a physical commodity (e.g. soybeans), shares in a company or foreign currency. Indeed, it is anything that could be the object of an agreement.

When the agreed date arrives, the contract is executed with the delivery by the seller and payment by the buyer. Let $F(t, T)$ denote the price agreed at date t for the delivery of the asset at date T. Note that the contract (which stipulates the price, among other things) is agreed at date t but is executed only at $T \geq t$. Full payment for the asset is not made until it is delivered, at T. There is no reason to rule out a *side payment* between the parties at date t (or any date before T), but, purely for simplicity, this is assumed to be zero.[1]

A *spot contract* is for delivery at, or very shortly after, the agreement of the contract. Let $p(t)$ denote the price agreed in a spot contract. A trivial arbitrage argument – hardly more than a definition – establishes that $p(t) = F(t, t)$.

Forward markets (together with their associated contracts and prices) have been in existence for as long as recorded history and for a wide range of commodities. Three categories of traders in forward markets are usually identified.

1. *Arbitrageurs* seek to exploit price differentials among spot and forward prices in order to make arbitrage profits (risk-free payoffs that require a zero initial outlay). Market equilibrium is usually defined such that arbitrage opportunities are absent – i.e. that arbitrageurs have successfully exploited any such opportunities, with the unintended consequence that their collective actions have driven arbitrage profits to zero.

2. *Speculators* have 'the object of securing profit from knowing better than the market what the future will bring forth'.[2] That is, speculators seek to profit by trading according to their expectations about the future. They bear the risk that their expectations may turn out to be wrong.

3. *Hedgers* trade in forward markets to eliminate (or, in practice, to reduce) the risks associated with other production or merchandising commitments. For example, a grain merchant may wish to sell wheat forward – adopt a '*short* position' – in order to guard against the possibility that the value of the stored grain will have fallen by

---

[1] Another way of stating the assumption is that the forward price, $F(t, T)$, is agreed such that the value of the contract to both parties at date t is equal to zero. Section 14.3.4, later in the chapter, studies the role of side payments when existing forward contracts (agreed in the past) are renegotiated.

[2] Keynes (1936, chap. 13, p. 170). Earlier (chap. 12, p. 158), Keynes defines speculation as 'the activity of forecasting the psychology of the market'.

the date at which it is sold. A miller, on the other hand, may wish to buy forward –
adopt a '*long* position' – in order to guard against a rise in the price of grain before
it is needed in the milling process. Here is the classic description given by Keynes in
1930 (Vol. II, chap. 29, sect. 5).[3]

> In the case of organized markets for staple raw materials there exist at any time two price
> quotations–the one for immediate delivery [spot price], the other for delivery at some
> future date, say six months hence [forward price]. Now if the period of production is of
> the order of six months, the latter [forward] price is the one which matters to a producer
> considering whether he shall extend or curtail the scope of his operations; for this is the
> price at which he can at once sell his goods forward for delivery on the date when they
> will be ready. If this [forward] price shows a profit on his costs of production, then he
> can go full steam ahead, selling his product forward and running no risk.

Although it is common to imply that arbitrageurs, hedgers and speculators
are different decision makers, such a distinction is naïve because the activities
listed above more appropriately apply to *motives*, not individuals. Motives reflect
decision makers' preferences, which may well be impossible to infer from public
information (the decision makers' actions) or even from any objective information,
public or private. Moreover, a blend of motives could be inextricably combined
in determining a given action. For example, all but the simplest hedging strategies
involve bearing some risk, and, this being so, the investor may be prepared to take
on more risk if compensated with a higher expected return – that is, there may be
a tincture of speculation in hedging decisions. Similarly, arbitrage strategies (in
the strict sense) may be infeasible, although *low-risk* actions approximating those
of arbitrage may be possible. Once again, the action may smack of speculation
as much as another motive. Despite these cautions, the distinction between the
motives behind arbitrage, speculation and hedging is worth preserving, and is
maintained in what follows.

Recall the distinction between *price risk* and *performance risk* (or credit risk)
introduced in chapter 1. Forward contracts allow investors to eliminate *price risk* –
the risk that prices will change between the date of a decision and the delivery
of the asset. But forward contracts accentuate *performance risk* – the risk that
one of the parties to the contract will fail to uphold the bargain when the contract
matures and payment becomes due. The parties to a contract commonly control
performance risk via the provision of good-faith deposits or *margins*, the role of
which is significant in futures markets.

Sometimes spot and forward markets are referred to as *cash* markets, to distinguish them from the *futures* markets, studied next. The reason for drawing the
distinction should become clear from the nature of futures contracts.

---

[3] Keynes developed his theory of forward and spot prices in a *Manchester Guardian* (newspaper) article in
1923.

14.1.2 Futures contracts

Futures contracts form a subset of forward contracts. They are legally binding forward contracts designed to facilitate trading in the contracts themselves at any time prior to the maturity date of the contract, T, specified for the delivery of the asset. ('Maturity date' and 'Delivery date' are used interchangeably in this context.) Futures, like forward agreements, commit the parties to the contracts to take specified actions at date T – that is, for the person who has promised to sell to deliver the asset, and for the person who has promised to buy to take delivery and to pay for it. Futures contracts, however, possess characteristics that enable the parties to 'undo' their commitments at low cost and without breaching any contractual obligations.

Where no ambiguity will result, in the remainder of this chapter the asset underlying any forward or futures contract is called simply 'the asset' or 'the commodity', as appropriate. Forward and futures contracts as financial instruments typically have value and are assets in their own right. Even so, the distinction between the derivative contract (forward or futures) and the asset on which it is defined should always be kept in mind.

Let $f(t, T)$ denote the price of a futures contract at date t for delivery at T.[4] Just as for a forward contract, the price is the amount per unit of the asset to be paid at date T when the asset is exchanged – if the contract remains in existence at T. A trader who adopts a *long* position at t on a contract specifying delivery at T promises to pay $f(t, T)$ at date T in return for receiving the asset at T. Similarly, a trader who adopts a *short* position at t on a contract specifying delivery at T promises to deliver the asset at T in return for $f(t, T)$ payable at T.

The marketability of futures contracts allows the possibility that only a small proportion of the contracts remain in existence at the delivery date, T. Most of the contracts are typically *offset* (or '*closed out*' or '*liquidated*') between t and T. A snapshot of the market at any instant of time reveals the total number of contracts – the *open interest* – that are outstanding. For every buyer there must be a seller. Hence, the total of long positions must equal the total of short positions – a condition sometimes called the 'bucket shop' assumption.[5] At any date t prior to delivery, T, the open interest could be greater or smaller than the total amount of the asset available for delivery. Certainly, there is no reason to require equality between open interest and the amount of the asset in existence for $t < T$. At date T, the stocks of the asset must suffice to allow delivery of the contracted volume; otherwise, default (or urgent negotiations among those holding contracts) will ensue.

---

[4] Futures contracts invariably allow an interval (sometimes as long as a month) during which delivery is permitted. This fact is neglected for simplicity.

[5] See Merton (1973) for the origin of the term, albeit in a slightly different context.

Until the contract delivery date draws near, the open interest often exceeds the volume of the asset that could conceivably be delivered. When the prospect for delivery becomes closer, many of the contracts are offset – the parties 'unwind their positions' – so that, at T, the amount of the asset exchanged is quite modest. For example, in 2003 the proportion of contracts in grain futures held to maturity was about 15.4 per cent of the average open interest, and much less than 1 per cent of all the grain contracts traded during the year (Commodity Futures Trading Commission, *Annual Report to Congress*, 2003).[6] Indeed, many financial futures contracts are written in such a way that delivery of the asset is not permitted, even if it were physically possible; how this can be so is explained in chapter 16.

14.1.3 Distinguishing between forward and futures contracts

Although forward and futures contracts share many common features, their differences are crucial for understanding the operation of futures markets.

1. A forward contract is typically a private agreement between two identified, named parties, one of whom takes a 'long' position (the buyer), the other taking a 'short' position (the seller). With futures contracts, the identity of the party who takes the other side of the contract is irrelevant. Futures contracts are traded on formal exchanges and involve a third party, the exchange *clearing house*, which acts as a guarantor for the contracts.[7]

   Once a futures contract has been agreed, the clearing house guarantee effectively makes the contract an *anonymous* agreement, thus facilitating further trading in the contract prior to the stipulated delivery date.[8] At the delivery date, a trader with short position must deliver the asset but would not know, until that date, to whom delivery should be made. In practice, even when delivery takes place, warehouse certificates are exchanged. Physical movement of the asset need not occur on the delivery date. Not surprisingly, exchange authorities impose obligations on the parties to ensure that the bargains are upheld. (See section 14.2.4.)

   By construction, futures contracts are *homogeneous*: for a given exchange, commodity and maturity date, one contract is identical with another. This is a corollary of the anonymity of contracts.

2. Futures contracts are *standardized*, in the sense that they are expressed in terms of stipulated quantities of a specified quality, or range of qualities, with a determinate

---

[6] Note that the open interest refers to the *stock* of contracts outstanding at the end of each month, while the volume of trade expresses the *flow* of contracts exchanged prior to delivery.

[7] The exchange authorities may very well be vigilant to monitor the identity of both parties to all contracts, in order to uphold compliance with exchange regulations and legal obligations. For example, many exchanges stipulate upper bounds for the number of contracts (long or short) that an investor is permitted to hold.

[8] Exchanges often allow the parties to a trade to know with whom they are trading – a concession that need not undermine, and that does not invalidate, the clearing house guarantee.

delivery date at a particular location. Neglecting some technicalities, the standardization is in terms of the following.

(a) *Quantity*: the contracts are written for a standard number of units; e.g. a wheat futures contract on the Chicago Board of Trade is for 5000 bushels.

(b) *Grade*: the quality (or acceptable range of qualities) is specified. For example, for wheat on the CBOT: 'No. 1 & No. 2 Soft Red, No. 1 & No. 2 Hard Red Winter, No. 1 & No. 2 Dark Northern Spring, No. 1 Northern Spring at 3 cent/bushel premium and No. 2 Northern Spring at par.'

(c) *Date*: the date of delivery is typically a calendar month, known as the 'contract month', delivery being permitted on any working day, though the time interval could be shorter. (Delivery may be permissible for a few days beyond the end of the contract month.) There is commonly a limited set of delivery months; e.g., for wheat in Chicago, the delivery months are July, September, December, March and May.

(d) *Location*: a list of the geographical locations (typically warehouses, grain elevators, etc.) at which delivery is permitted.

No obligation exists to standardize forward contracts, the terms of which are at the discretion of the parties to the contract. For this reason, forward contracts are often referred to as *over the counter*, in contrast with the standardization and anonymity of futures contracts.

3. Forward contracts are normally held to the date of delivery, at which time delivery takes place and payment is made. (It is at the discretion of the counterparties to renegotiate the contract at any time if they so choose.) Because futures contracts are easily tradable, delivery of the commodity in question need not (and commonly does not) occur, most contracts having been offset before maturity.

4. Unlike forward contracts, futures contracts are *marked to market* at the end of every trading day. To grasp what this means, suppose that an investor purchases ten futures contracts at a price of $1000 each and that the next trading day the price rises to $1050. The investor's margin account is credited by the exchange with a gain of $500 ($= 10 \times \$50$). It is *as if* the position is offset and immediately reinstated with ten new contracts. Note that the gain of $500 is a genuine profit if the investor sells ten contracts at $1050; otherwise, the trader begins the following day with a long position of ten contracts valued at $1050 (not $1000). If the price happens to fall below $1050 on the next day, the investor makes a loss, the margin account being debited with the change in price multiplied by the number of contracts.

Conversely, suppose that the investor sells ten futures contracts at $1000 each. If the price rises to $1050, the investor's margin account is debited with $500: the position is effectively offset and immediately reinstated, so that the investor has now sold ten contracts at $1050 (instead of $1000). Whether this constitutes an eventual loss for the investor depends on the price at which the position is subsequently offset (or the spot price if the commodity is delivered at the maturity of the contract).

Although with futures contracts there is much crediting and debiting of margin accounts during the life of the contract, it should be remembered that the futures contract price refers to a price at which the asset changes hands *upon delivery*. Prior to that time, the flows of cash into or out of margin accounts (described further below) exist to minimize performance risk, not as final payment for the asset itself.

The differences between forward and futures contracts reveal that they perform rather different functions for traders. Forward contracts can be tailor-made to meet the peculiar needs of those who deal in them. But, having been agreed, forward contracts may be costly to renegotiate, or to exchange with third parties. Futures contracts are designed to be easily tradable – *liquid* – but are not customized to suit the precise needs of those who seek to make, or take, delivery of the asset. Some assets, such as foreign exchange, are sufficiently homogeneous and liquid that the distinction between forward and futures contracts is of little economic consequence. For others, such as agricultural commodities, the distinction is more important because the asset may be heterogeneous in one or more relevant dimensions.

14.2 The operation of futures markets

14.2.1 Futures exchanges and their members

Some of the more well-known futures exchanges include: the Chicago Board of Trade (founded in 1848, a market in agricultural commodities and, since the early 1980s, financial futures); the Chicago Mercantile Exchange (CME, founded in 1874, a market in livestock futures and, since the early 1980s, financial futures, especially contracts in foreign currency and interest rate futures); the New York Mercantile Exchange (NYMEX, formed in 1994 from the Commodity Exchange in New York, a market in precious metals and energy futures); the London Metal Exchange (founded in 1877, a market in base metals); the International Petroleum Exchange (founded in 1980, a market for oil and natural gas products); and the London International Financial Futures Exchange (founded in 1982, a market in futures and options).[9]

While competition among traders on each exchange is normally taken for granted, exchanges themselves also compete for business. Copper futures, for example, are traded both on the LME and NYMEX. The contract specifications are not identical across exchanges; different contracts will suit different investors. Even so, exchanges have an incentive to make their contracts as attractive as possible. Also, investors may seek to exploit opportunities to profit from price discrepancies that they perceive among contracts traded on different exchanges.

---

[9] In late 2001 the Euronext group acquired LIFFE and renamed it Euronext.liffe. For convenience, the abbreviation LIFFE is used here and in the remaining chapters.

The exchanges are commonly owned and controlled by *member firms*, which may also be *floor traders* (acting as principals, on their own behalf) or *floor brokers* (acting on behalf of others). The exchange authority has an obligation to uphold the rules of the exchange in order to minimize dishonesty and to make the exchange an attractive place for trading in the contracts it offers. 'Investors' can be identified with principals (i.e. dealers acting on their own account), who instruct member firms or brokers to make deals.

The exchange clearing house is a legal entity separate from the exchange itself[10] (though, typically, there is an overlapping membership). All contracts must be registered with the clearing house; margins are deposited with it; it administers settlement (see 14.2.3, below); and it arranges compensation in the event of default.

14.2.2 Trading mechanisms

Most exchanges operate *order-driven* continuous auctions (see chapter 2). Instructions in the form of market or limit orders[11] to by or sell contracts are given by investors to their brokers (typically, members of the exchange). Each instruction is then communicated to a *floor broker*, who operates in the *trading pit* by engaging in an elaborate ritual of *open outcry* to make a trade. The trade may be with another broker acting on behalf of an exchange member or a floor trader acting as a principal. Many exchanges have now adopted various forms of computerized trading, such as the CME's GLOBEX or LIFFE's CONNECT *trading platform*, which provides an electronic limit order book for recording and executing orders. In some markets computerized trading has displaced open outcry altogether. In others it runs in parallel with open outcry, while in yet others computerized trading is allowed at times when the open outcry trading pit is closed. Open outcry may soon be consigned to history.

As already noted, the exchange authority determines the specification of each type of contract and the terms on which it can be traded. The *contract size*, or trading unit, defines the unit of measurement for the 'commodity' (e.g. for the FT-SE 100 index future one contract is equal to $10 *times* the value of the FT-SE 100 index). The *tick size* defines the minimum unit for price changes (e.g. 0.5 of each index point for the FT-SE 100 index). The *tick value* is the tick size multiplied by the trading unit (e.g. $0.5 \times \$10 = \$5.00$ for the FT-SE 100 contract).

---

[10] In London, for example, the London Clearing House (LCH) is the clearing house for the IPE, LME and LIFFE.

[11] These are the simplest types of order; most exchanges also allow other more complicated instructions to be executed.

Many exchanges impose *price limits*, which restrict the absolute magnitude of price fluctuations that are allowed in any one trading day. For example, for CBOT wheat futures the price per contract is allowed to change by at most $1500 (30 cents per bushel) each day, except that no limit applies during the delivery month.

Instead of price limits, some exchanges require trading to cease for a while if prices change by a large amount over a short interval. For example, on LIFFE, when a limit is reached trading is suspended for a one-hour recess – a cooling-off period. This sort of restraint is common for financial futures contracts.

Exchange authorities may also impose limits on the number of contracts held by any one investor. For example, for NYMEX oil futures each investor is allowed to be long or short in at most 20,000 contracts. Such a restriction reduces the scope for an investor to become dominant in the market (and, hence, to manipulate the price). Also, it limits the impact on the market in the event of an investor's default.

At the end of each trading day, the *settlement price* defines the price at which outstanding contracts are marked to market. Typically, the settlement price is set equal to the closing price – i.e. the price agreed for the last trade of the day. It is possible, however, that, when no trades have taken place towards the end of the day, the exchange authorities may decide that the last trade is unrepresentative for some reason and a different settlement price will be announced.

14.2.3 Terminating futures positions

If an investor has a position in futures, be it long or short, some action must be taken with regard to the contracts before or at the maturity date. How are futures contracts liquidated? There are three main ways.

1. *Offsetting trades.* The commonest form of settlement is for offsetting trades to be made sometime before the delivery date. An investor with a long position sells the same number of contracts previously purchased. An investor with a short position buys the same number of contracts previously sold. The gains or losses on the deal are then credited or debited to the investors' margin accounts. The process of marking to market ensures that the profit or loss is reflected in the value of the margin account when the offsetting trade is settled.

   The payoffs from futures positions, subsequently offset, are depicted in figure 14.1. Consider a long futures position, in which one contract is purchased at price f_0. If the position is offset (with the sale of one contract) at a higher price, there is a gain equal to the difference between the purchase and sale prices. Conversely, if the position is offset at a lower price, a loss is made, again equal to the difference between the purchase and sale prices – hence the positively sloped line with slope $+1$ in figure 14.1.

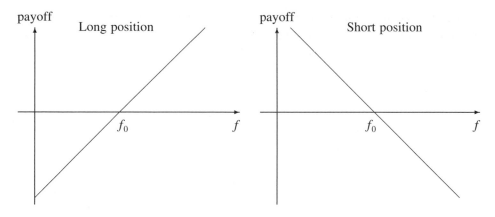

Fig. 14.1. payoffs from long and short futures positions

Suppose that the futures position is opened (contracts purchased or sold) at price f_0. When a *long* position is offset (closed), the contracts are *sold*. Hence, the payoff is positive if the price (at the date of offset) exceeds f_0, and negative if the price is less than f_0. Conversely, when a *short* position is offset, the contracts are *purchased*. Hence, the payoff is positive if the price is less than f_0, and negative if the price exceeds f_0.

Now consider a short futures position, in which one contract is sold at price f_0. If the position is offset (with the purchase of one contract) at a lower price, there is a gain equal to the difference between the sale and purchase prices. Conversely, if the position is offset at a higher price, a loss is made, again equal to the difference between the sale and purchase prices – hence the negatively sloped line with slope -1 in figure 14.1.

2. *Exchange of futures for physicals* (EFP). Two investors, one with a long position, the other with a short position, may agree to fulfil their obligations by the delivery of (and payment for) the commodity prior to the maturity of the contract. The clearing house must be notified of this agreement, upon which it cancels the contracts. The advantage of this procedure is that the parties can exchange a commodity that does not match the exact requirements of the futures contract. On some exchanges it is permissible to *initiate* futures positions via an EFP. For example, two parties may agree to trade a futures contract (one taking the short position, the other the long) as one component of an agreement involving, say, the exchange of the asset. Clearly, the parties to the EFP must inform the exchange authorities and deposit the necessary margins with the clearing house.

3. *Delivery.* Sometime during the stipulated delivery period an investor – say, A – with a short position submits a *delivery notice* to the clearing house signalling that delivery is to be made. The clearing house then selects (at random or according to a previously

determined rule) an investor – say, B – with a long position in the same contract to accept delivery.[12] Investor B must then make payment and receive the commodity, typically a *warehouse receipt*, from A.

For most *financial futures* (and also for some physical commodity contracts) exchange regulations may allow, or require, *cash settlement*, without any exchange of the asset. Cash settlement is accomplished by calculating the gain or loss on the contract, the amount of which is credited to the party that gains and debited to the party that loses; the asset underlying the contract does not change hands. For example, on LIFFE the FT-SE 100 index futures contract is settled in cash, whereas the British government long-term bond ('long gilt') contract can be settled in cash, or by the delivery of bonds from an eligible list specified, in advance, by LIFFE. It is quite common, both for commodity and financial futures contracts, that there is a range of 'qualities of the commodity' (for physical commodities known as the *contract grades*) or 'securities' that qualify for delivery; the investor who is short presumably chooses the cheapest eligible means of settlement. (Also, it is open to A and B, in the above example, to agree on terms for the delivery of the asset other than those specified in the original contract. This is known as an alternative delivery procedure (ADP), and is effectively the same as EFP.)

14.2.4 Margins

When an investor instructs a broker to buy or sell futures contracts, the investor deposits ('posts') an *initial margin* (or 'original margin') with the broker. Each trading day thereafter, until the investor offsets the position, the contracts are marked to market at the day's settlement price. Depending on the new, marked-to-market value of the contracts, the investor must hold at least a *maintenance margin* (normally somewhat less than the initial margin) with the broker. This may involve the broker making a *margin call* for the investor to deposit a *variation margin* with the broker, so that the credit balance does not fall below the maintenance margin.

Example

An investor purchases ten futures contracts on day 1 for $1000 each. The initial margin is $250 per contract and the maintenance margin is $200 per contract.[13] See the following table for a hypothetical sequence of price changes, together with the associated gains or losses.

On day 7 the position is reversed and the investor makes a profit of $100 = $10 \times (1010 - 1000)$. Notice that this is exactly equal to the increment in the

---

[12] Notice that only by chance would B be the investor to whom A sold the futures contract at the outset.

[13] Note that the details of the example will differ if the margin is specified as a *percentage* of the contract price rather than a given amount per contract. The principles are exactly the same, however.

Day	Price	Gain (Loss)	Margin account	Margin call
1	1000	—	2500	—
2	1020	200	2700	—
3	970	(500)	2200	—
4	930	(400)	1800	700
5	950	200	2700	—
6	980	300	3000	—
7	1010	300	3300	—

value of the margin account, including the margin call made on day 4: $100 = 3300 - (2500 + 700)$.

The variation margin on day 4 restores the margin account to its *initial* margin level. It is possible, depending on the rules of the exchange, for the margin call to restore the deposit to the maintenance level, in which case $200 would have been deposited at the end of day 4. The net gain or loss when the contracts are offset is, of course, unaffected.

The size of the margin deposit depends on the rules of the exchange and may differ among contracts for different commodities. Also, the required margin normally depends on each investor's entire bundle of contracts – that is, on the net exposure of the investor in the contracts. A market rate of interest is normally paid on margin deposits. Instead of cash, it may be permissible for an investor to deposit securities in fulfilling the margin requirement. For these reasons, the effect of margin regulations on futures prices, if any, is not at all simple or obvious. The obligation to hold a margin should be interpreted as a way of ensuring performance (good faith) rather than as a transaction cost, though there is an opportunity cost if investing the funds lodged in the margin account could earn a higher return elsewhere. Explicit transaction costs for investors typically take the form of commission charges levied by their brokers.

Not only do investors hold margin deposits with their brokers but the brokers also maintain their balances with the clearing house (or hold each investor's margin in an account at the clearing house). The rules vary according to the exchange, but may take the form of the broker paying a margin to the clearing house as a proportion of the *net* value of all the contracts made on behalf of the broker's customers. The principle at the root of all these margin regulations is that, in the event of an investor's default, the funds in the margin account plus the market value of the contract will be no less than the liability of the investor to the broker (and the broker to the clearing house). Default could occur either when there is inadequate response to a margin call or, at maturity, when the payment of cash (for a long position) or delivery of the commodity (for a short position) fails to take place. Exchange authorities tend to fix margin requirements according to the volatility of the relevant futures contract price: the more volatile the contract price, the higher the margin.

14.2.5 Bundles of futures contracts

Traders in futures contracts often package contracts together to serve investors (typically companies) with particular needs. Two of the commonest are *straddles* and *strips*.

Straddles

A straddle consists of a package of short and long positions in the same contract but with different delivery dates. Thus, for example, a straddle might comprise a short position in two pork-belly contracts for December delivery, together with a long position in two contracts, one for delivery in March and the other in June.

Sometimes straddles are known as *spreads*, though, strictly, a spread is the difference between the prices of the contracts that form the straddle. A straddle with a short position in one contract and a long position in another has two 'legs', referring to its component contracts. Straddles could also be constructed for contracts that differ not in delivery date but in some other dimension, such as the location at which the delivery of the commodity is to be made. When traded on the same exchange, straddles require smaller margins than for their separate components. Straddles can be attractive to investors for a variety of reasons – for example, to exploit beliefs that the gap between the prices will either expand or contract (without taking a view about whether the general level of prices will rise or fall).

Strips

A strip (or calendar strip) consists of a package of contracts, all long or all short, with different delivery dates. For example, an investor might acquire a 'long strip' by purchasing four contracts, one of which matures at each of the next four delivery dates. Why might the strip be attractive? Suppose that a trading company has a long-term supply contract that requires delivery to a customer of a commodity at a fixed price for a sequence of months. If designed carefully, the purchase of a strip could provide the company with protection against a rise in the commodity price during the life of the contract with its customer.

14.3 Arbitrage between spot and forward prices

Consider a homogeneous commodity that can be stored at zero cost, and the possession of which does not itself directly convey anything of worth. What is the relationship between the spot price, $p(t)$, and the forward price, $F(t, T)$, of this commodity for delivery at date T? The arbitrage principle provides the link.

Digression: borrowing and lending

Before establishing the link, recall the principle of compound interest.[14] Suppose that a loan of \$1 (i.e. one unit of wealth or unit of account) is made at date t. Let $R(t, T)$ denote the value of the loan (principal plus interest) at date T. For example, if $T - t$ equals one year and the annual rate of interest is 10 per cent, then $R(t, t+1) = (1+0.10) = 1.10$, with no compounding. If compounding takes place every six months then $R(t, t+1) = (1+0.05)^2 = 1.1025$. Slightly more generally, suppose that the rate of interest is r per period and interest is compounded once per period; then $R(t, T) = (1+r)^{(T-t)}$. The 'period' is commonly, but not necessarily, one calendar year. If there is continuous compounding, then $R(t, T) = e^{r(T-t)}$. These expressions assume that r is constant over the interval t to T; they are messier if r is non-constant, but no new principle is involved. The expression $R(t, T)$ is commonly termed the 'interest factor' or 'gross interest rate'. Note, finally, that the net present value at date t of \$1 to be received at T is just $1/R(t, T)$ – that is, the price at date t of a risk-free zero-coupon bond paying \$1 at date T.

14.3.1 Arbitrage: the simplest case

Suppose that $F(t, T) > R(t, T)p(t)$. Then arbitrage profits could be earned by borrowing enough money, $p(t)$, to buy one unit of the commodity at the spot price. Simultaneously, sell one unit of the commodity forward for $F(t, T)$. Store the commodity until date T. At T deliver the stored commodity, collect the cash – i.e. $F(t, T)$ – and payoff the loan (i.e. $R(t, T)p(t)$), leaving a sure profit of $F(t, T) - R(t, T)p(t) > 0$. This cannot be consistent with equilibrium in a frictionless market.

Suppose that $F(t, T) < R(t, T)p(t)$. Then arbitrage profits could be earned by, simultaneously, selling *short* one unit of the commodity at the spot price, investing the proceeds and purchasing a forward contract for delivery of the commodity at date T. At date T collect $R(t, T)p(t)$ from the investment, pay $F(t, T)$ for the commodity and return the unit of the commodity to its lender (i.e. from whomever it was borrowed at the outset, date t). This leaves a sure profit of

---

[14] This paragraph summarizes and extends the analysis of chapter 1, section 1.6, and appendix 1.3.

$R(t, T)p(t) - F(t, T) > 0$, and hence cannot be consistent with equilibrium in a frictionless market.

Thus, in the simplest case, the absence of arbitrage opportunities implies that

$$F(t, T) = R(t, T)p(t) \qquad (14.1)$$

This is the fundamental arbitrage relationship in forward markets. Note that each component – $F(t, T)$, $R(t, T)$ and $p(t)$ – can be observed at date t, when the bargain is struck. (Note, in particular, that the spot price, $p(t)$, is *not* the spot price at the date, T, when the forward contract matures.)

14.3.2 Complications

What determines whether (14.1) accurately predicts the relationship among $F(t, T)$, $p(t)$ and $R(t, T)$?

1. *Frictionless markets.* Transaction costs are assumed to be zero and there are assumed to be no institutional restrictions on trades. Also, it is taken for granted that performance risk can be neglected. To the extent that market frictions impinge on trading, $F(t, T)$ may diverge from $R(t, T)p(t)$.
2. *Storage* (or carrying) *costs.* For some assets (particularly physical commodities, such as grain or gold), the cost of storage (including insurance) may be significant, though for most financial assets such costs are negligible. Storage costs can be included by adding them to the right-hand side of equation (14.1). For later reference, let $c(t, T)p(t)$ denote the storage cost of one unit of the commodity, so that $c(t, T)$ expresses the storage cost of \$1 (one unit of account) invested in the commodity at date t and held until date T.
3. *Convenience yield.* The ownership of many assets confers benefits, merely by the fact of possession. Such benefits might take the form of *pecuniary* returns, such as dividends on shares or coupons on bonds. Alternatively, the benefits could be as intangible *utility* to the owner. Examples include: (a) a miller who finds it worthwhile to hold stocks of grain to facilitate the day-to-day scheduling of the milling process; (b) a miser who finds pleasure in gazing at a hoard of gold ingots; (c) an investor who finds some financial assets especially attractive because they can easily be sold for cash. In the case of (c), the benefit is sometimes expressed as a *liquidity premium*. (Keynes's enigmatic chapter 17 of *The General Theory* (1936) merits reading in this context.)

   The convenience yield is introduced by *subtracting* a term from the right-hand side of (14.1), or adding it to the left-hand side. For later reference, let $y(t, T)p(t)$ denote the convenience yield for one unit of the commodity, so that $y(t, T)$ expresses the convenience yield on \$1 invested in the commodity at date t and held until date T.
4. *Availability of stocks.* Restrictions in the availability of inventories present a complication that tends to be more relevant for physical commodities than for financial assets.

For agricultural commodities, stocks tend to be depleted immediately before harvests. It is also possible, though for different reasons, for the inventories of non-agricultural commodities (e.g. metals) to be limited at certain times and in some places. Even if inventories are plentiful, they may be held by firms or individuals who intend to process them, and, hence, not be readily available to trade.

When stocks available for trade are limited, the arbitrage principle fails to predict the equality (14.1). This is because there is not enough of the commodity in existence to allow it to be short-sold. Hence, $F(t, T) < R(t, T)p(t)$ may be consistent with market equilibrium, when inventories are low. This is especially likely to be true if T is a long time away relative to t.

Allowing for the complications outlined above, the market equilibrium condition, (14.1), becomes

$$F(t, T) \leqq [R(t, T) + c(t, T) - y(t, T)]p(t) \qquad (14.2)$$

where the inequality allows for circumstances in which stocks become so low that short-selling is infeasible. Neglecting possible restrictions on short-sales, and suppressing the date arguments of the interest factor, storage cost and convenience yield, (14.2) can be expressed more compactly as

$$F(t, T) = (R + c - y)p(t) \qquad (14.3)$$

Given its subjective nature, for most assets it is exceedingly difficult to measure the convenience yield, y, independently of the other components of (14.3). Consequently, sometimes y is defined to make (14.3) hold:

$$y \equiv R + c - \frac{F(t, T)}{p(t)} \qquad (14.4)$$

This is merely an identity, and predicts nothing. However, in the context of futures markets – replacing $F(t, T)$ with $f(t, T)$ – theories of storage have been constructed to explain y as defined in (14.4). It is postulated that the convenience yield varies inversely with the stocks of the asset. When stocks are low, y is high. As stocks increase, y falls, tending to some small constant value (possibly zero) when stocks are abundant.

14.3.3 When are forward and futures prices equal?

Suppose that two contracts are identical in every respect except that one is a forward contract and the other is a futures contract. If the rate of interest between dates t and T is *non-random* (i.e. known for sure) then the two prices are equal: $F(t, T) = f(t, T)$. (See appendix 14.1 for a demonstration.) The condition that the interest rate is non-random does not require that r is *constant* over the interval t to T but, rather, that its changes are known at the outset, date t.

Pairs of identical forward and futures contracts are rarely encountered in practice. The significance of the result is that it shows (a) why forward and futures prices may differ, and (b) the circumstances in which they are likely to be close approximations to one another. In particular, the result suggests that the difference between $F(t, T)$ and $f(t, T)$ is likely to be small if the interval between t and T is short (say, six or nine months), for then the prospect of large, unforeseen changes in interest rates is also small.

From here on, futures and forward prices are used interchangeably unless clarity requires otherwise.

14.3.4 Revaluation of a forward contract

Forward contracts, once agreed, typically remain in existence until the delivery date, at which time the asset is exchanged for cash. It is possible, however, that one or other party to the contract may seek to renegotiate the agreement before the delivery date. For example, a company with a long position in a forward contract for the delivery of heating fuel might decide that it no longer wishes to take delivery. This being so, it could propose to cancel the contract or try to sell it to a third party. Similarly, a company with a short position in a forward contract might find that it cannot deliver the asset and would, thus, be in breach of its contractual obligations. Consequently, it could seek to renegotiate the contract or try to offset its position by purchasing an identical contract from a third party.

The question of how to value a forward contract after it has been agreed, but before it matures, can be posed as follows. Suppose that the forward price for delivery at date T is given by $\widehat{F}$, where $\widehat{F}$ has been determined at a date, t', sometime before today, date t – i.e. $t' < t$. What is the value of the contract today, t (where $t < T$)?

For example, suppose that a contract is negotiated in January for the delivery of 1000 barrels of oil in December at a price of \$35 per barrel (thus, $\widehat{F} = \$35,000 = \$35 \times 1000$). The question is: what is the value of this contract at a later date – say, in March?

Let $V(t, T, \widehat{F})$ denote the value at date t of a forward contract agreed for delivery at date T with underlying asset price $\widehat{F}$. In a frictionless market and in the absence of arbitrage opportunities, the value, $V(t, T, \widehat{F})$, of the previously agreed forward contract is given by

$$V(t, T, \widehat{F}) = \frac{F(t, T) - \widehat{F}}{R(t, T)} \tag{14.5}$$

To interpret this result, note that $F(t, T)$ is the price as of today, date t, for the delivery of the asset at date T. The price $F(t, T)$ can, and generally will, differ from any previously determined price (e.g. $\widehat{F}$) for the same asset to be delivered at T. The expression (14.5) states that $V(t, T, \widehat{F})$ equals the net present value of the difference between the current forward price, $F(t, T)$, and the contract price, $\widehat{F}$, stipulated in the earlier agreement. (For a derivation of (14.5), see appendix 14.2.)

To continue the example, suppose that the forward price set in March for delivery in December is \$38.30 and that the interest factor for borrowing or lending between March and December is 1.10; then the value of the contract to deliver 1000 barrels of oil for \$35 per barrel in December equals: \$3000 $=$ $1000 \times (38.30 - 35)/1.10$. That is, it is worth paying \$3000 for 1000 barrels of oil at \$35 for delivery in December when the current forward price (in March) is \$38.30.

It is crucial not to confuse the value of the contract with the price to be paid for the underlying asset when the contract matures (at the delivery date). The value of an existing forward contract is not necessarily positive. Indeed, it will always be *non-positive* from the perspective of one party to the contract. To pursue the example further, a company that has *sold* 1000 barrels of oil at \$35 for December delivery would be obliged to *pay* \$3000 to cancel the contract if the current price for December delivery rises to \$38.30 (with an interest factor of 1.10).[15]

Another interpretation of the above analysis follows if *side payments* are permitted at the inception of forward contracts. Typically, it is assumed that side payments are zero. But there is no reason in principle why this must be so: one party to a contract could agree to pay a sum to the other at the outset. What equation (14.5) predicts is that the side payments and forward prices would be related in a precise way (not forgetting the conditions that the market is frictionless and arbitrage opportunities are absent). Returning to the example, if the forward price (with zero side payment) equals \$38.30, then a contract to deliver 1000 barrels of oil at \$35 will exchange for \$3000 (if the interest factor is 1.10).

If, as is typically assumed, no money changes hands at the commencement of a forward contract, then the value of a forward contract is said to be *zero*. In symbols: $V(t, T, F(t, T)) = 0$. With the passage of time, the forward price *on newly arranged contracts* rises or falls. Consequently, previously agreed contracts (arranged with lower or higher prices) become positive or negative in value.

Consistent with the earlier discussion, in section 14.1.3, futures contracts are forward contracts that are revalued each trading day. When a futures contract

---

[15] Alternatively, the seller would find it necessary to pay \$3000 to induce a third party to take over the contract (to deliver 1000 barrels of oil in December for \$35 per barrel) when the current forward price for December delivery stands at \$38.30 (and under the conditions already assumed – i.e. an interest factor of 1.10, frictionless markets and the absence of arbitrage opportunities).

is marked to market, it is just as if an existing forward contract is cancelled and immediately renewed at the current forward price, the change in price being credited or debited to the investor's margin account. The interest factor, $R(t, T)$, appears because the market interest rate is the opportunity cost of funds held in a margin account.

14.4 Arbitrage in foreign exchange markets

Arbitrage, speculation and hedging in foreign exchange markets operate according to the same principles as in other asset markets. Any differences are of form rather than substance – consequences of different terminology and different institutional arrangements.

The most important institutional feature of foreign exchange markets is that they largely involve OTC contracts in which agreements are negotiated by telephone amongst dealers operating from banks located around the globe. This feature, together with the fact that each currency is homogeneous (one US dollar is identical to any other), tends to favour *forward* foreign exchange contracts rather than *futures* markets, though foreign exchange futures contracts are traded – on the Chicago Mercantile Exchange, for example.

Arbitrage in foreign exchange markets operates in two distinct ways: (a) to link exchange rates among three or more currencies (see chapter 1 for a simple example); and (b) to link the spot and forward exchange rates between a pair of currencies. The latter link is expressed as the *covered interest parity* condition, found in international finance.

In order to state the covered interest parity condition, consider any pair of currencies, one domestic (say, pounds sterling, £), the other foreign (say, dollars, $). Let $p(t)$ denote the spot price of dollars (i.e. the price of \$1 in units of £). Let $F(t, T)$ be the price of \$1 (in units of £) for delivery at date T, the agreement being reached today, date t. Denote the interest factor in pounds by $R(t, T)$ and the interest factor in dollars by $R^*(t, T)$. The absence of arbitrage opportunities in frictionless markets implies that

$$F(t, T) = \frac{R(t, T)}{R^*(t, T)} p(t) \tag{14.6}$$

This is the covered interest parity condition. If (14.6) is not satisfied, it is possible to make positive arbitrage profits in a frictionless market. Hence, the equality must hold in market equilibrium.

To justify (14.6), examine the consequences of violating the equality. Suppose that $F(t, T) > R(t, T)p(t)/R^*(t, T)$. Note, for later reference, that this can be arranged as $FR^*/p > R$, where the date arguments are omitted for conciseness.

Consider the following investment strategy at date t: (i) £1 is borrowed (to be repaid, with interest, at date T); (ii) the £1 is exchanged for $\$1/p$, which are lent at interest; (iii) $\$R^*/p$ are sold in the forward market, to be delivered at date T in exchange for sterling. When date T arrives, the dollar investment yields $\$R^*/p$, which are exchanged (in fulfilment of the forward contract) for £FR^*/p. Also, at date T, £R are paid to discharge the sterling loan. The net payoff equals £$FR^*/p - R > 0$. This is an arbitrage profit, which is inconsistent with equilibrium in a frictionless market.

Conversely, suppose that $F(t, T) < R(t, T)p(t)/R^*(t, T)$. Now the arbitrage opportunity can be exploited as follows: (i) borrow dollars; (ii) exchange the dollars for pounds, which are lent at interest; (iii) sell pounds for dollars in the forward market. At date T the pounds that were lent are received (including interest), and are exchanged for dollars in fulfilment of the forward contract. Some of the dollars are then paid to discharge the dollar loan. Leaving the details as an exercise, it should be straightforward to check that the net payoff is necessarily positive. Once again, an arbitrage profit has been made.[16]

More frequently encountered in international finance is the *uncovered interest parity* condition, which can be expressed in the present notation as

$$E[p(T)|\Omega_t] = \frac{R(t, T)}{R^*(t, T)}p(t) \qquad (14.7)$$

where $E[p(T)|\Omega_t]$ denotes the spot exchange rate expected for date T, conditional upon information, Ω_t, at date t. A common error is to assert that (14.7) is a consequence of the arbitrage principle. While it is *possible* that $E[p(T)|\Omega_t] = F(t, T)$, its justification requires assumptions about investors' behaviour much stronger than needed in arbitrage analysis. If investors are risk-neutral and unanimous in their expectations about future spot exchange rates, then (14.7) could be regarded as a plausible prediction.

14.5 Repo markets

Repo is shorthand for 'repurchase' – more appropriately, 'sale and repurchase'. Repo agreements are typically negotiated for financial assets, though, in principle, they could be applied to any commodity.

Suppose, for example, that the 'commodity' is British government debt – i.e. gilt-edged securities. One party to the agreement, A, sells stock to a counterparty, B, for cash today and a promise to repurchase the stock from B at a specified later date for a specified price. Party A is said to *reverse out* of the stock. Party B is said to *reverse in* to the stock.

---

[16] Notice that, by suitable choice of the amount traded in the forward contract, the payoff can be denominated in either dollars or sterling.

The motives for repo agreements are many and various. One way of viewing a repo is as a loan, with the collateral being the asset underlying the agreement. In the example, A obtains a loan from B, the collateral being the stock that B holds until the loan is repaid (with repurchase of the stock).

Another way to view the repo is as the combination of a spot transaction and a forward transaction. In the example, A sells in the spot market and simultaneously purchases in the forward market. Both transactions are bundled together and made with the counterparty, B.

Notice that there is an implicit interest rate in the repo agreement. For simplicity, suppose that the agreement is to last exactly one time period, that the price A receives today is $100 and that the price A pays one period from now is $104. Then the implicit repo interest rate is $4\% = (104 - 100)/100$. Interest rates are quoted on an annual basis, so that when the time period is different from a year (it is normally much shorter) the rate is rescaled to allow for the duration of the loan. Also, it may be necessary to allow for the accrual of interest (forthcoming coupons) during the life of the repo. Neither of these refinements affects the basic principle. Hence, the repo agreement can equivalently be specified in terms today's security price ($100, in the example) and a repo interest rate (4 per cent, in the example).

Repo agreements can be used as vehicles for exploiting arbitrage opportunities. In the example, suppose that A can lend funds at 5 per cent. Then A could profit by borrowing at 4 per cent in the repo market and lending at 5 per cent. Whether or not this investment strategy should be interpreted as arbitrage depends, of course, on whether it is risk-free. If it is, equilibrium – in a frictionless market, with the absence of arbitrage opportunities – is attained only when prices and interest rates change such that the two interest rates are equal.

The assumption of frictionless markets is, of course, an idealization. Repo transactions are no exception to the impediments to trades and transaction costs that obscure the consequences of arbitrage. For example, regulations governing the borrowing of securities and tax laws can affect the feasibility and profitability of repo agreements. Reforms in the British gilt-edged securities market in early 1996 illustrate how institutions can impact on the operation of financial markets. In this instance, the liberalization of trading in securities enhanced the scope for an expansion of the repo market in government stocks.[17]

Just as with any forward transactions, performance risks can impinge on repo agreements: one or other party may default by failing to deliver the securities, or by neglecting to make the promised cash payment, when the contract matures. Thus, in the example, default would result if either A cannot afford to repurchase

---

[17] For details of the reforms, see Bank of England (1995).

the securities from *B* or if *B* is unable to deliver the securities (which *B* perhaps sold between the inception of the repo agreement and its maturity). However, much as in futures markets, mechanisms exist to minimize the risk of default. In particular, (a) the securities designated for repurchase may be kept in the custody of a reputable third party, (b) the parties may agree to deposit the funds in margin accounts, and (c) the process of marking to market ensures that the margin accounts reflect fluctuations in security prices.

The prospect of exploiting an arbitrage opportunity is only one of the motives for repo trading. For instance, security dealers use repos to maintain inventories of stocks when balancing the fluctuating trading flows with their customers. Banks use repos to replenish their cash reserves in the event of unforeseen withdrawals by their customers. In some financial systems repo markets are integral to the mechanism for conducting the central bank's monetary policy. The Bank of England, for example, implements monetary policy by trading in two-week repos at its policy-determined interest rate. The profit-seeking actions of banks then serve to transmit the policy throughout the financial system, and beyond into the rest of the economy.

14.6 Summary and conclusion

1. Forward and futures contracts enable agreements made at one date to be executed at a later date. Forward contracts are private, over-the-counter agreements negotiated between the relevant parties.
2. Futures contracts are exchange-traded contracts, the terms of which are controlled and guaranteed by organized exchanges. Forward contracts can be customized but are often expensive to renegotiate. Futures contracts are standardized but can be traded immediately and with low transaction costs.
3. The arbitrage principle links spot and forward prices at each date in frictionless markets. The principle can be applied to any market in which both spot and forward (or futures) contracts are traded. However, if ownership of the underlying asset provides a convenience yield or if storage is costly (or both), the absence of arbitrage opportunities plays a more limited role, as a guide to the measurement of convenience yields.
4. Forward contracts are normally constructed to begin life with a zero value. But, as time passes, the forward prices are likely to change, with the consequence that contracts acquire a positive value for one party and an equal negative value for the other. The arbitrage principle enables the revaluation of previously negotiated forward contracts at any date prior to their maturity.
5. Examples of markets for which the arbitrage principle links forward and spot prices include (a) foreign exchange markets (for which the covered interest parity condition expresses the absence of arbitrage opportunities) and (b) repo markets for the sale and repurchase of securities.

Futures markets have often been treated with suspicion, as arcane institutions that operate in mysterious ways. Some of the mysteries should have been illuminated, if not resolved, in this chapter. However, among the questions that remain are these. Why do futures markets exist at all? Why do futures markets exist for some 'goods' and delivery dates rather than others? What determines futures prices?

Apart from an inherent human propensity to bet on the outcome of future events (to speculate), futures markets facilitate the planning of actions that, for a variety of reasons, will be taken at a later date. Fundamentally, it is too costly – perhaps infinitely costly – for the supply of some goods to be changed instantly. Futures markets enable the planning of production and consumption across time to alleviate the uncertainties occasioned by supply inflexibilities. But it can be argued that *forward* markets perform this function just as well as futures markets. Thus, the existence of futures markets requires further justification: either that they perform the same functions as forward markets but more efficiently, or that they also serve some other purpose(s).

A distinctive role claimed for futures markets is that they facilitate *price discovery*; i.e. futures markets promote the dissemination of information about the equilibrium price for the asset underlying the futures contract. From this perspective, futures prices reflect the strength of demand and supply in circumstances when it would otherwise be difficult to obtain an accurate guide to the market price – perhaps the asset is heterogeneous in quality, or traded infrequently, possibly at widely dispersed locations. In the absence of futures markets for these assets, equilibrium prices would remain obscure, or even entirely hidden.

The effectiveness of markets' price discovery relies, partly at least, on the presence of active trading in contracts – accurate prices require market 'depth' (in the sense of many traders and many trades). Closely allied with price discovery is *liquidity* – the ability to execute trades swiftly (see chapter 2, section 2.2.3). But the liquidity of the market could also be deemed important for ensuring the attractiveness of futures markets in fulfilling the original function of forward markets.

Moreover, market depth and liquidity are relevant in determining the *range* of futures markets that exist. Only if there are sufficiently large volumes of demand and supply for delivery at specific dates is any market likely to operate successfully. This factor may help to explain why futures markets tend to be active for only a limited number of delivery dates, rarely with contract dates beyond eighteen months from the present. There may simply be too little potential demand and supply for delivery at dates further into the future – a consideration that begs the question of *why* there is so little demand and supply. For an answer, it is necessary to reflect upon the fundamental reasons, sketched above, to explain the existence of *any* futures market.

This chapter has explored one of the determinants of futures prices, namely the arbitrage motive that serves to link futures with current spot prices. The next chapter extends the inquiry to include the impact of speculation and hedging.

Further reading

Among the specialist texts on futures markets, those by Hull (2005) and, at a more advanced level, Hull (2003) are highly recommended. Chapters 1 and 2 in Hull (2005) are particularly useful to reinforce the subject matter of this chapter. Also worth consulting are the books by Duffie (1989, chaps. 2, 3 & 5), Luenberger (1998, chap. 10) and Edwards and Ma (1992, chaps. 1–3). For up-to-date information on contract specifications, access to the Internet is highly advantageous.

Williams (1986) explores important issues of economic principle and advocates the analysis of futures markets from the perspective of spreads among different contract prices. Also relevant is Holbrook Working's pioneering series of papers on the role of storage for futures prices; see, for example, Working (1949). More recent contributions that also merit attention include those by Houthakker (1959), Black (1976), Telser and Higginbotham (1977), Telser (1981) and Carlton (1984).

Appendix 14.1: Forward and futures prices

This appendix demonstrates that $f(t, T) = F(t, T)$: futures prices equal forward prices in frictionless markets with non-stochastic interest rates.

Consider, first, a *forward* contract for the purchase of one unit of the commodity at date t for delivery at date $T > t$, when it is sold for $p(T)$. The profit (which cannot be known until T) from this action is given by

$$\pi^\Gamma = p(T) - F(t, T) \tag{14.8}$$

Second, consider a strategy involving *futures* contracts for the same commodity (but not, generally, for the same *number* of futures contracts) that is initiated at t and that results in the sale of one unit of the commodity at T. Such a strategy must yield exactly the same profit (or loss) as that using the *forward* market; otherwise, arbitrage profits could be made by adopting, at t, a long position in one market and a short position in the other.

Let π^f denote the profit at date T on the futures strategy. The argument below demonstrates that the profits π^F and π^f differ unless the forward and futures prices are equal – i.e. $f(t, T) = F(t, T)$, where $f(t, T)$ is the futures price at t for delivery at T. Thus, even though π^f is unknown at $t < T$, unless the forward and futures prices are equal there is scope for making arbitrage profits by exploiting the difference between the two prices – both of which are known at date t.

To obtain the result, an appropriate trading strategy in the futures market is constructed. Let $R(t+1, T), R(t+2, T), \ldots, R(T-1, T)$ denote the sequence of interest factors for loans from $t+1$ to T, $t+2$ to T, and so on, beginning at each date between $t+1$ and $(T-1)$. By assumption (non-stochastic interest rates), these are known at t. Now, starting at date t, consider a sequence of futures contracts each of which is liquidated the following day and reopened (at a scale to be determined) such that, ultimately, one unit of the underlying asset is sold in the spot market at T. At each date it may be necessary to lend (or borrow) funds at the known rate embodied in the interest factor.

At date t suppose that the investor purchases $R(t+1, T)^{-1}$ futures contracts, which are liquidated at $t+1$ for a profit (or loss) of $R(t+1, T)^{-1}(f(t+1, T) - f(t, T))$. This essentially reflects the impact of marking to market, except that the contracts are not automatically renewed. The profit (loss) is loaned to (borrowed from) the capital market, yielding, at T, a payoff equal to $f(t+1, T) - f(t, T)$. At date $t+1$ the investor purchases $R(t+2, T)^{-1}$ futures contracts, which are liquidated at $t+2$ in the same way as for $t+1$, the preceding day. This sequence of trades continues until date $T-1$, when the investor purchases a futures contract for one unit of the asset at price $f(T-1, T)$. Finally, the asset is sold at the spot price, $p(T)$. The payoff (profit or loss) from the futures trading strategy is then given by

$$\pi^f = p(T) + (f(t+1, T) - f(t, T)) + (f(t+2, T) - f(t+1, T)) + \cdots$$
$$+ (f(T-1, T) - f(T-2, T)) - f(T-1, T)$$
$$= p(T) - f(t, T) \tag{14.9}$$

Thus, unless $F(t, T) = f(t, T)$, $\pi^F \neq \pi^f$ – as asserted.

Appendix 14.2: Revaluation of a forward contract

This appendix demonstrates expression (14.5) – i.e. $V(t, T, \widehat{F}) = [F(t, T) - \widehat{F}]/R(t, T)$. Begin by rewriting the equality as $VR = F - \widehat{F}$, where the t, T arguments are omitted for brevity.

If the equality, $VR = F - \widehat{F}$, does not hold, then there is an arbitrage opportunity in a frictionless market. Suppose, first, that $VR < F - \widehat{F}$, or, equivalently, $F - \widehat{F} - VR > 0$. Consider the following investment strategy undertaken at date t.

1. Borrow an amount V from t to T.
2. Use the funds to pay V for a contract that promises to take delivery of the underlying asset at date T in return for a payment of $\widehat{F}$ at T.
3. Negotiate a contract to sell the asset for F on its delivery at date T.

At date T the asset is acquired for $\widehat{F}$, and immediately delivered in return for F. Also, the loan, V, must be repaid, amounting to a payment of VR. The net payoff at T thus equals $F - \widehat{F} - VR$, which is positive by assumption. Hence, for zero outlay, the strategy yields a positive, risk-free payoff. Such an outcome is incompatible with equilibrium in a frictionless market.

Alternatively, assume that $VR > F - \widehat{F}$. Exactly analogous reasoning shows that an arbitrage opportunity is available. In this case, a contract for the delivery of the asset at T, in return for $\widehat{F}$, is sold for V at t. The proceeds, V, are lent at interest until T. Also at t, a contract is negotiated for the purchase of the asset for F at T. At date T the asset is acquired for F and delivered in return for $\widehat{F}$. Also at T, the funds lent at interest amount to VR. The net payoff is $VR - F + \widehat{F}$, which is positive, by assumption.

Therefore, in the absence of arbitrage opportunities, $V = [F - \widehat{F}]/R$ – as asserted.

References

Bank of England (1995), *Quarterly Bulletin*, 35(4), pp. 325–30.

Black, F. (1976), 'The pricing of commodity contracts', *Journal of Financial Economics*, 3(1–2), pp. 167–79.

Carlton, D. W. (1984), 'Futures markets: their purpose, their history, their growth, their successes and failures', *Journal of Futures Markets*, 4(3), pp. 237–71.

Duffie, J. D. (1989), *Futures Markets*, Englewood Cliffs, NJ: Prentice Hall.

Edwards, F. R., and C. W. Ma (1992), *Futures and Options*, New York: McGraw-Hill.

Houthakker, H. S. (1959), 'The scope and limits of futures trading', in M. Abramovitz (ed.), *The Allocation of Economic Resources*, Stanford, CA: Stanford University Press, pp. 134–59.

Hull, J. C. (2003), *Options, Futures, and Other Derivatives*, Englewood Cliffs, NJ: Prentice Hall, 5th edn.

   (2005), *Fundamentals of Futures and Options Markets*, Englewood Cliffs, NJ: Prentice Hall, 5th edn.

Keynes, J. M. (1930), *A Treatise on Money*, London: Macmillan (reprinted as Keynes, *Collected Writings*, Vols. V and VI).

   (1936), *The General Theory of Employment, Interest and Money*, London: Macmillan (reprinted as Keynes, *Collected Writings*, Vol. VII).

Luenberger, D. G. (1998), *Investment Science*, New York and Oxford: Oxford University Press.

Merton, R. C. (1973), 'Theory of rational option pricing', *Bell Journal of Economics and Management Science*, 4(1), pp. 141–83 (reprinted as chap. 8 in Merton, 1990).

   (1990), *Continuous Time Finance*, Cambridge, MA, and Oxford: Blackwell.

Telser, L. G. (1981), 'Why there are organised futures markets', *Journal of Law and Economics*, 24(1), pp. 1–22.

Telser, L. G., and H. Higginbotham (1977), 'Organized futures markets: costs and benefits', *Journal of Political Economy*, 85(5), pp. 969–1000.

Williams, J. (1986), *The Economic Function of Futures Markets*, Cambridge: Cambridge University Press.

Working, H. (1949), 'The theory of price of storage', *American Economic Review*, 39(6), pp. 1254–62.

15

Futures markets II: speculation and hedging

Overview

Two of the main determinants of futures prices are speculation (explored in section 15.1) and hedging (section 15.2). Hedging, although associated with risk reduction, rarely succeeds in eliminating price risk entirely. Hence, section 15.3 pursues the analysis further by deriving the degree of hedging needed to minimize risk. Also in section 15.3, it is argued that speculation and hedging may not be so easy to distinguish as first appears. Section 15.4 draws together the motives for trading in futures contracts to offer an overview of the determination of futures prices. Finally, section 15.5 explores how unscrupulous traders can render futures markets vulnerable to manipulation.

15.1 Speculation

In chapter 14 the motives for trading in futures contracts were grouped into *arbitrage*, *speculation* and *hedging*. If futures contracts are treated as financial instruments, it may seem odd to analyse the investors' decisions about holding them from the perspective of separate motives (speculation, hedging and arbitrage). Such an approach contrasts with that of portfolio selection, in which the investor's preferences are represented by a single objective function. The investor's objective (usually expressed by an expected utility function or mean-variance trade-off) can, in principle, capture all the relevant motives for asset holding.

Speculation and hedging both involve risk and, hence, could be treated as applications of portfolio selection, or, more generally, of choice under uncertainty.[1] Such an approach, while it yields insights, is sufficiently unconventional to be relegated to appendix 15.1. Hedging, though it almost invariably involves risk,

---

[1] Admittedly, arbitrage – at least in its strict form, being risk-free – does tend to be studied separately.

is associated with risk *minimization*. Thus, it is speculation that most nearly coincides with the activity of portfolio decision making.

Speculators in futures markets are typically viewed as highly specialized investors with a thorough knowledge of the market for a particular commodity (e.g. wheat) or a narrow range of commodities (e.g. grains, including wheat). These investors are assumed to seek to profit from their beliefs about price patterns in the future. It may be that some investors have access to superior information or perceive themselves as being better equipped to draw accurate inferences from information that is universally available. A narrow definition of speculation requires the speculator to trade in futures contracts only, not the underlying asset, but this view is more restrictive than needed here.

Speculators are often assumed to be risk-neutral, though an element of risk aversion is not incompatible with their activities. Given that (a) asset returns generally involve uncertainty about future payoffs, and (b) investors make decisions about how much of each asset to hold, speculation need not be regarded as unusual or exceptional behaviour. It is argued later (in section 15.3) that hedging decisions can be interpreted to involve an element of speculation, albeit perhaps small. Nonetheless, either for ease of analysis or because of the specialized knowledge required, speculators in futures markets are often treated as a separate class of investors.

The risk borne by speculators is that of adverse price fluctuations. A speculator who takes a long position (purchases futures contracts) is betting that the price will increase between the date of purchase and the date at which the contract is offset (sold). Conversely, a speculator who takes a short position (sells futures contracts) is betting that the price will decrease between the date of sale and the date at which the contract is offset (purchased). The presumption is that the speculator has no intention of taking, or making, delivery of the underlying asset (on which the futures contracts are written) – though, as already emphasized, this possibility need not be ruled out either in principle or in practice.

Hicks long ago noted the importance of speculation in futures markets (1939, p. 138). 'Futures prices are … nearly always made partly by *speculators*, who seek a profit by buying futures when the futures price is below the spot price they expect to rule on the corresponding date …'

Three points should be noted.

1. Hicks claims only that speculators are *partly* responsible for futures price determination. Hedging and arbitrage also play a role, though the consequence of arbitrage is for the link between futures and *current* spot prices, rather than on the general level of prices. The usual presumption is that speculators and hedgers inhabit opposite sides of the market (one group buying contracts from the other). This is a view discussed below, in section 15.4.

2. Hicks refers to the *expected* spot price at the delivery date (what Hicks calls the 'corresponding date'). Hicks has in mind that the futures contracts will be held to maturity when the speculator will either take delivery (or make delivery) of the underlying asset and simultaneously sell (or purchase) it at the spot price. The speculator's profit or loss is then the difference in the price at which the futures contract was acquired and the spot price upon delivery. Of course, in active futures markets the contract may well be offset before delivery takes place. But the principle is the same: the profit or loss depends on the change in price between the date at which the contract is acquired and the price when it is offset.

3. In the quoted passage, only speculation in the form of *buying* futures is mentioned. There is no reason, in principle, that speculation by selling futures should be excluded. The direction – purchase or sale – depends on whether the investor believes that the price will rise or fall. However, Hicks was describing a market in which most hedgers seek to reduce risk by selling futures contracts. Speculators take the other side of the bargain; that is, they buy the contracts sold by hedgers. This is the crucial feature of a theory of futures prices outlined in section 15.4.

Any theory of speculation requires a theory of expectations formation. Such a modelling exercise is inherently difficult, because expectations are almost invariably *un*observed. Even if investors could express definite estimates of their expectations (and they cannot), expectations are typically private and unique to the individual.[2] It is common in the modern literature to assume that price expectations are formed 'rationally' as predictions derived from a model of price formation. As always, there is no avoiding the necessity of constructing a model of prices, regardless of whether investors' expectations are formed rationally. This issue is discussed further in section 15.4, after the analysis of hedging.

15.2 Hedging strategies

15.2.1 Hedging in principle

Hedging exploits the following principle: *reduce the risk associated with holding one asset by holding a second asset so that, together, the payoffs cancel out across states of the world.*[3] The risk involved with holding one asset cancels out the risk associated with the other. In rare circumstances the hedge is *perfect* (risk-free). Typically, it is *risky* in the sense that the payoffs of one asset are not

---

[2] Surveys asking individuals to reveal their expectations are not uncommon. Whether the answers given bear any systematic relationship with the beliefs that genuinely inform investors' actions is another matter.

[3] Don't confuse hedging strategies with *hedge funds*. Hedge funds are collections of assets, rather like sophisticated investment trusts, designed to exploit specialized knowledge about capital markets, including markets for derivatives. While the objectives of the fund managers might be to reduce risks, hedge funds can turn out to be highly risky investments – as investors in Long-Term Capital Management found out to their embarrassment in September 1998.

exactly matched by the payoffs in the other. Note also that asset 'holding' is here used in a general sense: it could refer to either long or short positions.

Hedging: a simple example

Consider a world with two states (labelled 1 and 2) and two assets (labelled A and B) with payoffs as follows:

	Asset A	Asset B
State 1	-2	6
State 2	3	-4

Assets A and B are risky: their returns differ across states. But any strategy that holds A and B in the ratio 2:1 results in a payoff that is identical across states, thereby eliminating risk. Thus, asset A could be used as a perfect hedge for asset B, and conversely.

In many cases the motive for hedging is to insulate against the risk of changes in an asset's price between the present, t, and date, $t' > t$, at which the asset is to be traded (bought or sold). It is possible that the owner of an asset may not be committed to selling it at date t' but, instead, seeks to avoid exposure to fluctuations in the asset's price. It is as if the investor wishes to acquire the opportunity to sell for a guaranteed price – a price *known* today, t – at a date t' in the future, regardless of whether a sale is executed. Conversely, an investor may seek to have the security of buying an asset at t' in the future for a price that is determined today, $t < t'$.

Futures contracts provide one vehicle (though not the only one) for hedging against price changes. Historically, hedging has been applied to trading physical commodities (e.g. cotton, wheat or pork bellies), but now it is common to apply it in the context of a wide variety of financial instruments (see chapter 16 for examples).

In the remainder of this chapter futures contracts form the *hedge instrument* (or *hedge asset*). The hedge is adopted in order to avoid price fluctuations in what is referred to below simply as 'the asset'. Thus, for example, wheat futures contracts with maturity date next October could form a hedge instrument against fluctuations in the price of wheat ('the asset') intended for delivery in October. In principle, other financial instruments (e.g. forward contracts or options) could play the role of hedge instruments, though only futures contracts are considered in this chapter. (See chapter 20 for a sketch of options as hedge instruments.)

A *short-hedge* refers to the *sale* of the hedge instrument. A *long-hedge* refers to the *purchase* of the hedge instrument. Of course, whether or not any particular transaction in futures is part of a hedge strategy depends on the investor's other commitments or opportunities.

15.2.2 Hedging in practice

In an influential paper Working (1962) challenges the description of hedging outlined above. He points out that investment strategies in futures markets rarely fall into the neat categories of arbitrage, speculation and hedging – they often comprise elements of at least two, if not all three, motives. Here is Working's taxonomy.

1. *Carrying-charge hedging.* This is essentially an arbitrage strategy in which the investor chooses to hold stocks and then hedges against the risk of price changes in the future. However, in the presence of storage costs and convenience yields, the strategy is not entirely risk-free. (See chapter 14, especially page 349.) Thus, carrying-charge hedging constitutes an imperfect hedge.

2. *Operational hedging* 'normally entails placing and "lifting" hedges in such quick succession that expectable changes in the spot-future price relation over the interval can be largely ignored' (Working, 1962, p. 439). Here the main goal appears to be to design a strategy that enables the futures price to be used instead of the cash market spot price (which, given heterogeneity in the underlying commodity, may be difficult to determine with any confidence). Operational hedging reflects the 'price discovery' function of futures markets.

3. *Selective hedging* 'is the hedging of commodity stocks... according to price expectations' (p. 440). This appears to be just a respectable depiction of speculation. Working, however, would probably insist that the difference is that selective hedging is undertaken by traders who also hold stocks and, hence, who have some commitment to an industry that produces or consumes the underlying commodity. Speculation is treated as a pure gamble involving short or long positions in futures contracts. In this interpretation, speculators do not hold stocks of the commodity.

4. *Anticipatory hedging* 'is ordinarily guided by price expectations ... [and] serves as a temporary substitute for a merchandising contract that will be made later' (p. 441). From a theoretical perspective, there seems little to distinguish this from the previous category.

5. Pure *risk-avoidance hedging*. This is the residual category, studied in detail below.

The principles outlined below – distinguished by *motive* – are not inconsistent with Working's classification. Each of his strategies can be interpreted as an amalgam of the more narrowly defined concepts studied in this and the previous chapter.

In practice, hedging often seeks to reduce particular sorts of risk. For example, the payoff on a security might depend upon unknown future interest rates, among other sources of risk. A hedge strategy might then be designed to reduce or eliminate only the interest rate risk, without affecting the impact of other risks.

15.2.3 Perfect hedge strategies

Perfect, or risk-free, hedging completely eliminates an asset's price risk – the risk that the price at t' will be different from that agreed today, not the risk of changes in the spot price between today, t, and some date $t' > t$ (because the spot price today, being for immediate delivery, is irrelevant for delivery at t'). Perfect hedging is seldom found in practice, but it does provide a benchmark for more realistic cases in which price risk can be alleviated but not eliminated.

Example

Suppose that 'today', t, is a day in February. A company plans to sell a consignment of 100,000 gallons of crude oil for delivery in November, date T. The company may, or may not, own the oil today: it might be held in storage; it might be awaiting shipment from a distant port; it might not yet even have been drilled. For whatever reason, the company cannot, or does not wish to, wait until the oil arrives and transact at the spot price. Suppose that the futures price for November delivery is $f(t, T) = \$40$ per barrel. By selling 100 contracts (each of 1000 barrels) today, the company guarantees that \$4m ($= \$40 \times 100$ contracts $\times 1000$ barrels) will be received when the oil is delivered in November in fulfilment of the futures contract.[4]

In this example the underlying asset is the crude oil, and the hedge instrument is the futures contract. Given that – as implicitly assumed – the company can deliver the oil in accordance with the futures contract, a forward contract would achieve exactly the same hedging objective.

Suppose instead that, today, a company plans to acquire (for whatever purpose) crude oil in November. By purchasing the requisite number of futures contracts, the company can completely eliminate price risk. Having purchased the contracts, it waits until November and takes delivery at the price quoted in the previous February. This is an example of a perfect long hedge.

For the hedge to be perfect, it is crucial that either (a) the asset can be delivered according to the terms specified in the futures contract, or (b) – which amounts to the same thing – the futures price at maturity (date T, November) exactly equals the spot price of the asset. If either of these conditions fails, the hedge is risky.

Clearly, either the short-hedger or the long-hedger will have reason, in November, to regret the decision made in February. If the November spot price exceeds \$40 per barrel, the short-hedger could have received a higher price

---

[4] A complication that makes even this hedge less than perfect is described below under 'tailing the hedge'.

by waiting until November and selling in the spot market. If the November spot price is less than \$40, the long-hedger could have obtained the oil a lower price by waiting until November and purchasing in the spot market. But the spot price in November is unknown in the previous February. Price risk has, however, been eliminated. The hedge has achieved its objective.

Perfect hedges are rarely available in practice, for the following reasons.

1. A market in a suitable hedge instrument may not exist. Futures contacts (and options, for that matter) are traded for only a limited range of commodities or financial securities. Although in principle a forward contract could be negotiated, it may be too expensive, or impossible, to find a counterparty to accept the other side of the bargain.

2. Futures contracts, where available, are standardized. The specification of the futures contract may not correspond exactly with the requirements of the company seeking to acquire a hedge. For example, the grade of crude oil that a short-hedger plans to supply may not match that specified in the futures contract. Similarly, the date or location of delivery may differ from that of the futures contract: the company may wish to deliver in December for storage in New York, while the (NYMEX) contract specifies delivery to Cushing, Oklahoma.

3. The company adopting the short-hedge may not be certain about the date at which the oil will be ready for delivery. A futures contract maturing in November may be available but the short-hedger may not know whether the oil will have arrived at a designated location by then. Similarly, the company with a long-hedge may not know whether it will be ready to take delivery in November.

4. *Tailing the hedge*. Even if the company is sure to make (or take) delivery of the commodity according to the terms of the futures contract, a complication arises because futures contracts are marked to market. If the price of the futures contract changes on any day prior to delivery, outstanding contracts are revalued at the new market price, any gain (or loss) being credited (or debited) to the holder's margin account. Although interest accrues to the funds in the margin account, the gain or loss for any investor holding an open futures position (short or long) will depend upon the pattern of price changes while the position remains open. Hence, the amount of *interest* earned or forgone as a result of marking to market is unknown at the outset and may require some adjustment (rebalancing) of the futures position. This may seem trivial, but it may be significant for investors with large futures positions.[5]

Although a perfect hedge is feasible only in special circumstances, it is illuminating to study it formally, before turning to more realistic conditions that allow only risky hedging. To avoid complicated notation, denote today as date $t = 0$.

---

[5] The difference between forward and futures prices is at the root of 'tailing the hedge': see chapter 14, appendix 14.1, and Figlewski, Landskroner and Silber (1991).

Let $t' = 1$ denote the date at which the hedge is terminated (i.e. is 'liquidated', 'raised' or 'lifted'). In the example above, $t' = 1$ is a date in November, when the oil is delivered.

Let p denote the market price of the asset and f the price of the futures contract. Then $f_0 \equiv f(0, 1)$ denotes the futures price quoted at date 0 for delivery at date 1. Also, $f_1 \equiv f(1, 1)$. While p_0 and f_0 are known today, the prices p_1 and f_1 are not observed until date 1.

Let N denote the number of units of the asset to be delivered, or acquired, at date 1. Consider a company that is committed to making delivery at date 1. Without a hedge, the revenue from the sale, $p_1 N$, is unknown as of date 0, and hence is subject to price risk. The hedge is accomplished with the *sale* of M futures contracts at date 0. The position is offset with the *purchase* of M futures contracts at date 1.[6] At date 1, the gain (if positive) or loss (if negative) on the futures contract is $(f_0 - f_1)M$. Thus, the overall value of the hedged position, W_1, is

$$W_1 = p_1 N + (f_0 - f_1)M \tag{15.1}$$

As of today, W_1 is uncertain, because p_1 and f_1 are unknown. A perfect hedge uses the uncertainty about f_1 to *eliminate* the uncertainty about p_1.

If the asset is identical in every respect (grade, location and delivery date) to that specified in the futures contract, then $p_1 = f_1$. Hence, the choice of $M = N$ completely insulates the portfolio from price risk. The terms involving f_1 and p_1 cancel out, the value of the hedge strategy being known for sure at the outset: $W_1 = f_0 N$.

Pursuing the analysis further, define the initial value of wealth as $W_0 = p_0 N$. (This is the value of wealth if the asset could be sold at date 0 – perhaps purely hypothetical, because at date 0 the investor may not possess the asset to sell.) Now the *change* in wealth over the life of the hedge is defined as $\Delta W \equiv W_1 - W_0$, which, from equation (15.1), can be written as

$$\Delta W \equiv W_1 - W_0 = (p_1 - p_0)N + (f_0 - f_1)M \tag{15.2}$$

Equation (15.2) shows that the change in wealth stems from the change in the price of the asset and the change in the price of the hedge instrument. To make this more precise, define $\Delta p \equiv p_1 - p_0$ and $\Delta f \equiv f_1 - f_0$. The terms Δp and Δf are the price changes of the asset and hedge instrument prices between dates 0 and 1. (Note that they are *not* the price changes over some short interval of

---

[6] Note that the futures contract date could be equal to, but should be no later than, date 1. A *perfect* hedge to be liquidated in November could not normally be achieved using futures contracts that mature in the previous September.

time – say, a day – unless the life of the hedge just happens to equal the trading interval, a 'day'.)

Rewrite (15.2) as follows:

$$\Delta W = N\Delta p - M\Delta f \tag{15.3}$$

A *perfect* hedge requires the M to be chosen to cancel the effects of price changes over the life of the hedge. In symbols, M is chosen to eliminate the impact of Δp and Δf on ΔW. Hence, $\Delta W = 0$:

$$N\Delta p - M\Delta f = 0 \tag{15.4}$$

Hence, for a perfect hedge, M is chosen such that $M/N = \Delta p/\Delta f$. The value M/N is commonly known as the *hedge ratio*. Note that the hedge ratio takes this form only for a perfect hedge.

What matters for a perfect hedge is that there is an *exact* relationship between the underlying asset price and the hedge instrument price. Otherwise, the hedge ratio takes a more complicated form, as shown in section 15.3, below.

Long-hedges

The reasoning for a *long*-hedger – an investor who is committed to making a *purchase* at date 1 – can be adapted straightforwardly from the short-hedge. For a long-hedge, reinterpret (15.1) as the cost of acquiring the asset at date 1 rather than the value of the sale of the asset. That is, N is the number of units of the asset to be *purchased* at date 1, M futures contracts are purchased at date 0, and W_1 denotes the cost of acquiring the asset at date 1. As before, a perfect hedge eliminates the uncertainty in W_1. With the long-hedge, the asset is acquired for a spot price p_1 (unknown as of date 0) at the same time as the futures contract is sold at a price f_1 (also unknown at date 0). Given the exact relationship between p_1 and f_1, the uncertainty in W_1 vanishes.

15.2.4 Risky (imperfect) hedging

Expression (15.1) identifies the source of risk in non-perfect hedging: the prospect that the hedge instrument price differs from the asset price when the hedge is lifted – i.e. $f_1 \neq p_1$. For reasons already outlined, hedges are rarely perfect. Except when the asset is identical to that specified in the futures contract, f_1 may differ from p_1. As will be seen shortly, what causes the riskiness is not that f_1 differs from p_1 but rather that an exact relationship between the two is not known with certainty at date 0.

Risky hedging seeks to attenuate – because it cannot eliminate – the price risk associated with the value of an asset in the future. Risk reduction is achieved by taking a position in a hedge instrument the price of which is *correlated* with the price of the asset. In risk-free hedging the correlation is perfect; in risky hedging the correlation is imperfect.[7]

Consider again the example of a company that plans, in February, to deliver 100,000 barrels of oil in November. Suppose now that the grade of oil to be delivered does not correspond to that stipulated in any futures contract. Suppose also, to make the problem even more transparent, that no futures contracts are quoted for *any* grade of oil with a delivery date of November.

These circumstances do not imply that hedging is impossible, though it will be risky. Suppose that a futures contract for some specified grade of oil is available for delivery in December. If – an important 'if' – the price of oil to be supplied is correlated with that specified in the futures contract, then a hedge can be constructed. In this case, the company will sell futures contracts (though, as explained below, the volume of oil stipulated in the futures contracts is not necessarily equal to the volume of oil it intends to supply). Shortly before the company delivers its consignment of oil (say, in early November), it offsets its futures position by buying the same number of futures contracts (for December delivery, of course) as it sold in the previous February. The oil is then delivered and sold at the spot price on that date.

If oil prices fall between February and November, the decline tends be reflected in the futures price. Why? Because, in December, when the futures contract matures, the futures price equals the spot price for the grade of oil stipulated in the futures contract. The presumption is that in November, shortly before the delivery month, the futures and spot prices will be close, though not necessarily equal. The more accurate this presumption, the closer the prices and the less risky the hedge.

Conversely, if oil prices rise between February and November, the increase tends to be reflected in the futures price. There is no absolute guarantee that the futures price increases or decreases exactly in line with the price of the oil supplied by the company. However, being the same physical commodity – 'oil' – and with delivery dates close to one another, it is reasonable to assume that the two will be correlated, even if not perfectly. It is this less than perfect correlation that makes the hedge risky. But a risky hedge may be preferable to no hedge at all. Why? Because price risk is lower than without the hedge.

---

[7] Formally, risk-free hedging corresponds to a linear correlation coefficient (between changes in the asset price and hedge instrument price over the life of the hedge) equal to $+1$ or -1. Risky hedging corresponds to a correlation coefficient in between the extremes, with zero designating a strategy that fulfils no hedging purpose.

Summary

Risky hedging requires the choice of a hedge instrument the price fluctuations of which are closely correlated with the price of the asset (the greater the correlation, the lower the risk). The hedge instrument is sold or purchased according to whether the investor plans to sell or purchase the asset at a designated date in the future. The correlation between the hedge instrument price and the asset price then serves to attenuate the price risk associated with a transaction in the asset alone.

15.2.5 The basis

Risky hedging attains its goal if there is, at least, an approximate relationship between the price of the asset and the price of the futures contract (the hedge instrument). This relationship is often expressed in terms of the *basis*, defined as the difference between the two prices:

$$\text{basis} = \text{asset price } \textit{minus} \text{ hedge instrument price}$$

Beware: the basis is sometimes defined as the asset price minus the hedge instrument price, sometimes as the hedge instrument price minus the asset price. The former is, of course, just the negative of the latter. Also, the basis is often defined as a proportion of one of the prices. There is no standard usage in this regard.

In the examples above, the basis is just the spot price of the asset minus the futures price – i.e. at date 0 the basis is $b_0 \equiv p_0 - f_0$, and at date 1 it is $b_1 \equiv p_1 - f_1$. If the asset is identical with that specified in the futures contract, then the p_1 and f_1 are tightly linked to one another in a frictionless market and the absence of arbitrage opportunities.

The *basis* plays a crucial role when the asset differs from the asset underlying the futures contract. For example, the hedge instrument might be a futures contract for silver quoted on NYMEX, while the asset is silver coin in London.[8] In these circumstances, hedging is risky. It involves a looser association between the p_1 and f_1, and the scope for variation in the basis is greater than when the arbitrage principle binds the two together.

In order to understand the role of the basis in financial analysis, consider an investor who owns one unit of the asset and has sold one unit of the hedge instrument (a futures contract). Such an investor is said to be *long* in the asset

---

[8] The NYMEX contract requires the delivery of 'refined silver, assaying not less than 0.999 fineness, in cast bars weighing 1000 or 1100 troy ounces each and bearing a serial number and identifying stamp of a refiner approved and listed by the Exchange'. Also, delivery of the necessary warehouse certificates must be made at designated locations in the United States. Silver coin in London evidently does not satisfy these requirements.

and *short* in the futures contract. Over the interval between dates 0 and 1, the investor's wealth changes as follows:

$$\text{change in wealth} = (p_1 - p_0) + (f_0 - f_1)$$
$$= (p_1 - f_1) - (p_0 - f_0)$$
$$= b_1 - b_0$$
$$= \Delta b \tag{15.5}$$

(Note that, if the asset pays a dividend or provides any other services of ownership, these should be added to the right-hand side of (15.5). Similarly, the costs of holding the asset should be deducted.)

Equation (15.5) shows that the change in the value of the hedged position (the change in wealth) is equal to the change in the basis. If the basis increases (i.e. the asset price increases relative to the futures price), the investor gains, and conversely if the basis falls.

Consider, instead, an investor who has a *liability* for one unit of the asset (perhaps the asset has been short-sold) and has purchased one unit of the hedge instrument. Such an investor is said to be *short* in the asset and *long* in the hedge instrument. In this case, the change in the value of wealth is simply $-\Delta b$. If the basis decreases (i.e. the asset price decreases relative to the futures price), the investor gains, and conversely if the basis increases.

The 'basis' is a widely used term in futures markets and in studies of the determination of futures prices. However, caution is needed in its application to hedging: there is no reason, in principle, why the number of units of the asset and the hedge instrument should be equal (as is implicitly assumed in defining the basis).

15.3 Optimal hedging

15.3.1 Risk minimization

When hedging is risky, the number, M, of units of the hedge instrument sold or purchased generally differs from the number of units of the asset to be sold or purchased. To understand why this should be so, consider an investor who plans to sell N units of the asset at date 1 and who hedges by selling M units of the hedge instrument. Rewrite (15.3) as follows:

$$\frac{\Delta W}{N} = \Delta p - h \Delta f \tag{15.6}$$

where $h \equiv M/N$ is the *hedge ratio*.

The risk associated with the hedged position stems from uncertainty about Δp (because p_1 is unknown at date 0) and Δf (because f_1 is unknown at date 0). Given that Δp and Δf are unknown at date 0, it follows that no choice of h can guarantee to eliminate the risk of fluctuations in $\Delta W/N$.[9]

The hedge ratio that minimizes the variance of $\Delta W/N$ takes a simple form. From equation (15.6), the variance of $\Delta W/N$ can be written as

$$\text{var}\left(\frac{\Delta W}{N}\right) = \sigma_p^2 + h^2 \sigma_f^2 - 2h\sigma_{pf} \tag{15.7}$$

where σ_p^2 is the variance of Δp, σ_f^2 is the variance of Δf and σ_{pf} is the covariance between Δp and Δf. The value of h that minimizes the variance, $\text{var}(\Delta W/N)$, is found by differentiating (15.7) with respect to h and setting the derivative to zero.[10] The resulting value, h^*, here called the *pure hedge ratio*, is given by

$$h^* = \frac{\sigma_{pf}}{\sigma_f^2} \tag{15.8}$$

(Sometimes h^* is called the optimal hedge ratio, but, here, this term is reserved for a different concept, introduced below.) Another way of writing h^* is $h^* = \rho\sigma_p/\sigma_f$, where ρ is the correlation coefficient between Δp and Δf. The value of ρ^2 has been proposed to measure the effectiveness of hedging.[11] The closer the linear relationship between Δp and Δf, the less risky the hedge. In the limit as $\rho^2 \to +1$ the hedge becomes perfect.

The pure hedge ratio, h^*, is nothing more than the slope coefficient in an ordinary least squares regression of Δp against Δf. That is, the pure hedge ratio could be constructed from

$$\Delta p = \theta + h^*\Delta f + \varepsilon \tag{15.9}$$

where ε is an unobserved random error, such that $\text{E}[\varepsilon|\Delta f] = 0$, and $\theta = \text{E}[\Delta p] - h^*\text{E}[\Delta f]$. The presence of the random error is just another way of expressing the riskiness of the hedge – if the random error is identically zero, a perfect hedge could be constructed.

Given that, for a risky hedge, the relationship between Δf and Δp is not exact, it is also unlikely that h^* can be known for sure. The regression equation, (15.9), suggests a way, however, of estimating h^* from data on Δf and Δp. A graphical

[9] The analysis here ignores uncertainty about interest earned or forgone as a consequence of fluctuations in the funds held on margin in the process of marking to market. For an explanation of how *tailing the hedge* allows for such uncertainty, see Duffie (1989, pp. 239–41).

[10] The sceptical reader can confirm that the necessary first-order condition, $2h\sigma_f^2 - 2\sigma_{pf} = 0$, suffices for a minimum, because $\sigma_f^2 > 0$ ensures that the second-order condition is satisfied.

[11] The symbol ρ^2 expresses the coefficient of determination, or R^2, in a regression of Δp on Δf (i.e. ρ is the correlation coefficient between Δp and Δf). Ederington (1979) proposes the use of ρ^2 as an index of hedging effectiveness.

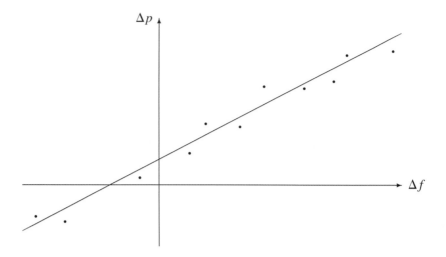

Fig. 15.1. The slope of the fitted line is an estimate of the pure hedge ratio, h^*

> Each dot represents an observed pair $(\Delta p, \Delta f)$ measured for a particular
> time interval. The line depicts the ordinary least squares 'line of best
> fit', the slope of which is an estimate of σ_{pf}/σ_f^2, the pure hedge ratio.
> The closer the observations to the fitted line, the more accurate the
> estimates and the less risky the hedge.

illustration appears in figure 15.1. Each dot in figure 15.1 denotes a pair of
realized values of $(\Delta f, \Delta p)$. The slope of the OLS line is, by construction, equal
to the pure hedge ratio, where sample values of the covariance, σ_{pf}, and variance,
σ_f^2, are obtained from the observations.

Suppose, for example, that h^* is estimated to be equal to 0.8 and that 1000
units of the asset are to be sold at date 1. Then, the variance-minimizing number
of units to sell via futures contracts, M, equals 800 $(= 0.8 \times 1000)$. While this
strategy minimizes the variance it does not completely eradicate risk, because
(a) the linear relationship between Δp and Δf is not exact and (b) the value of
h^*, being obtained from a sample of data, is subject to statistical error.

The hedging studied here is *linear*, in the sense that the relationship between Δp
and Δf is linear, so that h^* is constant. More complicated hedging strategies – for
example, using an options contract as the hedge instrument (see chapter 20) – may
result in *non-linear* hedging, for which the hedge ratio varies with respect to one
or more observed variables (e.g. the asset price). In this case, hedging becomes
dynamic, in the sense that the strategy requires continuous review throughout the
life of the hedge. Consequently, it may prove necessary to adjust the amount of
the hedge instrument held during the interval between the date that the hedge is
initiated ('date 0') and when it is lifted ('date 1').

15.3.2 Hedging as portfolio choice

In the choice of a pure hedge ratio, above, the objective is assumed to be that of minimizing risk, as measured by the variance of the payoff per unit of the hedged position, $\text{var}(\Delta W/N)$. More generally, in decision making under uncertainty, investors take into account the *expected return* as well as risk. In other words, investors may consider that they are not totally ignorant about future changes in asset prices, and, consequently, allow their beliefs to influence their decisions.

In the context of mean-variance analysis, the investor's objective can be expressed as follows. Choose h to maximize

$$\mathcal{U} = \text{E}\left[\frac{\Delta W}{N}\right] - \alpha \cdot \text{var}\left[\frac{\Delta W}{N}\right] \qquad (15.10)$$

where $\text{E}[\Delta W/N]$ denotes the expectation of $\Delta W/N$ and $\text{var}[\Delta W/N]$ denotes the variance of $\Delta W/N$. The parameter $\alpha > 0$ represents the investor's preference for risk minimization relative to expected wealth maximization: the larger is α the more weight is placed on risk minimization. (See chapter 4, section 4.4.2, especially page 103.)

It is shown in appendix 15.2 that the optimal hedge ratio, $\tilde{h}$ (i.e. the one that maximizes $\mathcal{U}$), is given by

$$\tilde{h} = h^* + \frac{f_0 - \text{E}[f_1]}{2\alpha\sigma_f^2} \qquad (15.11)$$

The first term, h^*, on the right-hand side of (15.11) is the pure hedge ratio, derived above. The second term is known as the *speculative hedge*, an oxymoron that highlights the entwining of investment motives. The speculative hedge measures the extent to which the investor trades in futures in order to gain from an expected change in the futures price. For finite values of α the investor is a *speculator* as well as a hedger

For an investor who is very sensitive to variance (i.e. for whom α is large), the second term in equation (15.11) is small and can be neglected. Then the optimal hedging ratio is merely the one that minimizes the variance of $\Delta W/N$. Thus, the pure hedge ratio, h^*, equals the optimal hedge ratio if α is arbitrarily large; variance minimization then dominates the investor's decision.

Equation (15.11) shows that optimal hedging can be viewed as an application of portfolio selection theory. An investor who holds a risky asset can benefit by holding a second asset (the hedge instrument) the price of which is correlated with the first. The correlation between the prices enables the investor to reduce the overall level of risk. Also, depending on the weight accorded to risk reduction relative to expected gain, the investor's decision can be interpreted as speculation in the hedge instrument, even though the motive to hedge is also present. The two motives, speculation and hedging, need not be mutually exclusive.

15.4 Theories of futures prices

This section turns from studying particular influences on futures trading – arbitrage, speculation or hedging – to theories of the determination of futures prices. Most theories seek to explain the price difference, $f(t, T) - p(t)$, or its negative, the basis (sometimes expressed as a proportion of $p(t)$).

One approach, introduced in chapter 14, focuses on the role of storage costs and convenience yields. To pursue this, write the condition expressing the absence of arbitrage opportunities (see expression 14.3, page 351) as

$$f(t, T) = (R + c - y)p(t) \tag{15.12}$$

where $f(t, T)$ replaces the forward price (assuming $f(t, T) = F(t, T)$).[12] Subtracting $p(t)$ from both sides of (15.12) and dividing by $p(t)$ makes the proportionate difference between the futures and spot price, $(f(t, T) - p(t))/p(t)$, equal to $R + c - y - 1$, which can be interpreted as the net opportunity cost of storage.

While the interest factor, R, is straightforward to measure, for many commodities estimation of the storage cost, c, and convenience yield, y, presents difficulties. In practice, therefore, models of futures prices based on (15.12) explore indirect proxy measures for the impact of c and y rather than attempting to construct immediate empirical counterparts for them. For example, the impact of c and y may be reflected indirectly, but clearly, in seasonal fluctuations in the price difference, $f(t, T) - p(t)$, for some agricultural commodities.

A second approach to futures prices focuses on the role of price expectations. To pursue this, rewrite the futures/spot price difference as

$$f(t, T) - p(t) = \{f(t, T) - E_t[p(T)]\} + \{E_t[p(T)] - p(t)\} \tag{15.13}$$

where $E_t[p(T)]$ is shorthand for $E[p(T)|\Omega_t]$ – i.e. the expected value of the spot price at date T conditional upon information, Ω_t, available at date $t < T$.

Although expression (15.13) is an identity with no predictive power, it identifies two sources of any observed discrepancies between futures and spot prices.

---

[12] Recall that $R(t, T)$ denotes the interest factor, $c(t, T)$ denotes the storage cost and $y(t, T)$ denotes the convenience yield. The t, T arguments of R, c and y are omitted to simplify the notation. Recall also that stocks of the asset must be sufficiently abundant if the arbitrage principle is to enforce an equality, rather than merely a weak inequality, in (15.12).

The first term in braces, $f(t, T) - E_t[p(T)]$, can be interpreted as a 'bias' or 'premium' reflecting the difference between the (known) futures price and the (as yet unknown) spot price at the futures contract delivery date. The second term, $E_t[p(T)] - p(t)$, denotes the expected change in the spot price between dates t and T.

Predictive power is often accorded to (15.13) by assuming that

$$f(t, T) = E_t[p(T)] \tag{15.14}$$

In words: the futures price reflects expectations about the spot price of the underlying asset at its delivery date. This assumption accords with the intuition that the futures price corresponds to an asset (a commodity, financial instrument or whatever) to be delivered at date T. If the futures price differs from the expected spot price, then there are opportunities for *speculative* profit. It is tempting to suggest that (15.14) represents the efficient markets hypothesis applied to futures markets. Indeed, it has much in common with the martingale hypothesis, introduced in chapter 3.

Given that futures contracts are traded prior to the delivery date, the reasoning underpinning (15.14) can be extended to futures prices at any date t', $t < t' \leq T$, so that the hypothesis becomes $f(t, T) = E_t[f(t', T)]$. For example, with $t' = t + 1$,

$$f(t, T) = E_t[f(t + 1, T)] \tag{15.15}$$

which asserts that futures prices (for a given delivery date) evolve according to a martingale process (if past and present prices are known at date t). Invoking the analysis of chapter 3, equation (15.15) implies that changes in futures prices, $f(t + 1, T) - f(t, T)$, are uncorrelated with any information available at date t (i.e. uncorrelated with every element of Ω_t, the information set at date t). Thus, it implies the testable prediction that changes in futures prices are serially uncorrelated.

Expressions (15.14) and (15.15) can be obtained from (15.11) when (a) $p_1 = f_1$ (i.e. the futures contract delivers exactly the same commodity as is traded in the spot market at date 1 (where $T = 1$)) and (b) $\alpha \to 0$ (i.e. when investors are speculators, and ignore the hedging motive implicit in utility-maximizing strategies).

More broadly, (15.14) and (15.15) can be viewed as a consequence of *risk-neutral* preferences held by investors. (An outline of the reasoning underpinning this result is offered in appendix 15.1.) Risk neutrality is, however, an extreme and stringent assumption. Once risk aversion (and, by implication, hedging) is permitted, (15.14) no longer expresses market equilibrium. As a result, *risk premia* become relevant and, if relevant, require modelling.[13]

Although they focus on different aspects of futures price determination, the approach via price expectations is not inconsistent with that via storage costs and convenience yields. They reflect different facets of the interdependences among futures prices, underlying asset prices and price expectations.

There is no reason, in principle, why models of asset prices (e.g. the CAPM, or APT) should not apply to futures markets. For instance, application of the CAPM to futures markets implies

$$\mathrm{E}[f_1] - f_0 = (\mu_M - r_0)\beta_f \qquad (15.16)$$

where μ_M is the expected rate of return on the market portfolio and r_0 is the rate of return on a risk-free asset. Equation (15.16) simply expresses the security market line for futures contracts. Notice that it differs from the standard SML because the return on the futures contract is expressed simply as the change in its price.[14]

If the CAPM is deemed too special, a more general approach would be to construct a multifactor model for futures prices, to which the APT could be applied. Models of futures prices based on the CAPM receive little attention in the literature. Why? Black (1976) offers two reasons: (a) futures contracts do not appear in the market portfolio (remember that the aggregate holding of any futures contract is zero by construction: the total of short positions equals the total of long positions, exactly); (b) evidence that beta-coefficients for futures contracts are close to zero. While these arguments do not imply that the CAPM – or a multifactor model – *cannot* be employed for futures contracts, any such approach needs to be justified on its own merits rather than merely with reference to the CAPM or APT.

15.4.1 Normal backwardation

One of the most celebrated and debated theories of futures prices was devised by Keynes, who proposed what has come to be known as the *normal backwardation* theory. Keynes – together with Hicks, who subsequently refined

---

[13] That is, it is necessary to address questions such as: are the risk premia constant? What do the risk premia depend on?

[14] The reason the return is expressed in this way is that futures contracts are peculiar in that payment for the asset does not occur until the maturity of the contract (or until the futures position is offset). Hence, the 'excess return' equals the difference between the price at sale and the price at purchase. The risk-free rate is ignored. Another approach, which leads to a different expression for the expected excess return, is explored in appendix 15.1.

the theory – applied their analysis to *forward* markets. Their ideas carry over, however, to futures markets, and it is these that are analysed here.[15]

Ignoring the special case of exact equality, $f(t, T) = p(t)$, there are two possibilities:

$$f(t, T) < p(t) : backwardation$$

$$f(t, T) > p(t) : contango$$

(The terms 'backwardation' and 'contango' originate in London Stock Exchange transactions, where 'backwardation' refers to a fee paid by the seller of securities for the privilege of delaying their delivery. 'Contango' refers to a fee paid by the buyer of securities for deferring delivery and payment.)

In its simplest form, the Keynes–Hicks theory asserts that backwardation is normally observed in futures markets. Hicks develops Keynes's argument as follows (1939, pp. 137–8).

... while there is likely to be some desire to hedge planned purchases, it tends to be less insistent than the desire to hedge planned sales. If forward markets consisted entirely of hedgers, there would always be a tendency for a relative weakness on the demand side; a smaller proportion of planned purchases than of planned sales would be covered by forward contracts [footnote omitted] ...

[This provides an opportunity for speculators, whose] action tends to raise the futures price to a more reasonable level. But it is of the essence of speculation, as opposed to hedging, that the speculator puts himself into a more risky position as a result of his forward trading ... He will therefore only be willing to go on buying futures so long as the futures price remains definitely below the spot price he expects; for it is the difference between these prices which he can expect to receive as a return for his risk-bearing, and it will not be worth his while to undertake the risk if the prospective return is too small.

The steps in the Keynes–Hicks theory are as follows.

1. In 'normal' conditions, futures markets are dominated by *short*-hedgers.

2. The sales of futures contracts by short-hedgers depresses the futures price relative to the spot price. The arbitrage condition allows for this to the extent that (a) the 'convenience yield' is high, or (b) stocks of the asset are limited.

3. Speculators seek to profit from the difference between the futures price and the *expected* spot price, $E_t[p(T)]$, at the maturity date of the futures contract.

4. The actions of speculators (in buying futures contracts sold by short-hedgers) constrain the extent to which the futures price can fall below the current spot price, $p(t)$.

---

[15] The reason for the focus on forward, as opposed to futures, markets by Keynes and Hicks is probably that futures markets were almost non-existent in Britain when they wrote in the 1920s and 1930s. No contentious issues are at stake in the substitution of futures for forward contracts in this context.

Unfortunately, as Duffie (1989, pp. 98–103) points out, Keynes is ambiguous in his use of the word 'backwardation'. Should it be

$$\text{(a)} \quad f(t, T) < p(t)$$

or $$\text{(b)} \quad f(t, T) < E_t[p(T)]?$$

It is the former, (a), that can be observed at date t (and that formally expresses the backwardation), but it is (b) that provides a *risk premium* for the speculators. The problem with using (b) is, as usual, that the expectations are unobserved. To highlight the difference between the two interpretations, consider the identity

$$f(t, T) - p(t) \equiv f(t, T) - E_t[p(T)] + E_t[p(T)] - p(t)$$

Clearly, the expected change in the spot price, $E_t[p(T)] - p(t)$, is pivotal to the distinction between the two versions of the theory. If spot prices are expected to increase over the life of the futures contract, then it is possible for normal backwardation to hold in the sense of (b) but not (a). As always, *expectations* of prices in the future are what matter for speculators.

The validity of the 'normal backwardation' theory remains controversial (partly as a consequence of the ambiguity described above). Several criticisms have been levelled at it.

1. Empirical studies are inconclusive. In an important sense the studies must be inconclusive. Why? Because $E_t[p(T)]$ is not observed and must be obtained as the prediction of a model. Tests of 'normal backwardation' can be implemented only in conjunction with a model of prices. Hence, it is possible to disagree about the plausibility of 'normal backwardation' as a result of disagreement about the model from which the prediction of the expected future spot price is derived.

2. Not all futures markets are dominated by short-hedgers. Keynes may have restricted himself to a special case. As Hicks perceptively remarks in the footnote omitted from the quotation above, the 'congenital weakness of the demand side of course only applies to forward markets in commodities, and will not apply (for instance) to forward markets in foreign exchange' (1939, pp. 137–8). For financial assets (including foreign exchange), reliance on the hedging motive of 'producers' makes little sense. Moreover, stocks of the assets specified in financial futures are unlikely to follow the systematic annual pattern associated with agricultural commodities. Even so, if the holders of assets seek to insulate themselves from subsequent price falls, they would tend to adopt short-hedging strategies.

3. The theory treats the market in question as isolated from other asset markets and, hence, ignores the covariances among assets' prices. Asset pricing theories such as the CAPM or APT imply that risk premia are determined by the covariance pattern of prices amongst all assets – idiosyncratic variability can, in principle, be diversified

away. As mentioned above, however, there is reason to doubt whether these theories are applicable to futures markets.

4. Lastly, according to one of the most respected analysts of futures markets, Hendrik Houthakker, 'the most telling argument of the critics of normal backwardation is that, as a body, small speculators tend to lose money rather consistently' (*The New Palgrave Dictionary of Money and Finance*, Newman, Milgate and Eatwell, 1992, Vol. II, p. 212).

15.5 Manipulation of futures markets

Futures markets are often considered to be vulnerable to practices that are regarded as 'unfair'. It is claimed that markets can be manipulated for profitable advantage by unscrupulous traders, who are judged to act in an 'improper' way. There is widespread disagreement about what constitutes 'improper' conduct in this context, and hence about how to determine whether manipulation has occurred. The disagreement encompasses everyone involved in making pronouncements about manipulation: market traders, exchange authorities, regulators, lawyers, judges, politicians and, of course, economists.

Commentators are usually confident in their ability to identify incidents of manipulation. Precise and generally acceptable characterizations are, however, unavailable. From an economic perspective, manipulation involves the exercise of monopoly power in the sense that at least one trader is a price maker, rather than a price taker, and can thereby act to influence the market price. Actions that take advantage of this influence are often regarded as improper, and may lead to the imposition of disciplinary sanctions by exchange authorities against the alleged manipulator, or to litigation instigated by regulatory authorities or aggrieved parties.

The most well-known form of manipulation is that of *cornering the market*. This works as follows, using – by way of example – the market for silver.

Suppose that a trader – say, *H* – succeeds in acquiring a substantial proportion of the stocks of silver bullion in approved warehouses. Also, *H* adopts a long position in a large proportion of the futures contracts outstanding for a narrow range of delivery dates.[16]

As the delivery dates draw near, traders with short positions ('short-traders' in what follows) purchase contracts in order to offset their obligations to deliver the underlying commodity (silver). But suppose that *H* declines to sell. Given *H*'s

---

[16] The anonymity of futures contracts implies that these trades can often be undertaken without other traders being aware that any one investor has taken such actions. Most futures exchange authorities restrict the number of contracts that any single investor is allowed to hold and may also have the discretion to require the identification of the counterparty to any contract traded on the exchange. In practice, the rules are hard to enforce. Even so, when the possibility of manipulation becomes a cause for concern, the finger of blame is commonly pointed at one investor, possibly acting in concert with collaborators.

dominant position, futures prices rise sharply as short-traders scramble to offset their positions. Short positions can also be settled by exchanges for physicals (e.g. by delivering stocks of silver coins to H), or by delivering warehouse receipts for silver bullion to H as specified in the futures contracts. But, here also, short-traders are in a quandary: H already owns much of the silver bullion and could dictate punitive terms for the delivery of silver coins in settlement of the contracts.

Investor H can thus exploit the discomfort of short-traders. They can (a) offset their positions by buying futures contracts at very high prices; or (b) negotiate with H to take silver coins, or delay delivery (on terms imposed by H), in order to be released from the obligations specified in the futures contracts; or (c) default (in which case H could seek redress from the futures exchange or take legal action for breach of contract). In common parlance, H has the short-traders 'over a barrel'.

The events described so far are often referred to as a 'squeeze' in the literature. The term 'corner' is sometimes reserved for the subsequent actions taken by an investor such as H, who can profit from the monopoly power as a consequence of owning a large proportion of outstanding stocks of the commodity, silver.

Should the squeeze, or corner, constitute a manipulation? Perhaps H genuinely wishes to accumulate large stocks of silver. Proof of manipulation requires evidence of H's *motive*. Preferences are not observed, and, hence, a crucial element of the evidence is necessarily circumstantial. Also, in practice, the trades alleged to constitute a manipulation may be much more complex than suggested by the description above. They typically involve different delivery dates, different markets, different grades of the commodity, non-standard private agreements, a multiplicity of trading accounts, and so forth. It may be difficult to determine *what* has happened, let alone to ascribe motives.[17]

Quite apart from whether manipulations can be proved to have taken place, there is doubt about whether the alleged perpetrators always profit from their actions. Ignore, for the moment, the futures market. In the market for the underlying asset, one trader may succeed in forcing the price up by purchasing a large proportion of the available supply. To profit from the price-making power this bestows the asset will have to be sold, and, when this is done, its price will tend to fall.[18] As a result, the price maker is not necessarily rewarded with high profits: the commodity is acquired at rising prices and disposed of at falling prices. Whether profits can be made depends on the pattern of the price over time, and this pattern cannot be guaranteed to favour the alleged manipulator.

---

[17] The example of H's operations in the silver market described here is a caricature of the events of 1979–80 drawn from Williams (1995).

[18] This is known in futures markets as the problem of 'disposing of the corpse'.

Now reintroduce the futures market. Here the prospect for profit from the 'squeeze' (as described above) is more transparent. Even so, are short-traders so naïve as to ignore the possibility of a squeeze? If they recognize it as a possibility, they should factor their beliefs about this contingency into their decisions. In particular, investors considering whether to take a short position will not sell until the price is high enough to compensate for the possibility that the market might be manipulated. This is not to suggest that manipulation never occurs, nor that it is harmless if it does occur.[19] Instead, it can be argued that manipulation is not, on average, a profitable activity (setting aside considerations of how well or badly the markets are regulated). The potential to make profits by manipulating markets thus remains a debatable matter.

The activities of the Sumitomo corporation in the copper market during the mid-1990s illustrate several of the above issues. In this incident there is evidence that the head of copper trading at the Sumitomo corporation, Yasuo Hamanaka, accumulated stocks of copper and long positions in futures contracts at the London Metal Exchange. Mr Hamanaka, acting in consort with a copper merchant (Global Minerals), was, it is alleged, able to drive up the price of copper over several years before mid-1996, to levels that would not otherwise have been observed. Shortly after accusations against Mr Hamanaka became public he was reassigned to other duties and the price of copper fell sharply.[20] Although Sumitomo incurred substantial losses as a result of the alleged manipulation, much of the company's copper trading involved non-exchange transactions at prices linked to those quoted on the LME. Given that commission fees on the transactions are commonly greater the higher the price of the metal, profits could thus be increased even if both purchases and sales were made at artificially high prices.

All legal decisions are open to error, either of acquitting the guilty or convicting the innocent. Although judgements about market manipulation may be particularly susceptible to error, regulatory authorities and courts of law in many jurisdictions are, nonetheless, obliged to address allegations of such wrongdoing. Evidence can take a variety of forms, including the results of statistical hypothesis tests. For instance, if the alleged manipulation focuses on a narrow range of delivery months, the futures prices for those contract months would be exceptionally high relative to prices for later delivery. Also, spot prices in the cash market tend to fall abruptly during, or shortly after, the delivery period for a manipulated contract.

---

[19] There could be social costs if futures markets are disrupted (become less liquid) because traders restrict their participation, fearing that they may be vulnerable to manipulation.

[20] Mr Hamanaka subsequently pleaded guilty to fraud and forgery in the Japanese courts and was sentenced to eight years' imprisonment. It seems that his actions were motivated by an attempt to recover losses made in copper trades in the 1980s and early 1990s. Mr Hamanaka's employers claim that he was a 'rogue trader', acting on his own initiative and not at their behest. However, many of the relevant facts remain confidential to the Sumitomo corporation. Consequently, the information needed to resolve the case may never enter the public domain.

With regard to quantities, abnormal volumes of the commodity would be shipped to the designated delivery points shortly before the contract matures and then away again soon after it matures. Markets for similar commodities (e.g. with different delivery locations, contract dates or standardized quality grades) that are not subject to the alleged manipulation would not exhibit such patterns, and, hence, could be used to provide a benchmark.

Pirrong (2004) develops and tests these hypotheses in the context of the alleged manipulation of the soybean market in Chicago by the Ferruzzi corporation, an Italian conglomerate, during 1988–89. He concludes unequivocally that statistical tests enable him to 'reject decisively the null hypothesis that Ferruzzi was acting as a price taker on the May and July 1989 soybean futures contracts, in favor of the alternative that the firm exercised market power' (p. 67). This being so, Pirrong goes on to argue that the *ex post* detection and punishment of manipulation is less costly to society than attempts to prevent its occurrence, for prevention imposes a heavy burden of bureaucratic regulations that can distort markets and reduce their effectiveness. If potential malefactors realize that their motives are likely to be revealed and punished, then, it is argued, the propensity to engage in manipulation will be much diminished. Episodes as apparently clear-cut as the Ferruzzi soybean manipulation may warrant such a view. However, the opportunities for market specialists to conduct complex manoeuvres that obscure their actions – let alone their motives – are manifold. And cautious market authorities, mindful of their responsibilities, may feel obliged to intervene before any suspected manipulation reaches its climax, thereby restricting the volume of data available for statistical tests (and thus limiting their reliability).

The cases outlined above describe classic forms of manipulation long known in futures and commodity markets. Various other types have been identified. For example, a trader may seek to spread a rumour that leads others (erroneously) to believe that the underlying commodity price will rise. The futures price then rises, and the manipulator seeks to sell before it is realized that the rumour is false.

A common feature of all types of manipulation is that a trader seeks to become a price maker – i.e. to take actions that influence prices. There is little doubt that traders can sometimes acquire this power. Whether they can be confident of profiting from their actions, whether their conduct imposes costs on society and whether prevention is superior to punishment are much more contentious issues.

15.6 Summary

1. Speculators in futures markets seek to profit from exploiting their beliefs – i.e. their expectations about subsequent changes in contract prices. In principle, the incentives

are no different from other investment activities, though knowledge about futures markets is often regarded as being of a specialized nature, available only to experts.

2. Hedging strategies are motivated by the aim to eradicate, or at least to mitigate, price risk in asset markets. Hedging involves buying or selling a hedge instrument (e.g. futures contracts) in such a way that the fluctuations in its price offset those in an underlying asset, which the investor is committed to buy or sell at a definite future date. Suitably chosen, the hedge attenuates the risks originating in ignorance about the future spot price.

3. Hedges rarely eliminate price risk altogether but can be chosen to minimize risk. More generally, hedging can be understood as a type of portfolio decision in which investors balance the expected return against risk. Consequently, hedging and speculative motives may both be present.

4. Hedging, speculation and arbitrage all affect futures and spot prices. One of the most well-known theories of futures prices is 'normal backwardation', a theory that, however, receives at best limited support from empirical evidence.

5. Futures markets are widely believed to be vulnerable to manipulation by traders who seek to influence prices to their private advantage. The extent of manipulation is difficult to establish, and doubts have been voiced about whether traders who seek to manipulate futures prices can systematically profit from their actions.

Further reading

Three particularly clear textbook expositions of hedging are those by Duffie (1989, chap. 7), Edwards and Ma (1992, chaps. 5 & 6) and Hull (2005, chap. 3).

In focusing on evidence from the silver market during 1979–80, Williams (1995) provides an attractive alternative to textbook expositions of futures trading. This fascinating book disentangles a notorious alleged manipulation and, in so doing, illuminates the operation of commodity markets.

Another exemplar of applied economics in unravelling evidence for market manipulation is that provided by Pirrong (2004). His earlier work, Pirrong (1996), is equally valuable, though from a broader perspective. Telser (1992) and Kumar and Seppi (1992) also provide noteworthy contributions to debates about futures market manipulation. Finally, see Gilbert (1996) for one of the few papers to illuminate the Sumitomo copper market manipulation.

Appendix 15.1: Futures investment as portfolio selection

Consider the fundamental valuation relationship, introduced in chapter 4. This asserts that an expected-utility-maximizing decision maker adopts an investment strategy such that

$$E[(1+r_j)H] = 1 \tag{15.17}$$

where r_j is the rate of return on asset j and H is the stochastic discount factor, a random variable dependent upon the investor's preferences (see chapter 4 for details). Strictly, the expectation should be conditioned on the set of information, Ω_t, available today, date t, so that (15.17) becomes

$$\mathrm{E}[(1+r_j)H|\Omega_t] = 1 \tag{15.18}$$

This complication is neglected until it is needed.

The FVR can be applied to futures contracts, though some reinterpretation is necessary. For simplicity, suppose that asset j is a *forward* contract agreed today, t, exactly one period before the delivery date T, so that $T = t+1$. The 'payoff' on the investment in the forward contract is the spot price at delivery, $p(T)$, while the price paid for that payoff is the forward price agreed today, $F(t, T)$. Hence, the gross rate of return – essentially, 'one plus the rate of return' – could be defined as $p(T)/F(t, T)$. This definition, however, ignores the fact that the investor pays $F(t, T)$ only at date T, not when the contract is agreed, at t. The investor has the use of the funds between t and T – funds with an opportunity cost equal to the risk-free interest rate, r_0. This being so, the gross rate on return on the forward contract, $(1+r_j)$, can be expressed as

$$(1+r_j) = \frac{p(T)}{F(t, T)}(1+r_0) \tag{15.19}$$

This definition asserts that the investment in the forward contract should be understood as an investment in the risk-free asset today, coupled with a commitment (the forward contract) to exchange (buy or sell) the underlying asset for $F(t, T)$ at date T. The market price of the asset at T – the payoff on the forward contract – is $p(T)$. Whether the investor actually invests in the risk-free asset at date t is irrelevant; what matters is that there is an opportunity cost of funds between the date at which the contract is agreed, t, and T, the date of delivery.[21]

It is straightforward to extended the analysis to forward contracts with more than one period before maturity. In this case, $(1+r_0)$ is replaced by a general interest rate factor $R(t, T)$, thus allowing for interest rate changes, if any, and compounding between t and T. Also, note that the stochastic discount factor, H, depends on both t and T, though this has been suppressed in the FVR, equation (15.17).

Application of the reasoning to *futures* contracts is also straightforward, because the process of marking to market requires the value of the futures contract to be

---

[21] Any good-faith margin deposit associated with the forward transaction is logically separate from the investment in the forward contract itself. Funds held in the margin account typically attract a market interest rate, and hence can be ignored in this analysis.

recalculated each trading day.[22] Consider two successive days t and $t+1$ such that $t+1 < T$, so that delivery is not an issue. Any contract (short or long) held at t and valued at $f(t, T)$ is revalued the next day at whatever the price happens to be then – i.e. $f(t+1, T)$. For notational brevity, define $f_0 \equiv f(t, T)$ and $f_1 \equiv f(t+1, T)$ (where, of course, $t+1 < T$).

If the investor's decision interval is one trading day, then the rate of return can be measured as for forward contracts, but replacing $F(t, T)$ with f_0 and $p(T)$ with f_1 so that

$$1 + r_j = \frac{f_1}{f_0}(1 + r_0) \tag{15.20}$$

A time-span between dates 0 and 1 different from the unit interval can be handled by replacing $(1 + r_0)$ by the interest factor, $R(t, T)$, as noted above for forward contracts. This complication is neglected here.

It is possible to express the excess return on the futures contract over the risk-free rate (i.e. $r_j - r_0$) by subtracting $1 + r_0$ from both sides of (15.20), to give

$$r_j - r_0 = \frac{f_1 - f_0}{f_0}(1 + r_0)$$

The expected excess return is then given by

$$E[r_j] - r_0 = \frac{E[f_1] - f_0}{f_0}(1 + r_0) \tag{15.21}$$

because f_0 and r_0 are known at date 0 and, hence, are non-random. Notice that the expression in (15.21) differs from that given in the text, (15.16). The difference reflects an ambiguity in how the return on a futures contract should be defined, given the peculiarity that (apart from the margin deposit) investment in a futures contract does not require any initial outlay of funds.

Returning to the analysis of the FVR, substitution from (15.20) yields

$$E[(1 + r_j)H] - 1$$

$$E\left[\frac{f_1}{f_0}(1 + r_0)H\right] = 1$$

$$f_0 = (1 + r_0)E[f_1 H] \tag{15.22}$$

where the final equality follows because r_0 and f_0 are known at date 0, and hence can be factored outside the expectations operator.

In principle, with assumptions about the stochastic discount factor, H, equation (15.22) could provide the foundation for a model of investment in futures contracts

---

[22] As with forward contracts, the margin deposit required to support the futures contract is logically separate from the payoff from the contract itself, although, of course, the margin account provides the bookkeeping device for recording the daily gains and losses.

and also of futures price determination. This is not attempted here. Instead, consider the extreme case of risk-neutral preferences – that is, $H = c$, where c is a constant, the same for all states. It follows from the FVR that $c = 1/(1+r_0)$.[23] Thus

$$f_0 = (1+r_0)\mathrm{E}[f_1 H]$$
$$f_0 = (1+r_0)c\mathrm{E}[f_1]$$
$$f_0 = \mathrm{E}[f_1] \tag{15.23}$$

Equation (15.23) asserts that, if investors are risk-neutral, the futures price today equals the *expected* futures price at date 1. To understand the relationship between this and $f(t, T) = \mathrm{E}[p(T)|\Omega_t]$ (equation (15.14) in the text), let date 1 denote the delivery date of the futures contract, so that $p(T) = f_1$. Finally, recall that the expectation in the FVR should be conditional upon currently available information. Thus, (15.23) and (15.14) amount to the same thing: risk neutrality implies that the futures price equals the spot price expected (as of t) to be observed at the futures contract delivery date. The equality will not generally hold if investors are *risk-averse*.

Appendix 15.2: Derivation of $\widetilde{h}$

From equation (15.6), $\Delta W/N = \Delta p - h\Delta f$, the expected value of $\Delta W/N$ is

$$\mathrm{E}[\Delta W/N] = \mathrm{E}[\Delta p] - h\mathrm{E}[\Delta f] \tag{15.24}$$

The variance of $\Delta W/N$ is obtained as follows:

$$\mathrm{var}(\Delta W/N) \equiv \mathrm{E}[(\Delta W/N) - E(\Delta W/N)]^2$$
$$= \mathrm{E}\{\Delta p - \mathrm{E}[\Delta p] - h(\Delta f - \mathrm{E}[\Delta f])\}^2$$
$$= \sigma_p^2 + h^2\sigma_f^2 - 2h\sigma_{pf} \tag{15.25}$$

Substituting from (15.24) and (15.25) into the objective function, $\mathcal{U} = \mathrm{E}[\Delta W/N] - \alpha \cdot \mathrm{var}[\Delta W/N]$, gives

$$\mathcal{U} = \mathrm{E}[\Delta p] - h\mathrm{E}[\Delta f] - \alpha\{\sigma_p^2 + h^2\sigma_f^2 - 2h\sigma_{pf}\} \tag{15.26}$$

The first-order condition for maximizing $\mathcal{U}$ with respect to h is found by setting the derivative of (15.26) with respect to h to zero:

$$\frac{d\mathcal{U}}{dh} = -\mathrm{E}[\Delta f] - 2\alpha h\sigma_f^2 + 2\alpha\sigma_{pf} = 0$$

---

[23] To see this, recall that the FVR holds also for the risk-free asset. Hence, substitute r_0 for r_j and c for H in (15.17). Because both r_0 and c are non-random, the expectation $\mathrm{E}[(1+r_0)c] = (1+r_0)c$. From the FVR, $(1+r_0)c = 1$, and the result follows.

The second-order condition is

$$\frac{d^2 \mathcal{U}}{dh^2} = -2\alpha\sigma_f^2 < 0$$

as required for a maximum of $\mathcal{U}$.

Finally, substitute $E[\Delta f] = E[f_1] - f_0$ and solve to give equation (15.11):

$$\tilde{h} = h^* + \frac{f_0 - E[f_1]}{2\alpha\sigma_f^2}$$

where $h^* \equiv \sigma_{pf}/\sigma_f^2$.

References

Black, F. (1976), 'The pricing of commodity contracts', *Journal of Financial Economics*, 3(1–2), pp. 167–79.

Duffie, J. D. (1989), *Futures Markets*, Englewood Cliffs, NJ: Prentice Hall.

Ederington, L. H. (1979), 'The hedging performance of the new futures markets', *Journal of Finance*, 34(1), pp. 157–70.

Edwards, F. R., and C. W. Ma (1992), *Futures and Options*, New York: McGraw-Hill.

Figlewski, S., Y. Landskroner and W. L. Silber (1991), 'Tailing the hedge: why and how', *Journal of Futures Markets*, 11(2), pp. 201–12.

Gilbert, C. L. (1996), *Manipulation of Metals Futures: Lessons from Sumitomo*, Centre for Economic Policy Research Discussion Paper no. 1537.

Hicks, J. R. (1939), *Value and Capital*, Oxford: Oxford University Press.

Hull, J. C. (2005), *Fundamentals of Futures, and Options Markets*, Englewood Cliffs, NJ: Prentice Hall, 5th edn.

Kumar, P., and D. J. Seppi (1992), 'Futures manipulation with "cash settlement"', *Journal of Finance*, 47(4), pp. 1485–1502.

Newman, P., M. Milgate and J. Eatwell (eds.) (1992), *The New Palgrave Dictionary of Money and Finance*, London: Macmillan (three volumes).

Pirrong, S. C. (1996), *The Economics, Law and Public Policy of Market Power Manipulation*, Boston, London and Dordrecht: Kluwer Academic Publishers.

(2004), 'Detecting manipulation in futures markets: the Ferruzzi soybean episode', *American Law and Economics Review*, 6(1) pp. 28–71.

Telser, L. G. (1992), 'Corners in organized futures markets', in L. Philips and L. D. Taylor (eds.), *Aggregation, Consumption and Trade: Essays in Honor of Hendrik S. Houthakker*, Amsterdam: Kluwer Academic Publishers, pp. 159–67.

Williams, J. (1995), *Manipulation on Trial: Economic Analysis and the Hunt Silver Case*, Cambridge: Cambridge University Press.

Working, H. (1962), 'New concepts concerning futures markets and prices', *American Economic Review*, 52(3), pp. 431–59.

16

Futures markets III: applications

Overview

The aims of this chapter are (a) to extend the analysis of futures markets with illustrations from non-commodity futures contracts; and (b) to study futures contracts for which the underlying asset is not an object that can easily be delivered – or, perhaps, is intangible and, thereby, impossible to deliver – when the contract matures. These contracts are essentially the same as commodity futures. Their specifications may at first sight, however, appear to be peculiar, especially with respect to the nature of the underlying asset, the process of contract settlement and, in some cases, the purposes of the strategies that make use of the contracts.

Much of the chapter focuses on financial futures contracts for which the underlying asset is a financial instrument that could (in principle, if not in fact) be delivered in fulfilment of the contract. The chapter begins, however, with an examination of weather futures contracts (section 16.1), for which 'delivery' of the underlying asset appears to be nonsensical.

Section 16.2 turns to financial futures with an outline of the characteristics of typical forms of these contracts. The following sections study three main sorts of financial futures contracts: (i) short-term interest rate futures (section 16.3); (ii) long-term interest rate (or, bond) futures (section 16.4); and (iii) stock index futures (section 16.5). Finally, section 16.6 illustrates the analysis of section 16.5 with a brief discussion of the failure of Barings Bank in late February 1995.

16.1 Weather futures

16.1.1 The CME degree day index

Forecasting the weather months in advance is a notoriously imperfect science – almost as imperfect as economic forecasting – yet it is of profound importance for some enterprises. For instance, the volume of rainfall in particular months of the year can make the difference between a bountiful harvest and crop failure.

'Weather', of course, has several dimensions (rainfall, temperature, humidity, wind speed, etc.), all of which are susceptible to wide variations across time and place. The futures contracts described here are based on *temperature*. Temperature variations would be of relevance, for example, to a company that supplies electricity, the demand for which tends to be unusually high during especially cold winters (for heating) and hot summers (for air-conditioning).

For a futures contract to be successful there must exist a pool of investors who would consider trading it. As always, this requires standardization of the contract. On the Chicago Mercantile Exchange, standardization is achieved with a '*degree day index*' (DD index), which is a measure – to be defined shortly – of extreme temperature variations at a stipulated geographical location. Investors (typically companies and professional traders) can then buy or sell contracts specified in terms of the magnitude of the DD index that will be realized during a designated time period (e.g. a particular month) in the future. At the end of the designated period, the 'weather' (i.e. the DD index) cannot be delivered. Instead, cash settlement closes all outstanding contracts at the maturity of the contract.

There are, in fact, several DD indexes embedded within the CME contracts. First, the DD indexes are location-specific: they are quoted for various cities in the United States and Europe. Second, contracts cover different time periods: months or seasons (winter or summer) – only contracts defined for designated calendar months are described below.

Third, separate indexes measure exceptionally high and low temperatures: cooling degree day (CDD) and heating degree day (HDD) indexes, respectively. The CDD index is defined as follows.

$$\text{Daily CDD} = maximum\{0, \text{daily average temperature}$$
$$minus\ 65° \text{ Fahrenheit}\}$$

Thus, if the average temperature during a day is 80° the CDD is 15, while if the average temperature is 58° the CDD is *zero* for that day. The daily CDD values are added up to provide an index of high temperatures (relative to 65° Fahrenheit) for each calendar month. Similarly, the HDD index is defined as follows.

$$\text{Daily HDD} = maximum\{0, 65° \text{ Fahrenheit}$$
$$minus\ \text{daily average temperature}\}$$

Thus, the HDD is an index of low temperatures while CDD is an index of high temperatures (both relative to 65° Fahrenheit). The labels 'CDD' and 'HDD' are chosen because high temperatures imply a demand for energy for cooling while low temperatures imply a demand for energy for heating.

As an illustration of how the futures contracts might be utilized, assume that 'today' is in February and suppose that the HDD index contract for December delivery in Boston, Massachusetts, is trading at 800. This means that profits or losses will be made on any contract purchased or sold today, according to whether the actual HDD index for next December in Boston turns out to be greater or less than 800 (assuming that the contract is held until the delivery date). Suppose that one contract is *purchased* at 800 and the realized HDD index turns out to be 880. This provides a *gain* of $8000 – i.e. 80 points each worth $100 (the contract terms stipulate that each point is worth $100). It is *as if* the contract has been offset (sold) at 880, the observed HDD index. Corresponding to each investor with a long position (who has purchased the contract) there must be an investor with a short position (who has sold the contract). In this example, any investor who took a short position at 800 loses $8000 per contract when the contract is settled at 880 – it is as if the investor offsets the short position by purchasing at the settlement price of 880.

Just as for any futures contract, positions may be offset before the delivery date. In that case, each position is settled at the HDD index value quoted in the market when the contract is offset. In the example above, suppose that the HDD index (for December delivery in Boston) stands at 900 in November. Long positions could be offset with a gain of $10,000 (100 points times $100 per point). Short positions taken on at 800 and offset at 900 would incur a loss of $10,000 per contract. Given that futures contracts are marked to market on a daily basis, the gain or loss when the position is offset is reflected in the investor's margin account, so that the final gain or loss will have accumulated in increments throughout the period the contract is open depending on daily fluctuations in the market value of the HDD index (see chapter 14, section 14.1.3).

16.1.2 Hedging with weather futures

Why might a company use weather futures as a hedge instrument? Suppose that an energy supply company's trading profits vary with the temperature in a city say, Boston The company could seek to protect itself against a mild winter (low energy sales) by taking a short position in HDD index contracts for December delivery in Boston. If the winter turns out to be mild, temperatures will be relatively high and the realized HDD index will turn out to be relatively low.[1] The company then offsets its short position by purchasing contracts at a

---

[1] Low relative to what? Relative to the quoted HDD index on the date at which the futures position is initiated. The quoted index will, presumably, reflect whatever information is available to investors at each date – information typically including evidence accumulated in the past about weather conditions during the delivery month. This evidence will influence trading in the contract and, thus, its market quotation. Towards the end of the delivery month, weather observations make it increasingly clear what the realized index value will turn out to be. Hence, the regular futures market prediction holds: as the delivery date approaches, the futures price (in this case the quoted index value) converges to the 'spot price' (in this case the realized value of the HDD index).

lower price than that at which it initially sold them, thus gaining from its futures strategy. The gain on futures will serve to offset its lower profits (or losses) as a consequence of the mild winter.

Conversely, if the winter turns out to be relatively harsh, observed temperatures are relatively low and the actual HDD index will be relatively high. The company offsets its futures position with losses that are compensated for by its trading profits (resulting from a high demand for the energy it supplies).

What determines the size of the company's futures position (the number of contracts it sells)? If the company seeks to minimize the variance of its net revenues, it will estimate the relationship between changes in its energy sales and the HDD index. This the company could do statistically, using data from past years, or from other information about the market it serves and weather predictions. Once estimated, the relationship enables the company to calculate the relevant pure hedge ratio (see chapter 15, section 15.3.1).

Winters are, of course, not confined to a single month. Typically, a company that seeks to hedge against a mild winter would acquire a *strip* of futures for a subset of contracts maturing in each of the winter months (say, from October to March in Boston).

By construction, hedging strategies smooth out profits and losses. In order to increase its profits, the company might be prepared to bear additional risks by not hedging to the extent required by the pure hedge ratio. It might even choose to *purchase* futures contracts if it has information suggesting that the realized HDD index will be higher than quoted in the market. By undertaking a policy different from that implied by the pure hedge ratio, the company adopts a speculative strategy – a strategy that presumably reflects (a) its tolerance of risk and (b) its beliefs about the future compared with the prices it observes in the market.

While the above discussion corresponds to the HDD index, exactly the same principles apply for the CDD index. For the CDD, the typical hedge strategy would be against average summer temperatures that turn out to be unusually high. In these circumstances, market quotations for the CDD prior to the summer months will tend to reflect normal temperatures. If the summer is abnormally hot, the realized CDD observations for the summer 'delivery' months (say, from May to August in Boston) will be higher than the market quotations (made earlier in the year, when the summer temperatures were expected to be normal). It is this divergence between the market quotations before the summer and the realized values when the summer arrives that provides scope for hedging.

16.2 Financial futures contracts

16.2.1 Spread betting

Spread betting on financial indexes resembles trading in financial futures contracts and, because it may be easier to understand, is outlined first. With spread betting, a company – the 'bookmaker' – quotes the price for a particular index at a particular 'delivery' (expiry) date. The investor (or 'client', or 'punter') can then bet on the index by buying or selling at the quoted price. When the contract expires, the client wins or loses according to the observed value of the index at that date. Just as with futures contracts, the spread bet need not be held until expiry, and can be offset at whatever price the bookmaker quotes on the day that the investor closes it.

A small, though significant, complication is that the bookmaker quotes not one price but two: there is a bid-ask spread. For example, if 'today' is a date in February, the bookmaker may quote 5550–5570 for the FT-SE 100 index in December. Suppose that a client *buys* by staking £10 per point on the December. This involves a starting price of 5570, the bookmaker's 'ask price'. Now suppose that the client closes the bet in October, at which date the bookmaker is quoting 5585–5605 for the December FT-SE 100 index. It is as if the client *sells* the index at the bookmaker's 'bid price' of 5585. In this case the client gains $15 = 5585 - 5570$ points times the £10 bet per point, a total of £150.

Alternatively, suppose that in October the bookmaker quotes 5525–5545, and that, for some reason, the client closes the bet. The client *sells* at 5525, a loss of $45 = 5570 - 5525$ points, thus incurring a loss of £450 (at £10 per point). As already noted, if the bet remains open at the expiry date, it is settled at the observed index value. The bookmaker may apply a spread around the observed value according to the terms of the agreement when the bet was initiated. (Bookmakers tend to have standard forms of agreement to cover such matters. In addition, clients are required to hold good-faith deposits with bookmakers for exactly the same purpose as for futures contracts.)

Evidently, an investor who expects the index to rise will bet on a rise by buying from the bookmaker (at the quoted ask price). An investor who expects the index to fall will bet by selling to the bookmaker (at the quoted bid price).

One of the main differences between spread betting and futures trading is that bets are not between punters but, rather, punters trade with the bookmaker, who quotes the prices.[2] In futures markets, contract prices are determined to balance supply and demand between sellers and buyers – the exchange authorities guarantee that the contracts will be honoured but do not initiate the buy and

---

[2] The exception is at the expiry date, when the realized index value is the value applied to close the bet.

sell orders. In general, spread betting is designed for private investors who can commit only small amounts of capital, compared with companies for which futures markets generally provide more favourable terms as a consequence of large outlays.

16.2.2 Contract specifications

Two aspects of financial futures that might seem perplexing, initially at least, are (a) that the underlying asset – henceforth, 'the asset' – may be harder to identify than for commodity futures; and (b) that, at the delivery date, contracts may often – for some contracts, must – be settled in cash, not by delivery of the asset. Even if delivery is permitted, there is typically a range of securities that satisfy the terms of the contract. (In this regard, financial futures are no different from commodity futures, for which several specified grades of the commodity may be delivered in settlement.)

In common with commodity futures markets, a high proportion of financial futures contracts tends to be offset before maturity. To review the principles, suppose that the price of a futures contract today (date 0) for delivery at date T is f_0 and that the contract is offset at date 1 where $T > 1$ (i.e. the position is closed *before* maturity).

Assume that M contracts are sold at date 0 ($M < 0$ corresponds to the *purchase* of contracts). At date 1 the M contracts are offset (purchased if $M > 0$, sold if $M < 0$). The payoff equals $(f_0 - f_1)Mv$, where v is the money value per unit of the futures contract price. For example, if the futures price is '5587' and $v = £10$, then the market value of one contract is £55,870 $= 5587 \times 10$.

The number v is known in advance – it can be calculated from the terms of the contract. In practice, v is the money value per unit of the contract price, defined by the *tick value* divided by the *tick size*. The tick size measures the smallest permitted change in the contract price, and the tick value measures the amount of money corresponding to the tick size:

$$v \equiv \frac{\text{tick value}}{\text{tick size}}$$

Thus, if the tick size is 0.5 (i.e. the futures price moves in half unit intervals – e.g. 5384.0, 5384.5, 5385.0, 5385.5, ...) and the tick value is £5.00, then $v = £5.00/0.5 = £10$.

What happens if the contracts are held to maturity ($T = 1$ in the above notation)? The only difference of principle, at $T = 1$, is that f_1 is determined according to the terms of the contract, not by the supply of and demand for futures contracts. In particular, for a cash-settled contract, f_T is set equal to the market value of the underlying asset at date T.[3] This is a value calculated from observations of the asset price, the method of calculation being made according to rules stipulated in the contract (examples are provided below).

For some financial futures it is permissible to deliver the assets (securities) underlying the contract, during the prescribed delivery period, in settlement of the contract. Subject to minor differences, the result is the same as for cash settlement – by construction, the delivered securities have a market value equal to f_T. The important point is that the futures price at the delivery date equals the price of the asset at that date. Sometimes there are technicalities that must be taken into account to determine precisely what constitutes 'the asset', but these do not alter the principle.

Lastly, it should be remembered that the gains or losses expressed by $(f_0 - f_1)Mv$ accumulate between dates 0 and 1 via debits and credits to the investor's margin account. The final outcome is the same, but the gains and losses accumulate daily through the process of marking to market.

16.2.3 Arbitrage, speculation and hedging with financial futures

The investment motives associated with arbitrage, speculation and hedging are exactly the same as for non-financial futures.

Arbitrage

A characteristic of many financial instruments is that they have a designated date of maturity. For example, the date on which a bond terminates is almost always stipulated in the bond indenture.

The maturity date for the bond must be distinguished from the delivery (maturity) date for a futures contract for exchange of the bond. The maturity date for the bond is never earlier (and is normally later) than the delivery date for the corresponding futures contract. Thus, a futures contract on a one-year bond requires the delivery of a one-year bond, when the futures contract matures. If the delivery date for the futures contract is, say, six months from the present, then *viewed from the present* the bond matures after eighteen months – i.e. one year from the futures contract delivery date.

The distinction between the maturity dates for (a) the futures contract and (b) its underlying asset is important for arbitrage strategies. Suppose again that the futures contract matures in six months from the present and stipulates the delivery of a one-year bond. In this example, the relevant comparison for arbitrage purposes is between the futures price and the price of a bond that matures

---

[3] f_T is just a less cumbersome way of writing $f(T, T)$. They denote the same price: $f_T \equiv f(T, T)$.

eighteen months from the present, for it is a bond with this maturity that could be delivered to satisfy the futures contract.

Speculation and hedging

The principles of speculation and hedging are just the same for financial futures as for other futures contracts. Speculation involves seeking to profit from beliefs that futures prices will follow a particular pattern, so that an investor who buys futures believes that the price will subsequently increase and one who sells believes that the price will fall. Hedging involves seeking to minimize the risk of loss associated with unforeseen asset price changes, realized only at a later date.

One notable feature of hedging with financial futures is that a hedge may be sought for an asset (or portfolio of assets) already in the possession of the hedger. This could, of course, be the case for any hedging strategy, but it seems especially common with regard to stock index futures. In this case the investor holds a portfolio of securities, the hedge being designed to limit the variability in the investor's wealth at a specified date in the future.

What is the criterion for the success of such a hedge? Given that capital is tied up in the assets, it is reasonable to suppose that a return is received even if the capital is successfully insulated from risk. Thus, in this circumstance, the criterion for a perfect hedge is that the rate of return on capital invested in the assets is equal to the risk-free interest rate over the life of the hedge. Most hedges are, of course, risky, but the risk-free rate provides an appropriate target, or benchmark, for appraising their success or failure. This principle applies generally when the investor owns the asset at the outset. A detailed illustration is provided for stock index futures in section 16.5. (Note that no capital is tied up in the hedge instrument – the futures contract – apart from margin deposits, on which it is reasonable to assume that the risk-free interest rate is paid.)

16.3 Short-term interest rate futures

16.3.1 Contract specifications

The defining characteristic of short-term interest rate futures is that the asset stipulated in the contract is a security with a short time period – say, three or six months – to maturity after the futures' delivery date. It is helpful to treat the life of the asset as starting at the delivery date for the futures contract. Thus, if the underlying asset is a three-month treasury bill and the delivery date for the futures contract is the end of June, then the treasury bill will mature at the end of September, three months after the futures contract matures. Contracts for '13-week US treasury bills' are traded on the CME; at the delivery date, investors with short positions deliver treasury bills with ninety-one days to maturity to investors with long positions, in return for the previously agreed futures contract price. As always with futures contracts, the market price of these bills as of the delivery date is exchanged in return for the bills. The funds lodged in margin accounts reflect the gains or losses on the futures position as a consequence of marking the contracts to market in the usual way.

Some short-term interest rate futures contracts, however, must be settled in cash. This is the case for the 'Three-Month Sterling (Short-Sterling) Interest Rate Future' traded on LIFFE. The asset underlying this contract is a notional £500,000 bank time deposit of three months' duration. The time deposit is *notional* because no time deposit changes hands at the delivery date; the contract is settled in cash, as outlined below.

The short-sterling contract price is quoted as $f(t, T) = (1 - r(t, T)) \times 100$, where $r(t, T)$ is the interest rate (expressed at an annual rate) that would be obtained on a three-month deposit starting at date T. The purchase of a contract at date t should guarantee a rate $r(t, T)$ for a three-month deposit initiated at T. (Complications are discussed later.) For example, if $f(t, T) = 96.50$, the implied rate of interest for three-month deposits made at T equals $3.50\% = 100 - 96.50$.

The tick size is 0.01 per cent, so that a change from 5.00 per cent to 4.00 per cent is equal to 100 ticks. The tick value equals £12.50, so that $v = £12.50/0.01 = £1250$ per contract. Why is the tick value set at £12.50? It is chosen to equal 0.01 per cent of £500,000 for three months (3/12 of a year):

$$£12.50 = £500,000 \times 0.01\% \times 3/12$$

As usual, many contracts do not run to maturity but are offset before maturity at whatever futures price happens to rule at the date when the position is offset.

Suppose, however, that a contract does remain open at maturity. How is it settled? As already noted, a three-month deposit is not exchanged. Instead, *cash settlement* occurs by terminating all remaining open positions at a contract price obtained from an average of observed three-month interest rates at date T. This price is called the exchange delivery settlement price (EDSP). It is calculated as 100 *minus* the average on the contract's last trading day of interest rates quoted by a designated list of banks for three-month deposits.

Suppose that the average interest rate is 4.21 per cent at date T. Then every existing contract – open position – is settled as if the futures price is $f(T, T) = 100 - 4.21 = 95.79$ (this is the EDSP). Although few contracts may survive to maturity, the EDSP calculation is important because the knowledge that it will be made in this way influences the actions of investors at dates prior to maturity.

To understand how this works, suppose that your rich aunt has just died (say, in February) leaving you £500,000, which you plan to deposit for three months when the money reaches you – say, at the end of June. If the futures price in February, for contracts maturing in June, is 95.00, you can ensure a rate of 5 per cent on your planned deposit by buying one contract (taking a long position) in February. Suppose that the three-month interest rate has fallen to 4 per cent at the end of June. The EDSP would then be 96.00, at which your long position is settled as if the contract is sold at that date. Hence, the difference of $96.00 - 95.00 = 100$ ticks yields a gain of $100 \times 12.50 = £1250$ – i.e. 1 per cent of £500,000 for three months. If you make the deposit, as planned, you will receive the going interest rate, 4 per cent. The gain on the futures contract (1 per cent of your deposit) means that, in total, you receive the 5 per cent 'locked in' when the contract was purchased in the previous February.

Complications and discussion

1. Given that the EDSP is calculated as an average of rates, a three-month deposit made to a particular bank on the maturity date might bear an interest rate that does not exactly equal the EDSP. In the example above, even though the EDSP is calculated from observed interest rates, the rate paid by the bank at which the deposit is made might be lower, or higher. Of course, there is no obligation for the investor actually to make such a deposit; what matters for the settlement of the futures contract is the EDSP, not any particular bank's interest rate.

2. If the futures position is offset before maturity, there is no guarantee that the observed three-month interest rate equals the rate implied by the futures price when the contract is offset. Although it is likely that the two rates will be correlated, that does not mean that they are equal.[4] Only at maturity is the contract price calculated using realized interest rates.

3. In the illustration above, if the three-month interest rate is higher than 5 per cent at the end of June there will be a loss on the position. But this will be balanced by the higher interest rate received on the deposit. For example, if the interest rate is 6 per cent there will be a loss of £1250 (i.e. 1 per cent of £500,000 for three months) on the futures contract, but the actual deposit yields 6 per cent, resulting in an overall net return of 5 per cent.

4. Although the trading strategy might be devised such that the gain or loss from the futures contracts matches the loss or gain from interest rate changes, there is a subtle difference between the two sources of income. The difference occurs because the gain or loss from the futures contracts accrues when the contracts are liquidated (perhaps at the contracts' maturity date, but possibly before), while the interest on the deposit is paid after the deposit has been made (typically, at the end of the three-month deposit period). Thus, if a gain is made on the futures contracts the investor can deposit the

---

[4] The quest for arbitrage profits links interest rates and futures prices so that, if the term structure of interest rates does not fluctuate wildly, changes in the futures contract price tend to be correlated with observed three-month interest rates.

gain and earn extra interest. If, instead, a loss is made on futures, the loss accrues before the deposit is made; the gain from a higher rate of interest on the deposit is received later on. Admittedly, the difference is likely to be minor (reflecting, as it does, interest on interest), but the power of compound interest is non-negligible if the capital outlays are large.

16.3.2 A short-term interest rate hedge

Consider a company that has borrowed £5 million on 1 February for six months at 8 per cent per annum for the first three months, the interest rate for the second three months of the loan being determined later, say on 1 May. Suppose that the company seeks to reduce or eliminate the risk of an interest rate increase for the second three-month period. It can do this by acquiring a short position in three-month sterling futures contracts. Assume, for the sake of example, that the price on 1 February for the June futures contract is 94.00.

Suppose that the overall level of interest rates rises between February and May, so that (for example) the company must pay 9 per cent for the second three months. Thus, the interest cost of the loan would increase by 1 per cent per annum – i.e. by £12,500 ($= 5{,}000{,}000 \times \frac{3}{12} \times 1\%$). The company could hedge against this contingency by recognizing that the futures price falls when the interest rate rises. Suppose that the futures price falls from 94.00 to 93.00 (100 ticks) between 1 February and 1 May. If the company sells ten contracts at 94.00 and offsets its position at 93.00, it gains £12,500 = 100 ticks $\times$ £12.50 $\times$ 10.

Thus, for a company with an obligation to refinance a loan in three months' time, a *short*-hedge is appropriate. This is consistent with the general principle of hedging, because a commitment to borrow in three months' time at an unknown interest rate is essentially an obligation to *sell* (i.e. to issue) a bond at that date. The appropriate hedging strategy is then to *sell* the hedge instrument, in this case the short-term sterling futures contract. Alternatively, an investor with a commitment to *lend* at some point in the future could hedge a fall in the interest rate by acquiring a long position in futures (by buying contracts).

Remarks

1. In the example, if the interest rate *falls* rather than rises, the company fails to benefit from the fall because the futures price tends to rise, inducing a loss on the futures contracts – a loss that must be set against the gain from paying a lower interest rate over the period 1 May to 31 July. As with all hedges, the benefit is that a price (in this case the interest rate) is locked in at the outset. But there will always be cause to regret the decision if the price moves in the wrong direction – in this case, if interest rates fall.

2. The illustration assumes that the interest rate paid by the borrower fluctuates exactly one for one with the rate implicit in the futures price. If this is not the case, so that for whatever reason there is some discrepancy between the changes, the hedge becomes risky (imperfect).

16.4 Long-term interest rate, or bond, futures

16.4.1 Contract specifications

There are many instances of bond futures. One is the thirty-year US Treasury Bond Futures contract traded on the CBOT. For this contract, the underlying asset is a coupon-paying bond that the US government has undertaken not to 'call' – i.e. redeem – for at least fifteen years from the futures contract delivery date.

Another example, which differs only in detail, is the Long Gilt Future contract traded on LIFFE. Here the asset is a notional British government bond with a face value (nominal value) of £100,000, paying a 6 per cent coupon over a period of 8.75 to 13 years from the maturity date of the futures contract.[5]

A number of bond issues satisfy the criteria laid down by LIFFE for inclusion in the 'list of deliverable gilts' underlying the futures contract. Investors who have open short positions when the contract matures are permitted to deliver any bonds on the list in settlement of the contract. Every investor who has an open long position at maturity must be prepared to take delivery of bonds on the list. (When an investor with an open short position signals to the exchange that a delivery will be made, the exchange authorities select an investor with an open long position, who is then obliged to take delivery and make the necessary payment.) Just as for all futures contracts, what happens to open positions at maturity is important because it influences decisions made at earlier dates.

Prices for gilt-edged securities are listed per £100 nominal value of the stock. If the price is quoted as 107.50, then £100,000 of stock costs £107,500 = $107.50 \times 100,000/100$. Futures contract prices are quoted according to the same convention.

The tick size for the futures contract is 0.01 and the tick value is £10.00, so that $v = £1000 = £10.00/0.01$. Thus, if one contract is sold at a price of 107.50 and offset (purchased) at a price of 107.35, the gain equals £150 = $(107.50 - 107.35) \times £1000$ (i.e. a gain of fifteen ticks, each tick being worth £10).

Now suppose that the maturity date is reached and delivery takes place. During the life of the futures contract, the daily price changes for the contract accrue as gains or losses, which are credited or debited to the investor's margin account

---

[5] Note that the specification of futures contracts changes from time to time at the discretion of the exchange authorities. The long gilt contract, for instance, was changed in 1998 from a bond with £50,000 paying a coupon of 9 per cent over a period of 10 to 15 years to one with a 7 per cent coupon maturing after 8.75 to 13 years, and then, in December 2003, to the specification described here.

(through the regular process of marking to market). At the date of delivery, therefore, the amount to be paid by the investor with a long position to the investor with a short position is the futures price shortly before the contract matures (two days, to be precise). This price is the EDSP for the long gilt future. The 'invoice amount' (i.e. the amount to be paid by the investor with a long position to the investor who delivers the securities) is calculated as follows:

$$\text{invoice amount} = (\text{EDSP} \times \text{price factor} \times 100{,}000/100) + \text{accrued interest}$$

The two adjustments are these.

1. *Price factor* (or *conversion factor*): the net present value (divided by 100) of the security to be delivered if the yield to maturity is set at 6 per cent. This accounts for the fact that none of the bonds on the 'list of deliverable gilts' exactly matches the terms of the futures contract. The price factor for each bond is published by the exchange authority.
2. *Accrued interest*: the amount of interest accruing to the delivered bond between the most recently paid coupon and the date at which the bond is delivered in settlement of the futures contract. Coupon payments made after the delivery date are paid to the holder of the bond at whatever dates are stipulated in the bond indenture (commonly, payments are made at six-month intervals).

   Thus, the adjustment for accrued interest compensates the investor who delivers the bond for that portion of the coupon that would have been received if coupon payments were made continuously rather than separated by discrete intervals of time.

During the period allowed for delivery, investors with short positions will be able to compare the market prices, price factors and accrued interest corresponding to bonds eligible for delivery. From among these it is possible to determine the bond that is 'cheapest to deliver', in the sense of being the least costly to hand over in settlement of the contract. Neglecting market frictions, this is the bond selected for delivery.[6]

16.4.2 A long-term interest rate hedge

Consider a portfolio manager who expects to receive a sum of money in three months that is to be invested in long-term interest-bearing securities. The manager could wait until the funds are received or acquire a long position in long gilt futures contracts. If the yield to maturity on long-term bonds *falls*, bond prices *rise*, and so does the futures price (assuming that the arbitrage principle operates and that market frictions can be ignored). Thus, when the position is offset – the hedge

---

[6] It is possible that an investor with a short position holds eligible bonds that are not the cheapest to deliver. In this case, transaction costs would be saved by delivering these bonds rather than buying, then delivering, those that are otherwise cheapest to deliver.

is lifted – a gain on the futures position compensates for the higher bond price. Conversely, if the interest rate rises, bond prices and the futures price tend to fall such that the lower bond price compensates for a loss on the futures contracts.

How many futures contracts should be purchased? If the manager intends to use the inflow of funds to hold bonds similar in specification to those that could be delivered at maturity, then the number of contracts can be determined by taking into account the price of the bond that is cheapest to deliver and its associated price factor (although these may change between the date at which the futures contracts are purchased and the maturity date). Alternatively, if the position is to be offset before maturity, or if the plan involves acquiring bonds other than those on the list eligible for delivery, a variance-minimizing hedge ratio could be estimated by regressing changes in the price of the bonds to be purchased on the changes in the long gilt futures price observed in the past. (See chapter 15, section 15.3, for the relevant hedging principles.)

16.5 Stock index futures

16.5.1 Contract specifications

The asset underlying a stock index futures contract is the bundle of shares the prices of which are averaged to form the index. Examples include the S&P 500 index futures traded on the CME, the Dow Jones Industrial Average futures traded on the CBOT, and the FT-SE 100 index futures traded on LIFFE.[7] All share the same general characteristics. For concreteness, it is the FT-SE 100 futures contract that is studied in detail here.

The FT-SE 100 futures contract essentially promises to deliver the bundle (portfolio) of shares that makes up the FT-SE 100 index, each share having the same weight as in the index itself. Positions remaining open at the contract's delivery date are, however, not settled by delivering the requisite package of shares: cash settlement is mandatory. The exchange delivery settlement price for the FT-SE 100 futures contract is the value of the FT-SE 100 index on the last trading day of the contract. In fact, it's not quite so simple as this, because the index fluctuates from minute to minute; consequently, the exchange prescribes a rule for calculating the EDSP as an average of the FT-SE 100 index over a specified time period on the last trading day for the contract.

The *tick size* is 0.5 of an index point with a value of £5.00. Hence, $v = £10.00 = £5.00/0.5$ per index point of the futures contract price.

---

[7] The S&P 500 index is a capitalization-weighted index of 500 stocks traded in New York, the DJIA is a price-weighted average of thirty large US stocks (the weights are adjusted to allow for stock splits, but otherwise the DJIA is equally weighted) and the FT-SE 100 index is a capitalization-weighted index of the shares of the 100 largest companies traded on the LSE. See chapter 1, appendix 1.1, and *The New Palgrave Dictionary of Money and Finance* (Newman, Milgate and Eatwell, 1992, Vol. III, pp. 582–8).

Stock index futures trading is exactly the same as for any other futures contract. For example, suppose that an investor purchases five contracts at 5304.5. If the futures price rises to 5319.0 the investor is credited with a gain of $(5319.0 - 5304.5) \times £10 = £145$ per contract – a total of $£725 = 5 \times £145$. The futures price is linked to the FT-SE 100 index by the rules governing settlement at maturity, even though many, perhaps most, positions are offset before maturity.

16.5.2 Arbitrage with stock index futures

The arbitrage principle links stock index futures prices with the underlying share prices in the same way as for any other asset. Recall, first, the arbitrage condition for forward prices (see chapter 14, section 14.3):

$$F(t, T) \leqq [R(t, T) + c(t, T) - y(t, T)]p(t) \qquad (16.1)$$

where $F(t, T)$ is the forward price at date t for delivery at T, $p(t)$ is the market value of the index at t, and $R(t, T)$, $c(t, T)$ and $y(t, T)$ denote the interest factor, storage cost and convenience yield, respectively, between t and T.

Now make the following simplifications.

1. Replace the forward price, $F(t, T)$, with the futures price, $f(t, T)$, on the stock index. This substitution is likely to be harmless for contracts with a delivery date less than about twelve months from the present. The maturities of exchange traded futures contracts rarely extend much beyond a year.
2. Replace the inequality with an equality, because there is unlikely to be any significant limitation on available stocks of the bundle of shares that comprise the index.
3. Assume that there is exactly 'one period' between t and T (i.e. $T = t + 1$), and that there is no compounding of interest within the period, so that $R(t, T) = (1 + r)$.
4. Set $c = 0$: the cost of holding the stock index is assumed to be zero.
5. Denote the yield, $y(t, T)p(t)$, on the stock index by $dp(t)$, where d is the dividend return on the stock index from t to $t + 1$. The dividend return is just the weighted average of the dividend rates of all the component stocks in the index, each with the same weight as in the index.

These simplifications imply that

$$f(t, t + 1) = (1 + r - d)p(t) \qquad (16.2)$$

Why might equation (16.2) fail to hold? Here are some possible answers.

1. The most prominent candidate is the impact of the transaction costs incurred when buying or selling all the component shares comprising the index. (Transaction costs for the futures contract are typically small and are neglected here.) It is, however, possible to trade in mutual funds (unit trusts) the composition of which tracks the commonly reported indexes – it is, in this sense, possible to 'buy the market'. The transaction

costs of dealing in such mutual funds are not zero but are significantly lower than buying and selling each individual company's shares.

2. The precise times at which the futures contract price is recorded in each trading day may not match the times at which the stock index is calculated. The difference is likely to be small except when intra-day price volatility is large.

3. Investors may differ in their expectations of the dividend yield for the shares comprising the stock index, or in their beliefs about the interest rate, r, relevant for borrowing and lending. These differences are normally tiny, again because the maturity date for most stock index futures contracts is usually within about twelve months of the present.

4. In practice, (16.2) is often written as

$$f(t, T) = e^{(r-d)(T-t)}p(t) \tag{16.3}$$

which allows for arbitrary time periods to maturity, $T - t$, and also for the continuous compounding of interest and dividends. The effects of these adjustments are typically minor, because $e^{(r-d)(T-t)} \approx 1 + (r-d)(T-t)$ for short periods of time if interest and dividend rates are small.

16.5.3 Hedging with stock index futures

Suppose that an investment manager controls a portfolio of shares quoted on the London Stock Exchange, the value of which is to be hedged with respect to a future date – say, twelve months from today. Let $t = 0$ denote the present and $T = 1$, twelve months from today. The manager could hedge the portfolio by selling FT-SE 100 futures contracts at date 0, offsetting the position at date 1. If share prices generally fall between dates 0 and 1, there is a gain on the futures contract that should balance the fall in the price of the shares in the portfolio. If share prices generally rise between dates 0 and 1, the increased value of the portfolio should balance a loss on the futures contract, assuming that the futures price reflects the rising share prices.

Why bother to hedge the portfolio at all? Instead, the shares could be sold, the resulting funds being deposited at the risk-free interest rate. However, there are circumstances in which a hedge might be needed. For example, stock markets are not as frictionless as assumed; transactions costs may be significant. Also, the investment manager may be legally bound to hold stocks rather than cash.

As remarked in section 16.2, a reasonable criterion for the success of this hedge is that the value of the portfolio should increase by an amount equal to the risk-free rate of return between dates 0 and 1. If such an increase can be achieved without error, the hedge would be perfect, in the sense that the capital value of the portfolio at date 0 earns exactly the rate of return that would be obtained by selling all the shares at the outset and investing the funds at the risk-free rate. Errors, however, do tend to creep in, as described below.

A challenge for the design of the hedge is that the portfolio is likely to differ in composition from the bundle of shares corresponding to the FT-SE 100 index. Hence, fluctuations in the market value of the portfolio are unlikely to be mirrored exactly in the FT-SE 100 index.

In order to use a stock index futures contract as a hedge instrument, it is necessary to establish a link between the return on the portfolio to be hedged and the return on the stock index. This relationship has to be modelled in some way – a fact that means that such hedges are rarely perfect. A common approach is to use a market model, with the stock index in question representing the price of the market portfolio (see chapter 6, section 6.3).

Example of hedging with a stock index futures contract

Suppose that the market value of the portfolio to be hedged is £2 million and that the portfolio's *beta-coefficient* is 1.2. In this example the FT-SE 100 index corresponds to the price of the market portfolio. Assume also that (a) the risk-free rate of interest is 6 per cent; (b) the dividend return on the FT-SE 100 bundle of shares is 4 per cent; and (c) the FT-SE 100 index equals 5000 today, date 0.

Assume that the arbitrage principle links the stock index and its futures counterpart: $f(t, t+1) = (1+r-d)p(t)$, so that $f_0 = (1+r-d)p_0$. Consider a futures contract that matures at date 1, exactly one year from date 0. This being so, the price of the futures contract today is 5100 ($= (1+0.06-0.04) \times 5000$).

Now suppose that the portfolio is hedged by selling 48 FT-SE 100 futures contracts maturing at date 1. A method for choosing the number of contracts sold, 48, is described below.

At date 1 the futures contracts are settled for cash and the value of the hedged portfolio is calculated at the prevailing market prices. Suppose that the FT-SE 100 index at date 1 is 4800 (i.e. a fall of 200 relative to its value at the outset). The value of each futures contract at date 1 is also 4800 (because the market value of any futures contract equals the value of the underlying asset when the futures contract matures: $f(T, T) = p(T)$). The payoff on the 48 futures contracts equals £144,000 $= (5100 - 4800) \times 48 \times 10$. Note that the number '10' appears because the futures contract specifies that each point of the index is worth £10. (As noted earlier, this is merely a choice of units. Any other amount could be specified without affecting the results, though the number of futures contracts traded does depend on this value.)

What is the return on the portfolio of shares worth £2 million at date 0? If the market model holds exactly, it can be shown that the portfolio *falls* in value (allowing for dividends received on the shares) by £24,000. The justification for this result is explained below.

Thus, the total payoff from the hedging strategy is equal to £120,000, which is 6 per cent of £2 million. The return on the hedged portfolio (stocks and shares together with the short position in 48 futures contracts) is equal to the risk-free interest rate.

Suppose that, instead of falling to 4800, the FT-SE 100 index rises to, say, 5300 at date 1. The payoff on the 48 futures contracts equals *minus* £96, 000 = $(5100 - 5300) \times 48 \times 10$ – a loss. But, if the market model holds, the portfolio of shares will increase in value (including dividends) by £216,000. Once again, the total payoff is £120,000 $(= 216,000 - 96,000)$ – exactly the same as when the FT-SE 100 index fell.

The reasoning underlying this illustration is that the change in the futures contract price reflects, in a precise way, changes in the underlying stock index. The rate of return on the portfolio is linked to the stock index via the market model. Thus, the rate of return on the portfolio is linked to changes in the futures contract price. The hedging strategy exploits this link so as to ensure that the fluctuations in the return on the futures position match those on the portfolio.

Analysis of hedging with stock index futures

A formal argument justifies the numerical example. First, the payoff on the futures contracts is given by

$$\text{futures payoff} = nv(f_0 - f_1) \tag{16.4}$$

where n is the number of futures contracts sold and v is the value of each futures contract per unit of the stock index ($v = £10$ in the case of the FT-SE 100 index futures contract).

Second, it is necessary to forecast the rate of return on the portfolio to be hedged. The market model predicts that the rate of return, r_P, on a portfolio, P, is related to the market rate of return, r_M, by

$$r_P = r_0 + (r_M - r_0)\beta + \varepsilon \tag{16.5}$$

where r_0 is the risk-free rate, β is the portfolio's *beta-coefficient* and ε is a random error (with expectation zero: $\text{E}[\varepsilon | r_M - r_0] = 0$).

The rate of return on the market portfolio can be written as the sum of its dividend component, d, and its capital gain (or loss) component, $(p_1 - p_0)/p_0$. Substitute these into equation (16.5) and simplify, as follows:

$$r_P = r_0 + \left(d + \frac{p_1 - p_0}{p_0} - r_0\right)\beta + \varepsilon$$

$$= r_0 + \left(d + \frac{f_1 - p_0}{p_0} - r_0\right)\beta + \varepsilon$$

$$= r_0 + \left(\frac{f_1 - (1 - d + r_0)p_0}{p_0}\right)\beta + \varepsilon$$

$$= r_0 + \left(\frac{f_1 - f_0}{p_0}\right)\beta + \varepsilon \tag{16.6}$$

Thus, the estimated return on the portfolio of shares is obtained by multiplying the expression in equation (16.6) by V_0, the market value of the portfolio at date 0.

The overall payoff from the hedge strategy (the portfolio of shares and the futures contracts) equals the sum of the payoff from the futures position, (16.4), and the return on the portfolio itself:

$$\text{hedge strategy payoff} = nv(f_0 - f_1) + r_0 V_0 + \left(\frac{f_1 - f_0}{p_0}\right)\beta V_0 + \varepsilon V_0 \tag{16.7}$$

where the payoff is expressed net of the initial value of the portfolio, V_0.

There arc two elements of (16.7) that are unknown at date 0: (i) the random error, ε; and (ii) the futures price at date 1, f_1.

The impact of f_1 on the payoff can be eliminated by choosing n as follows:

$$n = \frac{\beta V_0}{v p_0} \tag{16.8}$$

If n is chosen to satisfy (16.8), the return on the hedged portfolio equals $(r_0 + \varepsilon)V_0$. If the expectation of ε is zero, then, on average, the return is $r_0 V_0$ (the error can be neglected) and the average rate of return equals the risk-free rate.

Expression (16.8) establishes why, in the example above, 48 contracts were sold: $(1.2 \times 2{,}000{,}000)/(10 \times 5000) = 48$.

Equation (16.6) justifies why the portfolio in the numerical example is estimated to fall by £24,000 if the FT-SE 100 index falls from 5000 to 4800. From (16.6), setting $\varepsilon = 0$,

$$r_P = 0.06 + \frac{(4800 - 5100)}{5000}1.2 = -0.012$$

$$r_P V_0 = -0.012 \times 2m = -£24{,}000$$

where 2m is 2 million.

412 The economics of financial markets

Similarly, if the FT-SE 100 index increases from 5000 to 5300, the value of the shares increases by £216,000:

$$r_P = 0.06 + \frac{(5300 - 5100)}{5000} 1.2 = 0.108$$

$$r_P V_0 = 0.108 \times 2\text{m} = £216,000$$

Why the hedge strategy is risky

The hedge strategy, even if successful, is typically imperfect, for the following reasons.

1. Calculating the number of units of the hedge instrument to be sold relies on a model that generates forecasts of the return on the hedged portfolio. Models never give perfect results. Two obvious reasons for errors are these.

   (a) It is not possible to know the disturbance ε in advance (its expected value is zero but, almost surely, a positive or negative value will be realized). Models – even if correctly specified – never fit the data exactly.

   (b) The model's parameters (just β in the market model) are estimated, not known with certainty.

   Even worse, the model may be mis-specified, so that the forecasts are systematically in error. Possibly a more general, multifactor, model could provide better forecasts. Be that as it may, the risk remaining in the hedge strategy could be significant.

2. The conditions defining the available futures contracts may not match the requirements of the hedge. For example, there are only a limited number of maturity dates for which futures contracts are available, so that date 1 (one year from the present in the illustration) may not correspond to the maturity date of any contract.

16.6 The fall of Barings Bank

At the beginning of March 1995 Barings Bank, London's oldest merchant bank, collapsed and, being effectively insolvent, was taken over by the ING banking group. The losses incurred by Barings were a consequence of derivatives trading undertaken by one of its employees, Mr Nick Leeson. Leeson, operating from Singapore, achieved international notoriety when his role in Barings's predicament was revealed. While Leeson's activities were spread across several markets in both futures and options, the losses that proved fatal for the bank stemmed from long positions in the Nikkei 225 stock index futures contracts quoted on the Osaka and Singapore (SIMEX) exchanges. The Nikkei 225 is an index of prices for stocks quoted on the Tokyo stock market. The delivery date for the futures contracts was in March 1995, and subsequent months.

Sometime in late 1994 it appears that Leeson purchased Nikkei 225 index futures contracts on both SIMEX and the Osaka exchange. It seems that his superiors in London believed that Leeson was pursuing arbitrage opportunities from the small price differentials that occurred between similar contracts in Osaka and Singapore. Instead, long positions were taken in both markets, with ever-increasing volumes beginning in mid-January 1995. For such a strategy to be profitable, the futures price would need to have risen as the delivery date approached. As it turned out, exactly the opposite happened. The Nikkei 225 index fell, and – in accordance with the arbitrage principle – so did the futures contract prices. The increasingly volatile fall of the index was partly, at least, attributed to a devastating earthquake that struck the city of Kobe in the early morning of 17 January that year.

As the stock index and the futures contract price both fell in late January and during February 1995, Leeson increased the number of futures contracts he purchased on behalf of Barings. With the fall in the futures price, variation margin calls were made on the contracts – an implication of the daily marking of the contracts to market. The funds required to honour the margin calls were partly provided by the London head office and partly generated by Leeson's other derivatives trading – in particular, it seems, from the sale of put options. But by late February funds sufficient to fulfil additional margin calls were no longer forthcoming. Leeson then disappeared – he turned up in Frankfurt a few days later – and the regulatory authorities intervened to take over the administration of Barings. Leeson was arrested and returned to Singapore, where he was tried, convicted and sentenced to a term of imprisonment. (He was released in July 1999.)

In early 1995 the Nikkei futures contract was trading in the range 18,000 to 20,000, with each point worth ¥1000. Hence, each contract would have been worth ¥18 million to ¥20 million (then worth approximately £117,000–£130,000). It appears that Leeson purchased between 20,000 and 40,000 contracts. With a loss of about ¥2 million on each contract, as the index fell from about 19,600 to 17,600 the loss on 20,000 contracts amounted to about ¥40 billion. This was an exceptionally large position for any one bank to accumulate in a single futures contract. It appears that, by mid-February, Barings held almost 20 per cent of the open interest in the contract on the Osaka exchange alone.[8]

Leeson's motives for increasing the number of futures contracts held in January and February (the mortal blow for Barings) remains something of a puzzle, and is open to different interpretations. Of course, Barings would have made large profits had the futures price *increased*, but the Nikkei 225 index continued to fall and, with the approach of the contract delivery date, so did the futures price. One conjecture is that, by purchasing an ever-larger number of contracts, Leeson was

---

[8] The information in this paragraph is taken from the *Financial Times*, 27 February and 1 March 1995.

trying to force the futures price up, so that he could, at least, have liquidated his positions with only a small overall loss.[9] Usually, futures prices are treated as if they follow the price of the underlying asset (in this case the bundle of securities representing the Nikkei 225 index). But arbitrage between the futures contract and the underlying asset serves only to link the two prices. They are jointly determined, and, in principle, the causation could go in either direction. Hence, large purchases of the futures contract might drive up the price of futures contracts and, as a result, could induce the stock index to move in the same direction. If this was indeed Leeson's strategy, it evidently went badly wrong.

16.7 Summary

1. The analysis of commodity futures holds also for a broad range of agreements that differ according to the asset underlying each contract.

2. Weather futures provide an example of contracts linked to an index of the weather at a designated future date. Although it makes no sense for the underlying asset to be delivered when the contract matures, cash settlement provides a natural mechanism for closing contracts that remain open at the 'delivery date'.

3. With regard to financial futures, some of the terminology, measurements and accounting detail are different from commodity contracts, but the principles are the same. For example, hedging strategies can be devised to attenuate the price risk associated with positions in the underlying financial assets in the same way as for commodity futures.

4. Short-term interest rate futures are contracts on financial instruments with a time to maturity typically of three or six months measured from the delivery date for the futures contract. Some, such as for US treasury bills, can be settled with the delivery of the relevant security. For others, such as three-month sterling interest rate futures, cash settlement is mandatory.

5. Long-term interest rate futures are contracts for the delivery of bonds (of a specified type) at the maturity of the contract. A range of actual, traded bonds is normally available to satisfy the terms of the contract, though accounting adjustments are usually necessary to ensure compatibility between the bonds delivered and the hypothetical bonds stipulated in the futures contract.

6. Stock index futures may be interpreted as contracts for the delivery of a specified bundle of shares (those comprising the index) at the delivery date for the contract. In practice, the shares comprising the bundle are not delivered. The contracts are settled in cash, with the futures price at maturity set equal to the stock index on the delivery date.

---

[9] In addition, Leeson's positions in options markets would have benefited from an increase in, or at least stability of, the index.

The arbitrage principle can be used, with a high degree of accuracy, to predict the relationship between stock index futures contract prices and the relevant stock indexes. The relationship becomes vulnerable to error, however, when stock prices are highly volatile.

Further reading

A textbook treatment of financial futures is provided by Elton, Gruber, Brown and Goetzmann (2003, chap. 23). For a more detailed coverage, see Edwards and Ma (1992, chaps. 10 (stock index futures), 12 (short-term interest rate futures) and 13 (long-term interest rate futures)). Hull (2005, chap. 6) provides, among other things, a careful treatment of arbitrage in markets for long-term and short-term interest rate futures. In addition, Hull (2005, chap. 22, sect. 22.2) offers a short introduction to weather derivatives.

The books that chart the fall of Barings Bank tend to exploit the sensational dimensions of the incident. Most, though, do contain excerpts that aid an understanding of derivatives markets. In particular, Fay (1996) is worth consulting. Also see Hunt and Heinrich (1996), Rawnsley (1996) and Zhang (1995), and Mr Leeson's own self-justifying account in Leeson and Whitley (1996).

References

Edwards, F. R., and C. W. Ma (1992), *Futures and Options*, New York: McGraw-Hill.

Elton, E. J., M. J. Gruber, S. J. Brown and W. N. Goetzmann (2003), *Modern Portfolio Theory and Investment Analysis*, New York: John Wiley & Sons, 6th edn.

Fay, S. (1996), *The Collapse of Barings: Panic, Ignorance and Greed*, London: Arrow Books.

Hull, J. C. (2005), *Fundamentals of Futures, and Options Markets*, Englewood Cliffs, NJ: Prentice Hall, 5th edn.

Hunt, L., and K. Heinrich (1996), *Barings Lost: Nick Leeson and the Collapse of Barings plc*, Singapore: Butterworth-Heinemann Asia.

Leeson, N., and E. Whitley (1996), *Rogue Trader*, London: Little, Brown and Company.

Newman, P., M. Milgate and J. Eatwell (eds.) (1992), *The New Palgrave Dictionary of Money and Finance*, London: Macmillan (three volumes).

Rawnsley, J. (1996), *Going For Broke: Nick Leeson and the Collapse of Barings Bank*, London: HarperCollins.

Zhang, P. G. (1995), *Barings Bankruptcy and Financial Derivatives*, Singapore: World Scientific Publishing.

17

Swap contracts and swap markets

Overview

Financial *swaps*, like ice cream, come in a variety of flavours and packaging. An early flavour, popular since the 1970s, is the foreign exchange swap, an arrangement in which one currency is exchanged for another at regular intervals over an agreed time period. These foreign exchange (currency) swaps, together with several other sorts of swap, are described in section 17.1, where their affinity with forward contracts is explained. Also described here are 'swap futures', a sort of futures contract involving not the delivery of swap contracts themselves but, rather, cash settlements based on interest rate movements, which are relevant in many swap agreements.

Section 17.2 applies an elementary comparative advantage argument that provides a rationale – not the only one – for the existence of swaps. Although swaps are acknowledged to be low-risk financial instruments, they are not risk-free; the attendant risks are outlined in section 17.3. During the life of a swap, the parties to it may need to determine the swap's market value – i.e. what a third party would be prepared to pay for it. This is the subject of section 17.4. Finally, section 17.5 reviews the case of Metallgesellschaft, a large German conglomerate that incurred damaging losses from trading in derivatives, of which swap contracts were a significant component.

17.1 Swap agreements: the fundamentals

Swap contracts often include complicated provisions that tend to obscure their fundamental principles – principles that turn out to be simpler than they appear at first glance. Hence, it is instructive to begin with an example that, although unrealistic, focuses attention on the crucial aspects of swaps.

417

Suppose that two investors, A and B (they might be companies, financial institutions or private individuals), agree that, six months from the present, A will pay £1m (m ≡ million) in return for \$1.44m. The two investors have negotiated a swap contract between US dollars and pounds sterling. If this were all there is to swaps, there would be no need for further analysis: the agreement between A and B is nothing more nor less than a forward contract. Trivial though the example is, the intimate relationship between swaps and forward contracts should always be kept in mind.

Forward markets in foreign exchange are so highly developed that the swap, as a separate financial instrument, may not appear to serve any distinctive purpose. Forward markets are, however, not highly developed for all assets. Hence, swap contracts could simply be the form that forward contracts take when the relevant forward markets do not exist.

Alternatively, there could be other dimensions to swap agreements that distinguish them from contracts in forward markets. A relevant consideration might be that A and B, in the above example, cannot trade in the forward market, or, at least, cannot trade at the current market exchange rate. Perhaps the creditworthiness of A or B is such that neither could trade at the current market rate, and both would find a private agreement more attractive. Private or not, however, the agreement remains, effectively, a forward contract. The prospect that one of the parties to the contract may default introduces no new issues of principle, and, hence, the existence of performance risk is not in itself sufficient to differentiate swaps from forward agreements.

An aspect of swaps that does clearly distinguish them from other forward contracts is that each swap comprises a *sequence* of exchanges. To extend the example, the swap might require A to pay £1m to B in return for \$1.44m every six months for the next five years – the swap is a 'package' of ten forward contracts, two per year for the next five years. Slightly more formally, each exchange in a swap can be written as a '(*payment, receipt*)' pair. For A the swap is, thus, a sequence of ten pairs each equal to (£1m, \$1.44m). For B, each exchange equals (\$1.44m, £1m).

While many currency swaps are essentially no more complicated than this, they may often appear to be so. First, the swap is normally expressed as as set of interest flows on a *notional principal*. In the example, suppose that the notional principal is £20m and that the current spot exchange rate is £1 = \$1.60 (so that the dollar value of £20m equals \$32m). Now the swap could be expressed as an exchange of £10 per cent per annum in return for \$9 per cent per annum. Every six months, A pays £1m $(= 0.050 \times 20m = \frac{1}{2} \times 10\% \times £20m)$ to B in return for \$1.44m $(= 0.072 \times 20m = \frac{1}{2} \times 9\% \times 1.60 \times £20m)$. If the notional principal is denoted by $N = £20m$, then, from A's perspective, each exchange takes the form $(£0.05N, \$0.072 \times 1.60 \times N)$.

A second apparent complication is that swaps typically involve a financial intermediary (e.g. a bank) that collects a portion of the flow of funds between A and B in recompense for its services. The intermediary plays a role in bringing the parties together and may, according to the terms of the agreement, act as a guarantor in the event of default (see below, section 17.3). Intermediaries in swap markets often perform a 'warehousing' function in that they specify the standard conditions for swap contracts available to their clients. Consequently, the intermediary may end up being a party to a swap deal if it cannot find a client who will agree to become the swap counterparty.

It is helpful for later reference to express the example in a more general way. For any party to the contract, a swap consists of (i) a notional principal, N, and (ii) a sequence of the form

$$(x_1, y_1), (x_2, y_2), \ldots (x_i, y_i), \ldots (x_{n-1}, y_{n-1}), (x_n, y_n)$$

where n denotes the number of exchanges and where $x_i N$ is the payment in the ith exchange in return for $y_i N$.

In the example, for party A, $N = £20m$, $n = 10$, $x_i = 0.050$ and $y_i = 0.072$. From B's perspective, each exchange equals $(y_i N, x_i N)$ – i.e. ($\$0.072N$, $£0.050N$) – in the absence of an intermediary. In the presence of an intermediary, there will normally be a discrepancy between what one party pays and the other receives; the discrepancy constitutes the intermediary's fee.

The swap contract may require that specified payments are made at the outset, before the sequence of exchanges begins. For instance, currency swaps commonly stipulate that the notional principal is to be exchanged. In the example, A would pay £20m to B in exchange for $32m. In some swaps a *side payment* is made from one party to the other when the swap commences. The side payment reflects the swap's *value*: it expresses the present value of the difference between the two streams of payments. Commonly, however, the values of the streams, x_i and y_i, are chosen such that the initial side payment is *zero*.

Most swap agreements can be expressed in the general form outlined above. Thus, in a *plain vanilla interest rate swap*, fixed-interest-rate payments are exchanged for a stream of floating interest payments. For example, a company might agree to pay 9.25 per cent per annum on a notional principal of £10m at six monthly intervals for ten years in return for a floating rate on the same principal over the same time period.

How is the floating rate determined? This is a facet of the swap agreed between the parties, and is stipulated in the contract. A typical arrangement is to set the floating rate equal to LIBOR *plus* a specified number of basis points (b.p. – 1 b.p. = one-hundredth of 1 per cent per annum). LIBOR is an acronym for the London interbank offered rate, an average of rates that banks in London offer to lend to one another.[1]

In the example, suppose that the company agrees to pay 9.25 per cent and receive LIBOR + 40b.p. Applying the notation introduced above, the swap can be expressed in terms of the notional principal, $N = £10m$, and the sequence

$$(x, y_1), (x, y_2), \ldots (x, y_i), \ldots (x, y_{19}), (x, y_{20})$$

where $x = 0.04625$ (9.25 per cent per annum for six months) and $y_i = \frac{1}{2} \times$ (LIBOR$_i$ + 0.40)%. LIBOR$_i$ denotes the floating rate applicable for the ith exchange, a value not known until the time of the exchange.

Consider any one of the exchanges, say (x, y_4). This is a promise to pay a known sum, $xN = £462,500$, for an unknown amount, y_i, after two years (four six-month intervals) from the present. It is equivalent to a *long* forward position in which a promise is made to pay a known sum in return for an 'asset' (in this case a sum of money) the value of which is not known in advance. Thus, y_4 corresponds to a *spot* price, not realized until immediately before the exchange occurs.

In summary, an interest rate swap paying a fixed rate in return for a floating rate is equivalent to a sequence of *long* forward contracts. The swap counterparty, who pays a floating rate in return for a fixed rate, has effectively negotiated a sequence of *short* forward contracts – i.e. promises to deliver an asset the value of which is not known at the outset in return for an agreed sum, xN. For this sort of swap, as for many others, the parties would exchange *net* amounts at each payment date. Thus, the one party pays $(x - y_i)N$ (which is a receipt if negative) to the other party (minus any commission fees accruing to an intermediary).

There are many other flavours of interest rate swap contract. For instance, *roller-coaster* swaps involve changes in the notional principal over the duration of the swap. For *basis rate* swaps, floating rate payments with different bases (e.g. LIBOR and the prime commercial rate in New York) are exchanged. For a *forward rate* swap, the sequence of exchanges commences at a designated date in the future. For a *zero-coupon* swap, a sequence of floating rate payments is exchanged for a lump sum amount at the termination date of the swap.

It should be clear that swaps are contrivances that can accommodate a host of diverse cash flows. From among these, the following illustrate several distinctive features of swap contracts.

---

[1] There are several different LIBOR rates, corresponding to time periods of different length from overnight to a period of several years, though the three-month and six-month rates are the most widely quoted. LIBID is an abbreviation for the London interbank *bid* rate, an average of rates at which London banks bid for funds.

1. *Commodity swap.* Although quantities of two commodities could, in principle, be exchanged, in practice commodity swaps consist of financial flows that fluctuate according to stipulated commodity prices. Commodity swap agreements include provisions that cover: (i) the specification of each underlying commodity (e.g. grades of fuel oil at particular locations); (ii) the notional volume of each commodity; and (iii) the duration of the swap and the intervals between payments. For example, two companies might agree to swap prices for different grades of fuel oil on a notional volume of 50,000 barrels, every six months for the next five years.

   A common form of commodity swap is a fixed-for-floating swap, in which one party agrees to pay the other a fixed price – or, at least, a price that is determined, and hence known, at the outset – in return for the spot (i.e. float-ing) price of the same commodity. The commodity itself does not change hands. Rather, the price difference, multiplied by the notional volume of the commodity, is exchanged at each of the stipulated dates. Just as for other swaps, it is straightfor-ward to interpret a commodity swap as a sequence of forward contracts. The party that pays the fixed price in return for the floating price has effectively acquired a long position in forward contracts. The party that pays the floating price in return for the fixed price has effectively acquired a short position in forward contracts.

2. *Total return swap.* A total return swap commits one party to pay the flow of returns on one asset (e.g. a government bond) in return for the flow of returns on another (e.g. a corporate bond) from the counterparty. These swaps usually involve credit instruments, such as bonds, and the *total return* – coupon plus capital gains (minus capital losses) – changes hands. When one of the underlying assets is a company's shares (or a stock index), this sort of swap is often called an *equity swap.*

3. *Credit default swap.* In a typical credit default swap, one party makes regular payments but receives nothing in return unless default occurs on an asset specified in the contract. In the event of default, the first party (that made the sequence of payments) receives a lump sum amount from the counterparty, and the swap termi-nates. Thus, a credit default swap is a form of insurance contract for which each regular payment is effectively a premium and 'default' is the contingency against which insurance is obtained.

   More formally, suppose that the parties to the swap are identified as companies *A* and *B*. A third company (or sovereign state), *C*, has issued a debt instrument, *C*-bonds, which are risky in the sense that *C* might renege on some aspect of the bond contract (e.g. fail to make coupon payments, or to repay the principal). A credit default swap could specify that (i) *A* pays an *agreed amount* to *B* every six months during the life of the *C*-bonds, or (ii) *B* pays nothing to *A* unless a *credit event* occurs, at which time *B* makes a *one-off payment* to *A*. The *agreed amount* would be fixed in advance (it would depend on the notional number of *C*-bonds) or determined according to a stipulated rule (commonly based on the value of a floating rate of interest at each payment date). The *credit event* is typically defined to be the failure of C to fulfil some aspect of its contractual obligation with respect to the C-bonds.[2] The *one-off payment* by B to A triggered by the credit event is typically the payoff promised (but not delivered) in the C-bond contract. It could, for example, be the face value of the C-bonds if the credit event is a default at their redemption date.

As described so far, swaps are *over-the-counter* contracts. While financial intermediaries may quote standard terms and conditions, many swaps are customized, bespoke or 'tailor-made' to suit the needs of the parties. Consequently, swap contracts are, in general, not suitable for trading on organized exchanges.

Swaps resemble packages of forward contracts rather than packages of *futures* contracts. Even so, it is possible to buy or sell bundles of futures contracts that have swap-like features. For instance, the so-called *calendar strip* is a package of futures contracts written on the same underlying asset with a sequence of delivery dates (and futures prices) bundled together as a single transaction (see chapter 14, especially page 348). For instance, on NYMEX it is permissible to trade in calendar strips in 'light sweet crude oil' with consecutive delivery dates up to thirty months into the future. Note that thirty months is quite short by the standards of swap contracts, which not infrequently have lives as long as five years, or more.

Futures on swaps

In July 2001 LIFFE launched Swapnote[3] – a form of swap futures, or, more aptly, *futures on swaps* – for swaps denominated in euros. Swap agreements themselves are not traded. Instead, the contract is for a hypothetical swap of two, five or ten years' duration, commencing at the maturity of the futures contract.

LIFFE Swapnote contracts resemble bond futures contracts in the sense that the underlying asset (the hypothetical swap) is treated as a bond with notional principal of €100,000 paying a notional coupon of 6.0 per cent. What makes these contracts like swaps is the rule for calculating the exchange delivery settlement price, which depends on both fixed and floating interest rates. The EDSP is expressed as a bond valuation, the notional flow of fixed coupons being discounted using a set of *floating* Euribor rates (published daily by Reuters).[4]

Swap futures contracts were introduced on the Chicago Board of Trade in October 2001 (ten-year swaps) and June 2002 (five-year swaps). These contracts are effectively *bond futures* for which the underlying asset is a notional bond

---

[2] Although the swap agreement would seek to define the credit event as precisely as possible, ambiguity almost surely remains. That is, swap agreements are inevitably *incomplete*. What happens if, for example, C delays on payments rather than defaults, or makes payments in a different currency from that promised? Evidently, there is scope for complex and prolonged litigation.

[3] Swapnote is a registered trademark of Euronext.liffe.

[4] See chapter 12, section 12.4 for a description of bond valuation rules. Euribor is an acronym for euro interbank offered rate, compiled by the European Banking Federation (FBE – Fédération Bancaire de l'Union Européenne) and published daily in Brussels.

(with five or ten years to run, as of the date that the futures contract matures) that pays a fixed coupon of 6 per cent per $100,000. What links this bond to swap contracts is – once again – the way in which the EDSP is calculated at maturity. The EDSP is set equal to the value of the bond calculated by discounting the fixed stream of coupons at a benchmark rate, quoted by the International Swaps and Derivatives Association (ISDA) and published daily by Reuters.

All these futures contracts are *cash* settled. The value of each futures contract at maturity then enables investors to calculate the initial value of a hypothetical interest rate swap commencing at the futures maturity date.

By treating futures on swaps as bond futures with a fixed coupon discounted at a floating interest rate, the contracts mimic plain vanilla interest swaps. Hence, trading in LIFFE Swapnotes, or CBOT swap futures, provides ways for investors to hedge against, or speculate in, the uncertain value of a swap as of the date when the futures contract matures. (For more about swap valuation, see section 17.4.)

Swaptions

Swaptions are options on swap agreements. For example, a company may know that in six months' time it will seek to enter into a swap agreement but does not know, today, the terms of such an agreement (in particular, the level of the fixed rate or the mark-up over the the floating rate). The company could enter into an agreement (perhaps via an intermediary) to take an option on a swap, the terms of which are stipulated at the outset. The company would naturally pay a fee (premium) for this privilege. In six months' time the option would be exercised, or allowed to die, according to changes to interest rates over the intervening period and alterations in the company's plans.

A swaption is similar to a forward rate agreement (in which the swap is agreed today but begins at a future date), except that it can be allowed to lapse, whereas a forward rate agreement is an unconditional contract to implement the swap. The option premium is the payment for the freedom to let the swaption lapse at expiry. Swaptions, like swaps, are customized OTC agreements, not normally traded on organized exchanges.

17.2 Why do swaps occur?

Swap agreements – like all financial contracts – are negotiated because the parties perceive that it is in their interests to do so. Superficial though this remark is, it serves as a reminder that there is no intrinsic need to justify the existence of contracts leading to particular payoff patterns. One explanation for the exis- tence of swaps has already been implied, namely that swaps – interpreted as a sequence of forward contracts – could provide attractive hedge instruments

Another justification, rather more special to swap contracts, is that of *comparative advantage* (a concept commonly encountered in economics, where it is applied to explain patterns of international trade).

The theory of comparative advantage is invoked in this section as a device to illuminate the principles of financial swaps. Two illustrations are described: a plain vanilla interest rate swap, and a foreign exchange (currency) swap.

17.2.1 A plain vanilla interest rate swap

Suppose, for definiteness, that two companies, *A* and *B*, separately and independently of one another both plan to borrow £10m for eight years. The companies face different borrowing costs, however, according to whether the loan is obtained at a fixed rate or a floating rate:

	Fixed rate	Floating rate
Company *A*	10.00%	LIBOR + 80b.p.
Company *B*	8.50%	LIBOR + 30b.p.

There may appear to be no reason why a swap should be attractive to both companies, for *B* has an *absolute* advantage over *A*: *B*'s borrowing costs are lower than those of *A* at either fixed or floating rates. It might, for example, be the case that *B* is more creditworthy than *A*, and hence can borrow funds at a lower cost in both the fixed-rate market (say, by issuing bonds) and the floating-rate market (say, by negotiating a bank loan).

However, *A*, despite its absolute disadvantage, enjoys a *comparative* advantage in the floating-rate market, for it pays only 50b.p. more than *B* at a floating rate (LIBOR + 80b.p. compared with LIBOR + 30b.p.), while the extra cost of borrowing at a fixed rate is 150b.p. (10 per cent compared with 8.5 per cent). (Alternatively, *A* faces a higher comparative cost in the fixed-rate market relative to the floating-rate market.)

Assume now that, for whatever reasons, company *A* prefers to borrow at a fixed interest rate and company *B* prefers to borrow at a floating rate. The conditions for a mutually advantageous swap are now satisfied.

Consider the following three actions.

1. Company *A* borrows £10m for eight years in the capital market at LIBOR + 80b.p.
2. Company *B* borrows £10m for eight years in the capital market at 8.50 per cent.

3. An intermediary arranges a swap between *A* and *B* such that:

 – *A* pays 9.25 per cent in return for LIBOR + 45b.p.;
 – *B* pays LIBOR + 65b.p. in return for 9.25 per cent;
 – the intermediary collects 20b.p. for its services.

All of these interest rates are applied to £10m over a period of eight years. Thus, each year for eight years, *A* pays £925,000 in return for (LIBOR + 45b.p.)×£10m.; *B* pays (LIBOR + 65b.p.)×£10m in return for £925,000; and the intermediary receives a fee of £200,000 (= £10m × 0.20%). (If the payments are made at six-month intervals, these amounts must be halved. Nothing substantive is affected thereby.)

The payoffs are as follows:

Company *A*	Capital market	Pay	LIBOR + 80b.p.
	Swap agreement	Pay	9.25%
	Swap agreement	Receive	LIBOR + 45b.p.
		Net cost	9.60%
Company *B*	Capital market	Pay	8.50%
	Swap agreement	Pay	LIBOR + 65b.p.
	Swap agreement	Receive	9.25%
		Net cost	LIBOR – 10b.p.%
Intermediary	Swap agreement	Pay	LIBOR + 45b.p.
	Swap agreement	Receive	LIBOR + 65b.p.
		Net gain	20b.p.%

Both *A* and *B* gain from the swap. Company *A* borrows, in accordance with its preference, at a fixed rate. Moreover, it borrows at a rate equal to 9.60 per cent – i.e. 40b.p. less than the 10 per cent it would pay in the capital market. Company *B* borrows, in accordance with its preferences, at a floating rate. Moreover, it borrows at a rate equal to LIBOR – 10b.p. – i.e. 40b.p. less than the LIBOR + 30b.p. it would pay in the capital market.

From the perspective described here, two conditions must be satisfied for the swap to be attractive to both *A* and *B*.

1. The parties face different *comparative* costs of capital. In the example, the comparative cost of borrowing is higher for *A* in the fixed-rate market, and higher for *B* in the floating-rate market.
2. Each party prefers to borrow in the market for which its comparative cost is higher. In the example, *A* prefers to borrow at a fixed rate, while *B* prefers to borrow at a floating rate.

There is no reason to believe that these conditions will always be satisfied. If they are, a swap can be justified. If they are not, a swap is not justified – at least, not for the reason described above. Note also that the swap outlined above does not characterize the *unique* arrangement that would be attractive to both parties. The swap described is only one of many that would benefit both A and B. All that must be satisfied is that A ends up paying a fixed rate less than 10 per cent, and that B ends up paying a floating rate less than LIBOR + 30b.p.

Similarly, the payoff of 20b.p. to the intermediary is also by way of example. It might be higher or lower. Presumably, the intermediary will demand a fee for bringing A and B together. More importantly, part of the intermediary's payoff could represent a return to the risk it bears if the swap agreement obliges the intermediary to act as guarantor in the event of default by either A or B. In this case, the intermediary commits itself to continuing the swap with A if B defaults, or with B if A defaults.

17.2.2 Foreign exchange swaps

To illustrate a foreign exchange swap, assume that company A, for whatever reason, seeks to obtain a loan denominated in pounds sterling while B seeks to obtain a loan denominated in dollars. Perhaps A is located in London, while B is located in New York.

For the sake of example, suppose that the current exchange rate is £1 = $1.60, that A wishes to borrow £10m at a fixed interest rate for five years, and that B wishes to borrow $16m, also at a fixed rate for five years. The interest rates confronting the companies are assumed to be as follows:

	Dollar rate	Sterling rate
Company A	10%	12%
Company B	9%	8%

Company B has an *absolute* advantage over A in that it can borrow at a lower rate in both sterling and dollars. But A has a *comparative* advantage in the dollar loan market because its cost of borrowing is only one percentage point higher than that of B. By implication, B has a comparative advantage in the sterling loan market, where it pays $4\% = 12\% - 8\%$ less than A.

Because – by assumption – A seeks to borrow in sterling, while its comparative advantage is to borrow in dollars, and B seeks to borrow in dollars, while its comparative advantage is in sterling, a currency swap attractive to both companies can be designed.

Consider the following three actions.

1. Company *A* borrows $16m for five years in the capital market at 10 per cent per annum.
2. Company *B* borrows £10m for five years in the capital market at 8 per cent per annum.
3. An intermediary arranges a swap between *A* and *B* such that at the outset *A* exchanges the $16m it has borrowed in return for the £10m borrowed by *B*. Thereafter, for five years, the following happens.

 – *A* pays £11 per cent in return for $10 per cent – i.e. it pays £1.1m in exchange for $1.60m each year.
 – *B* pays $8 per cent in return for £8 per cent – i.e. it pays $1.28m (8 per cent of $16m) in exchange for £0.8m each year.
 – The intermediary pays a net $2 per cent and receives a net £3 per cent per year. That is, given the notional principal of £10m = $16m, it makes a net payment of $0.32m (= 1.60m − 1.28m) and a net receipt of £0.3m (= 1.1m − 0.8m) each year. At an exchange rate of £1 = $1.60, this amounts to a net gain of $0.16m (i.e. 1 per cent of $16m) per year.

The payoffs are as follows:

Company *A*	Capital market	Pay	10% ($)=$1.60m
	Swap agreement	Pay	11% (£)=£1.10m
	Swap agreement	Receive	10% ($)=$1.60m
	Net cost		11% (£)=£1.10m
Company *B*	Capital market	Pay	8% (£)=£0.80m
	Swap agreement	Pay	8% ($)=$1.28m
	Swap agreement	Receive	8% (£)=£0.80m
	Net cost		8% ($)=$1.28m
Intermediary	Swap agreement	Pay	2% ($)=$0.32m
	Swap agreement	Receive	3% (£)=£0.30m
	Net gain		1%

Notice that the intermediary is exposed to the risk of exchange rate fluctuations – i.e. the risk that the exchange rate will not remain at £1 = $1.60 throughout the life of the swap. In order to manage this risk, the intermediary could hedge using forward contracts in the foreign exchange market.

Both *A* and *B* gain from the swap. Company *A* effectively borrows in accordance with its preference (in sterling). Moreover, it borrows at a rate of 11 per cent – i.e. one percentage point less than the 12 per cent it would pay in the capital market. Company *B* effectively borrows in accordance with its preferences (in dollars). Moreover, it borrows at a rate of 8 per cent – i.e. one percentage point less than the 9 per cent it would pay in the capital market. Just as for the interest rate swap, the percentage gains of the parties to the swap are purely illustrative. (Insufficient information is provided above to determine the precise terms of the agreement.) The principle is that *A* makes a net outlay in sterling but at a rate lower than it would pay in the capital market, and that *B* makes a net outlay in dollars but at a rate lower than it would pay in the capital market. Also, the intermediary is compensated for its services.

17.2.3 Accounting for the interest rate differentials

For both the interest rate and foreign exchange swap examples described above, a necessary condition for the swaps to be mutually advantageous is that the companies face different *comparative* borrowing costs. While it will occasion no surprise that some companies must pay higher interest rates than others (e.g. as a consequence of different risks of default), it is more challenging to explain why the differentials should differ across markets.

   Why should such differentials exist? An overly superficial reply is to ascribe the differentials to capital market imperfections. Here are three less superficial responses.

1. *Asymmetric information* is pervasive in capital markets and could explain why the cost of borrowing varies among the sources of funds. For example, company *A* may choose to borrow at a floating rate from its local bank because the bank knows *A*'s business. A fixed-rate loan could be relatively expensive because it would involve issuing bonds in the capital market, where *A* is less well known. Company *B*, on the other hand, might be a secure investment bank with a high credit rating, and hence able to borrow at low interest rates in whichever market it chooses.
2. *Arbitrage opportunities*. The presence of interest rate differentials of the sort described could be a reflection of the existence of arbitrage opportunities. Swaps could then be interpreted as a vehicle designed to exploit such opportunities; that is, instead of assuming that arbitrage opportunities are absent, swaps contribute to the process by which such opportunities are competed away.
3. *Market frictions*. In the presence of transaction costs, institutional constraints on trading, tax differentials or regulatory obligations, some transactions may be less costly than others. Thus, it might be that swap contracts represent the least-cost way of achieving a desired pattern of payoffs on an investment.

17.2.4 Summary

A combination of differential borrowing costs across markets and different preferences among the relevant parties provides a justification for at least some sorts of swap (in particular, interest rate swaps and foreign exchange swaps). If (a) comparative borrowing costs differ among companies, (b) the companies seek to borrow similar amounts for similar durations and (c) each company prefers (for whatever reason) to borrow in the market for which it has a comparative *dis*advantage, then it is possible to construct a mutually advantageous swap. Swap contracts do not have to be justified in this way, however, and may be negotiated to fulfil other investment motives (e.g. such as hedging or speculation).

17.3 Risks associated with swaps

Swaps are susceptible to *performance risks*, in the sense that one or other of the parties may fail to honour one or more conditions of the contract. Given that swaps involve contracts for future delivery (typically of cash), it should occasion no surprise that the parties often agree to make *good-faith deposits* as collateral against default. Normally, the good-faith deposits are held with an intermediary, which, depending on the terms of the contract, acts as guarantor for the swap.

The risks associated with swaps are somewhat broader than default alone, and include the following.

1. *Credit risk*: the risk of default by one of the parties – i.e. the risk that one of the parties will fail to comply with some provision of the swap (e.g. premature termination of the payment sequence as a consequence of insolvency).
2. *Funding risk*: the risk that a party is unable to provide the necessary funds when it is required to increase its good-faith deposit. Typically, an intermediary guaranteeing the swap holds such deposits, the amount of which would fluctuate according to market circumstances. For example, suppose that a company has agreed to a commodity swap, which commits it to pay the spot price in exchange for a fixed price. If the spot price increases significantly for a sustained period during the life of the swap, the company would be expected to increase its collateral (the good-faith deposit) with the intermediary. If the extra collateral is not forthcoming, the intermediary might decide to terminate the contract (and possibly to seek legal redress).
3. *Market risk* (sometimes called *basis risk*): the risk of adverse movements in market conditions (e.g. a sustained change in LIBOR, or in a variable price that underlies a swap). It is exactly this sort of risk that swaps are designed to share between the parties to a swap. Hence, market risk is relevant for the viability of a swap only insofar as its occurrence is reflected in credit or funding risks.

17.4 Valuation of swaps

Although a large volume of business is transacted in swap markets, as OTC agreements, swap contracts can be customized according to the particular needs, preferences and opportunities of the parties. Hence, there is wide scope for differentiation in the terms of swap agreements. Benchmarks exist for common sorts of swaps (e.g. plain vanilla interest rate swaps), but, apart from these, there is no obvious package of ingredients to serve as a standard.[5] Most swaps are designed such that the initial value to both parties is zero – that is, so that no side payment takes place at the outset.

During the life of a swap, as information is revealed about the variable component of the sequence of exchanges, the swap contract typically becomes more valuable to one party and less so to the other. Consider, for example, a commodity swap in which the exchange of a variable spot price is exchanged for a pre-arranged fixed price. If the spot price falls, the party that pays the variable price gains relative to the party that receives it. This need not imply, of course, that the swap represents a bad decision, because the future spot price was unknown when the agreement was negotiated. However, when the spot price falls, the value of the swap contract tends to increase (from zero at the outset) for the party that pays the spot price, and decreases for the party that receives it. Strictly, the valuation of the swap depends upon *beliefs* about future changes in the variable component of the swap. The current, realized value is important only insofar as it informs beliefs about the future. The relevant point is that, after a swap contract has been signed, its value can become positive or negative at any time during its life.

If the swap continues in existence for the whole of the period agreed at the outset, then there is no compelling reason why it should be assigned a value, though each of the parties to the contract may continuously monitor its worth.[6] Valuation becomes necessary when one of the parties requests the premature termination of the swap or fails to comply with its obligations. In these circumstances, an existing swap contract may be taken over by another party, or the sequence of exchanges may be curtailed before the originally agreed date. In either case a side payment, equal to the swap's value, changes hands to compensate the party that is deemed to have lost out as a consequence of the revised arrangements.

The valuation of a swap is not a trivial exercise, depending as it does on beliefs about fluctuations in the variable component during the remainder of the swap's life and on an appraisal of the risks of default. A common practice is to associate each of the swap's payment streams with a security for which a market price can be observed. The value of the swap is then the difference between the market

---

[5] See above, page 422, for an outline of how futures contracts can aid the valuation of interest rate swaps.

[6] Also, if the contract is guaranteed by a third party, the guarantor may determine the level of collateral on the basis of a calculation of the swap's value. If default occurs, it will most likely be the party for which the swap's value is negative that reneges on the agreement. Hence, it is from this party that the guarantor is most likely to demand collateral (the good-faith deposit).

values of the two securities. For example, a plain vanilla interest rate swap could be valued as the difference between the price of a bond with fixed coupons and the price of a bond paying a floating rate. Clearly, the bonds used for the valuation exercise would need to be selected such that their coupon streams approximate, as closely as possible, the conditions that define the sequence of payments specified in the swap.

A commodity swap can be assigned a value equal to the difference between (a) the present value of the fixed payment stream and (b) the present value of the variable payment stream. The calculation of (a) should present no major obstacles. The calculation of (b) is, however, more problematical, as it relies on price expectations. A common practice is to use currently observed forward prices for the commodity to estimate each of the spot prices in the variable payment stream.

It should be unsurprising that there is scope for significant differences of opinion about the valuation of swaps. The prices of existing assets can, to some degree, provide objective information about the elements of a swap. Arbitration, or even litigation, may, however, be required to resolve disagreements about the terms of complicated swap contracts.

17.5 Metallgesellschaft: a case study

Metallgesellschaft A.G. (MG-AG), a large German industrial conglomerate, was brought to the verge of bankruptcy in late 1993, with losses estimated at $1.3 billion – an amount reckoned to be equal to about half the firm's capital at the time. The losses were attributed to derivatives trading by one of MG-AG's subsidiaries based in the United States, Metallgesellschaft Refining and Marketing (MG-RM). MG-RM's business centred on buying petroleum products (diesel fuel, heating fuel and gasoline) at spot prices, mostly in the open market, and selling to its customers on long-term contracts guaranteeing delivery at fixed prices. Many of the contracts were for delivery up to ten years from the date of agreement. Also, MG-RM traded in futures and swaps for which the underlying assets were oil products.

In the months prior to December 1993 the spot price of oil fell and MG-RM lost heavily on its derivatives trading. Its parent company, MG-AG, intervened to stem the losses by terminating MG-RM's derivatives contracts. Also, many of MG-RM's customers were offered the opportunity to renegotiate their contracts. Following these decisions, controversy ensued about the interpretation of MG-RM's policies and, consequently, about whether its parent's reactions were appropriate.

MG-RM's trading activities were complex but comprised three main components.

1. Long-term contracts for the sale of oil at fixed prices. The terms of these contracts varied but were such that approximately 160m barrels of refined oil products were to be delivered over periods of up to ten years. MG-RM's customers had, essentially, purchased packages of forward contracts for the delivery of oil. Subject to a caveat discussed later, MG-RM was thus guaranteed a known price for the oil it sold, promising to supply the oil whatever the spot price at each delivery date.

2. MG-RM acquired oil, in spot markets or by private agreement with refining companies, for delivery to its customers. (MG-RM had agreed to purchase the entire output of a company, Castle Energy, in the ownership of which it had acquired a large stake several years previously.)

3. MG-RM purchased – i.e. adopted 'long' positions in – oil futures contracts. It also negotiated swap contracts, agreeing to pay a fixed price in exchange for returns linked to the (floating) spot price of oil. It is estimated that underlying the contracts were about 55m barrels of oil in the futures contracts and approximately 110m barrels in the swap contracts.

There were effectively two branches to MG-RM's activities: a trading branch and a derivatives branch. The trading branch purchased oil at spot prices for delivery to MG-RM's customers at fixed prices over long periods of time. The derivatives branch purchased financial derivatives (futures and swaps) such that profits would be made if the price of oil increased, losses being incurred if the price of oil fell.

To what extent should the two branches be interpreted as part of an integrated strategy combining the two branches or, alternatively, as separate activities within the firm? The answer to this question is central to the controversy about the efficacy of MG-RM's policies.

The argument favouring MG-RM's management is that its activities should be considered as a whole and interpreted as a risk-reducing hedging strategy. The case against MG-RM's management is that it became exposed to excessive risks by speculating in derivatives and also, perhaps, by making long-term supply agreements with its customers.

17.5.1 The case for MG-RM

There is general agreement that MG-RM's business was risky. In favour of MG-RM is the argument that its actions were risk-reducing – i.e. could be interpreted as hedging. Simply stated, MG-RM had promised to deliver oil at fixed prices; it hedged these commitments by buying futures and making swap agreements to pay a fixed price in exchange for a floating price. If the price of oil increased, MG-RM's trading branch would make losses, as MG-RM bought oil at spot prices and made deliveries in return for the fixed prices agreed with its customers. But the derivatives branch would make profits, as the futures contracts were offset (i.e. sold) at prices higher than those at which they had been acquired, and as the swap contracts resulted in an increased inflow of cash (as a consequence of higher spot prices) in return for a fixed outflow.

Conversely, if the price of oil decreased, MG-RM's trading branch would make profits, as MG-RM bought oil at lower spot prices for delivery to its customers at fixed prices. But the derivatives branch would make losses, as the futures contracts were offset (i.e. sold) at prices lower than those at which they had been acquired, and as the swap contracts resulted in a decreased inflow of cash (as a consequence of lower spot prices) in return for a fixed outflow.

In the event, oil prices tended to decrease during the latter months of 1993.

Several complications obscure the simple interpretation of MG-RM's strategy as being one of straightforward hedging. The most important is that of a *mismatch* in duration between the trading branch contracts and the derivatives contracts. MG-RM's contracts for the supply of oil were of much longer duration (up to ten years) than for the swaps and futures (mostly, it appears, for less than a year).[7] MG-RM had adopted a so-called 'stack-and-roll' hedge. That is, it 'stacked' its derivatives contracts with purchases that approximated the *whole* of the 160m barrels of oil to be delivered over the subsequent years. But, because the derivatives contracts stipulated delivery in the near future, they had to be 'rolled over' – i.e. renewed at frequent intervals. If the strategy had been successful, the number of contracts rolled over would have gradually declined (at a rate equal to that at which the oil was delivered to MG-RM's customers), such that, after ten years, the mismatch in duration would have completely disappeared.

A stack-and-roll strategy involves two sorts of risk. Firstly, there is a 'roll-over risk' – that the outstanding contracts are renewed at a loss. MG-RM incurred such losses: the futures were offset (sold) at prices lower than those at which they had been acquired. (Contracts with later delivery dates were then purchased at the ruling market price.)

Secondly, the contracts remaining open were subject to funding risk as ever-larger good-faith deposits were demanded as collateral. For a company with a parent as large as MG-AG, there is scope for disagreement about the significance of the funding risk. If the parent had been satisfied with MG-RM's strategy, the necessary funds would, it is argued, have been forthcoming. On the other hand,

---

[7] There is also the question of whether MG-RM would have benefited from a different choice of hedge ratio – i.e. for the amount of oil underlying the derivatives contracts to differ from the total amount that it had promised to deliver. Edwards and Canter (1995) discuss this issue without offering a definite prescription. Pirrong (1997) concludes that the minimum-variance hedge ratio would have been much lower than the one MG-RM actually chose.

the costs of such liquidity, even for a conglomerate such as MG-AG, could have been prohibitive; so, it seems, MG-AG eventually decided.

The roll-over losses (though not the funding costs) could have been avoided had MG-RM acquired a 'strip hedge' – *calendar strip* – with payoffs matching its liabilities. This was not readily available, because futures contract prices are rarely quoted for more than about two years, and swaps for as long as ten years could have been so costly as to have eliminated MG-RM's trading profits.[8]

A complication

A complication, the existence of which helps to explain the stack-and-roll strategy, is that many of MG-RM's supply contracts included 'cash-out' options. These permitted MG-RM's customers to terminate their agreements in the event that oil prices increased above the contractually fixed price. MG-RM, which would have gained from premature termination in such circumstances, agreed to split the gain equally with any customer who chose to exercise the option. The gain would be calculated for the *whole* volume of oil promised for the remainder of the contract.[9]

Notice that the options could be exercised only if the spot price of oil had exceeded the contract price. This would have tended to occur only if the spot price had increased significantly, in which case MG-RM's derivative contracts would have yielded profits. In that event, the presence of the cash-out options could have justified MG-RM's stacked hedge: if the options had been exercised, the company would have needed to retain a smaller volume of outstanding derivatives as hedges for the remaining oil supply contracts.

As it happens, the spot price fell rather than increased. But that is not the point. Rather, it is that the *possibility* of rising spot prices favoured the adoption of a stack-and-roll strategy.

Summary

MG-RM's policies can be defended on the ground that the company was hedging, albeit imperfectly. Its supporters would claim that MG-RM's losses stemmed from an inevitable mismatch between its trading contracts and the derivatives it used as hedging instruments. Moreover, had MG-RM's activities not been

---

[8] Even if futures prices are quoted for periods in excess of about twelve months, the markets for distant delivery dates are notoriously 'thin', in the sense that only a small volume of trading takes place. Consequently, only contracts on disadvantageous terms are likely to have been available. Similarly, although OTC swaps with long durations might have been forthcoming, the relevant issue is the terms on which they would have been offered.

[9] Why would a customer have ever exercised an option to abandon a contract that allowed it to purchase oil at a fixed price below the spot price? One answer is that the customer might have decided, possibly for reasons unconnected with price fluctuations, to terminate the contract. Another is that the customer might have speculated that the spot price would fall in the future and, hence, sought to benefit from an immediate cash gain, and also to be released from its obligation to buy oil at the contractually fixed price later on.

interrupted by its parent, they would, it could be argued, have ultimately yielded profits (or, at least, much smaller losses). It has also been claimed that MG-RM's difficulties were exacerbated by German accounting rules – rules that effectively treated the trading branch separately from the derivatives branch. With such accounting conventions, hedging is bound to show a loss for some facet of the firm's activities. Why? Because, by construction, hedges are designed to offset losses from one set of transactions with profits from another; profits should not be expected from *both* branches.

17.5.2 The case against MG-RM

The case against MG-RM's management emerges from the reservations implicit in the defence, above. In short, MG-RM was gambling in derivatives contracts. By failing to choose the volume and duration of its futures and swap contracts more judiciously, MG-RM was incurring unnecessary and unacceptable risks. Also, MG-RM can be criticized for ignoring the magnitude of the funding that would have been necessary to maintain its derivatives positions if prices fell (as, in fact, they did).

From this perspective, if MG-RM's managers sought to act in accordance with hedging motives, they made a mess of it. Alternatively, if their motives were speculative, they were acting improperly (gambling with MG-AG's capital). Either way, the managers deserved to be fired.

It is tempting to conclude on a cynical note: had the price of oil risen, MG-RM's managers would have probably been rewarded with bonuses, rather than punished with dismissal. Less cynically, motives are always difficult to discern, and, especially when uncertainty is involved, the wisdom of hindsight is unreliable. In this context, the scope for reasonable disagreement remains.

17.6 Summary

1. Swap contracts are agreements to exchange flows of funds that vary over a specified period of time according to the terms of the contract. Typically, one party agrees to make a stream of fixed payments in return for a variable stream of payments linked to the price of an underlying asset.
2. Swaps can be interpreted as a package, or sequence, of forward contracts. Like forward contracts, swaps are traded over the counter, and can be customized in a host of ways.
3. Among the most common swaps are: interest rate swaps (e.g. the exchange of a floating interest rate for a fixed interest rate on a given notional principal); foreign exchange swaps (of one currency for another); commodity swaps (of the price of one commodity for another or for a sequence of fixed payments); total return swaps (of the total return on one asset for that of another); and credit default swaps (in which

a sequence of payments is made in return for a payoff in the event of default on a designated security).

4. Swaps can be justified on a variety of grounds, one of which is that comparative costs of borrowing and lending differ across investors. Alternatively, swaps can be viewed merely as extending the range of financial instruments available to satisfy whatever motives drive investors.

5. The experience of Metallgesellschaft in late 1993 illustrates how swaps can be undertaken for hedging purposes, but also how difficult it can be to achieve complex strategies, and why it is likely to be difficult to infer the motives for investment decisions from observed actions.

Further reading

Abken (1993) and Wall and Pringle (1993) together provide a concise introduction to swap analysis. An excellent textbook treatment of swaps is presented by Hull (2005, chap. 7), with a somewhat more technical analysis in his earlier book (Hull, 2003, chap. 6). These texts are particularly instructive with respect to the valuation of swaps. Marshall and Kapner (1993) give a comprehensive, but nonetheless straightforward and accessible, exposition of many sorts of swap contracts. A detailed analysis of some of the newer types of swap agreements is provided by Duffie (1999).

The experience of Metallgesellschaft is well covered by Culp and Miller (1995) and Edwards and Canter (1995), with both articles being reprinted, together with other contributions to the debate, by Schwartz and Smith (1997). For a statistical analysis and a critique of MG-RM's policies, see Pirrong (1997).

References

Abken, P. A. (1993), 'Beyond plain vanilla: a taxonomy of swaps', in *Financial Derivatives: New Instruments and Their Uses*, Atlanta: Federal Reserve Bank of Atlanta, pp. 51–69.

Culp, C. L., and M. H. Miller (1995), 'Metallgesellschaft and the economics of synthetic storage', *Journal of Applied Corporate Finance*, 7(4), pp. 62–76.

Duffie, D. (1999), 'Credit swap valuation', *Financial Analysts Journal*, 55(1), pp. 73–87.

Edwards, F. R., and M. S. Canter (1995), 'The collapse of Metallgesellschaft: unhedgeable risks, poor hedging strategy, or just bad luck?', *Journal of Futures Markets*, 15(3), pp. 211–64.

Hull, J. C. (2003), *Options, Futures, and Other Derivatives*, Englewood Cliffs, NJ: Prentice Hall, 5th edn.

(2005), *Fundamentals of Futures and Options Markets*, Englewood Cliffs, NJ: Prentice Hall, 5th edn.

Marshall, J. F., and K. R. Kapner (1993), *Understanding Swaps*, New York: John Wiley & Sons.

Pirrong, S. C. (1997), 'Metallgesellschaft: a prudent hedger ruined or a wildcatter on NYMEX?', *Journal of Futures Markets*, 17(5), pp. 543–78.

Schwartz, R. J., and C. W. Smith, Jr. (eds.) (1997), *Derivatives Handbook: Risk Management and Control*, New York: John Wiley & Sons.

Wall, L. D., and J. J. Pringle (1993), 'Interest rate swaps: a review of the issues', in *Financial Derivatives: New Instruments and Their Uses*, Atlanta: Federal Reserve Bank of Atlanta, pp. 70–85.

18

Options markets I: fundamentals

Overview

An option contract provides its owner with the discretion to buy or to sell an underlying asset. A call option confers the discretion to buy the asset, while a put option confers the discretion to sell. Unlike futures contracts, where the owner must either offset the contract or make delivery at maturity, the owner of an option can simply let the contract expire; that is, the option can be thrown away. This is the crucial distinction between futures and options.

Options form a subset of a broader class of 'contingent claims' contracts – financial instruments the payoffs on which depend upon the payoffs of some other underlying asset. Thus, for stock options the option to buy or sell a unit of a company's equity depends, among other things, on the market value of the shares. Options are, perhaps, the most commonly encountered sort of contingent claim, but, as shown in chapter 19, the basic ideas can be applied more generally.

This chapter is the first of three that explore option contracts and the markets in which they are traded. Chapter 19 studies option price determination, while chapter 20 applies the principles to a variety of contracts found in financial markets.

Section 18.1 defines call and put options, outlines their main properties and introduces some notation. The most commonly studied option contracts are options to buy or sell the ordinary shares of a publicly traded company – i.e. equity options. It should be assumed that these are the contracts being analysed unless stated otherwise. Section 18.2 outlines the many other sorts of option contracts that are traded in financial markets. In addition, some financial assets that do not appear to be options have option-like features. A brief commentary on these forms the subject of section 18.3.

Returning to the simplest option contracts, section 18.4 examines how the arbitrage principle can be applied to place bounds on option prices in relation to their underlying asset prices. The arbitrage principle is invoked again in section 18.5 to construct the put-call parity relationship. Section 18.6 illustrates put-call parity with one of the most famous results in corporate finance, if not in all of finance, namely the Modigliani–Miller theorem.

As with so much of financial theory, in what follows asset markets are assumed to be frictionless (a reminder is occasionally issued). The reason for the assumption is the same as elsewhere: it enables definite predictions in the absence of arbitrage opportunities.

18.1 Call options and put options

18.1.1 Definitions

This section introduces the main terminology and notation needed for the study of options. Little generality is sacrificed by studying the case of options on a company's ordinary shares. The shares represent the *underlying asset* for the option. For conciseness, the adjective 'underlying' is omitted wherever no ambiguity would ensue.

Call option: a security that gives its owner the right, but not the obligation, to *purchase* a specified *asset* for a specified price, known as the *exercise price* or the *strike price*.

Put option: a security that gives its owner the right, but not the obligation, to *sell* a specified *asset* for a specified price, known as the *exercise price* or the *strike price*.

The owner, or holder, of an option – who is said to adopt a *long* position – acquires the option by paying a *premium* (also called the *option price*) to the *writer* – who is said to adopt a *short* position. If the holder of a call option chooses to *exercise* the option, the exercise price is paid to the call writer in exchange for the asset. If the holder of a put option chooses to *exercise* the option, the asset is delivered to the put writer in exchange for the exercise price. In summary:

Call option

| Holder: | **may** *buy* asset for exercise price from writer |
| Writer: | **must** *sell* asset for exercise price, at holder's discretion |

Put option

| Holder: | **may** *sell* asset for exercise price to writer |
| Writer: | **must** *buy* asset for exercise price, at holder's discretion |

An *American* option can, by definition (i.e. as stipulated in the option contract), be exercised before or at the specified *expiry* (expiration) date. A *European* option can be exercised only at the expiry date, if it is exercised at all. Options that expire, unexercised, are said to die, and are worthless. Both American and European options are traded in financial markets across the world, not just in America and Europe, respectively. American options are more common but are more difficult to analyse than European options.

18.1.2 Trading in option contracts

As with other financial instruments, the option contracts that can be easily standardized, and for which there is a sufficiently large volume of business, tend to be traded on organized exchanges, such as the Philadelphia Stock Exchange, the Chicago Board Options Exchange (CBOE) or LIFFE. These *exchange-traded* options should be distinguished from *over-the-counter* options. OTC options, as their name implies, are customized contracts between investors (often arranged with the intermediation of a financial institution, which might itself be one of the parties to the contract).

Given that OTC options are constructed to satisfy particular needs, they may include non-standard, indeed esoteric, conditions. Consequently, market prices for OTC options may not be observed, implying that the parties must reach agreement about how to calculate their values. The commonest principle is to value OTC options such that, *if* they were traded in the open market, arbitrage opportunities would be absent; the resulting arbitrage-free value is referred to as the 'fair' value or price. The estimation of OTC option values in this way is not as easy as it might seem, especially when the assets underlying the contracts are not widely traded (so that their market prices are not readily observable).

While there are similarities between exchange-traded options and futures contracts, there are also some important differences. Perhaps the most important is that an option owner – an investor with a long position – can simply allow the option to die, unexercised. The same opportunity is not available to an investor with a long position in a futures contract, who must either offset the position before maturity or take delivery (and pay for) the asset on which the contract is written.

An option *writer* does not have the same privilege as an option owner and must accept that the option may be exercised, thereby imposing a loss on the writer. Thus, there is an asymmetry between long and short option positions – an asymmetry that is not present with futures contracts.

18.1.3 Margins

The asymmetry between buyer and seller affects the good-faith margin deposits that are required for option positions. When an option is purchased the buyer pays the premium, up front, at the outset, to the option writer.[1] The purchaser (i.e. with a long position) has no further commitment. Consequently, no margin deposit is needed.

A call option writer, however, will be obliged to deliver the underlying asset if the option is exercised. Similarly, a put option writer will be obliged to pay for the underlying asset if the option is exercised. Consequently, good-faith deposits are required from investors with short positions in options.

For call options, the good-faith deposit could take a very simple form, namely the deposit (with an intermediary, clearing house or exchange authority) of the asset on which the option is written. If the option is exercised, the asset is exchanged for the agreed exercise price (which is then paid to the option writer). In this case the option writer is said to have a *covered* position.

Option positions that are not covered are said to be *naked*, and, for these, margin deposits are obligatory. The purpose of the margin is to ensure that the option writer will not default (i.e. the deposit attenuates or eliminates performance risk). Given that the potential loss varies with the price of the underlying asset, so will the margin that is required. Exchange authorities stipulate rules to govern the size of margins. For OTC options, a bank or other financial institution typically guarantees against default and would negotiate terms for a good-faith deposit with the option writer.

18.1.4 Terminating an option investment

An option owner has three ways of terminating the contract.

1. Allow the option to die, unexercised, at the expiry date.
2. Exercise the option. Exercise occurs at the expiry date for a European option, or any time up to the expiry date for an American option.
3. Offset the position by selling an identical option before the expiry date. Offsetting is a routine operation for exchange-traded options, and can also occur for OTC options by the renegotiation of the contract.

For an option writer, the only legitimate way of terminating the contract before expiry is by an offsetting purchase. Such an action would be profitable if the writer makes the offsetting purchase at a lower premium than the initial sale. A profit equal to the value of the initial premium accrues, of course, to the option writer in the event that the option dies unexercised, though this profit is not realized until the expiry date.

---

[1] While this is typical, there are some options for which the purchaser makes only a margin deposit at the outset. The ultimate outcome is the same, though the bookkeeping during the life of the contract differs.

18.1.5 Notation

$C =$ American call option price, or premium
$P =$ American put option price, or premium
$c \ =$ European call option price, or premium
$p \ =$ European put option price, or premium
$S =$ current price of the underlying asset
$X =$ exercise, or strike, price
$T \ =$ expiry date
$t \ \ =$ current date, so that $\tau \equiv T - t =$ time to expiry
$r \ =$ rate of interest, assumed to be positive

Note that all of the prices C, P, c, p and S normally vary over time; i.e. they depend upon t. Their values at the expiry date are made explicit with a T subscript – e.g. S_T denotes the price of the stock at date T. For dates prior to T, the time subscript is omitted.

The interest factor, $R(t, T)$, depends on r (recall chapter 14, section 14.3). In the simplest case, for which the interest rate is constant, $T - t = 1$ period, and in which there is no compounding between t and T, $R(t, T) = (1 + r)$. Another common assumption is that of a continuously compounded constant interest rate, in which case $R(t, T) = e^{r\tau}$. Clearly, there are many other possibilities, which is why it is convenient to use $R(t, T)$ to include all of them.[2] Note for future reference that, if $r > 0$, then $R(t, T) > 1$ – a property that is assumed to hold throughout. Where no ambiguity is likely, $R(t, T)$ is written simply as R.

18.1.6 Payoffs from an option investment

Figures 18.1 and 18.2 depict the payoffs and net gains, upon exercise, for long positions (18.1) and short positions (18.2). In each case, the horizontal axis measures the asset price, S, *at the date of exercise*. For European options this date must be T, the expiry date. For American options it is any date before or at T.

Note that the payoff is gross of the premium paid by the purchaser to the option writer when the position was initiated. The net gain equals the gross gain minus the premium paid by the purchaser to the option writer.

On the innocuous assumption that more wealth is preferred to less, an option will never be exercised unless it is profitable to do so. Thus, a call option will

---

[2] A general case is that of continuously compounded but non-constant interest rates, for which $R(t, T) = \exp\left(\int_t^T r(\tau)d\tau\right)$.

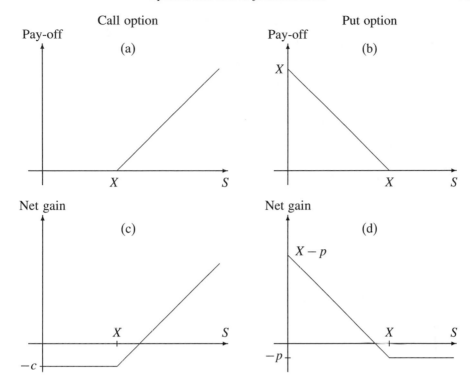

Fig. 18.1. Payoffs at exercise for call and put options: long positions

The exercise of a *call* option by its holder involves the *purchase* of the underlying asset at price X. The exercise of a call option would occur only if the market price of the asset, S, is at least as great as X: $S \geq X$. The payoff equals $S - X$ (panel (a)).

The exercise of a *put* option involves the *sale* of the underlying asset, by the writer to the option-holder, at price X. The exercise of a put option would occur only if the exercise price, X, is at least as great as the market price of the asset, S: $X \geq S$. The pay-off then equals $X - S$ (panel (b)).

Panels (c) and (d) show the net gains for call and put options respectively, found by subtracting the premium paid from the payoff.

not be exercised if the asset price is less than X, and a put option will not be exercised if the asset price exceeds X. The assumed absence of market frictions could be significant here. For example, the payoff from exercising a call option would be reduced by the transaction costs incurred from selling the asset acquired from exercising the option: if $S - X$ is smaller than the cost of selling the asset, then the option may be allowed to die unexercised. Conversely, an investor who intends to hold on to the asset following the exercise of a call option may be

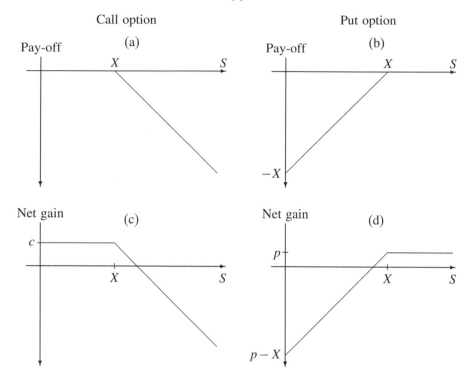

Fig. 18.2. Payoffs at exercise for call and put options: short positions

The exercise of a *call* option requires the option writer to *sell* the underlying asset to the option holder at price X. The exercise of a call option would occur only if the market price of the asset, S, is at least as great as X: $S \geq X$. The payoff then equals $X - S$ (panel (a)).

The exercise of a *put* option requires the option writer to *purchase* the underlying asset from the option holder at price X. The exercise of a put option would occur only if the exercise price, X, is at least as great as the market price of the asset, S: $X \geq S$. The payoff then equals $S - X$ (panel (b)).

Panels (c) and (d) show the net gain for call and put options respectively, found by adding the premium received to the pay-off.

prepared to exercise the option even if $S - X < 0$, because it might otherwise be more expensive to buy the asset in the open market.

The payoff for an option writer is the negative of the payoff to an option holder – it is a transfer from one to the other – as shown in figure 18.2. For a put option writer the maximum loss is the exercise price, X, per unit of the underlying asset (if the asset becomes worthless). For a call option writer, the potential loss is, in principle, unlimited.

Because European options can be exercised only at expiry, their values at expiry (date T) can be written

$$\text{call}: c_T = \begin{cases} S_T - X & \text{if } S_T > X \\ 0 & \text{if } S_T \leq X \end{cases} \qquad \text{put}: p_T = \begin{cases} 0 & \text{if } S_T > X \\ X - S_T & \text{if } S_T \leq X \end{cases}$$

More succinctly,

$$\text{call}: c_T = \max[0, S_T - X] \qquad \text{put}: p_T = \max[0, X - S_T]$$

where 'max$[A, B]$' means 'the larger of A and B'.

American options can be exercised early (before expiry). Consequently, their market prices cannot be less than the return from an immediate exercise; otherwise, it would be profitable to buy the option and exercise it immediately (a trivial arbitrage opportunity). Hence,

$$\text{call option}: \quad C \geq \max[0, S - X] \qquad \text{put option}: \quad P \geq \max[0, X - S]$$

Time subscripts on C, P and S, have been omitted to avoid clutter; for American-style options, these inequalities hold at each point of time (up to and including the expiry date).

18.1.7 In and out of the money

During the life of an option (before it expires or is exercised), the underlying asset price may differ from the exercise price stipulated in the option contract. The owner of a call option will not exercise the option when the exercise price exceeds the asset price – because the asset could be acquired more cheaply in the market at a price $S < X$. Similarly, the owner of a put option will not exercise it when the asset price exceeds the exercise price – because the asset could be sold at a higher price in the market, $S > X$. In such circumstances, the options are said to have zero *intrinsic* (or *parity*) value.

Even when options have a zero intrinsic value their market prices are likely to be positive. Why? Because there is a chance that the asset price will move in a 'favourable' direction (up in the case of a call option, down in the case of a put option) before the option expires. That is, all options are said to have a positive *time value* before expiry. Other things being equal, the time value of an option declines as the expiry date becomes closer (because, in a sense, there is less time for the asset price to move in a favourable direction).

This implies the following classification:

	Call option	Put option
$S < X$	Out of the money Intrinsic value $= 0$	In the money Intrinsic value: $X - S > 0$
$S > X$	In the money Intrinsic value: $S - X > 0$	Out of the money Intrinsic value $= 0$
$S = X$	At the money Intrinsic value $= 0$	At the money Intrinsic value $= 0$

18.2 Varieties of options

The range of available option contracts is limited only by the ingenuity of those who construct them. Such is the variety of contracts that have been observed that the non-standard options are sometimes grouped into a catch-all category referred to as *exotic* options. Rather than attempt to be encyclopedic, this section identifies the main ways in which options are differentiated and describes some examples.

Option contracts differ across several dimensions, including the *underlying asset*, the *date(s)* at which exercise is permitted and the rule used to calculate the *payoff* if the option is exercised. Some contracts even allow the holder to choose, at an agreed date, to stipulate whether the option is a put or a call. These are called *as-you-like-it* or *chooser* options.

18.2.1 Underlying assets

Exchange-traded options tend to adhere to the standard American or European puts and calls, and differ mainly in the assets underlying the contracts. Among the more common exchange-traded options are these.

1. *Equity options* (or stock options) written on the shares of publicly traded corporations.
2. *Interest rate options* to buy or sell securities that promise to pay fixed returns. These include bond options, written with government or commercial bonds as the underlying assets.
3. *Stock index options* for specified indexes; for example, Standard & Poor's 500 index on the Chicago Mercantile Exchange. On LIFFE, both European-style and American-style options are traded for the FT-SE 100 index.
4. *Foreign currency options*, such as the options on sterling traded on the CME.
5. *Options on futures* to buy or sell futures contracts. Most financial exchanges that list futures contracts also provide for trading in options corresponding to the futures contracts (see chapter 20, section 20.2).

For some options, the asset underlying the option contract is not uniquely defined. For example, bond options often specify a range of bonds that can be delivered (just as for bond futures).

Stock index options are effectively options on a bundle of securities (i.e. those for which the index is computed). Options such as this, which involve several underlying assets, are sometimes called *rainbow* or *basket* options. Yet another variant is the *exchange* option, in which one asset is exchanged for another (rather than cash in return for an asset).

The asset underlying an option could be another option. Such contracts are known as *compound* options.

18.2.2 Exercise dates

Some option contracts come into effect only at a specified date in the future. These are known as *forward start* options.

An American-style contract for which exercise is permitted only at a limited number of specified dates is known as a *Bermudan* option. More generally, exercise may be permitted for a restricted range of dates – a cross between American and European options.

18.2.3 Payoff rules

For regular contracts studied elsewhere in this and later chapters, the payoff when an option is exercised is just the difference between the exercise price and the value of the underlying asset at the exercise date. Other rules are often stipulated, including the following.

1. Instead of a fixed exercise price, the contract could specify that the payoff is the difference between the asset price at the exercise date and the maximum (puts) or minimum (calls) asset price during the life of the option. Thus, for a call, the option holder is able to purchase the underlying asset for the lowest price observed between the date at which the option is initiated and the exercise date. Similarly, for a put, the option holder is effectively able to sell the asset at the highest price observed during the life of the option. These contracts are known as *look-back* options.

2. In some contracts, it is possible for a European option holder to guarantee (or lock in) a minimum payoff at the expiry date. For example, suppose that a call option with an exercise price of \$100 expires at the end of June and that on some earlier date the asset price equals \$140. The option holder may be allowed to signal – 'shout' – that the payoff at expiry will be at least \$40 = 140 − 100. At the expiry date, if the asset price exceeds \$140, the holder receives the normal payoff

(the asset price minus the exercise price); otherwise, the payoff is $40. For these so-called *shout* options, the holder is typically allowed only one opportunity to shout a minimum payoff.

3. Instead of calculating the payoff using the asset price at the exercise date, it is possible to use an *average* of the asset prices over a specified period. This is a characteristic of *Asian* options. Another variant is for the *exercise price* to equal an average of observed asset prices rather than a fixed sum.

4. Options may have discrete payoffs. For example, the contract could specify a *fixed* payoff if it is exercised; here, comparison of the asset price with the exercise price determines *whether* it is exercised, not the payoff. These *cash-or-nothing* contracts are examples of *binary* options.

    Another variant is the *asset-or-nothing* option, for which the payoff is the value of the asset at exercise – i.e. the exercise price is zero.

5. Some contracts are written such that the option either comes into existence or ceases to exist according to whether the asset price rises above or falls below a specified level. These are called *barrier* options. One example is a *down-and-out* call option, which ceases to exist if the asset price falls below a stated level (normally set below the asset price at the inception of the option).

18.3 Option-like assets

In addition to contracts that are recognized as options, there are many securities with 'option-like' characteristics. Here is a selection.

1. *Warrants*. The commonest type of warrant is that issued by a company. The warrant holder has the right to buy shares from the company at a specified exercise price on or before a specified expiry date. Warrants differ from options in three ways: (i) warrants typically have long lives (with years, perhaps an indefinite number, rather than months before expiry); (ii) the exercise of warrants increases (or 'dilutes') the company's total equity; and (iii) complex provisions may be attached to the exercise of warrants (e.g. the company may include a clause allowing it to vary the expiry date according to changes in the share price).

    The effect of (i) is that standard models of option prices (such as those studied in chapter 19) are unlikely to make accurate predictions of warrant prices, especially for warrants with several years to expiry. The effect of (ii) is that dilution will, other things being equal, tend to reduce the value of each existing share. The effect of (iii) depends, of course, on the terms of the warrant itself.

2. *Callable bonds*. A bond indenture may grant its issuer the right to 'call' (redeem) the bond at some specified value (typically the face value, or 'par') before its redemption date. The issuer has an incentive to call the bond if its price rises above the specified value at which it can be redeemed. Commonly, the bond indenture restricts the opportunities for the issuer to redeem the bonds. For example, the indenture may

stipulate that the bond is not to be redeemed during the first twenty years of its life. Callable bonds can be viewed as *non*-callable bonds (i.e. without the call provision) bundled together with a *short* position in a call option on the bonds. A callable bond usually trades at a lower price than its non-callable counterpart, reflecting the premium corresponding to the implicit call option.

3. *Convertible bonds.* These are typically corporate bonds that include provisions permitting their holders to exchange the bonds for equity in the company according to stated conditions, on or at a specified date. A convertible bond can be viewed as a package of an *in*convertible bond (i.e. a bond without the conversion facility) bundled together with a warrant for shares in the company.

4. *Rights.* A rights issue gives existing shareholders of a company the opportunity to purchase additional shares in the firm, at a stated exercise price over a specified time period. The shareholders can then (a) exercise the rights; (b) sell them for cash; or (c) throw them away. (The rights become worthless if, at the expiry date, the company's share price is lower than the exercise price.) Rights issues can also be interpreted as a type of dividend (because the exercise price is normally fixed below the market price of the shares, thus giving the rights a positive market value).

18.4 Upper and lower bounds for option prices

18.4.1 The role of the arbitrage principle

Application of the arbitrage principle establishes limits, or 'bounds', on option prices relative to their underlying asset prices. That is, some combinations of option prices and asset prices can be excluded because they would permit unlimited, risk-free profits for zero capital outlay. In deriving each of the bounds described below, the logic follows identical steps: (i) suppose that the bound fails to hold; (ii) construct a portfolio with zero initial outlay that results in a non-negative payoff in every state (eventuality) and a positive payoff in at least one state; (iii) the existence of the portfolio contradicts the arbitrage principle. Hence, conclude that the initial supposition is false and the bound must hold.

As emphasized ad nauseam in previous chapters, the force of the arbitrage principle rests on the assumption of frictionless markets. In particular, it is assumed that (a) transaction costs are zero, (b) there are no institutional constraints on trades (so that unrestricted short-sales are permitted), (c) investors can borrow or lend at a risk-free (but not necessarily constant) interest rate, and (d) assets are divisible, as finely as needed, into small units.

For concreteness, the option is assumed to be written on a company's traded ordinary shares, or stock. For simplicity, it is assumed that one unit of stock corresponds to one option: this is merely a choice of units.

More importantly, it is assumed that the company pays no cash dividends during the life of the option, t to T.[3] The prospect of dividend payments during the life of an option affects the attractiveness of the option to investors and, hence, the premium that it commands.

Other things being equal, share prices fall upon the payment of a dividend as the quotation changes from *cum*-dividend (with the dividend) to *ex*-dividend (without the dividend). The greater the dividends over an interval of time, the smaller any increase in the share price (other things being equal, of course); effectively, a portion of the return to holding the share is in the form of a dividend. Given that options are not protected against cash dividends, a call option becomes less attractive and, hence, commands a lower premium than otherwise; and conversely for a put option.

A second implication of the payment of a dividend is that holders of American call options may find it profitable to exercise the options earlier than otherwise in order to collect the dividend.

18.4.2 Four simple bounds

1. *Option values are always non-negative.* This holds because it is not obligatory to exercise an option, which can be allowed to die if it is in the holder's advantage to do so.

2. *American options are worth at least as much as their European counterparts –* i.e. $C \geq c$ and $P \geq p$. American options provide the extra opportunity for early exercise (i.e. exercise before T). This opportunity can never have negative value (though, as shown below, the extra opportunity may have zero value).

3. *A call option is never worth more than the value of its underlying asset.* Suppose not. Then (i) write one call option, (ii) buy one unit of the asset and (iii) deposit the (positive) difference at the risk-free interest rate. The worst that can happen is that the option is exercised, in which case the asset is delivered in exchange for the option's exercise price. The net payoff is equal to either (a) the deposit plus the exercise price if the option is exercised; or (b) the deposit plus the value of the asset if the option is not exercised. Either way, an arbitrage profit is obtained and, hence, the stated bound must hold.

4. *A put option is never worth more than its exercise price.* Suppose not – i.e. $P > X$ (for an American option). Then write one option and deposit the cash at the risk-free interest rate. If the option is exercised, X is paid in exchange for the asset. The payoff is positive and equal to the value of the asset (non-negative), plus the excess

---

[3] Option contracts are typically protected against changes in the units in which the underlying asset is measured, so that, for example, the number of shares per contract would be changed automatically in accordance with a stock split if one occurs during the option's life. Normally, options are not protected with respect to the payment of cash dividends; i.e. it is possible to exercise an American call option immediately prior to a dividend payment, thereby collecting the dividend.

on deposit, $P - X$ (positive, by hypothesis), plus interest (non-negative). If the option dies unexercised, the payoff is the whole deposit, P, plus interest. Either way, an arbitrage profit is assured; hence $P \leq X$ – as asserted.

For a *European* put option the upper bound is more restrictive; a European put option is never worth more than the *net present value* of its exercise price.[4] Suppose not – i.e. $p > X/R$; $Rp > X$. Once again, write one option and deposit the cash. At the expiry date, if the option is exercised, X is paid in return for the asset. Because $Rp > X$, the value of the deposit, including interest, is more than sufficient to cover the exercise price. Hence, the investor's payoff is positive and equal to $Rp - X > 0$, plus ownership of the asset (which must have a non-negative value). Alternatively, if the option dies unexercised, the payoff is the whole deposit, p, plus interest. Again, an arbitrage profit is obtained; hence $p \leq X/R$ – as asserted.

18.4.3 Tighter bounds for option prices

The bounds established so far are quite loose. Further application of the arbitrage principle enables narrower bounds to be placed on European call and put option prices. These are depicted in figure 18.3, and explained below.

Lower bound for a European call option

$$c \gneqq \max \left[0, S - \frac{X}{R(t, T)} \right] \tag{18.1}$$

To interpret the bound, note first that it asserts that $c \geq 0$ – the value of an option is never negative. Next, it states that, if $S > X/R$, then $c \geq S - X/R$.

If the interest rate is positive, it follows that $R \geq 1$ and $X/R \leq X$: the present value of the exercise price is no greater than the exercise price itself. Hence, it certainly follows that $c \geq S - X$: the call option premium is at least as great as its payoff if exercised at asset price S.[5]

A justification for the bound is given here using a numerical example. (A more formal demonstration is offered in appendix 18.1.) Suppose that $S = \$110$, $X = \$110$, $c = \$5$ and $R(t, T) = 1.1$. (This will be the case, for instance, if the interest rate is 10 per cent per period, $T - t = 1$ and interest accrues, without compounding, only at date T.) This configuration clearly violates (18.1), for $\$5 < 10 = 110 - 110/1.1$.

---

[4] This more restrictive version of the bound does not hold for an American put option because early exercise is possible.

[5] A European option cannot, of course, be exercised before expiry, by which time the asset price may have fallen below X. But, as the argument in the text shows, this is irrelevant in establishing the bound. The reason why X/R appears in the bound rather than X is that the exercise price is not paid until T; the investor, in planning to exercise the option, can invest the funds at interest between t and T. For this reason, Merton (1990, p. 260) points out that the intrinsic value of the call option is more appropriately given by $S - X/R$, not by the conventional measure $S - X$.

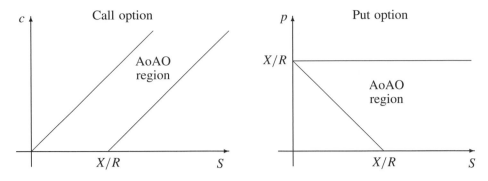

Fig. 18.3. Absence of arbitrage opportunities (AoAO) regions for European options

> The regions marked AoAO denote pairs of option and asset prices –
> c and S for calls, p and S for puts – such that it is impossible for
> investors to make positive arbitrage profits. If option and asset prices
> occur outside these regions, it is possible to design investment strategies
> (i.e. trading in options, the underlying asset and risk-free borrowing or
> lending) that guarantee arbitrage profits.

Construct the following portfolio: (i) short-sell one unit of stock for \$110;
(ii) buy one call option for \$5; and (iii) lend \$105 at the risk-free interest rate.

At the expiry date, T, the loan is worth \$115.50. The stock price at the expiry
date, S_T, may be greater or less than the exercise price, \$110. Suppose, for the
sake of definiteness, that S_T is either 120 or 100, and consider the following table:

	Initial outlay	Outcome: $S_T = 120$	Outcome: $S_T = 100$
Buy one call option	−5	120 − 110	0
Short-sell stock	110	−120	−100
Make a loan	−105	115.5	115.5
Net total	0	5.5	15.5

Suppose that $S_T = \$120$. In this event the option is exercised, the asset acquired
being delivered to redeem the short-sale. The cash deposited on loan more than
covers the exercise price of \$110, and the strategy yields a net payoff of \$5.5.

Suppose, instead, that $S_T = \$100$. In this event the option dies unexercised, but
the unit of stock is purchased (to redeem the short-sale) for \$100 – an amount that,
again, is more than covered by the deposit. A net payoff of \$15.5 is obtained.

It should be clear that, *whatever* the stock price at the expiry date, the chosen
portfolio (which requires zero initial outlay) yields a positive net payoff in *every*
state (though the *size* of the payoff depends on the S_T if $S_T < X$). Such an

outcome is incompatible with the arbitrage principle. Hence, the hypothetical violation of (18.1) is inconsistent with equilibrium in frictionless markets. The formal argument justifying the bound follows exactly the same steps, replacing the numbers with abstract symbols.

Lower bound for a European put option

$$p \geq \max \left[0, \frac{X}{R(t, T)} - S \right]$$

The lower bound for a European put can be demonstrated using the same reasoning as for the call option. No new ideas are needed and the derivation is omitted. (However, for completeness a formal justification appears in appendix 18.2.)

An American call option is worth more alive than dead: $C \geq S - X$. In words: it is not worth exercising an American call before its expiry date. Why not? Because the payoff from exercising the option is never greater than its market price. An investor who terminates a long position in American call options would always make at least as much profit from selling the options as from exercising them.

To understand why $C \geq S - X$, suppose not: $C < S - X$ (i.e. $S - C - X > 0$). Buy the option for C and exercise it immediately at a cost of X to acquire the asset. Sell the asset for S. The net payoff is $S - C - X > 0$. This is an arbitrage profit and, hence, incompatible with equilibrium in frictionless markets. Thus it must be that $C \geq S - X$, as asserted.[6]

While an American call *can* be exercised at any time to provide a payoff of $S - X$, it is more profitable to sell the option (for C) in the open market (assuming, as always, that markets are frictionless and arbitrage opportunities are absent).

If the market ensures that an American call option is not worth exercising before expiry, it follows that it is equivalent to an European option (for which exercise before expiry is disallowed). The corollary is that $C = c$; that is, an American call option is worth no more than a European call option.[7] The right of early exercise is worthless. This conclusion is guaranteed only if the asset does not pay a dividend during the life of the option. If a dividend is paid before the expiry date, it might be profitable for an American option to be exercised early in order to allow its owner to collect the dividend.

---

[6] Similarly for American put options: $P \geq X - S$. Suppose not: $P < X - S$ (i.e. $X - P - S > 0$). Buy the option for P and the asset for S. Exercise the option immediately by delivering the asset for X. The net payoff is $X - P - S > 0$. This is an arbitrage profit and, hence, incompatible with equilibrium in frictionless markets.

[7] For a formal justification, suppose that $C > c$. Then write one American call option for C, buy one European call for c and invest the difference, $C - c$, in a risk-free asset. It has already been shown that the American call will not be exercised prior to expiry. At the expiry date, either (a) both options will be exercised, in which case the loss from the American option exactly cancels the gain from the European, or (b) neither option is exercised. Hence, there is a certain net gain of $R(C - c)$ – an arbitrage opportunity inconsistent with market equilibrium.

18.5 Put-call parity for European options

The put-call parity relationship for European options states that

$$c + \frac{X}{R(t, T)} = p + S \tag{18.2}$$

In words: the price of a European call plus the present value of its exercise price equals the price of a European put plus the underlying asset price, at each date. It should be obvious that the relationship makes sense only for options defined on the same asset, for the same exercise price and with the same expiry date. Equation (18.2) also requires that the stock in question does not pay any dividend between t and T. The put-call parity relationship is sometimes called the *option conversion relationship*, because it can be used to construct put options from call options, and call options from put options. The put and call options must both be of the European type.

The put-call parity relationship is yet another implication of the absence of arbitrage opportunities. In this context, the familiar reasoning is applied twice: once to rule out $c + X/R < p + S$, and again to rule out $c + X/R > p + S$. The reasoning is illustrated with a numerical example. A formal demonstration involves the same steps, with symbols replacing numbers. (See appendix 18.3 for a formal demonstration.)

Case (A): $c + X/R < p + S$.

Suppose that $S = \$110$, $X = \$110$, $c = \$15$, $p = \$10$ and $R(t, T) = 1.1$. This configuration violates the put-call parity relationship:

$$115 = 15 + 110/1.1 < 10 + 110 = 120$$

$$c + \frac{X}{R} < p + S$$

Construct a portfolio as follows: (i) write one put option; (ii) buy one call option; (iii) short-sell one unit of stock; and (iv) lend the balance at interest.

Assume for concreteness that the stock price at expiry is either $S_T = 120$ or $S_T = 100$, and consider the following table:

	Initial outlay	Outcome: $S_T = 120$	Outcome: $S_T = 100$
Write one put option	10	0	$(100 - 110)$
Buy one call option	-15	$(120 - 110)$	0
Short-sell stock	110	-120	-100
Make a loan	-105	115.50	115.50
Net total	0	5.50	5.50

Suppose that $S_T = \$120$. In this event (i) the put option dies, costing the investor nothing; (ii) the call option is exercised, with payoff $10; (iii) a unit of stock is purchased for $120 and returned to its lender in fulfilment of the short-sale; and (iv) the payoff on the loan, with interest, equals $115.50. Thus, the net payoff on the strategy equals $5.50 ($= 10 - 120 + 115.50$).

Suppose, instead, that $S_T = \$100$. In this event (i) the put option is exercised, with a loss of $10; (ii) the call option dies unexercised; (iii) a unit of stock is purchased for $100 and returned to its lender in fulfilment of the short-sale; and (iv) the payoff on the loan, with interest, equals $115.50. Once again, the net payoff on the strategy equals $5.50 ($= -10 - 100 + 115.50$).

Notice that the magnitude of S_T (either $120 or $100 in the example) is irrelevant. In each case its value cancels out from the option that is exercised and the purchase of the asset at date T. (The singular case $S_T = X$ is trivial, both put and call options having exactly zero value at expiry.)

In summary, a portfolio has been constructed, with zero initial outlay, that yields a positive payoff in every eventuality. Such an outcome is inconsistent with market equilibrium for a frictionless market in the absence of arbitrage opportunities.

Case (B): $c + X/R > p + S$.

Suppose now that $S = \$110$, $X = \$110$, $c = \$20$, $p = \$5$ and $R = 1.1$. This configuration clearly violates the put-call parity: $\$20 + 110/1.1 = 120 > 115 = 5 + 110$.

Construct a portfolio as follows: (i) buy one put option; (ii) write one call option; (iii) buy one unit of stock; and (iv) borrow the funds needed for zero initial outlay.

Assume once again that the stock price at expiry is either $S_T = 120$ or $S_T = 100$, and consider the following table:

	Initial outlay	Outcome: $S_T = 120$	Outcome: $S_T = 100$
Buy one put option	−5	0	$(110 - 100)$
Write one call option	20	$(110 - 120)$	0
Buy stock	−110	120	100
Borrow	95	−104.5	−104.5
Net total	0	5.5	5.5

Suppose that $S_T = \$120$. In this event (i) the put option dies, unexercised; (ii) the call option is exercised, at a cost to the investor of $10; (iii) the unit of

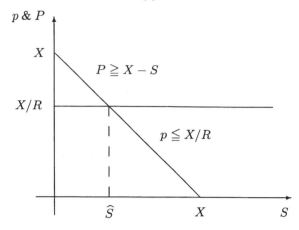

Fig. 18.4. Bounds for American and European put option prices

In the absence of arbitrage opportunities $P \geq X - S$ for an American put option, and $p \leq X/R$ for a European put option. Define $\widehat{S}$ by $X - \widehat{S} = X/R$. If $S < \widehat{S}$, then $P > p$: the price of an American put exceeds that of its European counterpart.

stock is sold for \$120; and (iv) the loan is repaid, with interest, at a cost of \$104.50. Thus, the net payoff on the strategy equals \$5.50 $(= -10 + 120 - 104.50)$.

Suppose, instead, that $S_T = \$100$. In this event (i) the put option is exercised, with a gain of \$10; (ii) the call option dies unexercised; (iii) the unit of stock is sold for \$100; and (iv) the loan is repaid, with interest, at a cost of \$104.50. Once again, the net payoff on the strategy equals \$5.50 $(= 10 + 100 - 104.50)$.

Yet again, a portfolio has been constructed, with zero initial outlay, that yields a positive payoff in every eventuality. Such an outcome is inconsistent with market equilibrium for a frictionless market in the absence of arbitrage opportunities. This justifies the put-call parity relationship for European-style options.

Why put-call parity does not extend to American options

While $C = c$ (subject to the conditions assumed in this chapter), it need *not* be the case that $P = p$. Hence, it is not permissible simply to replace c with C and p with P in the put-call parity relationship. This is because there are circumstances in which the premium for an American put strictly exceeds that for its European counterpart – i.e. $P > p$.

To show that there are patterns of S, X and R for which $P > p$, recall the bounds on option prices: $X \geq P \geq X - S$ and $X/R \geq p \geq X/R - S$. The relevant bounds here are $P \geq X - S$ and $X/R \geq p$. See figure 18.4.

For every $S < \widehat{S}$ in figure 18.4, $X - S > X/R$ and, hence, $P > p$, because $P \geq X - S$ and $X/R \geq p$. That is, $X - S > X/R$ implies that $P > p$. Given X and R, it follows that $P > p$ for sufficiently small S.

Intuition may be aided with a numerical example. Suppose that $S = 15$, $X = 120$ and $R = 1.20$. Now, in the absence of arbitrage opportunities, $P \geq 105 = 120 - 15$, and $p \leq 100 = 120/1.20$. If $P = p$, there is an arbitrage opportunity for trading in one of the options. For example, if $P = p = 95$, unlimited profits could be made by purchasing American options and exercising them immediately, with a risk-free gain of $10 = 120 - 15 - 95$ (i.e. $X - S - P$) per option.

18.6 The Modigliani–Miller theorem

Among the applications of the put-call parity relationship, the Modigliani–Miller (MM) theorem is perhaps the most prominent. The MM theorem, central to modern theories of corporate finance, asserts that the market value of a firm is invariant with respect to the composition of its financial liabilities.[8]

More precisely, the MM theorem states that, under certain conditions, the market value of the firm does not depend on its debt/equity ratio (i.e. its 'leverage' or 'gearing'). Thus, if a firm's equity is worth a total of $100m when it has zero debt, then, *all other of the firm's decisions remaining the same*, if the firm has debt with a market value of – say – $25m the market value of its equity will equal $75m. It should be no surprise that the MM theorem has given rise to immense controversy, not least because the 'certain conditions' demand careful statement. Also, a firm's financial decisions are rarely made in isolation from all the other decisions that everyone accepts will affect its market value. This makes it difficult to isolate the separate impact of financial decisions.

From the perspective of options theory, the essence of the MM theorem can be understood if S is interpreted as the total market value of the firm – *not* as the value of a unit of its equity, as in previous sections. Let X denote the face value of bonds issued by the firm. Assume that the firm will be wound up at date T in the future, the total value of its assets, S_T, being then distributed to those with claims on the firm – i.e. the holders of its bonds (debt) and ordinary shares (equity).

At date T the bondholders have first claim on the firm's assets: they are entitled to recompense up to X. Default occurs in those states (if any) for which the value of the firm's assets is less that its debt: $S_T < X$. In the event of

---

[8] Strictly, the MM theorem comprises a group of several propositions that collectively identify the relationship (or its absence) between the value of a firm and its financing decisions. See the entry on 'Modigliani–Miller theorem' in *The New Palgrave Dictionary of Money and Finance* (Newman, Milgate and Eatwell, 1992). For the original contributions, see Modigliani and Miller (1958), Miller and Modigliani (1961) and Modigliani and Miller (1963).

default the bondholders receive the whole value of the firm, S_T, and (in a world of limited liability) the shareholders receive nothing. Thus, the payoffs to the claimants are:

	Solvency $S_T \geqq X$	Default $S_T < X$
Shareholders	$S_T - X$	0
Bondholders	X	S_T
Total	S_T	S_T

These payoffs can be related to the payoffs on options expiring at T. It is as if shareholders possess a call option on the assets of the firm, with exercise price X at expiry date T. In the event that the firm's assets are sufficient to redeem its bonds (i.e. $S_T \geq X$), the shareholders exercise the option for a payoff of $S_T - X$. In the event that the firm defaults, $S_T < X$, the shareholders allow the option to die unexercised, with a payoff of zero.

The firm's debt is risky; bondholders are paid in full only if the firm does not default – i.e. if $S_T \geq X$. The payoff on the bonds equals $\min[X, S_T]$, or, more conveniently, can be written as $X - \max[0, X - S_T]$. The first term, X, is the payoff on *risk-free* bonds, while the second term, $\max[0, X - S_T]$, is the payoff at expiry (date T) on a put option, with exercise price X and underlying asset value S_T. That is, the payoff on risky bonds equals the payoff on risk-free bonds *minus* the payoff on a put option. Consequently, at any date, t, prior to expiry the value of the firm's bonds equals the present value of risk-free bonds, X/R, minus the value, p, of a put option. It is as if the holders of risk-free bonds have written a put option with exercise price equal to the promised payoff, X, on the bonds.

Let c denote the value of the call option on the firm's assets, with payoff at expiry equal to $S_T - X$ if the firm is solvent and zero if it defaults; i.e. the payoff on the call option equals $\max[0, S_T - X]$. Thus, the market value of the firm's assets, S, at each date, t, equals the value of its shares, c, plus the value of its risky bonds $(X/R) - p$:

$$S = c + \frac{X}{R(t, T)} - p \tag{18.3}$$

which is nothing more nor less than the put-call parity relationship. While (18.3) suggests that the total market value of a firm, S, is invariant with respect to the composition of its liabilities (equity and debt), it is not a proof. A proof, using reasoning similar to that of previous sections, is offered in appendix 18.4.

18.7 Summary

1. Options form one of the most important classes of contingent claims. The defining feature of an option is that it provides its holder with the right, but not the obligation, to take a specified action at a date, or over a range of dates, in the future.

2. Call options give their holders the right to buy an asset for a stipulated exercise price. Put options give their holders the right to sell an asset at the stipulated exercise price. European-style options can be exercised only at the expiry date. American-style options can be exercised at any time before or on the expiry date.

3. An investor who takes a short position is said to 'write' an option in return for a premium (the option's price) which the buyer pays up front. There is an asymmetry between long and short option positions. An option holder can always allow the option to die, unexercised. An option writer must stand ready to fulfil the terms of the contract until it expires.

4. The arbitrage principle can be applied to place upper and lower bounds on the prices of options traded in frictionless markets.

5. The put-call parity relationship for European-style options links the prices for put and call options on the same underlying asset, with the same exercise price and expiry date. Once again, the arbitrage principle is invoked to obtain the relationship. A notable application of put-call parity is the Modigliani–Miller theorem, which asserts that the market value of a firm is independent of its leverage (debt/equity ratio).

Further reading

The notation used here is close to that used by Hull (2005), who has produced one of the most accessible textbook expositions, covering the subject in more detail than here (see, in particular, chaps. 8 & 9). It is also worth consulting Edwards and Ma (1992, chap. 18) and Elton, Gruber, Brown and Goetzmann (2003, chap. 22).

For an appreciation of the fundamental principles of options as derivatives, see Varian (1987) and Rubinstein (1987). At a more advanced level, the seminal contribution of Merton (1990, chap. 8, pp. 255–81), though challenging, rewards diligent effort. Yet another thorough exposition of the principles of option price theory is provided by Cox and Rubinstein (1985, chaps. 1–4). Dixit and Pindyck (1994) present an analysis of options applied to the investment decisions of firms – that is, of 'real options', in contrast with the options on financial assets studied here.

For the Modigliani–Miller theorem, the entry with this heading in *The New Palgrave Dictionary of Money and Finance* (Newman, Milgate and Eatwell, 1992) provides a rare precise analysis of the theorem. Miller (1988) points out that the MM theorem takes precedence over the put-call parity relationship developed by Stoll (1969).

Appendix 18.1: Lower bound for a European call option premium

This appendix establishes the lower bound in a more formal way than in the text, using symbols instead of a numerical example. Recall that the bound states that

$$c \geq \max\left[0, S - \frac{X}{R(t, T)}\right] \tag{18.4}$$

The inequality is demonstrated by showing that, if it does not hold, arbitrage profits can be made in a frictionless market. Begin by supposing the contrary to (18.4):

$$c < S - \frac{X}{R} \tag{18.5}$$

where $c > 0$. Note for later reference that, because $R > 0$, (18.5) is equivalent to

$$(S - c)R - X > 0 \tag{18.6}$$

(By assumption $R > 1$, though only $R > 0$ is needed here.)

Now construct a portfolio, with zero initial outlay, by purchasing one call option for c, short-selling one unit of stock for S and lending $S - c$ (S_T denotes the price of the stock at date T):

	Initial outlay	Outcome: $S_T > X$	Outcome: $S_T \leq X$
Buy one call option	$-c$	$S_T - X$	0
Short sell stock	$+S$	$-S_T$	$-S_T$
Make a loan	$-(S-c)$	$R(S-c)$	$R(S-c)$
	0	$R(S-c) - X$	$R(S-c) - S_T$

At the expiry date, either $S_T > X$, in which case the option is exercised, or $S_T \leq X$, in which case the option dies.[9] Suppose that $S_T > X$, so that the payoff is $R(S - c) - X$. From (18.6) the payoff is positive.

Suppose instead that $S_T \leq X$, so that the payoff is

$$R(S - c) - S_T = R(S - c) - X + (X - S_T) > 0 \tag{18.7}$$

because $R(S - c) - X > 0$ and $X - S_T \geq 0$.

Thus, if (18.5) holds, a portfolio with zero initial outlay yields a positive return whatever the asset price, S_T, at date T. This is an arbitrage portfolio with a positive payoff in both states. From the arbitrage principle, it cannot be consistent with market equilibrium. Hence, (18.4) must hold in the absence of arbitrage opportunities in a frictionless market.

---

[9] If $S_T = X$, nothing would be affected if the option is exercised.

Appendix 18.2: Lower bound for a European put option premium

Recall that the bound states that

$$p \geq \max\left[0, \frac{X}{R(t, T)} - S\right] \tag{18.8}$$

The inequality is demonstrated by showing that, if it does not hold, arbitrage profits can be made in a frictionless market. Begin by assuming the contrary to (18.8):

$$p < \frac{X}{R} - S \tag{18.9}$$

where $p > 0$. Note for later reference that, because $R > 0$, (18.9) is equivalent to

$$X - (S + p)R > 0 \tag{18.10}$$

Now construct a portfolio, with zero initial outlay, by purchasing one put option for p, buying one unit of stock for S and borrowing $S + p$:

	Initial outlay	Outcome: $S_T \geq X$	Outcome: $S_T < X$
Buy one put option	$-p$	0	$X - S_T$
Buy one unit of stock	$-S$	S_T	S_T
Borrow	$S + p$	$-R(S + p)$	$-R(S + p)$
	0	$S_T - R(S + p)$	$X - R(S + p)$

At the expiry date, either $S_T < X$, in which case the option is exercised, or $S_T \geq X$, in which case the option dies.[10]

Suppose that $S_T < X$, so that the payoff is $X - R(S + p)$. From (18.10) the payoff is positive.

Suppose instead that $S_T \geq X$, with payoff

$$S_T - R(S + p) = S_T - X + X - R(S + p) > 0$$

because $X - R(S + p) > 0$ and $S_T - X \geq 0$.

Thus, if (18.9) holds, a portfolio with zero initial outlay yields a positive return whatever the price S_T at date T. This is an arbitrage portfolio with a positive payoff in both states. By the arbitrage principle, it cannot be consistent with market equilibrium. Hence, (18.8) must hold in the absence of arbitrage opportunities in a frictionless market.

[10] If $S_T = X$, nothing would be affected if the option is exercised.

Appendix 18.3: Put-call parity for European options

This appendix establishes the parity relationship in a more formal way than in the text, using symbols instead of a numerical example. Recall that the parity relationship states that

$$c + \frac{X}{R(t,T)} = p + S$$

The proof follows a familiar pattern, showing that, if the relationship fails, arbitrage profits can be made in frictionless markets. Given that the absence of arbitrage profits is a criterion for market equilibrium, the equality must hold. Two analogous arguments are needed: one if '>' replaces the equality, a second for '<'.

Suppose, first, that $c + X/R > p + S$ (where the arguments of $R(t,T)$ are omitted for convenience). For later reference, rearrange the inequality

$$X - R(p + S - c) > 0 \tag{18.11}$$

which holds because $R > 0$.

Consider the following strategy: buy one unit of stock for S, buy one put for p, write one call for c and borrow $B = p - c + S$, so that the strategy requires zero initial outlay.[11]

	Initial outlay	At expiry, T	
		$S_T > X$	$S_T \leqq X$
Buy one put option	$-p$	0	$X - S_T$
Write one call option	$+c$	$X - S_T$	0
Buy one unit of stock	$-S$	S_T	S_T
Borrow	B	$-RB$	$-RB$
	0	$X - RB$	$X - RB$

The table shows that, if $S_T > X$, the call option is exercised and the put option is allowed to die. Conversely, if $S_T \leq X$, the put option is exercised and the call option is allowed to die. The payoff is the same in either case. From (18.11), $X - RB = X - R(p - c + S) > 0$. Hence, the payoff is positive irrespective of whether S_T is greater than, less than or equal to X.

Thus, if $c + X/R > p + S$, a portfolio with zero initial outlay yields a positive return whatever the price S_T at date T. This is an arbitrage portfolio with a

[11] Note that B could be positive or negative. If $B < 0$, the strategy involves lending. In a frictionless market, lending is simply negative borrowing.

positive payoff in both states. By the arbitrage principle, it cannot be consistent with market equilibrium.

Suppose now that the put-call parity is violated with $c + X/R < p + S$. Rearranging the inequality, it follows that

$$-X - R(c - p - S) > 0 \qquad (18.12)$$

Consider the following strategy: short-sell one unit of stock, write one put, buy one call and borrow $B = c - p - S$, so that the strategy requires zero initial outlay. (Because B could be of either sign, remember that $B < 0$ is interpreted as lending.)

	Initial outlay	At expiry, T	
		$S_T > X$	$S_T \leq X$
Write one put option	$+p$	0	$S_T - X$
Buy one call option	$-c$	$S_T - X$	0
Sell one unit of stock	$+S$	$-S_T$	$-S_T$
Borrow	$+B$	$-RB$	$-RB$
	0	$-X - RB$	$-X - RB$

Once again, the table shows that the payoff is the same whatever the outcome. From (18.12), $-X - RB = -X - R(c - p - S) > 0$ by hypothesis. Hence, the payoff is positive no matter whether S_T is greater than, less than or equal to X. Consequently, if $c + X/R < p + S$, a portfolio with zero initial outlay yields a positive return whatever the outcome: there is an arbitrage opportunity.

In conclusion, if the put-call parity relationship is violated with either inequality, arbitrage profits can be made in frictionless markets. Hence, the put-call parity relationship holds under the stated conditions.

Appendix 18.4: The Modigliani–Miller theorem: a proof

Section 18.6, above, describes how the MM theorem can be illustrated using the put-call parity relationship, with the market value of the firm, S, equal to the value of its shares, c (a call option on the firm's assets at date T), plus the value of the risky bonds it has issued, $(X/R) - p$; i.e. $S = c + (X/R) - p$. In order to prove the MM theorem, it must be shown that S is invariant with respect to its debt obligation, X (the amount promised to bondholders at date T). That is, it must be shown that the value of S is the same for any value of X. It suffices to compare the outcomes for any two levels of X – say, $X_1 \neq X_2$.

An arbitrage argument proves that the value of the asset underlying the options is invariant with respect to the options' exercise price. Suppose not. In particular, assume that

$$c_1 + \frac{X_1}{R} - p_1 < c_2 + \frac{X_2}{R} - p_2 \qquad (18.13)$$

where c_1, p_1 are the option values corresponding to the exercise price, X_1, and c_2, p_2 are the option values corresponding to X_2.[12] For later reference, note that (18.13) can be rearranged as $X_2 - X_1 - R(c_1 - p_1 - c_2 + p_2) > 0$.

Consider the following strategy (portfolio): (i) write one call option for c_2, buy one put option for p_2; (ii) buy one call option for c_1, write one put option for p_1; (iii) borrow[13] $B = c_1 - p_1 - c_2 + p_2$, such that the initial outlay is zero.

Now, if it can be shown that the portfolio yields a positive payoff for at least one value of S_T and a non-negative payoff for all, there is an arbitrage opportunity, and the configuration of prices assumed in (18.13) cannot be compatible with market equilibrium (an absence of arbitrage opportunities).

To demonstrate that there is indeed an arbitrage opportunity, consider separately the three components of the strategy.

Payoff from (i): $- \max[0, S_T - X_2] + \max[0, X_2 - S_T] = X_2 - S_T$
Payoff from (ii): $\max[0, S_T - X_1] - \max[0, X_1 - S_T] = S_T - X_1$
Payoff from (iii): $-RB = -R(c_1 - p_1 - c_2 + p_2)$

Sum the payoffs from each of the three components, (i), (ii) and (iii), to give the overall payoff:

$$X_2 - S_T + S_T - X_1 - R(c_1 - p_1 - c_2 + p_2)$$
$$= X_2 - X_1 - R(c_1 - p_1 - c_2 + p_2) > 0 \qquad (18.14)$$

Notice that, before date T, S_T is the only unknown quantity in (18.14). As S_T cancels from (18.14), the payoff is certain (i.e. independent of the state of the world). From (18.13), the payoff is positive, implying that the strategy provides an arbitrage opportunity. This is incompatible with market equilibrium. Hence, the inequality cannot hold.

It is straightforward to establish the same conclusion if the '<' in (18.13) is replaced with '>'. For completeness, here are the steps. Suppose that

$$c_1 + \frac{X_1}{R} - p_1 > c_2 + \frac{X_2}{R} - p_2$$

---

[12] Thus, for example, c_2 is shorthand for the value of the call option with exercise price X_2 at date t and expiry date T: $c_2 \equiv c(X_2, t, T)$. More generally, $c_i \equiv c(X_i, t, T)$ and $p_i \equiv p(X_i, t, T)$. The arguments of $R(t, T)$ are omitted to reduce clutter.

[13] Lending corresponds to negative borrowing.

which implies that $X_1 - X_2 - R(c_2 - p_2 - c_1 + p_1) > 0$. Consider the following strategy: (i′) write one call option for c_1, buy one put option for p_1; (ii′) buy one call option for c_2, write one put option for p_2; (iii′) borrow $B = c_2 - p_2 - c_1 + p_1$, such that the initial outlay is zero.

The payoffs are as follows.

Payoff from (i′): $-\max[0, S_T - X_1] + \max[0, X_1 - S_T] = X_1 - S_T$
Payoff from (ii′): $\max[0, S_T - X_2] - \max[0, X_2 - S_T] = S_T - X_2$
Payoff from (iii′): $-RB = -R(c_2 - p_2 - c_1 + p_1)$

Sum the payoffs from each of the three components, (i′), (ii′) and (iii′), to give the overall payoff:

$$X_1 - S_T + S_T - X_2 - R(c_2 - p_2 - c_1 + p_1)$$
$$= X_1 - X_2 - R(c_2 - p_2 - c_1 + p_1) > 0$$

Once again, as asserted, the strategy's payoff is positive irrespective of the value of S_T: there is an arbitrage opportunity. Hence, the inequality cannot hold in market equilibrium.

The reasoning shows that the value of S in (18.3) does not depend on the value of X. In words: the market value of the firm is invariant with respect to the size of its debt, thus proving the MM theorem. Needless to say, the result depends on the assumption of frictionless markets; disputes about precisely how this is to be interpreted in the context of the MM theorem provide limitless opportunities for debate in the study of corporate finance.

References

Abel, A. (ed.) (1980), *The Collected Papers of Franco Modigliani*, Cambridge, MA: MIT Press (three volumes).

Cox, J. C., and M. Rubinstein (1985), *Options Markets*, Englewood Cliffs, NJ: Prentice Hall.

Dixit, A. K., and R. S. Pindyck (1994), *Investment under Uncertainty*, Princeton, NJ: Princeton University Press.

Edwards, F. R., and C. W. Ma (1992), *Futures and Options*, New York: McGraw-Hill.

Elton, E. J., M. J. Gruber, S. J. Brown and W. N. Goetzmann (2003), *Modern Portfolio Theory and Investment Analysis*, New York: John Wiley & Sons, 6th edn.

Hull, J. C. (2005), *Fundamentals of Futures and Options Markets*, Englewood Cliffs, NJ: Prentice Hall, 5th edn.

Merton, R. C. (1990), *Continuous Time Finance*, Cambridge, MA, and Oxford: Blackwell.

Miller, M. H. (1988), 'The Modigliani–Miller propositions after thirty years', *Journal of Economic Perspectives*, 2(4), pp. 99–120.

Miller, M. H., and F. Modigliani (1961), 'Dividend policy, growth, and the valuation of shares', *Journal of Business*, 34(4), pp. 411–33 (reprinted as chap. 2 in Abel (1980, Vol. III)).

Modigliani, F., and M. H. Miller (1958), 'The cost of capital, corporation investment, and the theory of investment', *American Economic Review*, 48(3), pp. 261–97 (reprinted as chap. 1 in Abel (1980, Vol. III)).

(1963), 'Corporate income taxes and the cost of capital: a correction', *American Economic Review*, 53(3), pp. 433–43 (reprinted as chap. 3 in Abel (1980, Vol. III)).

Newman, P., M. Milgate and J. Eatwell (eds.) (1992), *The New Palgrave Dictionary of Money and Finance*, London: Macmillan (three volumes).

Rubinstein, M. (1987), 'Derivative assets analysis', *Journal of Economic Perspectives*, 1(2), pp. 73–93.

Stoll, H. R. (1969), 'The relationship between put and call option prices', *Journal of Finance*, 24(5), pp. 801–24.

Varian, H. R. (1987), 'The arbitrage principle in financial economics', *Journal of Economic Perspectives*, 1(2), pp. 55–72.

19

Options markets II: price determination

Overview

In chapter 18 bounds were obtained on the range of option prices compatible with the absence of arbitrage opportunities. No attempt was made, however, to predict the level of an option price. This is the purpose of the present chapter. While attention concentrates throughout on the arbitrage principle, extra assumptions are required about the determinants of the underlying asset price in order to obtain the option price itself. Armed with these extra assumptions, the objective is to obtain a formula for an option price, where the arguments of the formula comprise a set of explanatory variables including, among other things, the option's exercise price and its time to expiry.

Very often the aim of the analysis is expressed in terms of determining the 'fair' option price, or of option 'valuation'. This approach typically makes most sense for an over-the-counter option that is not exchange traded, where the goal is to calculate the option's price *as if* the option were openly traded in the absence of arbitrage opportunities – and together with the other assumptions needed to make the calculation. It should be obvious that the 'fair' price depends on the assumptions of a model, but in practice it is often overlooked that the computed value may well be sensitive to the model on which it is based.

Section 19.1 outlines the assumptions common to most option price theories and describes the method of analysis. While the theory applies to any underlying asset on which options can be traded, there is no harm in assuming that the asset in question is a unit of stock (one ordinary share) issued by a publicly quoted corporation. Also, where no ambiguity would result, the asset underlying the option is simply referred to as 'the asset'.

Section 19.2 presents the simplest theory of option prices and shows how an arbitrage argument can be used to predict the price of a call option, albeit under an unrealistic 'two-state' assumption. Section 19.3 introduces the famous

Black–Scholes model, named after Fischer Black and Myron Scholes, whose famous paper in the *Journal of Political Economy* (1973) contains the original statement of the model. Although known as the Black–Scholes model, the theory was, in fact, developed jointly by Black, Scholes and Robert Merton in the late 1960s.[1]

The Merton–Black–Scholes analysis does not apply just to options, narrowly defined, but extends also to the broader class of contingent claims. An introduction to this analysis is outlined in section 19.4.

19.1 The fundamentals of option price models

The goal of an option price model is to construct a formula that expresses an option's price as a function of a small number of explanatory variables. The standard explanatory variables are (i) the asset's price, S; (ii) the option's exercise price, X; (iii) the option's time to expiry, $\tau \equiv T - t$; (iv) the interest factor, $R(t, T)$; and (v) a measure of the volatility in the rate of return on the asset.

For the simple model studied in section 19.2, the volatility could be measured as the difference between the asset price in the event that it rises minus the price in the event that it falls, divided by today's observed price. In the Black–Scholes model, volatility is measured by the standard deviation (or its square, the variance) of the rate of return on the asset. The index of volatility is typically denoted by σ.

The option price theories studied in this chapter apply the arbitrage principle to derive a function, $f(\cdot)$, such that

$$c = f(S, X, \tau, R, \sigma) \tag{19.1}$$

where c is the premium for a European call option. Each of S, τ, R and, perhaps, σ are functions of time, t, though this is not made explicit in (19.1). The formula for a European *put* option would have the same arguments and is obtained using the put-call parity relationship, or, from scratch, in the same way as for the call option.

It should be noted that equation (19.1) *links* the derivative (i.e. option) price, c, with the asset price, S. The option price is conditional on the asset price. The formula does not purport to represent a general theory of option prices. Here, 'general' refers to a theory that determines *both* c and S simultaneously as functions of fundamental influences, such as investor preferences and the stocks of assets. The principles upon which the pricing formula rests, as for all arbitrage reasoning, serve only to link security prices. Partial though it is,

---

[1] Merton's (1973) paper stands alongside that of Black and Scholes as the other seminal contribution to the theory of options. See Bernstein (1992) for an account of the pioneering research from which these papers emerged. Merton and Scholes were joint winners of the 1997 Nobel Memorial Prize for economics in recognition of their contribution (Black had died in 1995).

the model's strength is that it makes only a mild assumption about investors' preferences (that more wealth is preferred to less), and, consequently, it is widely applicable.

Every option held by an investor must have been written by another investor. In other words, the net total of options in existence must always be zero. It is reasonable, therefore, to postulate that the asset price, S, is independent of the option – the, so-called, 'bucket shop' assumption. Consequently it makes sense to interpret causation as going from S to c, rather than that the two prices are jointly determined.[2]

It is important to be aware that every option price model relies on assumptions about the distribution of S beyond the condition (essentially, frictionless markets) needed to apply the arbitrage principle. The nature of these additional assumptions is explored in sections 19.2 and 19.3. Predicted option prices are not solely an implication of the absence of arbitrage opportunities but depend also on the form taken by the distribution of S. The significance of this fact will emerge as the analysis unfolds.

Various methods of deriving option price formul appear in the literature. Although the methods may appear somewhat different, on closer inspection they are equivalent. Among the frequently encountered approaches are these.

1. Construct a portfolio of the option and the asset in such a way that the value of the portfolio is independent of S. (This is the so-called 'hedged position' in Black and Scholes, 1973.) Given that S is the only source of uncertainty, the value of the portfolio is certain. It is risk free. In the absence of arbitrage opportunities, the portfolio must yield the risk-free rate on the capital invested in it.

2. Construct a portfolio of risk-free borrowing or lending and the asset, such that the payoff on the portfolio in each state exactly equals the option's payoff in the same state – the payoffs on the portfolio *replicate* those of the option. In the absence of arbitrage opportunities, the value of the option must equal the value of the portfolio.

3. Direct application of the arbitrage principle. Construct a portfolio comprising (a) options, (b) the asset and (c) risk free borrowing or lending, such that the portfolio (i) requires zero initial capital outlay and (ii) has a non-negative payoff in every state. In the absence of arbitrage opportunities, the portfolio must yield a zero payoff in every state. The conditions that must be satisfied are sufficient to determine the option price.

Each of the three approaches results in the same option price, given the process assumed to generate the asset price, S, and for given values of the explanatory variables in the option formula, equation (19.1).

---

[2] This would not be true for warrants, the exercise of which increases the total number of the issuing firm's shares in existence. See Merton (1973, footnote 4) for the origin of the term 'bucket shop' in this context.

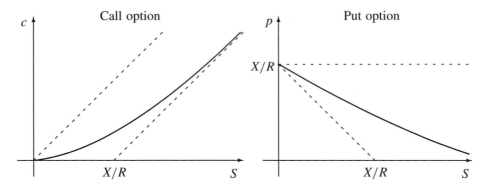

Fig. 19.1. Call and put option prices as a function of the asset price, S

The solid line in each panel depicts the option premium as a function of the underlying asset price (for given values of the other determinants of the option premium). Markets are assumed to be in equilibrium if, and only if, arbitrage opportunities are absent. Hence, the heavy lines appear in the regions (delimited with dashed lines) for which arbitrage profits are zero.

Figure 19.1 depicts European call and put option prices as functions of S. The diagrams indicate that c and p obey the bounds established in chapter 18, namely $S \geq c \geq \max[0, S - X/R]$ and $X/R \geq p \geq \max[0, X/R - S]$. The bounds serve to limit the admissible range of option prices in the absence of arbitrage opportunities. The additional assumptions, mentioned above, then determine the precise value of each option price (i.e. where it lies within the bounds).

The following assumptions are required in almost every model of option prices.

1. *Frictionless markets*: zero transaction costs and no institutional restrictions on trading. More precisely,

    (a) transaction costs are zero for trading in the option and in the asset;
    (b) borrowing or lending in unlimited amounts is possible at the same, given and constant (risk-free) interest rate;
    (c) it is possible to short-sell the asset without any penalties or restrictions; and
    (d) the asset is perfectly divisible, such that any fraction of a unit can be purchased or sold.

2. *Options contracts*:

    (a) the asset pays zero dividends during the life of the option, and the option is protected against stock splits;
    (b) the option is European: exercise is permissible only at the expiry date.

Although these assumptions can be relaxed to some extent (e.g. the interest rate does not have to be constant over time), it should be no surprise that frictionless markets are needed if the arbitrage principle is to make any definite predictions about prices.

19.2 A two-state option-pricing model

The model studied in this section is simple, because (a) there is exactly one unit time interval, $T - t = 1$, until the option expires, and (b) there are exactly two states of the world: at date T the asset price moves to one of two values, uS or dS, where u and d are positive numbers and S is the asset price observed at the outset (date t). It is not known *which* of the two states will occur. It is not necessary to assign probabilities, subjective or objective, to the states.

This approach can be extended to any number of unit intervals – hours, days, weeks, or whatever – between the present and the expiry date of the option. During each unit interval the asset price can move to one of two possible values. The result is the *binomial* model of option prices.[3] Although it may seem absurd to assume that the asset price can change to only one of two possible values each unit interval, the binomial model can be used as a starting point for other models, such as the Black–Scholes model. Also, the binomial model can be used as a practical device to obtain approximate option prices corresponding to more complicated contracts for which no explicit formula is available.

The reasoning outlined below is as follows: a portfolio consisting of call options, the asset and borrowing (or lending) is constructed such that (a) it requires zero initial capital, and (b) it is risk-free (in the sense of resulting in a non-negative payoff in every state). Given that market equilibrium requires the absence of arbitrage opportunities, the portfolio must yield a zero payoff in every state. Together, these conditions imply a unique equilibrium option price (given S, X, and r).[4] Any other option price would provide an arbitrage opportunity.

To grasp the reasoning, consider a numerical example in which the values of S, X, u, d and $R(t, T)$ are specified. The value of c is then derived in such a way that a portfolio with zero initial outlay yields a zero payoff regardless of whether S changes to uS (state 1) or dS (state 2). Suppose that $S = 80$, $X = 88$, $u = 1.6$, $d = 0.6$ and $r = 20\%$ per time period. Assume that interest is paid at T

---

[3] See Cox, Ross and Rubinstein (1979), the approach of whom is followed closely here.

[4] The exercise price, X, is chosen such that the option is worth exercising – it is 'in the money' – in at least one state (otherwise the option would be worthless at the outset). That is, for a call option, either $uS > X$ or $dS > X$, or both. For a put option, either $uS < X$ or $dS < X$, or both. If the same parameter values are to be used for both calls and puts, X would be chosen such that $uS > X$ and $dS < X$. Also, $R < u$ and $R > d$: otherwise, arbitrage profits can be made by trading in the asset and borrowing or lending alone, without involving options at all.

with no compounding, and $T - t = 1$. Hence, $R(t, T) = (1 + r) = 1.20$. Thus, the asset price starts at 80 and rises to 128 (state 1) or falls to 48 (state 2).[5]

The portfolio decision involves choosing the number of shares, N, to buy ($N > 0$) or to sell ($N < 0$); the number of option contracts, M, to buy ($M > 0$) or to write ($M < 0$); and the amount of borrowing, $B > 0$, or lending, $B < 0$.[6]

The goal is to choose N, M and B such that the initial outlay is zero. If the payoff is zero in each state (an absence of arbitrage opportunities), then the option premium, c, will be determined uniquely. Consider the table:

	Initial Outlay	State 1 $uS = 128$	State 2 $dS = 48$
Option contracts	$-Mc$	$(128 - 88)M$	0
Shares	$-80N$	$128N$	$48N$
Borrowing	$+B$	$-1.2B$	$-1.2B$
Total	$B - 80N - Mc$	$40M + 128N - 1.2B$	$48N - 1.2B$

From this information it is possible to determine the relationships that must exist among M, N and B to yield a zero payoff in each state. These relationships, together with the zero initial outlay, determine the equilibrium value of c.

Step 1: In state 2, $B/N = 40$.

Step 2: Using $B/N = 40$ from step 1, it follows that $40M + (128/40)B - 1.2B = 0$ in state 1. Hence, $40M + 3.2B - 1.2B = 0$, and $B/M = -20$. Also note that $N/M = -1/2$.

Step 3: Write the initial outlay as

$$M(-20 - (-1/2) \times 80 - c) = 0$$
$$M(-20 + 40 - c) = 0$$
$$20 - c = 0$$

Note that M cancels out, reflecting the arbitrary scaling of any arbitrage portfolio, and the option's price is $c = 20$.

---

[5] The units of measurement are dollars, pounds, euros, or whatever – i.e. the relevant unit of account. From now on the arguments to the interest factor are omitted: $R \equiv R(t, T)$, when $T - t = 1$.

[6] Each option contract is assumed to be for the purchase of one share. The amount of borrowing is measured in units of account.

To make the example more concrete, suppose that an investor writes two options, buys one share and borrows 40. The total initial outlay is $2c - 80 + 40 = 2c - 40$, and the payoff in each state is zero:

	Initial Outlay	State 1 $uS = 128$	State 2 $dS = 48$
Option contracts	$+2c$	$-2 \times (128 - 88)$	0
Shares	-80	$+128$	$+48$
Borrowing	$+40$	-1.2×40	-1.2×40
Net total	$2c - 40$	0	0

In state 1 the asset is worth 128, but the options are exercised against the investor, resulting in a loss of 80, and the loan is repaid at a cost of 48, resulting in a net payoff of zero $= 128 - 80 - 48$. In state 2 the share is worth 48, the option dies unexercised and the loan is repaid with a payment of 48, again resulting in a net payoff of zero.

Given that the payoff for the portfolio is zero in both states, in the absence of arbitrage opportunities it must have zero initial outlay. Hence, $2c - 40 = 0$ and the equilibrium option price must be $c = 20$.

It should be emphasized that, in the absence of arbitrage opportunities, *any* portfolio (N, M and B) that yields a zero payoff in every state and zero initial outlay results in an option price $c = 20$. In common with all arbitrage portfolios, there is an element of arbitrariness about the composition of the portfolio: buying two options, selling one share and lending forty serves to obtain the result equally well. Similarly, writing ten options, buying five shares and borrowing 200 also works. What matters is to *find a portfolio such that the payoff in every state is zero*. In the absence of arbitrage opportunities, the initial outlay for such a portfolio equals zero, and hence the equilibrium option price can be determined.

Interpretation in terms of a replicating portfolio

Consider a portfolio of the asset and debt that *replicates* the payoff from the option – i.e. the payoff from the portfolio equals the payoff from the option in each state. In the absence of arbitrage opportunities, it follows that the initial value of such a portfolio must exactly equal the market value of the option that it replicates.

This is exactly what happens in the argument above. The payoff from the portfolio in each state equals the payoff from the option with the opposite sign, positive or negative; together they add to zero. The option price is determined such that the initial outlay is zero; the initial value of the portfolio (of shares and debt) equals the value of the option, again with the opposite sign.

19.2.1 An option price formula

One way of obtaining a formula for the call option price in the simple model described above is to invoke the risk-neutral valuation relationship (see chapter 7). The RNVR states that, in the absence of arbitrage opportunities, there exists a set of artificial 'martingale' probabilities such that the price of each option can be written as the NPV of the option's expected payoff (where the discount factor is defined using the risk-free rate of return and the expectation is calculated using the martingale probabilities).

To understand how this works, begin by writing the payoff (expiry value) of the option in terms of uS and dS:

$$c_u = \max[0, uS - X] \quad \text{in state 1} \qquad c_d = \max[0, dS - X] \quad \text{in state 2}$$

Also note that $R = (1 + r)$ is the interest factor, so that expected payoffs are discounted by dividing by R.

The following table lists the two states, the martingale probabilities together with the payoffs on the option and the asset:

	Martingale probability	Option payoff	Asset payoff
State 1	π	c_u	uS
State 2	$1 - \pi$	c_d	dS

The RNVR implies that the option price is the discounted value of the expected payoff of the option:

$$c = \frac{\pi c_u + (1 - \pi)c_d}{R} \tag{19.2}$$

Notice that the only unknown argument in (19.2) is π.

The value of π is determined by applying the RNVR to the asset price:

$$S = \frac{\pi uS + (1 - \pi)dS}{R} \tag{19.3}$$

In (19.3), S can be cancelled from both sides. Solving for π and $1 - \pi$ gives

$$\pi \equiv \frac{R - d}{u - d}$$

$$\text{and} \quad 1 - \pi \equiv \frac{u - R}{u - d}$$

With π known, the option price, c, is determined from equation (19.2).

An inspection of equation (19.2) reveals that the pricing formula for options requires *no* information about investors' preferences (i.e. their attitudes to risk). Investors' beliefs are expressed via the values uS and dS to which the asset price moves in states 1 and 2, respectively. No assumption is needed about whether investors assign probabilities, subjective or otherwise, to the states. The irrelevance of investors' preferences should be no surprise given that the reasoning relies on the arbitrage principle. The assumption that the asset price changes to either uS or dS serves as a reminder that predicted option prices are not solely a consequence of the absence of arbitrage opportunities (i.e. the simple two-state assumption expresses the 'distribution of S' mentioned earlier).

The RNVR is, of course, not the only way to obtain (19.2). An argument from first principles can be made by rewriting the payoffs in the example using symbols rather than numbers:

	Initial outlay	State 1 Asset price $= uS$	State 2 Asset price $= dS$
Option contracts	$-Mc$	Mc_u	Mc_d
Shares	$-NS$	NuS	NdS
Borrowing	B	$-RB$	$-RB$
Net total	$B - NS - Mc$	$Mc_u + NuS - RB$	$Mc_d + NdS - RB$

The goal is to find an expression for c in terms of S, X, u, d and R, but excluding the chosen B, M and N. The steps are exactly the same as for the numerical example: find the set of values of the portfolio (B, M, N) such that the payoff in each state is zero. Substitute these values into the cost of the initial portfolio $B - NS - Mc$. Set this equal to zero and, hence, obtain the equilibrium value of c. Elementary but tedious algebraic manipulations result in equation (19.2).

19.2.2 *Price of a European put option*

Similar reasoning to that outlined above shows that the price of a European put option in the two-state framework is given by

$$p = \frac{\pi p_u + (1 - \pi)p_d}{R} \qquad (19.4)$$

where

$$p_u = \max[0, X - uS] \quad \text{in state 1} \quad \text{and} \quad p_d = \max[0, X - dS] \quad \text{in state 2} \quad (19.5)$$

There are several ways to obtain (19.4). One way is to apply the RNVR. Another is to reason from first principles, just as for the call option. Yet another is to apply the put-call parity relationship (see chapter 18, page 454).

19.2.3 Multiple time periods to expiry of the option: the binomial model

The analysis so far can be extended to cover circumstances where there are any number of unit time intervals between the present, t, and the option expiry date, T. Suppose that there are exactly two periods to expiry, with $t = 0$ and $T = 2$. The asset price changes, first, to either uS or dS and then, in the second period, either (a) from uS to u^2S or udS, or (b) from dS to udS or d^2S. See figure 19.2.

To understand how the call option premium can be derived, begin at date 2 and consider the ways in which each outcome can arise from date 1. Clearly, u^2S can occur only from uS at date 1; udS can occur from either uS or dS; and d^2S can occur only from dS. Now work back from date 2 to date 1, using the argument for an option with just one period to expiry. This provides a value (generally not zero) needed at date 1 in each of the two possible events such that the payoffs at date 2 would be obtained. Treat the date 1 payoffs as if they are the terminal values of the option, and then use the same principles to obtain the option value today, date 0.

More explicitly, write the three possible values of the option at date 2 as:

state 1: $c_{uu} = \max[0, u^2S - X]$, the value of the option when u^2S occurs;
state 2: $c_{ud} = \max[0, udS - X]$, the value of the option when udS occurs; and
state 3: $c_{dd} = \max[0, d^2S - X]$, the value of the option when d^2S occurs.

From equation (19.2), using the same definition of π, the option value at date 1 will have one of two possible values:

$$\text{at } uS: \quad c_u = \frac{\pi c_{uu} + (1 - \pi)c_{ud}}{R} \tag{19.6}$$

$$\text{at } dS: \quad c_d = \frac{\pi c_{ud} + (1 - \pi)c_{dd}}{R} \tag{19.7}$$

At date 0, today, using (19.2) again and substituting from (19.6) and (19.7), the option price is

$$c = \frac{\pi c_u + (1 - \pi)c_d}{R}$$

$$= \frac{\pi^2 c_{uu} + 2\pi(1 - \pi)c_{ud} + (1 - \pi)^2 c_{dd}}{R^2} \tag{19.8}$$

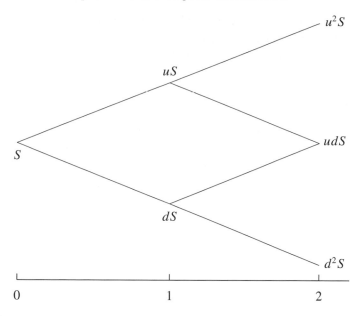

Fig. 19.2. The pattern of underlying asset prices: the two-period case

At date 1 the underlying asset price moves up to uS or down to dS. Starting from uS at date 1, at date 2 the asset price moves up to $u \times uS \equiv u^2S$ or down to $d \times uS \equiv udS$. Starting from dS at date 1, at date 2 the asset price moves up to $u \times dS \equiv udS$ or down to $d \times dS \equiv d^2S$.

Formula (19.8) has exactly the same interpretation as in the one-period case. The martingale probabilities corresponding to the three states (at date 2) are π^2, $2\pi(1-\pi)$ and $(1-\pi)^2$, respectively; the discount factor between dates 0 and 2 is $1/R^2$; and the RNVR implies that the option price today is the NPV of the expected payoff using the martingale probabilities.

Not surprisingly, the formula becomes more complicated as the number of periods is increased. But the principle remains the same. The result is the so-called binomial option pricing model. Cumbersome though it might appear, the method outlined above is commonly used in the construction of option prices, especially for complicated or non-standard option contracts that are not widely traded (or not traded at all) in organized markets. Computer algorithms for calculating these prices are often based on this approach.

The binomial model is also useful as a way of gaining insights into the Black–Scholes model, discussed below. In the analysis so far, no specific calendar time is associated with the unit time interval. That is, it is possible to interpret the entire period from 0 to T as being one interval of length T, or two intervals each of length $T/2$, or three intervals each of length $T/3$, and so on. More generally, suppose that there are n intervals each of length T/n. If the number of intervals is allowed to increase indefinitely, the values to which the asset price can move must be adjusted accordingly. This adjustment can be made in a variety of ways, with each leading potentially to a different limiting result. At this point the mathematical technicalities become delicate.

One limiting process corresponds to that in which the asset price does not change at all in most time intervals but experiences discrete changes (up or down) at infrequent instants of time. In this case, the limiting result is a so-called 'jump process'. Such an approach – assuming a Poisson distribution to model the jumps – has been the subject of research for circumstances in which asset prices evolve smoothly, except for occasional abrupt changes (the jumps).

Another limiting process leads to the crucial assumption on which the Black–Scholes model rests. Here, in each unit time interval the asset price is assumed either to increase by a constant amount or to decrease by a constant amount. (The values of the increase and the decrease are not necessarily equal.) As n, the number of unit time intervals, becomes large, the process can be understood to assert that the asset price changes in a continuous way without discrete jumps. It is as if a graph of S as a function of time can be drawn without taking the pen off the paper (whereas a jump process would require lifting the pen at the instant a discrete jump occurs). In plain words, this is, essentially, the assumption made about the evolution of the asset price in the Black–Scholes model.

Perhaps a more realistic assumption would be that S is continuous for most of the time, punctuated at isolated dates by discrete changes – i.e. the combination of a continuous process and a jump process, as mentioned above. Figure 19.3 shows example sample paths (i.e. hypothetical outcomes over a given time period) corresponding to the two assumptions. Panel (a) assumes that the asset price changes continuously (the limit of a sequence of 'small' price changes). In panel (b) the asset price jumps at dates A, B and C.[7]

While figure 19.3 results from two quite different assumptions about the random processes generating asset prices, in empirical applications the two are not so easy to distinguish. For discrete jumps, such as at A, B and C, might be approximated as steep – but nonetheless smooth – changes in a continuous sample path. Equally, some of the steeper changes in the continuous sample path could be more appropriately interpreted as discrete jumps. While the evidence may favour one assumption over the other, inevitably both are idealizations. It is never possible

---

[7] Strictly, the continuous lines shown in figure 19.3 are constructed as approximations to geometric Brownian motion – an assumption central to the Black–Scholes model (see section 19.3).

(a) Continuous sample path

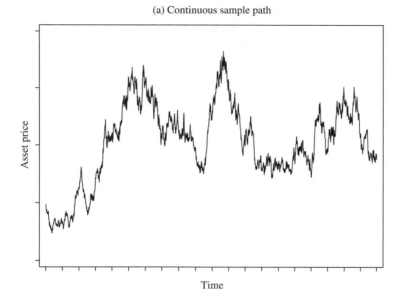

(b) Sample path with discrete jumps

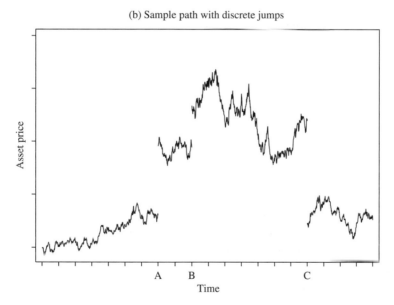

Fig. 19.3. Sample paths for asset prices in continuous time

Panel (a) shows the sample path (a hypothetical realization of the asset price over a given time period) for an asset price that changes smoothly, as an approximation to geometric Brownian motion. In panel (b) the asset price changes smoothly except at dates A, B and C, when it makes a discrete jump (up or down).

to know for sure which the true (whatever 'true' is supposed to mean in this context) random process is that generates the realized asset prices. Ultimately, the issue boils down to one of modelling tactics, namely to adopt the assumption that does least injustice to the data – always a formidable challenge.

19.3 The Black–Scholes model

19.3.1 Assumptions of the Black–Scholes model

Formally, the Black–Scholes model makes two assumptions in addition to those listed in section 19.1, above.

1. Trading takes place continuously throughout time. Obviously, this assumption cannot be taken literally, but it follows by allowing the number of unit time intervals (described at the end of the previous section) to become indefinitely large. The relevant issue is whether the assumption provides an acceptable approximation to trading in options markets.[8]

2. The asset price, S, evolves according to a *geometric* (or logarithmic) *Brownian motion* process with continuous sample paths. The formal statement of this assumption involves specialist mathematics and only a sketch is given here. The idea is, roughly, that the change in the logarithm of S over any short interval of time is identically and independently distributed with a Normal distribution, characterized by its expectation, μ, and variance, σ^2. In symbols, $\ln S_{t+\varepsilon} - \ln S_t$ is independently and Normally distributed for every $\varepsilon > 0$, no matter how small.

   Recall from elementary probability theory that the Normal distribution has the familiar, symmetric 'bell-shaped' density function completely characterized by two parameters, its expectation, μ, and its variance, σ^2. Assuming that the asset does not pay a dividend over the time interval in question, its rate of return is equal to its capital gain or loss.

   More formally, the asset's rate of return is equal to the proportional rate of change in S, written as $\ln S_{t+\varepsilon} - \ln S_t$ for arbitrarily small ε.[9] The expectation of this rate of return is denoted by μ. Its standard deviation, σ, is a measure of the variability of the rate of return on the asset.

   It is well known in probability theory that the Normal distribution can be deduced as the limit of the binomial distribution if the limit is taken in the way described, rather simplistically, in the previous section. What makes the mathematics difficult is that the time interval over which the price changes take place is arbitrarily short (infinitesimal).

---

[8] It can be argued that the assumption of continuous trading is really an *implication* of an earlier assumption, namely that of frictionless markets. From this perspective, transaction costs are what cause trading to take place only at discrete instants of time.

[9] For time intervals of finite length (e.g. a day), the rate of return is usually measured by $\dfrac{S_{t+1} - S_t}{S_t}$, where a day is of length '1'. This measure is closely approximated by $\ln S_{t+1} - \ln S_t$ if the rate of return is sufficiently small, as it will be under the assumption of geometric Brownian motion if the time interval is short enough.

A Normally distributed random variable can take any value between plus infinity and minus infinity. But, as a consequence of limited liability, most asset prices cannot become negative. The assumption that the change in the *logarithm* of the asset price is Normally distributed avoids this incompatibility.[10]

Is the assumption of geometric Brownian motion a good one? Does the assumption capture asset price movements as an acceptable approximation? This is an empirical issue: in many circumstances the assumption may turn out to be reasonably accurate. But there is nothing to ensure that asset prices *must* behave according to geometric Brownian motion. The assumption will have to be abandoned, or at least modified, if evidence appears that an alternative assumption better approximates the observed patterns of prices.

19.3.2 The Black–Scholes formula

Given the two extra assumptions together with those in section 19.1, Merton, Black and Scholes derived a formula for the price of a European call option on a company's stock with current price S, standard deviation σ, exercise price X, time to expiry $\tau = T - t$ and interest rate r. It is given by

$$c = S\Phi(x_1) - e^{-r\tau}X\Phi(x_2) \tag{19.9}$$

where

$$x_1 = \frac{\ln(S/X) + (r + \tfrac{1}{2}\sigma^2)\tau}{\sigma\sqrt{\tau}}$$

$$x_2 = \frac{\ln(S/X) + (r - \tfrac{1}{2}\sigma^2)\tau}{\sigma\sqrt{\tau}} = x_1 - \sigma\sqrt{\tau}$$

and $\Phi(\cdot)$ is the cumulative distribution function of the standard Normal distribution.[11]

The Black–Scholes formula can be derived as an implication of the arbitrage principle. Black and Scholes developed the argument along the following lines.

Consider an investor with continuous access in frictionless markets to (i) the asset (a company's ordinary shares); (ii) a call option on the asset; and

---

[10] Remember that the logarithm is defined only for positive values of its argument, and takes on values from minus infinity to plus infinity.

[11] The function $\Phi(z)$ expresses the probability that a standard Normal random variable, Z, has a value smaller than z – i.e. $\Phi(z) \equiv \mathrm{Prob}(Z < z)$. Formally,

$$\Phi(z) \equiv \int_{-\infty}^{z} \frac{e^{-v^2/2}}{\sqrt{2\pi}}\,dv$$

Two important properties of $\Phi(z)$ are (i) that it is increasing in z, and (ii) that it takes values between zero (as $z \to -\infty$) and one (as $z \to +\infty$). The curve of $\Phi(z)$ as a function of z is S-shaped, from zero at $-\infty$, through $\tfrac{1}{2}$ at $z = 0$ (a point of inflection) towards one as z tends to $+\infty$.

(iii) risk-free borrowing or lending. Using any given amount of initial capital, the investor forms a portfolio of the asset and the option. The portfolio weights are chosen, and continuously adjusted, to eliminate any risk associated with changes in the asset price from one instant of time to the next; the impact of changes in S on the market value of the portfolio is expunged. Such a strategy is feasible given the assumptions of the model, in particular that the asset price evolves according to a geometric Brownian motion and that continuous portfolio rebalancing (i.e. continuous trading) is possible. In the absence of arbitrage opportunities, the initial capital invested in risk-free portfolio must yield exactly the risk-free interest rate.

A crucial insight of Black and Scholes was to recognize that the equation they derived is the partial differential equation known as the heat-transfer equation in physics, the solution to which is given by (19.9).[12]

Another way of understanding the Black–Scholes reasoning is to notice that it is possible to construct a portfolio of the asset and risk-free borrowing or lending that replicates the pattern of returns of an option on the asset. The portfolio and the option must then, in the absence of arbitrage opportunities, be of equal market value. Once again, given the assumptions, the same formula is obtained. Merton concludes (1990, p. 293): 'The key to the derivation is that any one of the securities' returns over time can be perfectly replicated by continuous portfolio combinations of the other two.'

Notice that c does not depend on μ; the expected rate of return, μ, on the asset does not appear in the Black–Scholes formula. Hence, the predictions of the model will hold even if investors disagree about the expected return on the asset.

Merton (1973) shows that it is possible to obtain the Black–Scholes formula under less restrictive assumptions than those outlined above. For instance, volatility can be allowed to vary across time, albeit in a known way, and interest rates need not be constant. However, it is vital for the validity of the model that investors are unanimous in their beliefs that the asset price evolves according to a geometric Brownian motion, and also that they agree on the value of the volatility parameter. Samuelson is forthright in issuing the necessary caution (1972, footnote 6).

The market need not believe in the Black–Scholes formula in the way that it *must* believe in formulae that prevent [arbitrage opportunities] from being possible. Thus, how can a rational arbitrager 'know with certainty' what the σ is that he needs to do the arbitrage? [...] Query: what pattern of pricing, *if* it were known to hold with certainty (if, if!), would prevent the possibility of arbitrage? What pricing pattern will yield no profits to locked-in arbitrage strategy that must be engaged in until expiration time? Answer: the Black–Scholes pattern of pricing and no other.

---

[12] This differential equation, not reproduced here, can be applied to obtain valuation formul for many other financial instruments that differ from one another with respect to their so-called 'boundary conditions' – the conditions that must be satisfied when the instrument is created and when it expires.

If the Black–Scholes assumptions hold then the arbitrage principle implies their formula. But if the assumptions break down, say because investors disagree about σ, the validity of the formula is in doubt. Even then, the formula may provide an acceptable approximation, especially in the absence of a better alternative.

19.3.3 Measuring volatility

Apart from the parameter σ, the arguments of the Black–Scholes formula can be observed or calculated with a high degree of accuracy. Formally, σ is the standard deviation of the asset's rate of return.

As already noted, if the asset pays no dividends over the time interval in question, its rate of return can be written as $(S_{t+1} - S_t)/S_t$, the proportional rate of change in price (i.e. its capital gain or loss). Define $g_{t+1} \equiv (S_{t+1} - S_t)/S_t$. The standard deviation g_{t+1} can now be used to estimate σ.

Suppose that a sample of daily asset prices is available, $S_0, S_1, S_2, \ldots, S_N$.[13] The rate of return for each date is then given by $g_1, g_2, g_3, \ldots, g_N$, where $g_1 = \dfrac{S_1 - S_0}{S_0}$, $g_2 = \dfrac{S_2 - S_1}{S_1}$, $g_3 = \dfrac{S_3 - S_2}{S_2}$, and so on. Now σ^2 can be estimated by the sample variance:

$$\widehat{\sigma}^2 = \frac{(g_1 - \overline{g})^2 + (g_2 - \overline{g})^2 + (g_3 - \overline{g})^2 + \cdots + (g_N - \overline{g})^2}{N - 1}$$

where $\overline{g}$ denotes the sample average, $\overline{g} = \sum_1^N g_t/N$. The standard deviation, $\widehat{\sigma}$, is then obtained as the positive square root of the variance. For convenience, from now on the circumflex, $\widehat{}$, over σ is omitted, though it should not be forgotten that its value is never known with certainty.

Other methods of estimating volatility include assuming that $\overline{g} = 0$ (the mean is likely to be tiny for daily data) and assigning different weights to the g_t observations. In particular, it is common to assign a greater weight to the most recent observations, the weights declining for observations in the more distant past; the argument for this is, presumably, that recent observations contain 'more information', though the justification for this practice typically remains vague.

More important is the possibility that volatility is not constant; that is, σ may not be a fixed parameter but may change over time. Many sophisticated statistical studies have explored time-varying volatility.[14] At present, however, there is no generally accepted economic theory that predicts or can account for non-constant

---

[13] The unit time interval does not have to be a day, though this is commonly assumed.

[14] See Engle (2004) for an overview of the literature. Robert Engle shared the 2003 Nobel Memorial Prize in economics, partly for his pioneering econometric studies of time-varying volatility.

volatility. Hence, it is assumed here that σ is constant for the lack of any well-supported alternative.

Volatility, σ^2 or σ, has a time dimension: it is usually expressed at an annual rate. On the assumption that the daily g_t are independent of one another (an implication of the Black–Scholes geometric Brownian motion assumption), the *variance* for m days is equal to m times the variance for one day. Suppose there are 250 trading days per year. Then $\sigma^2_{\text{annual}} = 250\sigma^2_{\text{daily}}$ and $\sigma_{\text{annual}} = \sqrt{250}\sigma_{\text{daily}}$. For example, if the daily variance is 1.8 per cent, the annual variance equals $450\% = 250 \times 1.8\%$; the daily standard deviation is approximately 1.34 per cent, giving an annual standard deviation of $21.19\% \approx \sqrt{250} \times 1.34\%$.

Armed with an estimate of σ, it is possible to predict the arbitrage-free value of c given the other arguments of the Black–Scholes formula, namely the underlying asset's price, the option's exercise price, its time to expiry and the risk-free interest rate. If the option is actively traded, the observed price can be compared with that calculated from the formula. Alternatively, as mentioned earlier, the formula can be used to calculate the so-called 'fair' price for an over-the-counter, bespoke option.

Comparisons between option prices predicted by the formula and observed market prices can be used to test the Black–Scholes model. What, in principle, can be inferred from discrepancies between the observations and predictions? One, or more, of the following might be responsible.

1. The Black–Scholes formula may not be the correct rule to predict arbitrage-free prices. As already noted, the assumptions could be at fault. For example, transactions costs might create market frictions. Or perhaps the asset price does not evolve according to a geometric Brownian motion. Or investors might disagree about the value of σ.

2. One, or more, of the arguments of the formula may have been mismeasured. It is possible, for instance, that the asset price, S, may be observed at a different instant of time from that for the option price. Or errors may be made in approximating the risk-free interest rate.

   The most likely culprit is, however, an inaccurate estimate of volatility, σ. Black and Scholes themselves reported evidence that the formula predicts too high a price for options with high estimated volatilities relative to those with low estimated volatilities, for which the formula predicts too low a price. Later research tends to support their finding.

3. The market is in disequilibrium: arbitrage profits could be made by trading in the option and its underlying asset (together with borrowing or lending at the risk-free interest rate). In principle, it should be routine to determine whether arbitrage profits could be made. If even small market frictions are present, however, it may appear that potential arbitrage profits are available when, in fact, they are not. The evidence, cautiously interpreted, suggests that, for actively traded options, the magnitude of such profits is negligible.

19.3.4 Implicit volatility

Despite what may appear to be its dubious assumptions, the Black–Scholes model is widely accepted as the benchmark option pricing model, almost as an article of faith. Instead of being used to predict the option price, the formula is often invoked to calculate the *implicit*, or implied, *volatility* of the asset's rate of return. To compute the implicit volatility, the observed option price is substituted into the Black–Scholes formula, (19.9), together with all the right-hand-side variables except σ. The implicit volatility is then estimated as the value of σ that satisfies the formula.

Measures of implicit volatility can prove useful in practical applications, when standard deviation estimates are needed to assess the risk associated with holding an asset. An advantage of implicit volatility is that it is 'forward-looking' (i.e. based on investors' perceptions about the future), rather than based on the past realizations of asset prices used to estimate standard deviations.

Separate implicit volatility measures can be computed from each of several different option contracts with the same underlying asset. Given that volatility is a characteristic of the asset price distribution, the calculated volatilities should equal one another if the Black–Scholes formula holds. But there is evidence of systematic departures from equality. This is another way of expressing the finding, mentioned above, that there are biases in applying the Black–Scholes formula. The observed patterns of implicit volatilities have attracted financial jargon: 'smiles', 'smirks' and 'skews'. These terms are applied to graphs of implicit volatilities for options on the same asset but that differ with respect to exercise price, time to expiry, divergence between exercise price and asset price, or in some other aspect of the option contract. For example, there is evidence that implicit volatility is lower the longer the time to expiry.

Also, implicit volatility is commonly found to be lower for options with an exercise price close to the asset price and higher for large differences. The causes of these patterns is not well understood, though it is generally accepted that the assumption of Brownian motion requires modification. A topic of active research focuses on adapting Brownian motion to be compatible with volatility that varies over time. The challenge is to build robust models that identify the determinants of time-varying volatility.

19.3.5 Dividend payments and other underlying assets

If dividends are paid on the underlying asset before the option expires, the Black–Scholes formula, (19.9), no longer holds. Although a general formula for dividend-paying assets is not available, one special case is of particular interest. This is when the dividend on the asset is paid at a continuous and known rate, q, so that the dividend equals qS at each instant of time. If the other assumptions of the Black–Scholes model remain in place, it can be shown that the Black–Scholes formula also holds, except that S is replaced everywhere in the formula with $Se^{-q\tau}$.

While the special assumption of a continuous divided stream is, at best, a convenient fiction for ordinary shares, Black (1976) shows that the resulting formula is applicable to a range of other underlying assets, including futures contracts and stock indexes. (Options on futures contracts and on stock indexes are studied in chapter 20.)

When dividends are payable, an American call option will command a higher premium than its European counterpart, because early exercise may be profitable. In this circumstance no general formula for the call option price is available. An approximation is sometimes made by using the higher of two European option prices: one is the price of a European option with the same specification as the American option; the other is the price of a European option that expires just before the last ex-dividend date of the stock before the expiry of the American option.

19.4 Contingent claims analysis

An option contract is a special case, albeit a central one, of a derivative security – a security with payoffs that depend on the payoffs on another security, the underlying asset. A derivative security thus inherits its riskiness from the asset, and is more or less risky than the asset according to the function that maps the asset's payoffs to those of the derivative. If, as the previous sections have sought to explain, an option price can be linked to the market price of the asset, then it should be possible to extend the reasoning to a broader class of derivatives. This is the objective of contingent claims analysis.

A contingent claim can be interpreted as any contract the payoffs on which bear a precisely defined, but perhaps complicated, relationship with the payoffs on one or more other securities. Contingent claims analysis then seeks to assign a value to such a security by applying the arbitrage principle. If markets are frictionless, the value obtained is the one that will be realized in market equilibrium. This is the logic used to determine option prices. The result here is the same, namely a function that links the contingent claim value with the price of the underlying asset. Of course, the function itself will depend, among other things, on the relationship between the payoffs on the asset and the contingent claim. However, the reasoning is the same as for options.

A two-state example reveals the close similarities in the analysis with that for determining option prices. Suppose that a company's shares will be worth either 120 or 100 units of account each at date T (assumed to be one time period from today). Assume that the price of each share today is 80 and the risk-free interest factor, R, for one period from today is 1.20 (equivalent to an interest rate of 20 per cent per period with no compounding). Suppose that a contingent claim is available with a payoff (also one period from today) equal to either (a) 110 or (b) one of the company's shares, at the discretion of the claim's owner. In this example, the contingent claim could be interpreted as a convertible zero-coupon bond: the company promises to redeem the bond for 110 after one period or to provide the bondholder with a share in the company. If the share price is 120 (state 1) the bondholder will convert, while if the share price is 100 (state 2) the bond is redeemed for 110.

In this example, contingent claims analysis seeks to answer the question: what is today's price for the convertible bond? It is possible to determine the market price of the bond as follows. Construct a portfolio of the bond and risk-free borrowing or lending, such that the portfolio's payoffs exactly replicate the payoffs from holding shares. In the absence of arbitrage opportunities, the value of the replicating portfolio must equal the value of the shares. This equality determines the value of each unit of the contingent claim, the bond.

More concretely, suppose that an *arbitrage* portfolio is constructed from the shares, bonds and risk-free borrowing or lending. In market equilibrium, the payoff from the portfolio must equal zero in every state. Suppose, in particular, that one share is purchased, two bonds are sold at a price of Z each and a risk-free loan of 100 is made. The payoffs are as follows:

	Initial outlay	State 1 $S_T = 120$	State 2 $S_T = 100$
Shares	-80	120	100
Contingent claim	$2 \times Z$	-2×120	-2×110
Loan	-100	1.2×100	1.2×100
Total	$2Z - 180$	0	0

In the absence of arbitrage opportunities, the initial outlay that generates these (zero) payoffs must be zero: $2Z - 180 = 0$. Hence, the price of the contingent claim (convertible bond) must be $Z = 90$. Any other value of Z would provide an arbitrage opportunity.

It may not be obvious how the proposed portfolio was constructed. To see this, suppose more generally that N shares are purchased, M units of the contingent claim are purchased and B is borrowed.[15] The payoff table then becomes:

	Initial outlay	State 1	State 2
Shares	$-80N$	$120N$	$100N$
Contingent claim	$-ZM$	$120M$	$110M$
Loan	B	$-1.2B$	$-1.2B$
Total	0	0	0

Reasoning identical to that applied in the option example (section 19.2) shows that a zero payoff in both states implies that $M = -2N$ and $B = -100N$. Zero initial outlay then implies $0 = -80N - ZM + B = -80N + 2ZN - 100N = (-80 + 2Z - 100)N$, and $Z = 90$. (For every arbitrage portfolio there is an arbitrary scale factor. It is N in this application.)

The purpose of this example is to show how the reasoning that generated an option price formula in a two-state world can be applied directly to more general contingent claims. In practice, of course, it is necessary to allow for many more than two states. This is achieved using exactly the same methods as for options; that is, by assuming that asset prices are determined according to a more realistic process (e.g. geometric Brownian motion), or by constructing approximations using the binomial model with multiple states over a sequence of hypothetical time intervals. For some contingent claims (e.g. those equivalent to European options), it may be possible to obtain an explicit formula for the price; for others, a method of numerical approximation will be the best that can be accomplished.

Only a limited, though expanding, range of contingent claims are traded in organized exchanges. The scope for OTC (customized, or bespoke) contingent claims is much greater. For these, the method outlined above can be used to calculate a value deemed fair by the parties engaged in the transaction. Yet again, 'fair' in this context refers to the market price that would be predicted to hold in the absence of arbitrage opportunities in a frictionless market.

Elaborate investment strategies involving claims that are not traded in any market can be constructed by financial managers for their companies or on behalf of their clients. While the valuations implied by these strategies are consequences of the arbitrage principle, and hence may appear to be risk-free, caution is merited.

---

[15] As before, negative values of N and M denote sales, and $B < 0$ denotes lending.

Why? Because embedded within the calculations are assumptions about the probability distributions of asset prices. For example, an estimate of the volatility of each of the relevant asset prices is almost always required. By utilizing the technical skills of modern finance, the investment strategies work as predicted so long as the assumptions underpinning them are not violated. But if market frictions intervene, or if the volatility changes in unpredictable ways, disaster may befall. Witness the difficulties encountered by the hedge fund, Long Term Capital Management (LTCM), in September 1998.

LTCM was established in 1994, numbering among its founders Merton and Scholes. During the summer of 1998 LTCM's approaching collapse led to the intervention of the US banking authorities, which arranged loan support from a consortium of international banks in order to bail out, and effectively take over, the fund.[16] Although the details remain opaque, according to news reports LTCM had short-sold low-risk government securities and obtained loans, the resulting funds being invested in high-risk bonds ('junk' bonds and emerging country debt). LTCM would have made large capital gains if the spread between interest rates on low- and high-risk debt had narrowed. Instead, the spread widened dramatically when Russian bonds defaulted in August 1998. It appears that LTCM took a bet that spreads would narrow, and suffered the consequences when they moved in the opposite direction.

LTCM's investment strategies were much more complicated than conveyed by this brief summary.[17] Even so, they illustrate fundamental principles. One aspect that is sometimes overlooked is that the models on which investment strategies are based often assume that asset prices (and rates of return) change smoothly, thus approximating the geometric Brownian motion described in earlier sections. This may be a reasonable assumption most of the time. The trouble is that the models' predictions become inaccurate if asset prices change abruptly or if volatility changes in unpredictable ways. Essentially what happens is that, when asset prices change, the models signal that assets should be purchased or sold, but the models' prescriptions may not properly allow for abrupt – and large – changes in asset prices. Such abrupt changes tend to be rare, but, when they do occur, they can prove exceedingly costly.

---

[16] In the diplomatic words of Alan Greenspan, chairman of the US Federal Reserve Board at the time, 'Officials of the Federal Reserve Bank of New York facilitated discussions in which the private parties arrived at an agreement that both served their mutual self-interest and avoided possible serious market dislocations.' (Testimony before the Committee on Banking and Financial Services, US House of Representatives 1 October 1998.)

[17] See Edwards (1999) and *The Economist* (1998). For a discussion of the performance of hedge funds, see Edwards and Liew (1999).

19.5 Summary

1. Option pricing theory seeks to construct a relationship between an option premium and the price of the underlying asset. Information on the risk-free interest rate, the time to expiry, the exercise price and the volatility of the underlying asset price is also required.

2. The arbitrage principle is applied to obtain the option price formula. In common with all arbitrage arguments, the formula links the prices of different financial instruments. The analysis does not purport to determine the option price independently of the underlying asset price.

3. A simple arbitrage-free price formula is available if there is a single time period before the expiry of a European option, and if the asset price can take on one of only two values at the end of the period. The formula can be extended to allow for multiple unit time intervals to expiry, the asset price being assumed to move to exactly one of two values in each unit interval.

4. The Black–Scholes formula rests (in the absence of arbitrage opportunities) on the assumptions of (a) continuous trading in frictionless markets and (b) an asset price that evolves in accordance with geometric Brownian motion.

5. Apart from a measure of asset price volatility, the information needed to compute the option price is usually readily available (or can be approximated to a high degree of accuracy). One of the main problems in option pricing is that of estimating the relevant index of volatility.

6. Measures of implicit volatility are calculated by assuming the correctness of an option-pricing formula (typically, the Black–Scholes formula). The resulting measures can then be used in place of the estimates of volatility obtained more conventionally from historical data, or to reveal anomalies in the pricing of related contracts.

7. Contingent claims analysis extends option price theory to a broader range of financial instruments, namely all those with payoffs that depend on the payoffs of one or more other securities.

Further reading

Hull (2005, chaps. 11 & 12) provides an accessible textbook analysis of the determination of option prices. At a more advanced level, Cox and Rubinstein (1985, chaps. 5 & 6) and Hull (2003, chaps. 10–12) offer more detailed analyses.

From among the vast journal literature, the pioneering papers by Black and Scholes (1973) and Merton (1973) deserve close attention, but they are not easy reading. The excellent paper of Cox, Ross and Rubinstein (1979) provides a detailed treatment of the binomial model and shows how, by taking appropriate limits, the Black–Scholes model emerges. It rewards careful study. The brilliance of Samuelson's early (1972) tour de force will be appreciated only by those who have thoroughly grasped the later contributions. Merton (1998) and Scholes (1998) offer more readily accessible overviews of the literature.

For an illuminating discussion of the mathematics of continuous time in the context of finance, see Merton (1990, chap. 3). Among the textbook treatments of the relevant mathematical methods, beginners may wish to consult Ross (2003), while those with more confidence can proceed directly to Etheridge (2002). An elegant formal treatment of Brownian motion is provided by Pollard (2002, chap. 9). (The book as a whole is highly recommended for its rigorous, yet accessible, exposition of modern probability theory.)

Introductory expositions of contingent claims analysis are given by Fridson and Jónsson (1997) and Mason and Merton (1985). Lively descriptions of the fate that befell LTCM are provided by Lowenstein (2001) and Dunbar (2000).

References

Bernstein, P. L. (1992), *Capital Ideas: The Improbable Origins of Modern Wall Street*, New York: Free Press.

Black, F. (1976), 'The pricing of commodity contracts', *Journal of Financial Economics*, 3(1–2), pp. 167–79.

Black, F., and M. Scholes (1973), 'The pricing of options and corporate liabilities', *Journal of Political Economy*, 81(3), pp. 637–54.

Cox, J. C., S. A. Ross and M. Rubinstein (1979), 'Option pricing: a simplified approach', *Journal of Financial Economics*, 7(3), pp. 229–63.

Cox, J. C., and M. Rubinstein (1985), *Options Markets*, Englewood Cliffs, NJ: Prentice Hall.

Dunbar, N. (2000), *Inventing Money: The Story of Long-Term Capital Management and the Legends Behind It*, Chichester: John Wiley & Sons.

Economist, The (1998), 3 October, pp. 127–31.

Edwards, F. R. (1999), 'Hedge funds and the collapse of Long-Term Capital Management', *Journal of Economic Perspectives*, 13(2), pp. 189–210.

Edwards, F. R., and J. Liew (1999), 'Hedge funds versus managed futures as asset classes', *Journal of Derivatives*, 16(4), pp. 45–64.

Engle, R. F. (2004), 'Risk and volatility: econometric models and financial practice', *American Economic Review*, 94(3), pp. 405–20.

Etheridge, A. (2002), *A Course in Financial Calculus*, Cambridge: Cambridge University Press.

Fridson, M. S., and J. G. Jónsson (1997), 'Contingent claims analysis', *Journal of Portfolio Management*, 23(2), pp. 30–43.

Hull, J. C. (2003), *Options, Futures, and Other Derivatives*, Englewood Cliffs, NJ: Prentice Hall, 5th edn.

(2005), *Fundamentals of Futures and Options Markets*, Englewood Cliffs, NJ: Prentice Hall, 5th edn.

Lowenstein, R. (2001), *When Genius Failed: The Rise and Fall of Long-Term Capital Management*, London: Fourth Estate.

Mason, S. P., and R. C. Merton (1985), 'The role of contingent claims analysis in corporate finance', in E. I. Altman and M. G. Subrahmanyam (eds.), *Recent Advances in Corporate Finance*, Homewood, IL: Richard D. Irwin, chap. 1.

Merton, R. C. (1973), 'Theory of rational option pricing', *Bell Journal of Economics and Management Science*, 4(1), pp. 141–83 (reprinted as chap. 8 in Merton, 1990).

(1990), *Continuous Time Finance*, Cambridge, MA, and Oxford: Blackwell.

(1998), 'Applications of option-pricing theory: twenty-five years later', *American Economic Review*, 88(3), pp. 323–49.

Nagatani, H., and K. Crowley (eds.) (1977), *The Collected Scientific Papers of Paul A. Samuelson*, Vol. IV, Cambridge, MA: MIT Press.

Pollard, D. (2002), *A User's Guide to Measure Theoretic Probability*, Cambridge Series in Statistical and Probabilistic Mathematics, Cambridge: Cambridge University Press.

Ross, S. M. (2003), *An Elementary Introduction to Mathematical Finance: Options and Other Topics*, Cambridge: Cambridge University Press, 2nd edn.

Samuelson, P. A. (1972), 'Mathematics of speculative price', in R. H. Day and S. M. Robinson (eds.), *Mathematical Topics in Economic Theory and Computation*, Philadelphia: Society for Industrial and Applied Mathematics, pp. 1–42 (reprinted as chap. 240 in Nagatani and Crowley (1977)).

Scholes, M. S. (1998), 'Derivatives in a dynamic environment', *American Economic Review*, 88(3), pp. 350–70.

20

Options markets III: applications

Overview

Options contracts are used in a multitude of different ways for different purposes. For example, an investor who plans to acquire shares in a company but considers that the current price is too high might choose to write put options on the shares. If the share price remains high during the life of the options, the options are not likely to be exercised and the investor pockets the option premium, without buying the shares. Alternatively, if the share price falls and the options are exercised against the investor, the shares are acquired, as the investor intended, at the exercise price. (In addition, the investor keeps the premium, of course.)

Rather than attempt to catalogue all these policies, this chapter studies several applications that illustrate different aspects of options analysis. Section 20.1 begins with a review of stock index options. Sections 20.2 and 20.3 introduce options on futures contracts, together with a variety of applications. In particular, section 20.3 explains how options on interest rate futures can be used to construct caps and floors on the effective interest rate for borrowing or lending.

Section 20.4 outlines how the inclusion of options in portfolios can mitigate the impact of uncertainty about future asset prices. Hedging, introduced in chapter 15, is re-examined using options (rather than futures) as hedge instruments.

A successful hedge reduces the risks associated with asset price fluctuations. It is not designed to reap the benefits of asset price increases while also protecting the investor against losses when asset prices fall. Such protection is the goal of portfolio insurance, a class of policies designed to place a floor under the value of a portfolio, while not restricting its growth in the event of increases in the prices of assets held in the portfolio. Section 20.5 outlines several strategies that have been proposed to accomplish portfolio insurance, and discusses their strengths and weaknesses. Section 20.6 returns to more conventional options policies, with a brief overview of how option contracts can be bundled together to achieve particular payoff patterns.

20.1 Stock index options

Stock index options are almost identical to options on the shares of a single company. The main difference is what 'exercise' means for a stock index option. Suppose that a call option is exercised. This requires the exchange of the agreed amount of the underlying asset in return for the previously agreed exercise price. For a stock index option, exercise would imply that a bundle of securities, exactly matching the composition of the stock index, changes hands. The holder of a call would receive the bundle from a call writer, while the holder of a put would deliver the bundle to a put writer. Such exchanges would incur prohibitive transaction costs, and, for this reason, stock index options – like their futures counterparts – are settled in cash.

Consider, for instance, the FT-SE 100 index option traded on LIFFE. This option is available in both American and European styles. Expiry dates for the American option are at the end of June and December, together with other months so that options in the nearest three calendar months can be traded. Exercise prices are set at 25- to 100-point intervals close to the observed FT-SE 100 index. Quotations are made in index points, each point being valued at £10 (the tick size being 0.5 point, with value £5). The contract specifications for European options are similar, though, of course, exercise can take place only at expiry. A 'FLEX' contract is also available: this allows the parties to the contract (instead of the exchange authorities) to set the exercise price and the expiry date. Although more flexible, such contracts are likely to be less liquid (i.e. more expensive to offset).

Example (of the American-style option). Suppose that on a day in March the FT-SE 100 index is at 5100, and a premium of 150 is quoted for an American call option with exercise price 5000 and a June expiry date. An investor (who expects the index to rise above 5100) buys one call option for £1500. Suppose that in April the FT-SE 100 index rises to 5300 and the option premium increases to 380. The investor's position can be offset by selling one option, yielding a net gain of £2300, as shown in the table below.

Date	FT-SE 100 index	Exercise price	Expiry date	Premium	Action
March	5100	5000	June	150	Buy one call for £1500 $= 1 \times 10 \times 150$
April	5300	5000	June	380	Sell one call for £3800 $= 1 \times 10 \times 380$
					Net profit $= £2300$

What would have happened if the investor had chosen to exercise the option in April, instead of offsetting the position with a sale? An investor who had written one call option (with an exercise price of 5000 and a June expiry date) would be chosen at random by the exchange, and would have to pay £3000 = $1 \times 10 \times (5300 - 5000)$ to the investor who exercises the option. But, if an American option is worth more alive than dead, then it will be more profitable to offset the position with a sale rather than to exercise the option.[1] In this example, the investor gains £1500 = 3000 − 1500 from exercising the option, as against £2300 made by selling it. (Here, as elsewhere, transaction costs are neglected.)

Spread betting

Spread betting was outlined in chapter 16, section 16.2.1, where the bets were compared with futures contracts. The same ideas carry over to options contracts. Just as for the description of spread bets in chapter 16, clients trade directly with the bookmaker, who quotes bid and ask prices. In this context, the 'prices' are equivalent to option premia.

20.2 Options on futures contracts

On many organized exchanges it is possible to trade in *options on futures* contracts as well as in the futures contracts themselves. For instance, on NYMEX it is possible to trade in options on crude oil futures, where one option contract corresponds to each futures contract. On LIFFE it is possible to trade in options on the short sterling futures contract. There are many other examples.

Expiry date and delivery date. Options on futures are usually constructed in such a way that the option expires at, or shortly before, the delivery date for the futures contract on which it is written. It would be pointless for the option to expire *after* the delivery date on the futures contract, but there is no reason, in principle, why it should not expire *before* the delivery date.

A *call* option on a futures contract confers the right to take a *long* position in the futures contract. A *put* option confers the right to take a *short* position in the futures contract. The relationship between options and the assigned futures position can be summarized as follows:

	Call options	Put options
Long futures	long call (holder)	short put (writer)
Short futures	short call (writer)	long put (holder)

[1] Recall from chapter 18, page 453, that an American call option premium is at least as great as the payoff from exercising it early, in market equilibrium with the absence of arbitrage opportunities.

The *writer* of options on futures receives the option premium in return for an obligation to take a futures position opposite to the buyer in the event that the option is exercised. Thus, suppose that a call option is exercised: the holder receives a long futures contract with the price set equal to the option's exercise price, the corresponding short futures position being assigned to a call option writer. Similarly, suppose that a put option is exercised: the holder receives a short futures contract with the price set equal to the option's exercise price, the corresponding long futures position being assigned to the put option writer.

Options that remain in existence and 'in the money' at their expiry dates are normally exercised automatically. The futures position can then be offset, yielding an immediate gain (minus commission fees) for the option holder.

Example 1: a call option on a futures contract. Suppose that, in March, an investor buys one American-style call option, with an exercise price of $30 per barrel, on crude oil futures for December delivery. Each contract is for 1000 US barrels of oil. If, in September, the futures price for December delivery is $34 per barrel, the investor might choose to exercise the option. Exercising the option involves the receipt of $4000 = 1000 \times (34 - 30)$, together with a long position in one futures contract for December delivery. The futures position acquired in this way could be offset (sold) immediately, with no additional gain or loss (apart from commission fees, etc.). Thus, the result is a gain of $4000 *minus* the premium paid for the option in the previous March (and any transaction costs).

Notice that, when the option is exercised, the option writer (a) makes a cash payment to the option holder and (b) transfers a futures contract to the option holder. Given that the cash payment in (a) reflects the difference between the option's exercise price and the futures contract price, and that the futures contract can be offset immediately, it might seem unnecessary for step (b) of the transaction to take place at all. The gain from exercising the option appears to be captured in step (a) alone, while step (b) contributes nothing. In the absence of market frictions, this is true. However, in practice there is likely to be a discrepancy (possibly small, but non-zero) between the futures price used in the calculation of the option's payoff and the futures price at which the contract transferred in step (b) can be offset. This being so, the transfer of the futures contract can make a difference for both option holder and writer. It is possible, for instance, in the above example that the investor (option holder) may wish to take delivery of the oil in accordance with the terms of the futures contract. Thus, in the presence of market frictions, the exchange of the futures contract (when the option is exercised) is of significance.

However, if markets are frictionless, in the absence of arbitrage opportunities it would be more profitable to *sell* the option rather than to exercise

it early.[2]   The assumption of frictionless markets is, of course, an idealization. Acknowledging this, the example illustrates how the *magnitude* of frictions
impacts on the sequence of profitable transactions.

Example 2: a put option on a futures contract. Suppose that in May an investor
buys one American-style put option with an exercise price of $400 per troy ounce,
on gold futures for December delivery. On the COMEX exchange (a division of
NYMEX), each futures contract is for the delivery of 100 troy ounces of refined
gold. If, in October, the price of gold futures for December delivery is $390,
the investor might choose to exercise the option. Exercise involves the receipt
of $1000 = 100 \times (400 - 390)$, together with a *short* position of one contract for
the delivery of gold in December (i.e. a promise to deliver 100 ounces of gold in
December in exchange for $39,000 (= 100 \times $390 per ounce)).

Keeping in mind the caveat about market frictions noted above (example 1),
the futures position could be offset immediately, resulting in a gain of $1000
minus the premium paid for the option in the previous May. The purchase of a
put option with an exercise price of $400 thus means that the investor has bought
the right to sell gold (for December delivery) at $400 per ounce. In October this
right can be exercised when the futures market price is $390. The gain arises
from selling at $400 and buying at $390 per ounce. The investor could, of course,
hold onto the short futures position. Then an additional gain would be made if
the futures price falls before it is offset. (Obviously, a smaller gain, or even a
loss, would be made if the futures price rises above $390 before being offset.)
Although the early exercise of the option cannot be ruled out, it may be more
profitable to sell the option prior to expiry rather than to exercise it, just as for a
call option.

Example 3: options on weather futures. Weather futures contracts that trade
on the Chicago Mercantile Exchange were outlined in chapter 16, section 16.1.
Options on the futures contracts also trade on the CME, both for heating degree
day and cooling degree day contracts. One HDD option corresponds to one
futures contract (similarly for CDD options). The option premium is quoted
in HDD (or CDD) index points, each point being valued at $100 (so that an
option quoted at '12' has a premium of $1200). The options are European-
style, with expiry dates in November through to March (i.e. winter) for options
on HDD futures, and May through to September for options on CDD
futures.

---

[2] To see this, suppose that the option premium is *less* than the payoff from immediate exercise of the option:
$C < f - X$, where C is the option premium, f is the futures contract price and X is the option's exercise
price. Now an immediate arbitrage profit can be made from buying an option for C and exercising it
immediately, yielding a payoff of $f - X - C > 0$. This is ruled out if $C \geq f - X$, as asserted.

Option payoffs

The payoffs at expiry for options on futures can be described in the same way as for options on other assets, where now the futures price at maturity, f_T, replaces the underlying asset price, S_T. Hence, if the options are exercised, the payoffs c_T and p_T are

call option: $c_T = \max[0, f_T - X]$ put option: $p_T = \max[0, X - f_T]$

where X denotes the exercise price.

These results suggest that options on futures can be used to replicate the payoffs on the underlying futures contracts. To understand how this is achieved, recall that the payoff for a *long* futures position held to maturity is given by $f_T - f$ per contract – i.e. the contract is purchased at price f and offset by selling it for f_T at maturity.

Now suppose that the futures price today, f, equals the options' exercise price, X: $f = X$. Consider a portfolio comprising the purchase of one call option and the writing of one put option – sometimes called a 'synthetic futures contract'. If at maturity $f_T > X$, the call option is worth $f_T - X = f_T - f$, exactly equal to the payoff on the futures contract. (The put option is not exercised if $f_T > X$.)

Alternatively, if $f_T < X$, the put option is exercised with a (negative) payoff $f_T - X = f_T - f$, exactly equal to the payoff on the futures contract. (The call option is not exercised if $f_T < X$.)

Hence, the payoffs for the portfolio of one long call and one short put are exactly the same at expiry as for a long futures contract, when the futures contract is purchased at the option exercise price. (If $f_T = f = X$ both options and the futures contract have zero payoffs.)

Similarly, the payoff at maturity for a *short* futures position is exactly the same as for a portfolio comprising one *long* put option and one *short* call option, again assuming that $f = X$.

Suppose that $f \neq X$. In this case, the *put-call parity relationship* is helpful. With a futures contract as the underlying asset, the put-call parity relationship for European options is

$$c + \frac{X}{R} = p + \frac{f}{R} \qquad (20.1)$$

where R is the abbreviated form of $R(t, T)$, the interest factor.[3] (See appendix 20.1 for a derivation of (20.1).)

---

[3] Notice that it is not the case that f simply replaces S in the put-call relationship, $c + X/R(t, T) = p + S$, which appears in chapter 18, section 18.5. The reason is that the payment for futures is made only at the delivery date, T. Hence, the present value f/R replaces S, the underlying asset price.

Returning to the replication of futures contracts with options, notice that the put-call parity relationship implies that $f = X + R(c - p)$; the difference in the option prices compensates for any difference between f and X.[4]

Example. Suppose that $f = \$122$, $X = \$100$ and $R = 1.10$. The put-call parity relationship implies that $c - p = \$20$. A *long* futures position has a payoff of $f_T - 122$ per contract. Compare this with the payoff from buying one call and writing one put (i.e. a synthetic futures contract). The payoff at expiry on the portfolio of options is $f_T - 100$. (If $f_T > 100$ the call is exercised; if $f_T < 100$ the put is exercised.) However, the net cost of purchasing a call and writing a put equals $c - p = \$20$, an amount that must be borrowed at the outset and repaid with interest at date T: $R(c - p) = 1.10(20) = \$22$. Thus, the net payoff from the options portfolio equals $f_T - 100 - 22$, precisely the same as for the futures contract.

Valuation of options on futures

The theory of option prices can be extended to options on futures with an adjustment to allow for the fact that a futures contract requires zero initial outlay. Consequently, under the assumptions of the Black–Scholes model, the premium of an option on a futures contract can be determined by replacing the asset price S with $fe^{-r\tau}$ in the formula, where f is the futures price, r is the risk-free interest rate and τ is the time to expiry of the option, $\tau \equiv T - t$. Because the futures contract requires zero initial outlay of funds, the underlying asset price is replaced with its net present value, $fe^{-r\tau}$ (i.e. $f/R(t, T)$ in the notation used here, where $R(t, T)$ is a generalization of $e^{r\tau}$).[5]

20.3 Interest rate options

Interest rate options, of which there are many varieties, differ primarily according to the asset on which the options are written. The underlying assets include futures contracts as well as bonds. The bonds or debt contracts differ with respect to time to maturity, whether their coupons are fixed or variable, and the currency in which they are denominated.

A range of exchange-traded option contracts are available, but even more are created over the counter by financial institutions for their clients. Interest rate options introduce no new issues of principle, though the Black–Scholes model requires modification. This is because the volatility of the rate of return on the underlying asset, a bond, is not constant (as assumed in the Black–Scholes model) but diminishes as the bond approaches its redemption date.

---

[4] The reason for the presence of the interest factor, R, is that the option premia are paid at the outset, while the futures contract payoff occurs only at maturity, when the options are exercised.

[5] The opportunity cost of margin deposits is assumed to be zero because the depositor normally receives interest on the margin account balance.

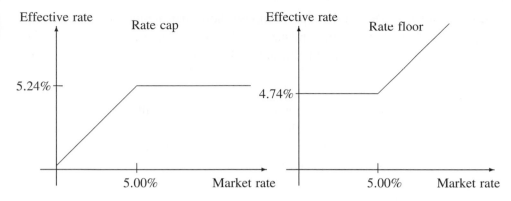

Fig. 20.1. Interest rate caps and floors

An interest rate *cap* (left panel) places a ceiling on the rate at which funds can be borrowed. Notice that the cap is not free: the effective interest rate (i.e. the cost of funds) exceeds the market rate at low market interest rates. An interest rate *floor* (right panel) places a lower bound on the rate at which funds can be lent. Again, notice that the floor is not free: the effective interest rate (i.e. the return on funds) is less than the market rate for high market interest rates.

The multitude of interest rate options is illustrated here with options on three-month sterling (short sterling) interest rate futures traded on LIFFE. American-style call and put options are available for trading.

An investor who buys a short sterling call option (a 'long call') acquires the right to buy a futures contract (i.e. to take a long position) at the stated exercise price any time up to the last trading day of the futures contract (at which date in-the-money options are automatically exercised on behalf of their holders). One difference between these option contracts and most others is that the premium is not paid at the outset. Instead, investors make margin deposits, which are marked to market on a daily basis so that gains are credited, or losses debited, until the position is offset or expires.

The motives for buying or selling short sterling options are much the same as for any financial instrument. Consider, for example, the construction of interest rate *caps* and *floors*, illustrated in figure 20.1. The following paragraphs describe how interest rate options can be applied to create an interest rate cap and a floor, respectively.

Example: interest rate cap

Assume that a company plans, in March, to borrow £500,000 for three months from 1 July at whatever market interest rate then rules. An option contract can be used to obtain an interest rate cap, with the objective of placing an upper limit on the interest rate paid on the loan. Suppose that a put option with an exercise price of 95.00, expiring at the end of June, currently trades at a premium of 0.24 (i.e. 24 ticks), where each tick equals 0.01 percentage points, worth £12.50 per tick.

One put option is purchased for £300 = 24 × 12.50. Now suppose that, at expiry, the futures price (i.e. the EDSP) is 94.00, calculated from a market interest rate of 6.00 per cent (94.00 = 100 − 6.00). The option is automatically exercised and the investor is assigned a short futures position.

The futures position is then cash settled with the sale of one contract for 95.00 at a date when the market price equals 94.00 (the EDSP), thus yielding a gain of 100 ticks – i.e. £1250 = 100 × 12.50. Consequently, there is a net gain of £950, equal to 0.76 per cent of £500,000 for three months. Hence, if £500,000 is borrowed at 6 per cent, the effective borrowing rate is capped at 5.24 per cent.

In essence, a futures contract has been sold at 95.00 and repurchased at 94.00. The purchase of the option ensures that no loss is incurred if the futures price is greater than 95.00 at the maturity date. This benefit is not free. Its cost is reflected in the option premium of 24 ticks.

Each one-point increment in the interest rate is matched by a different payoff on the option contract, as shown in the following table:[6]

Interest rate*	Futures price*	Gain (+) or loss (−)	% gain (+) or loss (−)	Effective borrowing rate*
9.00%	91.00	+4700	+3.76%	9.00 − 3.76 = 5.24%
8.00%	92.00	+3450	+2.76%	8.00 − 2.76 = 5.24%
7.00%	93.00	+2200	+1.76%	7.00 − 1.76 = 5.24%
6.00%	94.00	+950	+0.76%	6.00 − 0.76 = 5.24%
5.00%	95.00	−300	−0.24%	5.00 + 0.24 = 5.24%
4.00%	96.00	−300	−0.24%	4.00 + 0.24 = 4.24%
3.00%	97.00	−300	−0.24%	3.00 + 0.24 = 3.24%
2.00%	98.00	−300	−0.24%	2.00 + 0.24 = 2.24%
1.00%	99.00	−300	−0.24%	1.00 + 0.24 = 1.24%

(* Rates and prices realized at the option expiry date.)

If the interest rate (on the expiry date) is at or below 5 per cent, the option is allowed to die, unexercised. The company then benefits from lower interest rates but pays 0.24 percentage points above the market rate, the extra reflecting the option premium. But, if the interest rate (as of the option expiry date) exceeds 5 per cent, the company caps its borrowing cost at 5.24 per cent.

---

[6] Note that the compensation provided by the option for the interest rate rise is received when the option expires – i.e. before interest accrues on the loan.

In practice, of course, investors often need to adopt strategies that do not match the amounts or durations as neatly as in the example. In such cases it might be profitable to offset the position prior to the expiry date or to devise more complicated strategies, involving, say, a sequence of options with different expiry dates.

Example: interest rate floor

Assume that a company plans, in March, to make a deposit of £1m on 1 July for three months at whatever market interest rate then rules. An option contract can be used to obtain an interest rate floor, with the objective of securing a minimum for the interest rate received on the deposit. Suppose that a call option with exercise price equal to 95.00, expiring at the end of June, trades at a premium of 0.26 (i.e. 26 ticks).

Two call options are purchased for £650 = 2 × 26 × 12.50. Note for later reference that £650 = 0.26% of £1m for three months. Suppose that, at expiry, the futures price (i.e. EDSP) is 97.00, calculated from a market interest rate of 3 per cent (97.00 = 100 − 3.00). The option is automatically exercised and the investor is assigned a long futures position.

The futures position is then cash settled with the purchase of two contracts for 95.00, each at a date (the futures contract delivery date) when the market price is 97.00 (the EDSP), thus yielding a gain of 200 ticks on each contract – i.e. a total of £5000 = 2 × 200 × 12.50. Consequently, there is a net gain of £4350, equal to 1.74 per cent of £1m for three months. Hence, if £1m is deposited at 3 per cent for three months, the effective lending rate is 4.74 per cent.

Each one-point decrement in the interest rate is matched by a gain on the option contract, as shown in the following table:

Interest rate*	Futures price*	Gain (+) or loss (−)	% gain (+) or loss (−)	Effective lending rate*
9.00%	91.00	−650	−0.26%	9.00 − 0.26 = 8.74%
8.00%	92.00	−650	−0.26%	8.00 − 0.26 = 7.74%
7.00%	93.00	−650	−0.26%	7.00 − 0.26 = 6.74%
6.00%	94.00	−650	−0.26%	6.00 − 0.26 = 5.74%
5.00%	95.00	−650	−0.26%	5.00 − 0.26 = 4.74%
4.00%	96.00	+1850	+0.74%	4.00 + 0.74 = 4.74%
3.00%	97.00	+4350	+1.74%	3.00 + 1.74 = 4.74%
2.00%	98.00	+6850	+2.74%	2.00 + 2.74 = 4.74%
1.00%	99.00	+9350	+3.74%	1.00 + 3.74 = 4.74%

(* Rates and prices realized at the option expiry date.)

If the market interest rate (on the expiry date) is at or above 5 per cent (i.e. if the futures settlement price is less than or equal to 95), the option is allowed to die, unexercised. The company then benefits from higher interest rates but receives 0.26 percentage points below the market rate, the difference representing the option premium. But, if the interest rate, as of the option expiry date, is below 5 per cent, the company is assured of 4.74 per cent on its deposit.

Just as for the interest rate cap, the assumptions of the example are, at best, approximations in practice. Hence, more complicated strategies will be adopted, or the attainment of the interest rate floor will be imperfect.

20.4 Options and portfolio risks

20.4.1 Portfolios of options and their underlying assets

Portfolios that include options as well as their underlying assets facilitate the control and measurement of portfolio risks. To avoid unnecessary complications, this section focuses on a portfolio comprising N units of an asset (e.g. a company's shares) and M European call options on the asset (one share underlying each option).

The value of the portfolio at date t, W_t, is expressed as

$$W_t = NS_t + Mc_t$$

where c_t is the option premium and S_t is the price of its underlying asset. Hence, the change in the value of the portfolio between date 0, 'today', and date 1, in the future, can be written

$$\Delta W = N\Delta S + M\Delta c \tag{20.2}$$

where $\Delta W \equiv W_1 - W_0$, $\Delta S \equiv S_1 - S_0$ and $\Delta c \equiv c_1 - c_0$. For reasons that will become clear shortly, it is convenient to write (20.2) as

$$\Delta W = \left(N + M\frac{\Delta c}{\Delta S}\right)\Delta S \tag{20.3}$$

What makes the valuation of ΔW in equation (20.2) special is that, in the absence of arbitrage opportunities, an exact relationship is predicted between c_t and S_t (and hence between Δc and ΔS). In chapter 19 (page 468) the option premium was expressed as

$$c = f(S, X, \tau, R, \sigma)$$

Of particular interest here is the relationship between S and c.

If ΔS is sufficiently small, $\Delta c/\Delta S$ in (20.3) can be approximated by the partial derivative of c with respect to S, $\partial c/\partial S$. In addition, if the Black–Scholes model is appropriate for predicting c, it can be shown that[7]

$$\frac{\Delta c}{\Delta S} \approx \frac{\partial c}{\partial S} = \Phi(x_1) \qquad (20.4)$$

where $\Phi(\cdot)$ and x_1 are defined in chapter 19 (see page 481). The partial derivative of c with respect to S, $\partial c/\partial S$, plays such a prominent role in option price theory that it is given a name: the option's *delta*.

20.4.2 Hedging with options

The results in (20.3) and (20.4) show how options could be used in hedging strategies. Suppose that N and M are chosen such that the hedge ratio, M/N, equals $-\Delta S/\Delta c$. Now changes in the asset price, S, leave ΔW unchanged: a perfect hedge has been constructed.[8]

If the Black–Scholes model is appropriate to link c with S, then the hedge ratio becomes

$$\frac{M}{N} = -\frac{\Delta S}{\Delta c} \approx -\frac{1}{\Phi(x_1)}$$

Recall from chapter 19 that $0 < \Phi(x_1) < 1$ (in particular, $\Phi(x_1)$ is the probability that a Normally distributed random variable is less than x_1). Hence, to hedge against fluctuations in the value of a positive holding ($N > 0$) of the asset, it is appropriate to take a *short* position in call options ($M < 0$) – i.e. to write call options. Suppose, for example, that an option's delta is found to be 0.05; then the hedge ratio of $1/0.05$ requires 20 call options to be written for each unit of the asset, $M = -20N$.

Put options could, instead, be used to implement the hedge. Applying the put-call parity relationship for European options, it follows that the delta for a put option, with premium p, is

$$\frac{\Delta p}{\Delta S} \approx \Phi(x_1) - 1$$

This is a negative number between zero and minus one. Consequently, an investor who seeks to hedge a positive holding of the underlying asset would adopt a *long* position in put options:

$$\frac{M}{N} = -\frac{\Delta S}{\Delta p} \approx -\frac{1}{\Phi(x_1) - 1} > 0$$

[7] The result is not as obvious as it may appear from the formula, because x_1 and x_2 are themselves functions of S. Tedious calculations show that it is, nonetheless, correct.

[8] See chapter 15. Note that the negative sign in $-\Delta S/\Delta c$ appears because $M > 0$ is interpreted here as a long position (positive holding) in options, by contrast with a *short* position in futures contracts in chapter 15.

Suppose, for example, that a put option's delta is found to be -0.10; then ten put options need to be purchased for each unit of the asset, $M = 10N$.

Referring back to equation (20.3), the asset and the option appear symmetrically in the sense that either could be interpreted as the hedge instrument. It may be convenient to consider that the option is used to hedge against fluctuations in the underlying asset price. But it would be just as valid to interpret the asset as being held to hedge against fluctuations in the option price. Either way, the hedging strategy involves – as it always does – a reduction in overall portfolio risk through a cancelling of the price risks associated with the component assets.

20.4.3 Measuring portfolio volatility

Equation (20.3) can be helpful in measuring the volatility of portfolios including options, quite apart from hedging. Investors, particularly regulated financial institutions, often need to estimate the probability of 'worst-case' scenarios. In particular, *value at risk* (VaR) processes seek to estimate the largest loss that a portfolio would suffer with specified (small) probability over a specified period. For example, the holder of a portfolio currently worth £350m may need to forecast the lowest value to which it might fall over the next ten days with probability at most 0.05.

There are many ways of obtaining such estimates, several of which involve estimating the volatility of the portfolio's market value (volatility being measured by the variance or, equivalently, standard deviation of the portfolio's value). This estimate is derived from the price volatility of the assets comprising the portfolio. Given that the volatility of option prices is often even harder to estimate than that of the underlying assets, linking the option price to the underlying asset price (say, via the Black–Scholes model) can simplify the computations. This is what is implied in equation (20.3), where an estimate of the variance of ΔW can be made from an estimate of the variance of ΔS (the change in the asset price) and a knowledge of $\partial c / \partial S$ (which provides the link between the option price and the asset price).

Armed with an estimate of the portfolio's variance and an assumption about the probability distribution of the portfolio's returns (typically that it is Normal), it is possible to obtain measures of VaR.

The method outlined here need not, of course, be restricted to portfolios containing options, but can be applied to any portfolio in which derivative securities, the values of which can be linked to underlying asset prices, are represented. Reliable estimates of portfolio volatility can then be made, given estimates of the volatility of the underlying asset prices.

20.4.4 Some Greek letters and their purpose

So far in this section attention has concentrated on $\partial c/\partial S$, the response of an option price c to changes in S – that is, the option's delta. But option prices depend on other variables too, as indicated by the formula $c = f(S, X, \tau, R, \sigma)$.

The partial derivative of $f(S, X, \tau, R, \sigma)$ with respect to each of its arguments is crucial in designing strategies involving options. Collectively, the partial derivatives are known as 'the Greeks' – *gamma, theta, rho* and even *'vega'* appear, as well as delta.

The meaning ascribed to each term is as follows: gamma equals $\partial^2 f/\partial S^2$ – i.e. the rate of change of delta with respect to S; theta equals the rate of change of the option premium with respect to time, t, or $-\partial f/\partial \tau$, because $\tau \equiv T - t$; rho equals the rate of change of the option premium with respect to the risk-free interest rate – i.e. $\partial f/\partial r$ (where r denotes the risk-free interest rate, assumed constant, so that $R = e^{r(T-t)}$); and vega (not a letter in the Greek alphabet and sometimes known as *kappa*, which is) equals $\partial f/\partial \sigma$, the rate of change in the premium with respect to volatility.

The presence of gamma, $\partial^2 f/\partial S^2 \neq 0$, serves as a reminder that option prices are *nonlinear* functions of their arguments (at least in the context of the Black–Scholes model). That is, the magnitude of delta varies with the value of S.

One implication of the non-linearity is that the *gamma* should be taken into account to improve the accuracy in approximating $\Delta c/\Delta S$. This becomes of significance the larger is ΔS.

Another implication of the non-linearity is that effective hedging strategies employing options are 'dynamic', in the sense that the number of options held changes as the price of the underlying asset changes. Changes in option holdings should, in principle, be made continuously via a process sometimes called 'rebalancing'. Such a process can be expensive in transactions costs, consequently reducing the attractiveness of options as hedge instruments.

20.5 Portfolio insurance

'Portfolio insurance' encompasses a set of strategies that became popular in the 1980s among investment managers who sought to combine the opportunity for increased wealth when stock prices increase ('upside potential' in common jargon) with a limit on the losses incurred when prices fall. The goal is to find a strategy that succeeds in placing a 'floor' under the market value of a portfolio without at the same time imposing any ceiling on its value.

The benefits conferred by portfolio insurance should be distinguished from the reduction in risk achieved as a consequence of diversification. Recall that well-diversified portfolios are those for which idiosyncratic risks are negligible. Diversification protects against asset-specific (idiosyncratic) risks but not against market risk. Thus, when security prices are generally low, all well-diversified portfolios are adversely affected to a roughly equal degree. Portfolio insurance seeks to achieve the more ambitious outcome of obtaining positive returns when asset prices increase without incurring large losses when they fall.

The variants of portfolio insurance include the following.

1. Stop-loss selling and buying.
2. The purchase of put options.
3. Lending and the purchase of call options.
4. The creation of synthetic put options.

Stop-loss selling and buying

With this strategy, assets are sold when their prices fall to, or below, a specified lower threshold and purchased when their prices rise to, or above, a specified upper threshold. Stop-loss selling is likely to be successful when prices change smoothly and in an extrapolative way – i.e. when price falls tend to be followed by further falls, and when price increases tend to be followed by further increases. It is less satisfactory when there are sudden, sharp changes in prices or if the trading of assets is subject to delay. Also, the strategy is likely to incur significant transaction costs, because assets may be sold and repurchased on several occasions over any interval of time. Other portfolio insurance strategies share this drawback.

Portfolio insurance with put options

Suppose that the portfolio to be insured comprises a single risky asset for which a put option is available. Now the investor can place a floor under the asset's value with the purchase of a put option – a 'protective put'. The option can be exercised (or sold) if the asset's price falls below a specified value (the exercise price of the option). Let S denote the value of the security, and suppose that its value is insured using a put option with exercise price X and expiry date T. The market value of the asset at date T is denoted by S_T, and the value of the put option at T is $\max[0, X - S_T]$. Thus, the value of the insured portfolio is given by

$$S_T + \max[0, X - S_T] = \max[S_T, X]$$

Allowing for the option's premium, p, the net payoff equals $\max[S_T, X] - p$. In words: at date T the investor's wealth equals the greater of the value of the security or the exercise price of the option, minus the premium paid for the option.

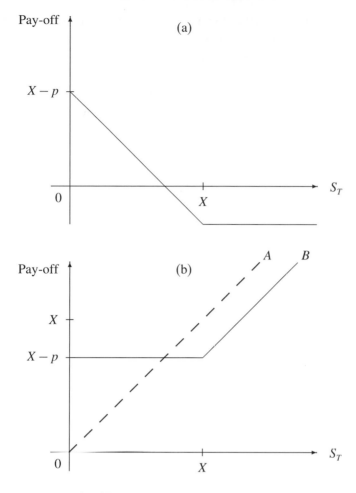

Fig. 20.2. Portfolio insurance with a put option

Panel (a) shows the payoff from a put option as a function of the underlying portfolio's market value at the expiry date, T. (The portfolio is assumed to comprise a single asset, with price S_t at T.) The dashed line in panel (b) shows the value of an *uninsured* portfolio; i.e. the payoff equals S_T. The purchase of the put option provides a lower bound of $X - p$ for the payoff when $S_T < X$. In the event that $S_T > X$, the payoff increases one for one with the market value of the underlying portfolio, though its level is lower by the amount of the option premium, p.

The outcome is shown in figure 20.2. In addition to the cost of the option, the strategy may prove unattractive because of the following.

1. Portfolios rarely consist of a single asset and normally contain many. When many assets are held, the purchase of options on all, or even some, of them could incur high transaction costs.

Options on stock indexes could provide inexpensive substitutes for options on individual shares. The effectiveness of this substitution depends on how closely the composition of the insured portfolio matches that of the index underlying the option – that is, on the correlation between the rate of return on the portfolio and the rate of return on the stock index.

2. Traded options tend to have a short time (typically weeks or months) to maturity, while the horizon for portfolio insurance may be much longer (several years, perhaps). This can make it costly – if, indeed, it is feasible – to obtain the desired floor to the value of the portfolio.

Portfolio insurance with call options

This strategy is similar to that using put options, except that, instead of holding risky assets and purchasing put options, the investor holds a risk-free interest-bearing bond (or makes a loan at the risk-free rate of interest) and purchases call options. Assume, again, that the risky portfolio comprises a single asset for which a call option is available. In this case the call option can be exercised (or sold) if the asset's price rises above a specified value (the exercise price of the option). Suppose that the call option has an exercise price equal to X with expiry date T. Each unit of the risky security can be insured at value X by lending $X/R(t, T)$ and buying the option for a premium c. The value of the call option at date T equals $\max[0, S_T - X]$, so that the value of the insured portfolio is given by

$$X + \max[0, S_T - X] = \max[S_T, X]$$

Allowing for the option's premium, c, the net payoff equals $\max[S_T, X] - c$. Again, at date T the investor's wealth equals the greater of the value of the security or the exercise price of the option, minus the premium paid for the option.

The shortcomings of the protective put option, outlined above, apply also to portfolio insurance using the call option. Also note that, in this case, the insured portfolio contains only risk-free bonds (or a loan) and options to purchase the risky assets – not the underlying assets themselves.

Portfolio insurance with synthetic put options

This form of portfolio insurance stems from the recognition that the put option needed to insure a portfolio is unlikely to be available, ready-made, in the market. Perhaps the portfolio to be insured comprises many risky assets, making it costly to purchase a put option on each. Or perhaps the time horizon for the insurance of the portfolio lies beyond the expiry dates of the available options.

The reasoning that results in the Black–Scholes formula serves to motivate the design of strategies based on synthetic options. One method for deriving the formula involves replicating the payoffs on an option via a portfolio comprising the underlying assets and risk-free lending or borrowing. If this logic enables the valuation of options, it should also permit the creation of *synthetic* options using, as raw materials, (a) the risky asset portfolio and (b) risk-free bonds. The idea is to mimic the payoffs of a put option on the portfolio and, hence, realize the protection that a put option provides. This seems too good to be true. Here are some of the potential drawbacks.

1. Although there is no explicit premium for creating a synthetic option, there is an implicit premium in the sense that a greater initial investment of funds is required to achieve the same returns in the 'good states' (high share prices) for an insured portfolio compared with an uninsured portfolio. The insured portfolio is protected against the losses suffered by the uninsured portfolio in the 'bad states' (low share prices), but more funds must be invested at the outset.

2. The strategy involves *dynamic replication*. Under the Black–Scholes assumptions, replicating the payoffs on an option requires continuous changes in the composition of the portfolio between risky assets and bonds. Such a strategy can incur high transaction costs as a result of frequent trading: the closer the approximation to the payoffs on a put option, the greater the number of transactions and the higher the costs.

3. The effectiveness of the strategy in replicating the option payoffs depends on exactly the same assumptions as made in the Black–Scholes model. These may or may not provide reasonable approximations to market conditions. The most sensitive conditions are (a) the absence of transaction costs (or, which can be interpreted as the same thing, the ability to trade assets continuously); (b) no sharp jumps in share prices (so that it is reasonable to assume that each asset price evolves according to a geometric Brownian motion); and (c) the ability to obtain accurate estimates of the volatility of asset returns.

   If, contrary to (a), transaction costs are non-negligible, they may overwhelm the benefits of portfolio insurance. If, contrary to (b), unforeseen jumps in share prices occur, then the portfolio manager may not have the opportunity to rebalance the holdings of risky assets and bonds so as to replicate the put option. If, contrary to (c), the volatility of share returns changes unpredictably, then the chosen combination of shares and bonds could fail to replicate the option payoffs. Consequently, it may be difficult – perhaps impossible – to create a synthetic put option on the portfolio with the required degree of accuracy.

4. The put option replication strategy requires the purchase of shares when their prices are rising, and the sale of shares when their prices are falling (see O'Brien, 1988). Counter-intuitive though it might at first seem, this strategy often forms a component of *programme trading*, in which stock purchases and sales are triggered automatically in response to observed changes in their market prices.

In view of the potentially high transaction costs incurred when trading in many assets, stock index futures contracts provide an attractive alternative for constructing a synthetic put option on the portfolio. Such a strategy resembles hedging the value of a portfolio using stock index futures, except that portfolio insurance requires the continuous revision of the position via the process of dynamic replication. If options on the relevant stock index are also readily available (i.e. widely quoted), these might incur lower transaction and administrative costs than synthetically created options.

Summary

The objective of portfolio insurance is to place a floor under the value of a portfolio without thereby restricting increases in its value. In the latter respect the strategies differ from hedging, which minimizes the risk of changes in the value of the portfolio, both up and down. The 'miracle' of portfolio insurance may resolve into a mirage when its costs are taken into account: (a) a premium has to be paid (either explicitly for traded options, or implicitly for synthetic options); and (b) continual rebalancing of the portfolio may incur high transaction costs. Active portfolio management in the form of portfolio insurance may yield benefits, but it is not free. Also, note two other reservations about portfolio insurance: (a) the time horizon is unspecified (different horizons could lead to different strategies and outcomes); and (b) except for special cases portfolio insurance is not implied by the principles of portfolio decision making, such as the expected utility hypothesis (i.e. the logical foundations of portfolio insurance could be construed as weak).

20.6 Combinations and spreads

Call and put options are often bundled together with the intention to create portfolios that have payoffs designed to achieve specific objectives. One objective might be, for example, to obtain a high payoff from extreme volatility (unforeseen sharp increases or decreases in an underlying asset's price), while tolerating a low payoff, or even a small loss, if volatility turns out to be lower than anticipated – see 'straddles', below. Another might be to obtain a certain payoff (the difference between two exercise prices) if an underlying asset price rises significantly, while incurring a small cost (the difference between two option prices) if the asset price falls – see 'bull spreads', below.

The bundles of call and put options constructed to satisfy these specific objectives can be classified in a variety of ways. Here they are grouped into 'combinations' and 'spreads', as follows.

Combinations comprise bundles, either all of long positions or all of short positions in call and put options on the same asset. For conciseness, only *long* positions are described here. Each corresponding *short* position entails exactly the opposite trade in each of the component options.

- *Straddles.* A long straddle consists of a long position in a call and a put with the same exercise price and expiry date.
- *Strips.* A long strip consists of buying one call and two puts with the same exercise price and expiry date.
- *Straps.* A long strap consists of a buying two calls and one put with the same exercise price and expiry date.
- *Strangles (or bottom vertical combinations).* A long strangle consists of a long position in a call and a put with the same expiry date but different exercise prices. The put exercise price, X_1, is lower than call exercise price, X_2: $X_1 < X_2$.

Spreads comprise bundles of long and short positions in either two or more calls, or two or more puts in the same asset. *Vertical* (or cylinder) *spreads* contain options with the same expiry date but different exercise prices.

- *Bull spreads.* A bull call spread involves buying a call with exercise price X_1 and writing a call with the same expiry date but higher exercise price, X_2 – i.e. $X_2 > X_1$.
- *Bear spreads.* A bear call spread involves buying a call with exercise price X_1 and writing a call with the same expiry date but *lower* exercise price, X_2 – i.e. $X_2 < X_1$.
- *Butterfly spreads.* A long butterfly spread consists of buying a call with a low exercise price, X_1, buying a call with a high exercise price, X_3, and writing two calls each with an exercise price, X_2, equal to the average of X_1 and X_3. All the expiry dates are the same and X_2 is typically chosen close to the current stock price.
- *Horizontal (or calendar) spreads.* A horizontal spread comprises a bundle of options with different expiry dates but the same exercise price. For example, a calendar spread could be achieved by (a) writing a call option and (b) buying a call option on the same asset, with the same exercise price but a later expiry date. The second option (with a later expiry date) is sold when the first expires.

The listed spreads refer to *call* options: each has an exact analogue using put options. Each of the listed spreads has a *rotated* variant for which the opposite position is adopted in each of the options (i.e. purchases become sales and sales become purchases).

While the above list is not exhaustive, it would be tedious and unilluminating to extend it further. To gain an appreciation of what can be achieved with spreads and combinations, it is instructive to graph their payoffs as functions of the underlying asset price. As an example, figure 20.3 shows the payoffs for a

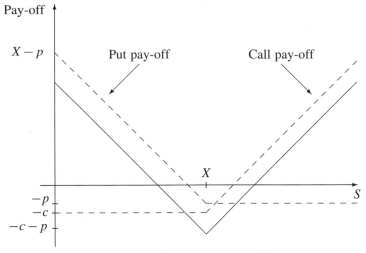

Fig. 20.3. A long straddle

A put option with exercise price, X, has been purchased at a cost of
p. A call option on the same underlying asset, with the same exercise
price and expiry date, has been purchased at a cost of c. The dashed
lines depict the payoffs (net of the premium paid for each option), at
exercise, for the put and call, respectively. The solid line depicts the
payoff of the combination of the put and call (i.e. a long straddle) as a
function of the underlying asset price at the exercise date. (While the
figure is drawn with $p < c$, there is no guarantee that this would be so;
p could be greater or smaller than c, depending on the asset price when
the options were purchased.)

long straddle. The construction of diagrams for the remaining cases is left as an
exercise for the reader.

20.7 Summary

1. Stock index options are written and traded for bundles of shares, the values of which
   are equal to commonly quoted stock price indexes. If a stock index option is exercised,
   settlement is in cash (not by the delivery of the bundle of securities underlying the
   stock index).
2. Options on futures contracts are options to acquire short or long positions in the futures
   contracts (including, for example, futures on stock indexes). Options on futures are
   written to expire on or before the futures delivery date. Normally, the options expiry
   date is shortly before the futures delivery date.
3. Interest rate options take a variety of forms (e.g. options on interest rate futures
   contracts). This sort of option is convenient for creating interest rate caps or
   floors.

4. Options can be used as hedge instruments in constructing hedge strategies. The relationship between changes in the option's price and the underlying asset's price provides the crucial link that determines the hedge ratio.

5. Portfolio insurance strategies seek to place a floor under the value of a portfolio while, at the same time, guaranteeing that the value of the portfolio increases in line with increases in the market value of its component assets. While trading in options can, in principle, achieve the objectives of portfolio insurance, the strategies normally involve the creation of synthetic options. Synthetic options are created by trading in the underlying assets and risk-free bonds in such a way as to replicate option payoffs.

6. Combinations and spreads are bundles of options packaged together with a view to achieving specific objectives. The components of the bundles differ according to the type of option (call or put), their exercise prices, their expiry dates and whether they are purchased or written (sold). As a consequence, it is possible to devise strategies that result in payoffs that are known functions of the underlying asset price realized at specific dates in the future.

Further reading

Hull (2005, chaps. 13–15 & 19) provides an excellent exposition of the material covered in this chapter but in greater depth. For a more advanced treatment, Hull (2003, chaps. 13–17) should be consulted.

Analyses of portfolio insurance include those by Leland (1980) and O'Brien (1988). The stock market crash of 1987 inspired much analysis, discussion and controversy about the role of portfolio insurance in the crash. On this topic, Rubinstein (1988) and Miller (1991, especially chaps. 3, 4 & 6) provide thoughtful assessments.

Appendix 20.1: Put-call parity for European options on futures

The put-call parity relationship for options on futures is a straightforward extension of the relationship for stock options, and is demonstrated here for completeness. Recall that the parity relationship states that

$$c_f + \frac{X}{R(t, T)} = p_f + \frac{f}{R(t, T)}$$

The proof follows the familiar pattern of showing that, if the relationship does not hold and if markets are frictionless, there exists an arbitrage opportunity. Given that the absence of arbitrage profits is a criterion for market equilibrium, the equality must hold. Two analogous arguments are needed, one when '>' replaces the equality, and the second for '<'.

Suppose, first, that $c_f + X/R > p_f + f/R$ (where the arguments of $R(t, T)$ are omitted for convenience). For later reference, rearrange the inequality

$$X - f - R(p_f - c_f) > 0 \qquad (20.5)$$

which follows because $R > 0$.

Consider the following strategy: buy one futures contract for f, buy one put for p, write one call for c and borrow $B = p - c$, so that the strategy requires zero initial outlay (f_T denotes the futures settlement price at date T).[9]

	Initial outlay	At expiry, T	
		$f_T > X$	$f_T \leqq X$
Buy one put option	$-p_f$	0	$X - f_T$
Write one call option	$+c_f$	$X - f_T$	0
Buy one futures contract	0	$f_T - f$	$f_T - f$
Borrow	B	$-RB$	$-RB$
	0	$X - f - RB$	$X - f - RB$

The table shows that, if $f_T > X$, the call option is exercised and the put option is allowed to die. Conversely, if $f_T \leqq X$, the put option is exercised and the call option is allowed to die. The payoff is the same in either case. From (20.5), $X - f - RB = X - f - R(p_f - c_f) > 0$. Hence, the payoff is positive irrespective of whether f_T is greater than, less than or equal to X.

Thus, if $c_f + X/R > p_f + f/R$, a portfolio with zero initial outlay yields a positive return whatever the price f_T at date T. This is an arbitrage portfolio with a positive payoff in both states. From the arbitrage principle, it cannot be consistent with market equilibrium.

Suppose now that the put-call parity is violated with $c_f + X/R < p_f + f/R$. Rearranging the inequality, it follows that

$$f - X - R(c_f - p_f) > 0 \qquad (20.6)$$

Consider the following strategy: take a short position in one futures contract, write one put, buy one call and borrow $B = c_f - p_f$, so that the strategy requires

---

[9] Note that B could be positive or negative. If $B < 0$, the strategy involves lending. In a frictionless market, lending is just negative borrowing.

zero initial outlay. (Because B could be of either sign, remember that both cases are covered if negative borrowing is interpreted as lending.)

	Initial outlay	At expiry, T	
		$f_T > X$	$f_T \leqq X$
Write one put option	$+p_f$	0	$f_T - X$
Buy one call option	$-c_f$	$f_T - X$	0
Sell one futures contract	0	$f - f_T$	$f - f_T$
Borrow	$+B$	$-RB$	$-RB$
	0	$f - X - RB$	$f - X - RB$

Once again, the table shows that the payoff is the same whatever the outcome. From (20.6), $f - X - RB = f - X - R(c_f - p_f) > 0$, by hypothesis. Hence, the payoff is positive no matter whether f_T is greater than, less than or equal to X. Consequently, if $c_f + X/R < p_f + f/R$, a portfolio with zero initial outlay yields a positive return whatever the outcome; there is an arbitrage opportunity.

In conclusion, if the put-call parity relationship is violated with either inequality, arbitrage profits can be made in frictionless markets. Hence, the put-call parity relationship must hold under the stated conditions.

References

Hull, J. C. (2003), *Options, Futures, and Other Derivatives*, Englewood Cliffs, NJ: Prentice Hall, 5th edn.
  (2005), *Fundamentals of Futures and Options Markets*, Englewood Cliffs, NJ: Prentice Hall, 5th edn.
Leland, H. E. (1980), 'Who should buy portfolio insurance?', *Journal of Finance*, 35(2), pp. 581–96.
Miller, M. H. (1991), *Financial Innovations and Market Volatility*, Cambridge, MA: Blackwell.
O'Brien, T. J. (1988), 'The mechanics of portfolio insurance', *Journal of Portfolio Management*, 14(3), pp. 40–7.
Rubinstein, M. (1988), 'Portfolio insurance and the market crash', *Financial Analysts Journal*, 44(1), pp. 38–47.

Subject index

3Com and Palm, 167

absence of arbitrage opportunities, 169, 224, 471
agency markets, 37
alpha-coefficient, 153, 202, 220
annuity, 284
anomalies in asset prices, 72
anticipatory hedging, 367
arbitrage, 20, 66, 126, 166–77
  arbitrage in forward markets, 337
  arbitrage opportunity, 169, 178, 316, 319
  arbitrage portfolio, 169
  arbitrage principle, the, 169, 468
  arbitrage profit, 169
  foreign exchange (forex) markets, 354–5
  forward and futures contracts, 349–52, 399
  market equilibrium, 169
  option contracts, 440
  proposition I, 170, 180
  proposition II, 173
  proposition III, 174, 177, 179
  role in option markets, 449–50
  term structure of interest rates, 326–8
arbitrage pricing theory, (APT), 194, 215–19
  APT and CAPM, 193
  bond markets, 327
  futures markets, 380
  risk premia, 190
  systematic risk, 187
  unsystematic risk, 187
Arrow security, 110, 174, 264
ask price, 17, 36
asset price volatility, 228–35
auction markets, 37

backwardation, 381
Bank of England, 308, 357
  Quarterly Bulletin, 356
Barings bank, 35
  fall of, 412–14
Bayes' Law, 51
BE/ME, book/market value of a firm's equity, 212
bear spreads, 515

behavioural finance, 10, 65, 75, 98–101, 235–7, 261
beta-coefficient, 129, 148, 203, 270
bid price, 17, 36
bid–ask spread, 36, 48–52
Black CAPM, 143, 157, 162, 205, 220, 270
Black Wednesday, 16th September 1992, 310
Black–Scholes model, *see* options
bonds
  annuity, 284
  average period, 294
  balloons, 284
  bond covenant, 286
  bond markets, 3
  bond rating agencies, 286
  bond valuation, 295–7
  bullets, 285
  callable, 283, 448
  clean price, 285
  collateral, 286
  consols, 284, 293
  continuous compounding, 303–4
  convertible, 283, 449, 487
  convexity, 288, 295, 300
  coupon, 224, 284–5
  coupon-paying bonds, 291–5
  coupons, 282
  credit risk, 297
  debentures, 286
  default, 283, 285–6
  definitions, 282–6
  dirty price, 284
  event risk, 297
  exchange-rate risk, 298
  face value (maturity value, principal), 282
  flat (current) yield, 292
  floating rate bonds, 285
  forward markets, 316–7
  holding-period yield, 287, 288, 314
  immunization (neutral-hedge) strategies, 298–300
  indenture, 283
  index-linked bonds, 285
  Macaulay duration, 293–5, 298, 303

519

Author index